D1559436

OCEANS OF WINE

The Lewis Walpole Series in Eighteenth-Century Culture and History

The Lewis Walpole Series, published by Yale University Press with the aid of the Annie Burr Lewis Fund, is dedicated to the culture and history of the long eighteenth century (from the Glorious Revolution to the accession of Queen Victoria). It welcomes work in a variety of fields, including literature and history, the visual arts, political philosophy, music, legal history, and the history of science. In addition to original scholarly work, the series publishes new editions and translations of writing from the period, as well as reprints of major books that are currently unavailable. Though the majority of books in the series will probably concentrate on Great Britain and the Continent, the range of our geographical interests is as wide as Horace Walpole's.

Oceans of Wine

Madeira and the Emergence of American Trade and Taste

David Hancock

Yale University Press
New Haven & London

Published with assistance from the Annie Burr Lewis Fund.

Set in Electra type by Tseng Information Systems, Inc.
Printed in the United States of America by Sheridan Books, Ann Arbor, Michigan.

Library of Congress Cataloging-in-Publication Data
Hancock, David, 1957–
Oceans of wine : Madeira and the Emergence of American Trade and Taste /
David Hancock.
p. cm. — (Lewis Walpole series in eighteenth-century culture and history)
Includes bibliographical references and index.
ISBN: 978-0-300-13605-0 (cloth : alk. paper)
1. Madeira wine—History—19th century. 2. Fortified wine industry—Madeira
Islands—Madeira—History—19th century. 3. Madeira (Madeira Islands)—
Commerce—Atlantic Ocean Region. 4. Atlantic Ocean Region—
Commerce—Madeira Islands—Madeira. I. Title.
HD9385.P83M334 2009
338.4′7663226094698—dc22
2009015934

A catalogue record for this book is available from the British Library.

This paper meets the requirements of ANSI/NISO Z39.48-1992 (Permanence of Paper).

10   9   8   7   6   5   4   3   2   1

For
G

CONTENTS

ILLUSTRATIONS

FIGURES

ix

PLATES

Following page 306

Plate 12. *The Toast*, by an unknown artist, c. 1810–1815
Plate 13. *A Country Wedding*, by John Lewis Krimmel, 1814
Plate 14. Wine bottle, with a "RW" seal, manufactured at
Caspar Wistar's Wistarburgh Glassworks, near Salem, New Jersey,
for his son Richard Wistar, c. 1745–1755
Plate 15. Thomas Jefferson's Madeira decanter, 1775–1800
Plate 16. Wine goblet, made and engraved by Henry William Stiegel
for his daughter's marriage to William Old, at his American Flint Glass
Manufactory, Manheim, Pennsylvania, 1773–1774

TABLES

Introduction: "An Unbounded Ocean of Business . . . Laid Open to Us"

Oceans of Wine was conceived seventeen some years ago, when I first visited the island of Madeira. For ten days at the end of what had seemed an inordinately long winter, I intended to enjoy the pleasures of a subtropical spa known for its warm, equable climate and dramatic, Alpine-like beauty. It was a glorious plan . . . until it began to rain. On the second soggy day, I meandered around the principal town, Funchal, and visited the Madeira Wine Company. Its tour was illuminating and the samples invigorating, but what piqued my interest most were the eighteenth-century ledgers that supported plastic grapes, antique brass measuring gauges, and iron brands once used to mark wine containers. Inquiring of the company's director, I learned there were many more such books tucked away in his "museum room," and "a few" others "up in a warehouse at the top of the hill."

Not one to dismiss such opportunities, I asked to see the collections. The records and papers in the company's museum, though fragmentary, whetted my appetite, and so the next day I climbed the hill to the stone warehouse. There on the top floor was a cavernous room, open to the elements, with wooden shutters dangling on rusted hinges and birds flying in and out. What surprised me most was neither the dead chickens nor the mushrooms the size of grapefruit growing from wooden boxes nor even the skeleton of what probably had been a goat, but the mountain of papers and books, probably twenty feet high and forty feet in diameter, cast there in abandon. The director thought my enthusiasm strange, and perhaps it was, but he let me excavate the mountain over the next few days. I soon found myself sympathizing with the narrator of Garcia Marquez's "Chronicle of a Death Foretold," who found "no [orderly] files whatsoever" but "a century" of records, "piled up on the floor of the decrepit colonial building,"

strewn about a room frequently "flooded" by the elements.[1] By the end of my
dig, I had uncovered letters and accounts of three wine export firms founded
in the mid-1700s. It appeared that nearly every outgoing letter and account had
been kept.[2]

The material challenged me to reconstitute a commodity chain that would
illuminate imperial and oceanic integration in the early modern world.[3] I could
narrate the life of a particular Atlantic commodity—Madeira wine—from grape
to table, and show how producers, distributors, and consumers all participated
in it. I could track the emergence of a particular transoceanic and interimperial
market that had not existed before and has only recently been appreciated by
scholars. Ultimately, I could wrestle with questions of increasing importance to
historians of the Atlantic-facing states in the early modern era: how did men
and women figure in and experience the transoceanic, interimperial market, and
how did their social worlds emerge and evolve in tandem and intersect with economic and political ones?

LINKAGES AMONG ECONOMIC ROLES
AND IMPERIAL GEOGRAPHIES

Oceans of Wine is a book about wine and the people who made, marketed,
sold, bought, and drank it in the early modern Atlantic world. The early chapters in parts 1 and 2 focus on the production of Madeira wine and its distribution around the world, especially to Europe's colonies in the Americas. The later
chapters, in parts 2 and 3, focus on wine in Anglo-America, Madeira's largest consumer market—its distribution to urban and rural drinkers, its place in stores and
taverns, and its social and cultural uses.[4] Combined, all these chapters transgress
a traditional division of labor among scholars: economists and economic historians emphasize production—cultivation, technology, manufacturing, labor, and
the demographics and politics of producers and merchants—while social and
cultural historians concentrate on consumption, diet, and meaning. Few of the
latter consider trade and distribution very much and, when they do, they exclude
other aspects of economic life.[5] A history that focuses on a single commodity can
highlight more easily the linkages among economic roles: producers produced
for consumers, and consumers consumed what producers produced for them;
distributors tried to serve these two masters and took a little off the top for their
effort.[6] Producers and distributors imposed constraints on consumers, especially
on what goods were available, their volume, and their quality; consumers influenced distributors and producers by favoring certain traits of goods and attaching
meanings to them. Neither producers nor distributors nor consumers were pas-

sive. All these people worked mightily to maintain networks of suppliers, financiers, agents, representatives, customers or friends; all constantly revealed what they thought, and listened in return.[7]

Thus, this book speaks to the adhesion of markets. It draws special attention to the work of distributors who were, alongside rulers, "the critical agents for the articulation of the supply and demand of commodities" but who have been less scrutinized than producers and consumers.[8] The core of the book focuses on the elaboration of distribution networks around the Atlantic, and in America from Nova Scotia to Jamaica and as far west as the Mississippi Valley. This is one of the great and as yet largely untold stories about the economic evolution of European and British America, part of which later became the United States. Ports were built and expanded, shops and markets set up, agency relationships formed, commercial tracts and newspapers published, roads and bridges built and improved. Distributors increased and spread out across the land, bringing an immense variety of goods from Calcutta, Hamburg, Mogador, Bristol, and Madeira to people in Boston, Savannah, Kingston, and Cincinnati. The fruits of their labors belie the models of "bounded" or sealed empire for Britain's global demesne and of rude self-sufficiency for America's economic development that historians have knowingly or unknowingly adopted.

Oceans of Wine is also about the porousness of empire: it examines the flow of Madeira wine across territorial empires and political orders. Madeira was produced in a Portuguese territory and distributed around the Atlantic basin by British, American, and Portuguese traders, and sometimes by French, Dutch, and Danish merchants, too. This western European import entered West African, Indian, and Asian settlements and the British, Portuguese, French, Dutch, and Danish American colonies, as well as (later) the United States. It linked Portuguese peasants, French brandy merchants, and Swedish lumbermen to an international group of traders working on Madeira, to English- and German-speaking commercial grandees and sea captains in Philadelphia, to tavern proprietors and storekeepers throughout Pennsylvania and the Ohio River Valley, and ultimately to drinkers in Illinois and Tennessee log cabins, where it played a supporting role in the elaboration of their complex social lives and cultures. The boundaries of empire were extremely permeable, and drinkers made the most of the situation.

In earlier research, I repeatedly encountered non-British imports in British America, and I wondered what they were doing there. It was surprising how little imperial historians, including the "new" British imperial historians who began publishing several decades ago, had considered them. Scholars working in this tradition—and I include myself among them—have written as if boundaries were seldom transgressed. Although scholars have been aware of the "unbounded" behavior of distributors and other early modern agents, they have rarely examined how it functioned in practice. By confining themselves to studying particular imperial and colonial constructs, they have developed neither the historiography nor the models to understand and fully explain the intertwined nature of the early modern Atlantic economy. It is not that they have believed in the separation of empires in reality, but that they have nonetheless subsequently created one historiographically. If one accepts their analyses at face value, the great age of transnational borrowing that was the "Age of European Discovery" declined into an "Age of Imperial Self-Sufficiency": in the latter, colonies traded mainly with their mother countries and received ideas and norms only from them; metropolitans exerted the most significant influences upon inhabitants of their empire's peripheries; interaction and negotiation with the center were the most important forces impinging upon early modern lives.[9] Yet the more I have studied the early modern Atlantic economy, the more I have come to realize that the seventeenth- and eighteenth-century empires are actually difficult to separate because they were intertwined; Europeans, Africans, and Americans constantly engaged each other across imperial boundaries in the years between the outbreak of the English Civil War and the fall of Napoleon.[10] Interimperial commerce, both legal and illegal, shaped everyday life in the Atlantic world to a remarkable degree by constituting much of the engagement. Trading and consuming the same goods—even when geographic or national communities laid particular, distinctive meanings on them—created a vocabulary for a cross-imperial Atlantic culture.[11]

A DECENTRALIZED, NETWORKED, AND SELF-ORGANIZED WORLD

How does a commodity history that crosses economic roles and imperial geographies confirm, complicate, or change our view of the early modern Atlantic world? In other words, how did the bridging of an entire oceanic market actually work, in detail, and to what effect? The study of Madeira shows how decentralized the early modern Atlantic was, with widely dispersed agency and frequent transgression of imperial boundaries. This complicates the standard historiography, which has largely remained in imperial channels or, worse, in the American case, treated North America as self-sufficient. At the same time, analysis of the Madeira wine complex shows that world as extensively linked by networks—family, ethnic, religious, business, and social—that participants created and managed. Historians have acknowledged this connectedness but have not appreciated its extent. Moreover, examining the Madeira case reveals that critical phenomena in that world emerged "self-organized," as lower-order relationships collectively created larger, useful economic and social institutions.

A DECENTRALIZED WORLD

The people whose lives and businesses and social projects are examined in *Oceans of Wine* lived in a largely decentralized world that allowed considerable room for individual agency. Contrary to both contemporary "mercantilist" thinking and some theoretically enriched understanding, this world was remarkable for a weak implementation of central governments' directives and a loose adherence to metropolitan behavioral and cultural trends.

The Madeira wine complex was never centered in England or metropolitan Portugal, nor even to a large degree in Madeira.[12] Rather, it was constituted by the actions of far-flung people who took advantage of the wine to further their own commercial and social goals in the context of their local situations. Producers and distributors responded to mercantilist master plans by taking advantage of the opportunities the plans created, if they created opportunities, and by tolerating, ignoring, or evading them if they did otherwise. Likewise, consumers modified and reinterpreted metropolitan styles, adapting them to their own situations rather than merely emulating them, or even invented styles of their own. Individuals and the "peripheral" institutions and networks they built mediated the influence of mother countries and dominant cultures. In extended imperial communities and porous interimperial markets, authority derived from what Jack Greene, writing about political communities, described as an extended and delicate process of negotiation, in which inhabitants in the peripheries were principals.[13]

The agent-negotiator who flourished in such a world—by seizing opportunities to achieve his goals—was a quintessential "entrepreneur." This role or something like it dates at least to the thirteenth century, but it acquired greater precision in the eighteenth century, when writers attached traits of self-employment, self-interest, and risk taking. Since then, three aspects of entrepreneurship have emerged as critical: a willingness to shoulder uncertainty and risk, management, and creative opportunism.[14] Among the overseas and inland traders who distributed Madeira wine, these features were common.[15] Trade was risky business in the early modern world. It was hazardous for traders along the Ohio River who ordered wine on their own accounts—the wine might not come, it might come with unexpected charges for transport and storage along the way, or it might not suit customer tastes. It was dangerous as well for those who left their homes and families for a remote Atlantic island with the hope, but not the guarantee, of sending back products that others would buy. Traders mitigated these risks by aggressively managing their businesses. Their letter books are full of descriptions of how they controlled operations and finances, and how they managed their customers—informing, importuning, flattering, cajoling, demanding, and all the time selling, selling, selling. In the second half of the eighteenth century, the island's merchant-exporters implemented numerous innovations that transformed the production of Madeira. These innovations spread from merchant to merchant; even today, Madeira wine is produced using their techniques. Across the ocean, Randle and John Mitchell, merchants who supplied wine to the Pennsylvania backcountry, devised a rudimentary version of the chain store just before the American Revolution—apparently the first in the English-speaking world. The Mitchells' operation did not last, and the chain-store form of organization would be reinvented later, but instances like this manifest the creative opportunism characterizing many of the agents in this decentralized era, while also revealing the pressure from customers and competitors that spawned such initiatives.

The reality of decentralization and the power of agency complicates the traditional understanding of states and empires that assumes the centrality of mother countries and their rulers, of institutions like law and empire, and of ideas like mercantilism.[16] This perspective colors the best scholarship, from John Brewer's analysis of the emergence of the modern state in England through changes in administration, logistics, and financing, to John McCusker and Russell Menard's argument for the centrality of trade and the increasing powers of metropolitan government in the development of the British-American economy.[17] By contrast, the Madeira trade shows that the influence of the state was considerably more indirect. For instance, although Britain's alliance with Portugal differentially affected the economic prospects of English-speaking traders doing business with Lisbon, Porto, and Madeira, and those trading with Bordeaux or Cadiz, it did not create a product or link distribution networks with commercial institutions or connect goods with their sumptuary displays, much less fix the mental associations of those displays. Central authorities—states, military and administrative structures, and metropolitan tastes and ideologies—affected the Atlantic worlds less than is often assumed or evidenced, and their dictates were much more subject to local interpretation.[18]

The power of individuals within the decentralized contexts in which they operated also complicates traditional views of action and structure in the lives of producers, distributors, and consumers.[19] Historians who study the agency of individuals, as compared to institutions and other social constructs, are often torn between two perspectives, one of which, exemplified by the long-lived fashion for biographies of influential people, emphasizes the role of strong, creative, *commenting on everybody every which way!*

or disruptive individuals whose actions determine events. The other, more influential in recent decades, shows actors and their actions embedded in their communities' social, economic, and legal structures, which both create and limit their freedom of action and thought. To understand the early modern Atlantic world of wine as a whole, both perspectives must be brought to bear, in part by noting that causality is reciprocal: individuals are embedded in a world and created by it; they also change the world by their actions and responses to their fellow members of the society and the nonhuman environment. Individuals produced and reproduced their worlds, which in turn produced and reproduced the people, activities, and attitudes of which they were comprised. Richard Hill, who founded one of the more successful eighteenth-century Madeira houses, left for Madeira to escape the stigma of bankruptcy in his Quaker community in Maryland, whose political-economic institutions of contract and forfeiture and social institutions of ostracism and opprobrium made exile an attractive option. Hill's actions reaffirmed the attitudes of his community—exile was more honorable than living in financial embarrassment—and reproduced the fortune-seeking aspirations that had motivated his forebears to leave Europe for America. At the same time, his actions created new economic and social contexts by improving commercial communication across the ocean, providing a model for commercial success, and instructing his customers (the same Marylanders he had just left in disgrace) on how to use wine to portray themselves as ladies and gentlemen. This is neither another "great man" story, nor one of an individual buffeted by his state or environment.[20]

Information gathering and problem solving for men like the Mitchells were dispersed processes, a reality economists have long appreciated. The Viennese-born economist Friedrich von Hayek was among the early proponents of the idea that markets succeed because they aggregate dispersed agents' local and particular information. "The most significant fact about this system," he noted, is "the economy of knowledge with which it operates, or how little the individual participants need to know in order to be able to take the right action" because they can rely on prices to convey others' knowledge.[21] Economists today are more skeptical of the informational efficiency of prices and markets than Hayek in the 1940s, but the picture he painted—of dispersed buyers and sellers, acting in ignorance of each other and each other's information, using prices to infer the relative value of goods, and making decisions for themselves rather than by referring to a central monitor or authority—remains the economists' canonical model. Even when the model only partially recapitulates historical reality, "decentralized decision-making processes" enabled "societies to maximize the efforts to explore alternative ways of solving problems."[22]

The seventeenth- and eighteenth-century markets for wine reveal the dispersal of information and its effect on decision making in operation. Individuals who solved problems with the resources and information they had at hand collectively created what might, somewhat grandly, be called an Atlantic wine system. Joseph Kershaw and his partners in an upcountry South Carolina store, for instance, gauged the demand for imported liquor by heeding the local increase in population, the danger of drinking water from polluted neighborhood streams, and the paucity of locally grown fruits and vegetables that could be distilled. Their buyers in Charlestown and, even more so, their suppliers in Madeira had no such information, but built customer networks based on the upcountry retailers' demand. Another part of the system, the road to the Ohio Valley over which much wine traveled, was laid in chunks and spurts by Indians, retailers and traders, army soldiers and militiamen, and settlers, all of whom contributed because they believed improving "their" stretch would promote their interest, business, or community. Once the new road was built, others could turn it to their own uses.

A NETWORKED WORLD

The individuals who populate *Oceans of Wine* did not live in an atomized, anomic world. Indeed, acknowledging the decentralized nature of Atlantic life sheds more intense light on the informal and far-reaching nature of the interpersonal connections among them. People linked themselves to one another, and the linkages formed networks. As historians like Chris Bayly and social scientists like Michel Callon and Bruno Latour suggest, networks facilitated the movement of people, objects, and ideas that crisscrossed the land- and marine-scapes of the early modern era. Atlantic-wide networks served as the integument of an evolving interimperial economy.[23]

In the last twenty years, scholars working in disciplines ranging from the sciences and mathematics to economics and sociology have paid considerable attention to networks as their investigations have shifted focus from individual atoms and discrete components to the universe of relationships. One of their most robust findings is that individuals connect to the world at large through others whose networks do not completely overlap theirs. The sociologist Mark Granovetter first observed this phenomenon, emphasizing how social networks generally, yet incompletely, overlap.[24] Duncan Watts and Stephen Strogatz formalized his insight, demonstrating how, if agents have partially overlapping networks, it takes only a handful of "super-connectors" to create a "small world," where each agent is connected to all or most of the others by a few intermediaries.[25] Many, perhaps most, eighteenth-century traders and buyers personally knew the relatively small number of people with whom they dealt. The Granovetter-Watts-Strogatz view highlights the importance of those who built more expansive links between suppliers, partners, correspondents, and consumers who were often physically remote and previously unacquainted with one another.

George Frey, a German redemptioner who ran a tavern, general store, and milling operation in Middletown, Pennsylvania, is a good example of such a trader. He managed his retailing businesses by building and nurturing connections to rural suppliers and patrons. He also developed and maintained links to suppliers and agents in Philadelphia, some of whom became customers for barter goods he had accepted in Middletown. Frey's connections reached back across the Atlantic to the Palatinate and people he had known in his youth, as he crafted a network that put Philadelphia wine importers in contact with Rhine wine shippers and linked wine exporters in Madeira to clients like the New York storekeeper who was the nephew of the New Jersey glassmaker who supplied Frey with window plate and bottle ware. Frey never met many of these people, although he was intimately linked to them. Like Frey, expansive traders of the long eighteenth century were more likely to leave records; so much of the story of the development of Atlantic distribution can be organized around them. They actively managed their suppliers, customers, and even competitors to create and maintain networks that connected drinkers in the Americas, Europe, Africa, and India with cultivators of grapes in Portugal, stave- and hoop makers and merchants in Scotland and Sweden, brandy producers and distributors in France and Spain, bottle makers in England and the Netherlands, and gesso manufacturers in Italy.

The network perspective focuses attention on people's contacts and the relationships that govern them, networks being "any collection of actors . . . that pursue repeated, enduring exchange relations with one another and, at the same time, lack a legitimate organizational authority to arbitrate and resolve disputes that may arise during the exchange relationships," in contrast to a textbook market's episodic relations and a hierarchy's recognized line of authority.[26] Ideas, institutions, and forces affect network members when they are brought to bear by the people with whom they interact. Thus, people's acquaintances and relationships created their identities: whom you did business with, whom you influenced, and who influenced you—that is, whom you talked to and corresponded with—was who you were. As participants in economic life, people responded to particular customers, employees, and suppliers. They created their social personae in reaction to specific characters they encountered in person or by repute.

is this about wine or int'l trade / hist theory?

This is a social conception of agents and agency, with people, their actions, and their institutions closely situated and embedded in webs of relationships and patterns of interaction. Some of the models already existed, and individuals adopted and adapted them. Others they constructed and improved upon anew to meet their needs.

In establishing links and building networks, the people of the seventeenth- and eighteenth-century Atlantic world created an infrastructure that bound them together—as each others' suppliers and customers, as partners, agents, and competitors, and eventually as compatriots. The networks they built were commercial, designed to sell goods from the inland settlements of North America to the eastern port cities and the world beyond, and vice versa. They built networks with growing numbers of correspondents, over lengthening distances and with increasing functionality. Once established, they turned these arrangements to extracommercial purposes as well. Because networks were composed of personal relationships and dealt with a wide range of subjects, they passed along both specific and general information; economic, social, and cultural norms; and commercial, moral, and political attitudes. When Londoners, Madeirans, and Philadelphians communicated about acquiring, transporting, and financing a cargo of wine, they also transmitted military and diplomatic news, shared their opinions on matters such as reform, independence, and revolution, and established guidelines for fiscal and moral probity, directly through instruction and indirectly through commentary on others. At their most intense, members' ties were ratified in contractual partnerships and marital alliances that cut across ethnic, religious, and national allegiances. Whatever the case, out of seemingly disconnected actors, impulses, conditions, and opportunities, the networks that members built created a dense, integrated, interimperial set of social, economic, and cultural institutions.

Network members reconfigured their networks between the early seventeenth century and the early nineteenth century. Transoceanic markets existed before 1640, of course, and producers, distributors, and consumers used networks to span them. In taking advantage of the innovations in shipping, communications, and finance over the period 1640–1815, they made the networks denser, connecting more people in more dispersed places, and carrying more and more varied information. The thickening of information along the networks propagated the Enlightenment explosion in investigating, printing, and reading that, in turn, facilitated shifts in production, distribution, and consumption. Wine was an early "site" for the increase in information density, as it was consumed all along the commodity distribution chain and consuming it was one of the age's more important forms of sociability.

key

A SELF-ORGANIZED WORLD

No state or person set out to create an interimperial Atlantic market or to articulate an oceanic wine culture. Nor did anyone plan to develop Atlantic-wide institutions or networks. Such structures were too grandiose and complicated—and too intangible—to have been imagined in advance. Yet they came forth, and contemporaries recognized them. They were "emergent" phenomena that no one designed or maintained; few were even aware of them in their entirety. They were created by decentralized individuals working out solutions to local problems and extending the solutions through their networks to places, personalities, and situations one step beyond, where they were adopted and adapted. Economies and societies like this can be called "self-organizing," and it is useful to think of the early modern Atlantic in terms of the self-organization of markets and cultures.

The idea of self-organization—that "the internal organization of a system, normally an open system, increases automatically without being guided or managed by an outside source"—is an old one, with its roots in Descartes' *Discourse on Method* and eighteenth-century naturalists' drive to comprehend universal laws of form. Its modern conception, reintroduced in 1947, defined a self-organizing system as an entity that "changes its basic structure as a function of its experience and environment," but by 1960 it was widely agreed that "only organisms and their environment taken together organize themselves" and evolve.[27] In its present incarnation, the idea is grounded in the work of late twentieth-century biology, chemistry, physics, computer science, and neuroscience, all of which have investigated the ordered behavior of large-scale aggregates as the result of complex interactions among many smaller-scale elements that operate according to simple behavioral rules. The focus on phenomena that result from interactions among individuals gives the concept its analytical value. It is less valuable if organization is imposed from outside or can be reduced to the analysis of individual elements. In science, the idea has been a response to the constraints of traditional disciplinary approaches, as practitioners begin to exhaust the explanatory power of the idealizations and assumptions that made the analysis of individuals in isolation tractable.

The idea of self-organization explicitly addresses the connections between higher-order phenomena and the multitude of individuals that create them or make them up. A canonical example in science is the state of a substance. A collection of H_2O molecules can be organized in one of three states: solid ice, liquid water, or gaseous steam.[28] However, this is not true of individual molecules: an isolated H_2O molecule does not have a state. This is because the state is an organizational dimension of the collection; it depends on the interactions among the molecules in the collection. The interactions differ when the collection is organized as ice, water, or steam. The collection is self-organized, as opposed to simply "organized," because the organization is the result of the internal relations among the molecules of the collection. The organization responds to its environment, but not uniformly. When heat is applied to a collection of H_2O molecules at room temperature, nothing happens to the substance's state; it is liquid. When the temperature rises beyond 100 degrees Celsius at sea level on Earth, however, there is a transition, from liquid water to gaseous steam. The internal relations of the molecules change.

This conception is useful for writing history because it allows us to switch focus when we consider people's actions, seeing them from their own points of view (isolated H_2O molecules), and also observing how the relationships among them create "higher-order" cultural, social, economic, and political phenomena (ice, water, or steam). Individuals' actions are specific to them and motivated by their proximate needs and goals. Social phenomena are organizational dimensions of groups of individuals; they result from the relations among them.

So dangerous
To simpli-
daun to
steam!

Turning the spotlight on self-organizing characteristics allows the historian to connect the emergent features of seventeenth- and eighteenth-century Atlantic life to the individual actors and actions that made them up. By the latter part of the eighteenth century, a Madeira wine culture had emerged in the Atlantic; it was multinational and interimperial, one of the first commodities to acquire these characteristics. The wine was drunk in cosmopolitan, coastal South Carolina and rustic, backcountry Virginia, in the East Indies and the West Indies, in polite circles in London and rude military messes along the Mississippi River, where it assumed similar meanings—with hints of luxury and cosmopolitanism—the heritage of their origin in a global conversation about the drink. The Madeira wine culture structured and constrained the possibilities for drinkers. It established whom Henry Hill of Philadelphia drank with in public and whom he invited into his home, which drinks connoted health or dissolution and which cosmopolitanism or patriotism, whether a toast at a dinner party showed courtesy or incompetence, and how to display one's wineglasses, decanting apparatus, and cellar. These cultural "rules of the (Madeira) game" were components of an apparatus of social status, meaning, and display with Atlantic scope. Its essential features came about without central design or direction, but not without individuals' thought and intent. Wine producers, distributors, and consumers engaged in intense personal conversations about wine culture: how to ascertain the quality of the wine, the right way to display and serve it, and how to make a proper toast with it. They carefully set out their decanters and corkscrews for respectable company to show their access to resources and their social acumen. In doing so, they connected their activities to each other, provisioned themselves, and made sense of their shared experiences. From this, a Madeira wine culture emerged.[29]

THE CASE OF MADEIRA

The decentralized, networked, and self-organized features of early modern transatlantic, transimperial markets emerge from the story of a single commodity—wine: how it was produced, distributed, and consumed, and how it was deployed in people's economic, social, and political projects. Madeira wine is particularly apposite: people in a province of Portugal produced it; a group of international traders residing there exported it; North, Caribbean, and South Americans and Europeans imported and consumed it. While it is not the only transimperial example well suited for the telling of such a tale—other commodities like ceramics and hardware flowed to communities around the ocean with little respect for borders—the island that produced the wine is geographically central, and so offers an unusually advantageous site for observing circumoceanic flows.[30] Madeira wine dominated wine imports into Anglo-America between 1640 and 1815, whereas Port wine dominated Brazilian and British imports. Madeira wine was important to the economy of North and Caribbean America and so to a significant portion of the Atlantic market. It remains relatively unstudied, at least from the standpoint of the interactions of its producers, distributors, and consumers.[31]

To manage this task, I pared down the inquiry's scope. (This may come as a surprise to those who find the book's size daunting.) The book focuses primarily on one island and its durable and desirable wine in the years from 1640 to 1815, the industry's golden age. In 1640, when the Crown of Portugal reverted to Portuguese control after sixty years of Spanish rule, and with the demise of Madeira's sugar trade, the island's wine trade began. It peaked 175 years later, when the security to Atlantic shipping channels returned after the conclusion of the Napoleonic Wars in 1815.[32] *Oceans of Wine* tracks the commodity's flow around the globe, examining the imports into numerous cities, while highlighting specific ports such as Philadelphia and New York whose records are better than, say, Kingston and Charleston, and focusing on a single consumer market, Anglophone America, this latter perspective being justified by the fact that half to three-quarters of Madeira's exports was consumed there. It is a question, in principle: How "Atlantic" is a commodity if four-fifths of it moves, even in complicated ways, between two subregions of the oceanic community? Yet such apportionment was the case of most commodities; moreover, exhaustive research reveals that there are few detectable differences in distributing Madeira (and other wines as well) to and consuming it (them) in other parts of that world.

The material available on Madeira and its wine is immense. My inquiries beyond distribution to production and consumption uncovered a vast array of records, far more than I had hoped for. Related documents fetched up as far east as Calcutta, west to Los Angeles, north to Copenhagen, and south all the way to Rio de Janeiro. Traditional and nontraditional sources, some well used and others unknown, traversed the globe like the wine whose history they narrate. Landowner/tenant-grower contracts, accounts of exchanges between growers and traders, and government and church records document the labors of producers and the amounts of wine produced in each parish. A treasure of distribution sources undergird this project, with registers for Madeira's port of Funchal providing a nearly unbroken run of import and export records, complemented by similar material for the ports of Brazil, British America, and the United States. In addition, there are the less-used but very rich papers of British, American, Portuguese, and Brazilian traders: at least a dozen collections of letters and accounts of Madeira's British and American exporters preserved by descendants or held in national or local archives and libraries, supplemented by two collections for Portuguese exporters, along with eight for British importers, and sixty-three for their American counterparts. The papers of many are remarkably complete, but they are only the proverbial tip of the iceberg, atop a mass of materials documenting the supply and custom of retail operations: from general stores and specialty shops to taverns and peddling concerns. Beyond personal and business papers is a wealth of related sources: architectural and archaeological surveys, advertisements, paintings and engravings, court cases, and probate inventories. Finally, newspapers, tavern and store registers, diaries, letters, menus, grocery and cellar lists, purchase invoices, and the like—anything that sheds light on what drinks people acquired and what they did with them—contribute to the measurement and interpretation of consumption.

OCEANS OF WINE

The story told by the manuscript and printed materials unfolds in eleven chapters. Chapter 1, "The Triumph of Bacchus," probes unused archival material to analyze the history of Madeira, the tiny island where "the strangeness of everything was interesting, . . . exciting," and often challenging, which figured as a point of encounter and articulation of peoples and cultures.[33] The place, the people, and their institutions—and changes to all three—provide a small yet powerful lens through which to glimpse the emergence and development of a transatlantic, interimperial community in the years between 1640 and 1815. This chapter also introduces the book's three substantive sections: production (chapters 2–3), distribution (chapters 4–8), and consumption (chapters 9–11).

Chapter 2, "The Culture of the Vine," looks at the agricultural producers of *✶ Ch 2 ✶* wine on Madeira, their social and economic institutions, and the process of cultivation as it played out year after year in the life of the vineyard, and relates how the fortunes of the island were closely linked to international trade via distributors and customers around the Atlantic rim. Chapter 3, "The Enlivening Grape," *✶ Ch 3* describes how the product so loved by George Washington was "invented" in the eighteenth century by a group of mainly Anglophone wine manufacturers and distributors. It focuses on the evolution of vinicultural practices, chronicling how innovation was introduced and implemented in the preindustrial Atlantic world—not from the center but from the periphery, and not through directives but from negotiation and conversation.

The story of distribution occupies center stage in any history of the emerging Atlantic market. Chapter 4, "'A Revolution in This Trade,'" describes the increasing scale and scope of Madeira wine distribution throughout the Atlantic and to the world beyond. Chapter 5, "A 'Commerce of Minds,'" looks in detail at one of the book's central arguments, that continual conversations among people around the oceanic rim created an Atlantic economy in the early modern period. After anatomizing the cohort of exporters, chapter 5 focuses on the central component of their trade—creating and maintaining customer networks—and sketches how exporters moved out from their initial reliance on kin, patronage, and peer groups to the cultivation of weaker, more impersonal ties in building their businesses. Chapter 6, "Merchants into Capitalists," highlights how these merchants evolved from just buying and selling to incorporate manufacturing, network management, and capital deployment within their expanding enterprises.

Chapter 7, "Strong Networks of Weak Ties," investigates the work of the American counterparts to Madeira's exporters: the importers and wholesalers in the large port towns of the Atlantic seaboard. In the course of managing distribution, these men on the ocean's colonial western shores took control of the businesses, pushed trade inland, specialized in commodities and markets and, thus, built capital. Chapter 8, "The Wet Goods Business," looks at drink retailers, whose work was transformed in the 1700s as the number of taverns and stores increased and the scope of their undertakings expanded. By 1800, wine retailers had become important distributors and wine retailing was now a specialty, not only in eastern ports but also at backcountry crossroads. Rural retailing is an

American story: Americans built the stores, supplied them from the coast, took inland produce to market, and provided the customers with credit. It is also a middleman story: opportunistic and creative intermediaries constructing yet another set of links in the decentralized and self-organized economy of the Atlantic world. Chapter 8 focuses on taverns and stores, documenting the development of economic life within "peripheral" markets and the creation and maintenance of their commercial links and networks, as well as showing how networks and the conversations around which they were constructed integrated backcountry and urban folk into a wine culture that spanned the Atlantic.

Part 3, chapters 9–11, deals with wine consumption. British Americans drank prodigious quantities of a growing variety of imported European wines in domestic settings between 1640 and 1815, endowing these wines with increasingly elaborate distinctions. Yet, whether one looks at drinking in the age of John Winthrop or of John Marshall, several features are not adequately explained by current economic and social writing on consumers, which part 3 seeks to redress. Chapter 9, "'Articles of Nourishment Both Mundane and Useful,'" reviews the wines available in British America and when, where, and how they were drunk. It also "recuperate[s] the home — the place of feminine and familial experience — as a site of meaning, history and knowledge" about the disseminating and drinking of alcohol.[34] The remaining chapters take a more qualitative, interpretative tack. Since food was not just "a system of alimentation . . . but also a system of non-verbal communication," these chapters analyze the meanings of wine. Starting with the proposition that historians have shied away from consequential materiality — that is, from connecting material practices and remains to past people's psychological, sociological, and cultural projects — they deploy insights from the study of dramaturgic performance and "boundary objects" to recapture how people used or made sense of terminology, behavior, and paraphernalia.[35] Chapter 10, "'Power to Give Sudden Refreshment' and Respect," looks inward, at the arts of consumption and the meanings associated with them, as Americans selected imported wines for increasingly elaborated purposes. Seventeenth- and early eighteenth-century Americans, for example, thought wine and spirits promoted physical health and social well-being. Chapter 11, "*Ars Bibendi*," extends this discussion to eighteenth- and early nineteenth-century American consumers, who expanded the conversation about wine beyond these two traditional uses; it now became part of their discussions about the ways their often increasingly commercialized lives were or should be lived. In doing so, it pays considerable attention to drinking artifacts. Such objects helped create the discursive links between producers, distributors, and consumers, offer exquisite examples of the material world of the Atlantic, and provide an appropriate conclusion to the narrative account.

Oceans of Wine begins on the Portuguese coast and ends along the banks of the Mississippi River. It tells the story of how a wine came to be made in Madeira; how, in distributing it around the world and particularly in America, individuals linked the markets and cultures of the Atlantic; and how Americans used Madeira and other wines to represent themselves and their cultures. It explains how a particular integrated market—of Madeira wine—grew and developed in the two centuries after England joined Spain, Portugal, Holland, and France in vying for a share of the riches of the Americas. And it shows a dense, integrated, interimperial set of institutions and ideas evolved within the Atlantic world out of seemingly disconnected actors, impulses, conditions, and opportunities. By the turn of the nineteenth century, Madeira the luxury drink was served when the parson came to visit in backcountry Ohio, during dinner on Jamaican and Curaçao plantations, in Army messes and hospitals throughout India, to patrons of London clubs and taverns, and at country houses and ceilidhs in Scotland. An Atlantic community existed that was linked by shared (perhaps stolen) production techniques, kinship and friendship relations, common consumption patterns—and conversations. Madeira was integral to that community. Conversations were neither grand nor philosophical nor even scintillating; they were plain, practical, and persuasive. But Madeira nevertheless created a common commercial, cultural, and conceptual space that pervaded the Atlantic basin, affecting people in Europe, Africa, the Americas—even India and China. Individually, Madeira's producers, distributors, and consumers conversed to take advantage of local opportunities; collectively, they invented a new world.

THE TRIUMPH OF BACCHUS

The Madeira that visitors found in 1815 was a tiny island that might have been an insignificant part of the Portuguese empire, except that, because of its location along major Atlantic wind and water currents, it became one of the principal provisioning nodes in a vast transoceanic trading web that had been spun during the seventeenth and eighteenth centuries. Even in 1640, Madeira was already a point of rest and refilling. Travelers stopped there to quell their appetite for food and drink, and captains to pick up shipping supplies. Over time, it became an increasingly desirable entrepôt for redistributing goods to all parts of the world, whether the other side of the island, mainland Europe, Africa, the Americas, or India and Asia. Chief among those goods was the place's principal product, wine.

The island also became a markedly cosmopolitan place in these 175 years, a point of encounter and articulation of peoples and cultures, an arena in which "the strangeness of everything was interesting" and challenging. In a place marked by a "combination of objects curiously, ay wonderfully novel to an English eye and certainly not [to] be met with at a similar distance in any other direction from Hyde Park Corner," nationalities met, traded, and clashed. Madeira emerged as a retreat for the peoples living around the Atlantic at the zenith of its wine's golden age: aesthetes desiring inspiration and consumptives seeking relief found in its scenery and climate escape from the grind of everyday life. Visiting in 1813, the novelist Theodore Hook sensed its appeal: "No place in the world . . . could have been [better] selected" for a "retreat, in which old associations and habits could so soon have been got rid of," and new ones adopted.[1]

More than anything else, Madeirans inhabited a richly textured crossroads community and mentality. Both were porphyritic and amalgamative in nature,

whereby elements combined but did not lose their own traits. This was a place
that was unabashedly provincial yet highly cosmopolitan, unquestionably Portuguese yet remarkably British, commercial yet religious, a market important for
world trade yet dominated by local agriculture, a node central to the elaboration
of global commercial and social networks yet possessed of only one real export
and a small population. The island, the inhabitants, and their institutions constitute a small yet powerful alembic in which to distill traits and changes that
shaped the wider Atlantic marketplace.

THE PLACE

The island of Madeira was situated at a crossroads in the Age of Sail: 32 degrees, 51 minutes north latitude, at its southern extremity, and 17 degrees, 16 minutes west longitude, at its western extremity. It is 1,457 miles south-southwest of
London, 559 miles southwest of Lisbon, 408 miles southeast of São Miguel in
the Azores, 340 miles west of Safi in Morocco, 216 miles north of Tenerife in the
Canaries, 2,619 miles northeast of Barbados, and 2,761 miles southeast of New
York.[2]

Geographers, traders, and mariners alike thought Madeira and its appendages
(Porto Santo and the three uninhabited Desertas), like the other Wine Islands of
the Azores and Canaries, belonged more to Africa than to Europe.[3] It lies near
the confluence of the North-East Trade Winds and the Rennell and Canary Currents. Since the prevailing Atlantic winds move clockwise in the Northern Hemisphere, and the currents move south-southwesterly, most vessels westbound from
Europe passed nearby, whether or not they stopped.[4] From London, for instance,
America-bound ships headed west out of the English Channel. At the Lizard
(the southernmost point of Britain), they steered WSW and, around 10 or 12
degrees W, set their course for Madeira's vicinity, accommodating the northwest-
erly winds that predominated off Portugal's coast. Near Madeira, relatively steady
winds and the Canary Current carried them southward, west of the Canaries,
and then into the North-East Trade Winds, which blew from April through September toward Bermuda. Given its comparatively temperate weather, constant
wind, and freedom from fog and ice, this southern shipping route was the preferred outbound route to America from the countries of northern and western
Europe. Thus, the island was perfectly situated for trade.[5]

Madeira is small—34 miles long and 14 miles wide, 90 miles in circumference,
286 square miles in area. It is smaller than Man, Guernsey, São Miguel, Tenerife,
Santiago in the Cape Verdes, Barbados, or Long Island. But it is—and was—impressive. From the initial reports of its discovery by João Gonçalves Zarco and

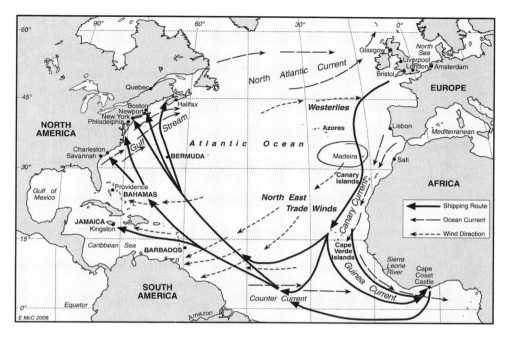

Figure 1.1. Madeira's placement in the prevailing Atlantic winds and currents.
Source: Drawn by Eliza McClennen, Cartographer.

Tristão Vaz Teixeira in the fifteenth century through the subsequent assessments of its resources by mariners and scientists to the impassioned romantic accounts penned by residents and visitors in the nineteenth century, it captured the imagination.[6] Centuries before, the ancients had written about an island that could only have been Madeira, believing this "Queen of Islands" to be the Elysian Fields—"an earthly Paradise"; their idea of a place dedicated to happiness reverberated throughout subsequent descriptions of the island. It was "the pleasantest Place" at the beginning of the seventeenth century, "fort agréable" at midcentury, and "the delightfullest Place in the World" at the beginning of the eighteenth century. Adam Gordon, on his way to North America, felt "pleasure" on the approach when he "could distinguish the uncommonly beautifull Landscapes with accuracy." George Washington's friend Robert Stewart found it "as charming as the imagination can well perceive," and the explorer George Forster thought it much like "a fairy garden." After the American Revolution, "the sublimity of the scenery" overwhelmed spectators: it was, the purser of the China-bound *United States* thought in 1784, "one of the most beautiful islands at present"; "nothing," one English nobleman admitted in 1792, "could be more picturesque and inviting"; and even the most dour Scotsmen were moved with "pleasurable" sensations on approaching it, the "Nature of the Country" being "peculiarly favorable to such impression, . . . picturesque to the greatest degree."[7]

Yet what was "picturesque and enchanting" to many was full of menace and imperfection to others: "huge perpendicular rocks, lofty precipices, prominent ridges, deep excavations and chasms, innumerable cascades, liberally supplied with rivulets, beautiful vallies, deep gullies and ravines, containing immense torrents of water" painted "a highly varied, sublime, and [a] no less alarming picture of nature." Drama and danger coincided. "The Queen" was not only beautiful and fertile but also powerful, capable of destruction, and "inaccessible." "Thick Fog" shrouded her, hiding small islands nearby, extremely rocky shoals, sometimes even the island itself.[8]

The artist John Greenwood captured what first struck the eye when the fog parted: Madeira's height (plate 1). It is as if some of the Alps had been set down in the tropics. Steep, rugged, and uneven, the island was formed some 20 million years ago during the Miocene Period, when lava spewed up from the ocean floor and built up a high east-west mountainous spine. Some peaks are "very high," higher by a thousand feet than any mountains in Portugal or Britain. Cabo Girão, west of Câmara de Lobos, is the second highest cliff in the world. The height evoked strangeness and unease. At a "distance of three leagues," the island bore "a very hideous appearance, occasioned by several vast mountains, the lower parts of which seemed of a red gravely colour and quite barren, and the summits" bore the "dark dirty green" captured by Greenwood. This vista was "odd almost beyond a possibility of description," though voyagers repeatedly made the attempt. It was "one ridge of mountains, of an amazing height, running east and west, rising quite from the water's edge to the summit"—a profile sketched by Thomas Prince in his 1710 ship log (figure 1.2). It was not "the least flat near the water" but rose "instantly from a rocky shore, to an horizon broke by the beautiful irregularity of the summit of the hills." Nor was the range one continuous slope, for its sides were "interspersed with an infinite number of smaller hills, and little hollows between them." The island was "one entire piece of irregularity." The only exception was an uninhabited "foggy plateau" to the west of the island's center, three and a half miles long by four miles wide, "not at all rocky, but [with] the soil of a stiff red clay," and encircled by a ring of hills from seventy to eighty feet high. Elsewhere, there was hardly a twenty-foot square of level ground anywhere. Even what was planted with vines was rocky land "rising up."[9]

The mountains were blanketed in woods and riven by streams. According to local tradition, the island was heavily forested in 1425, so densely that Zarco gave it the Portuguese name for wood—*madeira*—and then ordered it to be burned,

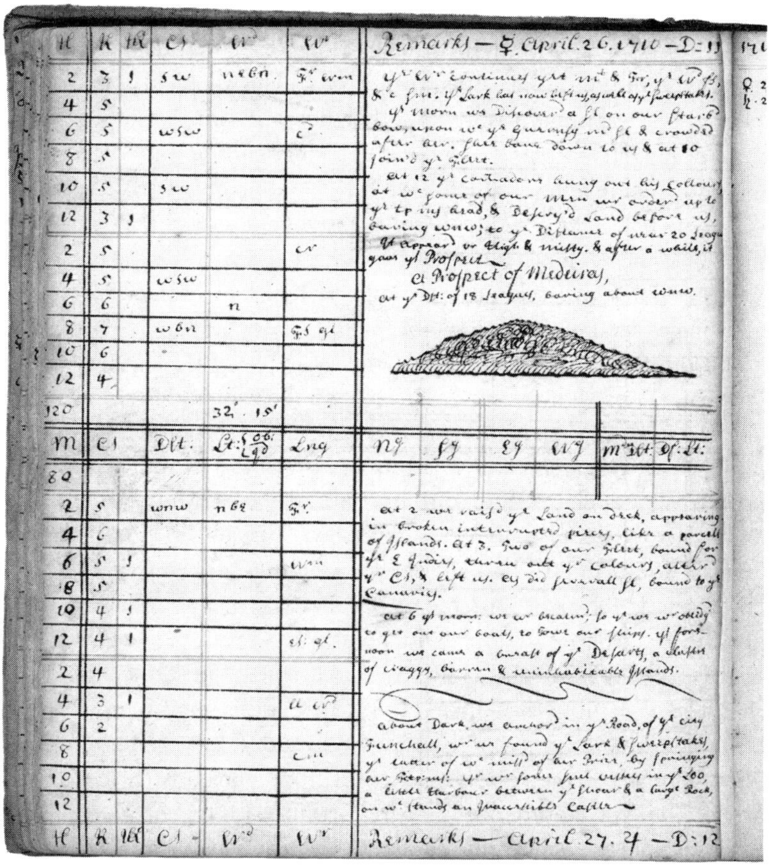

Figure 1.2. "A prospect of Madeira" in Thomas Prince's ship log, 1710.
Source: Courtesy of the Massachusetts Historical Society, Boston.

and burn it supposedly did for seven years. The fires, if real, did little to tame the place and, by the 1600s, heavy growth had returned. Father Antoine Jean de Laval, who passed through on his way to Louisiana in 1720, described the mountains as carpeted with trees up to their summits. Joseph Banks provided a more detailed picture nearly fifty years later: the lower reaches were covered in vines, above them stood "woods of chestnut and pine of immense extent," and higher up "wild timber of kinds not known in Europe."[10]

More to the point of its productivity, the "fertility and goodness" of the land were "very rich" and "uncommon," so fecund that it encouraged "everything almost spontaneously"; it was especially "proper for the vine." The most common soils were degraded pumice and a dark red earth, both of which were "mixed with a portion of sand and marl"; smaller hills possessed a dark red clay and "a black or gray sand"; other places enjoyed a very black mold.[11] Likewise, Madeira was blessed with abundant water, another necessity for grape growing. Eight rivers, numerous streams, and a plethora of springs carried water from the center of the island. "There fell from the Mountains," one visiting American sea captain noted, "many fine Rills of Water," which the inhabitants channeled into aqueducts (*levadas*) and used to water their vines.[12]

Soon after Zarco's arrival in 1425, colonists established a large town and several smaller villages on the more hospitable southern side, before harbors of varying safety and utility: Funchal, which became by 1640 the principal city and capital, dominated a bay between the Loo Rock to the west and the Brazen Head to the east; Marasylo, or Marsilia, lay to the west of Funchal, and Santa Cruz to its east; and Machico stood near the eastern tip. In time, new settlements arose. By 1791, when the merchant William Johnston's map was printed, there were also the towns of Madalena, Calheta, Ponta do Sol, Ribeira Brava, and Câmara de Lobos in the south and the hamlets of Faial, Santana, and São Jorge in the north. Except for the latter small settlements, the north remained relatively unsettled through the first half of the nineteenth century.

Climate not only assisted Madeira production but made it one of the Atlantic's more salubrious commercial hubs. "Healthy Air" was something visitors particularly remarked upon again and again, with "healthy" connoting temperate.[13] It was, they thought, "more moderate" than Europe, North America, or even the Canaries.[14] The "very Temperate" air was "refreshed for Nine Months of the Year by a Sea-breeze in the Day, from Eight in the Morning till Four in the Afternoon, and a Land-breeze in the Night, from Eight at Night to Four the next Morning."[15] Too, the sun was filtered. Between nine and ten in the morning, "a strong vapour" rose "like a cloud," screening the islanders for "the remainder of the day from the rays of the sun, without in the least obstructing the view, or rendering it less clear." Thus "freed from an inconvenient glare of sun-shine," one could work or relax "with greater ease and pleasure."[16]

Islanders enjoyed "a most delightfull Climate." The "extremes of heat and cold" were "never felt." Spring and summer were "the only seasons." Methodical observers all agreed. Dr. William Gourlay, a physician to the resident British, recorded that in 1793–1802 the temperature fluctuated between 74 degrees in the hottest months (August and September) and 62 degrees in the coldest months (December and January). Dr. Nicolau Caetano de Bettencourt Pita, a native, noted in 1812 that the thermometer averaged 72 degrees Fahrenheit in summer and 61 degrees in winter.[17]

There was "scarcely a single object of luxury" "growing either in Europe or the Indies that might not" happily flourish in such a climate. The environment was especially well suited to vines and grapes. Ushering in the planting season, the rains usually began in November and continued through late January or early February. The winds blew from the south and west, and the weather was quite stormy; fierce gales and heavy rains were frequent. "The winter was the only season of the year" when the sky was not "serene." Rainfall averaged about twenty-three inches each year, and most of it fell in the rainy season. Rain generally brought the worst of devastation. "Except on the top of the Mountains," snow and hail were unusual. Drier weather prevailed during late February, March, and April, when pruning was done before sap rose. The ensuing budding and flowering of the vines and the maturation of the grapes occurred at a time of year when the "sky was almost always covered by clouds." Not until July did high temperatures, cloudless skies, and the dry, irritating *leste* winds set in, in advance of a two-month harvest and pressing. Fog was not common on the island's lower reaches in these months, nor was dust, except when raised by the *leste*.[18]

Thus, situation, soil, and climate converged to make Madeira "the garden of the world," a place of contrast and continuity noticed by nearly all who touched there. The island was blanketed with trees. When the island was discovered, it was filled with cedar. By the 1740s, cedar was "seldom to be found," nor were oaks, elms, and limes: they had been replaced by poplars, pines, chestnuts, fruit and nut trees, and "several varieties of brush wood." Exotic specimens included the dragon's blood tree (whose sap was used as "a sovereign remedy for bruises"), the *lignum klodium* (which vied "with mahogany for domestic uses"), and the opuntia (a pear that turned urine red). When Captain Cook's party "botanized" in 1768, it found twenty-five plants previously unknown to science.[19]

As ships came for wine, foreign flora slowly began to complement native growth. Resident merchants aggressively imported and transplanted the stock of plants from both the Old and New Worlds. Grape vines and sugarcane were only the two most prominent. Sweet oranges came from China, while maize, sweet potato, and peanut came from the Americas. Hans Sloane, whose account of his 1687 visit is little more than a catalog of plants and trees, found apples, apricots, peaches, and pears originally native to Europe and Asia, walnuts originally belonging to many places in the Northern Hemisphere except Madeira, and oranges, lemons, citrons, bananas, guavas, figs, quinces, bays, limes, white and black mulberries, dates, yams, and plantains originally "common to . . . hotter parts of the world." In 1748, the pineapple, hardly "a native production," began to appear in "particular gardens," as did cinnamon and guava, which were brought from India via Brazil. More prosaic "vegetables produced by culture"—cabbage, corn, lettuce, and potato—had also been introduced from Europe and America and by 1800 become staples. The island, in short, was ever "fit for producing the Fruits of both Hot and Cold Countries." No "fruit, flower, grain, herb, nor root that growes either in Europe or Africa and great part of America" could not be successfully transplanted there.[20]

THE PEOPLE

GROWTH

"The Queen of Islands" grew from a small settlement with 2,310 inhabitants in 1455 to a substantial agricultural province with a bustling, cosmopolitan trading port and over 110,000 people in 1851.[21] Is population rose rapidly in the first fifty years for which data have survived, 1455–1505, at 3.8 percent per year, on average, and thereafter settled into a slower but fairly steady increase—between 0.5 percent and 0.9 percent per year for the next three and a half centuries, excepting during the period 1675–1760, when growth apparently temporarily stopped.[22]

Migration was quite heavy in the first two centuries of settlement. Europeans and Africans went or were brought to Madeira to take advantage of the island's central location and to exploit its rich resources. Most early settlers came from Portugal, and most subsequent arrivals came from Portugal and its dominions. The best modern estimates suggest that, from 1425 to 1700, 56 percent of all arrivals came from Portugal and its dependencies, another 12 percent came from Spain, and the remainder came from Italy, England, France, and Flanders.[23] Natural increase was great, as well, and it persisted longer than migration. Before 1740, early and widespread marriage, high rates of fertility, and a comparatively long life expectancy contributed to high internal population growth. That increase slowed somewhat in the second half of the eighteenth century. During the 1740s and 1750s, the incidence of marriage declined and the size of family decreased; in addition, child mortality rose, reaching an alarming 59 percent in the period 1759–66, a time in which population rose by only 1.4 percent. Such conditions persisted through 1815.[24]

Growth from immigration and natural increase was held in check by the persistence of these delimiting conditions through 1815 and episodic emigration after the 1660s. Only a third of the island was cultivable, and that was almost fully employed by 1640. Too, most cultivated land was owned by noble families and religious orders. This state of affairs impinged upon the opportunities and aspirations of the lower and middling sort, who earned their livelihood from working the land. Emigration from the island, minimal and sporadic before the 1660s, reached disturbingly unprecedented levels by the 1680s. The collapse of

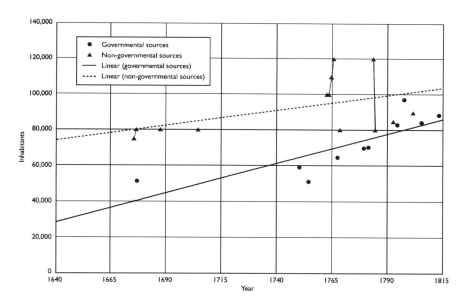

Figure 1.3. Madeira population, 1640–1815.
Sources: Phérotée de Lacroix, *Relation Universelle de l'Afrique, Ancienne et Moderne*,
(Lyon, 1688), 3:711; Shattocke, "Description," 1675, Eg. 2395, fol. 649, British Library,
London; Christopher Jeaffreson, *A Young Squire of the Seventeenth Century* (London,
1878), 1:170–72; Hans Sloane, *A Voyage to the Islands Madeira, Barbados, Nieves,
S. Christophers, and Jamaica*, (London, 1707), 1:9, 12; Thomas Howe, *The Annexed
Sketch* (London, 1762); James Gordon to Alexander Gordon, 1763, 1764, Gordon
of Letterfourie Papers, private collection, Preshome, Scotland; Thomas Cheap to
Secretary of State, 1766, SP 89, National Archives of the United Kingdom, Kew,
Richmond, Surrey, England; Robert Stewart to George Washington, March 10, 1768,
in W. W. Abbot and Dorothy Twohig, eds., *The Papers of George Washington*, Colonial
Series, vol. 8 (Charlottesville, 1993),75; J. C. Beaglehole, ed., *The "Endeavour" Journal
of Joseph Banks, 1768–1771* (Sydney, 1962)1:162–65; Inventario,1:144, 2:481, Arquivo
historico ultramarino, Lisbon; *Elucidário madeirense*, 2nd ed. (Funchal, 1946),
3:103–4; José Manuel Azevedo e Silva, *A Madeira e a construção do mundo atlântico*
(Funchal, 1995), 669.

Madeira sugar production—discussed at greater length below—left many families impoverished and landless, as consolidation of cane lands into vineyards and
transfer from insolvent tenants to solvent ones proceeded apace.[25]
    Emigration became an even greater problem in the eighteenth century, when
first gold and later diamonds were discovered in Brazil. Metropolitan and local

reaction to the exodus of workers to Brazil had to confront the countervailing need for labor there. At first, the Crown feared that emigration would strip Madeira and Portugal of laborers. To prevent this calamity, João V issued *alvarás* (charters or patents) in 1709, 1711, and 1720 to curtail significant exit. Yet emigration brought benefits to the kingdom as well, for it "relieved the pressure of an expanding population on resources and prevented declining yields, deepening poverty, and subsistence cases," and these benefits were increasingly recognized. So it was that in the late 1740s João's government offered free land and assistance to Madeirans who wished to immigrate to southern Brazil, and it authorized certain Lisbon merchants to carry at least five families from Madeira to Brazil on each of their ships. Some 1,277 inhabitants—2 percent of the population—left by such means in 1747–51 alone; most who did so were free men drawn largely by the prospect of economic gain, although religious freedom and social advance were also motivating factors.[26] After Brazilian gold exports peaked in 1755 and governmental incentives disappeared, private incentives persisted and individual departures continued. Exit was still substantial enough in 1779 for the governor of Madeira to consider measures to "prevent the emigration to foreign countries and to punish those who tried," to develop agriculture "to improve the miserable conditions of the population," to guard the coast better, and to institute a more rigorous auditing system. Those policies that were introduced were mostly ineffective, however, and the outflow continued. Many Portuguese boarded English vessels without passports, and such clandestine departures were only the tip of the iceberg. Plus an even larger group of Madeirans went to North America on account of Catholic persecution of Masons in the 1790s.[27]

MIX

The overwhelming majority of islanders—or "natives," in the parlance of the day—was tied to the land. Nearly all the land was owned either by "old & noble" Portuguese families, some of which had "princely Estates" outside Funchal and lived in their city mansions (*palacetes*), if they did not reside on the mainland, or by religious communities, like the Jesuits or Santa Clara nuns. The Jesuits, holding "precedence in Fortune" and place among the religious, had "secured the *Monopoly* of *Malmsey*," and so enjoyed substantial annual rents, even if the acreage they held was low, for Malmsey always fetched the highest prices. Natives were, thus, the owners (*senhorios* or *proprietarios*) of vineyards. The "owners" commonly rented their vine land on an annual basis to peasant "cultivators" (*colonos*) and in the eighteenth century also to semiprofessional "farmers" (*feitors*), who served as intermediaries between the landlords and tenants, renting from the former and to the latter. Tenants divided between *meyros* (who did not live on the land) and *caseiros* (who did). Under Portuguese law, tenants owned all but the land. After 1640, the bulk of the population was tied to the land in these three ways. True, a fraction lived in Funchal and traded the fruits of the island's agriculture or worked in servicing that trade. But that was always a small share overall. In the eyes of the natives, power, success, and upward mobility rose out of the land; trade would be entered into with an eye toward earning the means to acquire vine land and then exit commerce, which by 1815 had still not completely divested itself of its nonnoble taint.[28]

A small enslaved community of Africans worked for the natives. Black slaves were not heavily involved in wine production per se, but they played an important role in building Madeira's wine economy. Paradoxically, their numbers thinned in these years, when slave labor was on the rise in most other parts of the subtropical and tropical Atlantic plantation world. The importation of black slaves began around 1443, but became numerically significant only in the following century. In 1552, there were approximately 3,000 slaves, forming 15 percent of the island's total population. As cane cultivation declined during the late sixteenth century and gave way to grape growing, the need for labor (especially relatively expensive African labor) fell and the number of Africans decreased, cultivators either selling their slaves to Canary Islanders or setting them free. By 1598, there were roughly 1,150 slaves, forming 6 percent of the population, and their numbers continued to drop in the two centuries that followed. Indirectly, of course, blacks played an important role in the shaping of Madeira's market. The trade in slaves was central to the development of the trade in Madeira, for the former brought ships to Funchal demanding wine, fruit, and other goods to satisfy slave traders' personal, barter, and provision needs on the African coast. It was a one-way exchange, for few vessels returned with slaves directly from Africa; but the wine so exported was used as currency in slave-trading castles and depots by whites in their barter negotiations with African kings, in the medical treatment of whites and slaves, and as a sustenance and medicine for whites and sometimes slaves on the Middle Passage. Perhaps not so coincidentally, the rise of the Madeira wine trade roughly parallels the rise of the British and French slave trade.[29]

Notwithstanding the declining need, white Madeirans did not stop buying and selling slaves. In 1663, for instance, the English East India Company requested an islander to buy it two blacks "good, sober," and "well skilled in planting." Little is known about the slaves, but the request and others like it suggest there was still a vibrant market in black labor that survived the switch from sugar to wine, which had by the 1660s fully been accomplished. Registers of ships entering Funchal harbor between 1727 and 1768 record the importation of 1,337 slaves—an average of 33 per year. One-third of these slaves was brought from

Africa, one-quarter from Brazil, and one-quarter from the West Indies and North America. Whether most stayed or quickly moved on to other destinations is unclear, although church records indicate some remained for a time: Funchal's two central parishes baptized at least 556 slaves, constituting 3 percent of baptisms there, between 1750 and 1799.[30]

Blacks, whether slave or free, seldom worked the vine land. Grape growing being less labor intensive than sugar cultivation, there was less "reason" for them, or so it was felt at the time. The great amount of slack time in cultivation and manufacture and the comparatively minimal amount of exertion required even in heavy working times counseled against the year-round expense of providing food, clothing, and housing. So it was that Africans went from being primarily outdoor laborers to indoor or town laborers. By the middle of the eighteenth century, most slaves were domestics.

This state of affairs would likely have persisted, for there is little evidence that the abolitionist sentiment sweeping mainland Portugal inspired local support. It was the Crown that intervened. A royal *alvará* of 1761 banned the transport of black slaves from Portugal's dependencies to the kingdom and declared that those so transported would be freed. Unlike many royal decrees, this one stuck. Ships subsequently arriving at Madeira with slaves were refused entry. But the decree was confusing. Slaves already living in Portugal were not emancipated, nor were those arriving from non-Portuguese lands. The 1761 law was designed to prevent slaves being taken out of Brazil, where they were needed to work plantations and mines. When asked in 1768 whether the ban applied to slaves arriving from non-Portuguese lands, the Crown interpreted its edict broadly to include all lands. Five years later, it abolished slavery entirely, summarily freeing all blacks.[31] Even then, however, emancipation was only a principle, for slavery endured in places. Some Madeira exporters continued to use slaves in their Funchal operations, in their houses, offices, shops, warehouses, and on the harbor front through 1815.[32]

In terms of their share and their lock on goods traded between 1640 and 1815, the Portuguese controlled all of Madeira's professions and occupations but one—the export trade. "Strangers"—as natives referred to foreigners—dominated that branch of the economy. That they came to do so is remarkable given the restraints upon them. Strangers were essentially noncitizens whose allegiance and obedience were owed to the sovereigns of other states, and Madeirans' understanding of alienage was largely in sync with the canonical *ius gentium* of accepted private international law as articulated by Grotius and Vattel. In their view, foreigners possessed few property rights: they could not own property absolutely, they could not wage suits about property, and they could not inherit property. Moreover, they possessed no political rights: they could not vote, and they could not hold office. Madeirans' application of alienage, however, was less clear-cut. The category was used flexibly, strategically, opportunistically—there was in effect no fixed status for foreigners, only a shared sense of legal possibilities, and the parties drew on them as they saw fit.[33] Outcomes depended as much on the courts, judges, litigants, and issues as they did on law. About the only thing foreigners could do in Madeira was trade, and trading rights were spelled out in various commercial treaties signed by London and Lisbon between 1576 and 1654 and in the enabling legislation recognizing English consulships and factories and judicial advocates (*juizes conservadores*) designed to aid foreigners in legal matters. Complaints flowed to the English consul and the Portuguese advocate, but whether they would or could do anything about them and how the law would be applied were always unclear.[34]

Foreigners had long dominated the island's economy. Strangers were present soon after Madeira's settlement in the 1420s. Some, like William Annan of England and John Drummond of Scotland, arrived before 1500 and stayed. A handful of Englishmen and a like number of Europeans are known to have become permanent residents between 1547 and 1640 in the final century of sugar production and exercised significant governmental and social power. Scores of others traded no more than a decade or two and then left. Foreigners formed an influential group, but a small one, never comprising more than a fraction of the total population.[35]

Their small share of the population is deceiving. Foreigners concentrated themselves in Funchal, became active in its overseas export businesses, and drove the entire economy. Funchal's ruling body, the municipal Council, required merchants to register their imports into and exports from the island on a ship-by-ship basis, and the resulting lists are revealing of who the overseas traders were. Before the rise of wine in the 1640s, foreigners outnumbered natives directly involved in transoceanic distribution of sugar: between 1470 and 1500, some 24 foreigners worked in the city alongside 19 Portuguese; between 1500 and 1600, at least 246 foreigners exported sugar, wine, or other goods from Madeira alongside 121 Portuguese. After the eclipse of island sugar that occurred in the years 1575–1650, the shares were switched: more Portuguese than foreigners exported wine (17 out of 30 in 1682 and 118 out of 202 in 1815).[36]

But these numbers are also deceiving. With wine, foreigners together shipped out greater volumes than natives. In 1682, the foreigners managed nearly four-fifths of the export. It seemed to many as if they were the only traders, despite the fact that natives still comprised an overwhelming majority. While a wonderful example of inaccurate Protestant self-deception, there is some truth in the 1771 surmise: there were "a great number of English and French Roman Catholics

settled there," some English and French Protestants, and a smattering of Europeans—Russians, Swedes, Danes, Germans, Dutch, Swiss, Spaniards, and Italians—and North Americans. They dominated the economy's leading sector: in
1775, they managed over four-fifths of wine exported, and in 1815, just under
four-fifths. Their mix and importance gave a cosmopolitan flavor to the place
that few islands in the Atlantic—and, indeed, few cities on the Portuguese mainland but Lisbon—could boast of.[37]

Madeira's foreign export merchants came "from almost every part of Europe."
English-speaking traders formed the largest subcohort. At the beginning of the
eighteenth century, the fifty or so English people (merchants, plus their employees, families, and servants) probably constituted roughly 1 percent of Funchal's
population. In addition, they were served by an assemblage of fellow countrymen of roughly equal number who provided them with ancillary medical, food,
lodging, and other services; that group grew as the merchant body grew. The
records of the British Factory for 1774, for instance, reveal the presence of a doctor, a minister, a lawyer, his wife, an Englishman with no known occupation, an
array of bankrupt or senile pensioners, an Englishman and his wife who took care
of shipwrecked sailors, and a tavern keeper and his wife who ran an inn wistfully
named "The British." By the beginning of the nineteenth century, the British
probably numbered five hundred, or roughly 3 percent of Funchal's population.
They were the richest, most powerful of the foreigners, but they were not alone;
a dozen other foreign groups were at work as well. Combined, their presence
imparted a strong international flavor to the city—and, when they chose to band
together politically, they constituted a powerful mercantile lobby.[38]

Into this porphyritic world of largely cosmopolitan, largely Protestant foreign
traders was introduced around the beginning of the nineteenth century a small,
noncommercial group of foreign whites: invalids. Madeira had attracted the infirm since at least the close of the Seven Years' War, and probably before. In
1767, for instance, one Murray set down there specifically "for the recovery of
his health." The Scot did not find himself much improved by the experience,
and he returned to London. But the return of men like Murray did little to dis-
suade others from following in their footsteps. William Hickey's wife's maid was
just one among many who "benefited materially" from a stay in 1782. As the infirm reported back to families and friends, a reputation for Madeira's healthiness
spread throughout Britain and Europe. Some, like the sister of the Countess of
Glencairn, visited while traveling to other places and stayed awhile, but others
decided to remain, to return and settle permanently, or to return again and
again.[39] Those seeking a cure on the island were initially embraced by Madeira's
wine exporters, who offered "good wine, good victuals, and a good room with

tolerable society," seeing these visitors as potential customers and recommendations. Taking their cue from doctors, they suggested that, since their Tinta (a local red wine) was of "great service" healthwise to some of the natives, it would be invaluable to invalids.[40] The cure was further burnished by fashion and war. Prominent men and women found the island worth a visit, novelists sent their protagonists to it for their health, and news of their trips encouraged emulation, especially among the British: colonial governors and officials—even the future George IV—set out for Madeira.[41] After the British occupied the island in 1801, it acquired an even stronger appeal to English-speaking consumptives desiring not only "clear and salubrious" air but also a safe haven in time of war.[42] Not all physicians counseled a visit, even in peacetime, pointing out the unlikelihood of gaining advantage, and not all "foreigners" welcomed visitors from their homeland, resenting the disruption to business that converted "the island into a general infirmary and individual houses into sick wards." Yet it became a significant "*dernier* resort." Wine exporters could do little but profit from the growing fame of Madeira—both the island and the wine.[43]

RELATIONS

The Portuguese were famous for their sobriety and, natives forming the bulk of the population, this trait shaped their relations with the foreigners. On a material level, it manifested itself in bland food, temperate drinking, drab clothing, little color or decoration, and a paucity of public entertainments. There were no universities, and no academic, literary, or artistic societies or events, such as those found in Lisbon, Bahia, Charleston, or London. Few nonreligious schools existed before the early decades of the nineteenth century, when a school of art was founded to encourage local painting and design. There were neither lecture series nor reading groups before 1820, when a program of scientific talks was established. There was neither public library nor museum. There was no public press before 1821. Opera, ballet, and orchestra were not available. The offerings of the theater—first opened in the 1770s—were outmoded, and its schedule erratic. Public pleasures were rare: there is no record of boat races, horse races, cockfights, raffles, or lotteries. The only exceptions to the rule of sobriety were festivals and spectacles given by the governor. But even these were few.[44]

To say that the island's public life was sober is not to suggest socializing never occurred. Roman Catholics daily encountered their friends at Mass, even if attendance was driven primarily by devotion. Friendly calls among relatives and associates took place. Reading must have been an important form of personal amusement to the literate (admittedly a small group), given the books that merchant householders recorded in their inventories. Private parties were held. For men, as well, there were opportunities to overcome the restraint through membership in confraternities or brotherhoods—religious, charitable, or professional groups of pious men dedicated to good works whose meetings often ended with drunken revelries and militia musters.[45]

Portuguese restraint found its analogue in an adherence to purity of blood laws that had been in existence since the fifteenth century. Pure Portuguese, under such restrictive laws, should not mix with Portuguese Moors and Jews. Detailed inquiries were to be made "into the family and descent" of a suitor or matrimonial prospect before a marriage was entered into, in order to prevent any "affinity" with undesirable persons. After the marquês de Pombal abolished such laws and the distinction between "old" and "new" Christians in 1761, upper castes on Madeira began to relax their guard, allowing money and connection to ease remaining qualms. Still, for the island's middling and lower classes, customary separations remained intact.[46]

Denied public entertainments and any participation in native domestic socializing, foreigners grudgingly adapted, accepting some aspects of Madeira's native/stranger divide and working around others. They never admitted the place to be anything more than dull, and they dealt with the dullness by manically plying their trade. Business reigned, and the hours of the day marched according to its beat. Merchants tended to rise early, work all day—taking an hour or two for lunch—and go to bed early. "There were no recreations, diversions, or companions." The natives, one young Scots apprentice found, were "a very sullen, proud, deceitful people"; all but the priests and collegians lacked wit or conversational skill. The English were "much worse," for they were wildly competitive. There knew only "jealousy of one another's correspondents." Everyone tried to get "another's" trade. If they spoke to one another, it was "criticizing or telling stories" about third parties. It was "a bad time for new beginners," he groaned. "No place in the world" was "more convenient for business, or quicker in dispatch than this, especially for Englishmen who have nothing to divert them from it."[47]

Nonetheless, distractions came in off the ships, with the visits of friends, correspondents, and people who had been recommended to their hospitality by friends or correspondents: the height of the shipping season saw a continual stream of boarders and lodgers, all needing food, drink, chaperoning around the island, and explanation of its customs and manners. Yet, the hospitality was work for the merchants, and the camaraderie short-lived. Much more relaxing encounters took place among the foreigners themselves, both within national groupings and across national lines, who fostered a culture of sociability more or less unattached to business. An ambience of camaraderie, calls on each side, semiofficial receptions, and private parties glued foreigners together. Amateur theatricals, impromptu dinners, picnics, excursions, balls, and dances lightened their routine business schedules, making Funchal seem slightly more like the provincial capitals of Edinburgh, Dublin, Bordeaux, or Philadelphia. They tried "every amusement that a retired mountainous place will admit of." Some swam; others went horseback riding; still others favored shooting. Competitive games were common forms of amusement at home: whist, backgammon, checkers, and bowls.[48]

Chief among their outlets was "Bachelors Hall." Foreigners could not join confraternities, and clubs would not meet in the town's taverns, on account of their substandard appointment and fare. So the British combined the two in the Hall, which they founded by 1758. For ten years at least, they rented a villa, the Quinta do Val, which sat just beyond the city's walls, about a mile north of the harbor. It was here that James Cook, Joseph Banks, and Daniel Solander planted a tulip tree as a token of thanks for the Hall's hospitality. When a merchant bought the Val in the late 1760s, the bachelors moved to the Quinta dos Pinheiros, higher up with an even more spectacular view. Hall accounts suggest it was mainly a drinking and dining club for single men. One typical excursion required "cloths for country entertainments, 36 common knives & forks, 2 carving knives, 72 pairs candle snuffers, 72 small oval tin plates for tent table, and a japanned knife tray." The comfortable, genteel life led there was such a mark of the community that mere mention of the Hall among transatlantic travelers conjured up island hospitality and the quintessence of international camaraderie.[49]

Records of invitations to the Hall suggest that the English-speaking community was, socially, no respecter of nationality and religion among foreigners: many of the guests did not speak English. Social relations among foreigners were generally harmonious, if competitive. They invited one another to dinners and dances. They married one another. Typically, when American merchants had people staying with them and needed something to accommodate visitors, they borrowed it from Dutch or French friends.[50] Similar efforts served to bind individuals into a community where none had existed before: securing debts, witnessing deeds, providing guardianship, making beneficiary of estates, appraising estates. Across nationalities and among divisions of any nationality, ethnicity was not a very strong force; rather, it was malleable, and the gaps apparently easily bridged. The uprootedness and mobility experienced by most foreigners, atop the alienation of living in a strange, sometimes hostile place, broke down what might otherwise have been an obstruction to exchange.[51]

Interactions between strangers and natives, in contrast, were more restrained. Both believed that the groups should "not mix much together." They were segregated by religion, for the most part; by class, since few foreigners were of the lower sort and many were middling and upper; and by national allegiance. The Portuguese had "a strong aversion" to the British in particular, especially British Protestants, and the British held a similar view in reverse.[52]

"Much social intercourse between them" never arose. Recorded instances when the Portuguese interacted socially with foreigners neither correspondents nor partners are rare, as are times when the two groups allied themselves with one another for personal reasons. If a Protestant English merchant married a Catholic Portuguese woman, it was assumed he would "first renounce his religion." Of the roughly four hundred foreigners known to have worked in the wine trade between 1700 and 1815, some six married Portuguese women. Equally indicative of the avoidance of intermarriage: of the 3,350 marriages performed in the parishes of the Sé and São Pedro between 1750 and 1799, only 50 involved bonds between non-Madeiran Portuguese and foreigners; 8 of these 50 involved an English-speaking partner, and 2 of these 8 involved an English speaker and a non-English-speaking foreigner. Even fewer English women married Portuguese men.[53] In business, as well, natives and foreigners did not mix very much. The English allied themselves infrequently with the Portuguese as partners, and seldom turned to Portuguese for assistance. They did so with reason: entanglements with locals might end up before local judges who favored natives, whatever the strength of particular claims.[54]

The passage of time and the ascendancy of the British broke down some of the time-honored unwillingness of natives to assist and interact with foreigners, and vice versa. The two groups needed each other. That they could communicate was critical. Most resident English-speaking merchants (and this was nearly all of the foreigners) read, spoke, and wrote at least rudimentary Portuguese; all merchants whose records have survived kept some books in Portuguese, usually those having to do with growers and suppliers of wine. Although their records are scarcer, the major Portuguese merchants were able to speak and write English, although they were unwilling to exhibit their proficiency. Too, government officials, when called upon to converse with foreigners in their respective tongue, usually did so; when given a choice, they opted for French.[55]

As the British and Americans exporters became more involved in importing goods to be consumed on the island and in managing shops for their retail (both functions of a deepening engagement with wine), they tied themselves into the supply and credit networks of the Portuguese and into the natives' ability to repay. Conversely, as the Portuguese produced more wine for export, they became reliant upon consumer networks in the growing English-speaking world. Over the course of the "long eighteenth century," relationships developed that undermined the attitudes of the most genealogically proud Portuguese and most self-identified culturally superior Britons. This was unavoidable given the fact that space and business were not segregated.[56]

Mixing and assisting were not restricted to business. Apprenticeships, partnerships, and ventures of all sorts; marriages; kindnesses and loans; memberships in Masonic lodges; the provision of medical services; the relaxing of dietary rules to accommodate guests; a measure of religious toleration of non-Catholic or non-Protestant institutions and customs; the intervention of governors in legal process: all served in small ways to bind the native and stranger communities more tightly together by 1815.[57]

THE INSTITUTIONS OF A CROSSROADS COMMUNITY

The island so strategically situated tradewise at the head of the Canary Current and North-East Trade Winds and blessed with exploitable natural and human resources underwent a profound shift in economic orientation in the seventeenth century, moving from the Atlantic's premier producer of sugar to that community's premier producer of wine. The ensuing "Triumph of Bacchus" was assisted by the reworking of older civic institutions and the introduction of newer ones, institutions directly affecting wine and indirectly influencing the ways that native owners, cultivators, farmers, and laborers and foreign and native merchants interacted.

No part of the Madeira wine complex remained untouched by this reorientation. Not only did grape vines replace sugarcanes but the comparatively greater riches that accrued from vine cultivation to producers and exporters also freed islanders from using up more marginally arable ground or pursuing less lucrative alternatives. Increasingly, more money was made in an exclusive focus on wine; crops grown on the island for centuries, like wheat and corn, were procured more cheaply and easily from the Azores, England, and North America. Wine monoculture brought a relaxation in labor demands and a decrease in capital demands on owners and cultivators, wine being cheaper to produce than sugar. At the same time, though, an increase in output encouraged a widening in global distribution and, so, an increase in capital demands on exporters.

Development of what became Madeira's export-driven wine economy went through several broad phases. Initial experimentation coincided with initial settlement. Zarco, it was commonly believed, planted the first vines, in the 1420s, and vineyards and wines were taxed in the 1470s, but the production of wine remained primarily a subsistence undertaking. Sugar dominated this period.[58]

A boom in wine production and export began about 1600 and ushered in a second phase that endured for the next seven or eight decades and saw wine surpass sugar as the island's principal crop and export. This surge coincided with several developments. On the one hand, sources for Atlantic sugar grew. New World competition arose in the sixteenth century; by 1600, Brazilian sugar had bested that from Madeira, in terms of both quantity and quality. So, by the 1630s, there was simply more and better sugar coming out of Brazil, at a time when Madeira's canes were being ravaged by a plague of rats and insects. Thereafter other suppliers joined Brazil to crowd out any remaining share Madeira sugar might have enjoyed in European markets. Colonists first planted canes in Barbados in the 1640s, and in other islands in the Lesser Antilles in subsequent decades. Their export became significant enough within a matter of years to capture English- and French-speaking consumer markets, nailing the coffin on Madeiran sugar and confining the market for Brazilian sugar to Iberia. By the 1680s, then, there were "so many Sugar Plantations in Brazil and the West Indies" that it was not worth Madeirans' while to cultivate the crop, Hans Sloane reported, even if (as many believed) their type of sugar was superior to New World varieties. On the other hand, new demands for shippers emerged, independent of any supply change. The island's newest export could satisfy emerging Atlantic shipping and consumption needs: it filled empty holds in oceangoing vessels at a time when European vessels were increasingly involved in provisioning new settlements in America, and their holds were on average expanding; and it sustained many drinkers in North and Caribbean America and Brazil with a beverage that was neither successfully nor continuously produced in those markets. On top of this, moreover, the surge was built with infrastructure already laid down: Portuguese salt, fruit, and sugar traders cut numerous channels before 1640 through which wine could subsequently flow. Northwestern European traders, for instance, had long come to Portugal with grain and bought salt, fruit, and sugar, and to this mix could easily add both mainland and island wine. Early on, the ties and nodes of the sugar trade in particular formed the basis of the emerging wine trade.[59]

A long period, stretching from the 1670s to the 1810s, formed one last developmental period—in which slow and steady growth gave final shape to the production and distribution sectors. It constituted the age of the wine complex's great consolidation. Owners and exporters flourished as never before, even if the greatest part of the population, the growers, remained depressed. As chapter 5 discusses in detail, the number of ships departing Funchal each year (almost all of which carried some wine) increased tenfold between 1640 and 1815, and the quantity of wine they carried rose sixfold. Exports peaked at 20,400 pipes in 1805 (the pipe being the principal container of Portuguese wine, holding between 110 and 132 gallons, depending on the place of first export—in Madeira's case, 110).

Exporters reached the heights of their activity between 1800 and 1815—such levels were never regained.[60]

During this age of growth and consolidation, Madeira's exporters shifted away from reliance upon markets in Portugal and its dependencies toward cultivation of consumers in the English-speaking world. As they did so, their work became even more complex. From almost exclusively focusing on supplying ship provisions on demand to visiting captains in the mid-seventeenth century, exporters turned to supplying wine to repeat customers (American and Asian for the most part), to extending to those customers a more full-bodied commercial service, and to importing dry goods and grain stuffs from them for retail to islanders or reexport to Iberians. Participants thought this a "revolution in trade." It gained particular momentum between the 1740s and 1760s: while the possibility for exporters engaging in island retailing had long existed in the bringing to market of dry goods, fish, and grain, they only entered into it with any vigor in these decades. The value of such business was clear. Exporters wanted dry goods, fish, and wheat "in order to serve [their] customers," that is, the growers. The nature of this business was also risky. Doing well, however, required buying well, for better cloth, say, attracted better wine. Moreover, specialization to the point of relying on imported food, despite the disruptions of frequent wars, was an impressive instance of risk taking, but only for those most in danger of starving—the growers who formed the bulk of the population, who depended on the food and manufactures, and who had no control over the process run by the risk takers, who were never really much at risk. Given islanders' nearly absolute dependence on these imports in the post-sugar era, sales to the cultivators, farmers, and owners, especially credit sales, generally gave the exporters a stranglehold over them, which in the end allowed them to gain competitive preferences in the purchase of wine. Sales to local shopkeepers gave them similar powers.[61]

As the population of the island grew, the people transitioned from sugar to wine, and relations between natives and strangers became more intertwined and contested, so, too, did the capital city grow and its institutions evolve to meet the demands of the leading wine sector.[62] Supposedly named for the fennel (*funcho*) that flourished in its environs, Funchal had spread out over a square mile by 1600. A wall sixteen feet high and four feet wide protected it from the sea, its surf, and intruders. Three relatively wide streams formed the eastern and western bounds of the town. Eight east/west streets intersected at varying angles eight north/south streets coming down the mountain. Five clusters of buildings served as foci for the townsfolk: the Customs House along the harbor; the residences and offices of the governor and his troops further west; the cathedral; a square

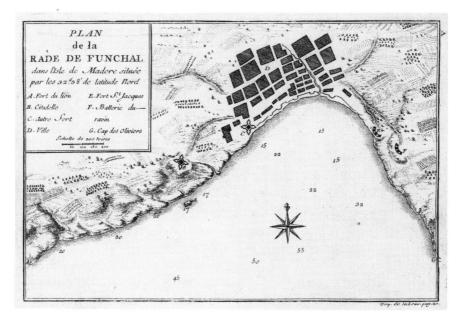

Figure 1.4. Plan of the road of Funchal, 1728.
Source: Antoine Jean de Laval, *Voyage de la Louisiane* (Paris, 1728). Courtesy of
the Houghton Library, Harvard College Library, Sci 2707,28*, Harvard University,
Cambridge, Massachusetts.

northeast of the cathedral bounded by the Bishop's Palace, Jesuit College and
Church, and Town Hall; and the principal marketplace and pillory to the east.[63]
    Although the city's area and layout remained more or less fixed from 1600 to
1815, the number of forts, offices, and residences and the range of services grew,
as the population rose and its trade burgeoned.[64] Population statistics for the
city are sparse and rather unreliable, but what survive suggest growth. In 1598,
Funchal had 2,279 hearths; in 1675, about 3,000. Its population remained stable
or fell slightly from 1675 to 1700. Later data for hearths have not survived, but
complementary information on inhabitants suggests that this halt or decline gave
way to growth. In 1687, some 9,836 people (one-eighth of the island's total population) lived in the city; in 1797, 18,892 did (one-fifth).[65]
    Within the eight-square-block city, a series of communities grew up after
1640—overlapping, intertwined, cooperative, and competing. Official, religious, and residential-commercial spaces rose up alongside one another. Imbued
as they were with a notion of property in which land was a foundation for power
and culture, visitors from Protestant Europe and Anglo-America paid close at-

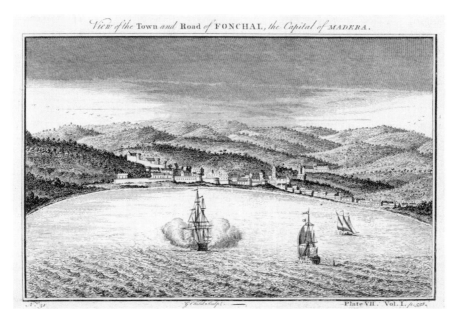

Figure 1.5. View of the road and town of Funchal,
engraved by J. Kyp and G. Child, 1745.
Source: "Supplement," in Thomas Astley, *A New General Collection of Voyages
and Travels*, vol. 1 (London, 1745), facing p. 20; this image is identical to the earlier
Prospect of the Town of Funchal, engraved by Johannes Kyp before 1722. Courtesy of
the Houghton Library, Harvard College Library, Geog 4157.45, Harvard University,
Cambridge, Massachusetts.

tention to these spaces, to what was owned and by whom: the sites, buildings,
uses, occupants, and contents all came under scrutiny.

STATE

For someone arriving by water, the most common landing place at Funchal lay
near the center of the beach that stretched before the city. After passing through
a thick, high wall that ran the length of the beach, the visitor first encountered
the Customs House (Alfândega) and a string of governmental buildings that left
no questions as to the centrality and power of the state and the state's reliance
on trade. The massive Customs House, shown in most contemporary paintings
and engravings, dominated this waterfront, with its three stories, "a large paved
court where the merchants walk as upon an Exchainge," and a battery of cannon
for protecting trade-based revenues.[66] Adjacent lay the Royal Treasury (Erário

Régio). Moving west inside the wall, one passed the small Health House (Casa da Saúde), the office of the chief health officer (*capitão da saúde*), and by 1703 the Product House containing the offices of the product master (*patrão-mor*) and quarters for his guards (*guarda-mores*)—all of whom had responsibility for examining incoming ships' state of health and granting passengers and goods entry warrants.[67] Further west stood the largest structures: the official residence of the governor and the castellated Fortaleza São Lourenço (plate 3), the island's principal defensive fort, housing troops under his command.[68] Along the northeastern bounds of the city lay the Town Hall (Casa da Câmara), which housed most of the executive and judicial offices of municipal government. A large market square (*praça*) was situated near the eastern edge of the bay in a triangle of land formed by the confluence of the Ribeira de Santa Luzeia and the Ribeira de Santa Maria. Lastly, scattered around the city stood several forts possessing varying degrees of defensibility, and these increased in number as the population expanded and perception of the need for its protection grew. Given the island's potentially vulnerable position in the Atlantic sea-lanes, defense was never far from the minds of Madeirans.[69]

What residents knew and what visitors discovered about these buildings and their occupants was that they constituted a labyrinth of overlapping and competitive royal and municipal institutions at work within the town. Government being grounded "upon the Plan of that of Portugal," an absolutist monarchical regime, all governance and property were in principle subject to the will of the monarch and his representative the governor and captain general (*governador* and *capitão geral*), who stood at the head of the island's military and civil departments. But to characterize Portuguese rule in Madeira as wholly absolute would be inaccurate. Actual control and administration always involved a contest among several powers, only one of which was royal. Considerable voice was exercised by city officials, landowners, and merchants whose main concerns were the promotion of personal authority, economic growth in the island's wine trade, and material well-being.

The governor's chief responsibility was to defend the island, and in this capacity he ruled supreme. Like the official who took charge after Portugal regained control of its dominions in 1640, each governor after him concerned himself primarily with the island's troops, forts, and militias as well as with visits by foreigners and their ships. That there were forts, walls, and cannon suggest the importance of security; that Madeira was never attacked attests to his success in maintaining it.[70]

The governor was less absolute and his authority more questioned in matters of finance. At the head of the Royal Treasury (Fazenda Real)—the most significant office in government—stood a comptroller (*provedor*) who answered not to the governor but to a Lisbon-based overseer (*vedor*) who had appointed him. From 1640, the comptroller sat as the president of a council (Tribunal do Alfândega), which after 1700 functioned independently of the governor and often thwarted his initiatives. Later on in 1761 was added a Royal Treasury (Erário Régio), over which the comptroller presided. Not until a council (the Junta da Real Fazenda) that the governor headed was inserted between the overseer and comptroller in 1775 did the governor regain some of his former influence in financial affairs.

The financial power of the governor was always limited, even after 1775. The comptroller managed revenues garnered from agriculture for much of the period, especially the tithe due to the king of all produce grown on the island (*dízimo*). In addition, he directed fiscal matters relating to shipping, like the authorization, levying, collection, and recalculation of duties, particularly the 10 percent import duties and the 11 percent export duties. Nearly all revenue flowing to the island government (as opposed to the Lisbon government) came from taxes and duties on or relating to wine that the comptroller's council (Tribunal) set, collected, and reset: the *dízimo*, the oldest tax, an imposition on agricultural exports levied to assist the Church; the *imposição do vinho*, a tax on retail sales; the *direitos de saída e entrada*, taxes on export and import; the *donativo*, another imposition on agricultural products; the *finto*, a wartime tax to subsidize government; the *subsidio literario*, a tax on wine, *aguardente*, and vinegar to aid schools and teachers; and the *imposição das estufas*, a tax on stoves used to heat wine during production. The comptroller used what revenues he could to pay for military and civil salaries, military supplies, and the upkeep of public buildings. Nor was his power limited to handling agricultural and commercial revenues. He set guidelines for wine measures used by growers and merchants, banned as it suited him the import of foreign products or the barter of goods in exchange of wine, and required merchants to submit dispatches that precisely listed the contents and destination of all cargoes. All in all, the comptroller and his officers wielded seemingly unlimited power, often in contravention of gubernatorial policy and royal law.[71]

Collecting revenue fell to the Customs. At its head sat a chief judge (*juiz da Alfândega*), an appointee of the comptroller and usually the administration's oldest judge. Among the more important of his staff was the "receiver of the king's duties" (*almoxarife*) and beneath him ranged an army of employees. Charged with collecting royal revenue, the Customs constituted the largest official cohort, working out of the large building that dominated the harbor.[72] Yet, while legally authorized to collect revenue, the Customs managed to do so only by bal-

ancing interests. On the one hand, it reconfigured many duties it had not initiated. Most taxes were established by other branches of government, like the 1772
impositions on wine, brandy, and vinegar, which were enacted by the Crown for
the creation and maintenance of primary schools. But the Customs found that it
had to recalculate and raise them, sometimes in accord with the dictates of the
king and governor, but just as often in opposition to them.[73] On the other hand,
the Customs did not manage all revenues. Collection of the impost on Brazilian
tobacco and snuff, for instance, was assigned to a contractor, usually resident in
Lisbon, who purchased the rights to sell such goods on the island, take payment
in wine, and reexport the wine to Brazil and India. About this, the Alfândega
could do little.[74]

Equally independent of the governor was the bureaucracy of judges and
courts that meted out justice to islanders. Law was the bailiwick of the chief
judge (*desembargador*), who resided in Lisbon, visited the island occasionally,
and acted as the judge of last appeal, and his deputy the inspector general (*corregedor*), who resided in Madeira and ran the island's judicial department. These
officers received their appointment from the monarch and held their places at
royal pleasure. In principle, they heard all causes on appeal from inferior courts
and judges; appeals from their decisions went to the king's court of appeal in
Lisbon.[75] Yet, in practice, justice in Madeira was as contested and problematic as
in most places. Law was not certain, property, as we have seen, being particularly
insecure for foreigners. Every six or seven years, the king dispatched a judge to
unravel "all causes that had not been well decided." In the intervening period,
those concerned with wine production and distribution waded through legal and
judicial process as if through a labyrinth, native and stranger alike. Jurisdictions
and regulations were complementary, overlapping, and competing; obtaining redress and fair treatment was intricate and complicated; and the rules and judges
were generally inflexible and rigid. Each of the three major geo-military divisions
of Madeira and Porto Santo, for instance, had its own law department officially
supervised by the chief judge and inspector general yet actually managed by a
judge elected by local senators in the captaincy's representative forum. Further
complicating royal jurisdiction, each municipality had its own courts and judges,
and military tribunals operated relatively independently of all courts.[76]

The law was less lenient and respectful to Britons and other foreigners than to
Portuguese. There was no need that it be, of course. As noncitizens, foreigners
were not extended the rights of property, in much the same way that a foreigner
had no rights under the Roman *ius civile*, or if they were allowed certain exceptions or privileges, such were extended so erratically and at such a high cost that
no right attached themselves and no precedents were established.[77] Foreign mer-

chants seldom felt they could "obtain justice in the courts at Madera" or from the Portuguese jurisprudential system in general; and, while the sentiment was what one would expect to be expressed by foreigners anywhere in this period, there is independent confirmation of their insecurity, and there was no attempt to ameliorate their disabilities as there was elsewhere.[78]

Legal problems for foreigners fell into one of three categories. First, the laws were complicated and vague, and the jurisdictions unclear. The laws relating to import duties were complex, and they became more so over time. Shippers and traders often experienced great difficulty in understanding, solving, or explaining them; the intricate interlacing of parts made it often impossible to grasp them separately.[79] Second, the laws were not equally applied to natives and strangers. Criminal laws were unequally administered. Commercial laws were peculiarly subject to the discrimination of those in power.[80] The comptroller could block the flow of goods and dispatch of ships to the Americas, and little help could be found in the courts. Or the product master who examined the quality of the fish imported from America could throw it into the sea if he thought it bad or could sell it to local fishmongers at a price much below that of the market, with no legal justification grounded in law ever being proffered. Or the Town Council could forbid foreign merchants to sell certain goods above certain prices and require grain importers to tender unnecessarily detailed bills of lading.[81] Finally, the resolution of local problems was elusive. In 1719, one merchant in Madeira fruitlessly complained of "appeals lying from thence to the courts at Lisbon," where the British ambassadors or envoys responsible for arguing them did "not concern themselves in those matters," thinking it "below their characters to apply to the judges of any of the said courts but only to the King and his ministers of state in the last resort." Fifty years later not much had changed. Lawsuits were still "very troublesome" for foreigners, as a determination in Funchal decided only "that the same thing, however clear & obnoxious, must be tryed" later on the continent and, in doing so, fall into a well of oblivion from which no final legal judgment was likely to emerge.[82]

With responsibilities intricately articulated, jurisdictions not clearly defined, officials nearly absolute in power vis-à-vis foreigners, and justice biased, certainty was elusive and property was highly insecure for those foreigners involved in the wine industry. Given the realities of the system, how could distributors obtain justice? They could avoid law altogether. They could use law at their peril. Or they could adopt intermediate approaches. It was the latter that the exporters generally favored. On an official level, they could cultivate the favor of the governor, since his attitude was critical to the conduct of or interference with trade. Drawing from the "contributions" English-speaking merchants imposed on themselves, the British annually made a 600$000 "donation" to the governor on the Portuguese king's birthday, in order to keep him "always amenable" to their business. Given the large size of this gift, the small annual income earned by the governor, and the precarious resources of his office, this donation usually succeeded in smoothing relations.[83] Exporters could also hire an advocate for their community on a semiofficial basis. Foreign merchants technically stood beyond the reach of royal, municipal, and military jurisdictions. Accordingly, from at least 1705, English-speaking residents hired a Portuguese trained in the law to act as their advocate—the *conservador dos Inglêses*—and handle disputes among themselves, disputes with Portuguese citizens, questions over the interpretation of treaty rights, disputes over specific duties, and debt cases. Yet his assistance went only so far, given the vague interpretation of law and the erratic dissemination of justice.[84] Finally, foreigners could resort to manipulation and bribery. There was, all knew, "no doing business . . . without being well with all the people in power," and that could only be "managed" with "a sum that is not worth consideration compared to the object attained."[85]

Alongside royal officials worked municipal officers. Each city and town had its own municipal council (*câmara*). Funchal's Council, the island's most important, met at the Table of the Propertied Men (Mesa da Vereações), northeast of the cathedral. The Council's main body—the Senate (Senado)—was made up of propertied managers (*vereadores*) elected by voters to pass legislation and spend revenue.[86] Another influential elected council (Conselho) approved all loans and taxes and set expenses; made up of voters who paid the highest municipal taxes, it served as a check upon the Senate.[87] The Senate approved municipal legislation and oversaw its implementation, managing Funchal's courts, police, and markets. It appointed officers, like municipal judges (*juizes ordinarios e pedãneos*), city and village magistrates (*alcaides*), bailiffs (*meirinhos*), inferior judges (*almotacés*), and city and mountain ridge guards (*guardas-mores*). It gathered municipal taxes, especially the tax on retailed wine (*imposição do vinho*). Most critical to the wine industry, the Senate set the floors and ceilings of prices to be paid to farmers and cultivators, decreed cultivation techniques and harvest times, and regulated imports and exports. Moreover, it guided the Health House and its Chief Guard, both of which worked with the Customs' health and police officers.[88] Yet, as in the examination of ships, so in most matters: municipal and Crown officers often worked at cross-purposes, and it was never clear whether the Funchal Council was independent of or subordinate to the governor. In principle, Portuguese municipal town councils had limited powers; the lines of authority were kept deliberately blurred and overlapping. In practice, however, Funchal's Council exercised a surprising degree of power, depending on its makeup, the personality of the governor, and the degree to which the Crown was worried about what was going on in Madeira—which was not often.

Religious institutions in Madeira raised similar challenges for natives and foreigners producing and exporting the island's wine. Entering the city from the harbor, one walked north along the side of the Customs House and into the heart of the city—the square before the cathedral that was the seat of the bishop—and into a community that was remorselessly Catholic.[89] In addition to the bishop and his establishment, the city at midcentury boasted the cathedral's own chapter, five friaries, three nunneries, two seminaries, and twenty-three parish churches and chapels.[90] After 1675, these numbers increased with the addition of three Franciscan communities, two Cordelier and one Carmelite. Madeira earned a reputation for Catholicity that has persisted to this day.[91]

Nevertheless, over the course of the eighteenth century, the island became more secularized and its religious communities declined. That decline set in before 1720, when the Jesuit College (plate 4) housed fewer ecclesiastics than it ever had in the past. It was certainly clear after 1759, when the expulsion of the Jesuits from Portugal and its dependencies that year removed one of the richest and most powerful orders from the scene. Massive exodus does not seem to have happened in Madeira; some Jesuits stayed on as secular priests. Still, officials blocked new Jesuits from settling and sold off long-held Jesuit properties. The decline of Madeira's religious institutions was not shaped solely by the fall of the Jesuits, however, for most orders were waning. By 1772, their total had dwindled to four friaries and four nunneries, half what it had been a century before. The clergy found it increasingly difficult to recruit new members, for fervor had greatly "slackened among the laity."[92]

The presence, dominance, and even decline of Catholics exerted a heavy influence on relations among participants in the Madeira wine complex. Religious communities were landlords, owning vineyards and countinghouses and setting rental and sale agreements; the Jesuits owned all the Malvasia land, for instance.[93] Catholic beliefs impinged on the religious practices of foreign Protestants, since they frustrated easy burial. The Church, allowing "no Charitable Thoughts to the Souls of Heretics," refused them "decent interment" before the 1760s; their corpses were "cast into the Sea." Only in 1761, after the intervention of the British consul in Lisbon, did Protestants gain land for burial. With financial support from the resident British merchants, a few acres in the northwest quadrant of the city were rented from the nuns of the Convent of Santa Clara.[94] True freedom of worship took even longer to arrive. The English-speaking "Nation" had to make do with itinerant ministers. Not until 1822 did Protestants gain their own church building and a full-time preacher.[95]

Outright persecution of Protestant believers, at least foreign Protestants, was, minimal. In large measure, the eighteenth-century Inquisition in Portugal took cognizance only of Catholic behavior. Moreover, international treaties explicitly safeguarded religious freedom, or at least freedom from harassment, to foreign merchants. Yet the oppressions perpetrated by the Portuguese from time to time on Protestant merchants were no less real, despite the legal safeguards. The Catholic Church's persecution of Freemasonry in the second half of the eighteenth century unsettled many merchants of all religions. Even if persecution and harassment became less frequent, its incidence and the Madeirans' unremitting Catholic zeal were powerful forces keeping foreigners and natives apart, should either group choose to emphasize their differences.[96]

SOCIETY

Public buildings so dominant on first landing were outnumbered by far more pedestrian, far less imposing structures—the houses, offices, stores, and warehouses of inhabitants, most of whom were involved in some way with the wine complex. The built environment they comprised was, en masse, a confusing amalgamation of metropolitan and provincial, cosmopolitan and pedestrian. Visitors seldom knew what to make of it.

The stock of residential and commercial buildings was permanent, and in style quite different from that inhabited by northern Europeans. It added to the strangeness of the place. The walls of the merchants' houses were made of "very thick" freestone or brick. The unglazed windows were "latticed, and the window frames . . . composed of a reddish stone." Flat and uniform roofs were covered with hard, smooth pantiles, and upon these were frequently set "large pebble stones to keep them from falling or being blown down." On either side of the narrow cramped streets, the houses, offices, lodges, and stores of the city's growing overseas merchant group and those who served it were visible.[97] Of the latter, there were thirty artisans who worked with wood, metal, and leather, shopkeepers who satisfied apparel and appearance needs, and manual laborers who provided construction and transportation services in 1700, plus an array of service providers like tavern-keepers, workers, and soldiers. A hundred years later, when another census was taken, the list had not changed much, except for an increase in the reach of the service group to include weavers, jewelers, and engineers and the expansion of the wine-support group to embrace seedsmen, vintners, coopers, carters, and tasters. Exhibited in the rise of shops was an Anglicization of everyday consumption. There were shops by 1700 that offered a wide range of international goods, like silks, jewels, chinaware, food, and drink. Yet few stocked British and American goods. By 1800, "most of the shops" had become "filled with articles of English growth and manufacture." Not surprisingly, many of the shops were established and run by exporters. By the time of the English occupation of the island in 1807, the city possessed a nearly fully developed economy capable of meeting the global demand for Madeira. Shops formed just one small but critical link in that transformation.[98]

One of the city's most striking features was that there were no obvious patterns to its layout. Merchants were scattered throughout the central town, symptomatic of the unavoidable interaction and interdependence of the island's dominant traders. There was no foreign merchant ghetto, as there was in many Atlantic port cities: native and stranger lived side by side, as did owner, farmer, merchant, and cooper.

The vernacular of Madeira's merchant homes was simple yet substantial. "The houses of the bettermost people" were large, "but those of the poorer sort very small." A typical house was 90 feet wide along the street and 180 feet deep. The doors to the street were "large, and the entries spacious," but neither were elegant, the former crudely constructed and the latter a space where men urinated in public. Most houses had three or four stories. No merchant lived on the ground floor, for this contained servant rooms, offices, stores, and warehouses. The "best apartments" were situated up "one pair of stairs," where the dining parlor and kitchen were placed. Inside, the rooms above were "large and lofty," and the ceilings wooden, coved, and "neatly wrought." Catholics nailed a wooden cross above the door of each chamber. Nearly every house had a garden and a lookout (*miranda*) on top — "a kind of Balcony" "to which in warm weather" the family retired to take in the "views of the surrounding country and of the sea."[99]

Funchal's vernacular merchant housing was a composite of differing styles, much as the commerce was made up of different nations, and this, too, changed, as foreign dominance grew.[100] In the second half of the eighteenth century, the simple Portuguese style of urban building begin to incorporate decorative motifs first introduced and popularized in England, the Netherlands, France, and America. With the introduction of good stucco at midcentury, rooms were enriched with plastered, paneled walls, and decorated and plastered ceilings. "Plain decoration" in the Portuguese style fell out of favor in the 1760s, while northern European windows with sashes and glass panes, for instance, became de rigueur; such was "the increasing wealth and taste for luxury" that few houses were found without them.[101]

The combination of styles and the porphyritic nature of Madeira's community are apparent in the early nineteenth-century house and office occupied by the

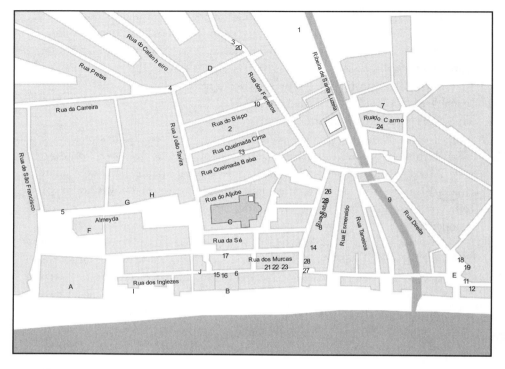

Figure 1.6. Map of public buildings and exporters' residences in Funchal, 1750–1815. Legend: A—Fort; B—Customs House; C—Cathedral; D—Jesuit College; E—Pillory and Plaza; F—Theater; G—Hospital; H—Orphanage; I—Health House; J—Câmara; 1—Henry Veitch; 2—Leacock & Sons; 3—Newton & Gordon; 4—Searle Brothers; 5—Hayward & March; 6—Blackburn & Co.; 7—Phelps & Page; 8—Gordon Brothers and Gordon Duff & Co.; 9—Charles Alder; 10—William and Thomas Haddock; 11—Duff Brothers; 12—Thomas and Arthur Ahmuty; 13—Robert Scott Jr. & Co.; 14—Scott, Pringle & Cheap; 15—Shirley & Co.; 16 and 17—Thomas and Arthur Ahmuty; 18—James Ayres; 19—Thomas Edward Watts; 20—Pedro Jorge Monteiro; 21—John Forster; 22—James Ayres; 23—Thomas Gordon; 24—John Searle; 25—Lamar, Hill, Bisset & Co.; 26—John Searle; 27—Alexander Gordon; 28—James Ayres; 29—Pedro Jorge Monteiro. Source: Drawn by Karl Longstreth. Maps created using software in the Map Library, University of Michigan, Ann Arbor.

American exporter John Howard March, who set up a firm in 1815. Situated along the tree-lined central mall that was the city's most prestigious address, next to the Misericórdia Hospital and opposite the Governor's Castle, it was large—90 feet by 260 feet (figure 1.7). One entered an arched gate piercing a high wall that fronted the mall, passing through a small room into a long hallway "paved with small stones" that was flanked on the right by a large, long interior garden and on the left by a smaller garden walk and garden in which were growing grapes, bananas, peaches, lemons, oranges, figs, cane, coffee, and yams. The house itself had four floors: the ground contained offices and stables; the first, the principal living quarters; the second, bedrooms; and the third, a lookout sporting cages of canaries, a table, and "a good telescope." Finally, behind this structure stood a poultry yard, a cooperage guarded by "two watch dogs chained in the daytime near their kennels" and, most important, "very extensive" wine stores.[102]

In the first-floor living quarters one engaged a space both foreign and native. Having climbed the steep stone stairs, one found on the left a sitting room that boasted "a balcony commanding a view of the ocean" and a smaller library off of it, straight ahead an entry hall, and to the right "a noble room" lit by "three windows, two with balconies, look[ing] upon the ocean." Opposite three windows were three doors that led to a parlor and a dining room. The parlor was "beautifully carpeted and furnished" and had two windows looking out upon a small interior flower and shrub garden. The ceilings and walls of these chambers were plastered, and the walls and chair rails were painted. From the dining room, one could descend to the garden via stone steps and admire a tank full of "small fish, some of a very deep red color." Service rooms lay beyond the entry hall: several keeping rooms and a kitchen with a chimney. The bedrooms above were large, with walls "nicely plastered and painted a lemon color" and nine-foot ceilings "of paneled wood, painted of a light blue color."[103]

The more enterprising foreigners appropriated native elements of decoration and furnishing, amalgamating or at least juxtaposing them with foreign detail. The tensions between integrating and separating were chronic, the former winning out more in town and the latter in the countryside. Indeed, in the villas (*quintas*) occupied by foreigners, one sees them using cosmopolitanism to reinforce separateness, even as they settled in on the side of the fanlike bowl forming the harbor and grew used to its ways. Given the poor road quality, the crude inland transport, and the incessant demand of their trade, it was only logical that merchants desiring to combine business and comfort would situate here. The villas usually lay within sight of the harbor (with a telescope, one could see the ships entering and identify nationalities by their flags) and within easy traveling distance to the city (one could cover the distance on horseback in three or

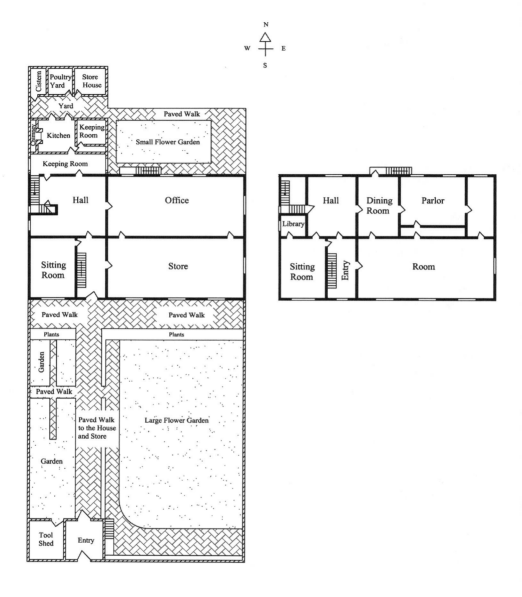

Ground Floor   First Floor

Figure 1.7. Ground and first-floor plans of the John Howard March House, c. 1815.
Source: Based on Edward Wells, "A Trip to Madeira, 1836–1837," in *Madeira Fragments*, ed. Graham Blandy (Funchal, 1971). Drawn by Donald Buaku.

four hours) (figure 1.8). The neighborhoods were breezier, cooler (especially in the warmer months), cleaner, and less congested, far closer to the Acadian ideal being lauded by the leading European literary and philosophical tomes that lined the merchants' libraries than the dirty, dilapidated squalor of their in-town neighborhoods. Moreover, the relative absence of houses and abundance of land on the mountainside allowed free rein to the foreigners' construction fantasies, far freer than was possible in town. As they pushed into the hills, untouched terrain let them build as they saw fit, to articulate their own identities and erect "floral temples" that were a microcosm of the world as they both saw and wanted it.[104]

Rural retreats arose in the last decade of the seventeenth century, according to visitors interested in architecture: there were no houses worth noting in 1687, but there were plenty by 1702, when "all along" the ascent from the town, "from the bottom to the middle," the land was "covered with quintas." As the 1750s watercolors of Richard Hill's Achada suggest, spacious quarters were surrounded by "beautiful gardens" graced with "pleasant fountains and running streams," "cool shaded alcoves of marble and various coloured stones," and orchards with "delicious fruits."[105]

The number of villas increased with each passing decade, although they did not reach critical mass until the 1750s, by which time several native families had begun to coalesce as a local gentry class, to appropriate northern European style, and to acquire a near-virtual monopoly of political, social, and commercial power. At that critical juncture, these families desired apposite expressions both visible and fixed of their newfound power. Such desires, too, aligned with those of the foreign elite: some foreign merchants, like Charles Murray (figure 1.11), had amassed enough wealth and prominence to announce their achievement—to themselves, fellow islanders, and passersby—and set themselves apart; other foreign exporters, like James Gordon (figure 1.10), had founded or joined firms spanning generations and settled in Madeira with the intention to stay and raise a family. A villa satisfied all.

All was not so Elysian, though. While the villas, townhouses, offices, and storehouses of the city's overseas merchant elite were comfortable and well appointed by the standards of the day, there were other aspects of social life that frustrated the persistence and push of the trading group and thereby the development of the international wine trade. The period 1640–1815 was an age of only limited civic improvement in Madeira, as many of the foregoing accounts have suggested, and most of that came only toward the end of the age. A want of structures and amenities retarded production and distribution and the pursuit of enterprise, and it reinforced the separateness of the foreign and native communities.

One glimpses this clearly in the port's commercial infrastructure. Funchal in 1640 was ill provided to meet the challenge of an expanding, exploding Atlantic,

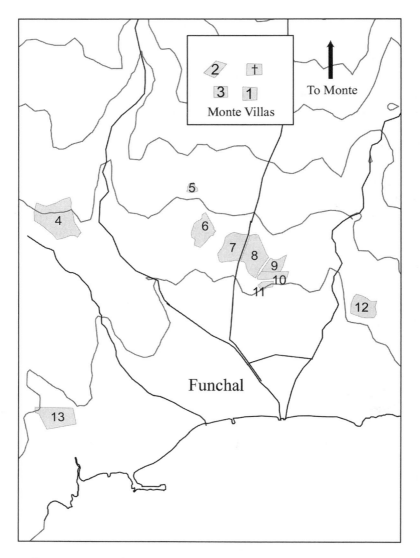

Figure 1.8. Map of exporters' *quintas* near Funchal, 1750–1815. Legend:
1—Quinta do Belo Monte (Charles Murray); 2—Quinta do Monte (James
David Webster Gordon); 3—Quinta Cova (Andrew Wardrop); 4—Quinta
da Achada (Richard Hill; William Penfold); 5—Quinta da Palmeira (Henry
Blackburn); 6—Quinta do Til (Alexander and James Gordon); 7—Quinta
dos Pinheiros (Bachelors Hall); 8—Quinta da Santa Luzeia (John Blandy);
9—Quinta da Levada (Andrew Wardrop); 10—Quinta San André (William
Casey); 11—Quinta do Val (Bachelors Hall, and later James Murdoch);
12—Quinta da Moedas Homens (Leitão); 13—Quinta Magnolia (Dr. Pita;
John Howard March)
Source: Drawn by Karl Longstreth. Maps created using software in
the Map Library, University of Michigan, Ann Arbor.

Figure 1.9. Richard Hill's Quinta da Achada, built 1750s–1770s.
Source: John J. Smith, ed., *Letters of Doctor Richard Hill and His Children*
(Philadelphia, 1854). Courtesy of The Library Company of Philadelphia.

Figure 1.10. James Gordon's Quinta do Til, built 1740s–1750s.
Source: Courtesy of Photographia-Museu "Vicentes," Funchal, Madeira.

Figure 1.11. Charles Murray's Quinta do Belo Monte, built 1780s.
Source: Courtesy of Photographia-Museu "Vicentes," Funchal, Madeira.

much less global trade in wine. Its exposed marine situation was troublesome, and there was little that the islanders could do about it. True, the fact that Funchal lay "open to the Atlantic" was something of a boon. The sea around it was deep: within one-half mile of the land, it was 300 feet and, within three-quarters mile, 600 feet; there, fishermen found plentiful stocks of albacore, dolphin, and bonito. But that depth created problems. There was no safe anchorage but at the western edge of the town, in 240 feet of water and at least a mile from the shore; even there a ship was always at the mercy of treacherous winds. In foul weather, when a gale blew from the south, southwest, or west and a great swell ensued, ships would have to slip their cables, raise their anchors, and put out to sea, "returning at a more favourable season for their lading." Other ships might "venture to ride out bad weather" by lying between the Loo Rock and the island, yet they did so at their peril, for frequently cables snapped and vessels crashed upon the "ragged steep rocky shore." In addition, the surf raised obstacles to easy shipping, as Greenwood captured in his 1783 oil painting (plate 5). Because of the depths and the winds, the bay had "so great a Surff" that those who rode or anchored offshore were in constant danger of capsizing. Broken hulls littered the bay and shore. In addition, rough surf made it difficult to get ashore or aboard without getting the passengers or goods soaked.[106]

Only gradually did islanders achieve some mastery over their "rode." About the fogs and clouds, they could do nothing. The changeable and fast winds could be partially managed with information. Elaborate sailing techniques were devised to accommodate wind changes, especially having to do with timing and direction. Local seamen imparted such wisdom to merchants, and merchants to visiting captains. Vessels arriving from the east "with the wind northeasterly" were told to go "through the passage between the Desertas and Madeira, keeping thence along to Madeira's shoar," since the northeasterly would "carry them as far as the Brazen Head" on the outskirts of Funchal. During the day, these ships were to "keep farther distant from the land, to avoid being becalmed under it, and to stretch into the stream of the sea breeze."[107] Similarly, to cope with the surf, mariners and merchants learned to turn "the stern towards it, and wait the rising of the surf," and then "endeavour to force in"; or, if that failed, they were to swim the pipes to the beach. Other steps, like innovations in boat design, were introduced to compensate for changeable weather, rough surf, and the relatively poor situation of the harbor.[108]

More physical, visible improvements were introduced only at the end of the eighteenth century. A true "quay or landing place" was needed to battle sea and sky and expedite shipping. During the 1750s, plans were formulated to enclose the harbor with a battlemented wall connecting the mainland to harbor islets. The king approved one design by a French engineer in 1757, but the project took years to finish and almost as soon at it was completed in 1775 a storm destroyed it. Alternate private schemes were floated in the 1760s "to join the Loo Rock at the Westernmost end of the beach" to the harbor's rocky point, but nothing was done with them. Construction of a true breakwater was not begun until 1885.[109] Second, a true lighthouse was needed to warn mariners of rock formations or weather conditions. But until the end of the nineteenth century seamen had to make do with a flag hoisted up a pole at the Loo Fort during the day and a lantern at night.[110] Third, unloading machinery was needed. The first real improvement came when an American wine exporter erected a column and a winch atop it near the Customs House in 1798.[111] None of these changes were revolutionary, of course, and only the column survived. Yet, through small, incremental, often unseen and certainly disconnected steps, they contributed to traders gaining greater control over the elements and ultimately over their trade.

Looking at Madeira's capital, one sees overlapping spaces in the built environment and in the activities unfolding within. Viewed together, one ascertains the

multiplicity of functions required for the buildup of a new wine market that occurred in these 175 years, and the degree to which one rather insignificant place
linked to and integrated with Portuguese and non-Portuguese networks and empires. One glimpses the extent to which the wine complex was decentralized,
organized by individual opportunists concerned primarily with the immediate
push and pull of the workday, concerned and frustrated more by local rivalries
and underdevelopment than central control and royal fiat, which they were willing to adhere to—but only when it served their purposes. One sees, as well, the
successful installation of a wine complex where none had existed before, largely
the work of a minority group of foreign traders who figured out how to work
with the native establishment. From much of the foregoing account, one could
conclude the natives had neither the commercial nor the organizational capacity
to develop an oceanic and eventually global trade in wine. A rural economy; an
uneducated populace; a work ethic that did not value education, record keeping,
and thrift, much less trade; nearly nonexistent capital: all these things stymied
the natives. Whatever their shortcomings—and they were legion—foreigners
had the capacity, although they had neither land nor laborers.

Yet facts belie such a conclusion. The two groups worked together to build
their market, and the improvements to their port are a case in point. Using the
time a ship spent in the harbor as a measure of the port's efficiency, one discovers
that that time fell from a high of twenty-three days in 1730 to eight days in 1775,
and to six days by 1815.[112] Thus, the greatest gains were made before the foreigners
began to lobby for change and introduce improvements on their own. A much
more efficient trade-based bureaucracy arose in the 1750s, in part a response to
the promptings of Pombal but more a function of the hawkeyed oversight of
several governors intent on maximizing the revenues flowing to themselves and
their demesne. At the same time, a much more tolerant approach to foreigners
set in, not only among officials like the governor but also among the natives.
Finally, again at the same time, a much more compliant group of marginal men
wholly obsessed with work arrived, intent less on asserting their Englishness and
rights (witnessed by a noticeable decline in complaints issued by the Factory and
consul) and more on gaining real profits and Atlanticizing the trade. That the
new wine complex emerged at all was the consequence of unrelenting human
endeavor among and between the natives and strangers.

Part I

MAKING WINE

2

The Culture of the Vine

"The culture of the vine" was "one of the most important means of support to the people of Portugal" for over a century, observed Henry F. Link, a professor at the University of Rostock who, with the German botanist Count Johann Centurius Hoffmannsegg, was touring France and Iberia and collecting plants between 1797 and 1801.[1] Viticulture engendered many of the ties to the overseas trading world that these kingdoms and their empires enjoyed between 1640 and 1815. This was the case not only on the mainland but also in Iberian dependencies. Certainly this was the case with Madeira in this period, when wine production was always for export.

Most of the island's agricultural land had been devoted to sugarcane in the sixteenth and early seventeenth centuries, but the success of sugar cultivation in the New World made sugar monoculture uneconomic for Madeirans, as we have seen. From the beginning of their oenological golden age, the islanders linked themselves to international trade and to distributors and consumers in Europe and other regions around the Atlantic basin. Accordingly, the Madeira wine producers "improved" their product and technique over the long eighteenth century with both local innovations and ideas and approaches previously adopted by continental European wine producers. Producers prospered because Atlantic trade routes were relatively free of fighting and because the trade policies of Britain and to a lesser extent Portugal favored the relatively free flow of the commodity; they suffered during war, when trade routes were blocked, and when government policy went against them. Yet, they prospered, too, by dint of hard work and incremental implementation of change in the way cultivation was done. The product that emerged increased in value in Atlantic markets and, as it did so, the producers reaped some of the rewards for this. These achievements were not foreseen and did not go uncontested: new varietals and techniques of husbandry were adopted by trial-and-error experimentation, and were stubbornly resisted by traditional practitioners. Moreover, these changes reflected and affected producers' engagement with distributors and consumers in the widening Atlantic-centered world of wine, responding to British, American, and Indian consumers' tastes as filtered back to them through what best may be described as "conversations" that island exporters had with the wider world—construing "conversation" in the early modern sense of the term to mean the action of dealing with others and things, an action not only spoken but also either written or performed: an "interchanging of thoughts."[2] Links to importers, sellers, and drinkers in London, Lisbon, Bahia, and Philadelphia made Madeira's producers critical agents in the emerging Atlantic economy. Indeed, they were so central that even readers of Ohio Valley papers in 1815 felt it necessary to keep abreast of the island's production levels.[3]

THE LAND

The islanders' annual production averaged roughly 25,000 pipes of wine between 1675 (when the island-wide crop was first tallied) and 1815. No annual production figure was compiled by the government, nor can one now derive such a figure from the related tax records that were kept. One must rely on eyewitness summations and, according to them, total production ranged as low as 5,000 pipes in 1770 and again in 1815 and as high as 60,000 pipes in 1794. But such extremes were rare. In most years, it fell between 20,000 and 30,000 pipes. Even so—and this is still a wide range—production levels swung sharply from year to year: for instance, 25,000 in 1783, 40,000 in 1784 and 1785, 13,000 in 1786, 26,000 in 1787, 17,000 in 1788, 24,000 in 1789, 12,000 in 1790, 20,000 in 1791, 1792, and 1793, and 60,000 in 1794.[4]

The physical environment constituted the strongest determinant of these levels, heavily influencing the cultivation of grapes, and Madeira was—and is— an island of numerous microclimates. For raising wine grapes, relevant aspects of climate include the orientation of the property and exposure to the sun, the height above the sea and the temperature, and the amount and timing of rainfall. These factors determined the types of grapes that flourished, the volumes, and the qualities of the raw juice or, as it is called, must (*mosto*). These were facts of agricultural life.

The cultivation of grapes depended, as well, on the soil itself. Most of the land used for vineyards was fertile, rich in nutrients and well drained, even if some terrain was "extremely rocky" and some ground rather shallow. Local experts and visiting scientists generally agreed on the fertility of the place, noting that the island was rich in much-needed nitrogen, phosphorus, and potash, even though most believed that that fertility had fallen consistently since the fifteenth century, the result of soil erosion and exhaustion.[5] Whether exhausted or not, the island enjoyed "one kind of soil more than another": decomposed red and yellow tufa. Soil analysts generally agree: Madeira's vineyard soils were a yellow, red, or dark tufa. This was "a free light sandy or gravelly" acidic soil that was generally free of chalk or lime. This was important because a mixture of tufa, marl, and sand feeding the vines allowed their roots "to spread wider, and to draw nourishment with ease from the extensive surface."[6]

Vineyards were scattered throughout the island, except on the very upper reaches of the mountainous peaks and in the cold, barren high central plains. Vine lands were variously categorized as being upper-, middle- or lower-ground, depending on their altitude and whether they lay on the northern or southern side of the island. The fifteen or so northern parishes generally produced twice the quantity of wine of the twenty-four or so southern parishes, although south-side vineyards produced higher-quality must. A census of the island's 1787 harvest, for instance, recorded that the southern parishes' vineyards produced 6,800 pipes, the northern 15,000 pipes. Volume-producing parishes all lay on the north side: Ponta Delgada (13 percent of the island's total production), Porto da Cruz (8 percent), and São Vicente (8 percent). In the south, no single parish dominated; the parishes producing the greatest amounts were St. Antonio on the northwestern outskirts of Funchal (5 percent), Câmara de Lobos to the west of Funchal (4 percent), and the inland and higher Estreito do Câmara de Lobos (4 percent). Other surviving island-wide censuses paint a nearly identical picture of quantity distribution.[7]

As to quality and price, the two sides also differed. "Good wines" were "all produced on the south side," one English merchant reported, "while those of the North are poor, pale, hungry wines, which are drank by the common people, as cyder is in England, or are made into Brandys." From one or two northern parishes, one might procure low "cargo wine," but as to "fine wine, not a drop." The more expensive musts flowed from south-side presses; in many years, south-side musts sold for twice that of north-side. Yet south-side vineyards faced a big problem: south-side growers cultivated primarily red or burgundy grapes, in contrast to the white grapes grown by their northern counterparts. Paler wines fetched higher prices, as consumers preferred them. When the best south-side wine was new, it was "not pale or white, but of a Claret or reddish cast." "Some, *the best of all our Wine*, and of course the dearest," fretted one exporter, was "darker than

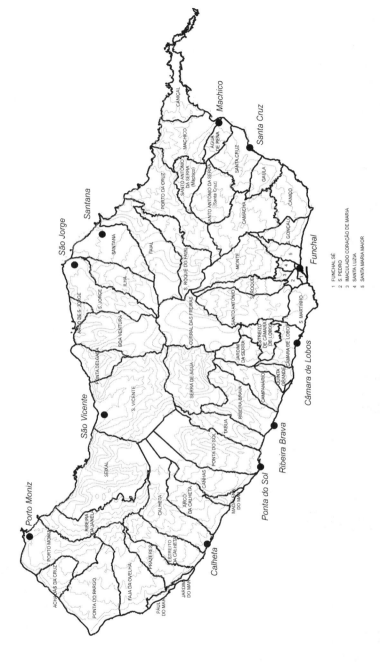

Figure 2.1. Map of island parishes and terrain.

Source: Drawn by Karl Longstreth. Maps created using software in the Map Library, University of Michigan, Ann Arbor.

Claret or Port." As a result, some blending with northern must was needed to lighten the product.[8]

Perhaps just as important as the distribution of vines was their extension into new areas of the island as the eighteenth century advanced. By 1700, over half of the arable land (one-third of the island) had been converted to the production of wine; by 1815, nearly two-thirds had been cultivated. Critical in this extension were the middle decades of the eighteenth century, when owners and cultivators began terracing and tilling the upper, hitherto uncultivated reaches of arable parishes and taking advantage of the declining prices of vine shoots to plant new vines in these areas. Isolated extension began to appear around the island in the 1750s, but large-scale introduction did not take place before the 1780s.[9]

OWNERS, CULTIVATORS, AND FARMERS

Three types of producers worked in the industry. The owners (*senhorios* or *proprietarios*) commonly rented their vine land "on an annual tenure" to cultivators (*colonos*). Such an arrangement originated in the fifteenth century with sugar cultivation. But a significant difference had emerged. By the middle decades of the seventeenth century, the owners were contracting directly with cultivators, as they had before, but the cultivators were gathering and pressing the grapes themselves, for black slaves were no longer much employed as manual laborers on account of the rising cost of slaves and the high seasonality of the work, plus the fact that absenteeism prevailed less among vine land than cane field owners.[10]

Cultivation (*colonia*) contracts did not change much over time: Iberians brought them to Madeira from the Peninsula in the fifteenth century, and the form they assumed generally persisted through the early nineteenth century. One typical contract of "lease and obligation" from 1646 ran for nineteen years. Under it, Ana Freitas leased from Senhor Palmeira e Massaptez "a site of vines and arbors of fruit," along "with a house and press." Freitas was entitled to receive irrigation water four days a week; in return, each year, she was obliged to tender two chickens and half of all crops reaped. After eighteen years, Palmeira e Massaptez would have to pay Freitas for all improvements (*bem feitorias*) she had made to the land, the house, the press, and the vines, if she had not already sold or mortgaged them (which she had the right to do by contract if Palmeira e Massaptez agreed). Sometimes an owner required the tenant to perform certain labors, and sometimes the work was detailed in advance, as when a 1757 contract stipulated that a tenant in Curral would have "to plant arbors, vegetables, yams, willows, meixieieras, etc." Sometimes a tenant paid the owner a rent in a fixed amount of produce or a certain percentage of production. Under traditional agricultural arrangements, the cultivator paid one-tenth of his produce as a tithe to the Church, another tenth as a tithe to the Crown, and four-tenths to the owner as rent, and he kept or sold the remainder. These tithes and rents were generally paid "in kind." The 1757 Curral tenant, for instance had, in the first three years of his contract, to tender only a chicken; during the succeeding three years, he had to tender a chicken plus one-third of all produce; for the remainder of the lease, he had to tender half of all produce.

The essence of the contract was a sharing of the product; a peculiarity of the arrangement was allowing the tenant to take ownership of improvements. Variations on the cultivation contract were endless; it was a "vague form that one cannot define with precision." Nonetheless, one can conclude a few things: it was a relational system in which almost all power ultimately rested with the owners. Under contracts that were more often than not oral and customary, a cultivator under contract and the inheritor of a contract had no absolute right to do with the land or improvement as he desired, even though he had agreed to work and improve it. The owner could refuse to sanction an improvement. Moreover, the owner could refuse to relet the land to the tenant or could wrest it from him at whim, changing tenants one year to the next. This threat of eviction served as a prod to the cultivator to maintain and increase productivity. Yet the threat was more voiced than executed: improvements would increase the buy-back costs borne by an owner; at the same time, they would enhance the value of the asset and so encourage stability of maintenance.[11]

A new class of "farmers" (*feitors*) emerged by the middle of the eighteenth century as important intermediaries between owners and cultivators. The farmers rented land from the owners and, in turn, sublet it to the cultivators. They also provided crude banking services to the ill-served cultivators, lending them the money to buy "necessities" and earning it back by taking their produce in repayment. Given the farmers' middling social status and their importance to the island's overall economy, noble families and religious orders preferred to deal with them rather than lower-sort cultivators. To both owners and cultivators, farmers injected greater security into land management, minimizing diachronic uncertainty and lowering transaction costs. Farmers eased the life of cultivators by granting them credit and, on occasion, supplying their needs. They eased the life of owners, as well, providing expert, on-the-spot information. Since it was all they did, they could acquire and deploy deep knowledge about the locality and capacity of the vineyards, the personalities of possible tenants, the quality of their wines, and the like—all matters which might be terra incognita to members of religious communities who had recently moved to the island or absentee land-lords who had long before moved away. In possession of the wine, the farmers also complicated wine's distribution, mediating between growers and exporters and thereby becoming immediate suppliers to the trade. Under this new system, the farmer paid the tithes to the Church and Crown; in addition, he sold the owner's four-tenths and sometimes the cultivator's four-tenths of the product and pocketed the difference between the price agreed with the owner or cultiva-tor and the price he could get in the market. This institution of farming sufficed for much of the eighteenth century, until at the beginning of the nineteenth cen-tury some merchants began going around farmers and "attaching" themselves directly to cultivators.[12]

THE VINEYARD

The "common vineyard" worked by cultivators generally consisted of three or four square acres, "in the center of which stands the family-house." It was, by all accounts, a "miserably built" structure—"little hovels," one visitor called them—constructed of large pebble stones without any cement, a thatched roof, a door, and sometimes a window. A small kitchen garden adjoined it. Elsewhere, the houses had "grapes, melons, gourds, & c. running all over them, so as not to be seen," and usually "on the south side two or three orange trees, bay trees, lemons, or such like." Each vineyard also had a press (*lagar*) and sometimes a press house (*casa do lagar*)—"a low stone building with high pitched roof, lighted by a couple of small windows, and shaded by the spreading branches of . . . the *Eriobotrya japonica*." A typical press house contained several presses, the largest of which was "capable of pressing four or five pipes of *mosto* at a time." Vines, presses, houses, and gardens were then surrounded by irrigation waterways and bramble, myrtle, pomegranate, prickly pear, or wild rose hedges.[13] The grapes of a Madeira vineyard were, by all accounts, "beyond all comparison, more large" than in most wine-producing regions of Europe; a bunch of grapes might weigh as much as six pounds or more; often, the weight of the grapes was heavy enough to break the stalks. Factoring in the acreage, they yielded voluminous quantities in a good year, although the vintage might vary dramatically from year to year.[14]

Little is known about how cultivators, farmers, and owners made the myriad of farming decisions affecting grapes and vines—from initial planning through vine treatment and crop sampling to final harvest—since few if any of them left personal, diaristic commentaries on point. Still, much can be gleaned from ref-erences made by those they encountered: island officials, resident merchants, and nosy visitors. According to these observers, viticultural practice was conservative or traditional. The choice of vine and grape variety was usually left to the cultivators, at least in principle. In practice, most cultivators continued to raise the vines already growing on the plots they leased. If more plants were desired, the vines were "generally propagated from cuttings, as the preferable mode of culture, rather than from seed," planted far apart, several feet in the ground and, as erosion advanced, in deeper trenches. Ideally, they would begin to bear in the third year, it taking a year to ripen the wood and engender bud development and another year to realize an adequate fruit set and fully developed bunches of grapes. In lands planted after 1640, most vines were propagated from "vine eye" cuttings—that is, small portions of the vine stem possessing a dormant bud and subsequently rooted in the soil. Some, however, were raised from hardwood cuttings—long pieces of stems. Still others were established through "layering," a form of propagating vines that placed a vine parallel to the soil, pegged the stem into the ground, cut it, and then covered the cut stem with soil. Vine propagation on Madeira, like elsewhere in Portugal, was most commonly conducted in the dormant growing season from early to midwinter.[15]

The biggest problem arising from this way of doing things was that the producers and exporters who bought the wine had little knowledge of what it was. Over the years, Madeira's vineyards had been planted with whatever variety presented itself and fruited prolifically. The "number of varieties of the vine is as great in Portugal as in other countries," one visitor noted in 1801, even if many were "often mingled together." Yet, as drinkers in the eighteenth century began to express their preferences for specific types of Madeira, and merchant distributors began to tailor the wines to specific tastes and markets, they came to desire particular varietals and to value consistency.[16]

Grafting from an established vine with desired characteristics was the best guarantee of consistency. But the cultivators initially resisted this approach as it could reduce the volume of wine vineyards produced. Even in the second half of the eighteenth century, when it was generally recognized that vines could be "frequently improved" by grafting, cleft-grafting, scutcheon-grafting, inoculation, and inarching, cultivators balked. The Portuguese, like producers along the Rhone and Moselle, knew of these methods and on occasion used them on the mainland. Madeirans generally did not. Refusing to graft, despite the inducements by exporters and the orders issued by the island government, of course, "spoild" the vine by allowing "different sorts of bad ones" to grow and be "taken as much care of as the best." While this was no secret, by 1768 (and then "with great difficulty"), only a few Madeirans had grafted their vines "and by this means bring all the fruit of a vineyard to be of one sort." Only gradually, late in the period, did cultivators embrace grafting, realizing they could grow grapes in new places where certain other crops might not survive. Nonetheless, "some of them still obstinately refuse[d] to adopt the practice" as late as 1812, even though they did graft their fruit and chestnut trees. Moreover, those who did adopt still clung to tradition, using a hearty domestic rootstock that descended from plants carried to the island by the settlers of the fifteenth century. Planting from seeds was "never practiced" on the island. Local rootstock was used until the onset of oidium in the 1850s.[17]

SELECTING THE VARIETY

racial tones overtones anywhere?

Agricultural and commercial experimentation encouraged a spirit of experimentation with respect to the proliferation and choice of varietals. In 1687, Hans Sloane listed only three sorts of grapes: white (probably Verdelho, the most plentiful grape, around two-thirds of the island's annual crop), black or red (Tinta), and muscatine (Malvasia). During Sloane's time and through the first quarter of the eighteenth century, the "great quantity of wine" was made from the juice of the white grape into which was mixed some of that of the red. As late as the 1790s, some commentators were still listing only five — white (Verdelho and Bual), red (Tinta), pink (Bastardo), and Malmsey (Malvasia) — because these varieties produced the tastes Atlantic consumers desired.[18]

Despite the apparent continuity, offerings actually expanded as Madeira drinkers reported back to island distributors that they preferred specific varieties to blended lots. American drinkers desired dryer wines, while British wanted sweeter. The divide spurred Madeira's exporters to produce new varieties with the requisite smoothness and sweetness. To get the cultivators to produce new varieties, as well as to produce them in pure lots, the merchants took the matter up with the island's regional government. The governors, convinced that the vineyards constituted "the principal wealth of the island," agreed and so intervened in the choice of varieties with greater frequency during the last quarter of the century. Certain varieties were to be preferred if the island's export was to be expanded, they had learned from hard experience. When it came time to promote the agriculture of neighboring Porto Santo in 1783, for instance, the governor ordered the planting of Verdelho, Bual and Tinta — but not Listrão, which he thought "tastes good" but did "not make good wine."[19]

So it was that by 1768 one British export house could send the governor of Montserrat a wide assortment of grapes filling ten tubs and a box. Most prominent were the Ferral ("a large black grape & very pleasant to eat, but not so proper for wine"), the Preta (a black grape that was "a wine grape"), the Malvasia or Malmsey ("a very luscious white grape"), the Alicante ("a large white eating grape"), the Verdelho (a white grape), the Bual (another white grape), and the Bastardo (which was a red grape that produced a pale white wine). These seven were "reckoned the best sorts" the island had to offer, but, the firm assured the governor, there were "a great variety" of others. To their customer Sir John Gibbons, the firm sent two additional types to be planted in his garden outside London—Amaretto and Terrantez—as well as two hybrids—the Alicante Preto and the Bastardo Preto—and to another customer they sent "the very high-flavored" Muscatel. These were but a sampling. In the same year, 1768, a friend wrote George Washington that the "rich Vineyards of Madeira" produced "no less than twenty three different species of Grapes." Some forty years later, when William Gourlay published *Observations on the Natural History, Climate, and Diseases of Madeira*, that was still the case.[20]

Of all the varieties, the four that were made into wine from largely unblended stock and favored by Atlantic consumers for their smoothness and flavor were subsequently dubbed "noble" in the nineteenth century: the dry Sercial, the less dry Verdelho, the medium-sweet Bual, and the sweet Malvasia.[21] The driest, the Sercial grape, produced a wine "superior to any dry wine," Gourlay noted, and "much esteemed on account of its scarcity and high flavour." Sercial grew best in the cooler higher vineyards of the South, roughly above one thousand meters, as at Jardim da Serra, or in the north at Porto Moniz and São Vicente. Unfortunately for the distributors, it was extremely scarce; in good years, it enjoyed only a small vintage and often it failed entirely, as in 1787. Sercial took "the work of many a long year to procure," since it could be grown on so few vineyards, and the lots were warranted to buyers through long-standing contracts. As late as 1807, this "scarce and dear wine," also known as "Madeira Hock," was "very difficult to obtain even 2 or 3 casks in the course of the year." Some firms considered giving up even offering it to purchasers.[22]

Verdelho flourished best on the north side, near Porto Moniz, Ribeira da Janela, and Santana. It had more sugar than Sercial and made a nuttier, peachier wine. It was, contemporaries noted, much sweeter, yet at the same time more acidic. Bual was grown in the warm areas of the south side: Calheta, Câmara de Lobos, and Funchal. It made a rich, sweet, spicy, dark wine. The last of what became the four "noble varieties"—Malvasia or Malmsey—was grown in the warmest, lowest altitudes along the southern coast, around Câmara de Lobos. Through the first two-thirds of the eighteenth century, Malmsey was a monopoly of the Jesuits, the order possessing the only lands on which it was grown; after the order's expulsion, the lands passed to the noblewoman and landowner Dona Guiomar. It appeared as two different types: red and green. It was always the last to ripen, and produced the island's darkest and sweetest must. Either red or green was "superior to any sweet wine." But Malmsey was always in short supply; in bad years, the failure could be total, as was the case in 1785, 1786, and 1787.[23]

Tinta (formally Tinta Negro Mole, or "Tent," as it was commonly known) was the island's staple grape, not one of the four "noble" varieties. It bore a taste "much the flavour of Burgundy" and was "commonly mixed with the other[s]," such as Verdelho and Bual, forming the base and coloration for most of the blends the exporters sent abroad. Throughout the period 1640–1815, it was common for traders to include a quarter-cask of red Tinta in an order for wine to give the wine "a deeper color if required" and, thereby, please the consumer better. The exporter William Bolton, for instance, sent to America in the early years of the eighteenth century some "old wines" "with their naturall collour," but he also sent three pipes of Tinta "soe that if [it was] thought fitt to putt any more couloring into them," the consumers "might doe itt" upon receipt. Tinta was "a very high-colored harsh wine" and was "seldom or never shipped off by itself, being chiefly mixed with very low thin pale wines." In many years, "all the *tinta*" was bought up for the purpose of mixing up and making parcels of blended wine.[24]

PREPARING THE SITE

In addition to selecting a variety, the cultivator bore direct responsibility for arranging the layout of the property, terracing the plot, trellising the plants, and channeling water to the vineyard. "The people belonging to the vineyards exert[ed] great skill and application in the management of their vines," according to a 1748 "Description of the Island"; indeed, this constituted "the principal subject of emulation among" them. This seemed correct despite the fact that, as late as 1815, the "instruments . . . with which their wine . . . is made, are perfectly simple and unimproved."[25]

As vines generally need a deep root run, careful trenching was essential. This was especially so on Madeira, where the slopes are extremely steep. Further compounding this need, the island experienced severe soil erosion; once the original forest cover was removed, the recurrent droughts and torrential rainfalls stripped dry soil from steeply sloped terraces. The decrease required cultivators to plant more deeply. Whereas in the middle of the seventeenth century they planted their vines twelve or eighteen inches deep, by the beginning of the nineteenth century they were placing them three to six feet deep. Furthermore, to protect them "from the hard ground at the bottom of the trench," they began placing a quantity of loose earth underneath. To make the most of the steep terrain, minimize the cascade of water down the sides of the hills, slow erosion, and retain the soil, they began terracing the hills as a matter of course by the second half of the eighteenth century. These terraces, constructed by hand and supported by stone walls, reconfigured the mountainside with a series of steps parallel to the horizon and shaped to the contour of the land.[26]

 Trellising, a subject that perennially fascinated visiting Americans and Europeans, was equally necessary. Early on in the south, and eventually all over the island, the "natives" fastened their vines "to poles about five feet high, sustained within squares, made of reed or cane," and "raised a little above the surface of the earth." The vines thus ran "all on a frame, about two feet or rather more from the ground, made of stakes drove down, and wild sugar canes in cross bars at topp; which covers therefore the ground." George Forster, who visited the island in 1772 while accompanying Captain Cook on his second voyage around the world, added detail. One or several walks, "about a yard or two wide, intersect each vineyard, and are included by stone walls two feet high. Along these walks, which are arched over with laths about seven feet high, they erect wooden pillars at regular distances, to support a lattice work of bamboos, which slopes down from both sides of the walk, till it is only a foot and a half or two feet high, in which elevation it extends over the whole vineyard. The vines are, in this manner, supported from the ground." The cultivators, thus, had room to climb under the trellises and root out the weeds and, later, during the harvest, cut bunches from below; in doing so, they escaped the rigors of the subtropical sun. In addition to easing the work of the laborers, "this method of keeping the ground clean and moist, and ripening the grapes in the shade" gave the wines "that excellent flavor and body for which they are remarkable." While this homemade "basket work" became the "usual mode" for training vines, Madeirans employed other methods in places. In some vineyards, especially on the north side, vines were "led up trees, or high poles"; on other lands, they were "cut down to the height of two or three feet, as at the Cape of Good Hope."[27]

Trellises dominated, nonetheless. Supplying the material for them sometimes proved difficult. The "finest poles in the world, for support of the vines," were "the long and strait branches of cedar trees," but as these were not always easy or cheap to obtain, chestnut poles (made from island trees) were common. Likewise, the lattices were made from sugarcane grown at the margins of brooks running down the mountains; decayed or useless reeds were usually replaced or refitted in February. Forster noted that "the owners of vineyards are . . . obliged to allot a certain spot of ground for the growth of bamboos; for the lattice-work cannot be made without them," and he was told that "some vineyards lay quite neglected for want of this useful reed." If they had none, they would have to buy them from neighbors or, more commonly, import them from abroad.[28]

Even as terracing and trellising demanded much of his attention, the cultivator could not ignore irrigation. Channeling water to a vineyard was always one of the more expensive and dependent operations undertaken. The water was collected from rivers and springs in the mountains and carried into the vineyards "by wears and channels" cut through the rock or by wooden pipes "suspended overhead." There, each cultivator had "the use of it for a certain time": some had "a constant supply of it," while others could use it only once, twice, or thrice a week. Those who did not have "a constant supply" were forced to purchase additional water from those who did, "at a high price." In all cases, the supply was spelled out in the cultivation contract or a separate deed detailing the frequency, duration, and volume of distribution. At an agreed-upon hour, a channel worker (*leva-deiro*) who managed the flow of the nearest channel (*levada*) sounded a horn, and the cultivator opened the sluices to receive the water. This system remained relatively unchanged through the nineteenth century, even though cultivators chafed at their dependence on the owners of the water. Water was never anything but "exceedingly scarce and exceptionally valuable."[29]

MANAGING THE CYCLE:
A YEAR IN THE LIFE OF A VINEYARD

Life on a vineyard had a routine largely dictated by the climate and crop, both of which ordered the daily lives of not only the cultivators but also the distribu-tors resident on the island and those carrying the wine across the seas. The year started for all in November, at the close of harvest. At that point, the cultivators stripped the vines of remaining fruit. Little pruning took place, although, "before the fall of the leaf" in the first three years of a vineyard's life, they dug a furrow "round each vine" in order to "cut the roots and afford sufficient moisture."[30]

In December, cultivators began digging and trenching to plant new vines and to replace diseased or dead ones. In January, they turned over the surface soil. The task was performed two times more during the rest of the cycle: early in the spring "before the leaves come out" and again "before the blossoms appear." Till-ing (*redrar*) was a "very necessary annual labour" whenever done, for it aerated the soil and allowed existing roots to breathe, promoted free or freer drainage of water to the roots, and killed harmful weeds that would otherwise sap nourish-ment from the vines.[31]

The cultivators applied manure in February, if they treated the land at all. Erosion not only thinned the soil of its nutrients but also destabilized vineyards clinging to the sides of steep mountains. These issues were not regarded as serious in 1700; but an urgency was apparent among those concerned by 1800: land re-quired "the frequent assistance of manure" — either animal dung or burnt ashes of wild broom—"for otherwise the plants soon decay, or produce very scanty crops." Manuring was especially critical in a time of transition, for older vineyards struggling to produce as before and for new vine stock struggling to gain a footing. Some proprietors did manure, but many more did not. Indeed, it appears that little was done on a regular basis to mitigate nutrient depletion: traditional approaches continued, and the vines suffered accordingly.[32]

In the rainy months of February and March, the cultivators cut back sprouts, shoots, or suckers to shape the vine, avoid tangles of unchecked growth, and "encourage regular and heavy cropping." As one Scottish exporter informed a customer to whom he sent some slips: Madeirans generally pruned vines "in Feb. & March, but the last is reckoned the most proper." The practice stood basically uncontested: unpruned vines would deteriorate in vigor more rapidly than pruned ones, and their crops would thin. The natives had "particular days" they favored for pruning—"the 3d or 5th day of the new moon of March or the 1st Friday of [the] same month"—which to the mind of the Briton bore "a strong face of superstition," but it was a custom that could not be shaken. One thing everyone agreed on: the vines had to be pruned before the sap rose. The manner of pruning depended "much on the skill of the gardener," especially in times other than the depth of winter. Superfluous branches were "lopped off" in a process known as *esladroar*, a "short time before and after" the vines were in bloom. On occasion, the leaves were "also taken off" (*esfolhar*) "to expose the grapes to the sun." In April, fields were cleared of weeds, grass, and herbs, shoots were tied up, and vines were topped. Superfluous shoots deemed unnecessary for the bearing of fruit were removed through May, and those deemed helpful were topped; most important, the vines were tied to the trellises or trees. It was in May that vines bloomed, and thus the care of the plants during this month was some of the most watchful, although from this point forward the rigor of daily routine lessened markedly for the cultivator.[33]

During the long lazy summer months, cultivators continued to trim the vines and remove new shoots. "Examination" of the foliage began on St. John's Day (June 24), if not before. At the same time, they began clearing the rows of unwanted undergrowth that would sap the vines of nutrients, and tended to fruits and vegetables like melons and gourds that they had planted in their shade. Weeding continued on into July. To allow for greater admission of sunlight into the vines, which would assist the ripening and facilitate the circulation of air (which would, in turn, decrease the likelihood of fungal mold), the leaves were plucked and the tops were nipped again. The summer months were some of the year's most critical, for this was the time that the grapes ripened. At this stage, the following substances are abundant in the berry: starches, tannins, chlorophyll, tartaric and malic acids. When the grape begins to swell, the starch and chloro-phyll contents diminish proportionately. Sugars now begin to accumulate in the berry and, parallel to their increase, malic acid decreases. At the end of August, the food supplies from the leaves become exhausted, but the grape continues to swell with the absorption of water from the roots. The cultivators were fully en-gaged in August and September with checking the bunches of fruit for ripeness, damage, and disease, readying the plot and labor force for the harvest, sharpen-ing knives for cutting the bunches from the stalks, acquiring new or cleaning old wicker baskets for collecting the plucked bunches of grapes, repairing the press, and readying goatskin receptacles to receive the new must.[34]

The harvest (*vindima*) could start any time after the middle of August, begin-ning at the water's edge and moving up to the highest cultivated elevations; it could last from four to six weeks, often through the end of October. When the harvest actually started was determined by the type, maturity, and location of the grapes. Verdelho grapes, for instance, ripened before Malvasia grapes; grapes grown on lower slopes, Malvasia excepted, were harvested earlier than those on upper slopes; and grapes grown on the south side were ready before those on the north side.

The harvest was a simple affair. The cultivator, members of his family and, if needed, unengaged neighbors, friends, and relatives willing to work for a small fee crept under the trellises, cut the clusters of grapes from the stalks, taking care to keep a piece of the stem attached to the bunch, and placed them in wicker bas-kets or clay tubs. The children removed the containers and carried them to the press. The process varied little from that deployed in other wine-growing regions: harvesters collected the grapes in "cool, rainey, dewey, misty or foggy mornings before [the] heat of [the] sun has exhaled moisture from [the] grapes"; then "cut the branches from vines as close to grapes as possible to have the less stalk, be-cause the more of the stalk goes into the press, the rougher and tarter the wine will be"; carried the bunches "to the press, without hurting or bruising" them; removed rotten grapes from the bunches; and placed the remainder in the vat. It generally took a Madeira household two weeks to clear a vineyard.[35]

During a typical year, it was not uncommon for the crop to fail in one part of the island. The natural hazards to production came principally from the weather. Early in the year, wind and hail could strip the vine of its flowers or halt fur-ther growth. Wind broke the vines and killed the grapes; hail broke the skin of the leaves and grapes, making the plant susceptible to disease or to drying and shriveling up. Either way, the flower was destroyed, and the fruit emerged small. One Madeira export merchant recounted a typical development: "When the vines were in flower, there was every prospect of an abundant vintage; but from

various causes"—primarily wind and hail—"much of the flower was destroyed &
the grapes which *escapared* have in general remained small." Heavy fogs block-
ing sunlight could similarly inhibit the efflorescence of the vine and maturation
of the fruit. As another exporter fussed to one of his correspondents, the foggy
weather in May 1760 had "done infinite prejudice to the vines," and islanders
feared there would be "a very short vintage." Thick fogs in June 1783 likewise hid
the sun for a month and did "great mischief to all the vines." The hot, dry *leste*
winds often did "a great deal of harm to the vines" in August. One particularly
severe *leste* "blew down some [vines] . . . & withered others" on most estates in
1774 and again in 1777. Two years later, a *leste* persisting six weeks burnt vines "to
a chip." The hot winds and extreme heat of August 1807, coming on top of "much
cold weather" in June and July, ripened the grapes before they had "attained a
proper size."[36]

Hail and wind were often accompanied by rain, which affected the growth
of the vines and the quality of the wines more than any other natural condition.
Lack of rain could shrivel vines and grapes. An "excessive hott" summer could
be especially destructive; dry weather "scorcht up" the grapes, and "excessive
heates" "dryed the grapes mightily." The "uninterrupted heat & long cloudless
sun" of August and September 1790, for instance, "indurated the skin of the
grape & thickened the pulp of the fruit so as to prevent its yielding the same
quantity of juice in proportion as usual"; this occasioned "a much greater breakage [shortfall] than was expected." A long, hot, dry summer might make the
wines too rich. Too much rain could be as problematic as not enough. Rain at the
right time was necessary. On the one hand, if the roots were "well soaked" during
the spring months, then the vines would "be in fine condition for budding." On
the other hand, the wine was "hurt by unseasonable rains in the vintage time."
"Misty drizzly weather" late in the maturation process rotted the grapes "very
fast" and made the wine "very thin & ticklish to be meddled with." The rules
could be contradictory. Malvasia grapes, which ripened in late September and
October, were made "much better" if it rained in early September, while the
opposite was true for Vidonia grapes, which were being harvested at that time.
During gathering and pressing, heavy rains caused the must to be "very thin"
and of "low quality." The rains of 1803 demonstrated the destructiveness of unseasonable weather. The season had been "remarkably fine, both for the Harvest
& Vines." The "vintage was going on favorably," and it "promised to be the largest
ever known." Half had been harvested when, on the last day of September, "the
rains began & continued with some intermission the ensuing week," culminating
in the flood of October 9. In that deluge, the city's three rivulets overflowed their

banks and washed away churches, offices, houses, and five hundred lives. Nearly half of the island's vintage was "destroyed or rendered unfit for shipping."[37]

Disease and infestation did little to interrupt the annual agricultural cycle—surprising since Madeira has come to be associated with the double wine scourges of oidium, or powdery mildew, and the aphid phylloxera, which decimated the island vines and roots in the 1850s and 1860s. Insects did not bedevil the Madeirans; not a single mention of insect devastation occurs in commercial correspondence or governmental files between 1640 and 1815. Diseases that severely handicapped grape growing were also rare. No fungal diseases were recorded. Horticultural invasions lay in the future.[38]

CONFLICT BETWEEN CULTIVATORS AND DISTRIBUTORS

Madeira's cultivators were the subject of frequent comment—and the object of constant derision—for foreigners working on the island. The latter complained to each other, to their partners and correspondents resident in Europe, Britain, or America, and to any guests who would listen. They complained about the Madeirans' tools, their agricultural methods, their conservatism with respect to agricultural practices, and their dishonesty. Looking back with hindsight, this is one place where the absence of the Madeirans' and especially the cultivators' voices leaves an unfortunate gap. Nonetheless, one can build up a partial picture of internecine struggle among participants in the island's wine complex.

Observers reported, for instance, that cultivators, inattentive to the deteriorated condition of the vines, failed to replace them often enough. Many vines were fifty years old, and some had been kept for over a century. Up to five decades, the older the better, but around that point the vines begin to dry out and produce fewer grapes. The management of plants fell on the cultivators, whose tenancy agreements often stipulated planting and care and whose agricultural improvements redounded to their credit upon eviction. Beginning in the 1770s, vine deterioration was on everyone's lips. The older cultivators "complain[ed] much of sickness among the vines"; the following year, they noticed that "sickness of the vines prevails more and more yearly." From these and similar observations, one can surmise that the "sickness" in question was soil and plant exhaustion. References to "the exhausted state" of the vines and soils became frequent in merchant correspondences and governmental files after 1750, but the situation was described as critical only in the 1770s, when a run of short vintages occurred.[39]

Compounding the distributors' sense of grievance was cultivators' (and often owners') conservatism with regard to new care techniques. New planting was

encouraged by the government from 1759, but its proposals were seldom implemented until the 1780s. The same was true with grafting. By 1768, as we have
seen, some cultivators had been persuaded "to graft their vines and by this means
bring all the fruit of a vineyard to be of one sort"; before this, good vine "had
been spoil'd" by allowing "different sorts of bad ones" to grow alongside it and
giving them "as much care of as the best, because they added to the quantity of
their wine." This was common practice, even though the islanders were "perfectly acquainted with the use of grafting, and constantly practised it on their
chestnut trees." Removing excess fruit also raised native ire: cultivators resisted
picking "off some of the grapes," one exporter observed with annoyance, despite
the fact that in June the clusters were full and the vines "so excessive weak that
the weight of the branches" was breaking the stalks.[40]

Distributors elevated their concerns over viticultural practice above mere
complaint when they detected the adulteration of south-side wines with inferior
north-side wines. Because the output of the north-side vineyards was greater and
comparatively untapped, it was profitable, albeit fraudulent, to mix north-side
and south-side must and pass the mixture off as the latter. This the exporters ab-
horred. From 1724, they lobbied successive governments to do something to curtail the practice. The Funchal Council responded from time to time. In 1737, its
Senate forbade the movement of wines from one side of the island to the other,
on the grounds that mixing these wines harmed the reputation of the island's
main export. Still, in 1756, on "the north side, they . . . had much more wine than
the south, which being of an inferior quality & much cheaper than the south
wines," certain trader-intermediaries "purchased great parcels" of north wine and
"made sad mixtures to make up their difference" in quality and "to sell them to
the English for south wine." This was a circumstance that the island's influential
exporters felt would be "attended with very bad consequences" for the economy.
Still, when southern vintages were small or unpromising, others felt there was
little choice but to mix, and "a great deal of north wine" was "brought into the
south."[41]

Another conflict also arose. Traditionally, the cultivators had set their own
harvest times, setting different dates for different grapes. As the demand for differentiated and finer wines rose around the Atlantic in the eighteenth century,
exporters began to demur on the correct time for harvesting. The cultivators, it
appears, did not sample their fruit; rather, they responded to surface color rather
than grape sugar in deciding when and where to harvest. The distributors felt that
the must from early-harvest, full-color grapes did not contain sufficient sugar.
Cultivators, however, believed that late harvesting courted risk: delay in an open-

air operation increased the likelihood of encountering rain, and they feared a watering-down of their must more than anything else at this point in the cycle. Distributors believed greater dangers arose not from delay but from "the grapes being gathered in too soone." The two were irreconcilably deadlocked.[42]

The government stepped in. The newly appointed governor João António de Sá Pereira revived in 1768 a Funchal Council's 1737 order forbidding the southward movement of north wines and issued a new set of regulations concerning the mixing of north and south wines. A few months later, he appointed inspectors to monitor adherence to these regulations. Their implementation in question in 1775, Sá Pereira reiterated the 1768 ban and also set May 1 as the date before which north wines could not enter the south, a time-honored means of frustrating adulteration and mixing, since most mixing occurred in the early months of the year. At the same time, he turned to the matter of the harvest being immature and disreputable, and found it an all too "general defect." He named vineyard "Inspectors in all the Parishes on the Southside to see that the grapes are not cut down before they are ripe"—an almost impossible task, inasmuch as the observation of such acts was "very difficult." The inspectors, not surprisingly, were extremely unpopular, appearing in the countryside from time to time, unannounced, whenever it struck the whim of the governor.[43] Sá Pereira's successor further tightened the system in 1784 and 1785. Believing the producers did not know how to cultivate vines for desirable wine, he authorized the island's inspector general to set dates for the harvest, and specifically ordered that Malvasia grapes should not be gathered before October 1. In the ensuing year's harvest, "the Commerce," finding that "the country people" were nonetheless "going to begin their vintage" at the beginning of September before the grapes were ripe, complained to the governor and asked him to "interfere." Their application was "attended with success," and he set four harvest dates for thirty-eight different parishes and ordered district inspectors "to increase their vigilance."[44]

THE CULTIVATORS' SALE OF WINE

Individual producers and vineyards traditionally forged long-term supply relationships with Portuguese and foreign exporters, granting them the rights of first refusal in buying their crops. The exporters visited the vineyards from time to time, watching the gathering and pressing, tasting the new wine, striking deals and finalizing transport arrangements, and advancing sureties to make delivery of the wine more certain. The producers brought wine to town after November, whenever required by the exporters. This arrangement was mutually beneficial, the exchange customarily being structured as barter. Exporters obtained wine, as well as year-round customers for retail imports, while the producers received foodstuffs and dry goods on credit and sometimes large sums of money as loans and made easier sales of their wine. The system did impose some burdens, however. On the one hand, it often fell to the exporters to take more wine than they needed from suppliers who had, from tradition, "some claim upon" them: exporters "did not like to let" these suppliers "sell to others," fearing they would thereby "lose them entirely." On the other hand, it was in most years "impossible for the country people to support themselves" without the assistance of the exporters, to whom they ran colossally in debt "in order to work" their vineyards.[45]

In an average cycle, sales to traditional buyer-exporters were finalized and future prices declared toward the end of the year, usually in the middle of December, after the wine had cleared in the producers' press houses. Weather permitting—and it frequently did not—export firms sent one or two tasters, usually trusted Portuguese employees, to sample the offerings of their traditional suppliers. Most merchants employed tasters—local Portuguese men with a "knowledge of wine" and regarded as "the best judges of it." A partner of an export house commonly joined the tasters out in the field, visiting traditional suppliers, free vineyards not yet committed to any exporter and, if one had what was regarded by foreigners as "Portuguese *scruple*," even suppliers already committed to others. If they found the wine satisfactory, exporters and traditional suppliers agreed upon its purchase and made arrangements for transport to Funchal.[46]

The exporter Robert Bisset recounted a typical foray in the field:

> I found all the Priest's old wine *danada* [tarnished] & 2 tons of his new wine & all the others very ordinary except the first ton on your right hand as you enter into his lodge & 1 or 2 more further on. José António's will not do. So they have all got a disagreeable taste joined with low quality that I was afraid to meddle with them. Therefore told him to dispose of them & I also told the Priest to do so likewise. The *Companhia Velha* have bought the *Muda*'s [Deaf Mute's] wine on which we depended. If an oppo. offers this year for Boston, I know not where to get wines to comply with their annual orders. I have seen M.l Franc.o [Manuel Francisco]. He has got about 8 casks that would do with better wine on account of their colors. I offered him 45$ [45 *milréis*] *encascado* [in casks] for his whole parcel, rejecting him only 2 *cascos* [casks, each roughly nine-tenths of a pipe]; he says less than 53$ he'll not take. Whoever buys them at that price must lay their account to lose 3 to 400$ by the bargain. I have been to see P. Pedro da Costa's wine on Sto Martinho; they are very good & would be of great service to us. He won't take less than 65$ the *caldo* [a kind of pipe] & 200$ bill, which would likewise be a losing bargain.

Visits such as Bisset's were a means of managing price, filled as they were with the cut-and-thrust of market haggling. They were also a way to control quality. Many times the exporters rejected what they and their traders regarded as "trash." Bisset expected to receive "a parcel of wines" from one long-standing supplier, but he was disappointed: "on tasting them," he "found them a parcel of low trash with a bad state & smell, full of *lyria* [a mildewlike growth], a thing I had no! seen on any wines this year and, to crown all, *arribada* [harvested too early]." He therefore told the cultivator to sell to someone else.[47]

At the cultivator's vineyard, exporters could buy wine straight from the press. Probably it was fermented, but little else was done to it. Such wine was known as *vinho a bica*, so named after the spout (*bica*) of the press. *Vinho a bica* was available from late September throughout October, depending on the vineyard and varietal, and it could be priced and measured out in small barrels or large pipes. At the vineyard, exporters could also buy a *vinho em limpo*, which was more manufactured. It had been fermented, clarified, mixed, and stabilized. Whether the wine was more manufactured or not, exporters usually purchased unbroken lots that were the produce of an entire vineyard. That is not to say that a vineyard's variety and grade were uniform. Most estates produced several grades. Yet the purchaser was generally required to buy all if he bought any. It was not uncommon for an export house to purchase the lower-quality wines that came with their traditional suppliers' other wines and, after the exchange, resell the lower grades at a loss.[48]

Purchases having been negotiated, exporters offered security for eventual payment and pickup or transport. Tax collectors, owners, and cultivators almost immediately carried away from the press what must and wine by law were due them, some with the help of porters and others by themselves, "sometimes in barrels, and sometimes in goatskin *borrachas* [bags]" like those depicted in plates 6 and 7. Exporters might either remove it to their lodges in Funchal or ask to have it set aside and moved at a later date, just before it was placed in the hold of a ship. Only when traders began to maintain lodges as a matter of course in the last quarter of the eighteenth century did they remove wine at the moment of purchase. Upon removal, the wine was transferred from the initial holding casks to goatskin bags, which were then carried to Funchal on the heads and backs of Madeirans; alternately, it was drawn by horses, mules, and asses, which were "yoke[d] in pairs to large sledges" on which the casks sat. The transport was managed by locals who operated independently of vineyards and contracted out their services to anyone who needed them.[49] The only interruptions to their work arose from the weather. In the 1767–68 cycle, for instance, when "bad weather" in winter "cut off all communication with the villages," the transport men could not get to town, nor could the exporters get to the vineyards. Little changed in the way they worked: the system that prevailed in the 1820s when William Combe depicted them was essentially that of two centuries before.[50]

Cultivators relied heavily on long-standing, often century-old relationships with the established export firms, and vice versa. Seldom was a firm cast aside; less often was a cultivator dropped from a list of suppliers. Scots exporter Francis Newton's several firms consistently drew from two dozen *fregueses* [suppliers/ customers] for nearly half a century. In 1759, Newton & Gordon purchased from fifty-three suppliers. All but one of them lived in the twenty-two south-side parishes, and most of the southerners lived in the southwest. More to the point, all but six had previously supplied Newton & Spence between 1748 and 1755. Moreover, sixteen of the forty-seven persistent cultivators in 1759 remained suppliers to the firm in 1815. The mutually beneficial system that buoyed Newton just as he set out in business gave his descendants in Newton, Gordon, Murdoch & Scott the wherewithal to ply their trade in the next century.[51] It was the same relation-based arrangement that William Bolton had deployed in the 1710s, and Richard Pickford before Bolton in the 1670s.

COMPETITION COMES TO THE VINEYARD

To believe supply relationships remained fixed would, however, be an error. The market for wine at the vineyard was competitive when Newton & Gordon made its purchases in 1759, and it became more so. Demand for Madeira wine was rising around the Atlantic, and new enterprisers were entering the export business. The new export houses that sprang up in the heady days of the 1760s and 1780s—because of the disruptions the American Revolution introduced, the 1770s were more stable—found themselves initially blocked from traditional sources of supply. So they had to build a base, and in part they feverishly strove to lure producers away from established firms and quickly replicate traditional relationships with north-side growers. Faced with this onslaught, the allegiance of long-standing suppliers to long-standing buyers eroded. In the harvest of 1763, Newton & Gordon purchased wine from the same number of suppliers as in 1759, fifty-three, but fewer than one-third of those producers were traditional sources; the rest were new to the firm. They bought from the same number of parishes as in 1759, but almost one-seventh of them were on the north side. Even highly resilient, successful firms like Newton & Gordon felt the pinch of competition, which they attributed to "the folly of the young houses as to what regards the extravagant prices they have given for wines."[52]

In this charged environment, cultivators could set their prices high and hold to them. Adding insult to injury, some went so far as to refuse to allow exporters to taste the wine unless they committed in advance to buying it. Negotiations with exporters grew barbed and, in the 1760s, established houses lost suppliers to "new men." The same thing happened again when a new batch of "mushroom merchants" sprang up after 1783. In 1784, for instance, the English Leacock firm learned there was no wine "in the country that is good" to be sent by people from their own vineyards, "except Sra. D. Anna Roza, who has her parcel on hand." Competing merchants had sought it but none agreed, on account of her high asking price and her desired form of payment, in bills of exchange. These were things the Leacocks, too, "cannot think of." The harvest of 1785, falling "miserably short of even the worst prognostications," exacerbated this erosion of traditional purchase. The paucity made suppliers and exporters alike more voracious and interfering:

> Dona Guiomar's parcel is not in the market nor has it been for several years past. Antonio João Correa's is next to nothing this year, and stands engaged to Scott's house for the supply of the young squire, as does Francisco Antonio's to Duff's house, to whom João de Carvalhal goes of course. Scott, Banger, and Gillis will most likely be competitors for the Nun's parcel. The Bishop's parcel being at the disposal of the Junta will most likely be given to Pedro Jorge as it has been bespoke by more persons than Murdoch, who we are informed met with a refusal. Our neighbor Jorge Correa very sensibly sold *a bica* for a high price, as many of them have done. Most other parcels of a middling size in common years are very small this year, and either bespoke or encumbered.

The exporter might be able to amass four hundred pipes of good south wine, but that was "certainly a very inadequate supply." The day the firm could rely on customary vineyards had passed.[53]

Newton & Gordon was a growing house, with an increasing appetite for product to sell. It responded to the increased competition by making its approach to supply more complex and expanding its base. Rather than clustering its purchases early in the new calendar year, as had been customary, it began buying in mid-November and persisted vigorously through May. By 1772–73, the firm had nearly tripled the number of its suppliers to 146, and quintupled the number of its purchases. Of the suppliers, only 15 percent had provided wine to the firm between 1759 and 1763. The number of parishes the firm dealt with had more than doubled from 1763, and more than before their suppliers hailed from northern and interior parishes. The obligation to buy unbroken lots had disappeared. It was no longer unusual to buy less than an entire lot and to buy from multiple vineyards in the neighborhood; several suppliers sold wine to Newton & Gordon on multiple occasions in 1772–73. But the most dramatic, because most expensive, action its partners took was to buy shares in vineyards. At least eighty-four pipes came from estates in which they had acquired an ownership interest. (Whether in doing so they acquired any rights sanctioned in local courts is doubtful, but they did solidify their supply.) Other foreign firms did the same. By 1815, competition had so eroded traditional patterns of buying that the time-honored system was in tatters: "acquiring good *freguesias*" became "an impossible task."[54]

Foreigners believed that natives like Dona Guiomar and the elder Pantaleão Fernandes—two prominent Portuguese landowners, both scions of powerful local families—instigated the poaching. Of course, what the established exporters regarded as "poaching" was viewed by the new distributors as making inroads into a closed market and by the producers as increasing opportunity and profit. Whoever started it, poaching was a significant manifestation of the marked increase in the global demand for Madeira wine in the last half of the eighteenth century, and Madeira's producers' and distributors' attempts to meet it. Alongside the reorganization of long-standing supply relationships and the reaction to it, two other phenomena also sprang from increased worldwide demand: a new group of intermediaries took advantage of the situation to buy cultivators' wine and sell it to distributors; and the prices and terms producers received for their wine improved substantially.

THE RISE OF *PARTIDA* MAKERS

One of the more intriguing developments in the history of Madeira's production was an undercutting of the farmers, who in the eighteenth century brought cultivators and exporters together. New enterprisers arrived on the scene during the Seven Years' War to perform many of the tasks previously undertaken by the farmers; and, in time, their work was eclipsed by the exporters themselves. Their new distribution system arose out of the success of the farmers and the breadth of their work on the one hand, and the competition among exporters on the other. These entrepreneurs were less interested in managing the land than in managing the flow of its wine. During the 1760s, a dozen or so natives began buying *vinho em limpo* directly from cultivators, breaking it into parcels (*partidas*) or lots, blending it, and reselling it to the exporters, usually well into the new year when the vineyards' stocks of wine were low or exhausted. Although they made up their lots in the countryside, these "*partida* makers" hawked their lots in the city, where "town wine" became synonymous with the "parcel." During the early days of the French revolutionary wars, shipping to and from the island was much "at a stop," and merchants reported "a good many" pipes full of wine "on hand for sale." These were mostly "*partidas* made up in Town," but they seldom contained desirable wine.[55]

Two problems inhered in the parcels, from the distributors' point of view: they were expensive, and they were uneven in quality. *Partidas* were "mixed & remixed" before they entered the distributors' town lodges. The Leacocks, for instance, believed that some of their competitors, "not knowing [the *partidas'*] composition," often deceived themselves "in the quality," which, "after their being kept on hand, instead of improving," degenerated and became "quite inferior." According to the elder Leacock, "the quantity of wines bought up by the natives to mix with low wines" raised prices, "besides entirely ruining the quality of the wines, as you don't know what you try, when they are mixed & made up into parcels." So, too, did the irrational speculations made and long credits given by upstarts and *partida* makers eager to meet rising demand from India. When Domingos Oliveira "propagated a story that he meant to buy 600 pipes of wine *a bica*," "saying he will" had the effect of "putting the people on asking exorbitant prices." Through the first quarter of the nineteenth century, parcel wine was always regarded by all but the newest, smallest houses as inferior. Still, every house used it.[56]

The benefits of patronizing the *partida* makers were substantial, quality notwithstanding. Resort to them increased the size of a firm's annual purchase. In 1759, Newton & Gordon bought on average 92 pipes, which was 1.7 pipes from each of their traditional suppliers. The firm preferred to spread its purchasing among a number of cultivators, rather than rely upon one or two, which was difficult at any rate, given the size of most island vineyards. In 1763, it purchased 148 pipes. Since it dealt with the same number of producers, the average purchase rose 60 percent to 2.8 pipes. By 1772–73, the average purchase from a supplier had risen to 8.6 pipes. The firm purchased lots above 10 pipes from nearly one-tenth of its suppliers, and some as high as 28 pipes. In 1772–73, its largest suppliers were *partida* makers.[57]

THE RISE OF PRICES

The year 1770 was a particularly "shocking year" for Newton & Gordon and other distributors seeking wine to buy. Pantaleao Fernandes had gone to Campanario parish

> & bought everybodies wine that would sell him without regard to price. Our customers could not resist the temptation & we are left without any wines from thence except 8 or 9 pipes. He gave Ant.o Glz 74$ *caldo* for his parcel of 80 or 90 pipes. Jarvis who sold us last year at 54$ insists on 70$. God knows [his wine is] very indifferent. João Francisco asks 80$ bill for his Quinta Grande wines, which are the only parcels we know of from that parish for sale. I never was so

undetermined in my days what to do. We can ill do without them & it is sacrificing everything to purchase at those prices. Upon consideration, I believe we shall be obliged to comply with their demands.

But 1770 paled in comparison to 1771, 1771 to 1772, and so on.[58]

Much had altered since 1748, when Francis Newton trained in the "common method [whereby] the English buy their wines." In the first place, modes of payment had changed dramatically. From the time of the rise of Madeira's export trade in wine in the preceding century, native cultivators bought provisions from exporters and, when the vintage was completed, paid for them with wine. The producers seldom bought imported goods from the producers on "present payment" with "reddy mony," as lucrative as that might have been to the exporters; instead, they bought on credit, usually during the harvest months of October or November, and they paid up in February and March, and "not in mony but in wines." However, this approach could supply but "a small quantity" of what natives needed and, accordingly, by the late 1740s, producers and distributors devised a more flexible exchange, buying wine on different terms. Distributors began buying wine not primarily with goods but increasingly with bills of exchange drawn upon either Lisbon or London. Distributors' bills had to be paid in full between two and six months if tendered in the Wine Islands and between four and seven months if tendered in Europe and Britain. The change was gradual. By 1760, it was still considered "extraordinary" for producers to accept commercial bills for must; by 1770, "everybody" sold "a great part" of their stock with such bills.[59]

The transformation in payment that occurred in the preceding half century continued. The increasingly assertive producers vis-à-vis increasingly competitive and insecure exporters were in such a strong position by the 1780s that they could insist on being paid in either bills or cash, at their discretion: North-side growers demanded "cash in hand," as did town parcel makers who "sold under engagements." Similarly, those who supplied the Indiamen required cash. But cash as a requirement presented "a most material disadvantage" since it decreased distributors' profits. The change was worrisome enough to Britain's consul Thomas Cheap for him to warn the Board of Trade in 1765. Within just two decades, the natives altered "the mode of payment, by insisting on having bills of exchange on Lisbon or London, for their best Wines," or cash, where previously they had received only bartered imported manufacture goods.[60]

Furthermore, wine prices had skyrocketed. The pricing of growers' wine was heavily influenced by the rise in competition, as Cheap also informed the board. The natives had made "their own prices," which were "extravagantly high" after the 1740s. They charged a *vinho o caldo* price, so named for the container that measured it (the *caldeiro*, or bucket) and the juice it contained (the *vinho a bica in mosto*); from at least the mid-seventeenth century Funchal aldermen had set a lower threshold for this price. The natives also charged a *vinho almudado* price, so named for the slightly larger container (the *almude*) that measured the newly manufactured must that had cleared *a limpa*. *O caldo* prices were always lower than *almudado* prices, given the greater measuring capacity of the *almude* and the greater manufacturing that had transpired before the wine was put into the *almude*. Another set of prices—those paid for parcels—was on occasion lower but more often higher than the other two, inasmuch as the parcels were often presented after committed lots had been exhausted.[61]

The levels of these three growers' prices were variously determined. Island government exerted some influence, since Funchal's Council Senate annually fixed minimum prices below which the growers could not sell their musts. More than anything else, however, grower expectations significantly shaped the outcome, especially when they were fueled by the behavior of merchants new to the scene and eager to wrest a share of the trade from more established exporters. As early as 1702, William Bolton, who often went to the field soon after the pressing began, was complaining that "noe man will offer a Pipe of Wine to sel, until they see the Ships in Port." Subsequent merchants tended to agree: "the price depends upon the demand," and by "demand" they meant what the growers thought both the distributors and the consumers would take. Growers were ever cognizant of both. In 1764, the "natives bought very dear of each other at the press, and will not like to sell them cheap, especially if ships come in soon." The hope for fleets bound to the West or East Indies fueled suspicion of a large call, whether or not their arrival was likely. So, too, did higher duties around the Atlantic, which led producers to expect a higher than usual demand before the law became effective. In 1764, for instance, the Portuguese began "demanding extravagant prices for their wines," thinking that "large quantities of wines will be introduced into America" before the Sugar Act kicked in. The nonarrival of ships might bring "the natives to reason in their prices." But reason seldom came. In 1770 a refrain first emerged, and it was repeated every year for at least five decades, only the names and the amounts changing. Robert Bisset learned from his traditional suppliers that their wines were "pretty good" that year. But

> the country people ask no less than 80$ and they are encouraged to hope they will obtain that price from a monopolizing spirit that possess[es] two or three of our monied men here. . . . Our Tobacco Contractor, Pedro Jorge Monteiro, . . . is said is to purchase 1,000 pipes, which is above ⅕ of the whole vintage,

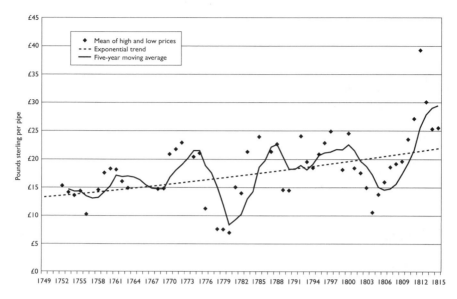

Figure 2.2. Mean of the annual average growers' prices for *vinho almudado*, 1749–1815. For each year, the highest and the lowest prices given to the growers were averaged together; since all available growers' prices fluctuated between the extremes, it is a reliable figure. A five-year moving average of these annual figures shows the trend in prices. In an agricultural cycle, there were big swings from year to year due to weather and other conditions; the moving average dampens the effect of any one year. The exponential trend line sketches the underlying rate of growth in the data. Sources: Newton & Gordon account books, Madeira Wine Company, Archives, Funchal; Leacock account books, Leacock Papers, private collection, Funchal; Factory minutes, Archives, Blandy Office, Funchal.

with a view it is said to get bill for them from the English. Pantaleão Fernandez has also given most extravagant prices, having purchased Ant. Glz [Gonzalez] of Campanario . . . at 74$ the *caldo*. By that & some other examples you may easily judge of the prices we are obliged to pay our customers for their trifling quantities.

In years when supply was short and demand (or possible demand) strong, growers found "they need only to lye by to get any price they choose to ask for their first wines."[62]

With growers increasingly emboldened, the prices they demanded of exporters rose, for the most part, between the 1690s and the 1810s. From a relatively constant price fluctuating around 22$159 (22,159 *réis* or £6 pounds sterling) per pipe of *vinho almudado* at the beginning of the eighteenth century (1696–1715), the mean of high and low prices offered to and accepted by growers rose to 33$750 (£9) per pipe in 1740–45, 55$368 (£15) in 1752–63, and 69$167 (£19) in 1768–74, then fell to 47$687 (£13) in 1775–83, climbed to 73$250 (£20) in 1784–92 and 76$063 (£21) in 1793–1801, fell again, this time to 67$015 (£18) in 1802–11, and finally rose to 106$438 (£30) in 1812–15. Thus, there were four bursts of increase—during the Seven Years' War, the American Revolutionary War, the early years of the French revolutionary wars, and the Napoleonic Wars. While growth was persistent, its rate somewhat slackened as the decades advanced: mean prices between 1696 and 1815 more than doubled in the first sixty-seven years of the period, moving from 22$159 (£6) in 1696–1715 to 55$368 (£15) in 1752–63, but less than doubled in the last sixty-three years of the period, rising to only 106$438 (£30) in 1812–15. If they needed it, here was clear evidence for island officials, producers, and exporters that the worldwide demand for their Madeira was outstripping the supply.[63]

As the eighteenth century came to a close, it became clear to islanders just how much the fortunes of their island and its producers of wine had been transformed by participation in the Atlantic wine complex. From the 1790s through the 1810s, exporters noted the changes obsessively. The 1790s were especially dramatic, for the average grower's price per pipe rose from roughly 51$500 in 1790 to 94$500 in 1800. Such prices had been previously reached, but they had been short-lived; now they remained for good. A "species of madness" possessed "all ranks" of growers and purchasers, who were "as eager after the wine, as if the vintage were a canny [short] one." What astonished the exporters most in January 1794 were "the enormous prices" they were forced to give for *a bica* wine. By September that year, a "most extraordinary change had occurred: the "natives" were getting "any price they demand[ed] for" any wine. This constituted a real and permanent "revolution." At the end of the century, John Leacock Sr. admitted that, in his fifty years there, he had never known "such exorbitant prices as have been demanded" recently.[64]

Such prices confounded island exporters, setting "common sense and calculation at defiance." They also roiled Atlantic consumers, who eventually had to pay higher prices or forego Madeira. Year in and year out and well into the next century, each season found growers demanding more and—almost always—getting more. Their lives had evolved considerably, for each season saw more farmers handling more of the legal and managerial work of production and more *partida* makers widening the range of pricing and sale options open to growers. Not surprisingly, when Francis Newton reminisced about prices in 1810, he looked back over a period marked by a doubling of prices since he had come ashore in 1748 and an entangling of participants. He found, in short, strong evidence not only of the transformed and enhanced role of the producer but also of the producer's linkage to the distributor and consumer.[65]

3

THE ENLIVENING GRAPE

Madeira is a manufactured product today. It is blended, fortified, agitated, heated, and aged, in addition to processes common to the production of all wines—pressing, fermenting, clarifying, and packaging. This was not the case in 1640. The original Madeira was a cheap, simple wine, made from a base of white must to which growers and exporters added varying amounts of red must in order to give it color and flavor. By the turn of the eighteenth century, producers and exporters were distinguishing among Malvasia (Malmsey), Tinta (Tent), and red and white Madeira wines as well as between new (freshly pressed) and old wines. By the 1760s, viniculture had become more elaborate, and Madeira's exporters were distributing six different grades of wine: Malvasia, London Particular, London Market, New York, Virginia (or Jamaica), and Common (or West India or Cargo). Product innovation and differentiation continued thereafter. By the turn of the nineteenth century, producers and distributors together had transformed Madeira into a complex, highly processed, expensive, and status-laden beverage. Its modern form had been "invented."[1]

This story of invention offers insight into early modern commercial life. The transformation of Madeira was both an economic act—carried out in response to commercial motives—and a social act—not invented by a solitary "genius" but by an Atlantic network of producers, distributors, and consumers in intense conversation with one another. Atlantic commerce—of which wine composed a not insignificant share—was a discursive system that in large measure sprang from a continual, complicated, often confusing exchange of information about goods—how they were made, packaged, and shipped; how they were distributed; and how they were stored, displayed, and consumed. These conversations, appearing in distributors' letters from, responses to, and visits with customers and producers, changed Madeira wine, its distribution, and its status; they built its market.[2] Much of the rest of this book examines the conversationally networked distribution and consumption of wine. This chapter focuses on its manufacture and the ways that product innovation was introduced, implemented, and re-shaped.

VINICULTURE AT THE VINEYARD

The first manufacturing steps took place at the vineyard and were taken by producers. Grapes were pressed, and wine was fermented. If natives sold *vinho a bica*, the must underwent no additional processing at the vineyard. But if they kept the must to make *vinho em limpo*, they also fermented, clarified, and mixed it. These were critical steps, for differences in body, color, and flavor owed "as much . . . to the different manner and time of" fermenting, fining, and mixing "as to any difference of the grape itself."[3]

PRESSING OR CRUSHING

The first step in treating newly harvested grapes was to extract the must through crushing or pressing. It began almost as soon as gathering commenced, and usually took place on the spot at the press house, although must was some-times extracted off-site in the press of the farmer or owner. The cultivator placed the grapes in "a machine of great simplicity in its construction." The typical Por-tuguese press (plate 8) had three parts: a long stone or wooden vat; a long chest-nut spindle at the head of the vat, with a screw at the spindle's higher end and a squared-off oblong block that rested upon a large stone at its lower end; and a lever that stretched across the length of the vat, extending beyond it about ten feet and connecting at the head end to the top of the spindle's screw. Portuguese presses varied in size: typical eighteenth-century vats contained between 80 and 550 gallons. They sat outside, usually underneath a covering.[4]

Little changed in the extraction process before 1815. When the vat was full of fruit, the growers began to crush or smash the grapes to liberate their sugars. Three or more workers would enter the vat and tread the bunches of grapes with their bare feet, for as "long as any juice can be expressed from them." Madei-rans did not usually remove the stalks, for, if they imparted an astringency to the must, it could be corrected for later. The must ran out through a sieved hole in the center, the middle, or a corner of the bottom of the vat and into a wooden cask or leather goatskin, the sieve separating the juice from the stalks, husks, and seeds. Workers next gathered together the pulpy mass that remained, surrounded it with a coil of rope several feet high, capped it with wooden planks, and pressed down on the nonscrew end of the lever and thereby on the mass; by the application of this pressure, they extracted additional juice. When the must stopped flowing, they removed the boards and ropes, broke up the pulp with hoes, resumed treading, and reapplied the lever to the mass for a second pressing. Third and fourth pressings were common. To the fourth, the workers often added water to the by then extremely dry mass; what resulted was *agua pé*, a drink served to the growers and pressers. All four pressings could be performed in a single day. "By this way and this only" did Madeirans make their wine.[5]

FERMENTING

Upon completing the pressing, vineyard workers took the product out of the vat and placed it in an adjacent fermentation cask. Chemically, one glucose molecule is converted into two ethyl alcohol molecules and two carbon dioxide molecules. Practically, internal enzymes of airborne yeasts spread around by insects and the bacteria in the must mediate the series of reactions involved in the conversion from sugar.[6]

In good weather, alcoholic fermentation—marked by the conversion of must sugar to ethyl alcohol and carbon dioxide by means of an oxygen-free metabolism of yeasts and observable in "the liquor rising" and emitting "a considerable quantity of fixed air, or carbonic acid gas"—began "almost immediately." If the grapes were ripe and yeasts were present, then fermentation proceeded rapidly. However, "damp or cold weather"—not unknown in Madeira's autumn—might slow the process. When the amount of produced alcohol vis-à-vis unfermented sugar was acceptable to the test and taste of the manufacturer, he arrested the fermentation by adding sulfur dioxide or an alcohol above 5 percent strength. The termination was critical, for the presence of small amounts of sugar made the wine prone to attack from bacteria, which in time demanded a different, second treatment after fermentation, which in turn gave wines like Madeira, Port, and Sherry much of their character. An insufficient anaerobic conversion created problems for distributors and consumers, as the wine continued to ferment in their lodges and cellars well into the year following the pressing.[7]

A variety of factors affected the process of fermentation and its speed: the ripeness of the grape, the presence of grape rot, the type of yeast, the temperature, the quantity of micronutrients in the must, the aeration of the must, and the addition of chemicals like sulfur dioxide. Usually, fermentation lasted a couple of weeks, although in the case of a rich, full-bodied sweet must, it might extend to several months.[8]

Some fermentations needed little help. "The wines from the north side of the island and those from some of the upper lands in the *Serra*" typically fermented "in the casks without any assistance or addition whatever." Other wines required assistance. Must from unripe grapes did not ferment well, nor did watery must pressed during rainy weather. Without a good fermentation, wine became "cloudy, thick and dusky" and would not "fine off" as other wines did. To avoid this outcome, Canary Islanders before 1670 began adding a fine white powder of heated gypsum called gesso or plaster of paris "to help the fermentation." Gesso's value was almost immediately appreciated, and it became the most common additive in continental Spanish and Portuguese viniculture, despite the fact that other ingredients, like quick lime, vinegar, and fir, oak, or beech shavings were available and known to be as effective.[9] By 1689, Madeirans were adding gesso to "feed" their fermentations, throwing nine or ten pounds of gesso into a hundred gallons of must. In the early nineteenth century, they were still adding "considerable proportions" of gesso to check the "aptness" of Madeira to grow "eager" (sour or acidic), "to break the coherence" of too "ropy" (viscid, glutinous, or slimy) a must, and to "introduce an alkaline balance" that would help it resist acidity.[10]

Tied to fermentation was a process seldom discussed but always present—aeration of the must. At the beginning of any fermentation, some aeration was required, inasmuch as yeast needs oxygen for growth. But the diachronic question was: how much aeration? Depending on the amount, the exposure of the must to air and its reactive component oxygen could improve or spoil it. Too much exposure could lead to oxidation of phenolics and a surfeit of acetic acid, while too little exposure could slow fermentation. To the eye, the sign of overexposure was a browning of the must, although oxygen worked more insidiously upon white juice: whites turned to an amber or brownish color, while in reds the change was less noticeable.

Madeiran producers may not have understood the chemistry of fermentation, but they appreciated the effects of proper balance. If oxidation was thought to be too great a risk, given the presence of rot among the grapes (the molds on the grapes introducing enzymes that accelerated reactions with oxygen), they added small amounts of sulfur dioxide during crushing to inactivate enzymes and counter the oxidation of phenolics. If oxidation was thought to be too free, they encouraged aeration at several points. They subjected the grapes to only one foot and lever pressing and, because of the different sieves that cultivators employed, they allowed the husks and seeds to pass into the must. Moreover, they let the must of some grades and varietals like Verdelho and Tinta Negro Mole stand in the open air for days after a pressing to achieve greater (or sufficient) aeration. Even if they initially placed the must in closed casks, they further aerated it upon racking, sometimes many times. If carefully managed, aeration allowed producers to develop a range of flavors other than those associated with the primary fruit aroma.[11]

CLARIFYING

When fermentation and aeration were finished and the producer achieved a sweetness level he desired, the wine was ready for the labor-intensive task of separating the liquid from the suspended and insoluble material in new wine as well as the lees or sediment that had already settled to the bottom of the container—clarifying.

To remove the detritus, the Madeirans racked and fined the wine. New wines, according to traditional guidelines, should have been clarified between mid-November and mid-December. Using a siphon, they "racked" the liquid into another container, leaving the compact of solid particles behind. They could produce the settlement of lees by holding the liquid in a vat or cask until solids settled. Or they could hasten it by fining or "forcing" it with the addition of organic or inorganic fining agents. Madeirans added agents that aided the agglomeration and settling of suspended colloids—microscopic particles, occasionally liquids or gases but usually solids, like molecules of pectins, phenolics, anthocyans, and tannins that contributed to viscosity. Clarification commenced soon thereafter, depending on the wine's quality and the container's size.[12]

As far as the producers and exporters were concerned, clarifying saved money and speeded sale. Most wines therefore received several rackings. Final racking at the vineyard usually occurred in December. Subsequent rackings took place upon arrival in the exporters' lodges, before transatlantic shipment, and upon arrival in the cellars of importers and consumers. The approach the exporter Scot, Pringle & Cheap adopted was typical. Its wines were constantly racked "every six weeks or two months"; it was a "constant rule" for the firm "never to move a pipe of wine without racking, tho it has only laid 8 days in the store." Its "method" was to combine the agent and the must in a pipe; "after some time, they fall & a good deal of clear wine may be taken off by a crane." When there was "little to attend to" in terms of business, workers in the firm passed the lees "through a canvas bag into a jug, by which mean only the grosser particulars remain & what goes through the bag will be as bright as amber." In addition to separating the new wine from the gross lees, multiple rackings added aeration, assisted in the formation of flavor compounds and the polymerization of tannins, and lightened the color.[13]

To fine a recently pressed, fermented, and racked wine, Madeirans mixed their musts with a variety of additives that formed insoluble complexes with unstable pigments and tannins and that allowed the whole complex to fall to the bottom of the solution: gesso, lead shavings, clay, isinglass or fish bladder, egg whites, and animal blood. While custom generally prevailed in selection, those interested could consult a handful of printed or manuscript treatises suggesting alternatives and outlining exact guidelines, formulae, and methods for selecting and using them. Some were more effective than others, and only lead was detrimental to health. Organic compounds were favored agents, especially gesso. Sale records of shops run by exporters suggest that gesso was the most common fining agent in Funchal. Wine and gesso were stirred until the liquid began "to have a vinous smell, and the carbonic acid" was evaporated. More gesso was added and the mix was stirred twice a day for several weeks. Islanders eventually turned to other agents. Isinglass ran a close second, with egg whites not far behind. Given that the waters around the island teemed with fish and many islanders kept chickens, there was no want of fish bladder or egg white.[14]

Exporters left more information about fining than did growers, but there is no reason to believe that the techniques of the former did not recapitulate those of the latter. Indeed, the evidence all suggests exporters copied their suppliers. What the partners of Newton & Gordon drank in the 1770s was fined with isinglass or eggs, and in this they followed their suppliers' advice and their own taste. One isinglass and blood recipe acquired from a grower they passed on to their customers: "Draw from the pipe two gallons of wine in a quart of which dissolve four ounces of isinglass. Take a pint and a half (not exceeding a quart) of kid's blood and . . . pour in the other seven quarts of wine at the same. Keep stirring well with a whisk. Then add the quart the isinglass was dissolved in and let them be well incorporated together with the whisk before it is poured into the pipe when done. Let the whole be mixed for 15 or 20 minutes by a stick." Years later, the firm suggested another supplier's formula to their Jamaica customers: "[Use] the whites of six or at most eight new laid eggs. Let them be well beat & mixed with about a gallon of the wine, & then thrown into the pipe, & the whole effectually mixed. The liquor should be carefully racked in ten or fifteen days; & after standing ten or fifteen days more, it will be fit to drink." Each recipe had its own merits, and a choice of one over another depended on the desired effect. Robert Duff weighed the pros and cons of the recipes of a long-standing supplier, but trusted more his own sense of things: "fining with eggs . . . reduces the colour more than with isinglass, and . . . milk or blood reduces the colour more than eggs." But with truly good wine, he did not want "to make tryal of either of the last mentioned finings" for fear of damaging the drink. Instead, Duff himself used gesso. Whatever agent was chosen, the key was moderation. Duff cautioned correspondents to avoid "too strong a fining," which would "impoverish & deprive it" of body, color, and flavor.[15]

Wines so fined were next mixed or, as exporters called it, "composed." "From the variety of grapes" grown on Madeira, one might expect "there would be a corresponding variety of wines" and, in fact, Madeira distributors were increasingly willing to accommodate consumers who wanted "a particular kind of wine." But any "particularization" was complicated by a far more thoroughgoing prior mixture that occurred at the point of production.[16]

Mixing began with cultivators at the vineyard, who in turn transmitted the art to the exporters. Most cultivators followed fairly simple recipes, blending either Tinta Negro Mole and another grape's must or two musts grown on the same or adjacent vineyards. Owners, farmers, and parcel makers mixed the wine of several vats to get a uniform product and to derive a wine marked by a specific body, color, or flavor. After 1750, such mixing became common and more innovative. Producers found they could add cheaper wine into the vat and sell it as their own. After north-side producers started making greater quantities of less expensive wine, south-side producers began to "top up" their batches with north-side wine. While storing new wine for exporters, the parcel makers also mixed the produce of different areas, vineyards, grades, and vintages. These practices disturbed exporters—rather disingenuously, for they would do much the same in Funchal—and government officials—who believed that mixing led to adulteration and fraud and tried regulating the flow of wine as a way of halting its debasement. But the mixers were sharp men, on whom the value of making poor products look better was not lost and on whom official and commercial opprobrium had little effect.[17]

VINICULTURE IN THE TOWN

BLENDING

To maintain and raise the character and quality of their product, exporters took up where cultivators left off—blending wines they acquired and improving them in the process. Such activity was not usual among exporters before the middle decades of the eighteenth century: it was the purview of producers, vintners, retailers, and consumers. Thereafter, it found acceptance with Madeira's wine distributors.[18]

Representative of those willing to blend, Robert Bisset shipped ten pipes of "fine" wine in 1764, wine that he knew well, as it came from a vineyard his firm had leased on the outskirts of Funchal. Yet, even so, he "mended" it by adding a half gallon of Tinta and "fine Campanario" that came from another estate farther west. Further, fearing "the Gentlemen in Virginia" might complain of their wine being "higher col.d [colored] this year than usual," he blended this stock more "on account of the greenness." Into every ten pipes, he put four pipes of "Antonio João's best Ribeira Brava or C. de Lobos, which made them of a beautiful color and gave them what they very much wanted—body and flavor."[19]

Exporters like Bisset also began combining "new" wine of the most recent vintage with vintages of previous years in roughly the same decades that they took to mixing varietals from different vineyards and regions. Before Bisset's fellow merchant Francis Newton shipped off some pipes in 1768, he put between eight and fifteen buckets of "old" wine in them; likewise, he "improved" three pipes he sent to London's Shakespeare Tavern with "10 buckets of new." Similarly, before Gordon Brothers sent two pipes in 1770, it gave one pipe "a dash of 6, 8, or 10 buckets old wine" and the other "a dash of 10 to 12 buckets of the oldest." When the vintage was poor, exporters felt "obliged to mix old" wines into "those of the first quality." Conversely, when old wines "not remarkable in quality" lay ready for export, they used good new wines to smooth them out.[20]

As blending became commonplace, exporters competed on blends. Occasionally, one finds mention of firm formulae in letters to partners. When James Gordon "concerted" three pipes of Malmsey, he took two pipes from his own stockpile and another pipe from the *senhoria* Dona Guiomar, added three buckets of French brandy to them, and "seasoned" it all with "a little boiling water." Similarly, before Thomas Murdoch sent wine to the Duke of York, he blended twenty buckets of fine pale wine from the 1788 and 1789 vintages with thirty-two buckets of Particular wine from the same years. Some pipes that the Leacocks exported to St. Kitts in 1796 contained "about 70 gallons each of Vintage '93, and 50 gallons each of Vintage '94," plus "1 gallon of brandy in each pipe." None of the partners, it was well understood, was to reveal the secret of the combination to another firm.[21]

Blending was a means to achieve various ends. Exporters blended in part to enhance wine's "body"—its perceived "weight," that is to say, the sensation of fullness that derived from the wine's density or viscosity. Body was the most perceptible trait to alter as well as the simplest alteration to effect. The more alcoholic a wine was, the more full-bodied. Perhaps the most common way to alter it was by adding brandy. (Since it also comprised a stage of production all its own, fortification with brandy will be treated more fully in subsequent pages.) However, brandy was only one among many means to add or enhance body. The chief gardener at England's Royal Botanic Garden and the principal expert on viticulture and viniculture writing in English before the middle of the eighteenth century catalogued other ways to induce this effect. One could mix in "Powders of burnt

Alum, Lime, Chalk, Plaster, Spanish white calcin'd Marble, Bay-Salt, and other the like Bodies" to induce "a Precipitation of the gross and viscid Parts of the Wine then afloat." One could mix seawater with must "to prevent the foulness and ropiness of wines." Certain remedies were connected with specific wines. To cure Claret's ropiness, for instance, one could clarify with a preparation of eggs, an infusion of the turnsole plant in good Sherry, or a fining with the turnsole-and-Sherry decoction after it had been strained. Alternately, one could add a heated compound of the ashes of vine branches or oak leaves, or insert some spirit of wine.[22]

Another reason for blending was to manipulate color, a trait that in the early modern era was central to the identity of any wine. Those familiar with the chemistry of winecraft knew that color was easily changed. The coloring was "contained in the pellicle [skin] of the grape," not the juice. As a result, "white wine may be made of red grapes, when the juice of the grape is expressed, and the husk [skin] thrown away." Older "wines lose their colour, a pellicle being precipitated [separated], which is either deposited on the sides of the bottles, or falls to the bottom"; if wines "be exposed to the heat of the sun during the summer, the colouring matter is detached in a pellicle, which falls to the bottom." By adding spirit of wine to the wine's lees, one could recapture the original color. Aware of such processes, producers and distributors knew that a wine "deprived of its colour is not perceptibly weakened." Accordingly, they willingly engaged in color enhancement. It was no exaggeration, either toward the beginning of the eighteenth century or a hundred years later, to observe that "the colour of wines are frequently artificial." Nor was coloring especially detrimental.[23]

Such practices were "no secret" to vintners in Europe and the Americas. If a wine was too pale or too dark, numerous additives could alter its appearance. The eighteenth century was especially rich in such inventiveness. Philip Miller's widely read *Gardener's Dictionary* provided an ample list of color-enhancing techniques, derived from interviews with growers, vintners, coopers, retailers, and consumers, and to this volume the exporters resorted again and again, keeping copies of it in their countinghouses for easy reference. To restore a white Spanish wine grown yellow or brown, Miller suggested adding milk, milk and isinglass, milk and white starch, or a compound of fleur-de-lis roots, saltpeter, egg whites, and common salt. To amend red Claret grown pale, he advised racking the wine "upon a fresh Lee, either of Alicante or red Bordeaux," then steeping it overnight in three pounds of turnsole "in two or three Gallons of the same Wine," straining the infusion, pouring the "Tincture into the Hogshead," covering the bunghole, and letting it stand. Exporters before 1750 adopted many of the prescriptions proposed by authorities like Miller, but in doing so they had to confront local ways of approaching the problem and also make do with local ingredients like "the very red" Tinta Negro Mole.[24]

Something revolutionary then happened with respect to color. As island prices rose around midcentury, exporters introduced their own particular colorations with greater frequency and creativity, drawing on their acquired knowledge and aesthetic. This change started on the margins of the winemaking and wine-consuming world. Many smaller, undercapitalized firms established themselves on the island in the early 1760s and, with less reputation to protect, they found ways to create and advance their business by imitating body, color, and flavor. Of the three, color imitations were the easiest and cheapest to effect. New firms began to "correct" the colors of the white north-side must, which they could afford. One newcomer added black-cherry juice so that his thin north-side must might bear the look of high-color, high-quality south-side wine, while another ground up almond bark and added it to his north-side wine.[25]

While "appropriate coloring" was accepted, counterfeit coloring was not. Indeed, a "correct" unadulterated color always was a point of pride among the Madeirans who peddled high-quality wine. High color (that is, a dark reddish or brownish hue) was a mark of good body and flavor. It is why the exporter Francis Newton expressed great surprise when his partner accused him of sending to London wines that were mixed with Tinta; in fact, what had been sent were "absolutely the best wines the island affords" — no creditable person "would put *Tinta* in good wines." The best export houses would add it only to very pale, poor wine. If customers wanted a different color for their best wine at midcentury, they had to color it themselves, and exporters supplied them with Tinta to do the job. Thus, beyond the simplest, most traditional approaches to coloring, quality-conscious islanders were loath to decolor or recolor their wines.[26]

A shift in attitudes toward coloring spread beyond the counterfeiters. As a craze for pale colors was sweeping through all parts of the Anglo-American consumer market under the sway of neo-Palladianism and neoclassicism and customers began demanding pale wines, even the most quality-conscious Madeirans acquiesced and altered the color of their wines in the fourth quarter of the eighteenth century. If the partners of Newton & Gordon were to choose wine for their friends, they would not "give up quality for color." But if their correspondents should free them "from blame" and buy "without brand mark," they would "send them as white as water." Loss or possible loss of customers precipitated this change in attitudes. Still, firms struggled for decades with coloring. Only in the late 1780s and early 1790s did most foreign firms agree that they would "give up" their still strong opinion "to please the palates" of their "employers" and give "no room for such complaints by satisfying them in color and lightness."[27]

Madeira's exporters, like producers, blended wine to elevate one last trait: flavor, or the overall sensory impression of aroma and taste. Flavor was the most complicated trait to manipulate, the decision to flavor most vexed, and the choice of inputs most contested. Competing considerations, like mouth and nose sensations and acidity, sweetness, alcoholic strength, fizziness, astringency, and bitterness all had to be weighed. The disguising of ill-flavored wines and the doctoring of "sick" wines with "improving" substances was pioneered well before the 1640s by doctors and quacks who recognized wine as a viable solvent for medicine and, later, a curative for disease. In time, the practice was taken up by wine producers and distributors whose business it was to enhance the product, and in their hands it spread with alacrity. Flavor manipulation received a spur in the English-speaking world when the flow of French wine to England was severely reduced. In response, Portuguese wine retailers in England started mixing their wines to extend their inventory.[28]

The possibilities for the flavoring of Madeira were seemingly endless, and they sometimes interacted with body- and color-enhancing techniques. "To help stinking Wines," one could rack them from "old and corrupt" lees. Alternatively, one could hang "in them little bags of spices," like ginger, cloves, cinnamon, and grains of paradise; one could insert elderflower or lavender; one could introduce a boiled decoction of "some of these spices." To help foul-tasting wines, there were "few other correctives, but what conduce to clarification." More were not needed, it was felt, since any "unsavouriness of wines" was removed when "their impurities [were] set afloat," and saline and sulfurous bits were separated from "the finer and sweeter" and "remov'd chiefly by precipitation." Practice was even more complicated than the confusing contemporary descriptions suggest. Urban retailers, vintners, cellar men, and householders devised and adapted all kinds of "specifics" to palliate "the several vices of wines of all sorts" and to copy the virtues of others. To correct "rankness, eagerness, and pricking of Sacks and other sweet wines," some stirred in white limestone; to help "pricked" French wines, some added powders of Flanders tile and roche alum; to ameliorate Rhenish wines, some racked it "into a clean and strongly-scented cask or vat" and mixed it with a concoction of beaten honey and skim milk. Adulterations and fabrications occurred along the entire commodity chain; one could never be entirely clear what one was acquiring or drinking. Each set of practitioners had its own favorite additives. Portuguese producers and exporters consistently put alkali or salt of tartar into sour wine to "absorb the acidity, and give it the taste and smell of new wine," and into this concoction they mixed "a quantity of the acid liquor," so as to avoid the blackness and muddiness of too much alkali. Over the course of the eighteenth century, Madeira's exporters and producers learned about these practices and copied them. The island being such an important commercial cross-roads, these possibilities made a stew of European practice.[29]

One of the more contested aspects of altering flavor by Madeira export houses was the addition of sweeteners. Producers and merchants who had hoped to "improve" degraded wines had for a long time sweetened them after the several fermentations had ended. Most traditional was a blending with a sweet must like Malmsey. Objectionable yet still not uncommon was the introduction of sugar. Five pipes of Malmsey that the Leacocks had purchased from a grower would only be fit for export "after being *concertada* with an additional arrove of sugar," they predicted.[30] Every producer and distributor in Madeira seems to have had his own additive to sweeten the wine, whether it be sugar, sloes, wild plums, raisins, mustard, or nettles. Some adulterations, like sugar, were harmless. "In order to make wines stronger and more pungent, a variety of spices" were employed, like galangal, cardamom, and mace, and these were benign. Other items were less so. Sage leaves used to give to wine the flavor of a sweet Muscatel imparted "a strong stupefying smell and very pernicious effects." But it was the diachronic and widespread infusion of lead or alum—commonly used to sweeten food and drink—that was most pernicious. As the eighteenth century advanced, the custom came under attack. Public dissatisfaction with gross wine adulteration first surfaced in the 1710s, with a blistering satirical attack waged by Daniel Defoe, Joseph Addison, and Richard Steele. By the 1780s, complaints about it had reached such a fevered pitch that no writer on wine could ignore it. By then, experts were publicly proclaiming that "horrid deleterious compositions which are sold for wine and manufactured by members of the wine merchants" that were "littell more than a mixture of unfermented vegetable juices mixed with cyder, brandy, and sugar of lead, or some other saturnine preparation . . . ought to be ranked in the class of poisons." Yet, despite the mounting scientific and medical evidence against the use of such poison, it remained common practice through 1815 to add lead to "sour wines in order to sweeten" and "render them agreeable to the palate."[31]

FORTIFYING

In addition to blending their wine, the islanders began to fortify it with brandy, a form of mixing that enhanced its body but was considered a stage of production all its own. Indeed, fortification is often singled out as one of the hallmarks of Madeira. For Madeira was multiply fortified. After producers placed the must in the vat, they introduced brandy according to their discretion and thereby stopped the first alcoholic fermentation. A "second or insensible fermentation" from lactic acid bacteria often ensued. After three or four months of letting the concoction settle, the producer added more brandy. Finally, "at the time of exportation," the shipper introduced yet more. Multiple fortifications made for an exceptionally potent drink. So, too, did Madeirans' practice of using a brandy a "full 10 per cent above London proof by Clarke's Hydrometer" as the fortifying agent, and 10 percent was the islanders' lower limit! Sometimes the brandy's strength ranged as high as 29 percent above proof. On average, the percentage of absolute alcohol in Madeira, a drink that had gone through at least three fortifications before it reached the consumer, was 22 percent, well below that in whisky, rum, brandy, and gin (about 52 percent), roughly the same as Port (23 percent), but well above all other wines (between 13 percent and 20 percent), ale (7 percent) and small beer (1 percent).[32]

The road to deliberate, systematic, multistage fortification by the distributor was not clear-cut. The first mention of someone counseling the addition of brandy to wine appears in the advice of a physician in England in 1633. Other "experts," usually vintners, began suggesting its inclusion in the late seventeenth century as a means to cure muddiness and ropiness and to restore body and flavor. In the intervening years, the Dutch were actually manufacturing "burnt wines," that is, French table wines of the Charente region that they had either fortified with brandy or further distilled. By the turn of the century, most Portuguese wine producers probably agreed with the chemist Caspar Neumann that "weak wines are improved by an addition of spirit, particularly before the fermentation is complete." Porto's producers and exporters may have been adding brandy to their wine as early as 1724, but if so they did it erratically.[33] With respect to Madeira, it was actually North Americans who most consistently implemented European prescription or copied European models. The first recorded instance of an American suggesting the addition of brandy to Madeira appears in the 1743 edition of *Poor Richard's Almanac.* The first recorded mention of an American actually doing it occurred in 1761, as Garrett Beekman informed John Searle. As the letter from Beekman to Searle suggests, American shippers and retailers backwards-influenced Madeiran cultivators and merchants. The first reference to island growers and exporters deliberately and consistently adding brandy appears in 1753; it noted almost in passing that the American practice was gaining acceptance on the island.[34]

But to what effect? Most exporters believed fortification "helped" "very indifferent and clear" grades. It imparted a smooth taste to acidic, rough, or full-bodied must. "A stronger dose of brandy" strengthened "weak and pale" "thin juice" that had a small proportion of black grape. It ate "off the sweetness" and thereby "prevent[ed] fretting"; since Madeira had a "sweetish" must, it needed more brandy "than was common" with a wine. Today, we know adding brandy

ensures microbiological stability, rendering impotent most bacteria and strains of
yeast and thereby precluding further fermentation. Then, they knew it stopped
fermentation . . . and added alcoholic strength, thereby pleasing consumers who
liked "everything that is powerful and heady."[35]

However contemporaries described or justified it, fortification appears to have
been quickly adopted by a majority of Madeira's exporters by 1762. In that year,
a partner on the island could write with little fear of rejection that the recipient
might "discover a taste . . . not usual" in the wine he was sending him. In taking
over the management of another firm, the exporter Henry Hill decided to overturn tradition and add "double distilled brandy." By 1764, his firm was putting
a half bucket of such brandy into every pipe it shipped overseas. The craze for
brandy was great enough that it and other houses soon bemoaned its absence. As
one exporter told his brother, many of their wines were "on the fret" because they
"did not give them brandy enough"; the wines that year were "sweetish," which
consumers would "no more endure than green wines," and, since these wines
required "more cordial than common to eat off the sweetness," more brandy was
required. Unfortunately, Madeira's supply was exhausted.[36]

Even as many exporters embraced fortification, some firms initially balked,
especially those dealing in high-grade wines; as late as 1815, they were still decry-
ing such "spoilage," arguing for its use only as a last resort, and refusing to fortify
as a matter of course. The debate pitted distributor against producer, distributor against distributor, and official against distributor. The exchange reached a
fevered pitch in 1794, when brandy was in particularly short supply, and usage
was heatedly endorsed by men "deeply interested in the admission of French
brandy." Consumer satisfaction slowly overpowered exporter scruple, however. If
adding brandy would "anyhow aid the sale," then distributors became willing to
fortify. By 1800, the "brandy doctrine" was upheld by all. The Leacocks were typical. Agreeing that brandy was "an essential help to wine," they made it a rule "to
give all wines that go round a sufficient portion. We find that all those houses who
are most noted for putting an extra quantity of it in their wines meet with more
success in pleasing their correspondents than those who ship much better wines
that do not. . . . Indeed in the course of eight or nine months continual agitation
on board a vessel, the extra fire and spirit of the brandy must be much exhausted
and softened and the wine receive the strength, which is quite different when
the wines remain quiet and undisturbed in our stores." There was "no such thing
as making any quantity of wine tolerably good without having good brandy to
do it with." Brandy became the "indispensable" component of all grades but the
highest. Even the previously reluctant Newton & Gordon felt that its "real good
wines require[d] . . . a very small portion of brandy," although the brandy had

to be "exceedingly fine," "the oldest & [the] best without regard to price." The practice became "universal." Some like the Gordons used less, others like the Leacocks used more, and still others like many a cultivator threw it in indiscriminately, often using it as a substitute for gesso as well. But everyone used it.[37]

The most important aspect to the adoption of fortification was the Madeirans' customer responsiveness. There were many palates in the English-speaking world (their wine's biggest market), and firms altered their formulas to suit, negotiating them with American distributors and consumers in response to the preferences of drinkers in particular regions. The correspondence between Madeira's exporters and overseas customers shows this process at work. Foremost in buyers' minds were questions of color and flavor, not brandy. But brandy was never irrelevant. Without treatment, new wine bore a reddish color and sweetish taste; having experienced additional fermentation and climatic heating, old wine bore a lighter hue and drier taste. Adding brandy directly altered both traits, and these were traits on which consumers weighed in constantly.

In the West Indies and southern regions of North America, where there was no worry about Madeira spoiling from cold, a love of wines of a darker hue and sweeter taste was able to flourish. To satisfy hot-climate customers who wanted to avoid the lightening and intoxicating effects of adding alcohol, distributors put less brandy in the wine they shipped; sometimes, in response to requests from Caribbean planters, they left it out altogether and sent along a quarter-cask of brandy and another of Tinta, so that the customers could strengthen and color it to taste. In contrast, more northern consumers asked for a paler, drier wine, and shippers responded by adding one or two gallons more brandy than they put in Caribbean wine. South Carolinians and Virginians preferred extremely pale, dry wine as "white as water" that had been heavily fortified; Philadelphians requested golden wines with slightly less brandy and slightly more sweetness; and New Yorkers wanted an amber, somewhat reddish drink that was even less brandied and more sugared. Distributors learned about these differences, and honored them. If it had known certain wines were destined for the London market, one firm acknowledged, it would "have brandied them accordingly." "When they are shipt [for the West Indies market], we put in only one gallon, & that of weak Guernsey brandy, thinking they might be tasted & exposed to sale four or five weeks after shipment & that they would be smoother & more palatable from having little brandy." But when wines were shipped to northern climes, distributors added much more. Each market demanded a certain brandy and flavor and, after rounds of negotiation (for producers' responses to consumers were never simply acquiescence), each market received its own drink.[38]

That the islanders could satisfy customers was a function of not only their inclination but also their placement in a global commodity chain. Not just any brandy would do. True, early modern producers, distributors, and consumers were nowhere near as clear as moderns in the distinctions among distilled spirits. Distillers were quite content procuring anything distillable, distilling it, and calling it by whatever name would appeal. True, too, the Madeirans had sugar and wine available from which to distill a spirit—the dregs of both would suffice—and they distilled both, probably as early as the fifteenth century. The product was always small in quantity, never reliable, and low in quality. There was, for instance, "none to be had" in 1785. But 1785 was not unique. In any short vintage, "when wines are dear, brandys are so also," as the locals "make but little." Yet it was available. These things are all true, but to an extent that is surprising, the distributors involved in manufacturing Madeira were neither easily satisfied nor easily fooled. They endlessly discussed the merit and supply of brandy from various sources among themselves and with their customers.[39]

The exporters largely preferred French brandy from Armagnac, Gascony, and Cognac. French "spirit was 20 p cent above proof, old, mellow & a perfect nosegay in flavor." These qualities and speedy dispatch kept Madeira firms returning to France.[40] French brandy was not always available, however; so, alternative sources had to be explored: Andalusia, Jerez, and Catalonia in Spain; Lisbon and Porto in Portugal; Holland; even Guernsey and Jersey. The Guernsey stock was in some respects appealing. "Truckers" from that island took in the always difficult to sell "low wines" of Madeira and found vent for them in the Caribbean. But the brandy they exchanged for wine was "detestable trash." It was, in fact, seldom from Guernsey; rather, it hailed from Barcelona, Valencia, and other Spanish ports. Such stocks were easier, quicker, and cheaper to import. Still, there was "no comparison between the quality" of what they imported and the good brandy from France.[41]

French brandy persisted as the fortifier of choice, but it was always a problematic one. The continental war in Europe that began in 1792 raised new challenges to its supply and forced Madeira's exporters to look farther afield. In 1793, firms possessing only a few pipes of brandy relied upon British cruisers to bring more from England; little came. In 1794, needy firms began scouring suppliers in Lisbon and Porto; but how far, they wondered, could they "depend upon Portugal for a supply in case this infernal war continues?" Late that year, the large Newton & Gordon firm was in an especially precarious position: their stock of French was "very low." "Much, very much" did they "wish to have it a little augmented" with more but they could not "point out nor hint at any source of supply." In the end, Lisbon brandy had to suffice. "Perfectly new from the still" cost half the price of other brandies and, given its proof, was worth double as much; too, it was easily obtained. Following Newton & Gordon's lead, other big export firms began ordering brandy from Lisbon. But Lisbon's ships were likely targets for the French. In the bind created by the war, some firms set up their own brandy distilleries on Madeira and, initially, they boasted that their liquor was "not much inferior to French" in flavor and "greatly superior" in strength. But soon their spirits were dashed. It was seldom satisfactory. Thus, whatever the source, problems with non-French brandy bedeviled island manufacturers. One crisis succeeded another, each affecting the quality of supplies. Brandy coming through London and Guernsey was adulterated; that coming from France and Portugal for the most part was not, but it was constantly taken prize by the enemy. Not until the fall of Napoleon did easy supply of French brandy return.[42]

AGITATING

Solutions to one set of problems created another set: a clarified and fortified wine could be quite rough. The addition of gesso induced a "hot and burnt taste and twang"; furthermore, the addition of a lower-density alcohol like brandy left the spirit floating on top of the wine and produced a harsh, bracing, and often uneven taste. To remedy these defects, the Madeirans systematized yet another vinicultural innovation: deliberate agitation. "Extraordinary agitation in the cask" wore off the sometimes erratic taste of the brandy by distributing the spirit, and worked off the aftertaste left by gesso. In addition, it removed any remaining insoluble materials suspended in the must.[43]

The innovation was uneven. Agitation occurred naturally in the course of transport. Given unavoidable seaborne carriage, wine-filled pipes lying in the hold rocked to and fro as the ship rode out high waves en route to distant markets. These benefits were recognized soon after exporting became significant. The "wearing out" of undesirable flavors "by incessant commotions at sea" especially worked in the "favour of Madeira wines" when compared with those wines transported coastwise or overland within Europe. By making such comparisons over the course of the eighteenth century, Madeira's exporters deepened their understanding of the link between agitation and its effect. Any exporter of consequence was told time and again by his correspondents that in "the course of eight or nine months' continual agitation on board a vessel, the extra fire and spirit of the brandy" was "exhausted and softened, and the wine receive[d] the strength, which is quite different when the wines remain[ed] quiet." Such information also flowed in reverse. Responding to calls for direct shipment to London, distributors reminded customers there that it was "an advantage to ship wine on board of vessels that have protracted voyages as the motion of the vessel is of great service to the wine."[44]

But customers, distributors, and producers learned something else from these epistolary exchanges: all voyages were not alike. Some vessels experienced greater agitation, others less, and, as a result, quality varied greatly. "Consistence" being highly desirable, islanders acting on the knowledge gleaned from both agents' reports and consumers' requests pushed to force agitation in the late 1780s. There was some precedent for this step in both ancient Roman and recent French viniculture.[45] But the influence on Madeirans was probably more pragmatic. Deliberate agitation was inspired by the islanders' fining procedures. By custom, cultivators poured egg whites into a pipe of wine at the vineyard and stirred it well "by inserting a stick at the bung hole" and keeping "the liquor in motion for a quarter of an hour." Increasingly aware of the general benefits of agitation accruing from ship transport, some exporters also got their suppliers to stir the mixture with a stick after brandy was added, much as they did after fining agents were introduced. Other firms assigned employees to rock the casks manually in their own Funchal storehouses and thereby induce the effect of stormy seas. Later, at the turn of the nineteenth century, in dialogue with American consumers who were reporting back that they found artificially rocked wines as acceptable as naturally rocked wines, islanders employed new steam-powered machines to perform the racking. As with any early modern innovation, it is difficult to know who precisely drove the process of change; yet it is not insignificant that continual implementation occurred only after consumers started praising the effects of agitation.[46]

HEATING

Heating wine, like fortification and agitation, was introduced in isolation, in stages, and in concert with customers' views and distributors' reworking. Heating affected fermentation, clarification, and stabilization. It quickened oxidation and destroyed fungi. If ambient heat was raised, interactions among natural organic chemicals occurred faster, speeding up the reaction of harmful bacteria as well as the aging. Moreover, it affected certain wines more than others. Understood in terms of the science of the day, which held that wine's response to heat was a function of its chemical makeup, Madeira's combination of "the more active and noble principles of sulphur and air" was "fixt to such a degree" that it actually required "a considerable degree of warmth . . . to keep it in order, and give it . . . taste."[47]

The heating of wine was not restricted to Madeira production, of course. It had a long history. The technique was favored by the ancients, Cato, Columella, Pliny, Theophrastus, and Galen all tell us. Romans in particular placed their wine in a south-facing room "in the highest Story" of their country villas, where containers would be subjected to "the Heat of the Sun" as well as "warmed by fire."[48]

The technique was also utilized by early modern winemakers. In the middle of the seventeenth century, French producers preserved wines by putting them "in a stove" or in front of "a good fire made round about the Vessel," and allowing them to come to a boil. A century later, French vintners corrected acidic grape juices by adding sugar and rapidly fermenting the brew at the highest possible temperatures, placing the wine in a fermentation room fitted out with stoves, and using ovens to produce high-quality wines. German producers in Alsace and the Moselle Valley similarly put the must of unripe grapes into wooden casks and placed them in cellars warmed by fires in order to render them "more palatable and agreeable."[49]

Inasmuch as the usually chatty exporters wrote nothing of ancient or modern practice, one can safely assume Madeira's heating arose independently, not in imitation of ancient or continental technique but a response to Madeira's chemistry, the point of production, and the dictates of transport. "No sort of Wine" better agreed with "hot Places" than Madeira. Indeed, it had "one very particular and odd Property" — "the more 'tis expos'd to the Sun-beams and heat, the better it is." Given Madeira's geographical situation and the simple, almost crude manufacture of its wine, some heating arose naturally. The early blended wines received a treatment of natural heating, first from direct exposure to the sun during the open-air harvest and later from indirect exposure while sitting in Funchal's clay-tile-covered attics awaiting export.[50] Additional heating occurred in the hold of the ship. On voyages to Africa, the Americas, and India, wine cargoes were subjected to extremely high temperatures in ships' holds, often 110 and 120 degrees Fahrenheit (in contrast to storage cellars, which were kept between 70 and 90 degrees). The wine might lie in the hold for all the time a ship stayed in tropical climes, cooking.[51] It was this treatment that Francis Newton warned a partner about in 1754, when he wrote that the time of a certain brig's stay at Barbados was so short that the new wine in it would improve but little and that it "would answer much better to ship them in another vessel that will be some months in the West Indies." Alternately, cargoes might be removed from the ship and lodged with a resident in a subtropical or tropical port for any number of months or years, as were two pipes of wine that Newton's firm sent to a Jamaica merchant, who was asked to hold on to them for two or three years. Brazil, Barbados, Jamaica, Florida, and India all provided the requisite warm cellarage.[52]

Buyers and consumers began reporting — and producers and distributors began noting — that consumers liked wine that had made a long voyage to hot places. For consumers, there was the benefit of a more palatable drink. For Madeirans, there was the attraction of further improvement and heightened sales. For retailers in England, there was the lure that wine that had come round via the West

Indies would sell for £10 or £12 sterling more than a wine direct from Madeira. By 1775, it was a "general rule" among exporters: "new wine" would always be "more suitable to a warm than a cold northern climate," for there it would it would improve more rapidly.[53]

Upon hearing about heat's great benefits from consumers, shippers began intentionally sending the wine on long circuits, even when quicker, more direct routes were available. The first mention of a distributor deliberately sending wine the long way round via the West Indies occurs in 1749, and via the East Indies in 1772. Thereafter, shippers experimented aggressively and competitively with heating routes. Through numerous trials, a circuit of "floating ovens" came to be established by 1775. Gentlemen around the Atlantic were encouraged "to allow their private supplies to make the Tour." Madeira wine would improve "more in a few months in the Bengal," Brazil, or Jamaica climate "than it does in years in Madeira."[54]

During the American Revolutionary War, when wine was piling up in Madeira for want of a draw from the States (for Britain's ally Portugal had banned American vessels from entering its ports), producers and exporters shifted the process of heating to land. After 1775, one begins to find exporters writing about stoves, ovens, and hothouses being used for warming pipes and cellars, both overseas and on the island. Much like ancient Romans and contemporary Alsatians, the English sometimes put their Madeira "in stoves or hot-houses" and the Anglo-Americans kept them "in cisterns on the tops of the houses." One Charlestonian kept his Madeira, Port, Burgundy, and porter "in [a] cask loft" as early as 1773. New Yorkers performed their own variation: they "frequently boil[ed] it, or parboil[ed]" their wine "in decanters, or jugs [probably glass demijohns], by the fireside."[55] Whether they influenced Madeirans is unclear, but such practices were known to the exporters and were consonant with subsequent on-island innovation in the mid-1790s, when a ninety-year-old Portuguese landowner and merchant named Pantaleão Fernandes the Younger constructed a stove (*estufa*) into which he placed casks of the most recent vintage. Fernandes's stove was little more than a room filled with barrels lain on trestles and warmed by wood fires to 90 or 100 degrees Fahrenheit. By all accounts, the nonagenarian erected his stove for the sheer love of tinkering. But, for all the trial's naiveté, its merit was recognized by younger growers and exporters, and his stove-heating (*estufagem*) process initiated another frenzy of experimentation.[56]

Every major export firm rushed to rent a stove or build its own, despite lingering doubts about the applicability of heating to all grades.[57] What were employed were fairly simple structures—not the multistoried hothouses (*armazéms de calor*) used a century later, with pipes on the ground floor and vents in the attic. Stoves came in various formats, shapes, and sizes. One large quality firm built itself a one-room, freestanding *estufa* in the yard behind its countinghouse in 1799 and began work on another beside it. Another firm built large tanks for holding new wine, into which it placed coils through which passed hot water. Most firms built stoves for their own use exclusively, but some houses rented them out to others "at a certain rate per pipe." Indeed, while finishing plans for their own stove, the Leacocks rented space in another owned by a Portuguese exporter, as well as experimented with the niceties of a complementary technique—immersing pipes of wine in heaps of dung. It had become "general practice to put wine into Dung that it may improve by the Heat." "We have made the Experiment," they wrote a consumer, but as far as they could "see at present, we don't think it answers the purpose intended; however, we shall give the Wine a fair chance & let it remain to see how it turns out." Other firms like that of the Searles had "practiced this Method uniformly for a number of years," and the Leacocks supposed it had answered, otherwise the Searles would not have continued it. The smell was fine, the Leacocks were happy to report back to their American customers, and the look pretty, the wine "having lost all its color," but the taste was somewhat rough![58]

Whatever the inspiration or influence, whatever the innovation discarded on the road to heated wine, the decision to allow, encourage, and control heat had a profound effect on the process of production. By 1815, warming rooms had won out over dung heaps. It was the stove that most fired the imaginations of exporters, and nearly every quality and midrange house was using one. Almost everyone concurred: "heat must be of benefit, & we must make a climate."[59] A wine that would be palatable to Americans only after four or five years in England, three years in Madeira, or one year in the East or West Indies could be readied in a stove in three or six months. Considerable savings in time and money accrued from shortening production and avoiding long-distance cargo fees. Moreover, in mellowing the wine, producers and distributors mitigated undesirable traits and increased the quality of low-grade export.

Ultimately, what guaranteed the success of the technology were the reports from the men and women who drank the wine in America, India, and Europe. Their "candid opinion" was unanimous and positive. Oven-heated wines did not sour as quickly as unheated or traditionally heated wines; consumers could depend upon its flavor. Just as important, oven-heated wines possessed the same essential traits of body and color, and heating imparted a patina of age. Thus, it was a reliable "manufactured" luxury known for its drinkability—the product of a love of experiment, cost- and resource-saving imperatives, and the desire to satisfy well-articulated customer concerns—that men and women in the wider

Atlantic world chose to drink in the salons of fashionable London and taverns of provincial Bahia and New York and to buy in the chaotic auction houses of Calcutta or crude general stores that sprang up throughout frontier North America.[60]

AGING

Aged wines were nothing new to Madeira, nor to its golden age. Well before Madeirans appreciated the effects of heating, producers in ancient Mesopotamia, Assyria, Greece, and Rome recognized that aging improved certain wines. More recently, seventeenth-century doctors and connoisseurs in Europe regarded "old" and "new" wines differently: "wines that are new, are unwholesome," Thomas Venner reported in 1620, "and the more new, the more unwholesome, for they have in them little heat, and consist of a grosse and excrementall substance." Such awareness, which Venner acquired while working as a wine cooper and later a Madeira trader, came to be shared by many in the ensuing century. Aging wine, they reckoned, wrought significant benefit. It made it "fit for drinking much sooner." It diminished the harsh taste and yeasty odor of new wine. It imparted to Madeira in particular a smooth, mellow, nutty flavor and a clear, pleasing, often invigorating odor. Moreover, it allowed the wine to fare "better"—that is, not sour as quickly—in "colder climates." As one prominent Madeira exporter knew from his own trials, "a full high flavored wine with a true & simple taste will improve & mellow to excellence, & age will give it the pale color so much esteemed by those who drink."[61]

But if aging per se was not new, intentional aging by the distributor was. If it occurred at all at the beginning of the eighteenth century, it took place in the cellars of consumers. In 1700, when Madeira distributors described wine they shipped to America or Britain as "old," they meant wines of eighteen months or so, the product of the previous year's vintage that they had been unable to sell. The relative youth of the old wine persisted for decades and was not restricted to the island. Indeed, the writer of the *Encyclopédie*'s 1765 article on wine allowed even less time in defining "old": new wine was "that which has aged two or three months, old is that which has aged a year."[62] Whatever the time allowed for "old," Madeira's distributors "seldom or never" had old wine in store before 1775. Francis Newton was quite clear on the matter: old wine would "not at all answer." The leakage from it was "very considerable," and the island's climate too changeable and cold; besides, Madeirans had "no proper stores to keep" it in. When distributors like Newton did ship old wine, and a few began to send very small amounts in the late 1750s, they sent a fairly young wine (eighteen months from harvest), in a small amount, and to particular favored customers who requested it. "Unless old wine" was requested, firms like Newton's "never ship[ped] it, as it is somewhat dearer."[63] Older wine was typically aged by the purchaser. So, when Dean Swift was cracking open a bottle in 1730, he was pouring wine he had purchased at least seven years before; when Warren Johnson was padding about New York in 1761, he was able to buy fourteen-year-old Madeira that city wholesalers and retailers had acquired in 1748; when Thomas Jefferson was making a gift of thirty-six bottles to an old science professor in 1775, he was giving Madeira that his family had placed in its cellars eight years earlier. Only very occasionally did an exporter send three-year-old wine or older before the 1760s, and, if so, it was remainders or returns. Purchasers were the ones who "keep the wine by them till it becomes old."[64]

Not until the American Revolution did Madeira's exporters begin intentionally and systematically holding on to wine for longer than a year or two. The Gordon Brothers firm began acquiring old wine at this time to keep its customers "in good humour," although it was not without cost. A "great stock of wine," the proprietors found, "employs much of our money. Others who do not do the same are more masters of their capital, and can employ it some times to greater advantage." "The gain on old wine" did not correspond "as it ought to do," for they could not charge "proportionally as it deserves." Even so, other firms followed suit. The Hills looked back at the end of the war and found that much of their attention had been "employed in getting fine wine," having bought "upwards of 400 pipes of that quality from 5 years old downwards."[65]

Madeirans' acquisition and distribution of aged wine can be dated with some precision. In official shipping prices set by the island's British Factory of exporters, it was only in 1781 that Madeira's merchants began to charge £1 more per pipe for every additional year of age. After 1785, they began to charge "what they think the old wine is worth"—prevailing custom adding 20s. for every year of age. But the Factory was a conservative body, loathe to embrace innovation unless it had long been sanctioned by the market. Export firms' records suggest that age pricing had risen slightly earlier. In drawing up its 1774 inventory, Newton & Gordon first recorded stocks of "old wine." In that year, the firm was charging £1 more for each year of age. By 1777, it was shipping three-year-old wine. By 1782, it had in its lodges twenty-two and one-half pipes of vintage 1775 wine and twenty-seven and one-half pipes of vintage 1780.[66]

The introduction of aged wine had three main causes. First, American consumers began to plead with the islanders in the 1760s for "some old," since "the older it is the better" and not all customers had cellars for aging new wine.[67] Second, the islanders experienced a run of bad harvests between 1768 and 1772, when vintages fell below one-third their usual level and exporters almost ran out of wine to satisfy long-standing buyers. To forestall further incapacity, the exporters began restocking their wine in earnest after harvests returned to average levels in the mid-1770s.[68] Finally, just as normalcy was returning to the island, the American Revolutionary War commenced, and access to the exporters' largest customer base was cut off (which a call from India did not yet match). The amount of wine shipped to Anglo-America fell by two-thirds. To store what remained on hand, distributors bought or rented lodge space. At the same time, frightened by the specter of bad harvests, they continued their restocking, purchasing more pipes, hiring more coopers, and buying more wine.

While wine sat and aged in Madeira, the stores and cellars of revolutionary America were depleted. When at war's end the sizable American market for Madeira gradually reopened, the exporters took advantage of the situation: they not only off-loaded their aging supply but also segmented the market and stratified their customers by wealth and taste, introducing a vocabulary of age distinctions that postwar consumers in Kingston, New York, and London could use to describe more precisely what they were drinking and distinguish themselves from those who drank younger wine.[69]

Aged wine made more than just good short-term business sense, though; it also became necessary practice, incumbent upon any aspiring quality trader. Once begun, old stock had "to be kept up." By the late 1780s, it was apparent to all exporters that a "large stock of old wines requires much capital and is attended with much expense," but it was "extremely desirable" — no, it was "absolutely necessary." "Taste for old wines" among drinkers around the Atlantic had become so demanding that it was "next to impossible to execute their orders" without a large old stock. Snooping about other houses, Newton & Gordon learned that the merit of the wine flogged by its chief competitor in the quality-wine market was "its great *age*." Accordingly, it decided that its future shipments would all possess this quality as well. It became "scarce possible" for any firm to please "private customers" "without being possessed of a stock of old wines." The "great and essential superiority" of a firm depended on "the age of the wine more than from any other circumstance." "Age, age is the grand *sine qua non*."[70]

This is not to say that Madeira's exporters introduced aged wines and age distinctions without apprehension. A high-quality characteristic like age invited wide imitation and created real problems. Old stock was quite costly, and it took up a lot of space, which was also quite costly. But the costs were incurred, for the rewards were substantial. "The demand for our wines in America increases daily . . . with the opulence of the country," merchants believed. "The taste for fine old wine" in particular "extends more & more" there, where, "to procure the best," customers were willing "to give the highest price & to pay the premium." Profits slowly broke down the resistance of even the most obdurate traditionalist, but what fixed the minds of the majority were the reports on old wine sent by customers of such wine in America, Britain, and India. These were largely favorable. "The taste for old wines" was in 1787 "so general" in English-speaking America that "none but old wines" of five years' age "would please" connoisseurs. By 1793, many firms were shipping eight- and ten-year-old wines. In 1815, the dispatch of fifteen-year-old wines was commonplace. By then, no exporter could deny that "a reserve must be kept adequate."[71]

PACKAGING

Madeira's exporters continued to improve their wine and create an altogether different product by lavishing considerable attention on packaging. Native carriers (*borrachãos*) delivered goatskin bags filled with wine to Funchal stores, lodges, and warehouses. Once there, care for the product fell to the exporters, and much of the work involved repackaging. To package wine correctly, exporters had to tend to a plethora of details and draw upon a global commodity chain that ultimately allowed them to enhance the quantity and quality of the commodity.

An exporter's typical customer was usually content if his wine arrived on time, the quantity was that which had been agreed upon, and the quality was good. Not surprisingly, it was a challenge to see that these things transpired. Accurately building wine containers to hold "correct" quantities was a task that consumed considerable entrepreneurial energies, and in no trade excepting perhaps that in sugar was the practice more vexed than the wine trade. What size should Madeira's casks be? How should they be constructed? How should they look? The containers into which the wine was transferred had to be constructed at the spur of the moment from available materials, properly built, and appropriately sized for and geared to the product and its market. Madeira's containers, in their material, size, and composition, were examples of the efficacy of the workings of the Atlantic market. In their evolution and assemblage, one sees the distributors drawing from many points around the ocean and encountering and yet overcoming global and local obstacles to any integration of that community.

Exporters transferred the wine from bags and barrels to various containers. The most common was the pipe (*pipa*), so named, it is alleged, because it resembled the barrel of a musical pipe. A round, slightly bulging vessel of greater length than breadth, it was usually made from long staves, ringed with hoops and closed at the ends with flat circular heads. Typically, there was at least one hole for a stopper, known as the bung. But commonality was elusive. From a production standpoint, variations and discrepancies were almost legion in the pipe. From an analytical perspective, discrepancies were encouraged, indeed manufactured.[72]

The matter of a container's size is deceptively simple. The pipe, according to Madeira law, contained so many *almudes*. But the *almude* varied over time. For much of the 1640–1750 period, Funchal's Council defined, for tax purposes, Madeira's pipe as containing twenty-six *almudes*. Around 1750, the Council downsized it to twenty-three *almudes*. Finally, in 1800, it raised it to thirty *almudes*. These volumes, it should be noted, were volumes of account; they affected only Portuguese taxes. The standard for "common" export pipes maintained by foreigners and adopted by most natives remained stable at 110 English gallons. Confusion really arose only when other markets adopted different measures. Lisbon's pipe contained roughly thirty-one *almudes* before the 1830s (140 gallons). Porto, too, had its own size pipe (138 gallons).[73] From the time of Henry VI, England maintained a 126-gallon pipe measure and that standard was reaffirmed for Britain in 1706. Some colonies incorporated England's standard into their law, like Pennsylvania at its founding and Barbados in 1744, while other colonies like New York and Virginia legislated a 120-gallon pipe in 1750.[74] Further confusing the matter, Madeirans themselves had different pipes: after Barbados adopted its standard, they proffered a "Barbados" pipe of 126 gallons, whose sole raison d'être was "to ease the impact of freight and duty charges," since the same tax fell on a pipe of 126 gallons as on one of 110; when the English East India Company insisted on pipes containing 115 gallons, Madeira's exporters complied almost a decade later with a container that size. Moreover, Madeirans produced containers smaller and larger than pipes. Smaller casks were common, most notably the hogshead (*quarto*, a half of a pipe), the quarter-cask (*quartola*, a quarter), the barrel (*barril*, an eighth), and the tierce (between a half and a quarter). Larger containers—like the *tonel* (or tun, twice the size of a pipe) and the butt (sometimes the size of a Barbados pipe but usually between it and a tun)—were constructed, but they were for use in the lodges only.[75]

The range of containers and measures seems dizzying in retrospect.[76] Yet it was the pipe that was the unit of the Madeira and Portuguese wine industry. To handle it properly was ultimately to enhance the product and please the consumer. In making the most of the pipe, the exporters had to decide first whether to use ready-made containers or to assemble new containers from "pipe packs" (containing staves, heads, and a bung plug) compiled elsewhere. Ready-made pipes had appeal, especially when a crush of business slowed dispatch, for such casks, manufactured in London or Lisbon, usually brought flour or flax to Madeira on the voyage to the island. Indeed, from the start of a significant overseas trade for Madeira's wine in the middle decades of the seventeenth century, exporters gained a supply of previously constructed containers through the food-for-wine barter that prevailed. Both cost and convenience counseled use. So did "the difficulty of getting them made" due to a paucity of coopers, a situation particularly chronic on Madeira.[77]

Exporters never felt completely comfortable with ready-made casks, however. They consumed a lot of space in the hold of a ship, yet, relative to other items, provided little weight as ballast. Furthermore, the wear and tear that casks were subjected to in the hold of an oceangoing vessel required continual dismantling, cleaning, and rejoining. Finally, casks came relatively infrequently; the one Atlantic trade that utilized the greatest number of usable casks—the Caribbean sugar trade—sent little of its commodity to Madeira. As a result, if an exporter had a choice, he opted to assemble pipes on-island. This option brought the added advantage of not having to predict in advance the quantities and sizes that would be demanded. One did need coopers, of course, but they were never in abundant supply. Still an exporter did not have to employ one full time—he could share with another exporter who did employ one or could procure the services of an independent artisan in Funchal.[78]

Assembling pipes in situ also raised other, more far-flung challenges. Chief among them was maintaining flexibility in procurement. Wooden container parts came from a number of settlements rimming the Atlantic Ocean. What mattered most to the islanders was that the wood for these parts be durable and free from sap, knots, flaws, or wormholes. The staves, the principal component, were always made from white oak; no other material, even red oak, has surfaced. White oak was hard, supple, and watertight—one of the strongest of the common hardwoods growing in the temperate Northern Hemisphere. It was physically easy to work worth. Too, it held liquids remarkably well. Most critically, for those intent on maintaining body, flavor, and taste, it promoted clarity and stability in red wine and added new layers of complexity to white.[79]

White oak staves could come from a number of places, depending on the vagaries of war, quantity, and price, and exporters who would be well supplied had to juggle all of them. Local wood supplies existed, we know, but they were easily exhausted and never matched foreign staves in quality. The same was true of British supplies. Hamburg was exporters' favorite source. "Hambro" staves were unsawed and workable, as well as thick and durable. But they were also the most expensive. When Hambro staves were in low supply or at high price, the islanders looked elsewhere. American staves provided the most reliable and best alternative. They came cheaper. Besides, the American white oak (*quercus alba*) had certain beneficial features: it had a much more palatable vanillin flavor, more astringent than the smoother, subtler oaks of Germany and France; it was richer in tyloses than European counterparts—that is, richer in structures that plug the vessels and fibers running parallel to the trunk—and therefore was better at holding wine, as the path of the liquid was blocked by the structures. But even the American supply was uncertain. When the ports of Portugal and the United States were closed to each other during the American Revolutionary War, exporters began looking to the markets of Danzig and Stettin. Polish staves proved thin, however, and Madeira's coopers returned to working with American staves after the war.[80]

Once procured, parts would have to be dried, if necessary (dry wood was essential if the casks were not to leak), assembled, and finished.[81] During final coopering, special care had to be taken in fitting the pieces together to prevent leakage. Exporters became almost obsessive about such matters when they began to hold on to aged wine after 1770. Leakage was all too frequent. If full containers lay long in their courtyards or lodges, the wood would dry and split in the sun or heat and the casks ooze, losing as much as 4 percent. Similarly, if the containers lay too long in the hold, the casks would require recoopering on landing, as the heat was "apt to loosen the hoops." To stop more efficiently the bunghole, they covered it with a tin plate made in Cornwall. Likewise, they replaced chestnut hoops with iron ones. Vigilance was continual.[82]

Finished casks then had to be protected, for pilferage plagued the trade. Accordingly, the islanders devised a number of countermeasures to protect what was a growing on-island investment. First, they inscribed particular marks on the insides of containers. To "guard against change or improper treatment, a thing too common," Newton & Gordon stamped "the private mark S" on the inside of their bungs. Sometimes distributors placed seals over the bungholes. To "discover if any deceit should be practiced," other exporters "put the same seal" as they used in private correspondence on "the bung below the tin and upon the plug . . . in the head." Second, they started noting quantities differently than before. Exporters had marked casks for centuries, usually with chalk, in order to tie the cargo to items previously ordered and then being sent. Such marks were a help to both sellers and buyers: they imparted information not only about origin and capacity but also about how parts fit together, critical in a trade that employed differently sized containers and regularly dismantled, reassembled, and reused them. Because it was often "utterly impossible" to distinguish the parts of a common-gauge pipe from those of a slightly larger container, firms in the last quarter of the eighteenth century began to carve or paint the number of gallons in the cask on each stave and to indicate its connection to adjacent staves. Finally, they began to inscribe their names on the heads and near the bungholes and numbering or otherwise identifying the pipes, further solidifying an association between firm and product. Traditionally, distributors had chalked their names on the outside of the cask. This was not only good marketing but also good protection—advertising the firm to all who saw the cask, somewhat minimizing the possibility of confusion during shipment, and appealing to the desires of status-conscious customers who wanted to possess and display desirable brands. Even so, as the value of inventories and the cost of wine rose, chalking fell from favor. Exporters began searching for alternatives. Ever attentive to the desires of buyers, distributors carved their names on the heads of the casks. Some time later, they started to carve the names of the buyers. Smaller firms like Leacock & Sons generally found branding easier and cheaper than carving. For these reasons, it ordered two "LEACOCK" irons from London, plus "a set of letters of the alphabet," "screws for fixing them in the groove," and four scribes for marking pipes, and commenced branding in 1800.[83]

Ordering the parts and assembling the pipes were only the first stages of package management, a task to which the exporters turned with increasing zeal in the last decades of the eighteenth century. Before shipment, they washed, seasoned, painted, and marked the pipes, the charges for which were added to the cost of the container. They reused casks and complementary parts when they could. With a reused container, a more vigorous washing was needed. Traditionally, they used cold water: they filled the cask with it and then shook it, knocking off rough tannins that clung to the wood and revealing leaks. By midcentury, they started to scald with boiling water. Scalding cleansed old containers and seasoned new pipes; it was particularly good at extracting "the disagreeable taste" and "the high color" of new wood. Initially, the water was boiled in large caldrons standing in the countinghouse yard. But as new boiling and pumping technologies came on the market—Newcomen's 1712 engine and especially Watt's 1769 improvement—most exporters acquired them. Hill's firm, which had always lost "a great deal of time" and money "in bringing up water to wash the pipes," acquired a boiler in 1765. Newton & Gordon bought one of the newer Watt's models in the 1770s; it was "more effectual, more expeditious, and less expensive" than the caldron method it had previously employed. By 1815, no firm of any size did without boiler and pump.[84]

Painting was another cask preparation challenge to which the importers rose in the last half of the eighteenth century. The idea emanated from the Caribbean, where planters repainted sugar and wine casks. The reason, customers argued, was to keep the pipes "free from the worm." But initially Madeira exporters balked: the paint "would impregnate the liquor," and it would have to be removed when the cask was rebuilt. By the 1770s, however, they had become convinced of the relatively low risk of taint and so struck a compromise with consumers: the firms would not paint pipes for high-grade wine but would paint their heads, since it "pleases the eye, has a neat and attentive appearance to the owners of the Liquor, & is of real service to the cask"; in contrast, they would paint entire casks for lower-grade wines. They would, of course, charge more.[85]

Much of wine's manufacture did not stop at the borders of the vineyard, as the foregoing pages suggest. Full-service, beginning-to-end, vineyard-to-wharf care of wine and casks became standard operating procedure among quality and middling export houses in the several decades preceding 1815. Fining, racking, agitating, and fortifying formed a nearly continuous set of activities, and the chain continued once the wine was deposited in the lodges. The distributors seasoned new pipes by letting them stand unused for months. After cleaning the pipes, they filled, bunged, painted, marked and, if buyers wished, cased them. Furthermore, although the heating of wine naturally began in the open-air vineyard and some producers artificially heated it in stoves there, stove-heating was a maintenance and stabilization task more closely associated with exporters.

Given the work done by exporters in town, storage became a more serious post-manufacture concern. Early on, distributors left the wines in the vineyards and claimed them only right before shipment for much of the period. They began to make more complicated arrangements after the middle of the eighteenth century, however, bringing the wine to town in advance of shipment, storing it there, and maintaining it themselves. The Quaker firm of Lamar, Hill, Bisset & Co. was in the vanguard of this shift; its movements reveal one final way that a new and different product was invented.

In want of fine wines in August 1763, Robert Bisset approached the *partida* maker Manoel da Silva, who led him on a tour of town storehouses. In Silva's own lodge in the Rua dos Ferreiros, thirty pipes lay ready for purchase. Bisset was aware of their quality; his expectations and concerns rose "to a great degree," particularly because da Silva told him "another house of credit had spoken to him about purchasing them." Bisset then went to taste them. But to his "great surprise [he] found them all" damaged: they were "so low in quality . . . they would only do for a Dutchman." On leaving, Bisset next visited Antonio Vidella's lodge, where he found wines his partner Henry Hill had previously chalked as worthy of examining. Vidella complained of Hill's "not having taken them out" immediately when Hill had marked them. Bisset demurred: "marking them could be of no prejudice" to either the owner or the wine, for Hill "only went with a view of knowing the quality." Bisset told Vidella that he would "continue to claim his supply till Jany next & would then look at his wine." If the exporter liked it, he would buy it and close the account; if not, Vidella might sell it.[86]

What Bisset was describing was a lodge system in the making. *Senhorios, par-*

tida makers, and exporters with wines to sell or ship placed them in town lodges or warehouses. If an exporter like Bisset needed to sample a parcel, he would visit a lodge, taste the wine, strike a deal, and mark his pipe; if he needed to store some wine before shipment, he would rent a lodge or use one of his own. These lodges were newcomers to the island, having been devised at the same time as a new wine was being invented — indeed, they were part of the same larger processes of product improvement, innovation, and differentiation. The lodges were scattered about the town. A typical export firm might manage a dozen lodges at a time. With its roots deep in grain-rich Maryland and Pennsylvania, Bisset's firm rented six lodges for grain, five lodges for hoops, oil, flour, wax, and cables, and thirteen lodges for unnamed commodities in 1767. It also possessed significant storage space in its countinghouse. But the bulk of its capital was tied up in wine, which it placed in two lodges on the ground floor of the countinghouse and nine other lodges in Funchal.[87]

The Madeira lodge system emerged only in the final third of the eighteenth century, when competition among exporters was rising, the differentiation in grades that accrued from innovation in the product was making its mark among Atlantic consumers, and business was becoming more heavily capitalized. The system employed a variety of spaces. A small lodge might be no bigger than a large residential room (20 by 24 feet), as was the case with "the lodge below the midwife" that Bisset's firm rented. A larger lodge room, like one of those under Bisset's own residence, probably ran 45 feet along the street and 90 feet back into the lot. A large undivided building solely dedicated to wine storage might be 90 by 180 feet; its lower floors could be used for work, its upper floors for storage. Since high temperatures favored the wine, it was under the upper-story eaves that wine usually found temporary respite. There, wooden pipes sat on their sides on curved racks, stacked two or three pipes high. Given the cost of the commodity stored in them, lodges were usually secured with "the best and strongest patent pad locks" that London or Lisbon could provide.[88]

Bisset's firm's investment in and use of lodges and storehouses was hardly extraordinary. After the Seven Years' War, most exporters acquired and managed at least some buildings for this purpose. They increased exporters' control and ultimately effected real savings in effort, time, and money. It was with real entrepreneurial pride that one exporter puffed to his partner that the "greatest part, if not all, of our business, [is] within our doors."[89] One could no longer hope to do any business without storage.

The often-intense focus on the monumental increases in human productivity that followed the Industrial Revolution makes it is easy to forget just how innovative the immediately prior centuries were. The invention of Madeira wine helps to bring this preindustrial inventiveness back into the picture, displaying the social—that is, the decentralized, discursive, reciprocal, and personal—nature of the process, and the Atlantic stage on which it took place.

Each aspect of Madeira's invention unfolded over time and through discourse. Producers and distributors continually "looked over their shoulders" to see what customers wanted; and consumers paid close attention to what producers and distributors were telling them about the proper use of what was gradually becoming a status symbol. Innovations in selecting, fortifying, agitating, aging, heating, packaging, and storing were not mainly responses to new technologies but, more important, ongoing negotiations among producers, distributors, and consumers. The enterprisers who developed the Madeira product started small, eventually forming a network that linked producers on their little island to consumers around the world. They had to persuade consumers that changing varietals, agitating, heating, aging, packaging, and storing were valuable improvements. The goals of Madeira consumers were probably more cosmopolitan—to show their familiarity with a transatlantic luxury diet and discourse. Yet by the end of the eighteenth century, they had convinced producers to "improve" the product by aging and fortifying it and by packaging it in more ways more appealing and useful to customers. Through rather mundane communications, producers and distributors provided and obtained information about consumer needs and product problems: they created understandings among parties, and they built organizations. They made consumers partners in product innovation, enlisting their aid in design, assessment, and dispersal. Consumers expected to be heard and heeded. They were. Small, sometimes seemingly insignificant interactions wrought great change.

Part II

SHIPPING AND TRADING WINE

4

"A Revolution in This Trade"

Madeirans planted vines in the 1440s and exported some wine as early as 1455, but the great age of their wine industry began in the seventeenth century and reached its zenith in the beginning of the nineteenth century under the management of English-speaking merchants. English merchants commenced wine trading by 1640, satisfying overseas partners' and customers' needs by exporting wine to English settlements in the New World. Portugal effectively turned the Madeira wine trade over to the English in the 1640s and 1650s by requiring trade with Portuguese America to be channeled through ports on the mainland. This biased the economics of supplying wine to Brazil against island traders in favor of mainland merchants. Soon thereafter England allowed wines produced in Madeira and the Azores to enter its colonies directly, exempt from Crown duty under the 1663 Navigation Act. This opened British North America, the Caribbean and, later, India as markets for the islanders, and wove Madeira into Britain's imperial mercantile institutions. Funchal functioned as a privileged port for Anglo-America, although it never formed part of Britain's formal empire.[1]

The market increased dramatically in the years between 1640 and 1815: the number of ships departing Funchal each year increased tenfold, and the quantity of wine they carried away grew sixfold (figure 4.1). Most of the expansion occurred after 1775, when ship departures more than doubled, wine exports almost tripled, and export prices nearly doubled. In the New World, the volume of Madeira delivered to the English-speaking colonies in Caribbean and North America increased through the 1770s, although more slowly than the white population living there. The ensuing revolution in America was a watershed event for them. Because the newly independent states were no longer part of the British Empire, Spanish and French wines that had been handicapped by British mercantile regulation became competitive with Portuguese wines. The emergence of competition led to a marked and permanent reduction in the volume of Madeira shipped to Anglo-America for the first time since the middle decades of the seventeenth century.

Over the 175-year period, Madeira producers, distributors, shippers, and consumers staged what they described as "a revolution in this trade."[2] The revolution was partly the increased scale and worldwide direction of Madeira exports; this chapter delineates these changes. It was also a revolution in the organization and business methods of the traders. That revolution was made necessary by the increases in scale, and, in turn, made them possible. It hastened the development of peripheral agents, organizations, and institutions exempt from metropolitan control, allowing the American distributors to continue trading independently of Britain after independence. The next three chapters explore the people who wrought the transformation, how they did so, and what they made of what they did.

OPPORTUNITIES FOR MADEIRA TRADERS

The Atlantic Madeira wine trade was so successful because it solved a number of economic problems. European shippers in the early modern era were plagued by empty holds on the America-bound legs of round-trip voyages. At the same time, European settlers in most parts of America needed a palatable wine to drink but were unable to produce it in commercially profitable quantities until the nineteenth century. Supplying Americans with Madeira wine—which, exporters discovered, improved rather than deteriorated en route—was a profitable response to the problems.

THE PROBLEM OF EMPTY HOLDS

Before the age of steam, European vessels on the long transatlantic passage westward more often than not called at one of the Wine Islands for water and wood, unless they took the more northerly route over Scotland and Ireland open to them in the summer. As Madeira was "not much out of the way going down to the West Indies," it was regarded as "generally worth a ship's while in peaceable times (or, in war-time, if a ship of force) to touch" there, as they could frequently find some freight or provision that was of "great service."[3] At first, the principal freight was sugar. When cheap Caribbean sugar undercut Madeira's sugar, islanders substituted their wine.

Captains who went from England to the Caribbean or Chesapeake carried bulky products away from America—fish, flour, tobacco, rice, and sugar. As

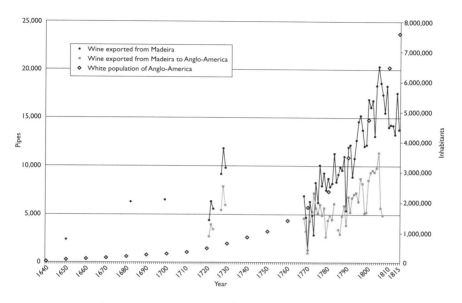

Figure 4.1. Wine exported from Madeira, 1640–1815.

Sources: For wine exported from Madeira, see Livros dos direitos por entrada (e saída),
Cobrancas, old codex 1503 and nos. 306–9, 311 (1620, 1650, 1682, 1687, 1699, 1709),
Alfândega do Funchal, and Livros dos direitos por saída, 1721–23, 1727–29, 1768–1815),
livros 272–326, Provedoria e Junta da Real Fazenda do Funchal, Alfândega do Funchal,
both at Arquivo Nacional da Torre da Tombo, Lisbon. For Madeira wine imported
into Anglo-America, see Naval Office Shipping Lists, CO 5/1446–1447, 510–511, 710,
573, CO 106/1, CO 142/15–19, CO 243/1/15 and T 1/512), National Archives of the
United Kingdom, Kew, Richmond, Surrey, England, for the following jurisdictions—
New Hampshire (1724–25, 1727, 1742–43, 1745–49, 1751–55, 1757–64, 1766–69),
Massachusetts (1716–19, 1752–65), New York (1713–43, 1748, 1751, 1753–55, 1763–64),
New Jersey (1723–27, 1733, 1739–41, 1743–51, 1754–55, 1757–59, 1763–64), Virginia
(1700–1704, 1726–59, 1768–69), South Carolina (1717–18, 1724, 1731–32, 1734–38,
1758–60, 1762–63, 1766, 1768–72), Georgia (1755–57, 1760–67), East Florida (1764–
69), Jamaica (1705, 1709–15, 1717–21, 1724, 1727–29, 1743–49, 1752–47, 1761–69,
1782–88, 1795–98), and Barbados (1718–21, 1728–38, 1747, 1752–53, 1782, 1784–88,
1797–1806); *American State Papers: Documents, Legislative and Executive, of the
Congress of the United States*, vol. 1 (Washington, DC, 1832), vol. 2 (Washington,
DC, 1834), 1–81; and for population estimates, see John J. McCusker and Russell R.
Menard, *The Economy of British America, 1607–1789* (Chapel Hill, 1991), tables 5.1,
5.3, 6.4, 7.2, 8.1, 9.4; Michael R. Haines and Richard H. Steckel, eds., *A Population
History of North America* (New York, 2000), 307, 373; and Stanley Engerman to David
Hancock, December 10, 2007 (Caribbean data from 1790 to 1815 include free persons
of color as well).

transatlantic sailing vessels grew larger (on average, they increased fivefold between 1550 and 1800) and more expensive to operate, it became important to fill the holds with high-value commodities instead of low-value bulk ballast like brick and other building materials.[4] Cloth, England's principal manufactured export, was neither bulky nor weighty enough to fill holds. Even if it had been, most dry goods cargoes were unloaded in Madeira and reexported to southwestern Europe, where consumer demand for dry goods was greater than in England's plantation colonies. Shippers might have routed their vessels through West Africa and carried slaves to America, but the increase in time and special outfitting required for slave voyages, and the constant demand for frequent-return sugar vessels, generally kept the dry goods fleet distinct from the slave fleet.[5] On voyages that began in British America, similar predicaments arose: fish and, in the eighteenth century, grain could fill a vessel bound to Europe, but a return commodity was needed to avoid an empty hold or low-profit ballast. No one ever wanted a vessel to "come dead freighted." Wine was sizable, needed in America, and profitable. By loading wine in Madeira, shippers could recover some of the costs on two-thirds of an outbound trading leg from Europe or on a return voyage to America. Voyagers from both sides of the Atlantic saw good reason to stop there.[6]

THE CHALLENGE OF VIABLE ALTERNATIVES

Anglo-American settlers wanted wine. Not until the early nineteenth century could they drink a palatable wine that was manufactured on their own continent. This was not because of "ignorance of established methods" or for want of trying. Rather, climatic extremes, insects, bacterial infections, rot funguses, and mildew killed European vine stock in America. Until the development of hybridized varieties, Americans had no viable grape alternative to imported wine.[7]

Wine was woven deep into the initial settlement dream. In 1565, the pirate Captain John Hawkins visited the French colony of Huguenots at Fort Caroline, at the mouth of the St. John's River in Florida, and noticed the colonists had been able to manufacture twenty hogsheads of wine. Some twenty years later, Sir Walter Raleigh's voyagers arrived on Roanoke Island and confronted a sea of grapes rising and falling with the surging tide. Twenty years further on, the Virginia Company's Jamestown was launched with the hope of finding a marketable commodity, whose "ambitious vine" and "purple masse" the poet Michael Drayton predicted would "kisse the sky" atop native cedar. Indeed, nearly every early account of England's American settlements described riverbanks overflowing with native grapes, as George Percy fantasized, and a "great store of Vines . . . in Great abundance." Publicists of these adventures praised this gift of grapes, and on it built an edenic vision of great abundance and wealth that persisted for centuries.[8]

Enterprising Americans doggedly pursued the dream of a wine that could sustain English shipping, augment royal revenue, provision metropolitan tables, make wine more accessible, and at the same time provide the colonists with an exportable staple commodity and their government with much-needed revenue. Both John Smith and William Strachey alluded to wine being made in the first years of the Virginia settlement.[9] But early efforts produced little; what was produced was sour; and the quantity was never enough to call it an industry.

As went Virginia so went the rest of Anglo-America. Governor John Winthrop went so far as to accept a grant to an island in Boston Harbor that required him to establish a vineyard on it; he could not. The proprietor of Maryland ordered his son the governor to plant a vineyard on the St. Mary's River and to expand its acreage; within a decade, every plant had perished.[10] The experiment in Georgia during the 1730s was only the most high-profile disaster. James Oglethorpe intended wine and silk to provide the economic basis for his new philanthropic community. The Scottish botanist that the Georgia Trustees hired died en route in Jamaica. The Spanish captured his successor. The gardener who finally made it to Georgia turned out to be profligate and quit within a few years. The experiment, with no reliable management, collapsed.[11]

Despite the obvious failures, metropolitan officials and colonial assemblies continued to offer encouragements, and private societies and individual gentlemen undertook experiments. The 1750s, 1760s, and 1770s saw an efflorescence of planting schemes, often as a means of mitigating the effects of economic downturns. The poet and enterpriser John Leacock (distant cousin of the Madeira exporter) gladly received "Directions from Mr. Henry Hill," scion of another Madeira house, "for the culture of vines of the natural produce of this country" and struggled to implement them.[12] But not until the turn of the nineteenth century did they bear significant fruit. Jean Jacques Dufour, who had studied viticulture in Switzerland, arrived in the States in 1796 and organized the Kentucky Vineyard Society in Lexington in 1798 and 1799. Nearly all the vines at his "First Vineyard" failed, but he established another vineyard in 1802 along the Ohio River near the town of Vevay in southeastern Indiana. His "Second Vineyard" was "the first practical success in American wine-growing," producing vendible quantities. Dufour succeeded where others had failed because he planted the Alexander grape, a native *labrusca* hybrid that was the offspring of "an unknown native and a *vinifera* vine." The resulting hybrid was immune to black rot. Swiss vinedressers harvested a vintage in 1806 or 1807 and continued to do so through 1820, when approximately 110 pipes were made. By that time other Americans were doing the same, but the amounts were small.[13] Even if commercially viable, domestic stock would not make serious encroachments on European wine for another 175 years.

Madeira wine minimized the problem of an empty or only partially filled hold, but it was by no means the only solution — good as it was — to the challenge of a viable alternative. Other European wines existed for importing, and they figured as not insignificant imports from time to time. But these wines were less reliable in two senses. First of all, they did not possess the same capacity as Madeira to benefit from heat, and high temperature was a constant companion on board voyages to Anglo-America, trade winds and ocean currents generally dictating travel through subtropical and tropical waters, as we have seen. The response varied according to the must in question and its management at the point of production. But as a general rule, apart from Port, Sherry, and some Canary, wine degraded long before it arrived in America. Well through Jefferson's day, French wines soured horribly, for instance, if they even arrived intact, for the French tended to ship in bottles and the bottles often broke. Second, Spanish and French wines did not enjoy the privileges that accrued from alliance. As Britain's oldest and most constant ally in the seventeenth and eighteenth centuries, Portugal never once saw its wines proscribed by the British or their colonists. France and its frequent ally Spain did, especially as the Anglo-French struggle for continental and oceanic hegemony erupted after 1700 into at least five major wars, with a not insignificant Atlantic dimension to each. In times of peace, their wines could flow to Anglo-America without significant restriction; in times of war, however, they would be seized by privateers and prohibited by laws and regulations. Madeira was always more fortunate and, with the privileges bestowed by the 1663 Navigation Act on it and wine from the Azores, doubly so.[14]

THE SEVENTEENTH-CENTURY TRADE

With no homegrown competition in Caribbean and North America, European wine dominated the market there. Between 1600 and 1700, the reported exports of wine from Madeira rose more than fivefold, from 1,200 pipes to perhaps 6,500 pipes. Most of the growth occurred after 1640 when the Portuguese monarch granted a monopoly of Brazil's markets to Lisbon's growing merchant community. In this post-Restoration era, the trade in Madeira's principal commodity shifted to non-Portuguese distributors and non-Portuguese-speaking markets. It is the rise of the English that most significantly marked this century.

While there are stray references to Madeira being exported in the last few decades of the sixteenth century, the earliest surviving records documenting a sustained export trade in wine are the letters of a Funchal distributor working between 1649 and 1652 and a Customs House register for 1650. Over the three and three-quarters years that he detailed his activities, Diogo Fernandes Branco observed 3,339 pipes being exported from the island, almost 900 pipes each year. Of the recorded destinations, 41 percent of the wine went to Angola, 7 percent to London, 4 percent to Brazil, and 3 percent to Lisbon; the remaining 45 percent went to other or unstated places. Branco noted only 21 pipes going to English America, mainly the island of Barbados.[15]

Interpreting Branco is difficult, since it is unclear whether he writes of the island's trade or solely of his own trade business. The Funchal Customs House register for 1650 documents that the government levied export duties on roughly 2,800 pipes of wine that year, slightly more than three times Branco's yearly average of 900 pipes. His numbers probably represent one firm's business and indicate the dominance and a focus on a particular region of the empire that an individual could achieve in the early years of the trade, when the Portuguese were still influential. Contributing to his dominance was the fact that war broke out between England and Portugal in the second half of 1650 and exports by the English were lower than normal and exports by the Portuguese relatively higher. Complicating understanding further is the fact that the government did not levy duties on wines exported by Portuguese merchants on Portuguese vessels before 1801, and in some years the share they carried appears (from complementary government sources) to have been nearly a quarter of all wine, recorded and unrecorded. So the actual total export may have been as high as 3,800 pipes. In addition, the 1650 customs register contains some hints as to destination—1,011 pipes were freighted by the Companhia Geral do Brasil—and these, too, complicate Branco's tally. In contrast to the 4 percent that went to Brazil in Branco's letters, this was roughly 40 percent of the stated export and just over a quarter of an export estimate that takes unstated shipments into account.[16]

From such records—and there are only a handful of volumes for the first eighty years of the trade—one can draw several conclusions. Island exports certainly rose. The total number of recorded exports more than doubled, to 6,500 pipes by 1699 over 1650. Most dynamically, exports to English-speaking America nearly tripled between 1650 and 1699, from 1,378 pipes in 1650 to 3,920 pipes in 1699, at a time when that region's white population more than tripled, suggesting that per capita consumption was falling, a message heard by the exporters as a call to pay close attention to American tastes and to convert Madeira wine from an affordable, popular drink into a more exclusive beverage.

Brazil's and Angola's share of Madeira dramatically declined toward the end of the seventeenth century. Then, in 1712, a royal edict ordered that only "three

Table 4.1. Ship departures from Funchal mentioned in
William Bolton's letters, 1695–1713

Destination	1695–1700		1702–1713	
	Number	Percentage	Number	Percentage
British West Indies	127	43	285	52
British North America	19	7	89	16
Total for British America	146	50	374	68
European America	19	7	38	7
Britain	35	12	43	8
Continental Portugal	13	4	13	2
Other European states	27	9	14	3
Total for Britain and Europe	75	25	70	13
Other regions	52	18	63	12
Total recorded	292	100	545	100

Sources: For 1695–1700, see André L. Simon, ed., *The Bolton Letters: The Letters of an English Merchant in Madeira, 1695–1714*, vol. 1 (London, 1928); for 1702–13, see Graham Blandy, ed., *The Bolton Letters, 1700–1714*, vol. 2 (Funchal, 1960). There are no letters for 1701, the second half of 1710, and 1711. Bolton has been analyzed by José Manuel Azevedo e Silva in "A navegação e o comércio vistos do Funchal nos finais do século XVII," in *Actas III — Colóquio internacional de história da Madeira* (Funchal, 1993), tables II–III, pp. 363–64, and figs. 1–2, pp. 381–82; and Alberto Vieira, "A vinha e o vinho na Madeira nos séculos XVII–XVIII," in *Os vinhos licorosos e a história* (Funchal, 1998), 100, 107–9.

ships in a year shall be permitted to go" from Madeira to Brazil carrying island produce.[17] The edict confirmed the decades-long trend toward Madeirans being cut out of the Portuguese-Brazilian trade, and severely restricted the markets that were easily accessible to the Portuguese merchants on the island. The foreign exporters in Funchal cast their entrepreneurial eyes on the English plantations as markets to be developed, and they co-opted other enterprisers in the process. Increasingly, Madeira was carried not only by European and American sea captains but also by American merchants, American planters, and metropolitan agents who handled the affairs of Americans.[18] According to the scholar who has studied seventeenth-century Madeira most closely, the "opening up of new markets in the English American colonies, with . . . steadily rising demands" from shippers and drinkers, gave "strong support to the Madeiran wine economy, which formerly had depended almost exclusively on the Portuguese colonial markets." "The growth and prosperity" of Virginia, New England, Maryland, New York, and Pennsylvania lined the exporters' coffers. English "expansion in the West

Indies, particularly after the conquest of Jamaica in 1655," also helped build "a significant new market for heat-resistant wines" like the Madeirans'.[19]

Letters of a resident English merchant, William Bolton, confirm the Madeirans' reliance on Anglo-America at the end of the seventeenth and beginning of the eighteenth centuries. Bolton's observations of Funchal shipping suggests that a majority of vessels were already leaving for English-speaking ports by 1695–1700. Bolton was scrupulous in his observation; one gets no sense he favored the recording of the English and foreign vessels over Portuguese ones; indeed, since he saw the Portuguese as the competition to beat, he wanted his partner in London to appreciate the threat in its fullest dimension. By 1702–13, Bolton recorded two-thirds of the ships as leaving for the British West Indies or New England, in contrast to 5 percent to 10 percent as departing for Portuguese and other non-British colonies in America and the east. Only 26 percent in the earlier period and 13 percent in the later period were bound for mainland Portugal, England, Ireland, and other European states. Islanders were expending their greatest energies on British America by 1700.

ANGLO-AMERICA FROM THE PEACE OF UTRECHT TO THE PEACE OF PARIS

Strong ties between Madeira and British America marked the first three-quarters of the eighteenth century. The British Caribbean and North American colonists were consistently the largest takers of Madeira, and Madeira was consistently the largest-volume wine imported into those regions. Surviving records do not report the amount of wine exported, but the Customs House arrival records (*entradas*) also document the numbers of vessels leaving the island. Nearly all of them carried wine, so it is possible to draw some conclusions from this information and complementary information about imports into the wine's largest market. An average of 70 percent, and never less than two-thirds of departing ships, left Madeira for the European colonies in the Americas from 1727 to 1738, the earliest years for which the records survive. The British American settlements there received the vast bulk of Madeira's shipping and wine. Some 65 percent of vessels leaving the island stated they were bound for the British West Indies and British North America: an average of 40 percent went to the Caribbean colonies, while 25 percent went directly to Britain's colonies to the north.[20]

Ships with North America as their stated destination dropped in both absolute and relative terms after 1739 and remained anemic through the end of the Seven Years' War. At first this was a function of the disruption and blockage of shipping lanes in the West Indies, which bore the brunt of Atlantic fighting during the

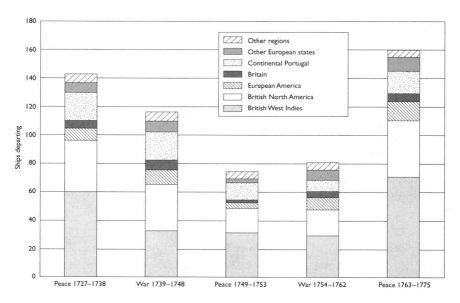

Figure 4.2. Ship departures from Funchal mentioned in Funchal *entradas,*
annual averages, 1727–1775. During the American Revolution, recording
of destinations in the *entradas* becomes erratic.
Sources: Livros dos direitos por entrada (1727–75), nos. 146–56, Provedoria e
Junta da Real Fazenda do Funchal, Alfândega do Funchal, Arquivo Nacional
da Torre da Tombo, Lisbon.

American-theater Wars of Jenkins' Ear (1739–43) and King George's War (1743–
49) and the European-theater War of Austrian Succession (1739–48). During the
Seven Years' War (1756–63), fewer than half of all ships leaving the island went
to British America. This conflict was especially disruptive to Madeira's shipping.
France and eventually Spain declared war against Britain, and Portugal, as Britain's ally, declared war against France and Spain. Fewer vessels came to Madeira
from Europe on account of the high freights, high seamen's wages, and high
insurance premiums imposed to deal with the threat of capture or destruction
on the high seas. Exporters complained bitterly that the trade from America was
"very inconsiderable" because of the costs of shipping and the America-based
"vessels being forced into transport service."[21]

The close of the Seven Years' War in 1763 brought a return to shipping patterns
that had prevailed a quarter-century before. Of ships leaving Madeira with wine
in 1763–75, 68 percent reported that they were sailing for British possessions in
the Americas, a larger share than in the years before 1739. The share going to

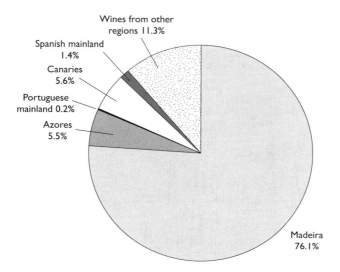

Figure 4.3. Wine imported into Anglo-America,
by origin of wine, 1700–1775.
Source: See source note to figure 4.1.

the British West Indies reached a new high—43 percent—and the share going to British North America returned to its former level—25 percent. (Another 10 percent went to the American colonies of other European powers.) While commercial letters imply that more ships actually went to the North American colonies in the 1760s, British customs officers' reports suggest the shares calculated from Funchal's customs records are fairly accurate. According to British compilations of colonial customs for 1768–72, 1,530 pipes arrived on average each year in the thirteen colonies. Funchal's entry books show thirty-seven ships on average leaving for ports in those colonies, so a typical vessel would have carried a load of 41 pipes.[22]

In Anglo-America, Madeira was one of several imported wines, and wine was one of several imported alcoholic beverages that, alongside domestically produced alcoholic drinks, were drunk by American inhabitants. Of these drinks, Madeira was usually the single biggest selling, although as it became more expensive its share shrank and gave way to other drinks. Its share in overall consumption is harder to gauge, given the paucity of household accounts recording such matters and their silence on the consumption of water, milk, and fruit juices.[23]

An imported wine portfolio can be reconstituted for all the colonies by com-

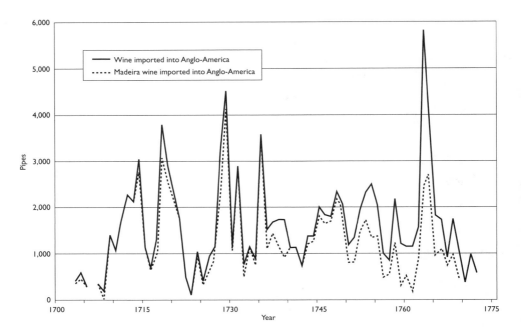

Figure 4.4. Wine imported into Anglo-America, by volume of wine, 1700–1775.
Source: See source note to figure 4.1.

bining data from the Naval Office Shipping Lists (hereafter NOSL) and complementary sources like colony-kept shipping manifest books. Figure 4.3 shows wines from the Wine Islands dominating British North American markets in the first three-quarters of the eighteenth century: 76.1 percent of wine imports came from Madeira, 5.5 percent the Azores, and 5.6 percent the Canaries. Little wine (only 0.2 percent) came from Lisbon, Oporto, and the Portuguese mainland, which is surprising since Port wine dominated Britain's home market; mainland Portuguese wine even ranked below the 1.4 percent that came from the Spanish mainland. Other wines, like French, Rhenish, Italian, and those simply designated as "wine," comprised 11.3 percent. Madeira reigned chief among wine imports in the British colonial period in terms of quantity and value in all but four years (1754, 1761, 1762, and 1765).[24]

Two new factors began pulling in opposite directions in the wake of the Seven Years' War. On the one hand, the Treaty of Paris (1763) opened new lands to the British in the Caribbean and parts of North America. The resulting land rush included many Madeira drinkers who took their habits with them into the "new" American frontier. To protect its recently expanded demesne there, the Crown

stationed an army of occupation of America for its western edge. Both governmental and personal expenditures associated with the flow of migrants westward
encouraged wine and spirit distributors, who saw in the move a relatively low-risk
opportunity to extend their custom by supplying and sometimes owning stores
and taverns on the frontier.

On the other hand, the soldiers and sailors arriving in America were charged
with implementing reforms designed to tighten loopholes in the imperial trading
system and pay for the military's maintenance.[25] Whereas previously the central
London government had levied no duties on wines imported directly into British
America from Madeira and the Azores (indeed, it had specifically exempted
them since 1663), it now imposed duties on these wines via the 1764 Sugar Act,
setting them at £7 sterling per tun (a tun was double the size of a pipe) if they
were imported directly into British America from Iberia or its dependencies; if
the wines were routed through Britain, they were assessed £3 10s. sterling per tun
on entry into Britain and 10s. sterling per tun upon subsequent importation into
the colonies. Thus, the colonists could save nearly half the duty if they imported
through the mother country.[26] The direction of Madeira shipping was little affected, however. The cost of doing business in London probably amounted to £3
sterling per tun, so it saved little money to route the product there. While American distributors signed and presented petitions to Parliament and staged protests
in opposition to the new duty, importers acquiesced in paying the duty, imported
it through neutral channels like Curaçao, disguised it as other wines, or ignored
the law by outright smuggling. The volume that flowed from Madeira to British
North America remained fairly constant. Contrary to what Benjamin Franklin
told the House of Commons in 1766, the colonists could neither produce nor
eschew the commodity. Some groups, like Virginia planters and Massachusetts
merchants, may have altered their buying habits briefly, but they were unwilling
to do without Madeira for long. Imports were affected, however, by the price increases engendered by the new duties. In the five years after the act's passage, the
prices of customary grades of Madeira rose high enough that some Americans
refused to buy them, preferring cheaper grades or lesser wines like false Madeira
(adulterated Canary), Canary, Rhenish, or domestic grain-based alcoholic substitutes.[27]

The Townshend duties that were imposed three years later raised additional obstacles to importing Madeira, and they heightened a widening constitutional debate that among other things questioned the right to tax. Attempts to use Madeira
politically as the target of nonimportation actions were less than effective.[28] But
an important precedent was set. So, when in October 1774 the First Continental Congress was looking for symbolic commodities to attack, the Americans

resolved to prohibit "the importation into British America" of all "wines from Madeira or the Western Islands" after November 1774, until the repeal of the duties they thought most deleterious to their Atlantic trading. Madeira distributors first began to feel the pinch of independence that December.[29]

ANGLO-AMERICA AND THE GLORIOUS CAUSE

America's separation from Britain and the closing of Portuguese ports to United States' vessels from 1776 to 1783 permanently weakened Madeira's hold on the American market and brought to an end the economic integration of the island's economy into the British imperial trading system. The conflict's early years witnessed a drastic decline in wine exports to British North America because of the port closures. Exports continued to the British Caribbean, but they did not flow in the same quantity as before the war because of the interruptions in communication and hazards to shipping. Exporters were caught in the middle. Uncertainty became immediate and personal within months, as Americans began to boycott Madeira and other Portuguese wines after November 1774. By April of the following year, usually the busiest time of the year for filling requests, islanders began complaining that Americans were sticking to the terms of their nonimportation agreement and "coming in & going away without wines," which made "matters very quiet." By autumn 1775, it was clear that the problem was more than just sluggishness: "the distractions in America" brought about "a very considerable diminution in our demand." The large vintage of that year did not help. Nor did Parliament's passage later that year of the Prohibitory Act barring traffic to and from the rebellious colonies and, several months later, authorization of naval cruisers and privateers to seize ships ignoring the prohibition. Wine prices started tumbling early in 1776. The "unhappy disturbances" interfered with exports to North America, even to "such colonies as may have returned to their obedience." Making matters worse, the Portuguese monarch entered the fray in support of her ally George III and in June 1776 forbade any entry of American ships into Portuguese ports. "Times" became "Very Bad." North American shippers, for reasons of principle or safety, stopped calling.[30]

Madeira's distributors responded to constrictions in American markets by supplying the two armies in the conflict, smuggling the wine to their customers and pursuing markets that did not exist or were less important before the war. Most of the thirteen mainland British colonies imported no Madeira during the war, yet as a whole they resumed taking 25 percent of Madeira's exports by the latter years of the conflict. The 25 percent reflects the large exports to New York City for the use of the British army and navy stationed there during most of the conflict. British contracting began early in the war. In summer 1775, General Howe sent the transport *British Hero* to the island, and a consortium of five firms filled its hold with "a good quality" wine "not less than three years old." Two years later, in autumn 1777, four of the five firms that had supplied Howe again loaded a transport, the *Lady Gage*, with thirty pipes: twenty-four of high-quality "Old Particular" and the remainder cargo wine for hospital use. Two prominent and vocal holdouts to supplying the British that year were the largely American firms of Lamar, Hill, Bisset & Co. and Searle Brothers, which instead shipped wine to American officers and soldiers and customers in American-occupied towns. Their shipments were minor; their opportunities were severely curtailed by the closing of the port of Funchal to American captains and vessels after 1776. Between 1777 and 1783, only two private ships each year left Madeira and entered New York Harbor.[31]

Some wine was also brought into America through the non-Portuguese, non-British colonies in the Caribbean. That region was not exactly new to the Madeirans, but new markets opened up there during the war. Madeira distributors targeted the Dutch and Danish free ports such as Curaçao, St. Croix, and St. Thomas, which could be used to launder wine and smuggle it into North America. In 1776, Nowlan & Leacock made use of the Dutch loophole: "In order to cover the interest of our mutual friend Mr. Richard Yates of New York in the present unfortunate & precarious times," the firm "made out the necessary documents for his ship." The vessel was loaded with about three hundred pipes of wine and dispatched to St. Eustatius and Curaçao. From there it would move on to New York. Madeirans exported 17 percent of their wine in 1779–82 to the Dutch and Danish islands. Even though North Americans could not legally import the alcohol during the war, they had not lost their taste for it, providing the neutral traders in the Caribbean a lucrative middleman role, just such as they had in the wake of the 1764 Sugar Act.[32]

Madeira's distributors also directed their energies toward the British West Indian and Canadian colonies. Being theaters of action, they saw volumes fall early in the conflict. In some years, exports to Caribbean and Canadian colonists dropped by half, the NOSL tell us, although the interruptions never lasted longer than nine months. The supply of troops in the West Indies and Canada partially made up for the disruptions in custom. By the latter part of the war (1779–82), the British West Indies received 26 percent of Madeira's wine exports, according to Funchal's *saídas*, which survive without significant gaps from 1779 onward. This was much the same share they had received in the 1740s and 1750s. Once fighting ceased, exports to the British islands resumed with gusto. To Barbados, distributors saw a return to prewar export levels in the 1780s and a tripling of customary levels in the 1790s and 1800s. Something similar happened with Jamaican exports: a return to 1760s levels in the 1780s, and a doubling of 1780s levels in the 1790s. In the years spanning the close of war and the establishment of federal government in the United States, exports to the British West Indies averaged 2,500 pipes per year, whereas those to the States averaged 1,800 pipes. In the ensuing decade, when Madeirans began reviving their American opportunities, the markets grew at different speeds: annual averages to the British West Indies increased by 43 percent, to 3,600 pipes per year, whereas those to the States rose only by 9 percent, to 2,000 pipes per year.[33]

ANGLO-AMERICA FROM YORKTOWN TO WATERLOO

Although the new United States resumed importing Madeira in the aftermath of the Revolution, the wine never regained the place it held in American life before 1776. Island distributors made overtures to the Anglo-Americans — writing letters and sending consignments on their own initiative — but many, in some cases most, of their efforts foundered. Now that "these obstacles" were "removed & peace again restored," many Madeirans hoped that matters would be "on the same footing . . . as formerly." They were disappointed. Americans had been cut free from the British imperial trading regime and had developed a taste for continental wines.[34] Whereas 25 percent of Madeira had been sent to the thirteen colonies during the war, only 16 percent was sent to the new United States in its aftermath (1785–89). Exports to the British West Indies — still regulated by British law — grew, reaching 31 percent. Wine exports to the non-British colonies in America, which had buoyed the island's overseas trade during the conflict, fell by over two-thirds, to 5 percent of Madeira's exports. Canada took 2 percent.[35]

In the years for which import data for all states have survived, Madeira wine as a share of the wine imported into the United States slid from 31 percent in 1789–90 to 5 percent in 1798–99. Its share revived only slightly in the nineteenth century. Madeira accounted for an annual average of 11 percent of American wine imports in 1800–1804, 6 percent in 1804–08, and 17 percent in 1808–12. The War of 1812 saw dramatic cuts in Madeira imports (to less than 1 percent), but they rose again thereafter, to 13 percent by 1814–15. Quite noticeably, variations in Madeira levels were no longer driving changes in the American wine market after 1789. As figure 4.6 shows, Madeira imports remained fairly constant, at least from 1795 to 1807.

Changes in other wine mattered more. In particular, wines from France and Spain were now regularly imported. Freed from British mercantile restrictions on trade with France and Spain, the former thirteen colonies diversified their

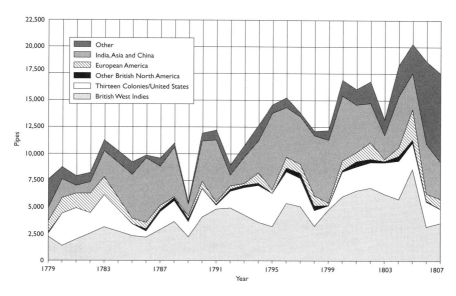

Figure 4.5. Wine exported from Madeira, 1779–1807. A total for 1784 is available, but individual shipments are not; the shares for 1784 are the average of the 1783 and 1785 shares. The Funchal *saídas* after 1800 are marred by a large number of unrecorded destinations: between 4 percent and 47 percent of post-1799 export registers make no mention of destination. This may reflect opposition to new laws imposing higher duties on certain destinations or the sloppiness of new clerks. However, since all countries are represented in the 1800–1807 *saídas*, there is no reason to believe that the unrecorded entries do not mirror the recorded entries.
Source: See source note to figure 4.1.

sources of wine. The value of wine and vinegar imported directly from France into the United States rose twenty-seven-fold between 1787–90 and 1803–06 (indeed, the dramatic spike in all wine imports in 1802–05 resulted from a significant increase in French wine imports, all other wines remaining fairly constant in these years). Moreover, Sherry and St. Lucar wines came into vogue; in half of the years between 1793 and 1807, the quantity of Sherry imports exceeded that of Madeira.[36]

While direct voyages from Madeira to America did not revive and grow as Madeira's exporters had hoped, indirect and illegal operations filled some of the gap. Departures to the Caribbean revived to one-third of all departures in the nine years between the issuance of the July 1783 Order-in-Council and the beginning of the French Revolution. Much of this wine was for reexport to the United States. The dominant British exporters in Madeira came to see Jamaicans

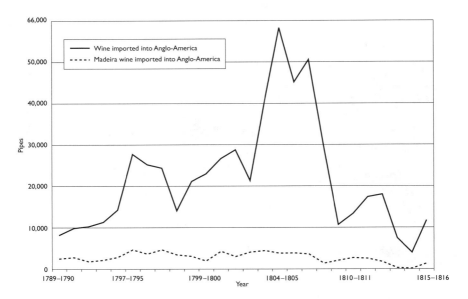

Figure 4.6. Wine imported into Anglo-America, 1789–1816.
Source: *American State Papers: Documents, Legislative and Executive, of the
Congress of the United States*, vol. 7 (Class IV): *Commerce and Navigation*, vol. 1
(Washington, DC, 1832).

as a way "to introduce" themselves "to many substantial people" in the States,
and Jamaicans, in turn, depended upon neutral Danish, Dutch, and Swedish
shippers to do the carrying, frustrated as Anglo-Jamaicans and Anglo-Madeirans
were by Great Britain's requirement that British and British American shippers
carry cargo in British vessels and, for several years at least, the states' discour-
agement of British entry into their ports. Despite the greater variety of wines
now sold in the marketplace and the stiff competition raised by the occasionally higher quantities of Spanish Sherry being imported, the island still supplied
"America's wine." Given the high price of Madeira—highest of all wines—its
value remained unmatched.[37]

BRAZIL

Like Anglo-Americans, Brazilians did not manage to produce wine commercially before the late nineteenth century (in fact, the Crown forbade such industry to protect metropolitan producers), yet they did not lose their taste for it.[38]
Madeirans supplied them with small amounts of wine at least as early as the 1580s;

indeed, Brazilians were probably Madeirans' first overseas customers. Toward the middle of the seventeenth century (1638–55), Madeira merchants shipped 370 pipes on average each year to Bahia, Pernambuco, and Rio de Janeiro—perhaps 10 percent of total exports. By the end of the seventeenth century (1687–95), average shipments to the Brazils had risen to 1,100 pipes, or roughly 15 percent of total exports.[39] Yet, even as the shares were rising, the dynamics of the trade to Brazil and the interests of the Madeiran wine traders were diverging. The Crown in 1649 granted a monopoly right to the Companhia Geral to supply Brazil with all kinds of provisions and "help national merchant houses accumulate sufficient capital to compete more effectively with British merchants in the colonial trade as a whole and, by extension, in Portugal proper." Since the Companhia was based in the capital, the costs of bringing island wine to Lisbon for reshipment to Brazil predisposed its directors (many of whom owned vineyards near the capital) to favor Lisbon wine. The Crown diminished the monopoly somewhat in 1650 by allowing two Madeiran ships, each bearing 300 pipes, to be sent directly from the island to Brazil; from 1712 to 1735, it allowed three. Allowances notwithstanding, the monopoly checked the development of a Brazil market for Madeirans. No island-privileging monopoly company was founded, although Pombal considered establishing one in the 1760s, and the Madeirans were not able to break the stranglehold of the mainland monopolies with respect to wine.[40]

The exports of the monopoly companies sketch some of what Madeirans never gained. The Companhia Geral do Grão-Pará e Maranhão was founded in 1755 and lasted twenty-three years. During the three years from 1762 through 1764, it sent thirty-nine ships from Lisbon to Atlantic ports, fourteen of them to Pará or Maranhão. All but one of the fourteen carried Lisbon wine, on average fifty barrels each year, as well as large volumes of *aguardente* (distilled wine between 29 and 45 percent alcohol). The Porto-based Companhia Geral da Agricultura das Vinhas do Alto Douro, founded by Pombal a year later, enjoyed the similar privilege of supplying other Brazilian settlements with wine. In 1761–73, Porto exporters shipped 23,800 pipes to Brazil—more than 1,800 pipes per year, or roughly 39 percent of their total annual exports—in the same years that they sent fewer than 6,000 pipes to Britain.[41] Each of the thirty-eight ships that arrived in Brazilian ports from Portugal in 1791—from Lisbon (twenty-two ships), Porto (fifteen), and Figueira (one)—came laden with wine. Not one came from Madeira.[42]

So constrained, Madeira only trickled to South America; in the years 1796–1807, Madeira's annual exports to Brazil averaged only half a pipe, compared to Lisbon's and Porto's combined annual exports of roughly 11,500 pipes. After the Crown and Court moved to Rio de Janeiro in 1807, the restrictions were relaxed, and departures from Madeira for Brazil rose to twenty-five vessels per year. Madeira's temporary success was assisted by the decimation of mainland vineyards and ports in the Spanish and French invasions of the wine-producing areas. The restoration of calm and the ouster of the French returned Madeira to its second-class status compared to Lisbon and Oporto.[43]

INDIA AND ASIA

Although Madeirans did not develop markets in the South Atlantic, they were more successful in the Indian Ocean and beyond. At least as early as 1703, Madeira merchants were expecting English East India Company ships to anchor, although it is not clear whether the vessels arrived. One Indiaman captain definitely called at the island in 1707 and loaded one hundred pipes of wine for India; two years later, another did the same. According to William Bolton's papers, 3 percent of Madeira's shipping in 1702–13 left for the East. Bolton probably understated the size of the Anglo-Indian trade, since East India Company men often bought wine from vessels anchored off the Cape Verde Islands.[44]

A routine English East India Company trade began only in 1718, after several experiments with wine as a cargo. In that year, the directors named the Madeiran Joseph Hayward their agent for supplying their forts in India; the agency remained with his firm and its successors for nearly fifty years.[45] By the 1740s, a regular procurement system had emerged. The forts placed orders with the directors, who commanded the captains of one or two company ships to call on their agent on the island for wine. Usually three hundred pipes were ordered each year, which the agent directed to the two India Presidencies in equal lots. In addition, each ship could carry a "wine indulgence" of twenty pipes freight-free on the captain's or his men's own accounts. On shore in India, company officials divided the official company wine among the garrisons and allowed military officers the privilege of purchasing more at 25 percent below the invoice price.[46]

The fortunes of exporters improved markedly after Robert Clive's 1757 victory at the battle of Plassey, when the company assumed de facto territorial rule over large parts of the subcontinent. The directors began ordering from three to six company ships to pick up wine at Madeira each year. India became the destination for 2.4 percent of all vessels departing Funchal, and was more significant in terms of wine traded, for India-bound vessels possessed three times the tonnage of other ships leaving the island. They could load from 350 to 600 pipes of wine each clearance. About the same time, the company employed a second agent on the island, granting a contract to Thomas Cheap's large firm. The two agent firms maintained a lock on "the whole Company business" until 1785, when the agency system was discontinued. Other houses did not think it worth their while to vie for official orders, although they supplied India captains on an individual basis.[47]

The rapidly growing number of British servants and military men after Plassey and the grant of the *diwan*—the right of receiving the revenue of Behar, Bengal, and Orissa—to the British in 1765 enlarged the pool of drinkers. The Presidency of Bengal complained in 1763 that it did not have enough to satisfy current uses and annual dividends even though "the quantity sent" it in 1762 had been "more than usual"; the excess had been "put up at public sale." Again in 1764 it found its allocation "very inadequate to the wants of . . . servants alone, exclusive of the inhabitants of the settlement." The "number of servants both on . . . civil and military lists" had "so much increased" that at least three hundred pipes were needed to satisfy just army demand. "Enlarge the export of this article as far as you possibly can," it begged the directors. The company tried to augment its offerings with Canary Vidonia, but the settlements reported their "general dislike" to London: it was "much inferior to the Madeira," which had "more body" and was "esteemed" as "a more healthy and pure wine." Other wines, not all European, were available to military consumers: Claret, four other types of French wine, four types of Cape wine, white, red, Rhenish, Moselle, Spanish, Sack, Malaga, Canary, Vidonia, Muscatel, Palm, and Persia. But it was Madeira that gave "the best Tast."[48]

Tapping into this opportunity, civil servants engaged in a "Private Trade" that grew up alongside the official "Company Trade." Captains were entitled to take wine "sufficient for their own use," their 20-pipe "indulgence," and "present wine" allowed the Presidencies. Some captains also began reexporting wine to London for resale, in contravention of company regulations. Combined orders rose dramatically in the 1760s, with private orders eventually outstripping company orders. In January 1764, for instance, island merchants were told by their London partners to expect six ships to take 2,000 pipes, considerably more than the four ships and 209 pipes ordered by the directors. A similar call came two years later when, two months into the new shipping season, another 2,000 pipes were dispatched on the outbound India fleet. In time, during the 1770s, the company stopped trying to control the trade and allowed anyone to take wine to India.[49]

Portuguese merchants also supplied their own and non-Portuguese colonies in India with wine. Madeira was occasionally taken to Portuguese India and Asia by the Portuguese East India Company fleets and private merchants who had licenses to ship directly to the subcontinent. The licenses were granted in Lisbon and the wines loaded in Lisbon, Porto, or Funchal. In 1700, private merchants trading to Portuguese India (usually Goa) were infrequent, but the trade grew,

especially after 1770, when the royal licensing agency allowed Portuguese merchants to go to Portuguese and British India.[50] The British merchants noticed
the Portuguese activity. Late in the 1770s, one British trader reported that the
Portuguese "got much into the spirit of trading"; he claimed they annually sent
"no less than 4,000 pipes . . . in Portuguese ships & shipped by Portuguese," to
British and Portuguese India alike. Dona Guiomar Madalena de Sá Vasconcelos
Bettencourt Machado de Vilhena, a great Madeiran landowner, was one such
merchant. Moving into trade in 1776 after the death of her husband, she sent
twenty vessels to India between 1782 and her own death in 1789; half of them
carried wine from Madeira. For only a few of these shipments does she seem
to have bothered with procuring licenses, but when she did she drew upon the
services of Mayne & Co., Thomas Horne, and José António da Fonseca, all of
Lisbon, and on Charles Murray, England's consul in Funchal who frequently
traveled to the capital and did her bidding. Nonetheless, her exports were considerable. One vessel, departing the island in April 1784, carried seven hundred
pipes of wine. Throughout, she supplied Bengal's burgeoning marketplace, directing her shipments to two Scottish firms working in Calcutta, to which she
was introduced by Murray.[51]

The war brought American "correspondence" to "a stand" and forced the
British firms to employ "almost the whole of" their "attention . . . in getting fine
wine" and sending it to India and other points in Asia. They cultivated markets in
the Persian Gulf (Gombroon on the Straits of Hormuz, and Basra), India (Calcutta, Madras, and Bombay), Sumatra (Bencoolen), and China (Canton, Macao,
and Limpao). Conservative firms that had been reluctant to enter eastern markets found themselves in the 1770s accepting contracts for India and working to
develop customer bases there and to the east. Britain's eastern settlements provided a sizeable new group of customers, who soaked up 16 percent of the exports
between 1776 and 1782.[52] During the 1770s and 1780s, the directors ordered four
hundred pipes of wine on average to be laden on noncompany "chartered ships"
bound for Bencoolen's Fort Marlborough (present-day Indonesia) and beyond.
The company's main focus in the Revolution years, after India, was on China,
however. To facilitate the acquisition of silk, porcelain, and especially tea as well
as silver and opium, it supplied wine to the men stationed at Canton, the only
Chinese port open to foreign traders, sending six or more pipes of Madeira each
year after 1776. The company's push into China succeeded for, by the late 1780s,
the London sale of China goods outstripped that of India goods.[53]

Between the American and French revolutions, the share of ships departing
Madeira for India, Southeast Asia, and China climbed to 40 percent and the
share of wine to 37 percent. The East India Company, which had left the trade

to private traders in previous decades, now got back in the business. Its directors were ever "more desirous of increasing" their consignments of wine to India and Asia, inasmuch as "the Portuguese and other European nations" derived "great benefit by what they sent there." The East Indians were good customers: they paid more for their wine than Europeans and Americans, and they paid for it faster. But they were discriminating; India customers "made a larger demand for old wine" than other customers. The directors accordingly began ordering more wine and more aged wine after 1785.[54]

To do this the directors dismantled the agency system they had used for nearly a century and established an annual auction, requiring wine suppliers to tender written bids to them in London. In the first year, the American John Searle III won with a low bid of 536 pipes at £20 sterling per pipe. Two years later, six different firms received contracts to supply a total of 510 pipes at £25 sterling per pipe. The auction quickly injected more competition into the Madeirans' India business. Several years later, in response to the Charter Act of 1793, the directors changed course again, sanctioning up to three thousand tons of "private" cargo each year—previously none had been allowed on company vessels, excepting the indulgence wine. This fueled the Madeirans' ambitions, drawing them farther down "the India road." Then, in 1799, Governor-General Lord Mornington opened the trade fully by granting leave "to individuals unconnected with the East India Company to take up & load ships directly for London upon their private account." Thus, at the turn of the nineteenth century, anyone could use India as a route to Europe, giving "a totally new turn" to "the Commerce" of Madeira.[55]

Early nineteenth-century British India was a place where the "European inhabitants of respectability certainly love wine." Thomas Williamson, whose *Wild Sports of the East* thrilled thousands of India enthusiasts, reported that the Britons there kept "as good tables as the seasons may enable them to furnish," and they drank "none but the best of wines." Madeira, Port, and Claret were all "in general use." Madeira exports to Asia surged. Nearly one-quarter of Madeira exports went to India, Southeast Asia, and China through 1815.[56]

BRITAIN, PORTUGAL, AND THE REST OF EUROPE

Britain and Europe never emerged as major markets for Madeira wine. In Britain's case, this is something of a surprise, because Portuguese wines dominated British imports during most of the eighteenth century. The trade depended largely on international political rivalries, which whipsawed Portuguese imports in the seventeenth century. When it was legal to import French wine, the En-

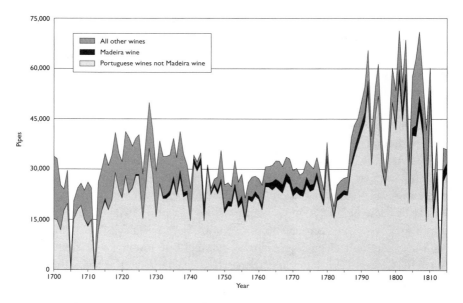

Figure 4.7. Wine imported into England and Wales, 1700–1815.
Source: Elizabeth B. Schumpeter, *English Overseas Trade Statistics,*
1697–1808 (Oxford, 1960), tables xvi–xvii.

glish drank a lot of it. For instance, men in the metropolis imported thirty thousand pipes of wine in 1675, nearly half of it French; less than 1 percent was Portuguese. In contrast, during the embargo on French wines in 1679–85, wine imports were more than forty thousand pipes per year, of which 34 percent was Portuguese. Some of this was undoubtedly Madeira, which was being reexported at least in 1683. At his accession James II lifted the embargo on French wine, and the share comprised by Portuguese wine fell back to pre-1679 levels. When the embargo was reintroduced upon James's fall in the Glorious Revolution of 1688, Portuguese wine's share of wine imports rebounded to 36 percent in 1690–96.[57] Between 1697 and 1815, mainland Portuguese wine, principally Carcavelos from Lisbon and Port from Oporto, dominated British imports: nearly two-thirds of wine came from continental Portugal. Spain was the source of another quarter: Sherry, Mountain, Malaga, Alicante, Benicarló, and Vidonia. Other wine-producing countries played an insignificant role.[58]

  Although some Madeira was imported into England in the early 1600s, the British began the eighteenth century importing little of it. The volume rose over the century until, by the first decade and a half of the nineteenth century, Britain imported 2,500 to 5,000 pipes each year. Still, Madeira constituted only 3.3 percent of wine imported into Britain from 1700 to 1815, and it never exceeded 7.4 percent in any one year. On the Madeira side, the British never took more than 7 percent of the island's exports directly, although a small additional amount was imported via British America and India.[59]

Neither did a market for Madeira materialize in Portugal. Mainland Portugal imported little wine because it produced its own. The Customs House entry books that survived the earthquake of 1755, post-1755 port books, governmental reports and memos, and merchant letters all suggest that Madeira was almost invisible in mainland Portugal's wine market. Island wines were expressly barred from importation into the mainland in 1683, at the same time that Castilian and Catalonian wines were barred.[60] One hundred years later, the exporters shipped only eighty pipes to the mainland each year, barely enough to keep a large New York wine wholesaler afloat. The only liquors that Madeirans exported to the mainland were the sweet Malvasia, the brandy-like *aguardente*, and the sweetmeat *casquinha* made from the rind of citron, and much of that was later reexported to northern Europe and Italy.[61]

Apart from legal reasons, the people of the mainland seldom imported alcohol because local wines were produced in greater quantities and retailed for less than Madeiran, Azorean, Spanish, or French wines. Nearly three-quarters of the Douro Company's Port output in 1761–69, for instance, was retained for home consumption. The same was true for the wine of Lisbon-area producers. Lisbon (white Carcavelos), Beira, Setúbal, Alentejo, Algarve, Porto (red and white port), Minho, and Trás-os-Montes wines found vent in the taverns and shops of Lisbon, Viana, Porto, and the smaller agricultural towns of the mainland to those who did not drink homemade concoctions. The average price to mainlanders of a pipe of Douro table wine in the 1760s was 23$595, just over half what it cost to buy a pipe of Madeira.[62]

Exports to other European states were more important for their network value than as substantial destinations, for they allowed islanders to acquire supplies like brandy and iron, and manage commercial matters like banking and financing.[63] France, Spain, and Italy—all wine-producing countries—understandably took little of Madeira's wine, except for the occasional shipment of Malvasia.[64] The Dutch thought Madeira an "excellent wine," and sometimes imported it through London.[65] The Baltic states were a more common destination. Mid- and large-sized firms doing business with those countries generally corresponded through the Hamburg firms of John Scotland, Frederick St. Paul, and Kloefeder & Pashen as well as through Danzig and Stettin houses. From time to time, they sent Copenhagen a shipment or two of Madeira, and by the 1760s they exported wine to Norway, Sweden, Hamburg, adjacent German principalities, and Russia as well.[66] Although the quantities involved were small, the Baltic trade was significant because Madeira's wine exporters needed Baltic wood and iron for pipes, Baltic isinglass for finings, and North Sea fish for laborers; in turn, the Baltic states wanted a liquor less strong than vodka.[67] While the long-hoped-for "great consumption" never arrived before the fall of Napoleon, the region was important to their business.

Madeira was known as "America's wine" in the eighteenth century, and the characterization is apt. Stopping at Madeira was convenient for provisioning ships on the westward leg of the Atlantic trades. Transporting Madeira wine to Anglophone America filled the ships' holds profitably. It provided a potable drink to European settlers in the New World who were frustrated in developing viniculture in America. British mercantile policy encouraged it, and Portuguese mercantile policy discouraged the alternative of taking the wine to Brazil, where Port was privileged. From this perspective there is something almost inevitable about the development of an extensive Madeira wine trade to America.

Yet the participants called it "a revolution in this trade," and the revolution was more than simply the sum of increases in the scale and scope of distribution. Exploiting the opportunity to sell Madeira wine in America required changing the ways market participants did business—increasing the density and complexity of arrangements for buying, marketing, selling, and transporting goods around the Atlantic basin and beyond. As the volume of wine, the frequency and regularity of shipping, and the extent of the wine's dispersal increased, the organization of the enterprises became more extensive and complex; this was true of both the Madeirans' production and export enterprises and the importing, wholesaling, and retailing enterprises on the receiving side of the Atlantic. The revolution in organization transformed not only the conduct of the Madeira trade but also the workings of the entire Atlantic marketplace, moving it from a congeries of metropolitan and frontier economies with sparse links, many of which were characterized by European exploitation of their peripheries, to a more or less interdependent system in which "the gains from trade were not always distributed to the European power with sovereignty over its colonies." In the new regime, returns "flowed to providers of goods and services that were determined not by the flag of the imperial power but by economic relations on a broader scale."[68] What islanders and their customers did to increase the trade and complicate its organization lies at the center of the evolution of wine's world.

5

A "Commerce of Minds": Madeira
Distributors and Their Customers

The link between grape growers and wine drinkers was the collection of distributors, typically the forgotten or ignored characters in any commodity's history. On Madeira, the distributors began as exporters, performing the functions of merchant, agent, consignee, agent-consignee, and representative.[1] As the eighteenth century progressed, they integrated backward, becoming manufacturers concerned with production processes and techniques, and forward, becoming sophisticated marketers. As the population of consumer societies in America exploded in ways that intrigued Europeans, Madeirans, like other European exporters, made forays into the Atlantic wine market and, in networked conversation, seized the chance to make money from their drink.

THE MADEIRA MERCHANT EXPORTERS

In the earliest days of the Madeira wine trade, the number of island merchants active in overseas commerce was small. During the seventeenth century, the group of commercial strangers hovered between one and two dozen. Native merchants, who had been overshadowed by foreigners during the heyday of sugar, continued to be outflanked after wine replaced it. Although they always outnumbered foreigners, natives lost in terms of share of exports with each passing decade (table 5.1). In 1620, there were approximately 40 exporters: 28 Portuguese and 12 foreigners (including 6 Flemish and 3 English). In 1650, there were 66 exporters: 48 Portuguese, 10 English, and 8 other foreigners. By 1687, there were 80 exporters: 56 Portuguese and 24 foreigners (of which at least 13 were English). In 1699, the total had grown to 95, including 80 Portuguese, 8 English, 4 French, and 3 Danish or Dutch.

In the golden age of distribution that ensued, the number of exporters increased substantially. Between 1703 and 1807, at least 925 men and 4 women assumed responsibility for buying wine from growers, packing it, finding overseas buyers and placing it aboard ships. In the six years between 1721 and 1727, the size of the wine export community exploded from 63 to 160. By 1768, the group had grown to 216. After the American Revolution, it dropped, falling to 202 by 1807 and 177 in 1815.[2]

Foreign traders grew apace: from 15 in 1699 and 10 in 1721, they increased to 76 by 1807. Because the movement of the seat of government from Lisbon to Rio in 1807 and the opening of Brazil's ports to British traders in 1810 rendered Madeira a less useful transshipment point for goods going to either Portugal and Spain or Brazil, their number fell to 48 in 1815, from just over one-third (36 percent) of the island's merchant community to just under one-quarter (24 percent). Even if one included the five English-speaking Americans in the 1815 British count, English speakers' share constituted only just over one-quarter (27 percent). While the majority of exporters were always Portuguese, in 1815 as before, the Funchal commercial community included "merchants from almost every part of Europe." Of those working in the island's export sector between 1703 and 1807, 542 (58 percent) were Portuguese, 295 (32 percent) were British, and 38 (4 percent) were American, along with a few Danes, Dutchmen, Frenchmen, Italians, and Spaniards. English-speaking enterprisers increasingly dominated the foreigners. Of the 25 British merchants in Madeira in 1727, 19 were English, four Irish, and two British Americans. Forty years on, in 1768, quite a few Scots had entered the market, constituting more than one-third of the 34 Britons; the Americans had risen to 6. Other foreigners comprised only 4 percent of the exporters. Soon after 1800, the proportion of Britons and Americans among the foreign merchant community rose; 72 of the 76 foreigners were English speakers in 1807, and all but one of the 48 (a Frenchman) in 1815.[3]

The number and share of foreigners cannot convey with accuracy their strength. While Spain ruled Portugal and wine vied with sugar, the ten largest wine exporters of 1620 comprised 56 percent of the island's wine exporters and paid 92 percent of export taxes (probably shipping most of the wine). Portuguese were among the top ten exporters, paying 18 percent of the export customs duties between them. They worked alongside three Flemings, two Englishmen, two Frenchmen, and one German. The largest, English merchant William Ray, and his nearest competitor, the Fleming Guilherme Dinis, together paid 38 percent of all island wine export duties.[4]

As wine eclipsed sugar, the number of participants increased, and non-Portuguese merchants increasingly dominated the trade (table 5.2). By 1650, the

Table 5.1. Madeira merchants known to be exporting wine, 1620–1815

Year	Portuguese	British	Other foreign	Total foreign	Total
1620[a]	28	3	9	12	40
1650[b]	48	10	8	18	66
1687[c]	56	13	11	24	80
1699	80	8	7	15	95
1721	53	9	1	10	63
1727	125	25	10	35	160
1768	173	34	9	43	216
1807[d]	126	72	4	76	202
1815[e]	129	42	6	48	177

Sources: T. Bentley Duncan, *Atlantic Islands: Madeira, the Azores and the Cape Verdes in Seventeenth-Century Commerce and Navigation* (Chicago, 1972), 54–57, based on old codex no. 1503 (1620), Alfândega do Funchal, Arquivo Nacional da Torre do Tombo, Lisbon; Livros dos direitos por entrada (e saída), Cobrancas, nos. 306, 308–9 (1650, 1687, 1699), Alfândega do Funchal, Arquivo Nacional da Torre do Tombo; Livros dos direitos por saída, nos. 272–326 (1721–23, 1727–29, 1768–1815), Provedoria e junta da Real fazenda do Funchal—Alfândega do Funchal, Arquivo Nacional da Torre do Tombo. Cf. Blandy, *Bolton Letters*, vol. 2, for 1702–10 and 1711–13; Petition, December 15, 1706, fol. 140, Blenheim Papers, vol. 410, British Library, London; Livros dos direitos por entrada, nos. 7–8, 21–22, 146–55, 177–91, 220–21, 469 (1717–18, 1727–1815), Arquivo Nacional da Torre do Tombo. Note: These numbers probably overestimate slightly the share of foreigners. The Livros dos entradas e saídas, like the books of export taxes, in particular, do not usually record Portuguese merchants using Portuguese ships to export sugar and wine as such enterprisers were not taxed. Their numbers were small, however, as most Portuguese utilized foreign shipping as well, and so appear in the tally. Duncan tries to correct for undercounting, but his estimations are no more convincing than actual tallies.
a. All British are English; foreigners are 6 Flemish, 2 French, and 1 German.
b. All British are English; foreigners are 6 Flemish, 1 French, and 1 Italian.
c. All British are English. 1699: All British are English.
d. The 72 British include 8 Americans as English speakers.
e. The 42 British include 5 Americans as English speakers.

ten largest exporters—comprising 15 percent of the entire merchant community—paid 79 percent of all wine export duties. Some fifty years later, by 1699, the ten largest exporters—comprising one-tenth of the entire export group—paid 82 percent of all wine export duties. Two of these men, when their work is combined, shipped 55 percent of all wine. In 1727, the ten largest exporters—6 percent of the community—managed 6,420 pipes—70 percent—of it. Thereafter, the share exported by the top ten trended slightly downward through the early nineteenth century but remained high; in 1768 the ten largest exporters exported 68 percent of all wine, and in 1807 63 percent of a much larger volume.

Table 5.2. Ten largest exporters of Madeira wine in five different years, 1650–1807

Year	Merchant	Number of pipes	Share of exports (%)
1650	Matthew Da Gama	107	21
	Richard Pickford	55	11
	Manoel Thomas	53	10
	Duarte Zormans	43	8
	Captain Diogo Gueirreiro	39	8
	Antonio Lopes Maciel	37	7
	Antonio Camacho	33	6
	Manoel Fernandes Mondim	18	4
	Antonio Gonçalves d'Araújo	15	3
	Antonio Peronel	10	2
1699	Richard Richbell	1,823	28
	William Bolton	1,766	27
	Samuel Barquim	425	7
	Pedro de Faria	320	5
	Sebastiao Pinto Lobato	185	3
	Eusebio Da Silva Barreto	153	2
	Alexandre Sauvaire	143	2
	Joseph Caire	141	2
	Benjamin Homem	132	2
	João Phillippe	124	2
1727	Charles Chambers Sr.	3,085	34
	Marcos Gônçalves Rocio	1,137	12
	James Pope	559	6
	Richard Miles	510	6
	Benjamin Bartlett	304	3
	Pantaleão Fernandes	291	3
	Anthony Lynch	194	2
	John West	169	2
	William Goddard	96	1
	John Bisset	76	0.8
1768	James Denyer	899	13
	David Taylor	851	12
	Thomas Loughnan	606	9
	James & John Murdoch	405	6
	James Ayres	368	5
	Paulo Teixeira Pinto	358	5
	James Duff	325	5

continued

Table 5.2. Ten largest exporters of Madeira wine in five
different years, 1650–1807 *continued*

Year	Merchant	Number of pipes	Share of exports (%)
	Joseph Gillis	320	5
	John Searle	294	4
	Andrew Donaldson	273	4
1807	Newton, Gordon, Murdoch & Scot	1,985	11
	Gordon, Duff & Co.	1,880	10
	Phelps, Page & Co.	1,548	9
	Murdoch, Yuille & Wardrop	1,043	6
	Colson, Smith & Robinson	1,039	6
	Monteiro & Co.	951	5
	George & Robert Blackburn	788	4
	Correia de Franca	768	4
	Scot & Co.	763	4
	Christopher & William Lynch	685	4

Sources: See source note for table 5.1.

Nonetheless, the top ten exporters were the substantial, dedicated wine merchants on the island at any time. A large proportion of the other exporters seems to have been occasional—traders who sold wine only from time to time as an accommodation to customers to whom they sold other goods or opportunistically. In 1650, for example, fifty-six out of sixty-five exporters (roughly 87 percent) shipped 10 or fewer pipes of wine that year—in such a small amount and in containers of a pipe or less that one doubts they would have regarded themselves as being "in the trade." Indicative of the increase in scale since the middle of the seventeenth century, wine exporters shipped more as the decades advanced. Out of the twenty-eight exporters named in a surviving *saídas* volume for 1807, only two (or 7 percent) shipped 10 or fewer pipes and fourteen exported fewer than 348 pipes (roughly 2 percent of total exports, and the equivalent of 1650's 10 pipes). While the 1807 records do not list all exporters, what survives suggests a winnowing of the ranks and a decreasing involvement of "small fry."[5]

Breaking down these shares by ethnicity, one learns that, in 1650, there were five Portuguese merchants among the ten largest, and they managed 45 percent of all exports. The largest wine exporter—Matthew Da Gama—was Portuguese, and he handled 21 percent. Two English merchants, two Flemish, and an Italian all competed, and it is to men like them that natives like Da Gama lost out in

the ensuing seventy-five years. In 1699, there were again five Portuguese merchants among the top ten exporters, but now they garnered only 14 percent. The
largest two exporters were English—Richard Richbell, who managed 28 percent
of all exports, and his compatriot William Bolton, who managed 27 percent.
The remaining top exporters were Dutch, Portuguese, French, and English, but
none handled more than 7 percent of all exports. By 1727, only two Portuguese
men—Marcos Gônçalves Rocio and Pantaleão Fernandes—ranked among the
ten largest. All other significant exporters were English; one of them, Charles
Chambers, Sr., dominated the trade, shipping one-third of all wine exported.
Over half (55 percent) was managed by the eight largest British merchants.

Forty years later, no individual trader dominated as Chambers once had. Between 1748 and 1774, many British and American "small fry" swarmed to the
island to establish a house, and many a British or American sea captain thought
himself capable of acting the merchant. English-speaking foreigners continued
to dominate. Of the top ten exporters of 1768, Paulo Teixeira Pinto was the only
Portuguese, and his share was a mere 385 pipes (5 percent). The nine British or
British diaspora traders among the ten largest managed even more of the exports,
63 percent, than they had in 1727. Scots and Americans now figured prominently: the former managing 29 percent of the exports, and the latter 9 percent.

By 1807, the French and Napoleonic Wars had seriously disordered the trade
and led to a realignment in dominance. Two Portuguese firms—Monteiro & Co.
and Correia de Franca—now ranged among the top ten, sharing 9 percent of
the trade between them. In addition, the British had stopped the advance of the
Americans, returning the "balance of trade . . . much in favor of the English."[6]
Many American firms that had mushroomed in the heady days of the 1760s
and 1770s had since joined British firms. As well, some of the older American
firms unraveled, most notably the Hill and the Searle and Pintard houses. Other
American concerns faltered from fiscal imprudence. By the 1810s, the British
were resurgent. Of their firms, four were primarily Scottish, three English, and
one Irish. Together, they managed 54 percent of exports.[7]

While the British retained the upper hand, citizens of the new United States
remained active participants in the trade, despite encountering severe obstacles
to their continuance in it. In 1727, some 52 percent of the ships whose entries
and exits included listings for the nationality of ownership were British ships, and
40 percent Portuguese. By 1768, some 87 percent were British; only 5 percent
were Portuguese. In the prerevolutionary shipping registers of Funchal, colonial
British American vessels were included in the British imperial total, and it is
not possible to distinguish metropolitan from colonial ownership. But by 1807,
after record keepers started making such distinctions, the Portuguese, British,

and Americans had almost equal shares: the Portuguese owned 31 percent of the fleet, and the Americans edged out the British, 32.9 percent to 32.5 percent, for the largest volume of shipping. The nationality of the captains underscores the important place that Americans had come to hold in the Madeira wine trade. In 1727, of the fifty-six ships that dropped anchor in the harbor and reported the nationality of masters, some twenty-two (39 percent) had British captains, and another fourteen (25 percent) British American captains; only nine (16 percent) had Portuguese captains. By 1807, captains from the Azores, Madeira, and Portugal constituted 30 percent of the group, in witness to the increasing strength of the Portuguese, whereas 32 percent hailed from Britain and the States in equal measure.[8]

"FOUNDING PARTNERS": NECESSITY, EDUCATION, AND RELIGION

The dominant British exporters came from the middling ranks of their birthplace communities, which stretched from Aberdeen, the Spey Valley, and Glasgow in the north to Norwich in the east, London and Plymouth in the south, and Bristol, Cork, Dublin, and Liverpool in the west. To a man, they were younger sons, having come from middle- or, in a few cases, lower-income families that, if they could help at all, provided only for their eldest. Distant experiences and nonfamilial resources became imperative.

Many escaped from the lack of opportunity in the places of their births and the farms and villages of their childhood and spent time in large port towns, regional capitals like Dublin and Edinburgh, and even the great metropolis London. Thomas Loughnan was one such man on the move—the son of a modest Wapping brewer of Scottish origin, who could do little but wish him well when he married in 1770.[9] Joseph and William Phelps of Dursley, about twenty miles northeast of Bristol, were born in the 1740s into a fairly comfortable family that had long been active in the Gloucestershire woolen industry, but by the time they came of age that industry had been wracked by the transition from household to factory production and the family was left with nothing. Joseph and William found it more advantageous to make a go of it elsewhere: Joseph went to London in the early 1770s, while William moved to Madeira later that decade.[10] Walter and Robert Scot, who came to the island in the late 1720s, were younger sons in a branch of one of the Borders' largest clans, the Scots of Lauder, Berwickshire, although in their case an older brother, John, preceded them by several years.[11] John Barrett was an impoverished only son languishing in Brosely, Shropshire, when his uncle James Pope made a place for him in his countinghouse on the island. John Leacock was even less well provided for by family: his father, a weaver, died in 1736 and he had no "useful" relatives, so his mother enrolled him in Christ's Hospital, a school for orphans. Five years later, the only option open to the penniless "Blue Coat" boy was a seven-year apprenticeship to William Murdoch and John Catanach in their Madeira wine house—that is, a long apprenticeship with the friend of a friend in a land he had never seen. The four Duff brothers left their family farm alongside the Spey to toil as clerks in Edinburgh and London in the 1760s before joining their uncles James and Alexander Gordon in Madeira.[12]

Some of the distributors were refugees who had fled their homelands for religious reasons, like the Huguenot Pierre Vallette, who left France after the Revocation of the Edict of Nantes in 1685, went to England, where he was naturalized, and subsequently established a business in Madeira, which he plied through the 1710s. Others sought safe haven for political missteps, like support of the Stuarts. Dominick Sarsfield was harried out of southern Ireland for the part he played in the Williamite wars of the late seventeenth century. Francis Newton and Alexander Gordon of Letterfourie (plate 9) fled Scotland, where they had fought for the Young Pretender at the battle of Culloden (1745).[13] Other distributors found in the island not political but economic refuge. Newton and his brother Thomas were younger sons of a penniless minister in Aberdeen. On coming of age at the time Francis moved to Madeira, Thomas set himself up as a dry goods merchant in New York, until near-bankruptcy "encouraged" him to join his brother several years later. There he found another New Yorker, the improvident George Spencer, who had left the colony in embarrassment in the 1740s and the house of Isaac Gualter Bradick.[14]

Itinerancy, education, and religion united most founding traders in the work of establishing a business. Their movements are clear. But their education is difficult to ascertain precisely. British traders were literate, having received some primary instruction back home. Of the 333 English-speaking foreigners working on the island between 1700 and 1815, some 23 received secondary education and 8 attended university. At least two received medical training and worked as doctors. Three more acquired an education through the British army or navy. Distributors' religion is even more difficult to identify, yet the little surviving information we have suggests that it made Madeira comfortable for the Catholics among them and gave the rest a reason to band together against the dominant Catholic culture. Most of the 542 Portuguese, barring the handful of *converso* Jews, were schooled in Catholicism. Of the 333 English-speaking foreigners, there were at least two dozen Catholics. The wastrel George Spencer "became a Roman Catholick to serve his own particular Interests," and there were probably more like him, inasmuch as aspiring but unattached young men often lodged with "a Roman Catholick Family." The rest, one surmises, were Protestants of one stripe or another, who felt a need to cohere. There were at least a dozen Quakers and Huguenots. But this was loose Protestantism: the lack of regular Protestant services and a wide adherence to the principles of Freemasonry irrespective of religion or nationality suggest a weakening of religious ties among both Protestants and Catholics.[15]

"LEGACY MERCHANTS": INHERITANCE AND OPPORTUNISM

In the seventeenth and first half of the eighteenth centuries, Madeira's trade was dominated by foreign bachelors. One of the more prominent, James Pope, died single in 1743 and bequeathed his business to his nephew John Barrett. When Barrett died three years later, he, too, had never wed. Nor had James Smart by the time he was found dead in his bed, having "overloaded his stomach" with lobster. Early on, most foreigners remained single: Benjamin Bartlett, James Gordon, and Francis Newton, to name just three, all enjoyed "the stile [of] a bachelor." This entailed living above the countinghouse or in meagerly furnished rented rooms and partying at Bachelors Hall, a spa up in the hills above Funchal that was open only to single men and their guests. The amenities of the island or the religion and xenophobia of the natives discouraged the raising of foreign families in the first century of the wine trade.[16]

Over the course of the eighteenth century, however, the export of wine came to be dominated by married men, as did many early modern trades, and for these men passing on a legacy in business was easier than for bachelors; indeed, it was imperative.[17] New entrants often married the sister, daughter, or heir of a fellow British or American merchant and established a household, while other enterprisers brought wives and sometimes children with them and raised families. John Leacock Sr. was among the former. After his apprenticeship to Catanach & Murdoch expired in 1749, Leacock remained with the firm as a salaried clerk. On the death of Murdoch in 1757, he left it to form a wine-trading partnership with George Spence—a move in large part facilitated by his marrying Murdoch's "housekeeper," a widow who had inherited substantial property from him. Leacock's competitors Robert and John Scot had done much the same a decade before, if more traditionally: Robert married Elizabeth, the sister of his partner John Pringle, while John married American exporter Dr. Richard Hill's daughter Harriet. Other exporters brought wives with them. Hill had married Deborah Moore in Maryland, and she bore him three children there before relocating with him to Madeira in 1739 and bearing four more. Several generations later, William Phelps briefly traveled to London to wed in 1783 and quickly reembarked with his new wife for Madeira, where they raised seven children.[18] It was rare for foreign exporters to marry Portuguese women.[19]

Merchants begat merchants. Upon foundations of family, the English-speaking merchants started erecting multigenerational houses the same way enterprisers did throughout the Atlantic world: bringing up "their own relations to business in preference of others," unless, of course, "a handsome fee accompanies a stranger, or he happens to be recommended by a particular address & experience in affairs, or known accuracy & fidelity within the counting house."[20] What constituted "relations" was an issue, of course, and the meaning broadened. By the middle of the eighteenth century, through a rather porous system of preferences, many of the houses that were built on close family relationships had become larger, more loosely affiliated. Although many partners were still related by blood and marriage, as often as not they were connected less directly.

Close connections between firm and family were a prominent mark of most export wine houses before the American Revolution. Many firms were built by one family, with the partnership being divided among fathers, brothers, sons, sons-in-law, and cousins, as were Lamar, Hill, Bisset & Co., Searle & Co.,[21] Gordon & Gordon,[22] Hayward & Co., Haddock & Co., Nowlan & Burgess, Leacock & Sons, and Phelps & Morrissey. Many others were founded on the union of two or more families and, as the century progressed, their numbers increased. An instructive if extreme example is that of the firm established by Thomas Loughnan, who was linked by blood and money to at least five different firms. Loughnan surfaced in Madeira as early as 1753, when he apparently began trading in the island on his own; his father, the proprietor of the Fox Brew House in Wapping, acted as his London agent. In 1770, Thomas returned to England to marry Philadelphia Fergusson, the daughter of the Irish sea captain Robert Fergusson of Cork and the granddaughter of the Scots land magnate Alexander Fergusson of Craigdarroch. Loughnan fathered four daughters in Britain before moving back to the island in the early 1780s. Through his wife, Loughnan became connected to her grandfather Alexander's cousin Charles Fergusson, a London wine merchant, who in the late 1750s had formed Fergusson, Murdoch & Co. and who later worked through Shirley, Banger & Co. In addition, Loughnan became tied to Thomas Gordon, one of the principals in Newton, Gordon & Murdoch, for Charles Fergusson's daughter Jean had married John Hamilton Dempster of Skibo, whose sister married Thomas Gordon. Furthermore, through his wife, Loughnan became linked to James Fearns of Fearns Brothers, James having married Philadelphia Loughnan's younger sister. The only firm Loughnan ever officially joined was Scot, Pringle & Cheap, which he did in the 1780s, and that tie was tightened when Loughnan's daughter Zepherina married its partner Henry Veitch in 1796.[23]

The commercial union of two families often included intermarriage, but that was not necessary. Francis Newton never allied himself through marriage to any of his many partners. On escaping from Culloden, he found work as a book-keeper in Alexander Johnston's London countinghouse. There he prospered, and three years later Johnston offered a generous salary should he continue in the work. He refused. Instead, he accessed Johnston's global network of correspondence and secured a place in the Madeira firm of one of Johnston's contacts, João José de Vasconcelos, "the great[est] man on the island." Johnston arranged for Newton to receive a decent salary, bed, board, washing and, most important, "free liberty to trade" for himself. In time, Newton found the setup restrictive and left the post to partner with a dry goods merchant—George Spence of London—who agreed to procure orders for wine in Britain and handle exports of cloth to Portugal. "Jealousy" slowly insinuated itself into the operation. Sensing the likely demise of their relationship, Newton began building yet another firm. He brought into the house his younger brother Thomas, working independently in New York, naming him his agent there. He also employed his nephew David Young as his clerk, and his older brother Andrew Newton of Norfolk, Virginia, as his Chesapeake agent. Having thus strengthened the organization, he broke with Spence and, within five months, entered into a new partnership with his brother Thomas Newton and with Johnston's nephew Thomas Gordon of London, who had recently come out to Madeira. Johnston provided nearly all the capital for the new operation. The Newtons, Spences, and Gordons never intermarried, but their firms nonetheless prospered; the connections between the Newtons and Gordons remained close through the end of the nineteenth century.[24]

Marriage alone could not have sufficed to build an enduring business, of course. Whatever the external conditions and relationships that pushed them from their homeland and caused them to pursue trade, Madeira's dominant exporters were essentially opportunity seekers. If they lacked inherited wealth or economic opportunities at home, they possessed "strong" ties of kin and "weak" ties of kith, and they doggedly deployed both to their advantage in building businesses. They never cut themselves off from families and friends, even those who had nothing to offer them in their early years, and they used their time in Madeira to knit together whatever connections they could, calling for startup capital, seeking suppliers, offering work, and seeking customers.[25]

Newton's case is instructive on the manipulation of ties, for it took the Scot three tries to find among friends of friends and other "weak" relationships a partner he could respect and remain with. The importance of weak extended non-familial ties to an operation founded on strong intertwined family relations characterized the opportunistic construction of the house managed by the Scots and Pringles. Walter and Robert Scot came to the island in the late 1720s and established the firm of Scot & Scot; several years later, their older brother John (who had gone out to Madeira before them) joined as a partner. In 1731, when Walter decided to go it alone, Robert and John combined forces with John Pringle, an erstwhile Borders neighbor. Marrying Pringle's sister, Robert moved to London in 1737 to manage Scot, Pringle & Scot's growing affairs in the metropolis. Thereafter, the firm was managed by Walter Scot (who had returned to the fold), John Scot, and John Pringle for about twenty years, until John Scot settled in Yorkshire in 1755, Walter Scot retired to London two years later, and John Pringle returned to Scotland three years after that to claim an inheritance. With only Walter Scot making occasional visits to Madeira, the firm joined forces in 1761 with an "outsider," Thomas Cheap, whose family had connection neither to the Borders nor to the Scots and the Pringles, yet whose value was undeniable. Cheap had previously worked for a competing house in London, and he had ties to the British legal world (for he was a relative of the Scots jurist Alexander Wedderburn). The alliance with this nonrelative proved advantageous. In 1763, he gained the island's British consulship, and the post brought the firm more than an ordinary share of business. Several years later, the firm took on Charles Murray of Philiphaugh, John Pringle's first cousin and Robert Scot's son-in-law, and, before Cheap resigned as consul, he arranged for Murray to replace him. But the value of intertwining blood and connection through a lock on the consulship was not lost on the new generation; by maintaining a balance, the firm continued to dominate the foreign community for the next fifty years.[26]

CREATING CUSTOMER NETWORKS

The must and production goods needed to manufacture wine could be bought; the knowledge of how to combine them could be learned. The wherewithal to begin in business could be provided by those with whom the exporter shared blood, membership in some group, experience, or expectation. Often, components and know-how could be obtained from competitors. But customers — people who purchased the wine and the most important asset of each trader — could not be bought or borrowed. Finding them, cultivating them, and satisfying them comprised an exporter's most important challenge, and the one to which wine distributors turned most of their attention.

Madeira's exporters approached the difficulty of creating a customer base as a network task. It is probably senseless to try to define yet again "network" — the idea is so vast, and so little precision can actually be attached to it in an early modern business context. It should suffice to consider it "any collection of actors . . . that pursue repeated, enduring exchange relations with one another and, at the same time, lack a legitimate organizational authority to arbitrate and resolve disputes that may arise during the exchange."[27] A successful trader was someone who could build and manage such ordering structures. Madeirans approached the linked challenges of finding, cultivating, and satisfying customers as a network matter: they made use of the preexisting networks they brought to the business; and they built new networks. This was a requirement not just for them but anyone working over oceanic-scale distances using the transportation and communication technologies of the day. Madeira's networks are significant for presenting three main traits possessed by other operatives, in and out of the economic realm, in bold relief: relationships were personal, ties were nonhierarchical, and participation was voluntary. Moreover, they are equally valuable as they help distinguish networks from other forms of commercial and social organization, such as markets, hierarchies, and formal institutions; additionally, they focus on the realities confronting network members—the achievement of success and the avoidance of failure.[28]

Founding partners of Madeira's wine houses began by appealing to personal contacts: to their families and to the patronage and peer groups from which they had come. Almost always, these groups were based on shared ethnic or religious background. Hardly a week went by in the career of an exporter when he or his correspondent did not appeal to fellow members in ethnic and religious groups. In this, he was typical of Atlantic merchants everywhere. Yet, over the course of his career and especially after 1750, the successful Madeira distributor broadened his networks. He extended them beyond personal connections, building new customer relationships with more impersonal—what are now thought to be more "businesslike"—attitudes. By 1815, decisions were based less frequently on whom someone knew and more often than before on whether the decision made sound business sense, as determined by third-party calculations. Even so, the networked business approach never faded.

KIN, PATRONAGE, AND PEER NETWORKS

Deploying defined kinship connections—interpreted loosely to include fellow members of an ethnic group or religious minority—was the most important way to establish a business and develop a correspondence. A sole reliance upon them was seldom if ever depended upon, although it was useful as a springboard. Dr. Richard Hill's first customers in the early 1740s were his son and son-in-law back in Philadelphia; consignments of provision goods from there and Maryland that is, from "the family of our relations," who were all Quakers—kept him from failing in his first three years on the island. Hill's contemporary Francis Newton counted his older brother Andrew in Virginia among his first buyers after he moved to the island in 1748. Of the roughly fifty correspondent relationships his firm struck in its first ten years in the trade, over three-quarters were with blood relatives or fellow Scots. Toward the end of the 1750s, it targeted doctors and lawyers trained in Scotland, "playing the Scottish card" with men of like experience. Similarly, the Nowlan & Burges firm received its first orders in 1759–62 from family members, especially those still residing in Burges's native Ireland. Family constituted the lifeline for entrants, even as late as 1815, when John Howard March set up business and relied primarily upon his brothers Joseph and Clement in New Hampshire and his cousin Thomas in New York for capital and orders for several years.

Madeira exporters also called on their patrons. These individuals might bear kin affiliation, but just as often did not. Usually, a patron was someone who had previously nurtured the merchant, granted him protection, and lent him support to advance the interests of both men. Frequently, patrons were former employers, yet from time to time they were current correspondents, albeit far more influential politically, commercially, and socially than the rest. In the middle of the seventeenth century, for example, Diogo Fernandes Branco regularly sold wine to two merchants: João Fernandes in Barbados and José Ferreira in Newfoundland. Whether either had once been his master or were now simply correspondents or agents is unclear, but the three men had known each other from the time they had all previously worked together in Brazil. No kin relationship is discernible. What is clear is that the two used their money and continuing influence in Brazil to advance his interests there in commercial and noncommercial ways. Resort to such men was common. In 1695–1714, William Bolton found business in Barbados through William Heysham, a brother of his friend Robert Heysham of London and a promoter of Bolton's Caribbean interests. The same was true of Bolton's contemporary Duarte Sodré Pereira, whose agents—Aaron Lamego in Jamaica, Joseph Ward and Benjamin Mason in Barbados, and Manuel Alves Correia and Miguel de Crasto in Curaçao, all of whom he had met during his stay in Brazil—lent support to his operation and built his business.[29]

The house of Newton & Gordon offers some of the best examples of the extension of networks. When Francis Newton began shipping wine in 1749, he shipped first to Jamaica, to Samuel Johnston, a leading Jamaica merchant and planter who was also the brother of his former London employer. Newton would later trade with another Johnston brother, Patrick, a Barbados planter. Several former friends in the Borders, coming from more elevated families, found it of value to extend Newton their favors: Walter Hunter, William Ellworthy, and George Lawder. All had settled in Jamaica and in the 1750s Newton began drawing on them for orders, advice, and recommendations.[30]

Peer networks, of necessity, gradually emerged in the evolution of any firm's trading. Wine was commonly sent, distributors reported, "for the use of *particular friends.*" In effect, almost all existing ties were utilized. "Early attachments" were often regarded as "the most lasting," noted one schoolfellow of Thomas Gordon: "They often reap much a happiness in point of society, business or advancement in life." There was "vast advantage," many thought, to boys "being sent to publick school," for it brought them business down the road. Certainly, Gordon used contacts previously made while attending the Mercer's School in the City's Old Jewry in his search for customers. John Corrie of Charleston, James Plunderleath of Roxburghshire, Andrew Robertson of London, and Basil Cooper of London bought from Gordon and funneled him their suggestions as to other potential customers. In the same way, Christ's Hospital in Hertfordshire—not a "hospital" in the common sense of that word but a school that prepared the orphaned or homeless children of London freemen for apprenticeship or university—funneled consignments to John Leacock for sixty years until his death in 1799. Such ties were both emotional and instrumental.[31]

Overlapping sets of relationships with peers also gave shape to emergent business. After Thomas Newton joined his brother in Madeira in 1756, he wrote a volume of letters to men with whom he had no more tie than that he had once dwelled among them, having worked in New York for eight years as a dry goods merchant in the 1740s and 1750s. He wrote twenty letters a day, all with the same pitch. Evan Cameron had been Newton's partner in a dry goods firm, and so Newton wrote Cameron almost immediately. He had rented rooms with Malcolm Campbell, and, based on their *"intimate friendship,"* he begged Campbell to use his "utmost endeavours to procure" him "the consignment of a vessel & to speak to all" his "friends & acquaintances to give" him "the preference." "Old acquaintance" with Dr. Robert Knox and *"intimate friendship"* with his brother, as with Anthony Sarly, were enough to win an order. Cameron, Campbell, Knox, and Sarly were all immigrants whose company Newton had kept in New York. More to the point, they were all equals—at least in standing and rank. Whether mates or just members of the same age or social set, Newton had little hold over them—they had to be wooed.[32]

The value of all three bonds—kin, patron, and peer—was immense, at least in the early stages of building a business. Merchants with such connections knew each other and communicated independently of commerce. Because of these more full-bodied ties, information about product quality, reputation for adhering to the ethical standards of the commercial community, responsiveness to customers' wishes, and fair dealing traveled fast and far. Communication was generally easier in networks built with such links, where the parties implicitly shared premises regarding interaction. In uncertain times and ventures, trustworthiness was enhanced by these structures, in which all parties assumed they had shared interests and predispositions.

EXTENDED NETWORKS

Yet firms that succeeded found they had to move beyond the base of familial and ethnic connection. It was a lesson learned by exporters in most midsize and large firms, although a reality that has been ignored by most network historians. In some sense, the traders' reorientation grew out of their reflections on the extent to which kinship ties did not always work for them. Fathers fought their sons, and vice versa. Brothers squabbled and failed one another. Rivalry among siblings was as strong then as it always is. Cousinage was a concept so vast and loose to at times be almost content-free, despite the nearly constant, closely affectionate salutation of "dear cousin" that opened many a business letter. As Henry Hill knew from years of frustration—despite Quaker relatives' insistence on brotherly love—"no disputes are so disputable as those between relations."[33]

And so the channels for distributing wine became less personal. Typical was Newton & Gordon's development of a relationship with the New Yorker John Burnett. Thomas Newton was "well acquainted" with Burnett and, responding to a request for contacts, Burnett "promised" Newton that he would ask his brother in Antigua—the planter David Burnett—to give "preference" to the firm. For over two decades, Newton & Gordon made the most of this more remote type of connection. Their correspondent in Norfolk—the merchant John Riddell, a friend of Gordon from childhood—sounded yet another variation on the theme. When Riddell quit trading to return to Scotland, he suggested that Newton & Gordon transfer the handling of their Norfolk business to Logan & Gilmour, a stranger to the Madeirans; having dealt with it for over twelve years, however, Riddell could vouch for the Virginia firm's veracity and connectedness.[34]

Thus, slightly more impersonal connections, although not necessarily more formal, were forged by encounters with and approaches to acquaintances, friends of friends and, increasingly, strangers. As the decades passed, most firms grew "ever ambitious" of extending their network to "gentlemen of character." "Character" often consisted of having numerous friends and a willingness to share them. Two groups were especially desirable to expansively minded traders: sea captains with contacts in port towns and merchants with correspondents in regions surrounding those towns. Newton & Gordon had long dealt with sea captain Alexander Stupart, whose vessel had regularly called at Funchal and Kingston, and, pleased with his handling of affairs, the firm made its reliance upon him annual. It did so primarily because it did not "know a man better calculated for . . . picking up orders among his friends in Jamaica." Similarly, Captain Stephen Singleton was "extensively engaged in the Madeira trade" in the 1810s, and, as a result, John Howard March found him ideal and wanted to "structure an engagement with him," as he could "obtain many orders for wine." Friends of correspondents and of friends—increasingly very attenuated ties—often passed through the island with "a friendly letter of introduction," and the exporters exerted influence on them to buy or promote their wine as recompense for being treated so well. Even without a visit, the power of a common acquaintance was great. Alexander Johnston of St. Kitts, for instance, urged his neighbors the traders Unwin & Neech to procure wine from Newton & Gordon, and the latter did so in 1783 and for the ensuing two decades. Most remote but over time hugely significant were total strangers. Many visitors called without warning or introduction. Charles Manly, who arrived without letter of introduction but plenty of initiative, ingratiated himself with John Howard March; given March's kind reception, Manley's brother in Gran Canaria subsequently bought Madeira from March and, in turn, sold Canary wine to him. "Entertaining such strangers as we have no connection with" exposed exporters to new customers and emergent tastes, as well as to new ways of making goods or dispersing products.[35]

IDENTIFYING WITH CUSTOMER NETWORKS

What does this combination of kin, patron, and peer relations and more extended, seemingly impersonal ties suggest about how commercial lives were conducted? It is no exaggeration to say that a Madeira trading house—indeed, any circum-Atlantic commercial operation—was defined by its customers. In many senses, an Atlantic merchant's identity was his customer portfolio. This is not the way individual identity has usually been conceived. Historians, anthropologists, and other scholars have more often than not presented family, ethnicity, and religion, as well as class and gender, as the chief determinants of personal identity. These factors were certainly at work in Madeira trading, and in very explicit ways. But successful merchants expanded their horizons beyond their communities of origin and built customer networks that supplemented, if they did not supersede, their families and backgrounds. These networks defined the merchants to themselves and to their peers. It is impossible, of course, to be certain how historical personages exactly thought of themselves; one cannot interview them, and the relatively unreflective, action-oriented people who became wine exporters left little personal commentary. But one can divine some perceptions through their behavior and from oblique references in their letters.[36]

Family, nationality, race, and religion were all important ingredients of the

Madeira merchants' identities. Identities were grounded in kinship, and kinship brought real benefit to the merchants. Partnership formation was often
faster among blood relatives, and contractual issues—who could provide initial
resources, who was responsible for firm direction, and how gains would be divided—were often easier to negotiate. Members of a family participated because
it was a tontine of sorts—surviving relatives might benefit and inherit. Moreover,
family played these roles because members remained connected over long periods of time, pursued varieties of activities, and, it was presumed, shared goals
and ideals; often, they did not have to specify the range of activities and assumptions in the detail they had to when associating with strangers. The elements of
affiliation generally existed as part of a package, and usually the participation of
members did not demand a balancing of parties in any exchange.[37]

Family association also gave entrée to nonfamily members—potential partners
and customers—by aligning Madeira's merchants with people who already knew
the reputations of the strangers. It created, in doing so, "social capital" for both
exporters and strangers who were unfamiliar with each other but who recognized
each other's smaller family or larger clan. "The role of family affiliation vis-à-vis
others relies partly on its value as a signal of personal traits—honesty, fidelity,
skill, and so on—and on the degree to which the family takes responsibility for
the obligations and actions of its members." That is, family affiliation signaled
authority, discipline, altruism, and solidarity to the rest of the world. Families
constituted recognizable collective characters, which became embedded in the
identities of members. All this made them especially valuable in forming a network.[38]

At the same time, family ties held no monopoly on understanding, sharing, or
trust; "the benefits of the ideal family were ephemeral," particularly "when internecine strife was common." Limiting oneself to family, even extended family,
limited opportunities for achievement. As a result, savvy merchants expanded
their bases of contacts, customers, and correspondents. As their commercial activities grew and became less centered on their initial circles of relatives, patrons,
and peers, their identities—their senses of who they were—expanded. The various links among acquaintances, friends of friends, and strangers were what sociologists call "weak ties," in contrast to the "strong ties" of friends, neighbors, and
relatives. Common religion and ethnic links could function as strong or weak,
depending on the degree to which they injected similar or dissimilar points of
view into the relationship, although a shared moral vocabulary probably made
them more strong than weak, given the penchant of fellow religionists and eth-
nics for avoiding in-group criticism. Weak ties are more exchange-oriented and
less intimate, intense, and time-consuming than relations with relatives, neigh-

bors, or friends. Weak ties have strong informational advantages, for someone to whom one was weakly tied was "more likely to move in circles different from" one's own and have "access to information different from that which" normally one receives. Because people with strong ties are usually similarly situated, they often did not have access to the information about different peoples, places, and resources that was needed in transoceanic business.[39]

Madeira merchants' weak ties often arose from contacts with ship captains, visitors who stopped at the island, and second-, third-, and even fourth-hand links to friends of friends. These ties imprinted commercial identity as powerfully as did strong ones. A merchant's customer portfolio certainly reflected and summarized his origins, yet moved beyond them. It is this understanding that Thomas Lamar conveyed to Henry Hill when reminding Hill that the "interest" of their firm lay "naturally in America." Its founder and two of its partners came from Maryland and Pennsylvania. But a customer base should be "pursued [there] by every eligible method," to wit, by moving far beyond recognized ties of consanguinity.[40] The Searles likewise pursued New Yorkers, and the Brushes Bostonians, whether they knew them personally or not, and in time pushed well beyond the bounds of each. Predominantly British firms like the Leacocks and Gordons turned to England and Scotland. Such men built their portfolios of customers by integrating the emigration patterns of their families and friends, their own various travels, their choice of partners, and the like—fundamentally, by aggressively pursuing tenuous, often distant commercial opportunities.

This expanded, almost symbiotic identification with customers revealed itself in a number of ways. Table 5.3 details the geographical distribution of three firms' customers in the second half of the eighteenth century. Newton & Gordon (and its successors) focused on England and the West Indies: 171 of its 210 customers during the early 1770s lived in one of these two places, as did 246 of its 273 customers a decade later, and 303 of its 404 customers at the end of the century. In the late 1750s, Newton & Gordon's first correspondent in Barbados was Patrick Johnston. In Jamaica, it served Philip Pinnock, James Nasmyth, Donald Campbell, James Kerr, and Nathaniel Beckford—some of the more important landholders there. By 1782–85, it had at least 33 regular Jamaica customers, more than any other Madeira firm: 7 individuals and firms in Kingston, another 7 in Spanishtown, 2 in Savanna-la-Mar, and 17 on undisclosed plantations. In addition to regular customers on which it relied for annual orders, Newton & Gordon shipped to a large number of more occasional, irregular buyers; there were 67 such customers in three years in the early 1780s. Consistent with their English and West Indian interests, Newton & Gordon sympathized with the British at the outbreak of war.[41]

Table 5.3. Geographical distribution of three firms' customers in the eighteenth century

Geographical area	Newton & Gordon			Leacock		Lamar, Hill, Bisset & Co.		
	1770–1772	1782–1785	1797–1798	1763–1765	1797–1798	1762	1767	1796–1797
England	79	121	112	27	19	9	11	1
Of which London	71	111	102	26	17		9	1
Scotland	7							
Ireland	1	2	1			1		
Holland		3				1		
Spain		1				1		
Portugal	1	5	7			2		
Madeira	1	1			1			
British Canada			3					1
New Hampshire			3					
Massachusetts			3	1		16	6	
Connecticut						3	1	2
New York	1	3	3	1	1	2	18	
New Jersey						1	1	

Pennsylvania	1	7	3		22	13	2
Maryland	1	1	2		4	9	
Virginia	4	5	14		33	39	16
South Carolina	1	29	1	1	1	12	2
Georgia		5					
West Florida	4						
West Indies	92	191	33	22	9	13	6
Of which Jamaica	67	116	13	3	2	3	
Of which eastern West Indies	25	52	18	19	7	9	5
Of which Barbados	1	4	2				
Africa		11					
India and Asia	9	20					
Unstated	1	3	1		24	9	9
Total	210	273	83	44	129	132	39

Sources: Newton & Gordon Bills of Lading Books, 1770–72, 1782–85, 1797–98, Cossart, Gordon Papers, Madeira Wine Company, Funchal; Leacock Bills of Lading Books, 1763–65, 1797–98, Leacock Papers, private collection, Funchal; Lamar, Hill, Bisset & Co. Inventories, July 1, 1762, July 1, 1767, 1796–97, folders 3–4, Lamar, Hill, Bisset & Co. Papers, Edward Wanton Smith Collection, 4 folders, 1762–1802, Historical Society of Pennsylvania, Philadelphia. The 1796–97 Lamar, Hill data, in a List of Outstanding Debts, is partial, but no more complete accounting has survived.

John Leacock's firms were likewise identified with England and the West Indies, but they never matched the scale of Newton & Gordon's engagement. Between the 1760s and 1790s, he saw his firms increase the number of shipments managed and nearly double the number of pipes exported. Although Spence, Leacock & Spence shipped extensively to British North America in the 1760s, 60 of their 83 customers lived in England or the Caribbean. In the latter region, it supplied customers in Antigua, where Leacock's brother lived, Barbados, Grenada, Jamaica, St. Kitts, and Tortola. By the century's end, the firm's successor, Nowlan & Leacock, had moved farther afield, having added the Bahamas, Demerara, Martinique, Montserrat, St. Croix, St. Vincent, and Santo Domingo to its Caribbean portfolio, plus new destinations in India and England. Like Newton & Gordon, the firm was slow to return to prerevolutionary customers in the United States market; when it did, it discovered that American-identified firms—those firms with American partners and British firms whose correspondence with the self-conscious "Americans" emphasized their respect for the new country—had saturated the place. The Leacocks' customer base, and so the firm's attention and identity, became imperialized, turning more to India and to lands that Britain annexed or occupied in the 1780s and 1790s, like Demerara. While they had no customers per se residing in India, as table 5.3 notes, they began to fill ships that went there on a regular basis so that their cargoes could be reexported to London after a stay in the subcontinent. They began to supply as well a large London intermediary, Cleland, White & Co., which first bought several hundred pipes in 1798 for resale in India and the next year another 500. Given such large orders, India loomed larger in their sense of who they were as businessmen.

Lamar, Hill, Bisset & Co., in contrast, was a North American firm heavily engaged with the mid-Atlantic and upper South colonies and states, especially Pennsylvania, Maryland, and Virginia. Before the Revolution, Richard Hill leveled his sights on Philadelphia, where his family was established. During the Revolution, the firm, headed by his son Henry, attempted to run the British blockade of the North American coast and supply the colonists. By heritage, ideology, and business interests, it always identified with a place it thought was "rising fast to wealth & consequently to luxury," and it stood well positioned to answer the "call for much" of Madeira's wine after the war. This shows in its customer lists. In 1762, 82 of the firm's 129 customers lived in what became the United States, 59 hailing from Pennsylvania, Maryland, and Virginia alone. Five years later, 99 of 132 customers were from the future States, including 61 from the same three jurisdictions. Even after the firm's business had been intentionally downsized at the end of the century, its distinctive focus remained: 1 customer hailed from

England; 1 British Canada; 2 Connecticut; 20 Pennsylvania, Virginia, and South Carolina; 6 West Indies; and 9 undesignated markets.[42]

With respect to identification with customers, it was not just that the distributors dealt with buyers in a greater number of places around the world as the century advanced and, perhaps paradoxically, that they specialized in serving customers in certain regions. They also showed sympathy with the areas with which they traded and often took on their causes as their own. They sometimes advocated the political causes of their customers, even if the support contravened their own national allegiance. The Leacocks and the members of Gordon, Duff & Co. became expert not only in East India Company affairs but also in governmental administration of the subcontinent, and constantly supported efforts—in England and India—to open up the country and reform its legal system. The Americans—the Hills and the Searles—were almost slavish in support of the colonists during the revolutionary agitation of the 1760s and 1770s. But the pro-British Newton & Gordon, which initially supported Britain's fight against its colonists, adopted a more moderate tone as the conflict evolved; during the 1790s, it staunchly defended the Americans against the quasi-military assaults of the British. In the last third of the century, most firms in Funchal also began to express concern and lobby actively for the passage of Portuguese and American laws that eased their trade with their customers and protected customers' commercial property.

In other ways, too, the identity of exporters became intertwined with that of their customers. Some distributors became poachers, stealing customers from other traders. Such behavior was anathema to them before 1763. But, by the final third of the century, customers had become critical to the profile of any firm, and so were vigorously fought over. Nor would just any customers do: distributors became more "class conscious," in the sense that whom they served became a "brand" of their firm. Whom an exporter supplied—regardless of family or ethnic tie—became more important to its image than where its partners came from. In this way, the idea of "a quality house"—not a term exporters used or a concept they fussed about in the 1690s—emerged at the end of the eighteenth century. The "first houses" did not deal in adulterated, mixed, north-side, and low wines. They tried to avoid India or navy business. For them, "the quality of the wine is the chief thing." In short, they aggressively, obsessively pushed the plan of providing quality to quality. Scot, Pringle & Cheap was perhaps the leading house in purveying quality wine in the 1760s, joined by Newton & Gordon, whose pursuit of the niche began in the 1780s. The Hills earned a reputation for shipping "nothing but wine of the first quality" in that decade, too, although they always had difficulty meeting the demands of their customers, at the same time that the

Leacocks also struggled to enter the tier of "quality houses." What each of these firms did or tried to do was ship only London Particular and perhaps New York grades, plus rarer varietals like Malvasia and Sercial. Not surprisingly, those who adopted this approach prided themselves on a higher than average percentage of customers regularly taking a pipe or two each year and in a personal knowledge of their customers.[43]

MANAGING MADEIRA'S CUSTOMER NETWORKS

Madeira exporters struggled to build a business and make a profit by constructing customer networks. Once built, how were they managed? In essence, they handled these structures by carrying on multiple sets of interactive, transoceanic conversations about the wine—how it was made and packaged, how it was shipped and distributed, how it was displayed and consumed. The conversations, as we have already seen, were not limited to verbal communications. Nor were they restricted to offering products, filling orders, arranging financing and shipping, and negotiating prices. Rather, they were full and frank exchanges about the improvement of the product, the elaboration of distribution channels to suppliers and consumers, changes in tactics, clients, and venues, what constituted fair prices, the construction of a drink made to the taste of a new market, and the like. Such conversations, at a deep level, were coordinating mechanisms whereby transatlantic businessmen determined what was a saleable product, who was a good partner, and what was a satisfactory transaction.[44]

"Conversation," in the early modern sense of the term, was the action of dealings with others or things. It need not have been public or oral, although modern scholars have inexplicably reduced it to speech acts. It embraced not only what was spoken but also what was done in complement to words. It might have taken a few minutes or hours; but it also might have spilled over days, months, or years. It need not have involved just two parties. The important ingredient was an "interchanging of thoughts" with another—a "commerce of minds" the poet Cyril Tourneur called it—and this was something that could be effected in writing and across water. Conversation construed in this manner had to exhibit two characteristics. There had to be a subject: participants had to have a focus for their talk, a center around which to exchange their ideas. Such was the gist of Samuel Johnson's bon mot that he had "had *talk* enough, but no conversation," for there had been "nothing *discussed*" by the two parties. Second, the conversation had to be collaborative: each participant had to have the opportunity to offer his knowledge and articulate and rearticulate his position. As Henry Fielding acknowledged, conversation was "that reciprocal interchange of Ideas, by which

Truth is examined. Things are, in a manner, *turned around* and sifted, and all our knowledge communicated to each other." Conversation, then, was, among other things, a highly nuanced, enlightened metaphor for the Atlantic commercial world. It drew together the ideas of learning with exchange, truth with commerce. Throughout, it implied the triumph of civil discourse, with the insistence that reason, courtesy, and articulation could explicate the world and reconcile differences. Merchants who wrote about wine to others across the seas might have been surprised and flattered to have their letters and accounts labeled "conversations"—a rather fanciful word for their earnest, mundane discussions!—but they would have recognized why the label fit.[45]

Madeirans' conversations were not part of a metropolitan master plan. Rather, they were nonhierarchical, voluntary, and self-organized discussions among complementary goal seekers working mainly around the Atlantic basin, each responding to the opportunities in his local market and at the same time connecting to multiple, other, similarly motivated yet differently influenced correspondents residing in different places. Fortunately for the twenty-first-century observer, a great deal of this discourse was epistolary, and a large portion has survived. In addition, the conversations were increasingly intense, as exhibited in the rising volume of correspondence and growing deployment of agents and partners to the customers' localities. By means of correspondence, wine exporters, uncoordinated but certainly copying each other's successful moves, inculcated the ideas and aspirations of customers.

CONVERSATIONS CREATE NETWORKS

Transatlantic trade networks—indeed, transatlantic trade—sprang from conversations. In recent years, social scientists have proliferated typologies of networks—some useful for certain purposes, some for others. At least four properties that they ascribe to networks quite broadly are applicable to the exchange structures that emerged in the early modern Atlantic wine trade: information flow between members, conflict resolution, increased flexibility, and the enforcement of norms. Conversations were the mechanisms that enabled these properties to be fully realized.

Nonhierarchical conversations with customers, suppliers, agents, and friends provided Madeira traders with information about the opening of markets, the good or "miserable state" of credit, the presence of disease that would close a port to their wine, the tactics of other exporters, the bankruptcies of correspondents, the progress of vessels around the globe, the passage and enforcement of restrictive regulations in consumer markets, the tastes of specific communities, and so on. When Newton & Gordon first pushed into Georgia, it approached the

Savannah firm Inglis & Hall. "We should be glad to hear from you & know something of the trade & produce of your province, if any quantity of wines could be disposed of to advantage, what qualities," it wrote, "with every other particular which may occur to you necessary for our information." As few Georgia vessels had come to Madeira, it was "in the dark with regard to the qualities or prices of your produce" or the colonists' call for wine. In doing so, the firm acknowledged the importance of information flow to itself and to would-be customers.[46]

Much of the conversation passed on rumor or speculation of a sometimes intimate, personal, and sensational nature. By letters from noncustomers and word-of-mouth reports from captains and passengers, the partners of Newton & Gordon in Madeira heard in July 1772 "the melancholy news of sundry great failures in London" that "in general" ran "much among the Scotch houses," and that their erstwhile patron Johnston's sometime partner Thomas William Jolly was "gone in the common wreck." The insinuation was that Johnston, their metropolitan agent, might also be embarrassed. Before hearing from Johnston or their own London partner, the Madeirans wrote to another firm in London, asking for confirmation of Jolly's business and cutting their losses with correcting orders. Decades later, hearing a rumor that "immense quantities" of brandy had been captured and carried to England, without waiting for verification, the firm changed its plans for supplying itself with spirits, canceling orders from continental sources and ordering supplies to be bought in London instead. Some of the reportage, as of Johnston's supposed 1772 insolvency, was groundless, yet exporters were forced to deal with it as if true and to clear the slate. They strove to correct the misinformation whenever possible. In this Johnston succeeded. Not all were so fortunate. At one point, "some *wise* men" in Madeira, "who journalize[d] other men's business and behavior to their friends in London and who also receive[d] journals of what their friends in London hear, see and imagine," averred that Thomas Murdoch planned to ship five hundred pipes on a certain vessel (figure 5.1). There was no truth to the allegation, and Murdoch did his utmost to dispel the rumor. But most islanders never believed him, and the high prices that persisted among the growers as a result persisted through the year.[47]

Conversations with customers also helped resolve conflicts. The expanse of water separating them restricted the ability of Old World sellers and New World buyers to track and observe each other directly. In order for trade to occur at all, base levels of trust had to be established. Disagreement potentially threatened trust, because, if unresolved, it cast an almost immoveable shadow of sharp dealing on at least one party and resulted in loss of business. Accordingly, even before any action was taken and any accusation was made, a pointed conversation

Figure 5.1. Thomas Murdoch
(1758–1846).
Source: © Royal Geographical Society,
London.

with clear meaning held in extenso from far away, if skillfully managed, might cool hot tempers. In effect, a conversation figured as something like arbitration before a lawsuit. If an importer proffered questionable bills or exhibited suspicious creditworthiness, the exporter would ask a correspondent or agent in the importer's community to encourage the individual in person or through writing and thereby effect repayment. Vice versa, as well: if a Lisbon house was treated falsely by a Madeira firm, that house might approach another Madeiran to effect reconciliation, as was the case when John Parminter of Lisbon approached Newton & Gordon about questionable bills tendered by Smith & Ayres, and get the former to write or talk to the latter. Persuasion, exporters instructed junior partners, was central to profit making.[48]

Once divisions became public, distributors minimized any damage by making conversation personal and face-to-face. This tactic was particularly useful when the exporter wanted to remain on good terms with the correspondent. In the 1760s, for example, Newton & Gordon's Boston correspondent John Rowe, a highly regarded merchant, questioned the amount he owed the company. With such a magnate, getting "the proceeds . . . out of his hands" was tricky and had to be done "with the greatest caution & prudence"; accordingly, the firm chose not "to affront him or show him any reason that" it was "dissatisfied with his usage" but rather to order its own Thomas Newton in New York to visit Rowe in Boston. In the end, Rowe still refused to pay: the approach did not work this time. But often it did. Sometimes when a correspondent refused to pay for wine delivered, a distributor brought a new party into the conversation, drawing on a local with whom the offender had a more intimate acquaintance or who could apply pressure to him. Firms frequently found occasion to adopt these less aggressive, more conversational tactics. In 1803, Newton & Gordon asked its New York agent Robert Lenox to recover money *"with delicacy"* from two Virginians, which he had to do via the post.[49]

Conversations between commercial correspondents could increase firm flexibility and speed in handling trade. A network of customers helped a distributor ride out hard times in overseas markets. When a market was glutted with wine, an exchange of letters with a customer on the spot informed the distributor of excessive supply and made the case for shipping the wine elsewhere. Such was the situation when the master of a Salem vessel found "dull sale" in Georgia for wine acquired from Scot, Pringle & Cheap. He wanted to send his cargo to Carolina. Since the Madeirans' agent there could give "no encouragement to that idea," their correspondent in Salem redirected the cargo to himself. More dramatically, correspondence with the East India Company, India-bound captains, and members of the military and civil establishments on the subcontinent facilitated many exporters' sending their wines to fresh addresses in South Asia when the North American ports were closed to British ships during the Revolution.[50]

Conversations were, lastly, a powerful means of exerting transoceanic control. Because the relationships among sellers and buyers were multiple, overlapping, and noncoercive—that is, because they were a network, as opposed to a hierarchy or a single link—accounts of infractions of economic and social norms spread rapidly to all network members. In relating such infractions, participants in the Atlantic wine trade articulated their own norms and implicitly committed themselves to them, at the same time that they reported on and warned about others' lapses. Early in his career in Madeira, Francis Newton unabashedly disclosed to correspondents that another exporter was, in a most untraditional manner, begging from any supplier for imports into Madeira and in turn offering wine at prices settled in advance before the imported goods were seen. Newton warned that this was a "way to make a man bankrupt in this business."[51] Newton's was a complex communication. The Scot was making his correspondents aware of the risks incurred by trading with such an imprudent gentleman, and this was valuable advice. The gentleman in question did go bankrupt five years later, and the correspondents who heeded Newton's suggestion avoided entanglement. At the same time, Newton was committing himself not to offer prices on imports before he had seen them and ascertained their quality, and was telling his correspondents, many of whom were his suppliers, not to ask him to do so.

Traders did not distinguish strongly between business/professional and social/personal infractions, and so there was often a strong moral tone to their description of wrongdoers, as Newton's ire suggests. When John Leacock notified customers that his former partner Spence had overextended himself through land speculation in America and thereby bankrupted himself a second time, his breathless, horrified tone left no question whether he believed this reflected badly on Spence's character. When Richard Hill wrote a Philadelphian about the looseness of a competitor's practice, he felt it threatened the competitor's ability to honor his commitments. Not honoring one's commitments was one of the gravest commercial sins where oceanic distances were in play. In predicting his competitor would fail in this way, Hill was attempting to insulate himself from the economic ostracism and social opprobrium that would ensue by establishing a different set of standards for himself. Hill may have particularly needed to establish standards, as he had himself gone bankrupt back in Maryland, yet such pronouncements were not peculiar to men with his past; all distributors used them to assert and inculcate correct rules of deportment. James Duff's 1802 bankruptcy was explained to correspondents as a matter of evil over good: it was a "contemptible sin," one "solely owing to his extensive and very imprudent engagements as an insurer, which is a vile gambling trade." Marien Lamar's rejection as a partner could be easily accepted by his confederates given his "wrong behavior"—which in his case was lethargy and a fondness for "the baneful practice of immoderate drinking." Pointing out or commenting on good or bad character or behavior became an important way to maintain network control. Thus were commercial codes of behavior replicated. No one reading epistolary exchanges would have missed either the message or the goal.[52]

CUSTOMERS TALK BACK

Much of the extant record for Madeira wine traders' exporting and marketing appears in the letters they wrote to others. As a result, most of what we can reconstitute is the traders' side of the conversations, and, sadly, in the case of Madeira, since only a handful of Portuguese traders' letters or accounts have survived, most of that side is the foreigners.' But, of course, customers were actively managing their suppliers, even as the suppliers were managing them and, luckily, some of the customers' letters have survived as well. Through the conversations they participated in, customers were actively involved in the design, assessment, and distribution of the product. The exporters constantly asked customers to give their opinion on the wines previously sent. The buyers talked back. In doing so, they participated in the invention of the modern Madeira wine, as we have seen, providing opinion that helped turn a cheap, simple table wine into an expensive, complex, and highly processed luxury product.

Customer interaction and conversation pressured distributors in a myriad of ways, many of which were unrelated to the product's manufacture. One sees this in bold relief in the negotiations that led to a late eighteenth-century shift in payment arrangements. Distributors as early as 1640 had required as compensation for wine of the first quality either specie or a bill of exchange drawn on London. "Great sacrifices" on the part of the customer "& much advance of capital" were expected if an exporter was to send "so scarce & valuable an article." But "few houses" in Atlantic consumer markets, "except those of the first capital & connections," could pay in this way. After the American Revolutionary War, awareness grew that commercial life had changed in ways that weakened the hands of distributors and strengthened those of the customers. In particular, American consumers began demanding new terms for compensation. By the early 1790s, Madeira exporters began allowing unheard-of payment periods and locations and interpreting discharge more flexibly. They would in future allow buyers

> from 12 to 18 months credit on the amount if payable in London, according as the order might be limited or extensive. But if instead of drawing at this extended period upon London, it should by you be preferred that we should receive our payment in America, we would allow the same credit, with this additional circumstance: that when the amount should become due instead of its being paid or remitted, we would request you to invest the sum in such produce as would suit our market, that the commission on the shipment, as also the opportunity employing your own vessels might be derived to you from the transaction.

This was a transatlantic commercial relationship that had integrated considerably: the parties were each the other's suppliers *and* customers; they relied on each other's judgment; and they were frank about each other's gains. Overall, they trusted each other. Yet, this was not a disposition that Americans found congenial and, over several years and in countless letters, the two groups whittled down a more acceptable arrangement, one where customers prevailed. The exporters would allow credit of up to two years and the choice of bills upon London, Lisbon, Philadelphia, or New York. In return, the customers acquiesced in matters of product and cargo, waiving final say over the makeup of the cargo and the taste of the wine. "In order to maintain long-term cooperation, repeated sequential communications, decisions and negotiations" over credit were staged, and significant concessions were granted to Madeira's overseas contacts.[53]

SENDING OUT VISITORS TO AND ESTABLISHING
AGENTS IN CONSUMER MARKETS

By the late eighteenth century, most middling and large firms were intensify-ing whatever conversations they were having with customers by sending partners to America and Britain "to settle a correspondence." The practice had long oc-curred. Benjamin Bartlett, for one, stopped at New London in 1717, but did so mainly because it lay on his way home to England. Many others did likewise. Pur-posive, designed trade missions did not become commonplace until the second half of the century. Competition for buyers made them necessary. Dr. Richard Hill went expressly to America to "drive all before him" in the 1750s—to pro-cure wine orders from old and new customers and arrange for American con-signments—or, less politely, to trounce the competition. He first sallied forth in 1754, calling on friends where he landed, in Lower Marlborough, Maryland, in his hometown of Londontown, in Baltimore, and in Philadelphia, from which he departed. In all, he spent three months on his journey. His appetite whetted, he returned two years later. Hill landed at Norfolk, Virginia, and moved on to Williamsburg and then his native Ann Arundel County. Intending to return in two years, he left from Norfolk, but near shipwreck caused his vessel to turn back and forced on the exporter a more extensive foray lasting another year, during which he called on acquaintances and strangers in Virginia, Maryland, and New Jersey.[54]

The 1750s saw others rushing to do the same. In 1754, Gedley Clare Burges left his sometime partner Robert Jones in London and, with Jones's letters of recom-mendation in his brief, set out on an elaborate "visitation of the counties," taking in Liverpool, Dublin, Cork, Waterford, and Bristol. Early the next year, George Spence made a journey to Scotland to drum up orders. Spence's partner made it clear what his goal was to be: "Your principal study," Francis Newton hectored, "ought to be to procure orders and consignments." After Newton parted with Spence and aligned himself with Thomas Gordon, the latter traveled to Bristol and Liverpool "to procure a good deal of business" for the house in 1758. In America, Newton's brother Thomas, the third partner in their newly reconfig-ured firm, secured the support of New York general merchant John Provoost, and the two traveled throughout New York and New England, where, in addi-tion to prospects, they encountered the Madeiran John Searle and an agent of the Madeiran Andrew Donaldson, who were also working to procure "an open-ing to a larger correspondence." Charles Murray, sweeping through most cities between St. Augustine and Boston, drummed up business for Scot, Pringle & Cheap in 1765. Ten years later, he repeated the itinerary. The success of Murray's trips in particular raised such envy that, on the eve of the Revolution, at least four other firms were planning "a Tour through America & the West Indies," "with the sole purpose" of acquiring "some more friends in those quarters." All hoped such "tours" would "make . . . many good correspondents & obtain many orders for wine."[55]

As the size of the island export community grew after 1750 and competition heated up, export houses appointed agents in London, Philadelphia, and New York. Eventually, some settled partners in Britain and Anglo-America to monitor commercial developments and secure new correspondents. When Francis Newton arrived in Madeira in 1748 and allied himself with George Spence, he relied on his partner to handle affairs in London, which largely meant procuring orders for wine and financing the outbound cargo. After about a decade, Newton parted company with Spence and turned to an erstwhile London employer, Alexander Johnston, to handle his affairs on a part-time basis. This new arrangement persisted even after he allied with Thomas Gordon in 1758. Within three years, there were "so many partners residing in London" who were able to devote more time and procure more orders than Johnston, a representative with other, often conflicting interests, that Newton & Gordon began to worry. Like other firms of its size and ambition, it eventually sent a partner to reside in the metropolis. It was not enough to cover only London, however; American ports needed personal management as well. Newton & Gordon had already sent Thomas Newton to New York in 1758. When he died in 1766, it appointed John Provoost its agent; four years later, when Provoost's efforts began to flag, they appointed Waddell Cunningham.[56] Lamar, Hill & Bisset's Henry Hill, and Searle Brothers' James Searle likewise settled in Philadelphia (figures 5.2 and 5.3). Although "having partners on the spot" was not a feature of transatlantic trade early in the century, it became one after 1750. It was at the century's end the sine qua non of doing business "in the Madeira Way."[57]

In the aftermath of the American Revolutionary War, every house of any size or pretension had to have an agent in Britain and the States. Their proliferation seems to prove the opposite of Philip Curtin's sweeping claim that, as cross-cultural commerce grew and evolved, the need for agents subsided. What drove the push in Britain was the growth of a London-based India business for wine when, in the 1780s, the East India Company opened up the competition for supplying the subcontinental forts, troops, and civil servants. In principle, a distributor could have placed bids from afar, but most firms found it helpful to wine, dine, wheedle, and cajole the directors on the spot. By 1785, there were at least ten resident partners all clamoring for the lucrative supply contracts. "Every foreign establishment ought and must have a partner to reside in London."[58]

Figure 5.2. Henry Hill (1732–1798).
Source: John J. Smith, ed., *The Letters
of Dr. Richard Hill* (Philadelphia,
1854). Courtesy of The Library
Company of Philadelphia.

Figure 5.3. James Searle (1730–1797).
Source: Courtesy of The Historical Society
of Pennsylvania (HSP), Philadelphia, The
Stouffer Collection, vol. 10, fol. 66.

The push for agents in America came from a different quarter—demography and wealth. "The importance of the American trade"—a function of the remarkable growth in its population during the eighteenth century—made Madeirans think it "superior" to their trade with any other place. Accordingly, many firms appointed not just resident agents but also supracorrespondents or supra-agents. Before the war, it had been customary to have a correspondent in each of the major port towns; this person handled goods, procured orders, managed finances, received remittances, paid drafts, and dunned tardy debtors. After the war, as security seemed assured and population continued to expand, all firms who were heavily engaged in "the America way" appointed a single agent across all states to handle most of their American affairs. Newton & Gordon, for instance, first employed Jeffrey & Russell of Boston in 1791 and Robert Lenox of New York four years later to oversee all of its American affairs. Lenox, a twenty-five-year-old Scot, was the consummate intermediary. At the time of his appointment, the firm's need for consolidation had grown immense—not only were its customers more numerous and its exports more voluminous but American banking and insurance had developed to such an extent that one needed an American to realize and negotiate the rapidly proliferating commercial and financial possibilities. By 1802, although the firm still corresponded directly with a few large wholesalers, its "chief reliance" was on Lenox. It did "not allow any cargoes except what Mr. Lenox sends to be drawn for upon"; all the firm's transactions in America—indeed, any request "for any information concerning us"—went "more or less through that Gentleman's hands."[59]

CARING FOR ISLAND VISITORS

One final way that the Madeirans managed a network was to attend to any and all comers, whatever the likelihood of eventual custom. Given its geographical position, Madeira evolved into a natural way station for travel to Africa, the Americas, and India. Passengers stopping there had to stay somewhere if their ship lay at anchor for more than a few days. The flea- and rat-infested vessels, stinking of rancid food and human excrement, held little allure. Foreign travelers stayed with the exporters, most of whom were British and Protestant, the latter an advantage to Protestants passing through a Catholic land. Even at the beginning of the nineteenth century, there was "not a tolerable Inn, nor a decent lodging to be had in the town." One inn dignified with the name of "the British Hotel" was open, but it was in reality "little more than a miserable ale house." So the houses of Madeira distributors became hotels, and "the great hospitality" of the distributors made the want of comforts "less felt." But reception and entertainment were not entered into out of altruism; they looked upon it as work—as a way of procuring orders and consignments.[60]

Care of island visitors was not restricted to commercial men and their companions. Mere tourists came to be regarded as likely targets for sales. As we have seen, the island became an Atlantic attraction in its own right, not merely a staging post for overseas settlements. Scientists came to investigate the production of the wine, voyeurs the "Gothic" practices of Portuguese Catholics, and aesthetes and budding Romantics the drama of the landscape. In addition, as the Atlantic medical community popularized the benefits of Madeira's climate for the consumptive and of its wine for the gouty, invalids floated to the island in droves.

To all these visitors, the exporters opened their doors. There were some costs, of course. Long-term patients and convalescents might rent villas, but until they did so they stayed with exporters and, often, the sick were so far gone that removal to a rented villa was impossible and so they stayed with the merchants until they were buried at the merchants' charge. More willingly, merchants opened their homes "for the reception of the passengers stopping for refreshments . . . in their way to Asia or America." This was a considerable undertaking but a fruitful one. Providing a refuge gave merchants a link to individuals with new information and correspondence; it brought them in contact with people from different backgrounds and empires and with different social and economic networks; it facilitated the initiation of trust relationships. Cross-fertilization went both ways, of course. It exposed Atlantic sojourners to new ideas, too, and the distributors made sure that among them was the practice of drinking a wine that perhaps the consumers had not considered before and in a manner they might not have seen. By physically creating an environment of openness, distributors could more easily access new information sources and consumer contacts as diverse as the empires they inhabited. Many a future customer or correspondent began with a merchant providing a room or a meal to a visitor who arrived at his door with the flimsiest of introductions.[61]

The importance of forging customer contacts among noncommercial types so as to better bridge distinct groups and distant markets was immense, even if it is hard to calculate today. Not all merchants were as enterprising as James Murdoch, who gave printed cards to his guests telling them "to apply" on their return to London to Murdoch's agent, whom Murdoch had instructed "to be attentive & solicit" business and "find out" whether they had "any friends or connections that can be serviceable" in terms of generating orders for wine. Yet, taking care of onetime visitors and treating them—as well as established contacts—as potential customers was considered just another part of doing business, another way of creating social capital. All firms consciously extended their reach in such a way. Most merchants shared Murdoch's zeal and seized the chance to extend their network. It was not uncommon in a busy week for an exporter to feed two dozen at dinner and to offer a bed to half that number. Newton & Gordon and Leacock & Sons frequently hosted as many as twelve visitors at a time, even in slow months, and most guests were not established correspondents. That is not to say that hospitality imposed no bother. The extra expense and extraordinary diversion "which breaks in upon" a house and "its management of business" were privately grumbled at as intolerable. Yet the hospitality persisted through the nineteenth century, for the "behavior & attention" that a distributor lavished on "all Madeira visitors" enabled him, "by his acquaintance, to enlarge & benefit his mercantile connections."[62]

MARKETING TO WINE CUSTOMERS

Madeira exporters built, extended, and managed customer networks through extensive conversation. Their goals in using such talk were commercial: to sell Madeira wine to larger numbers of customers at rising prices. Consequently, much of the conversation can be described as "marketing," as the merchants set out to stimulate demand, adopting the techniques emerging in other sectors of the Atlantic consumer market and inventing a few of their own. They sensed via research emerging trends among drinkers. They shaped new products that satisfied drinkers' tastes and determined the most effective ways to seize their imaginations, whether through advertisement or outlet. Over the course of the eighteenth century, the talk proved fruitful, achieving its desired end: Madeira, as we have seen, became a sought-after luxury product commanding high prices. Exporters made Madeira the most expensive wine of the day, as customers used product and price to validate personal successes.[63]

The distributors stimulated demand by raising their prices and introducing new varietals and blends, as we have seen, and by devising new terms to accompany the grades, as we shall see. To the same end, they deployed more explicit marketing techniques. Naming the wine became an art few traders could resist. "From interested motives," exporters and their agents began "to give whimsical appellations" to the wine in the late eighteenth century, calling it after the ship that carried it, like the "U.S.S. *Constitution*," or the family or group that ordered it, like "The Supreme Court." While "a Madeira merchant stares & smiles" at the terms, knowing them "to mean nothing," such monikers and others, like "Pedro," "Brazil," or "Conventicle," imparted to customers the sense of a limited edition or exotic origin and persuaded them "that unusual excellence in the liquor accompanies those appellations."[64] Similarly, exporters also tried tying their wine to famous customers. Some merchants wooed buyers by boasting about famous military and political customers—a ploy that both amused and irked competitors. John Marsden Pintard bragged "much of shipping General Washington's wine," one partner in the Lamar, Hill, Bisset firm fumed, even though the Hill firm "used formerly to supply him . . . to his satisfaction." General Washington's or Lord Nelson's purchase and praise of a wine or the fact that a firm's wine had graced the table of a dinner for Alexander Hamilton or the Prince Regent was used to recommend a pipe of the same lot to future purchasers. Never without an agenda, John Howard March, who had learned from the best while a clerk in the Newton & Gordon house, constantly dangled before would-be buyers the names of his best customers, including President James Madison, Secretary of State Monroe, and Justice Bushrod Washington. It was, March presumed, an honor for Americans to have their wine drawn from the same vats.[65]

Madeira distributors also used material props to support their conversations about wine, marketing both the alcohol and a style of drinking to accompany it. They adopted and encouraged the use of elaborate paraphernalia to differentiate its grades and distinguish it from other wines. Corkscrews of increasingly intricate and fanciful designs, silver bottle and decanter "tickets" (wine labels) etched with the word *Madeira*, two sizes of crystal decanters also etched with the word, small crystal glasses suitable only for heavily fortified drinks like Madeira, and the like: the distributors introduced these into their own households and recommended them to visitors and correspondents as the indispensable trappings of a knowledgeable wine connoisseur. After the 1760s, island firms began ordering "low, round decanters for the table while at dinner" from English glasshouses and, to go with them, "low, heavy glasses for them to hold as little as possible." On occasion, tumblers might be used instead of stemmed glasses, but, they had to be fit "for seeing [the] wine." Making use of the proper glassware at their own tables, exporters introduced visitors to "the art and mystery of drinking Madeira" and then sold them the glassware that they carried in their Funchal retail shops so that wine novices could replicate the rituals when they returned home. They thus provided their contacts a basis for selecting and using accoutrements, conduct, and attitudes and for constructing references and comparisons.[66]

Along the same lines, the distributors later in the century turned to "prestige packaging." They constructed special pipes, painted customers' names on them, and decorated them with personalized insignia and crests. They took their cues from Ceded Islands' planters who needed pipes immune to the attack of the worm and who requested painted casks and iron hoops. Exporters acquiesced, happily charging them extra. In time, they realized that what was born of necessity was growing into "general fashion" and so promoted the decoration as if it had been their own idea. In the same vein, they cut purchasers' surnames into the staves and purchasers' initials into the bungs. In customizing the package this way, they enhanced its value: a pipe that "pleases the eye, has a neat and attentive appearance to the owners of the liquor, & is of a real service to the cask" was more easily marketed to consumers. To safeguard buyers' interest "against change or improper treatment" shipboard or wharfside, some firms even started stamping "a private mark" unique to each customer on the inside of the bung.[67]

Madeira distributors conversed with their customers over oceanic distances. They deployed a variety of narrative devices in their conversations: reports of events and data, analysis of the effects of the events and data on the direction of business and social life, appeals to third-party authorization and validation, offers of business relationships and, later, debates about their management, authoritative pronouncements on the product and how it should be used and enjoyed, cajoling and solicitous expressions of interest in correspondents, and flattery, to name just a few. The immediate goal was to sell wine; the longer-term goal was to establish relationships with people who would buy wine repeatedly and recommend it and the firm to others.

Customer networks emerged from these conversations. The structures were not phenomena of individual traders or customers, still less individual transactions, but properties of the relationships among the individuals: that is to say, the actions out of which the relationships rose were conversations. The economic and social trading system that resulted was genuinely a system of networks— of sets of relationships with many nodes. Distributors were connected to each other; customers were connected to each other; distributors were connected to consumers; and both groups were linked to other merchants, agents, correspondents, and customers around the Atlantic. This form of economic and social interaction dominated oceanic trade before 1815, in contrast to arm's-length trading or hierarchies of power relationships. Arm's-length trading always raises the issue of trust, which is why mercantile dealing flourishes in direct, eyeball-to-eyeball exchange societies where goods can be inspected and services validated. At the same time, hierarchical relationships require monitoring and feedback, which are information-intensive in their own way. Networks, at least Atlantic-scale networks such as those the Madeira trade engendered, succeeded where these other two forms did not because they conserved on information. This may seem unusual, because the foregoing has emphasized how participants spread information through networks. But while they did spread information and exchange services, the knowledge and action required of each actor was reduced, and most of the information an actor required was local to him.

More specifically, transatlantic trade emerged from customer networks that in turn emerged from continual, complicated, often confusing conversations about commodities—how they were made, improved, and packaged; how they were shipped; and how they were stored, displayed, and consumed. Conversations built and maintained the networks that bound people together between firms and across roisterous waters and imperial divides, transforming a collection of dispersed operatives into a commercial infrastructure that was larger than the sum of its parts. Conversations spread information, created understanding—sometimes misunderstanding—among parties, and gave common cause to widely dispersed agricultural producers, distributors, and consumers. The geography of Madeira's distribution suggests that commercially minded people were almost "encoded" to converse.

Madeira's exporters held conversations first with preexisting, personal relationships: kin, patron, and peer. When these ties ran out or failed them, they made up new personal relationships, for example, with dinner- and houseguests, even strangers, and conversed with them. Some connection was needed, if only a general one. If there was a sufficiently important business reason, they engineered a relationship with a stranger and gave it the appearance of the personal. The hint of personal connection told all relevant parties that the participants were abiding by the rules of the game.

What were the effects of conversations with strong and weak network members? In short, Madeira flowed. It flowed to nearly every place in the world where European powers were extending their reach: regional markets for consumption opened and thickened in the West Indies, North America, the East Indies, and northern Europe. Desired prizes were the large port cities of British America, the capital cities and forts of the Presidencies of India, Britain's largest cities and, to a lesser extent, Lisbon, the larger Brazilian ports, and Portuguese settlements in India and Southeast Asia. But they were not all. Worldwide destinations for the exporters' wine doubled between 1700 and 1815. In sum, the world received "more & more . . . the attention of a Madeira concern" as the Madeira exporter became more adept at conversing with it.[68]

6

MERCHANTS INTO CAPITALISTS

Madeira wine exporters changed their business practices substantially over the course of the period 1640–1815. At the beginning of the period, their principal tasks were buying low and selling high. Their associations were simple and their capital requirements modest. By 1800, successful men "organized" the trade. They refashioned the product, inventing a substantially new drink over the course of the long eighteenth century by developing new production technologies and participating in production. They built networks of buyers who, in turn, gave statuses and identities to the distributors, managed chains of product and conversation directed toward them, and insinuated themselves into their customers' personal lives and social projects. They moved from selling on the spot to captains (the norm in the seventeenth century) to filling the orders of correspondents and agents overseas, and then to sending partners to live and trade in consumer communities. They also managed supplier networks and used their geographical position to engage in a reverse trade from America to Madeira and a forward trade to southern Europe. The new business practices required more capital than simple trading did, and by the end of the period successful distributors were capitalized at three or four times the levels of early in the time frame. While the capital levels of Madeira firms never approached those of the British monopoly companies such as the Bank of England and the East India Company, nor even of the great London or Lisbon mercantile houses, they were massive compared to the commitments required by the family-based trading that preceded them.

Did this make them capitalists? "Capitalist" denotes an enterpriser who amassed his own and other people's capital and used it to produce more capital, taking economic risks in the process. Capitalists, in this sense, took initiative to organize suppliers, competitors, and customers to create an economic environ-ment that would produce more returns to the capital. They were not passive or sleeping investors; rather, they were the entrepreneurs who used the sleeping investors' funds. This emphasis on the managerial and organizational aspects ad-heres to a Weberian conception of capitalists as carriers of rationality, in contrast to a Marxist conception that emphasizes the relationship of capital and capital-ists to labor.[1]

The argument made here about the changes in merchants' work does not ad-dress the issue of the origins of capitalism. In fact, it presupposes that some forms of capitalism existed by 1640 and asks how merchant groups got recruited or co-opted into them. Thus, the principal concern here is with the contagion of *contagion* capitalism—about which historians know little—rather than its origins. Most *of* historians seem to agree with Marx and other theorists that the sources of the *capitalism!* transition from feudalism to capitalism lay in increases in rural productivity. This consensus unduly privileges the production side of the story. When the entire commodity system is examined, from production through distribution to con-sumption, markets emerge out of marketplaces, capitalists evolve from traders, manufacturers grow from artisans and growers, and consumer culture emerges from agrarian culture—and they do so together, in continual interaction.

ORGANIZING THE TRADE

Because letters to and from customers dominate extant records, those conver-sations are the best-known aspects of distributors' work. But the same organiz-ing, improving mentality was at work in less frequently discussed aspects of their business. They organized networks of suppliers using conversational techniques similar to those they used with customers. They increased their oversight and management of the condition of the wine after it left their hands. They height-ened their control over shipping and imports into the island by taking interests in ships and cargoes. By the early nineteenth century, a Madeira wine trader man-aged suppliers, shippers, customers, and products over multiple years and vast distances. In executing these three important tasks, they, lastly, became more systematic, standardized, and "professional" in their enterprise.

SUPPLY NETWORKS

A distributor needed goods, both exports to sell and imports to resell. Madeira distributors carefully constructed supply networks toward these ends. Their supply networks fell into a class of asymmetric or centralized social networks "characterized by the presence of a central agent," in this case, the distributor himself. The networks coordinated "vertical or transactional interdependencies between firms" and entrepreneurs, usually linking them by oral or epistolary agreement, although occasionally by legal contract. Few of their network relationships were full-fledged joint ventures; their agreements generally specified only "the terms of goods and service exchange and not the organization of the relationship between the firms" or individuals. Yet these networks were able to internalize important externalities: they provided "a flexible organizational solution for joint specialization," offered "some protection for property rights of intangible assets," and lessened "the capital accumulation constraint on the division of labor and growth." Moreover, the exporters managed these networks using many of the same personal, voluntary, and nonhierarchical techniques they used with customers. In particular, they came to rely upon conversations as the preferred mechanisms of network management, and upon fewer, more regular, longer-term supply relationships, rather than a multitude of ad hoc ones.[2]

Wine distributors, we have already seen, imported manufacturing and packaging ingredients into Madeira, and this required ongoing relations with merchants in the Baltic countries, northern England and Scotland, the Channel Islands, western France, mainland Portugal, southern Spain, and North America. Wood for barrel staves, hoops, and bungs; iron for barrel hoops; gesso for fining down the must; and brandy for fortifying the wine: to have wine available for export, a merchant in Madeira needed to procure all these inputs simultaneously.[3] Wine distributors also imported "distribution goods" to balance wine exports. Such goods outfitted the islanders and oiled their barter economy; thus indispensable, their procurement had to be carefully handled. They imported cloth and dry goods from England and Europe, for example. But flawed or spoiled cloth and clothing could cost more than the wine that they were exchanged for. When they could, merchants relied on relatives and employees they trusted to buy and pack the goods, but even when trustworthy agents controlled their movement and the goods came safe to hand, there was no guarantee they were suitable: English-speaking distributors experienced chronic difficulty intuiting which textures, colors, and patterns the Portuguese on the island and mainland and in the Brazils would find attractive.[4]

The largest distribution item imported into Madeira was food for basic needs. Madeira harvested only a minor crop of wheat each year in the best of times, and Porto Santo and the Azores, where harvests were larger, did not produce enough to satisfy Madeira's growing demand. The same was true of fish: local stocks never sufficed. One rather imperious Englishman, invoking the principle of comparative advantage (without seeming to notice), pointed out that "were the Natives to apply themselves with common industry," "the demand would be much smaller"—but they "had little interest in doing" so. At the same time, importing foodstuffs served wine consumers well by providing them an outlet for their own New England fish, mid-Atlantic grain, and South Carolina rice. The reverse trade also provided Madeira merchants with currency. American customers who took wine of greater value than the foodstuffs they exported paid the balance in cash. "It was only by importing food" that the distributors could "command [the] cash" they needed for their "immense payments" to the growers and the government. Well into the nineteenth century, "the importation of food" was the only reliable means they had of supplying themselves "with money to pay for . . . wines." Those exporters who did "not import grain or flour" were "often disappointed for want of conveyances" to wine-consuming markets.[5]

Importing food into Madeira required careful, constant management in three areas. Successful distributors paid close attention to their sources: of fish in Newfoundland, New England, and the North Sea; of wheat in the New England, mid-Atlantic, and Chesapeake regions of North America; and of rice in South Carolina and Georgia. At the same time, they monitored demand in multiple reexport destinations in southern Europe, Africa, and South America. Further, when they could, they exerted control over quality, timing, and price in order to best lure the customers, whether they were on or off the island. It was possible to procure a supply on an ad hoc basis, but, as with their relationships with overseas buyers of wine, Madeira exporters increasingly found it in their best interests to ally with one or a few suppliers as their businesses grew. Fuller engagement with the provisioning of the island and southern Europe and tighter control over the process of procurement both attracted "handsome freight" to their houses and earned them "handsome profit."[6]

Supply networks at work are best revealed in Madeirans' procurement of fish. Dried and salted cod from colonial New England had been a barter item in the wine trade ever since Portuguese, English, and Anglo-American ships began plying the waters between New England and southern Europe in the 1640s.[7] The principal import into Madeira from North America was cod, usually salted cod, for much of the ensuing 120 years, and firms strove to maintain a sufficiency, although they did so in a one-off, highly idiosyncratic fashion. Smaller catches of fish in the late 1750s and early 1760s, occasioned by both natural causes and the depredations of the Seven Years' War, increased competition, however, and led many of Madeira's firms to establish more formal supply alliances. Such drove the formation of the agreements that Newton & Gordon struck with Jeremiah Lee, Robert Hooper, and John Rowe of Massachusetts for cod and with Scot & Co. of Sweden for herring.[8]

The inclusion of herring and Sweden suggests that firms began thinking constantly about alternatives, obsessed as they were with interruptions to traditional channels. Prior to the Seven Years' War, the island's relatively small herring supply had rested "entirely in the hands of the Glasgow merchants," who got their fish from the Baltic, and "hardly any" other herring "came from any other port." But during that conflict, as their American correspondents faltered or were prevented from supplying them with cod, Newton & Gordon and other firms looked to other ports for North Sea herring, which was larger and cheaper (Glaswegian herring being small and expensive). Gordon Brothers, Newton & Gordon's competitors, began devising schemes to flood Madeira's market with fish from Scotland, Norway, and especially Sweden. In one lucrative venture of 1760, Gordon Brothers joined Scot, Pringle & Cheap to bring a shipload of red herring from Bergen to Madeira. The vessel then bore what remained unsold, together with wine, to the Canaries and South Carolina and consigned it to an agent in Charleston; on return, it carried rice to Lisbon. When war or the depletion of fish stocks frustrated these newer schemes, as they invariably did, distributors settled for smaller, rounder, and cheaper southern European pilchards. The type of fish mattered as much as the source. Exporters, who knew their customers, generally favored cod or herring—not pilchard: firms with American origins favored cod; those more rooted in Britain did what the Gordons did and favored herring. But ultimately practical constraints and considerations shaped selection. As cod ran short in the 1770s and the larger, cheaper herring did not keep well, they resigned themselves to pilchard. Between the Seven Years' War and the American Revolution, exporters with North American origins dominated cod imports into Madeira, while those of British allegiance controlled herring imports; with independence, the American exporters' control of cod importation lapsed, annual exports to Madeira falling to one-sixth of what they had been at the end of the Seven Years' War. This left the British exporters "with no other rival" in the herring and cod market.[9]

Thus, the Madeira firms diversified, adding other products to their core raison d'être of shipping wine to the Atlantic world. Although business diversification is a modern concept, and usually used in the context of industrial enterprise, it is apposite here. A firm could "continue to administer both . . . old and new activities with the same personnel, using the same channels of communication and authority and the same types of information." Sales in various products—wine, fish, and wheat, for instance—were in that sense complementary. In addition, they were complementary with respect to the networks of customers they had built, at least in the Americas: Madeira exporters sold the crops of the Americans who bought their wine. Dr. Richard Hill's constant complaint in his first year on the island was not that he lacked buyers for his wine, but that he was miserable "for want of wheat, bread, or flour" to sell on Madeira. "I have not a single friend to consign to me," he wailed. Product diversification and geographical expansion "added new resources, new activities, and an increasing number of entrepreneurial and operational actions and decisions" to the work of men like Hill.[10]

QUALITY CONTROL

At the same time they were developing and managing supply networks, Madeira's distributors were increasingly attentive to the quality of their wine all along the distribution chain. From the mid-seventeenth century, exporters personally tasted and tested the wines before placing them on board ships, discarding bad wines when necessary. They visited the vineyards, usually late in the year, taking with them a native Portuguese "taster" employed both for his skill in language and his palate. Usually a particular taster was tied to a particular house. "Most merchants trust[ed] to their Tasters, Portuguese, who" were "the best judges of" the wine and best able to train the merchants in a "knowledge of wines."[11]

Madeira's distributors also began instructing their agents to taste and test the wine upon its arrival overseas toward the close of the Seven Years' War. The first recorded injunction toward this end was issued in 1763 when Robert Bisset advised Henry Hill, who had just returned to Philadelphia as the firm's resident partner and agent there: "If you should [travel] . . . near any of these gentlemen's [customers'] houses, I wish you could taste the wine and advise me how they prove, for I can assure you they were not entirely to my liking, having an *aspereza* [roughness or harshness], [and] smallness." After 1775, personal oversight near the point of consumption became commonplace. Indeed, it bore to the heart of a firm's ability to compete. When John Leacock Sr. lectured his son on how to handle their firm's London business, he was simply expanding upon what Bisset had urged nearly three decades before: pay "particular attention" to the quality of the wines arriving in the market, so that the firm could "succeed in giving general satisfaction." An agent was to "strain every nerve" and gain "a knowledge of the kind of wines which are imported into London." Doing this ensured firm quality but also snooped on the competitors. It would not be going too far, Leacock supposed, "to attend on the quays when the West India ships arrive, both to hear the character of the wines shipt" and, "if possible, to taste them yourself" and thereby gain "the fullest information respecting their quality," for that "may be the means" of the firm's "improvement in what" it ships. If its wine was wanting, or the consumer "obstinate & tenacious" in insisting it so, most firms agreed they should reclaim it. It would not do to have unsound wine with one's brand affixed to it flowing around consumer markets.[12]

The attention to quality at an increasing number of distribution and consumption points occurred as Madeira distributors began changing the makeup of the beverage—fortifying it with brandy, rocking it in barrels, heating it, and remaking its packages. Their focus on product quality was as conversation-based as the outreach to customers and suppliers that reinvented the product. They conducted these conversations not only with their partners and agents but also with their neighbors. Exporters were intensely interested in what their competitors were doing. They picked up a lot informally, in the course of idle chitchat, spontaneous visits to one another's countinghouses and homes, meetings of the merchant community, and social events at Bachelors Hall. Given how small Funchal was and how much exporters' correspondences overlapped, it was difficult to keep secrets for very long; with respect to product innovation, few firms even tried. The Leacocks regularly monitored the progress of the larger Newton & Gordon firm, for instance, "to see how they proceed" before they made major decisions. Similarly, they knew when the Murdochs were beginning to heat their *estufa*, and what Phelps was doing with his. Exchanges of information about technology and quality required limited, often tacit grants of cooperation, contribution, and sometimes long-term commitment among firms. In turn, they fostered future exchanges and established deeper levels of trust.

For quality control to pay off, Madeira distributors also had to educate their customers in the art of connoisseurship. "Quality" was wasted if customers could not discern it. Consumer education became crucial as blended and heated wines came on the market in greater volumes in the 1790s, and their arrival drove extensive conversations on the nature of the wine: its color, odor, taste, and strength. During that decade, firms expressed heightened concern about whether a "palate . . . accustomed to drink *genuine* and *unsophisticated* wine" would be able to detect bad vintages and wines wrongly "improved" by mixtures. Accordingly, they took steps to articulate to buyers in detail how to tell the good from the bad, defining "quality" together with their customers.[13]

GREATER ENGAGEMENT WITH SHIPPING

Madeira distributors principally acted as agents through the end of the Seven Years' War—filling orders and accepting consignments from customers and allowing the owners and captains of vessels to assume the risk and control the property in transit. A principle of prudence from the onset of an overseas wine trade guided most firms: to "adventure deeply . . . very rarely" for their own account, "whether sending out wines or taking in provisions." Merchants began to depart from such caution and participate more fully in shipping and trading in the 1760s. In short, they became active principals, taking shares in both ships and cargoes. Many of the shares they entered into jointly, each merchant or firm taking ownership of up to one-third of a ship or a cargo. Joint ventures ensured them provisions and orders and divided costs and risks. Furthermore, they encouraged a measure of cooperation among distributors, property-based incentives being necessary "where uncertainty and opportunism are particularly prevalent," as they were in the mid-eighteenth-century wine trade.[14]

Several exporters had resolved as early as 1749 "to buy a small vessel to send to North America," seeing the "scheme" as "the only method in the world" to force consignments—that is, "to push business [gain orders] from America," which by that time comprised "half of this trade." By owning a few vessels, Lamar, Hill, Bisset & Co. early on "made a great advantage of their grain," which "turned out to better advantage than if consigned" the normal way. Joint ownership of vessels was more common, as when the Gordon Brothers agreed to keep a 140-ton vessel constantly sailing among Madeira, St. Kitts, and Virginia by owning it in thirds with a Leewards Island trader and a Norfolk merchant.[15]

During the Seven Years' War, as wine firms began to compete more vigorously for Anglo-American consumers, investing in cargoes grew in popularity. Firms took shares of American goods on their own accounts, "authorizing the shippers to draw for their reimbursement" "upon London at the usual sight"; they paid for the freight of the goods with bills of exchange on the delivery of the cargoes; wines were shipped "by the return of the vessel." In 1757, even Richard Hill's firm began taking shares in cargoes, in its case goods imported from Philadelphia, making "a great hand of their grain and turn[ing it] to better advantage than if [it was] consigned to them by Americans." Its competitors grumbled, but quickly followed suit. After the close of the war, intent on copying the Hill model, the Madeiran John Searle and the Philadelphian Thomas Riche took halves in grain cargoes from Philadelphia; likewise, Newton & Gordon ordered and bore all risk for "a small quantity" of Massachusetts fish. Such ventures, exporters reasoned, would bring them not only supplies of fish or grain but also buyers of wine: the shippers who came to the island to deliver cargos would carry wine from their partners' houses back to America. Owning vessels and cargoes came to be seen as the best method for controlling trade, and so the "entire plan for American correspondences" was rewritten. As they always had, the firms continued accepting consignments of staple articles like fish, wheat, or rice and "made return" in wine. But more commonly they now brought goods to themselves, adventuring "in cargos of American commodities" on their own account and, with increasing vigor, they acquired shares in vessels to take their wine to customers. This was always "according to circumstances," of course, for the expense of owning vessels and freighting space and the probability of loss were still high.[16]

Assuming a principal's risk was a major change for the distributors of Madeira's wine, further enmeshing their operations with those across the ocean. Even more than receiving each other's goods on consignment for resale, taking ownership of commodities required trust. It has always been useful, the economist Kenneth Arrow once noted, "for individuals to have some trust in each other's word." Absent trust, "it would become very costly to arrange for alternative sanctions and guarantees and many opportunities for mutually beneficial cooperation would have to be forgone." In the expanding world of the Madeira exporters, the "parallel creation of trust between the firms" or enterprisers in question was effected by interpersonal affiliation, expressions of shared values and norms (usually articulated through transoceanic communication), and histories of consensus and repeated performance over extended periods along supplier and customer networks.[17]

Trust developed in this manner made it possible to turn simple, seemingly unimportant communications and interactions into enduring patterns of association. Trust was important, yet, the Madeirans' motto was more "Trust but verify" than simply "Trust." They monitored and regulated their principal ventures with a scrutiny they did not apply to consignment operations. At an obvious level, at the venture's outset, they required an up-front, personal financial commitment from overseas partners in joint ventures (on purchase of vessels and outfitting materials, or on acquisition of goods properly packaged). They demanded from fellow adventurers more frequent updates on all aspects of a voyage and adventure, asking for more letters and more information than was customary. They required, as well, more frequent and better accounting. Finally, they expected a more meticulous insuring of their own cargoes and ships than was the norm with others who consigned goods to them. With trust and control intertwined, joint ventures became common.[18]

PROFESSIONAL APPROACH

The increased scale and complexity of transatlantic trade in the eighteenth century required an increasingly coordinated, "professional" approach to business. Between 1750 and 1815, firms midsized or larger acquired customers on at least four continents, and so the need for coordination was great. One discerns the trend toward professionalization most clearly among the foreigners. They specifically ordered account books as needed from London, often in batches. The books they bought were basic before the middle of the eighteenth century and sometimes even later, if a merchant was launching himself. A few years into his first partnership, in 1753, Francis Newton ordered "a Journal & Ledger, the same as last, & a Cash Book pretty broad," besides post paper and wax. But by the time Newton & Gordon added a partner two decades later, it ordered a full run of books directly from London stationers. The list gives some indication of the requirements of a growing, successful firm:

1 ledger, containing 7 quires [a quire commonly forming 16 pages], of fine, super-royal paper, bound in vellum, covered with buckram and lettered;
1 alphabet to the ledger;
1 journal, similarly constructed;
2 books, each containing 3 ¼ quires, each of fine royal paper, bound in vellum, covered in buckram and lettered;
1 book, marked "Invoices, Bills, & C."
1 book, marked "Cash Book";
1 book, marked "Bill Invoice Book";
1 book, marked "Wine Entry";
1 book, marked "Borrador & C., for payments and disbursements to the men who carried wine from the countryside in goat skins;
1 book, marked "Island Accounts";
1 book, of demi-paper, marked "Copy of Letters";
1 book, marked "Merchandise Expenses";
6 books for memorandums, unruled, with marble covers;
6 alphabets; and
3 titles for books.

The labels of books were marked in English and Portuguese, depending on the activity being recorded. Certain books were dedicated to the accounts of island suppliers, island customers, and house expenses, others to overseas correspondents, suppliers, customers, and ventures. More extensive and varied office supplies were to be sent as well, including six pasteboards, two reams of quarto letter paper, two reams of fine foolscap, a half ream of blotting paper, twelve papers of ink powder, a bottle of red ink, a tin pen, six pencils, a ruling brass, two sand boxes, four ivory-handled penknives, two pairs of scissors, two ivory folders, and a dozen pieces of red tape.[19]

As account books and office supplies multiplied in countinghouses, so standards of accounting improved. Before 1750, accounts were balanced infrequently, it appears—at the death of a partner, the termination of a partnership, or the whim of a resident partner—say, once every seven years. No standard prevailed—annual balancing was not part of the exporters' lexicon. But by the end of the century, as the exporters purchased and read (and required that their clerks also read) a handful of how-to manuals published by a variety of British and Anglo-American experts—which told them that "the merchant should be perfectly acquainted with all the departments of writing, arithmetic, and the keeping of books"—annual inventory taking and account balancing became routine for firms of any size or with overseas partners. The exporters made up annual accounts every June 30. They routinely copied portions of the accounts and forwarded them to nonresident partners. Typical was one enclosure that John Leacock in Madeira sent to his son William in London in 1796. It contained an inventory, a balance sheet, a list of bad debts, accounts for the several partners, a statement of profit and loss, "wine accounts," and the London partner's account for countinghouse and related expenses incurred overseas (such as membership at several coffeehouses allowing admission to the firm's partners and clerks, India House and other public office fees and gratuities, and postage). What was to be reported on was also increasingly hammered out with vigor by the partners, and items relating to accounting became some of the most important detailed in articles of copartnership. Newton & Gordon, restructuring itself in 1814, specified that each year, on June 30, "an inventory of all goods, and effects on hand shall be taken, and a general balance of the books and accounts made, as soon after that period as the same can be accomplished." Copies were to be transmitted to the London partner and "to lie in his counting house for the information of himself and of the other partners." The partners set the accounting principles for valuing inventory "to prevent trouble, and guard against possible differences in opinion, concerning the valuation of effects and property." "All wines, brandies, casks, and materials for making casks shall be valued at first cost & charges, as nearly as the same can be ascertained," for instance. "All property in houses and buildings" was "to be taken at the original cost, except some circumstances should have occurred to enhance or depreciated the value, in which case as much be left to the discretion of the persons on the spot." Finally, all "debt known and ascertained to be lost beyond doubt should be expunged from the account to prevent the copartners being deceived as to the amount of their gains, from the business, or of their capital in the house." It was not just annual accounts that needed to be submitted in a neat and orderly fashion. Exporters demanded and sent weekly and monthly letters updating overseas partners. By 1815, many firms were starting to do what one American house was hoping to do—have the partners adhere to a "plan of numbering" correspondence, "so that all . . . letters shall be regularly noticed." Numbered letters may seem small matters to more business-complicated generations, but to men in the early modern wine trade, "particularity in numbering and forwarding letters" regularized the flow of information and reduced the costs of giving the dispersed partners duplicated information.[20]

Keeping records and regularizing methods of managing correspondence and accounts were more widespread by 1815, not only among the foreigners but also among the Portuguese. It is hard to be precise, because not all firms' records survive and most of those that have are those of foreigners. Before 1750, foreigners continually complained that even substantial native firms or traders kept poor records, if they kept them at all. When William Halloran joined Manoel da Campos in the 1730s, he found the latter's accounts a mess. "What little business" da Campos had "was ill attended," his partner "trusting entirely to a Portuguese clerk & serv.ts whom he never was at the trouble to call to an accot, nor did he ever look into the house's affairs, having at that time a pretty good estate of his own to live upon." "All the books," Halloran described, "were a confused blotter or a sort of waste book in the Portuguese language & an Invoice book with some accots of Dr & Cr in English." What Halloran then introduced—the full range of double-entry books, ledgers, journals, and complementary sets and forms, all "in order to . . . proceed in a more regular manner than they had done"—stood in stark contrast.[21] While one might want to discount such diatribes as xenophobic and imperialist rant, Portuguese wine exporters' records suggest there was some truth to the accusation, certainly to the charge that they did not adhere to more complex European standards of the day. The Portuguese were certainly familiar with commercial forms—they commonly used bills of exchange for international trade, for instance—but they were less consistent in recording them for comparison later on. Many Portuguese wine exporters kept no records; but, then, their annual wine exports were so relatively small that rigorous accounting may have hardly seemed warranted. Other natives kept some books, but these were decidedly simple when compared to northern Europeans' books. Jesus Maria José of Funchal, we know, kept a book of current accounts, but in it he only listed the item sold, the unit rate, and its total value; there are no cross-references to other books and no identifications of account holders.[22]

Early in the history of the Madeira wine trade, the Portuguese approached record keeping differently. Not until the marquês de Pombal established the Aula de Commercio in 1769 (a commercial school whose first teachers were, tellingly, not Portuguese but Genoese and Swiss) and specified what a merchant needed to know in order to be worthy of his "noble" calling did Portuguese practice improve across the board. Pombal's initiative raised the esteem of the profession. His use of the word *noble* is noteworthy, for hitherto commerce had not enjoyed a favorable social status, its members often confused with members of "mechanical" professions and, given the number of *conversos* in the merchant community, with untrue Christianity. As a result, merchants had abandoned the trade when they could, regarding it as a temporary way station on the road to landed respectability. Due in part to Pombal's initiatives, many large Portuguese firms, at least on the mainland, adopted British-style record keeping in the second half of the eighteenth century. Turn-of-the-century records left by Tome José Pereira Araújo and Domingos Oliveira are every bit as full and regular as those of Newton & Gordon, although there still remained a fair amount of variation in Portuguese houses.[23]

In addition to accounting methods and record books, participants in the Madeira wine trade adopted common standards. The pipe was one standard that cut across national lines. Island firms came to insist on 110-gallon containers for all but the India market. This standard probably hardened because 110 gallons was also the volume of the British Caribbean sugar and rum container, and West Indian sugar planters, important buyers of wine, could reuse the casks and thereby reduce the cost of the wine to them. Similarly, mid-Atlantic Anglo-American wheat and corn exporters could reuse wine pipes for grain cargoes. Common standards also attached themselves to business methods. Exporters increasingly demanded that partners and clerks speak, read, and write Portuguese. As well, they came to pay their correspondents commissions and their agents salaries with greater frequency, whereas agents had previously seldom received regular compensation, apart from expenses. Most intriguingly, the larger, more successful export houses began insisting that agents and clerks adhere to the same prices for wine, terms of barter, and standards for product quality.[24]

CAPITAL

Organizing the wine trade was expensive, and became more so over the course of the eighteenth century. It is not much of an exaggeration to say that, in the early days of Madeira's industry, if a young exporter had contacts that would direct their orders for drink toward him, he could make a go of the business. By the turn of the nineteenth century, exporters maintained networks of producers whom they supported with advice and credit; manufacturing and storage facilities to transform the product; and extensive customer outreach apparatuses. These things took capital and, over time, larger amounts of it—for equipment, supplies, space, and credit to producers and customers. As the anonymous author of *The Book of Trades* noted in detailing the work of the merchant in 1807: "To carry on the business," a man should possess "a large stock of general knowledge, and a considerable capital."[25] In so building their transatlantic wine businesses, the exporters became "capitalists." The Madeira wine merchants increased the capital in their businesses, taking additional partners and expanding their firms if they deemed that necessary.

The amount of equity paid in by partners or patrons rose dramatically after the middle decades of the eighteenth century. Detailed records of capital requirements are rare for Madeira houses, as for firms in any trade of the age. But a dozen or so accounts have survived in business archives, and they allow us to chart the increase in the demands upon partners for both start-up and operating capital. The experience of the operations run by Michael Nowlan, John Leacock, Francis Newton, and Thomas Gordon show the trend.[26] In 1756, Michael Nowlan and another Irishman, Gedley Clare Burges, entered into partnership; to initiate their trade, they and two sleeping mainland partners pooled 12:000$000 (£3,250 sterling). Nowlan & Burges lasted for six years, after which Nowlan decided to go it alone. When in 1774 he joined forces with John Leacock, they deemed 17:000$000 (£4,604) sufficient to carry on work nearly identical in scale to that of Nowlan & Burges. In 1791, four years after Nowlan died, Leacock reset the stocks of the firm and took his two sons into the business. They opened with a capital of 26:250$000 (£7,100). Even this was not enough to meet the mounting demands of the trade, however, for, five years later, they increased the amount to 36:000$000 (£9,800). In less than forty years, the capital requirements for a midsized wine-trading firm had tripled.[27]

The stocks of Newton & Gordon best represent the requirements for a larger operation. In founding the firm in 1758, Francis Newton contributed half the capital, Thomas Gordon one-third, and Thomas Newton one-sixth, but it is unclear exactly what the total was. From allusions in correspondence, it appears it probably lay between £3,000 and £6,000 sterling. In the mid-1760s, on the death of Thomas Newton, the remaining two partners "augmented" firm capital "considerably," probably raising it to £20,000. Two years later, when William Johnston joined them, the books show £17,469 (64:500$000) of capital, although the demands of increasing inventory caused them to raise their investment the following year to £23,833 (88:000$000). According to Gordon, "the average capital employed" at the time of balancing in 1778 and 1782 amounted to £29,792 (110:000$000) and of this just over half "existed on the island." After the war, the firm reconsidered its capital needs because one of the London partners wanted to take some of his money out of the firm. The partners discussed reducing capital to as little as £15,000. In the end, they concluded that that would "be scarcely sufficient" for a firm desiring to regain lost ground; at least £20,000 was needed so that "every advantageous object may be pursued," with the excess distributed to the partners. After Johnston departed and Thomas Murdoch IV replaced him in

1794, the partners rewrote their articles, increasing the capitalization to £21,000. On this occasion, the partners projected growth poorly, for the amount was not sufficient to maintain inventories and make increasingly large shipments of aged wine to America. Accordingly, four years later, they doubled it to £40,000. By 1805, after old Gordon died and a new five-man partnership was formed, stock was set at £64,000; three years later, even that was found insufficient, and so it was reset at £90,000, where it remained for the duration of the Napoleonic Wars. Thus, in the first fifty years of Newton & Gordon's history, the stock of a typical large firm rose nearly twentyfold. On Madeira, as elsewhere, an extensive, increasingly Atlantic and global trade "required an extensive capital."[28]

INVENTORY

Much of the increase in capital supported increases in inventory. Three firms' total inventories between 1753 and 1815—those of Newton & Gordon, Lamar Hill, Bisset & Co. and Leacock & Co.—detail the buildup, the run of these firms' inventories being greater than of most firms. Although it varied from firm to firm, inventory accounting generally included wine (including brandy) and "charges on wine" (gesso and brimstone for fining, preparation implements—funnels, cranes, pinchers, and corkscrew—wooden and glass containers); merchandise (like dry goods, fish, wheat, and rice) and "charges on merchandise" (wooden casks and cloth bags, machines for cleaning wheat, and weights, beams, and scales); office utensils (such as books, papers, and writing supplies); house furniture; house expenses; and cash. (In Newton & Gordon's case, it also included the amortized values of leased and owned property, but this was unusual.) Inventory fluctuated quite a bit from year to year and even decade to decade, depending on weather, harvest, vintage, war, and consumer demand, but the trend toward larger inventories is evident in two of the three companies.[29]

Newton & Gordon, especially, grew dramatically in the last half of the century. The only record of inventory we have of Newton's early partnership with Spence is a list of combined stocks at the end of 1753: 8:081$790, or £2,189 sterling. After Newton split with Spence and allied himself with Gordon, recording became more frequent and regular. There exist seven inventories from the first eight years of their partnership. The itemizations were subject to wide swings, but their average was just shy of 9:000$000, or £2,435. The average of 1790 and 1791 was 58:600$000, almost £15,900, a nearly sixfold increase; if the increase had been steady over the thirty years, it would have been nearly 7 percent per year. The greatest rise, however, occurred over the next decade (1796–1805), as firms adopted the more expensive *estufa* heating process. In the ten accountings between 1805 and 1815, total inventory averaged 297:815$238, or £80,658, a fivefold increase over the 1790s. Although not as dramatically, the comparatively small two- and three-partner Leacock firms saw comparable increase: from an average 14:631$000 (£3,963) in the early years of the American Revolutionary War, total inventory rose to 25:593$872 (£6,932) in the middle years of the French Revolutionary conflict (1796) and more than doubled to 59:836$000 (£16,205) in the early years of the Napoleonic conflict (1800–1803). Between 1805 and 1815 they nearly doubled once more, to 100:000$000, or £27,000.

As with Newton & Gordon, the era of *estufa* heating unleashed a dramatic rise. But differences existed in the Madeira firms' buildup of inventory. The mid-sized American firm Lamar, Hill, Bisset & Co.'s inventories did grow but did not increase as clearly. The extant records are sparser than for the Newton firms and the Leacock firms; Lamar, Hill, Bisset seems to have accounted for its business only every five or six years between 1762 and 1792, and then ten years later in 1802. The records show considerable variability in inventory levels. However, the two lowest inventory levels occurred before the outbreak of the American Revolution—in 1762 they were 29:238$093 (less than £8,000 sterling) and in 1772 they were 22:754$921 (just over £6,000). Between 1782 and 1802, inventories bounced around between 33:000$000 and 50:000$000 (£9,000 and £14,000) without a trend. The stagnation in the firm's business is reflected in these inventories. After 1761, the firm's principals lived in Philadelphia and London and were mainly concerned with providing a living for relatives overseas. Unlike Newton & Gordon and the Leacocks, the firm did not retain earnings and plow them back into the operation in the last four decades of the century but paid them out to the founding partner's heirs.

Much of the growth in inventory came from investments in the finished product, wine. Before the 1750s, smaller commercial draws, technologically primitive production, and limited storage facilities created little incentive to store wine. Large wine inventories became commonplace only in the 1770s, when abundant vintages and the reduction in demand from Anglo-America because of the war left Madeira merchants with an excess of product. Firms responded creatively to the "crises" of the 1770s by keeping old wine and aging it themselves, where earlier they had left storing and aging to customers, and they used these changes to solidify the idea of Madeira as a luxury drink. The most detailed picture of the buildup appears in Newton & Gordon's records: between 1769 and 1775, wine stocks averaged 12:210$196 (£3,307 sterling); by 1805–15, they had risen tenfold to 142:335$104 (£38,549). The Leacocks' wine account had grown over fifteen-fold between 1790 (4:264$034, or £1,155) and 1815 (64:640$742, or £17,507). For Lamar, Hill, Bisset & Co., the increase was more gradual. Wine stocks rose by two-thirds to 26:054$890 (£7,057) in 1777, up from 17:242$250 (£4,670) in 1767.

In 1792, the firm valued its wine account at 29:968$595 (£8,117); by 1802, after the firm began storing heated wine, stocks had risen to 38:143$350 (£10,330).

Inventories show other increases in the cost of doing business in addition to the cost of building and maintaining wine stocks. As firms moved into the retailing of imported goods, they leased Funchal shops and stocked them with dry goods and foodstuffs; these show up in the records. More notably, as Madeira's wine was "invented" after 1750, the expenses incurred in producing the improved product mounted. Wine traders required additives like brandy, stoves, engines, pumps, additional pipes of all shapes and sizes, tools (funnels, gallon pots, bung and tap borers, pincers, and bung screws), supplies, and especially buildings and warehouses for heating, aging, and storing the wine. The equipment was recorded on the books, and consumables (brandy and other supplies) were capitalized, in the accounting language of the day, as "charges on wine." They grew significantly, especially after the onset of *estufa* heating in the 1790s. Lamar, Hill, Bisset & Co.'s 1802 inventory reveals 586$006 added to the already considerable 32:000$000 laid out in wine to accommodate the copper boiler, the share of a pump it owned jointly with another firm, the coal for heating the boiler, and tile and pine gantries—all required by *estufa* heating. "Wine Expenses"—not just "Wine"—came to be a regular item in any inventory after the American Revolutionary War. Whereas before that conflict they constituted only 6 percent of inventory, by the 1805–15 period they had risen nearly 100-fold in value and as a share of inventory to 18 percent. As one exporter mused in 1787, "a large stock of old wines requires much capital and is attended with much expense, but it is extremely desirable & . . . absolutely necessary."[30]

PARTNERSHIPS

What happened to the exporters themselves, caught up as they were in these institutional changes? Over the 150 years in which an Atlantic and then global distribution system developed, the work required to participate in the Madeira wine trade increased dramatically. Firms had to manage supply sources and customer relations more intensely. Trading activities encompassed not only the sale of wine to more and farther-flung parts of the globe but also procuring equipment and other inputs into Madeira production as well as reverse trade goods for sale in Madeira or reexport to southern Europe. Manufacturing processes had to be organized and overseen, quality control monitored, and accounts drawn. These activities required more capital and more hands. Accordingly, firms grew in size over the period: trading concerns managed by lone proprietors and single families gave way to larger firms managed by partners who more often than not were unrelated.

In the second half of the seventeenth century and the beginning of the eighteenth century, firms usually consisted of two merchants closely related — brothers, a father and son, or an uncle and nephew. Such was the case with the two Miles brothers, the three Scot brothers, and James Pope and his nephew John Barrett. Occasionally, two or three unrelated albeit well-acquainted merchants pooled their talents and resources and shared risks, as did Obadiah Allen and Richard Pickford in the 1670s and 1680s, Richard Miles and Richard Richbell in the 1700s, and William Bolton Sr., Marmaduke Darrell, and John Morgan in the 1700s and 1710s, but they were exceptions. Relations between nonrelatives were less close. When, in the 1670s, Allen & Pickford joined with William Freeman of Nevis and London, they did so as correspondents, not partners. Similarly, when the later, somewhat larger Bolton, Darrell & Morgan joined with Robert Heysham of London and his brother William Heysham of Barbados, they did so as agents, not partners, and when the governor of Madeira and wine exporter Duarte Sodré Pereira allied with Aaron Lamego of Jamaica in the 1710s, he did so as a correspondent.[31] By the first quarter of the eighteenth century, the English-speaking export community — forty-three strong — had only four or five partnerships and firms — Bolton, Darrell & Morgan (which evolved into Bolton & Darrell on Morgan's demise), Lynch & Lynch, Miles & Richbell (which evolved into Miles & Miles at Richbell's death), plus James Gordon's brief alliance with Manoel Da Costa Campos and, when that broke up, Campos's partnership with William Halloran. All other British traders appear to have operated as sole proprietors, as did the Portuguese merchants, excepting of course Campos.[32]

As the eighteenth century unfolded, Madeira distributors acquired a greater number of partners, many of whom were nonrelatives and nonresidents. The importance of family, kin, friendship, and ethnicity notwithstanding, the exporters around 1750 brought in many nonresident sleeping partners to command greater financial resources or metropolitan expertise; such was the reason Michael Nowlan combined with Gedley Clare Burges in Madeira, James Archbold and Domingos Francisco Guimaraes in Oporto, and Robert Jones in London. A common type of agreement was the one that Robert Ayres struck in 1761: he kept a third share, gave another third to working partner Edmund Smith of Madeira, and divided the remaining third between Samuel Smyth of London and James Sedgeley of Bristol, sleeping partners who provided capital and acted as agents in England. By 1768, at least ten English-speaking firms, with fifty partners among them, traded out of Funchal.[33]

By 1815, at least eighteen British and American firms had establishments there. What this number means is that sole proprietorships had ceased to play any major role in the island's export sector. Not one of the top ten exporters in 1807 worked alone. The nineteenth-century wine firms that dominated commonly had from four to five and sometimes six active partners—at least one who resided in London and, for the American firms, another who lived in the States. Blood ties still bound firms together, but, with greater frequency, relative strangers with much-needed capital and connection were brought into the business. Over the course of the preceding century, the average size of foreigners' firms had doubled, and firm makeup had diversified.[34]

The Portuguese, in contrast, avoided partnerships. Pantaleão Fernandes Sr. and nine other natives joined firms: Pantaleão Fernandes & Francisco de Ornelas de Brito, Nicolau Soares & João Telles, Lucas Teixeira & João de Vasconcelos, Francisco Theodor & Benito Perreira, and Manuel Pacheco & Manuel Rocha. (Fernandes at various times formed short-term alliances with James Gordon, Richard Hill, and Robert and John Scot, and Pacheco also partnered with Robert Scot.) But these men constituted at most 5 percent of the island's Portuguese traders. Why this was so is unclear, for there were no legal or institutional constraints on the Portuguese becoming partners; indeed, Portuguese law was, if anything, more encouraging and accommodating of partnership than the English common law or the emerging commercial law of Anglo-America. Under Portuguese law, the liability of partners depended on the nature of the contract, which could and often did stipulate limited liability, something that was not yet a fixture of English law.[35] While a boon in some respects, this allowance also reflects the strong Portuguese perception that their opportunities in the Madeira trade were not as great as those of English speakers, and so not worth the effort of building firms. Few Portuguese ever went into a partnership, even at the end of the Napoleonic Wars, when the natives were making a comeback among the island's exporters.

A COMMUNITY OF TRADERS

The merchants responsible for shipping Madeira around the world collaborated with each other on the island even as they competed. This should not surprise: traders of similar products often work together, especially when they are concentrated geographically or socially, as were the islanders. Sometimes the collaboration in Madeira was overt, sometimes subtle, sometimes even covert. Merchants shared most when matters of general welfare were affected, especially if allied against outsiders. They shared least when getting or keeping customers was at stake; indeed, they were downright proprietary about customers. Some subjects, like loans, lay in a gray middle area.[36]

Collaboration did not eradicate competition. Firms were always suspicious of one another, especially where customers were concerned. Certainly, there was "nothing but jealousy of one another's correspondents" when Francis Newton arrived in 1748. Everybody was "trying all he can to get another's, that they scarcely speak to one another"; when they did, it was mainly "criticizing or telling stories." Newton's observation could just as easily have been noticed by Branco in 1650 and March in 1815. Yet, collaboration continually checked or recast the competition, for it was an enabling device for trade. The exporters on Madeira routinely rented warehouse space in their town lodges to other export merchants and provided stabling and provisions for their animals. When extraordinary commercial demands fell upon neighbors, they funneled one another alum for fining, *aguardente* for fortifying, bags for storing grain and flour and, on occasion, wine for filling orders. They sold peers staves, hoops, and pipes when supplies ran low, and they loaned coopers to assemble or rework the pipes. The demand for wine was so large and the scarcity of casks so great in 1764, for instance, that many firms were "obliged to borrow" both; three years later, a similar state of affairs returned, and again borrowing and lending came to the assistance of those in need.[37]

Exporters and firms also provided one another with cash or credit when individual coffers ran low. Thomas Cheap offered to "stand forth as far as" he could so that Thomas Gordon's "credit suffer not" in the disorienting commercial turmoil produced by the Ayr bank crisis of 1772–73. Gordon's credit had been seriously questioned, for his patron and most prominent London correspondent—Alexander Johnston—was under an even greater cloud of suspicion and heavily scrutinized by governmental authorities. (Scot, Pringle & Cheap's reputation, too, was threatened, for it also did business with Johnston.) If such questioning continued, Cheap offered to underwrite Gordon more fully. The following year, Lamar, Hill, Bisset & Co. agreed to lend Johnston £2,000; at one point, the partners appeared to pull back, offering only half that amount and imposing unusually strict conditions (demanding that Gordon provide a letter of credit), but they recanted and claimed a miscommunication. The loan went through as originally planned. As both their positions make clear, this was not altruism: merchants charged interest on the loans; moreover, they borrowed from others on the assumption that in the future they would "spare some to [the lender] if required." The process was recursive. When Yuille, Wardrop & Co. asked Gordon, Duff & Co. in 1790 to provide some assistance, Yuille reminded Gordon that Yuille had helped Gordon four years before, and lent it brandy the previous year. Island exporters knew each other's business situations better than anyone else and so were in the best possible position to decide to whom lend money and on what terms.

Of course, they did not always lend, and, when not, they sometimes wrote letters detailing how imprudent the would-be borrower was, which in effect translated as an indictment of asking for money when unlikely to repay.[38]

The distributors also worked together in short-term joint supply adventures, as when a number of them in the 1760s coordinated their imports of Swedish herring, an arrangement that made the fish cheaper for all. During this decade, every recorded midsized house sent ventures to the North Sea for herring. Success required beating most—but not all—of the competition back to the island to meet the demand for fish during Lent and the long dry summer. In the 1760s, Robert Bisset and William Murdoch banded together to send a ship to Gothenburg and to return with herring early to the island, where they also "agreed to be of one price." Similarly, in the 1770s, a handful of merchants who acquired too much rice devised a scheme for raising market prices of Philadelphia flour, since high flour prices were, they thought, "the only thing that can prevent a great loss" on their rice; they predicted their rice would sell high, "as there is not a grain of corn at market."[39]

The most extreme form of cooperation involved the sharing of suppliers. This, of course, is what Bisset and Murdoch did, although in their case the Gothenburg supplier required it. In any case, if there were few sources, a distributor could not monopolize them. But sharing generally exceeded necessity, and exporters often offered their sources freely to others. As late as 1816, Scot, Loughnan, Penfold & Co. gave a letter of introduction to John Howard March, who was just settling on the island, to its brandy supplier in Bordeaux. No less extreme, firms shared agents, as when Lamar, Hill, Bisset & Co. asked its Philadelphia partner to perform some work for Newton & Gordon in the city and its hinterland—in his case, "to ask, demand, sue for and settle" accounts.[40]

Initially, cooperation moved along ethnic lines. Through the middle decades of the eighteenth century, Englishmen turned to Englishmen, Scots to Scots, French to French, Americans to Americans. Subsequent collaboration replicated these patterns. Scot, Pringle & Cheap and the Gordon Brothers consistently answered the call of British Newton & Gordon for pipe materials and vice versa, while Thomas Loughnan and William Phelps had a continuing supply relationship with Leacock & Sons, which regularly loaned them ten-year-old brandy. Likewise, Americans—the Hills, the Searles, Pintard, and March—tended to help each other with greater regularity than they did non-American enterprisers. But as the decades passed and the trading community grew in size, new ties were formed. Those from all parts of the English-speaking British Empire turned to one another for help; common language became a more powerful bond than shared ethnicity. The island was too small to hide when one denied help to another. More important, the economic and legal position of the expatriates was too besieged by the "native" officials to ignore requests for help from other "strangers."

In the small and somewhat claustrophobic environment that was Funchal, some foreigners eventually cooperated with the largest and most secure Portuguese merchants—and vice versa. Early in the eighteenth century, Richard Miles borrowed from the Portuguese distributor Duarte Sodré Pereira when Miles ran short; at the same time, Benjamin Bartlett shipped wine and brandy as a favor for Pereira. Still, one combs records in vain for many such instances of straddling the native/stranger divide. Later in the century, the level of interaction was much the same, even if there were fewer reservations about foreign merchants working with established Portuguese traders. Pantaleão Fernandes led the way in the early decades of the century with several alliances with Britons. Thomas Blackburn and the Pennsylvanian William Jenkins (a clerk in the Hill firm) "became connected" at some point in the 1770s with Joaquim José Sanches and his brother Luis Vicente Sanches and carried on "a long commercial intercourse of many years" as their partners; when, in 1784, their work demanded metropolitan representation, Blackburn left "a considerable part of his capital in their hands (which they were to reimburse him by stated installments)" and moved to London, agreeing to act as their agent "at a stipulated allowance." There was, therefore, some Portuguese/non-Portuguese cooperation, but it was rare, and it remained so through 1815.[41]

OFFICIATING RELATIONS AMONG FIRMS: THE CONSUL AND THE FACTORY

Two quasi-governmental organizations on Madeira—the Consulate and the Factory—institutionalized cooperation among islanders and, whenever possible, eased the more dire effects of interaction and competition. These establishments grew alongside an overseas trade for Madeira's wine. Although England had some form of commercial representation in Portugal as early as 1578, the institution of consulship was not legitimized by treaty until 1642. Resident in Lisbon and supervising England's trade with that city, the first English consul general in Portugal was also responsible for the trade of the outports and islands. A vice-consul for Madeira first appeared in 1666, when an established Funchal exporter, John Carter, was appointed. In the final third of the seventeenth century, Madeira's resident English merchants elected the vice-consul; by the second quarter of the ensuing century, the consul general in Lisbon appointed him, upon the advice of Madeira's residents and the approval of Britain's monarch. As the number of the British on Madeira grew, the value of their exports rose, and effective competition emerged in Lisbon, Porto, and the Azores, the residents gradually concluded they needed their own independent representative. But only in 1754 did White-hall acquiesce, granting the Madeirans the right to their own representative and the privilege of electing the vice-consul.[42] Other countries also maintained consulates in Madeira alongside the British. By the first decade of the nineteenth century, Russia, Sweden, Denmark, Holland, France, the Holy Roman Empire, Naples, Italy, and the United States had all stationed commercial representatives there. Yet these officials never sat atop an association of merchants as vigorous and efficient as the "Factory" formed by the British and never moved beyond commercial agency to price-fixing and social organization.[43]

A factory was an association of traders that promoted the business of English-speaking merchants at work in foreign countries.[44] From its formation in the first decade of the eighteenth century to its dissolution in 1812, the Factory functioned as a means for safeguarding the shipping and trading interests of its members and similarly situated British and American traders who visited the island by promoting cooperation with island officials, and thereby easing the flow of wine, and by resolving conflicts that arose both among the resident exporters and between the English-speaking residents and visitors and the Portuguese government. It protested abrogations of commercial and social privileges, acted as an advocate for members' complaints against governmental policies, and arbitrated business disputes among the British. It managed relations with the island government to ensure a relatively smooth functioning of the island entrepôt. It maintained a "National Duty Fund" from a tax euphemistically called the "Contribution" that it levied on the captains of British ships exporting wine, sugar, and citron. With the fund's revenue, it annually "augmented" the salaries of the governor, *procurador, provedor,* and *escrivao* of accounts and retained the services of a *conservador.* Gifts, salaries, and presents deducted, the bulk of the fund was then divided among the community. Many of the objects of its largesse were commercial in orientation: the fund rented a house for the consul, kept a shed near the Customs House for the use of members, and maintained a road from the shed to the landing place.[45]

Over time, the Factory added price-fixing to its trade-management functions. This manipulation of the market, not usually associated with the rise of the market but nonetheless one of the inherent capacities of emergent capitalism, stood as the ultimate expression of merchant collaboration. From at least 1753, Factory members met together at the end or beginning of every year—preferably December 31 or January 1, but sometimes not until the middle of January—to set shipping prices for the wine that had been harvested the preceding September and October. The size and quality of the previous vintage weighed most heavily in their decision making, although expectations of demand, information about gluts in some markets, prices charged by the growers, and the presence or progress of war in the Atlantic also influenced their deliberations. The Factory affirmed prevailing prices or set new ones for the seven or eight different qualities of the wine, with Malvasia at the high end and Cargo at the low. These prices were generally adhered to during the Factory's heyday, not only by members but also by nonmember foreigners and even many Portuguese exporters. When a foreign merchant did circumvent established prices—through, say, discounts on an invoice—this breach was met with vigorous discussion followed by stern reprimand and commercial sanction from his fellows. Members refused to extend the offender credit, loan him staves, or supply him with wine or brandy when his supplies ran low. The community was too small, the needs of its members too intertwined, and the dominance of the large British firms too great, it was generally felt, for a merchant to go it alone and charge what he would.[46]

The Factory also served several key social functions bridging foreign and native cultures, and these grew more prominent over the course of the eighteenth century, as the population of resident Britons and Americans and their domination of the economy increased. One of these functions was to provide a bulwark against the inroads of the Catholic Inquisition. As early as 1722, the Factory intervened when an overzealous Franciscan and his novice baptized ten unwary Englishmen traveling to Gambia to work in the slave trade and then incarcerated them in the Misericordia Hospital under the guise of protecting them from "wicked heretics" and "the Infidel Moors" in Africa. On the Factory's insistent lobbying, the traders were released. Years later, in 1761, the Factory requested permission to build a cemetery for Protestant burial and on succeeding erected and maintained "The Nation's Burying Ground" on land rented from the nuns of Santa Clara on the outskirts of town. Throughout its long history, the Factory paid for the services of itinerant Protestant ministers and showered them with gifts, and in the early 1800s began agitating for "a proper place of worship."[47]

More to the thrust of commerce, the Factory took care of English-speaking traders and sailors who were stranded in the course of their voyaging, as well as of British subjects who became sick or infirm while staying on the island. By 1774, it had established a hospital, stocked it with medicine, and installed a doctor. It supported merchants who had gone senile, paying room, board, and medical expenses, in addition to providing pensions to other resident Britons rendered incapable. Widows and orphans of Factory members received pensions, as did members who had gone bankrupt and their survivors. Lastly, the Factory assumed responsibility for rescues in the aftermath of shipwrecks, and it auctioned salvaged goods. When foreign vessels foundered in the harbor or near the island, it provided meals, lodgings and, if the need arose, burial.

The cooperative factory system worked well through the middle decades of the eighteenth century, when the size of the foreign community was still small. Factory prices were not set high enough to tempt established merchants into deviating from them, given the economic and social sanctions the Factory could bring to bear. But they were high enough that new entrants interpreted them flexibly. One area in which one finds some "creativity" is in Factory members' handling of growers' prices. Previous to the 1760s, always unofficially, most members had adhered to the same range of prices offered to the producers and had respected the long-standing agreements between exporters and growers. Nonetheless, as on-island competition among distributors heightened, small British and American firms not represented in the Factory began offering growers higher prices for their must in the 1760s, even before the state of the vintage was known. Frequently, these firms paid cash for wine, rather than tendering the customary bills of exchange or bartered dry goods, and they allowed eighteen months of credit, rather than the customary nine. These "small fry" acquired large stores of new wine in their lodges in this way and used them to undercut Factory prices in overseas markets, like those of the West and East Indies, that had a tolerance or taste for inferior wines. As the century drew to a close, nonmembers gained in assertiveness.

The voluntary collaborative institution that had operated more or less as a cartel and whose members controlled the bulk of island exports began to fall apart after the American Revolution. Technically, it lost only its North American–born members, who now owed allegiance to the United States, but the exodus reduced the Factory's revenues, authority, and influence. Others members began to see themselves as free to opt in or out, pay dues, and follow norms as they chose. At the same time, Portuguese merchants began reasserting themselves, setting up their own partners in London and adopting British-style competitive behavior. Domingos Oliveira, for example, garnered a share of the India trade—not just the Portuguese East India Company's business but also the English Company's custom, and he dominated the exports to Brazil that revived after 1796. At some point, it became no longer worth even the British merchants' while to belong to the Factory or to acquiesce in its pricing schemes. Factory minutes note that its deliberations over pricing became exceptionally bitter after 1790. One resolution of late December 1791, in particular, created a furor, for to many it seemed "to have been carried by combination, secrecy & surprise." Increasingly, members of the Factory were "actuated in their resolves by their own private commercial occurrences in business" and, "whenever that is the case, the original compact & design of a Factory is dissolved and every house must govern themselves according to their own opinion & interest."[48]

Serious disagreement among members came to a boil in 1806, when the Anglo-Irish firm of Colson, Smith & Robertson refused to pay the "Contribution" tax. The house alleged that "such mode of levying the duty" was contrary to the 1722 act of Parliament ordering the work of factories, arguing that the tax preceded the law and that the law dictated other ways of raising the duty; the Factory countered that, since the act was designed to organize the trade of the mainland, it could continue a duty upon exports that had prevailed before the act. Only the "friendly" intervention of General Beresford, acting governor during Britain's occupation of the island, "convinced" the firm to contribute "voluntarily" their 670$700 in 1808. In contrast to the 1791 dispute, this imbroglio confirmed the irreversible impotence of the Factory as an institution, laying bare as it did the limits to cooperation and collaboration. "Daily dwindling from its ancient respectability & consequence," it experienced the episode as a preliminary death shudder. Internal relations continued to sour, notwithstanding the face-saving voluntary contribution of 1808, and the Factory dissolved itself in 1812.[49]

The Madeira wine distributors accumulated savings from past labors, their own and others,' and invested them in the trade. They took risks, with the expectation of reaping profits. They engaged in trade that was "roundabout," in the sense that the end-of-century manufactured product required labor and other inputs to heating, agitating, and fortifying, plus those required to barrel and ship. But the change that really stands out is how they managed their business as their investment grew. They organized suppliers and employees. They elaborated consumer networks to reach out to customers who were no longer individuals, but themselves distributors. Their relations with customers and suppliers were developed and cemented by multiple layers of interest and connected to infrastructures of partners and agents around the world. They organized their own community, too, to provide mutual aid and to restrict undue competition. Their principal sources of profit moved away from simple trading forms to the more complex, integrated, and controlled management of supplier, shipping, and customer relationships around the world.

It is hard to identify a moment when the Madeira traders "started" being capitalists. When they were introduced, few of their business innovations were perceived as dramatic departures from business as usual.[50] Most of them were adaptations of well-known habits and practices. New arrivals on the island brought ideas and observations from the metropolises; they were modified and integrated or dismissed as unhelpful. Furthermore, the change was not universal; as late as 1806, the young Richard Brush made his way from Boston to Funchal to set up a long-distance trade with his countrymen in the simple way his grandfather had done a century earlier. But the change was inexorable; there was too much to be gained by regularity and consistency, by ongoing relationships with suppliers and customers, by the carefully maintained networks. Brush failed and returned to Boston. By the end of the eighteenth century, their organizing, together with taking the risks and receiving the profits, marks the Madeira exporters as capitalists and makes their work notable in the construction of a transimperial Atlantic economy.

STRONG NETWORKS OF WEAK TIES:
IMPORTING AND WHOLESALING WINE
IN EARLY AMERICA

Taking the waters at a fashionable New York spa in 1816, the Savannah wine trader Robert Mackay wrote to his wife, Eliza, in amazement: "What will this immense Country come to in the End, when at this early day, all the Luxuries of the World appear to have become necessary to the people for their common comforts?"[1] Importer and purveyor of Madeira, Port, and Claret, Mackay was one to comment, for men like him provided the luxuries—a lot of them.

In the seventeenth century, European wines were commonplace in Atlantic diets—maybe not a staple, yet not a rarity, either. Some were expensive, in time coming to be regarded as luxuries, others almost as cheap as beer. Most drinkers bought wine from tavern keepers. Some bought it from retailers or wholesalers, who imported directly from overseas suppliers, as did those who were wealthy enough. Supply chains were short and fairly simple; there were few intermediaries between wine exporters and consumers. By the nineteenth century, European wine was regarded as a necessity. Europeans and Americans—as the European-descended population of the colonies and former colonies now referred to themselves—had been aggressively settling the interior regions of North and South America for over a century, carrying wine and the custom of drinking it with them. Drinkers' links to wine distributors were now longer and more indirect. Wine importing was dominated in the major American cities by dedicated importers and wholesalers, "merchants," who had become the principal suppliers of wine and spirits to storekeepers and tavern proprietors; some of them had begun to specialize in particular product lines. Although a few wealthy people continued to import directly from Europe—it was seen as a marker of status—for the most part even retailers had foregone direct importing in favor of buying from importers.

In parallel with the development of opportunistic, capitalistic exporters in Madeira who built sophisticated intercontinental networks for their businesses, a group of importers and wholesalers with similar characteristics arose on the American side of the Atlantic to be their counterparts. Approaches to business diffused around the Atlantic world like the goods being traded. The American importers and wholesalers increased their connective capacities by building networks of customers, suppliers, and competitors on the basis of "weak" connections. The Americans, however, had the advantage that they could usually meet their customers in person. Because of this they constructed specialized spaces for displaying their wares and meeting and courting customers. This chapter teases out who the American importer-wholesalers were in British America and the early United States and how they did their business; the next discusses their principal customers: the tavern keepers and retailers who distributed wine to the drinkers of urban and inland America.[2]

"ALL THE PEOPLE" THERE "ARE TRADERS"

In calling someone a "merchant," contemporaries usually meant to distinguish him from a "retailer."[3] Over the seventeenth and eighteenth centuries, merchants' economic and social roles developed in every substantial English-speaking port; the word came to refer to those who imported European, African, and Asian goods into America, exported American goods to Europe, and undertook ancillary finance, storage, and wholesaling tasks.[4] Yet, with respect to any individual, the distinction was not always as clear to contemporaries as it has been to historians, since many individuals held a number of occupations. To seventeenth-century observers, "all the people" in America "are traders."[5] Even by the middle of the eighteenth century, "merchant" was still a portmanteau occupation. The greater, more extensive "interests and material accomplishments" of the "few eminent merchants" (some called them "greater merchants") of places like New York distinguished them from "other colonists whose lives were shaped by city commerce" ("lesser merchants"). Yet, both groups occupied themselves with imports and exports, and both groups often sold directly to consumers.[6] In a city like Philadelphia, they constituted "a large occupational group embracing both wealthy traders and many petty capitalists who lived no more sumptuously than a successful cooper or grocer."[7]

The merchants in Anglo-America were men. In New York, for instance, women "were never officially designated merchants, granted a freemanship as such," nor have any records of a female importer or wholesaler been discovered, although women were shopkeepers and artisans. Merchants were, by and large, "new" men, newcomers with unimpressive backgrounds. Entry to the group was easy, compared to entry into British and European merchant communities. Ease of entry was facilitated by the fact that business was precarious: failure through loss or bankruptcy was common, and the sons of successful merchants were often lured into landownership as a more socially desirable activity. These men congregated with other merchants at the heart of the city; they clustered their houses and places of business next to one another. New York importers in 1700 lived and worked along the East River, for the most part, where they enjoyed easy access to the city's main wharves; nearly a century later, they were either still there or had moved a few blocks to Queen, Dock, and Smith streets and Hanover Square. They were also comparatively wealthy: "merchant" was the wealthiest occupation on the 1789 New York tax lists, with £1,870 current in assessed wealth per person on average, compared to storekeepers (the thirteenth wealthiest, with £645) and tavern keepers (the twenty-ninth wealthiest, with £240).[8]

The cohort of merchants who imported and wholesaled wine at any particular time was small. In the last third of the seventeenth century, only a handful of Boston firms and individuals, like John Hull and Thomas Jefferies, actively traded wine. They engaged in a direct, bilateral commerce, exchanging area fish and wood for wine, usually from the Canaries and the Azores, although occasionally from Madeira.[9] Even in the early years of the eighteenth century, only ten Bostonians advertised importing or wholesaling wine. They sold by the pipe, barrel, or quarter-cask—or more vaguely by the "parcel." Only the vendue master and one other trader distributed "per gallon" or bottle. In addition, twenty-nine sea captains imported wine into Boston and probably engaged in wholesaling, too. Their voyages usually traced a circuit, either Boston, Europe, and the Wine Islands or Boston, the Wine Islands, and the Caribbean, and returned via another North American port.[10] Their interest in wine was opportunistic; they were generally more interested in higher-value commodities. Jacob Leisler of New York was fairly typical in his trading activities and the range of his interests. Leisler imported wine, whale oil, tobacco, slaves, salt, and pantiles. On at least one occasion, he sent one of his own vessels to the Azores, but this was rare, for he preferred to import wine on other men's ships. He was also a tapster and imported wine for his tavern alongside the wine he brought in for wholesalers and other retailers. Accounts for his mother-in-law Marritje Jans, Reinier Willemse, John Tatham, and a company of militiamen under his command reveal him selling large quantities of Madeira, Malmsey, Canary, and Fayal at the time of his "rebellion" in 1689–91.[11]

For parts of the eighteenth century, port records for New York and Boston survive that allow a more detailed look at the wine-importing communities. They show a few individuals importing the bulk of the wine and a great many others small quantities, presumably for their own use or that of their families. The New York Customs House ledgers from 1703 to 1709 record fifty-two arrivals of forty ships containing 1,935 pipes of dutiable wine consigned to ninety men; 95 percent of the wine was Madeira or "wine" noted as coming from Madeira. Three men—Stephen DeLancey, Abraham De Peyster, and Thomas Wenham—paid duty on 58 percent of the wine. Each of them imported more than 220 pipes; the fourth largest importer paid duty on only 94 pipes. Ten importers paid duty on 25 pipes or more; together, they handled just over three-quarters of the wine. Most merchants were small, occasional traders of wine. Of the ninety men who paid duty on wine, sixty-seven did so in only one year, and thirty-nine did so on two pipes or fewer over the seven-year period. The merchants among them traded dry goods, wines, spirits, and furs. Englishmen dominated. While over a quarter of the ninety bore Dutch surnames, only DeLancey and De Peyster stood among the top ten importers.[12] While they are not exactly comparable, New York's Naval Office Shipping Lists for 1715–22 show a larger number of traders responding to a growing market. Some 4,600 pipes were imported, and 130 traders owned shares in wine cargoes, anything from a sole (with the trader importing or receiving the lot), the most popular, to a seventh (sharing it with six others). Stephen DeLancey remained the largest importer; Abraham De Peyster was fourth largest. But many more traders were serious importers; by this time the top ten traders imported less than half the total. DeLancey's share was less than 14 percent.[13]

Naval Office Shipping Lists have also survived for Boston and Salem for 1714–19. While the import records are sketchy, their companion export registers are more complete and show the major Anglo-American ports beginning to support a reexport trade in wine. In 1716–19, just over half of the wine imported into Boston and Salem was reexported to colonies from Nova Scotia to Surinam. The average reexport lot was only about three pipes, considerably smaller than the typical import shipment. The market structure of reexporting was similar to that of importing: a few traders seem to have reexported regularly or in largish volumes, alongside a substantial fringe who exported once or twice in small quantities. In these five and a half years, 160 sea captains took 560 pipes away from Boston and Salem. The four largest reexporting captains left with 29 percent of the total; thirty-six "important" reexporters together took 73 percent. Of the twenty masters recorded as importing wine into the colony's two main ports, five also appear among the exporters, including Richard James, the largest recorded exporter.[14]

By midcentury, wine trading had become a much bigger business. The group of wine traders had grown dramatically, and so had the volumes imported and reexported. Many of the New York manifest books from 1743 to 1760 have survived, as have the Naval Office Shipping Lists for Boston and Salem from 1752 to 1765. In these years, 653 individuals or partnerships imported 8,400 pipes of wine into New York; 17 of them were women. Some 110 merchants accepted consignments of 5,400 pipes of wine imported into Boston and Salem; none was a woman (figure 7.1). The quantity of wine imported into Anglo-America seems to have fallen substantially in the early 1750s, but a spurt in trading occurred halfway through the Seven Years' War and continued into the next decade. Interestingly, in these years (1757–63), reexports considerably outpaced imports (figure 7.2). It is unlikely that the traders had enough wine in storage for this to represent a drawing-down of inventories. In 1759, for example, exports were 700 pipes greater than imports. It is more likely that they had procured wine illegally, a supposition that supports the Crown's contention late in the war that smuggling was out of control. If the degree of smuggling was great, this means our evidence for the volumes of wine traded is only partial; true imports of wine into Anglo-America must have been substantially greater.[15]

The structure of wine importing and wholesaling communities did not change as dramatically as the size. Importing continued to be dominated by a small number of principal traders, with a much larger number of secondary and tertiary participants (table 7.1). The largest importers, recorded as importing a hundred pipes or more, brought in more than one-third of New York's wine and more than a half of Massachusetts'. On the other hand, the substantial fringe of importers — more than half of all importers in New York's case — who brought in fewer than two pipes each accounted for only 4.4 percent of imports. For purposes of analysis, one can isolate a group of "important" importers in each colony: those who imported eighty pipes or more over the period plus the most frequent importers. In New York, fifty-six "important" men brought in just under two-thirds of the wine; in Massachusetts, thirty "important" men brought in just over two-thirds.[16]

Only a few merchants might have been recognized as carrying on a trade in wine, focusing on it more than on other items, inasmuch as they persistently imported and reexported over a number of years. Eleven Massachusetts traders were among both the major wine importers and the major wine reexporters. By far the most important was Richard Derby. He was the largest importer and the largest reexporter as well as the most frequent, importing in eight of the thirteen years and exporting in ten of them. Most traders were small, however. Of the 110 merchants recorded as importing, only 19 imported in more than one year. Exporting was considerably less concentrated than importing. There were almost

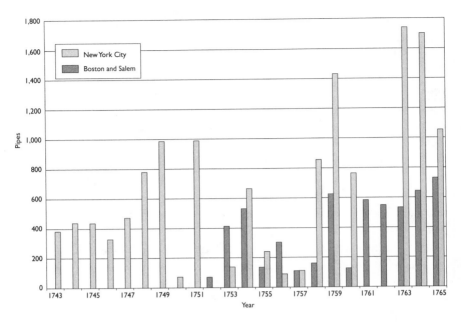

Figure 7.1. Massachusetts (Boston and Salem) and New York City wine imports, 1743–1765. New York's Manifest Books show imports into the city for forty-seven quarters over the period from the second quarter of 1743 through 1751 and the third quarter of 1754 through the third quarter of 1760. Many of the manifests have been burned or damaged by fire and severe discoloration. When in doubt, a quantity of one pipe was assigned the importation. There were eighty-seven importations on twenty-nine vessels for which the name of the person paying the duty was unclear. The most seriously ravaged records were those from 1757 to 1759. The Massachusetts NOSL are extant for forty-seven quarters for Boston and forty-five quarters for Salem over the thirteen-year period from the last quarter of 1752 through the third quarter of 1765.

To make data comparable from year to year, data have been interpolated in the quarters where there are gaps; the interpolation is a product: (average percentage of imports for that quarter) × (volume of imports for that year).

Sources: New York Naval Office Shipping Lists, 1743, 1748, 1751, 1753–55, 1763–65, CO 5/1226–1228, Massachusetts Naval Office Shipping Lists, 1752–65, CO 5/849–851, National Archives of the United Kingdom, Kew, Richmond, Surrey, England; New York Manifest Books of Entries, 1743–51, 1754–60, New York State Library, Albany.

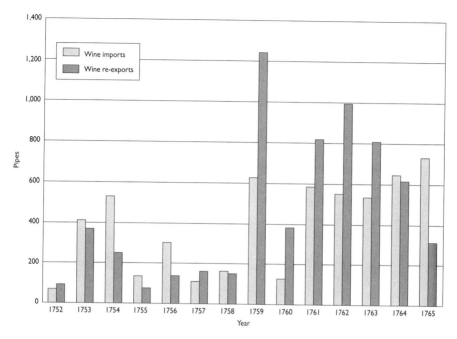

Figure 7.2. Massachusetts (Boston and Salem) wine imports and reexports, 1752–1765.
Sources: See source note for figure 7.1.

three and a half times as many people recorded exporting as importing; the nine exporters who each took away a hundred pipes or more collectively exported less than one-third of the wine shipped out. More exporters than importers traded regularly, and a much larger fraction of them exported in small quantities: 100 of the 357 traders exported in more than one year; 118 of them exported fewer than two pipes.

Contemporary New York records show a wine business that was slightly more concentrated than that which prevailed in Massachusetts. Few merchants were in the market for the entire period. The four largest traders show the variety in the time pattern of trading. New York's largest importer, Lawrence Reade, did not get started in the business until 1754, although he then imported in all but one year from 1754 to 1760, averaging more than 100 pipes per year when he did import. The second largest trader, George Foliot, traded in only three years; he is among the largest traders because he imported 388 pipes in five shipments in 1759. David Van Horne was the most frequent importer into New York; he imported wine in twelve of the sixteen years for which some records have survived. John Beekman began importing in 1749, and imported in eight of the last

Table 7.1. Market share of wine imports, 1743–1765

| | Importers of | | | | |
City	100 pipes or more	20 pipes or more	2 pipes or less	"Important" importers	Total importers
New York City (% market share)	17 (39)	75 (71)	349 (4.4)	56 (60)	652
Boston and Salem (% market share)	14 (51)	60 (94)	13 (0.3)	30 (67)	110

Sources: See source note for figure 7.1

ten years for which there are data. But Beekman's presence among the largest importers is due not to the regularity of his importing but to the fact that in two years, 1755 and 1759, he imported more than 100 pipes. In 1755, he accounted for more than 40 percent of the wine imported into New York. (In six of the sixteen years, the market share of the largest importer was over 25 percent.) Each of these four men imported more than 250 pipes. Family groups were important, apparently more so than at the beginning of the century. The large Van Horne clan, six of whom imported some wine, collectively brought in 5 percent of the total, four Beekmans 4 percent, and the Livingstons 3 percent. (At least eight and possibly as many as eleven Livingstons imported wine; it is difficult to be certain because of similar names within the family.) A few women, like Cornelia Rutgers and Madeleine Debrosses, served as importers, probably as a way of making investments and securing some financial independence from their fathers, brothers, or husbands.[17]

What do we know about the kind of person who traded wine on the eve of the Revolution? Consider the nearly four hundred individuals who distributed wine in Massachusetts between 1752 and 1765. Of these, nearly half worked and lived in Boston, and of them nearly half left evidence of how they described their occupation. Four dozen and some described themselves as merchants—importers and wholesalers. It is impossible to determine whether these men acted on their own account or as agents of Madeirans: no formal agency relations have surfaced, although a dozen maintained regular correspondences with Madeira houses. Some fourteen of the merchants were also retailers, while two more were also tavern keepers and innkeepers. At midcentury, importers and wholesalers could still wear several hats.[18]

The four dozen and some Boston wine merchants at midcentury were remarkably ordinary. Many appear to have been born in the city's vicinity, if not in the city itself. Seven are known to have been born in Britain—one in Ireland, two in Scotland, and four in England—and, given what is known about the place of birth of most people—little—and the extent of migration in the eighteenth century—high—this is certainly a minimum. Many also appear to have been born into families of middling rank with some previous connection to overseas commerce. The wit Joseph Green was the son of a sea captain, for instance, while Joseph Lee was the son of a shipbuilder. Many were sons or nephews of merchants, like Nathaniel Bethune, the son of the trader George Bethune, or Samuel and Arnold Welles, the sons of the merchant Samuel Welles. Only three merchants were members of commercial dynasties spanning three or more generations. Few appear to have received extensive education. Although it would be surprising to discover Boston's merchants did not receive some form of primary and secondary education before they went into the countinghouse, as Joseph Green did at the South Grammar School, most did not attend college: only seventeen attended Harvard, and none went to Yale. None attended an Inn of Court or a university in Britain, or took the Grand Tour in Europe. In the realm of religion, wine merchants remained firmly fixed in Boston's establishment. Nearly all professed traditional creeds: two-thirds Congregational and a third Anglican. In the realm of politics, they ran the gamut. The revolutionary agitation that drove a wedge in Boston's and Salem's dynamic commercial society found them on both sides of the major issues of the day: of the ones for whom a political stance can be ascertained, two-thirds opposed the general trend of imperial legislation in the 1760s which, among other things, imposed a duty on wine imported directly from Madeira and the Azores, and supported the war effort as "Patriots." The remainder declared themselves to be "Friends of the Government" and took Loyalist positions. Only three are known to have remained neutral, although, in the light of the silence of so many, the number was likely much greater. Only in their wealth were wine merchants extraordinary. Most importers and wholesalers enjoyed a significant degree of comfort. In 1771, the Boston wine traders for whom records have survived owned, on average, £544 sterling in assessed taxable wealth, roughly twice the amount owned by the average taxpayer. At the same time, they owned, on average, 172 tons of shipping, the approximate equivalent of three ships. None went bankrupt, although many fell on hard times, especially as the Revolution advanced. In 1774, wine merchants on average died with estates valued at £2,068 sterling, four times the wealth of Bostonians probated that year. Although the socioeconomic dimensions of Boston's non-wine-trading merchants and of merchants in other Anglo-American port towns have not been studied enough to allow detailed comparisons, the information we have suggests that Boston's wine merchants were a cross-section of the town's trading class, and probably representative of wine merchants throughout Anglo-America. From unimpressive families but ambitious and with a few connections, they pursued opportunities and entertained risk with a vigor less common among members of the established merchant community. Indeed, at the outset, all they really had were their connections, and these they used with alacrity to open up new areas of trade.

For the years during and after the Revolution, the evidence is less complete, as port registers of entries and clearances have not survived. Many of the records compiled by Crown officers were destroyed at the time; similar records were not always kept by the new states; many of those that were kept have been destroyed or lost. The New York merchant community in the revolutionary era can be divided into two groups: those working before the war, from 1768 through 1775; and those working during it, from 1776 through 1783. In the earlier period, among the 173 advertisers selling liquor in the city, there were 47 "merchants," another 46 wholesalers (some of whom also managed retail operations), and 44 retailers (not including the retailing wholesalers). Surprisingly, neither importers nor wholesalers suffered during the war in terms of the size of their cohort: 387 different sellers advertised wines and spirits, including 52 merchants, 196 wholesalers and wholesalers/retailers, and 76 retailers. In an equal amount of time (eight years), under very different economic circumstances (British occupation, the need to service Britain's army and a burgeoning Loyalist population), the number of enterprisers advertising wines and spirits more than doubled. Less easy to quantify but not insignificant was the growth in the numbers of foreigners, especially Portuguese, who moved to New York after 1783 and began importing and wholesaling there.[19] No import and export records survive for the 1765–1800 period to facilitate a reconstruction of the top ten distributors' share. But Alexander Mings's 1815 *New-York Price Current* affords a final glimpse of the structure of his city's merchandising. In that year, there were 137 importers listed, including importers, wholesalers, retailers, and auctioneers. Most were clustered at the island's tip, not far from the East River. But firms were now as common as lone enterprisers. The top ten — 7 percent of the cohort — took half of all wine imports.

Boston's postrevolutionary wine-trading community likewise cast much the same profile that it had before the war.[20] It was still local, maritime, and middling in origin, small in size, and geographically concentrated. Advertising in the 1807 *Boston Gazette* were eighteen wine importers and wholesalers in the city, alongside thirty retailers, and most of the eighteen also dealt in spirits. The wine importing and wholesaling cohort had declined from the numbers in the 1760s, but it was small then, and it was small in 1807. Those who traded wine were still based in the central commercial zone. More than half of the operations spread out along seven different wharves; some sixteen lay on Long Wharf and another eight on India Wharf. Established religions and established ideologies predominated, although no great issue like independence rose to test the divisions.[21]

Interestingly, some specialization had emerged. Five of the eighteen merchants focused consistently on wine. Nathaniel Bartlett was one who styled himself a "wine merchant." From a store beneath the Old South Meeting House, he sold a full range of wines and spirits, which he kept "constantly" and sold for cash: "Choice O.P. Madeira, Lisbon, Sherry, Vidonia, Port, Claret, Malaga, Wines— *free from adulteration.* Old Cognac Brandy—Holland Gin; Old Jamaica Spirits, and all other kinds of LIQUORS—London Porter; Philade. Do.; 600 dozen best Bottled CIDER; 20 hhds and bbls Cider, for family use; Strong Beer—first chop Havana CIGARRS, much approved of." All these goods were available as "cheap as at any other place in town." James Dennie focused on wine, spirits, and related items in a store on Broad Street, where he stocked Sherry, Catalonia, Claret, stout, and sugar, while his brother Thomas Dennie kept a more extensive selection of wines and spirits as well as corks, jugs, lead, bottle baskets, and bottle cases at his wholesale store a few blocks away on Merchant's Row: "Best Old London Particular Madeira imported from the first houses in Madeira," other Madeira, Tent, Fayal, Lisbon, Port, Vidonia, Sherry, Malaga, Bordeaux Claret, De Grave, and Cape wines, Cognac and Bordeaux brandy, Holland gin, Jamaica spirits, Antigua rum, arrack, London porter, brown stout, cherry brandy, and "a general assortment of Bottled Liquors." Israel Munson and Cornelius, Coolidge, & Co. likewise focused on the wholesaling and retailing of wines and spirits to the near exclusion of other goods. The *Boston Directory* of 1807 listed two wine wholesale stores—one run by David Bradlee, Merchant's Row, and another by his brothers Thomas and John Bradlee, on the south side of the market. Still, self-styled "wine and spirit merchants" remained something of a rarity; most advertisements placed by wine importers listed wines and spirits alongside "a variety of goods too tedious to mention."[22]

DIRECT IMPORTS BY CONSUMERS

To appreciate the work of Anglo-American importers and wholesalers, it helps to understand the consumers who did not buy from them but instead enjoyed a direct relationship with wine-trading houses on Madeira or another wine-producing area. Nearly two-thirds of Newton & Gordon's consignees in 1770–

72 were individuals ordering for personal consumption, although their orders comprised less than one-third of the volume. For the Leacocks the story was the same. In 1763–65, 56 percent of their consignees were direct purchasers, but they took only 17 percent of the wine. In every case for which there is a full record of shipments by exporters, direct purchases constituted over half of the orders. On the receiving end, "private persons" went "much . . . in[to] ordering single pipes of wine . . . for their own use," and the large number of small importers in the import records confirms this.[23]

Direct importing was most important in plantation colonies with few cities and few and bad roads, and where the richest inhabitants lived along wide, navigable waterways. Such proprietors preferred annual standing orders, which ensured them a regular supply, usually of a better quality of drink, without repetitive correspondence. Exporters also favored such orders, as they constituted a reliable draw. Regular customers were treated with deference; when stocks ran short in Madeira, standing orders were filled first, regardless of the fact that they were usually smaller.

The riverine communities of Virginia, Maryland, and the Carolinas were perfect for direct supply. William Byrd and his cousin Colonel Harrison, both of whom owned shares in vessels that traded between Virginia and Madeira, imported directly for their own consumption at the beginning of the eighteenth century. So casually as to suggest routine in 1733, Colonel William Randolph Jr. asked for two pipes of wine from Hayward & Chambers of Madeira, and Sir John Randolph sent to James Pope for a similar lot. Many Virginia planters in the 1760s depended on their relationships with Dr. Richard Hill, himself an erstwhile tobacco planter; in his words, he "cleaned up" by answering their private orders. Even as late as 1803, by which time so much else distribution-wise had changed, Virginia planter John Wickham's wine book shows him buying directly from four different Madeira houses for his capacious James River cellar. All these planters generally took one or two pipes each year to fill their cellars and satisfy their drinking and medicinal needs. The distance between settlements and the paucity of retail outlets in their respective colonies explain regular private orders.[24]

Similarly, Caribbean colonists often bought direct. In the second half of the eighteenth century, John Leacock's house shipped nearly two-thirds of its "private orders" to planters, merchants, and officials living in the West Indies. Newton & Gordon sent more than half of its private orders there before, during, and after the Revolution. For Caribbean buyers, the choice of a supplier was more influenced by blood relationship than it was for North American consumers. Leacock's older brother William and other relatives settled in the Leeward Islands, and they called on John in Madeira; Leacock's firm never sent less than seven-tenths of its private orders to the eastern Caribbean. Newton & Gordon, too, was patronized by a myriad of relatives, schoolmates, and friends living in Jamaica, in addition to Samuel Johnston, a brother of its London benefactor and agent. The firm never sent less than three-quarters of all its private orders to the island.

Communities bound by religious ties, such as the Quakers and Catholics, also turned to fellow or former believers for buying direct. Although his own religiosity had lapsed, Richard Hill made the most of Quaker connections, as did the exporter George Lawrence. Both called on Friends throughout the years they were building their Madeira businesses. In reverse, Quakers wanting wine approached Lawrence and Hill more readily than they would non-Quakers, introducing themselves on that basis alone.[25]

Direct supply was a largely elite phenomenon: the Hancocks of Boston, Browns of Providence, Beekmans of New York, Carters of Virginia, and their ilk routinely ordered two to four pipes from Madeira each year in the 1750s and 1760s. Most of it was for their personal consumption. They also frequently procured a pipe or two of "the very best Madeira wine" for friends and colleagues. The merchant prince Thomas Hancock of Boston bought some wine as a gift for his colony's governor. His nephew John Hancock did the same in 1767, ordering wine for its treasurer and two pipes for his friends John and Jonathan Amory, wealthy merchants who had no ties to Madeira's houses. The "Best Company" deserved a regular quality supply, and that came only direct.[26]

In addition to ordering for their own accounts, individual buyers also procured wine for others—merchants and retailers, and also friends and people of influence. In 1704, for instance, the mayor of Philadelphia, Richard Hill, the uncle of the Madeira exporter, ordered several pipes of Madeira from the island exporters Miles & Richbell for Timothy Kayzer of London, and Isaac Norris Sr. ordered seven pipes of Madeira for other Philadelphians, even as he ordered twenty-five pipes for himself. The merchant could either charge the others a commission to cover the costs of handling, as Norris did, or absorb those costs in the interest of friendship, as Hill did.[27]

THE BUSINESS OF WINE IMPORTING AND WHOLESALING

Importers' and wholesalers' most valuable contribution to connecting Madeira producers to American consumers was building contacts with suppliers, fellow traders, and customers and sharing products, services, information, and credit with them. Wine merchants maintained networks of traders in Europe and elsewhere who needed North American products and who could supply European goods wanted by Anglo-American customers. They built such networks to satisfy local needs, generally calling on one supplier for one product, although, in order to capitalize on shifts and opportunities as they arose, they also maintained relationships with other suppliers of different products. Only toward the end of the eighteenth century did American merchants import the same product from a number of suppliers. In addition, they drew upon networks of peers at home. A pipe of wine might go through several importers' and wholesalers' hands before it wound up in a retailer's tavern or shop or a family's cellar. The fluidity and open-endedness of the personal, voluntary, and nonhierarchical networks they built allowed them to forge new connections quickly and use them creatively.

Before the early nineteenth century, there was seldom enough business to specialize by commodity or type of goods, so merchants traded whatever they could. "To be a merchant . . . in 1660 meant to be engaged, wholesale and retail, in the exchange of a great variety of goods, to be ready to accept payment in all sorts of unexpected commodities and currencies, always to be seeking new markets in which to sell new kinds of goods and new kinds of goods to satisfy new markets." Related to buying and selling was the oversight of goods: unloading and loading ships, storing and monitoring cargo before sale, and transporting goods to buyers. While the daily operations of a large London countinghouse might have been left to junior partners or clerks to manage, American businesses were small enough that senior partners seldom delegated important oversight activities to underlings. After acquiring some capital, these entrepreneurs integrated downstream, buying shares in ships and cargoes. This pattern persisted through the launch of the new Republic. By then, a few wet goods, dry goods, and provisions merchants had become savvier and begun to specialize in the commodities or regions they traded with. Still, they remained the exception, and their business practices did not differ significantly from the generalists.[28]

The experience of John Van Cortlandt, a grandson of the patriarch of Van Cortlandt Manor and, in his own right, a prominent New York sugar refiner and general merchant, provides an example of a trader who opportunistically found his way into the business of wine importing and wholesaling and then aggressively used his networks to pursue it. From his "sugar house" on a corner of Trinity Churchyard, Van Cortlandt managed a far-flung commodity empire that encompassed England, Europe, the Wine Islands, settlements in Africa, the West Indies, and the Chesapeake and mid-Atlantic regions of North America. He turned to wine because it promoted his sugar trading and rum manufacturing. From time to time, he ordered Madeira or accepted some either as freight or on consignment as a way of making his West Indian voyages more profitable. He exchanged the wine in the Caribbean for sugar and molasses, which he refined, distilled, and sold in New York. If he could not sell all the wine to Caribbean planters and merchants, he sold it alongside his rum to New Yorkers. Either place, wine was in demand among retailers, householders, and medicos.

Then, in 1764, he took a dramatic step, taking advantage of Britain's reform of its empire in the wake of the Seven Years' War. Parliament passed the Sugar Act, imposing unprecedented Crown duties on wine from Madeira and the Azores when imported directly into the British colonies after September 1764. Learning of the legislation well before it went into effect, Van Cortlandt commanded his factor in Virginia to hire a ship, load it with grain, and consign it to Newton & Gordon in Madeira. He chose Newton & Gordon largely on the basis of having worked with Thomas Newton a few years before in New York. Van Cortlandt asked the firm to dispose of the grain to "best advantage" and "remit the net proceeds in good Madeira wine"; in addition, he asked it to send several pipes of "good old wine" for his family's use. He also advised Newton's house to ship to New York "as much . . . good New York & London wines," since he could find buyers. The vessel arrived in Manhattan well before the legislated deadline. Van Cortlandt sold thirteen of the nineteen pipes to four prominent citizens at his small store near the North River: Peter DeLancey, Nicholas Bayard, Henry Beekman, and Patrick McDavitt. None were family members, but they were all family friends and one was an occasional business partner. Moreover, they were all competitors, part of New York's wine-importing "class": Bayard and Delancey imported extensively between 1743 and 1760 and, although Henry Beekman had not, four other Beekmans had.[29]

Pleased with the results, Van Cortlandt ordered another ship to Madeira the following year, to be laden with Virginia corn or, if that was unavailable, New York wheat. The corn came through and this voyage turned a profit as well. The success spurred him to seek out other, larger wine ventures, in which he owned one-third or half of the return cargo of Madeira, sharing it with competing merchants. In 1767, he dispatched a vessel with 3,500 bushels of corn; but the ship suffered mishap and bad weather, forcing him to reroute it to the Caribbean. Not one easily thwarted, he authorized two more Madeira voyages in 1771. In less than a decade, Van Cortlandt backed sixteen voyages to Madeira in addition to selling wine consigned to him by Madeira exporters and other American entrepreneurs. Once he had found suppliers who would reliably tender wine, competitors who would trade with him in New York, and customers who would turn to him for products other than sugar, he combined them to smooth out his Atlantic trading. Suppliers, peers, and customers were his greatest assets. Without them, he could not expand, shift, and adapt as the larger Atlantic marketplace evolved around him.[30]

NETWORKS OF SUPPLIERS

To manage their businesses, merchants maintained correspondences with customers and suppliers in Britain, Europe, Africa, and the Americas. Wine importers and wholesalers established relationships with Madeira exporters to obtain
wine from them. Variations on the business relationship emerged, depending on
who managed it and assumed the risks. The risks were substantial. A cargo owner
could lose the cargo to piracy or privateering, as did Isaac Norris Jr. when some
of his ships were taken by privateers during the War of Jenkins' Ear, brought into
Havana, and stripped of their goods. He could also lose the venture to nature, the
most common obstruction. Ice on the Delaware and East rivers and in Boston
Harbor—threatening from December through March—could bring shipping to
a halt in the winter months, causing "a general stagnation of business," and leave
"the price of everything . . . unsettled." Disease stopped traffic. The smallpox that
devastated the northeastern colonies in 1752, which "deter[red] all cuntry people
of coming to market," deprived the importers and wholesalers of outbound cargoes as well as of customers for wine. Similarly, the yellow fever that struck Philadelphia in 1792 prompted officials to bar incoming vessels and impose a quaran-
tine on ships already lying in the harbor.[31]

The most common business arrangement was for the importer-wholesaler to
accept wine on consignment from an exporter. In this case, the exporter bank-
rolled the voyage, provided the shipping, and bore the risk. Sometimes the merchant was responsible for selling the wine, but other times the exporter had already sold the wine and it came with instructions for delivering it. The importer,
as agent or consignee, managed the unloading and sale or delivery of the wine,
charging the consignor for expenses incurred and a commission for services rendered. The considerable wine merchant Abraham De Peyster did much business
this way in the early 1730s when he accepted Madeira from the exporters Walter
and Robert Scot and John Day, with the understanding that it would be delivered according to the exporter's instructions.[32]

As American merchants became more familiar with oceanic trade and better
capitalized, they began ordering wine on their own accounts, financing voyages
and assuming the risks and the profits. In 1703–08, William Trent Sr. kept at least
six vessels plying the waters between Philadelphia and Madeira, carrying grain
and flour to Madeira and returning with wine supplied by Miles & Richbell, despite the War of Spanish Succession that was then raging in Europe. Each year,
he sent one or two of his ships. He coordinated his dispatches with other merchants, renting the cargo space in halves, thirds, or quarters. Trent owned at least
one of the vessels outright, a ship that he and Isaac Norris Sr. had designed for a

bilateral trade in Pennsylvania flour and Madeira wine. Later, in the 1720s, with his son and the Madeiran Richard Miles, the elder Norris used a sloop he owned to shuttle between Philadelphia and Madeira, making at least seven such voyages between 1724 and 1727. Similarly, Gerard Garret Beekman concerned himself in a New York-to-Madeira sloop during the 1740s and 1750s. Like Trent, Norris, and Beekman, most substantial American importers and wholesalers who were interested in the trade engaged in one or two such investments in the course of their careers. The control over oceanic distribution that ownership imparted—no longer were they at the mercy of other merchants who might delay, or shady or irresponsible captains who might imperil the cargo—was valuable enough to outweigh the risk of losing the wine through seizure or shipwreck.[33]

The interests of the Americans and Madeirans became most heavily intertwined in joint ventures, which increased in frequency as the eighteenth century advanced. When the Norrises offered Miles & Richbell a share in a vessel two years after its launch, they also offered the Madeirans the assurance of future business. Joint ownership helped the chronically cash-poor Norrises, who "want[ed] money in Madeira and could not so easily . . . forepay in England." Joint vessel ownership led to joint cargo ownership and importation. Sharing helped the Madeirans, too. The Pennsylvania legislature had reduced duties on wine imported on vessels owned two-thirds by colonists; the proposed joint venture allowed Miles & Richbell's wine to enter at the reduced rates.[34]

From the Seven Years' War onward, American merchants grew more aggressive in "managing" suppliers. Rather than accepting what was consigned them, they began to specify the amount, grade, and quality of wine. Gerard Garret Beekman once requested a wine that the Hills had sent to his neighbor, "as fine a parcel of wines as e'er come to this market." Such requests did not always achieve their ends, so even more specific requests were sent. In sending John Searle "a small bottle" with some "yellow rich sweet" Madeira that had been sent to a friend, Beekman insisted that Searle procure him a pipe of the same. By the 1760s, American tastes were developing and differentiating, and American importers demanded that Madeirans send them the wine that would sell in their particular locality. Some good-quality wine arrived in New York in 1764, for instance, but it was "neither old nor high coloured enough" for the market; neither tavern keepers nor retailers would "buy any wine" that was for domestic use, since neither could "afford to let it lay by." Philadelphia merchant John Baynton insisted the islanders supply an erstwhile partner who had moved to Jamaica. He ordered them to send "good old Madeira Wine . . . mellowed by being long at sea [and] in a warm climate" for his own private consumption and the "very best London old wine of a light amber color" for his firm's sale account. He instructed the wine be "kept on board the vessel" until its arrival in Philadelphia. As they became more demanding, American importers grew more willing to alter long-standing supply relationships to get what they preferred. When Beekman began trading wine in a big way in the 1750s, he did not merely continue with the house his forebears had used; instead, he asked three houses—Hill, Lamar, & Hill, Chambers, Hiccox & Chambers, and Searle Brothers—each to ship him two pipes of the best London wine so that he "may judge who ships the best."[35]

Despite entrepreneurial aggressiveness, enduring supply relationships were grounded in trust. Because of the distances and delays, the reliability of a correspondent to deliver goods, provide information, and pay debts—and to be truthful—had to be established, in many cases beforehand. American wine importers and wholesalers who did not go themselves or send supercargoes had to delegate to others at the point of shipment the selection and packing of the commodity; trusting them was a critical business decision. An independent, on-the-spot delegate knew more "about the quality gradations," the supplier's financial state, and "which of their goods" was "best suited" for overseas travel and marketing. But that delegate could also take advantage of his superior information. So reliance upon suppliers was still extremely critical. The rules for exchange were usually malleable, even for the highest-quality wines, to which the most rigid rules of exchange attached. Leniency was usually allowed to trusted importers and wholesalers. "It was not our custom to ship best wine in large quantities," wrote John Searle in 1763, but his firm always complied with a request from "a trustworthy friend." New York's Peter Stuyvesant sent 600 *pistareens* to Scot, Pringle & Scot in 1757. He hoped there would "be enough to purchase a pipe and half of ye very best," but if not, he asked the firm to "advance a small" amount of wine, reminding them, by recounting a decade of history, that they could "depend on having" their money "very soon." Stuyvesant had to trust Scot, Pringle & Scot to send him "ye very best," or anything at all. Scot, Pringle & Scot had to trust Stuyvesant to grant him credit.[36]

Once trust was established, importers and suppliers generally remained allies. Few Americans bought from more than one supplier in any period; only very late in the eighteenth century, due to the growing competition among islanders and their unprecedented disregard for Factory pricing, did it become common for importers to buy from more than one supplier at the same time.[37] In the early decades of the eighteenth century, William Trent Sr., Isaac Norris Sr. and Isaac Norris Jr. remained loyal to Richard Miles's various firms in Madeira. They approached other firms for wine only in special circumstances. On one occasion, Isaac Sr. had a personal if unexplained falling-out with Miles and struck deals with Benjamin Bartlett, Vasconcelos de Bettencourt, and Francisco Luis de Vasconcelos. But the displeasure was short-lived, and the breach repaired. Isaac Jr. wandered from the Miles fold only once. Even so, serious concern over performance could drive a wedge between firms. At midcentury, Samuel Galloway dispensed with Richard Hill Sr.'s services on the suspicion that Hill had not worked hard to sell Galloway's wheat. The most common cause of rupture was the inability of a supplier to provide enough wine or accept all of the barter goods tendered.[38]

On the other hand, few Americans restricted themselves to dealing in one kind of wine. Seventeenth-century merchants imported French wine until the onset of England's anti-French wars and the passage of laws aimed at destroying the power of Louis XIV. They acquired Azores and Canary wines until Britain blocked Spanish imports during the War of Spanish Succession. Geographically blessed like Madeira, Canary was the second most easily obtained Atlantic wine, with Azorean wine running a close third. As early as the 1680s, Jamaica importer-wholesalers handled wines from Malaga as well as Madeira. North Americans sold wines from the Canaries and Azores as well as Madeira between the 1690s and 1710s.[39] By the middle of the eighteenth century, importers had further diversified their suppliers. Philadelphia's Baynton, Wharton & Morgan corresponded with Lamar, Hill, Bisset in Madeira for Madeira, but they also bought Port from Holdsworth, Olive & Newman in Oporto, Lisbon from Mayne & Co. and Parr & Bulkeley in Lisbon, and generic Portuguese from Lampriere Brothers in Faro. During the mid-eighteenth century before the American Revolution, most suppliers hailed from Portugal and the Wine Islands. American merchants seldom traded with either the French or non-Canary Spaniards.[40] During that conflict, however, commercial ties to Spain and France were substituted for those to Britain. American merchants returned to Portuguese suppliers after the war, yet they also maintained their new correspondences with Havre de Grace, Bordeaux, Jerez, and Cadiz. Willing, Morris & Swanwick made this shift, importing Château Margot and Cognac through Bordeaux while replenishing its stocks of Madeira and Canary. In the early nineteenth century, Claret and Sherry were as easy and cheap to procure as Madeira and Port, and it was a rare import firm between Halifax and Kingston that did not simultaneously deal with L'Orient, Nantes, Bordeaux, Cognac, Porto, Lisbon, Cadiz, Funchal, and Tenerife.[41]

NETWORKS OF PEERS

In addition to their networks of suppliers, Anglo-American merchants traded among themselves. Unlike those of the Caribbean sugar merchants, North American peer wine networks remained commercial; not until much later and well into any particular relationship did they evolve into a common political stance. Wine importers and wholesalers appealed to their peers to get wine when they did not have enough, or to sell it when they had too much. Most trading was close to home: a merchant would take a pipe or two from a competitor whose stock was not selling in town. Importers also acquired wine from merchants in other ports, particularly wines like Mountain or Bordeaux that were never easily acquired and always in short supply. When Jonathan Dickinson of Philadelphia could not find "any good wines" around him in 1718, he applied to his "particular friend" Stephen DeLancey in New York. The traffic between Philadelphia and New York was always active but, as the eighteenth century advanced and coastwise connections throughout America improved, port-to-port assistance occurred farther afield.[42]

Importers and wholesalers supplemented buying and selling among their competitor "friends" by opportunistically trading with others. One day in 1748, needing some good wine to sell to a regular customer, Gerard Garret Beekman found Claret "by chance" "in two Persons' hands"; he later found more on the street, on the carts of two draymen. This almost accidental mode of procurement is hard for us to recapture, because so much of it went unrecorded; but it was common. Similarly opportunistic but better recorded was the kind of trading that ensued when merchants used each other as agents, as when, in 1763, Eleazer Trevett in Newport sent Beekman some Fayal to sell for him. The wine was unsaleable in New York, however, being new and not colored. "Fortunately, a Vessel" bound for Halifax weighed anchor in New York with instructions to approach the merchant William Francklin and secure eight pipes of Fayal. When Beekman heard the news, he "Immediately Applyd" to Francklin and sold him the liquor—"as they was[,] without filling up, tho' they wanted from 2 to 3 gallons each[,] at £17 round[,] which was the most" he "could obtain."[43]

Glutted markets were among the most persistent vexations merchants complained of, and they took it upon themselves to move their stocks rather frequently. Much of this was classic arbitrage: low prices in one place and high prices in another prompted them to ship the wine to the higher-price markets. Not only could the wine be profitably sold in the new port, it could also give "an advance to the remaining quantities" in the original market. When some wine proved unsaleable in Maryland, for example, John Searle instructed Samuel Galloway to order "any vessel" to proceed to the Caribbean so that "the wines may be trucked there for rum, &c., which in the end would probably be attended with good profit & a more speedy sale [than] at Maryland." Given the ease of transport and communication, both of which improved over the eighteenth century, Madeira wine could be kept in motion until it found a market.[44]

But not always profitably. Sometimes importers and wholesalers could not move their cities' surpluses because other cities were also glutted. Such a case arose in Halifax in 1754 when it had a surfeit of Fayal.[45] Worse, they might move the wine and still not be able to sell it in the new market. Very early in the century, Isaac Norris Sr. sent a ship to Madeira, where it took in as much wine as it could stow, and then directed it to New York, where Rip Van Dam was to sell ten pipes. But Norris's wine did not sell well there, the tastes of the place differing from those of Philadelphia. Later in the century, New Yorker Peter Stuyvesant tried selling Robert Tucker's wine in New York. Stuyvesant gave it "all . . . assistance" in his power, but Tucker's captains' stay in New York was so short that Stuyvesant was obliged to sell "to a disadvantage." Peers could generally be relied upon to shift product between ports, to seek greater profit, but there were limits to their abilities.[46]

Merchants also bought and sold wine at auction, where city vendue masters hawked the wares of failing enterprises. As successive commodity gluts buffeted the American market after the Seven Years' War, many took advantage of the vendue. It was not problem-free, of course. In 1785, for instance, most wine consignments to New York were disposed of at public vendue, although at "little or no profit." But it was still better than holding the wine in inventory, with the cost of capital and storage included. The situation was different for buyers, for the prices were good. Beekman often bought at vendue, especially when he was buying for customers in adjacent colonies. The problem with auctioned wines was that, "generally," they were "very low" in quality. Worse, the quality was difficult to ascertain. They were generally "put up 5 and 6 [barrels] in a lott"; as a result, one sometimes procured "a very good cask among them," but that left four or five "very indifferent."[47]

Trade among distributors eventually grew great enough to support brokers who negotiated the transactions. Appearing on the scene in the years following the Seven Years' War, they proliferated rapidly after the War of Independence. Some brokers accepted fees for matching buyers to sellers and vice versa, while others—in a more advanced operation—bought from sellers, held on to the goods as inventory, and sold from a "broker's store," usually "cheap for cash." Whatever the particular setup, the goods so managed were general, much as were an auctioneer's goods. Boston's Edmund Quincy Jr. characteristically announced the sale of two pipes of Madeira alongside large quantities of sugar, beef, and other goods in 1764, while Philadelphia's William Smith offered old Lisbon, dry goods, sugar, and ginger. The broker's main task was "to maintain a 'market' in a particular product." He collected goods and news "from retailers or other potential customers" with whom he had close ties. He then tried to "transform that information" or possession "into purchasing actions directed at competing" merchants. The contribution to commerce of brokers like Robert Ross and Peter Lohra of Philadelphia lay not just in receiving "to sell on commission on all kinds of merchandise"—and there was no broker who consistently advertised who did not at some point in his advertising history before 1800 dispose of wine—but also in "knowing what goods will be needed sometime in the future and placing anticipatory orders, in judging where that desire for goods will be largest or strongest, and in directing the flow" there.[48]

NETWORKS OF CUSTOMERS

The most important asset of any importer and wholesaler was his customers. In contrast to their supply networks, wine merchants' customer networks were extensive. A midsized American trading house needed between ten and thirty regular customers as a base for its sales, for most customers did not rely on only one source. Urban merchants normally dealt with customers in their own towns, but they also supplied backcountry retailers, dispensers, and householders. As a particular merchant or firm succeeded, the lines to customers stretched far along the coast and deep inland along rivers.[49] The principal customers included wine-related artisans—vintners who blended the wine, cellarers who blended and stored it, and coopers and bottlers who packed it—as well as lesser merchants, storekeepers, shopkeepers, innholders, tavern keepers, and consumers. American enterprisers built associations with their customers in much the same way Madeira exporters were doing—through conversations and flexible terms— although their networks were simpler. As the decades passed, customer expectations of performance grew, and the importers' and wholesalers' approach to them became more complicated and nuanced: more prepared, more restless and competitive, more investigative and solicitous, and more buoyant (because more heavily capitalized). One manifestation of their more aggressive outreach to customers is the premises they constructed for displaying their wares and for entertaining and soliciting customers.

Especially in the first century of wine trading, most sales were small, even to retailers. Masters of such exchanges, William Trent Sr. and Alexander Paxton of Pennsylvania procured sixty pipes of Madeira from Miles & Richbell in 1709. As soon as customs officials authorized unloading, Trent and Paxton commenced sales. They sold the first pipe on November 3 and another seven days later. Thereafter, sales quickened. Half of the pipes were sold between January and March, in fifty lots to thirty-seven buyers. The buyers all lived in Philadelphia City and County and paid in cash; three were women. Only two bought more than a pipe; those two bought two pipes each.[50] Three decades later, a few customers of the Norrises took larger quantities and more speedily, but most transactions were still small. One ship owned by the Norrises, the *Bona Vista*, brought thirty-four pipes from Richard Miles (who owned three-eighths of the vessel); it landed part of its cargo at Barbados, exchanging it for sugar and molasses, before returning to Philadelphia with the rest of the wine. Back home, in just under a month, the firm sold twenty-seven pipes to thirteen Philadelphians, mainly storekeepers and tavern keepers. Only two purchasers bought more than two pipes: the proprietor of the Crown tavern took three, and a storekeeper seven.[51]

Abraham De Peyster of New York was another merchant who traded in wine, and his much fuller accounts give us a rare glimpse into the extent of customer networks. De Peyster sold wine and spirits as a complement to other goods throughout the greater New York City area, and he owned or held shares in at least seven New York/Madeira vessels. From 1723 to 1733, De Peyster acquired more than forty-seven pipes of Madeira from four island houses, plus one New York importer, and he sold eighty-eight pipes, the difference made up by incidental purchases in New York and drawing down his stocks. Some twenty-four identifiable New York City inhabitants bought almost two-thirds (fifty-five pipes) of his sales; ten transactions involved anonymous buyers who paid cash. The rest went to those who worked or lived along the two main roads going down the Jersey coast toward Philadelphia. One customer was significant: Perth-Amboy tavern keeper William Maxwell took ten pipes of wine in April 1728, and half of another cargo the next month. But for Maxwell's custom, which persisted for a decade, out-of-town purchasers were all De Peyster's relatives or friends, who seldom bought more than a pipe for personal use.[52]

Importers and wholesalers became more aggressive at the time of the Seven Years' War, not only acquiring wine for established customers but also undertaking speculative ventures. One sees this at work in the operation that Philip Cuyler devised for the supply of the British and colonial forts in western New York. Early in the conflict, with a partner and a factor, Cuyler built four bateaux and filled them with goods needed at Fort Oswego, on Lake Ontario, north of present-day Syracuse. The cargo included Madeira, which was a favorite of the officers, as well as rum, sugar, molasses, tea, coffee, chocolate, butter, pepper, tobacco, and dry goods. But Cuyler could not survive with soldiers as his only customers. He had family ties to Albany and Schenectady (his father, several siblings, and cousins lived there), so he focused some attention on the upper reaches of the Hudson and the Mohawk. For similar reasons, he cultivated buyers in Rhode Island, where his wife's family lived, and in New Jersey, where friends had settled. Cuyler made use of his family ties and extended them to associates far beyond.[53]

The Seven Years' War was a watershed in wine wholesaling for many more merchants than Cuyler. Wine-drinking settlers began pushing into the new western territories with a renewed vigor in the 1750s and 1760s, and suppliers stretched their distribution lines to meet them. At the same time, the number of individuals engaging in importing and wholesaling back east rose, increasing the competitive pressure on merchants in the port towns, much as the "mushroom" merchants were increasing the pressure on exporters in Madeira at the same time. The rise in merchants led to increased efforts to please customers, by calling on them, offering packages of goods they wanted, tailoring the wine to their tastes, and extending credit. One detects this new commercial aggressiveness in the circuits that merchants made during and after the Seven Years' War. Urban importers and wholesalers, who for the most part had been content to wait for customers to come to them, started visiting surrounding counties and towns in search of business. The Philadelphian George Morgan was one of the merchants who redrew his map of interest. Unlike his older partners before him, he took a tour of the New England colonies in 1764 to drum up sales. A few years later, he floated down the Ohio and as far west as Kaskaskia doing the same.[54]

To meet with success, importers and wholesalers had to provide a full range of services: accepting, inspecting, tasting, repairing, handling, and storing the liquor; transporting it to customers; securing payment; exporting the customer's goods; and providing customers with contacts among traders in other goods. They began to take care of quality, packaging, and price—all matters that had previously been dictated or handled by European exporters.[55] They became obsessed with the wines customers desired. A type of wine might go out of fashion. In New York in the 1750s, Claret was in "no demand" and there was "very little Burgundy or French wines"; Sherry, likewise, was "in very little esteem"; Madeira and Canary, on the other hand, were the "chief wines drunk." Merchants therefore stocked them first. Or, the taste might put consumers off. When buying in bulk, customers usually tasted the wine they were considering. They shunned sour wine. They also disliked new wine, which possessed a rough flavor. When they could not return ill-tasting wines to Europe, merchants doctored them, making them sweeter or darker, depending on the palate to be satisfied. In some markets, richer, darker hues were valued and accordingly would "sell much sooner," as would white wines that were blended with Tinta or "red, to coulor them." If wines were "new and not coulered," they would be "the very poorest articles you can send to this market and will not sell" except "at a very poor rate."[56]

Extending the effort to draw customers into their fold, merchants also allowed better—meaning more liberal—terms of credit. "A real scarcity of money," plaguing all of Anglo-America, often obstructed consumers' wine purchases; so, too, did the suspect nature of locally issued paper money. Barter goods like fish, beeswax, wheat, and corn were acceptable as payment, but only for lesser wines. For better grades of wine—and over the course of the eighteenth century the quality of wine was improving—cash alone sufficed. But cash was scarce. The situation forced the merchants into what they felt was an excessive but unavoidable "commercial liberality": when money was scarce, they offered customers more relaxed credit terms, from three to nine months; when cash was at hand, they discounted their prices for cash payment. The traders of Anglo-America negotiated such policies with care, taking into consideration individual cases and relationships, but over time their liberality became a required feature of the wine trade.[57]

THE SITES OF WINE TRADING

Wine importers and wholesalers needed places to meet suppliers, competitors, and customers, to handle and store their liquor and its paraphernalia, and to keep letters and accounts tracking their increasingly complex businesses. These were their residences, countinghouses, and warehouses. In mid-eighteenth-century parlance, a "countinghouse" usually denoted a "room appropriated by traders to their books and accounts," although over time the room and building became conflated. American countinghouses did not differ much from British ones, except that they were usually smaller, a reflection of colonial merchants' smaller operations. In the last half of the eighteenth century, an established but not grand importer's or wholesaler's home, office, and store occupied a three- or four-story brick building. The ground floor was devoted to business, with a semipublic reception room and work area in front and a more private room for the merchant or partners in back. Private quarters lay above. Greater merchants might separate the functions architecturally, residing in one building and working in another, although unmarried partners and clerks usually lived in the countinghouse.[58]

Wine merchants' countinghouses had discursive and display uses as well as practical ones. They stood open to the public: customers, suppliers, competitors, and friends could come by. There merchants could conduct intimate conversations and forge personal relationships. Their furnishings revealed the accoutrements of the trade and their expertise, as well as their place in society. One of the most important aspects of display was the degree of separation between business life and private life. Most enterprisers did not have the wherewithal to own multiple establishments, and so their residences doubled as workspaces. Small- and midscale merchants usually lived behind or above their offices. If successful, a merchant could own or lease a separate residence, testifying to his entry into the subcommunity of elite merchants. But even then he could not separate from trade completely, for the greater merchants still usually kept an office in their dwelling and a warehouse of sorts in their cellar or backyard.[59]

BUILDINGS

Three increasingly grand buildings built or occupied by Philadelphia wine importers and wholesalers suggest the role that architectural space played in connecting merchants to their networks in a decentralized Atlantic commodity marketplace.[60] The wine importer Samuel Neave's house on South Second Street near the corner of Spruce Street was built in 1760. It is probably the most representative of the three as it was neither undeniably grand nor stridently Georgian. The house was originally thirty by forty-four feet with three and a half stories above a raised basement that served as cellar, a three-bay front, a brick facade with marble trim, a pedimented frontispiece, and a single-story gabled lean-to wing in the rear (figure 7.3). A fourteen-foot-square verandah and pantry connected the main house to a long, narrow (thirty-five by eighteen feet) outbuilding, with a kitchen below and nursery above. At the back of the property lay a greenhouse and a stable. Inside, the house's layout adhered to the fashionable London side-hall townhouse plan. In many respects, Neave's house was similar to the more genteel homes of its day. What marked it as the home of a merchant was the ground-floor store at its front and the counting room office behind.[61]

Another merchant who dabbled in wine, Charles Stedman, built a house a few blocks away on South Third Street, between Spruce and Walnut, several doors down from the house occupied by William Byrd III. Stedman's house was by design more sociable, set farther away from the wharves. It had many elements in common with Neave's: three and a half stories, a three-bay front of brick trimmed with stone, a Doric frontispiece and fanlight, a three-story lean-to in the rear, and a gabled roof; it was also laid out in the side-hall townhouse plan (figure 7.5). Yet it was grander. It boasted a high Georgian style, in contrast to the simpler vernacular style of Neave's house, and at thirty by fifty feet was larger. Each of the two floors had three rooms, trimmed with wainscoting and cornices. A slanting wooden bulkhead provided street-side access to Stedman's cellar, which by the 1760s was a necessity for a gentleman. From the front walk, one saw not a storefront or display window, but three floors with twelve-over-twelve sashes on the first- and second-story windows, eight-over-eight sashes on the smaller third-story windows, dentilled cornices decorating the facade, and arched dormers on the top floor. Lead spouts and electrical rods made by Benjamin Franklin graced the residence.[62]

Stedman made his house more of a familial preserve by erecting a separate two-story office building in back where he met customers. But even one as ambitious and successful as he could not easily separate social and business pursuits; in fact, he worked out of both spaces. The fairly traditional residence in front appears elegant and removed from the cut and thrust of everyday business, but that has more to do with changes that the city has undergone in the nineteenth and twentieth centuries. When the merchant moved in, it sat on the edge of a busy commercial zone, easily accessible to customers. Even at a leisurely pace, it took Stedman only six minutes to walk to the closest wharf and another eight minutes to get to the London Coffee House.

Three blocks from Stedman's home and two decades after Stedman built it, the importer and scion of the Madeira house Henry Hill erected a residence on South Fourth Street in the new Federal style. Hill bought the property in 1782 (it was previously the home of wine merchant George Meade) and in the ensuing years rebuilt and refurbished it. This insecure and obsessive trader—a birthright Quaker who attended Meetings but never joined any Meeting and had some sort of stutter—occupied the existing two-story brick house on the property and tirelessly managed the construction of something new. With a profusion of high-style English detail, the latter met "the general approbation of those of good taste," even if it did not lie "in the best part of the City"[63] (figure 7.7). It boasted a Flemish bond brick facade and a front entrance that demanded attention. It was larger than Stedman's and Neave's at forty-eight by fifty-one feet, with three and a half stories set atop a raised basement and a three-bay front. Hill imported the large front fanlight from London. He decorated the cornice with acanthus leaves and fret-band motifs, and inserted a reedlike band between the double doors and stairs—both all the rage in London. Inside, he introduced a commodious center-hall floor plan. The entrance, tiled in black and white Italian marble squares, led to a handsome carved staircase with mahogany rails. He added white marble fireplaces and decorated them with floral, foliar, and shell motifs and putti. He placed elaborate acanthus motifs on the ceilings.

By the time the house was ready to occupy, Hill was more a man of parts—a fixture in Pennsylvania society, a director of the Bank of North America, and an ardent Federalist partisan—than a man of commerce. From his home office, Hill could differentiate his treatment of customers: he could decide how intimate and deferential to be . . . or allow them to be. To gain greater familiarity, he could share wine, spirits, tea, or something more substantial with them in addition to transacting business. He could invite some people into his home office and, in extraordinary circumstances, into his home; others he did not.

Despite his gestures toward Georgian serenity, Hill did not eschew the cut and thrust of commerce, the source of his wealth and power. The house was an

Figure 7.3. Front facade of Samuel Neave house,
Philadelphia, built c. 1760.
Source: Courtesy of The Library of Congress—
Historic American Buildings Survey, Washington, DC.

important site for his firm's wine trading, as it was for his political maneuvering. He installed a large working cellar, which was accessible, along with his private study, through a door opening off a side street. In the cellar, he stored and displayed wine he and his partners brought from Madeira, and he offered samples to correspondents, neighbors, generals, and fellow club members who came to taste the wine that bore the brand of "Hill's Madeira." His last mention in Philadelphia's newspapers occurred in an announcement postponing the "Sale of Madeira Wine" that was to be held in this very space.[64]

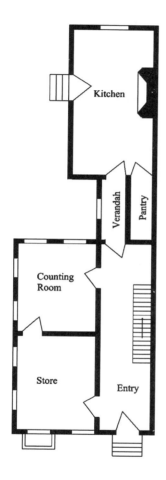

Figure 7.4. First-floor plan of Samuel Neave house, Philadelphia, built c. 1760. Source: Based on Insurance Policy Minutes, August 5, 1760, The Philadelphia Contributionship, The Contributionship Companies, Philadelphia. Drawn by Donald Buaku.

Figure 7.5. Front facade of Charles Stedman house,
Philadelphia, built 1765.
Source: Courtesy of The Historical Society of Pennsylvania,
Philadelphia.

CELLARS

Storage was essential to merchants, and wine merchants needed it more than most; so it became a mark of the wine trade. By itself, a 110-gallon wine pipe was a sizeable beast. Six or twelve such creatures took up a large amount of space. A cellar or "a large vault" under the street before one's house was a common feature of dwellings, countinghouses, and warehouses in European and American cities. Sometimes it extended under the entire house: sale announcements singled out "a commodious cellar under the whole" as worthy of notice. Henry Hill and Samuel Neave had their own. Others rented cellar space if they did not have it, or if theirs was not capacious enough, under the Exchange (as in

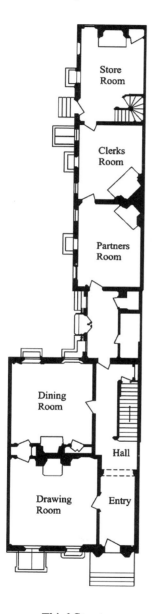

Store
Room

Clerks
Room

Partners
Room

Dining
Room

Hall

Drawing
Room

Entry

Third Street

Figure 7.6. First-floor plan of Charles Stedman
house, Philadelphia, built 1765.
Source: Based on Nicholas B. Wainwright, *Colonial
Grandeur in Philadelphia: The House and Furniture
of General John Cadwalader* (Philadelphia, 1964).
Drawn by Donald Buaku.

Figure 7.7. Front facade of Henry Hill house,
Philadelphia, built 1783–1787.
Source: Courtesy of The Historical Society of
Pennsylvania, Philadelphia.

Charleston) or a under a competitor's house. Although he had his own, Neave
needed more space; so he rented "convenient CELLARS for Wine Stores, under
the Dwelling House of Doctor MORGAN," a few blocks from his own countinghouse. As the wine-trading business grew, resort to rented cellars grew more frequent. A good cellar needed to be dry and either hot or cold, depending on the
wine stored. One New York cellar in 1773 was deemed particularly suitable for
Madeira, which needed heat, because it was "half above ground," half below, and
so benefited from the sun shining on it "most of the day." Toward this end, many
subterranean cellars were heavily plastered. A good cellar was also sturdy: heavy,
usually two-inch planking on floors withstood the wear and tear of moving heavy
barrels around, while liming them softened the contact of wood upon wood. It
should also be fireproof and, above all, commodious.[65]

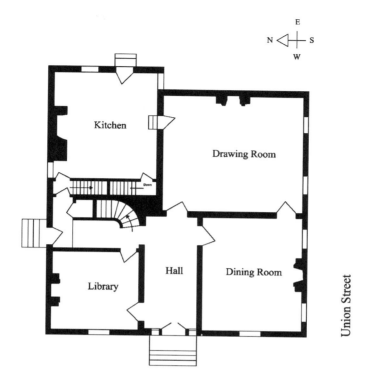

Fourth Street

Figure 7.8. First-floor plan of Henry Hill house,
Philadelphia, built 1783–1787.
Source: Based on materials kept by The Society for the
Preservation of Landmarks. Drawn by Donald Buaku.

As the eighteenth century advanced, demand for more and more varied wines, increasing competition among retail outlets, and growing awareness of wine maintenance increased the amount of wine wholesalers kept in inventory— some kept upward of several hundred pipes—and this required that a larger part of the premises be devoted to storage. When Henry Hill rebuilt the house on South Fourth Street in Philadelphia in the 1780s, he added an arched wine cellar in its basement to store his firm's Madeira imports. In the same decade, the merchant John Deas Jr. installed a shelf-lined wine cellar under the whole of his new countinghouse on East Bay Street in Charleston. Some importers and wholesalers dedicated special buildings to wine storage. Charleston wine and dry goods wholesaler Thomas Simons in 1805 kept his stock—nearly 675 gallons of ten kinds of wine and five kinds of spirits—in one of the outbuildings behind his main house, in addition to a much larger cache of wine-filled pipes he stored in a warehouse nearby.[66]

Wine merchants and customers alike viewed cellars and warehouses as evidence of the scale of the business and the knowledge and skill of the businessman. They became proud possessions. In the years preceding the Revolution, one wholesaler and importer in Philadelphia invited the public into his cellar to select "wine at very reasonable prices." Another firm likewise directed interested buyers to the cellar it had rented "under the Friends' Meeting [House] in Pine Street," where they would find wines "Just Imported" from France and Italy. Charleston importers boasted about the capacities and capabilities of their "very good" cellars. There merchants displayed different types of wine and spirits and the paraphernalia for blending and packaging them. One needed the full range of wine containers, from pipes, hogsheads, and quarter-casks down to bottles, to be ready to sell "from a quart to any quantity," and the full range of vintners' tools to perfect or improve the blend. In the cellar customers could find the wine "ready packed" or have it mixed and casked or bottled before their arrival. The cost of a wine cellar was considerable, but by 1800 no importer or wholesaler of any expectation could trade without one. It became the sine qua non of a competitive wine-trading operation.[67]

INTERIORS

Little is known about how merchants' houses and offices were outfitted—odd, given their prominence in the early American cityscape. A contemporary English watercolor depicts a single room with several chests; account books and ledgers grace shelves; clerks work on slope-front desks; and pigeonhole cabinets line the wall behind. A contemporary American sketch from 1795–1805 (figure 7.9), perhaps of Stephen Girard's Philadelphia countinghouse, shows much the same: a space suffused with light, with a large fireplace, unadorned walls, and the clerks separated from visitors by a rail. It is safe to assume that most business spaces were not so grand, not lit by such a large Palladian window, and not so uncluttered.[68]

Probate inventories fill out the rather sketchy picture, confirming the separation between business and personal lives.[69] A typical counting room or countinghouse contained the wherewithal for business. Most obvious were correspondence materials: writing desks, stools, candlesticks and candles, pencils, pens, ink and inkstands, sand and pounce boxes, paper in several qualities, and ac-

Figure 7.9. *A Merchants Counting House*, by Alexander
Lawson, c. 1795–1801, possibly of Stephen Girard's
countinghouse in Philadelphia.
Source: Courtesy of The Library Company of Philadelphia.

count books. Newspapers and magazines kept the occupants abreast of news. Here, too, one found tools of the wine merchant's calling. Charleston commission merchant John Walter Gibbs, who traded heavily in wine in the late 1780s from a countinghouse behind his residence, kept a wine crane for siphoning wine, a hand pump, funnels, measures of various quantities, a mortar and pestle for pulverizing fining agents, and weights and scales for weighing them. Carpenters' tools for breaking down, repairing, and reassembling casks were also a necessity. Since hours were long, personal needs intruded into the workspace, and the office served as a second kitchen and shed at times, with coffee mills, coffeepots, teakettles, cheese toasters, wine and rum containers, corn mills, and a full array of rakes, hoes, and spades. Assigned to the countinghouse were at least one clerk, perhaps two, and a slave. The artifacts and occupants "convey a sense of the command of the human and material resources" needed to carry on interimperial exchange and local sales.[70]

Countinghouses were not always so plain and utilitarian. When the Charleston wine wholesaler Thomas Simons died in March 1805 at the age of forty, fully engaged in trade, the contents of the large front room on the ground floor of his 13 Legare Street residence show that he used it not only for conducting business—bookkeeping, negotiating, and some displaying and selling—but also for reading, dining, and sleeping. This room was dominated by two hundred books set in a case; scattered around them were two spyglasses, a portable writing desk, and a straw floor covering. Such elements were the stuff of overseas trade. But in his letters, Simons said he desired to make his customers and suppliers feel "at home," and thus more willing to do business and cooperate with him. So the room where Simons entertained and dunned customers was also the dining room and game room, with six Hogarth prints, a pair of dining tables, fourteen straw-bottom chairs, a small tea table, two sideboards, a wine cooler, two knife cases filled with knives, and a backgammon board. The room "offered an important venue for face-to-face negotiations, where the competitive culture of trade coincided with hospitality," even as it served as a family dining room. It allowed Simons to display familiarity and equality, should he deem it fruitful, "render[ing] personal and private experience sensible in the larger situation" of an ever-shifting commercial world.[71] At his death, the room also contained three beds, three mattresses, three pillows, two bolsters, four basins, a basin stand, a looking glass, and a medicine chest. Simons's final illness may have forced him to remain on the ground floor, which would account for sleeping and medicinal articles not usually associated with the countinghouse. In the yard behind the residence, an outbuilding housed wine containers, carpenters' tools, barnyard animals, and garden implements. The dividing line between professional and personal in Simons's world was at best imprecise—and he liked it that way, for it allowed him to expand his trade.[72]

Countinghouse rooms sent a number of messages to those who entered. They expressed the merchant's bona fides: he had a cellar, wine to sell, and tools for treating and tasting the wine. These implied, although not always correctly, that the importer or wholesaler understood the arts of wine. They expressed his commercial success: an office, a clerk (or, better, two clerks), a separate back room, a stockpile of wine, and a cellar and warehouse suggested that the merchant was good at his business. They expressed his allegiance to merchants' habits and norms: a countinghouse in a central location at the heart of the city's commercial zone, easy to get to, and usually open. Most houses with clerks stayed open from 5 or 7 in the morning to 9 at night. "Constant attendance" was these merchants' watchword. Rows upon rows of ledgers showed that they kept written records in an orderly fashion; this inspired confidence that they treated customers diligently and lawfully. Being invited deeper into the countinghouse conveyed a message of intimacy to the customer. Being ushered into the back room was an honor, even greater if merchant and client later removed to the living quarters of the house. These were small spaces but they conveyed subtle variations on the themes of professional skill, allegiance, and respect—all the better because they were automatic and in the background—supporting the merchants' conversations with customers, competitors, and suppliers and fixing the integument of their trade.

BAYNTON'S NET

Many of the ways that wine importers and wholesalers constructed and maintained connections in a decentralized and porous transimperial economy are summed up in the work of the firms founded by Peter Baynton. Born in Philadelphia in 1697, Baynton entered the world of business in the 1720s; the dynasty he founded spanned much of the eighteenth century. He married a Charlestonian. At least as early as 1721, he captained a coastwise trading vessel that shuttled between Philadelphia and Charleston, selling wood and lime to planters in Carolina and acquiring rice and rum for Pennsylvanians. After his first wife died, he married a Philadelphia woman in 1723 and settled there the following year. Baynton imported and sold sugar, rum, clothes, sea provisions, whale oil, and "sundry European and West India Goods" from a small house at the lower end of Front Street. Like any West India sugar trader, for that is how he styled himself, he also offered wine. He traded small volumes, usually Canary, although he occasionally offered Madeira, Claret, Florence, and generic "wine." In 1728–31, for instance, he sold 386 gallons to twenty-two customers, all but two of whom lived and worked in the city. Few buyers were related to him by blood or marriage. Baynton had two large customers in these years: James Sykes, an assemblyman for Newcastle County, who bought 160 gallons of Canary, and Edward Hatton, who bought 110 gallons of Madeira and 25 gallons of Florence. Like other importers and wholesalers, Baynton also retailed wine. Aside from Sykes and Hatton, his customers took smaller amounts, on average 4.6 gallons of wine over four years, and half of them bought two gallons or less. All but two chose Canary, although that may simply reflect that Baynton, like other wholesalers, sold what he had on hand and did not buy more until he had depleted his stock.[73]

When Peter drowned in the Delaware River in 1744, his eldest son, John, inherited the business. John Baynton's trade focused more on the import and sale of wine than his father's. During the late 1750s, he began investing in various ad hoc general merchandising voyages to Newfoundland and Jamaica, in company with Peter Bard. They eventually parted ways, and John joined forces in 1758 with a more prominent merchant, Samuel Wharton, to sell a "large and neat assortment" of imported "European and East Indian goods" "very cheap" "for Ready Money, or short Credit."[74] Baynton & Wharton and its successor built and deployed links to eastern suppliers, local competitors, and western customers.

John Baynton and his partners aggressively built new bridges to suppliers. Noting that his firm dealt "pretty constantly in Madeira wine" and had done so from the time of his father, Baynton proposed to Madeira suppliers Lamar, Hill, Bisset & Co. that he and his partners "frequently address" the Madeirans on condition that they would "in like manner make the correspondence nearly-reciprocal." By this, Baynton meant that the exporters should "from time to time" consign to his firm in Philadelphia parcels of their wine, which would be "as well disposed of" by it as by any firm there. At the close of the Seven Years' War, Baynton became even more adventurous and issued a volley of proposals. He asked Lamar, Hill, Bisset & Co. to join him in buying a vessel or two, but the Madeirans squelched this idea. He next proposed that the exporters supply his firm with as much wine as the Americans "could advantageously vend"—in essence, that the Madeirans grant him an exclusive agency contract, cutting off his competitors in Canada. This would, he argued, aid Philadelphians eager to break into the Newfoundland fish trade. The scheme probably sank, as there is no subsequent mention of it, and the Hills continued to export to Canada. But Baynton & Wharton was not checked. It strove "to engross the future" of the Atlantic wheat trade two years later, proposing to "ship as much from hence as all other persons whatsoever" to the Hill firm. Multiply rebuffed, Baynton & Wharton and its successor, Baynton, Wharton & Morgan, started searching for more supportive correspondents and alternative supply systems that involved cooperating with competitors in Philadelphia.[75]

The lure of the frontier and an interest in western and Indian trade turned the partners' attention inland, even as they were scheming to engross the trade in Atlantic wine. Baynton & Wharton sold provisions to the troops at Quebec in 1760 and at Forts Pitt and Detroit two years later. When the firm's erstwhile apprentice (later junior partner) George Morgan became a senior partner in 1763 (he would marry John Baynton's daughter the next year), the newly reconfigured firm of Baynton, Wharton & Morgan returned to the possibilities of supplying frontier customers. From 1763, when it opened a store at Fort Pitt, the small, residential countinghouse and store on Philadelphia's Water Street served as the center of a widening, well-financed web of commerce. By 1765, the firm had committed to an "Illinois Bubble" that Morgan concocted with the Indian agent and fur trader George Croghan. The Fort Pitt store supplied people at the head of the Ohio River for over five years with everyday necessities—clothing, wine, and spirits to whites and liquor, jewelry, and weapons to Indians. Eager to push into undominated markets, the firm began supplying travelers on the Ohio and Mississippi from three additional stores, near Fort Kaskaskia, near Fort Chartres, and in the shadow of the Cahokia Court House, and that work quickly dwarfed provisioning Fort Pitt and its environs. The firm drew on suppliers as far east as Amsterdam and as far north as Boston; by 1766 it had brought roughly £40,000 sterling in goods to "the several Posts in the Indian Country" that supplied soldiers and civilians. For five years during the 1760s, the Fort Pitt store stood as the most significant provisioning post for the Ohio Valley journey, remaining dominant by placing agents in the western field and insisting upon constant reports from them on how commodities such as Madeira fared.[76]

Merchants were, with rulers, "the critical agents for the articulation of the supply and demand of commodities" in Anglo-America and elsewhere.[77] The transatlantic wine merchants were critical agents of articulation in the movement of Madeira wine from grape to table. Their networks had a particular geometry, characterized by one major link across the Atlantic for each product they imported and a multitude of links to customers, most of whom were nearby. Until late in the eighteenth century, the American-side merchants usually maintained relationships with one Madeira house at a time, using them to sell American grain, fish, and furs to Europe and to supply them with wine for resale in the towns and on the frontier of the New World. They dealt with houses in other places for other goods, including other wines and liquors. Exclusivity in a relationship arose from two sources: trust and lack of competition among the

Madeira exporters. Oceanic distances required trust. Building it with a correspondent took time and effort; as long as Madeira exporters adhered to Factory prices a single supplier was enough. This system began to fray as the nineteenth century approached and competition among Madeira exporters encouraged them to compete on price. By this time, Americans imported a greater variety of wines, and they were able to deal with several Madeira exporters to take advantage of the price competition.

At home in the New World, the importers and wholesalers cultivated a range of customers. They particularly sought out tavern keepers and storekeepers who bought larger quantities, but most continued to sell by retail to individuals as well. These relationships were usually local, so buyers could see their suppliers face-to-face. They transacted business on the street, in coffeehouses, and in lawyers' chambers, but the most important venues for encounters with customers were the merchants' countinghouses, which were designed as "conversation spaces" to personalize the exchange. A countinghouse often had a back room, more private than the front, furnished with chairs, a dining table, a tea table, decanters, wineglasses, tumblers, biscuits, nuts—and wine. The room could be devoted to business or co-opted by family socializing. Inviting customers into this and other private rooms allowed merchants and customers to step out of their customary commercial roles and inject a personal tone that solidified relationships. From there the wine was dispersed into the country and into consumers' hands.

8

The Wet Goods Business

Importers and wholesalers dominated the commercial communities of early Anglo-America, but retailers—tavern keepers, storekeepers, shopkeepers, and artisans who sold the wares they made or improved—were far more numerous, and also essential for getting liquor to customers.[1] Often considered "rather lowly creatures in the social hierarchy" of the English-speaking world, whose occupations afforded them "an easy life," they affected consumers more directly than importing merchants.[2] In the wine trade, they served as indispensable intermediaries between the distributors tied to the oceanic marketplace and consumers.[3] In the 150 years preceding the outbreak of the Seven Years' War, taverns were where consumers bought wine and spirits for both off- and on-premises consumption, excepting very prominent individuals who purchased directly from suppliers in the Wine Islands and mainland Europe and sometimes attempted to cultivate grapes. Most consumers bought wine from taverns or, occasionally, vintners, distillers, and coopers who imported it or, more likely, bought it from importers and other retailers when stocks ran low.[4] After the middle of the eighteenth century, stores came to dominate the off-premises liquor trade. Much of the surviving evidence comes from the ledgers and papers of a group of entrepreneurs who were principally, but not only, storekeepers. They combined liquor sales with sales of other goods, and sometimes very different businesses such as ship repair and milling; they pushed the trade out from their initial bases of operation; they traded wine with their peers; occasionally they even imported. They connected Atlantic and coastal distributors to inland consumers, incorporating the latter into transatlantic conversations and further articulating and shaping supply and demand. Toward the end of the eighteenth century, some of them began to see the opportunity to sell wine as a specialty business.[5]

THE TAVERN KEEPER'S TRADITIONAL TRADE

It was widely held among European settlers of the Americas that "the first thing the English" did was "set up a Tavern or drinking house," "be it in the most remote parts of ye world or amongst the most Barbarous Indians."[6] Taverns were the most common nondomestic buildings in Anglo-America in 1640 and still in 1740. They were the principal sites for alcohol acquisition before the Seven Years' War and, alongside homes, the main sites for alcohol consumption through 1815. They were common commercial and social structures not only in America but around the Atlantic.[7] Even in the 1800s, when stores and shops sold plenty of liquor, it would have surprised no one that Mother Hubbard went "to the Tavern For White wine & Red" and to "the Alehouse" for beer.[8]

Anglo-Americans erected drinking establishments with particular relish during the seventeenth and eighteenth centuries. In Boston, New York, and Kingston, even in Quaker Philadelphia, city dwellers "were generously supplied— perhaps over-supplied—with licensed taverns." Taverns were usually centrally located, erected along waterways and the main thoroughfares crisscrossing commercial districts. In New York, taverns flourished along the East River, in the East and Dock wards containing Dock Street, Hanover Square, Wall Street, Water Street, Beekman Street, and on numerous slips, docks, and quays. In Philadelphia, they hugged Water and Front streets, especially near the center of the town just south of High Street, and then, as the town grew westward, High Street itself. In Boston, taverns abutted harbor wharves. Charleston's taverns lined the bay.[9] In the countryside, tavern keepers opened their doors where river crossings intersected roads. From the opening of each new region in Anglo-America, taverns were among the principal ways Europeans gained an economic foothold. Within a year of the opening of the public house in Philadelphia in 1682, another opened in neighboring Germantown. Lancaster to their west had its first tavern by 1717, Harrisburg by 1719. The first public house opened in Carlisle in 1731, in Chambersburg in 1732, in Bedford in 1762, and in the shadow of Fort Pitt in 1765.[10] Moving down the Ohio River, travelers found a tavern at Martin's Ferry in 1770, at Marietta in 1784, and at Cincinnati in 1788. North of the river, there was a tavern along Zane's Trace at Chillicothe in 1796 and at Zanesville in 1800. By 1815, Chillicothe had fifteen taverns and Zanesville eleven. As the population in these areas grew, tavern keepers kept up with demand.[11]

The tavern business was a simple one. Few proprietors were full-time keepers; most had other jobs. They sold a small range of drinks from relatively simple, often crudely constructed vernacular buildings that usually doubled as their homes. Most of their suppliers were local or, in the case of imported liquor, resident in the nearest port. Most of their customers were friends and neighbors.[12]

Little distinguished most taverns from residences except for the signs out front, stables behind, and patrons at the door.[13] Urban tavern keepers were usually tenants, renting the building for as short as one year or as long as seven, and living in it as well as operating the tavern. In the early 1700s, for instance, George Emlen, his wife, four sons, four daughters, and a "Negro Woman Quasheba" all lived in and provided the staff for Philadelphia's Three Tuns. Its layout was largely the same as other family dwellings; only particular furnishings differed. Emlen's ground floor was divided into two rooms, separated by a central staircase, fireplaces, and chimneys. One of the two rooms was a larger "public room" with a built-in bar that was caged to protect the liquor and dispenser. Several rooms on the floors above were available for meetings; there were also two large bed-chambers on the first floor and three smaller ones on the second. Garret space was undoubtedly also used. Bulk liquor and food were stored in the cellar and in four of the five outbuildings: a kitchen, a brew house, a bake house, a storage "out house," and a stable. Any Atlantic visitor would have felt at home. The tax rolls valued the Three Tuns at £150 current money in 1693; by 1710, it was valued at £326 current. The increase is mainly due to Emlen's acquisition of an alley lot abutting the tavern, some pastureland, and adjacent tenements with a bake house behind them.[14]

Tavern rooms were simply finished and relatively unadorned, and owners and tavern keepers did little to improve them. In this they adhered to metropolitan models, although they were usually smaller.[15] They spent little on furnishings and comforts before 1763, as figure 8.1 and plate 10 show, and poorly maintained what they did acquire. Even in 1710, most of the Three Tuns's pieces were "ould." Rooms were sparsely furnished. No pictures adorned walls. The furniture was bulky, the fabrics durable. The main public room had a "large square table," a "small square pine table," six "ould" rush-bottomed chairs, an old chest, and an old chair. The other room, probably used for dining, contained only an "ould Square oak Table & Bench." Nor were the chambers upstairs luxurious. The "best" chamber had a sack-bottomed bed with curtains and valance, a "large new table," a black walnut oval table, a large oiled chest, and four black rush-bottomed chairs, plus a mountain of cotton and linen bedclothes. In this room, probably Emlen's, were stored the household's linens. The other large chamber contained four beds, furnishings for them, a cotton hammock, two chests, six chairs, five blankets, three coverlets, and five old rugs. Bed linens were either "finer" or, more commonly, "ould & cours." If the other third-floor rooms had

Figure 8.1. An eighteenth-century tavern interior, by Justis Junker,
after Charles Spooner, c. 1732.
Source: Courtesy of Collection of The New-York Historical Society,
New York, New York.

anything more than beds, blankets, rugs, chests, chairs, and trunks, it was not
noted. All in all, the tavern had a dozen beds, but that was hardly high given the
size of Emlen's family. The cellar was commodious, but it did not constitute significant investment: it contained a pipe of wine, three barrels of beer, and seven
casks of cider. It appears that Emlen began providing provision services; that is
why he acquired the stable yard, pasture ground, bake house, and brew house,
the last two doubly useful as he could supply himself and sell the beer and bread
he made to others. This was innovative of Emlen, but his relative neglect of the
tavern proper was more typical.[16]

The simplicity of the early Anglo-American tavern business is captured in the
tavern keepers' relations with suppliers and customers. Early tavern keepers' suppliers were few, usually local, and their relations relatively uncomplicated. Most
tavern keepers bought one type of spirits, usually rum, from a sea captain or local
distiller, wine from a merchant in a nearby port, beer from a local brewer, and
cider from an area farmer. Locally made drinks such as beer, cider, and sometimes
rum came to the tavern in the course of settling accounts or barter exchanges

with customers. Tavern keepers also bought supplies ad hoc — on the wharf off incoming vessels, at the houses and warehouses of importers and wholesalers, and
at the tavern itself, when peddlers called on them. They bought as need arose:
casks were generally used up before replacements were purchased.[17] Shipwright
and tavern keeper James West of Philadelphia sold only rum, beer, and cider at
the Pennypot in the last decade of the seventeenth century, for instance. The
narrow range reflected the fact that his suppliers were largely his customers and
employees: sea captains and merchants who were buying ships from his yard
or having their ships repaired there, and who often paid in Caribbean spirits,
and neighbors and laborers who were indebted to West and paid him in locally
brewed beer and fermented cider.[18] To the north in Massachusetts, the Rehoboth town moderator and tavern keeper Daniel Smith likewise procured drink
a decade later from only a few suppliers. Occasionally they resided in large port
towns nearby but, more commonly, they lived in Rehoboth itself. Some patrons
were distillers and paid Smith with rum for wine and other goods they bought
from him.[19]

Early tavern keepers' customers were neighbors, and local tastes drove the
business. The customers at West's Pennypot in the 1690s were, by and large, customers and employees of his adjoining shipyard. In the 1707–11 "diary" Smith
kept of sales in Rehoboth, he recorded that 72 percent of his customers resided
in his township, and they placed 78 percent of the orders for drink. Smith sold his
patrons what they wanted, as long as he had it, but sales were small and buyers
relatively easy to please. Smith's account with townsman Edward Glover shows
this. Glover preferred wine. One evening, Smith sold Glover an unspecified volume of wine in exchange for two pounds of sugar; several weeks later, he repeated the transaction. On both occasions, Glover probably carried the wine
home, since on-site consumption was usually accompanied by the consumption
of additional drinks, light snacks, or meals. On two subsequent occasions, Smith
sold Glover a quart of "common wine," poured Glover a gill of it, and watched
him drink it on the spot. Like Glover, Smith's other customers tended to stick to
their favorite beverages: wine drinkers ordered wine, spirit drinkers spirits. But
a want of inventory occasionally forced Smith to pour them other beverages.
Instead of providing William Corbett Jr. with his usual, a half-pint of wine for on-
the-spot consumption, Smith sold him four gills of liquor at the end of September 1710, when the tavern's stock of wine was exhausted. Most patrons appear to
have tolerated such substitutions. They did not stop frequenting the tavern when
they could not obtain their favorite drinks, but usually they were not long out of
stock.[20] Every three or four months, regulars paid their accounts, often tendering
homegrown provisions and home-manufactured items in lieu of what they owed

Smith, in barter for past drink or on consignment to Smith, who would sell them and credit their accounts with any overplus after the debts were extinguished. Strangers paid in cash.

Toward the middle of the eighteenth century, particularly in densely settled communities through which travelers passed, the practice of tavern keeping began to change. Managing a tavern demanded more of proprietors than it had in West's or Smith's day. As tavern keepers focused more intensively on the business, they pursued other occupations less frequently; when they did, they often combined the tavern with lodging or a store. They began offering a greater variety of drinks and ancillary services to a growing list of customers. They drew less on their customers for drink, turning to an expanded list of suppliers, although they did not usually procure imported drink from more than one or two individuals in a year. They visited the suppliers to taste and select wine and spirits; if the samples pleased, they brought one or two pipes or barrels home with them. They often shifted their patronage, coming to view purchases as one-off transactions. By the 1750s, it was unusual for tavern keepers to maintain long-term procurement relationships.[21]

The evolution of Anglo-American taverns accelerated after the Seven Years' War. Many communities gave up licensing and the attempt to use it as a form of relief for widows and the poor. New entrants flooded in, jostling with traditional dispensers for a growing population of drinkers. The more adventurous "endeavored to please" by cultivating novelty. All found themselves "challenged to find new ways of attracting patrons."[22] At the heart of these "new ways" lay what retailers described as "versatility." They expanded their offerings of drinks. They provided space for services and attractions that had not typically been offered before 1750: fencing schools, painting and tracing studios, health centers, hair salons, reading rooms, wax museums, animal showrooms, and stagecoach depots, to name just a few. They invested in new, expanded, and refurbished premises and upgraded the furnishings to attract drinkers who could now choose from a greater number and wider range of dispensers. To these ventures, they pitched the new language of gentility and respectability then sweeping the Atlantic world.[23]

In tandem with the improved wine, spirits, food, and services, tavern keepers competed on price. After the Seven Years' War, they began keeping abreast of competitors' prices, not only in the tavern in the next street but also in the next town or city. Few distributor-consumer exchanges survive, but some that do show competitive pricing at work. In 1759, the proprietor of Philadelphia's British Punch House learned that New York taverns "afford a Bowl of Punch for a Shilling [12 pence]," while ones in his city charged 50 percent more. With an eye to drawing the thirsty within and assuming that New Yorkers were reckoning a bowl at two pints, he offered to "make three pints of Punch for Fifteen Pence" and to make it of "the best Spirit imported here." The proprietor thought it smart, too, to announce "choice Madeira Wine, at three shillings a Bottle, and other Liquors in Proportion," and "all sorts of Choice, comfortable, and wholesome Cordials, wholesale and retail, at the lowest Prices." "At the lowest prices" was a constant refrain in the 1760s and 1770s. When one of his patrons told George Frey in 1776 that he could buy a glass of wine more cheaply at Wolfley's than at Frey's, Frey dropped his price immediately. A decade later Thomas Allen, proprietor of a New London, Connecticut, tavern, learned that the price of the highest-quality Madeira was lower in New York taverns; he lowered his price. Such moves suggest competition among tavern keepers that had not operated in previous years, when proprietors' pricing generally went uncontested. Keeping patrons happy became a more complicated and expensive task during the era of independence.[24]

THE STOREKEEPER'S NEW WORLD

In 1761, two Philadelphians, Benjamin Mifflin and Samuel Massey, opened a "Large convenient, and well accustomed Store . . . situated near the Drawbridge, fronting both Front and Water Streets." In it, they sold several sorts of wine, "Rum, Sugar, Melasses, Bohea and Green Tea, Pepper Alspice, Ginger, Rice, Coffee, Cotton," salt, corn, and "sundry other Articles, as usual." Madeira, Tenerife, Vidonia, Fayal, and red wine were important enough for the storekeepers to keep separate, named accounts of them in their books, and this was a minimum, for individual customers' accounts detail even greater variety.[25] Newman Swallow's bay-side store in Charleston, not far from the public Vendue House, was a similar operation a decade later. Swallow sold wine and spirits, beer, vinegar, water biscuit, flour, and salt, as well as consumer goods such as glassware and hats. To manage the liquor inventory, he acquired six "horses for liquor" (wooden supports to hold wine and spirit casks), a bottle rack, a scale, beam, boards and weights, three other pairs of scales and weights, pewter measures and funnels, and wicker bottles. He outfitted himself and his clerks with a desk, two Windsor chairs, and a bookcase to lure and impress customers. His store's two counters and six glass cases were laden with glasses and utensils ready to provide samples to those who stepped within.[26]

Wine and spirits other than rum were unusual in stores before the Seven Years' War. Only occasional mention of Madeira, Azores, Canary, Portuguese, or Spanish wines surfaces in ledgers, day books, and waste books. The few stores that included wine in their offerings did not feature it prominently.[27] After the Seven Years' War, storekeepers embraced the sale of wine and spirits more fully. One

sees this in their ledgers, inventories, and advertisements. Wine seldom constituted a separate accounting category for retailers before the conflict, but it often
did afterward.[28] Four times the number of storekeepers in Boston, New York,
Charleston, and Kingston carried wine, from a little more than 10 percent of the
group before 1765 to 40 percent after it.[29] Seven times the number of retailers
advertised wine in Philadelphia in the 1770s as in the 1730s.[30]

Little direct evidence reveals why storekeepers added wine to the products
they sold after the mid-eighteenth century, having mostly avoided it before.
There does not seem to have been a change in consumers' buying habits; for
example, there was no temperance movement that would have led them to avoid
taverns in favor of more discreet places to purchase liquor or a shift in the gender
of the family liquor buyer—and even this presumes women felt less comfortable
in taverns than men, which does not seem to be the case. On the sellers' side,
storekeepers and tavern keepers had access to the same importers and, as will be
discussed below, the same networks of retailers who traded wine among themselves as they had it or needed it. The most likely impetus to the shift in wine
sales was the increased availability of family-sized containers, which made selling
small amounts of wine much more convenient for store operations. Early in the
century, ceramic and glass containers were hard to come by in British America.
The glass ones had to be imported, with the costs of breakage taken into account.
Some ceramic vessels were produced locally, but ceramics degraded more easily
than glass. Taverns were set up to buy wine in bulk and dispense it from a tap,
but most stores were not. Taverns bought wine in pipes of 110 gallons or barrels
of 31 ½ gallons and kept small containers to rent to customers. A family could
rent a jug or bottle, bring it in repeatedly to be refilled, and eventually return it to
the tavern. By the time of the American Revolution, Philadelphia retailers could
buy containers at John Elliot Sr.'s Philadelphia Glass Works, Caspar Wistar's
glass factory in New Jersey, and Henry Stiegel's glass factory in central Lancaster
County, as well as at their in-town showrooms and the specialty wine-and-spirits
and glass-and-china specialty shops, brokerage houses, and warehouses that were
beginning to mushroom in the 1760s and 1770s.[31] With small containers cheaper
and more available, stores could broach a pipe or, better, buy wine from a wholesaler who broached it for them, and sell smaller amounts in closed bottles and
jars, just as they did other products. This reduced the investment in wine inventory as well as the demands on store operations from maintaining open pipes.
Reduced quantities of wine created an additional advantage: stores could afford
to keep more varieties in stock than most taverns, which still bought in bulk. This
increased their attractiveness to customers who were buying for off-premises consumption.

MANAGING A STORE

Storekeepers were originally general merchants who kept premises where customers could buy and sell goods. It was relatively easy to enter the business; the first stores were extensions of the storekeepers' houses. Once a place was chosen, the retailer needed goods to trade and customers. In an age that lacked the record-keeping and information-accessing capabilities that arrived with the nineteenth-century expansion of banks, postal services, railroads, and telegraph companies, this required networks of commercial relationships. Men and women like Mifflin, Massey, and Swallow built and maintained them with an intimate, almost familial style of doing business that persisted well into the nineteenth century. They obtained wine to sell on credit or consignment from wholesaler-importers and other retailers; they sold it to people who lived and worked nearby, and to their family and ethnic relations at greater distances. Sometimes they combined their stores with other employments: George Frey, for example, ran a store as an adjunct to his grain mills and taverns in Middletown, Pennsylvania. Often they took their customers' grain, furs, and manufactures in exchange. They sold or bartered the goods they received from their customers to other customers and to their suppliers who ran export houses. Organizing, managing, and servicing the people a retailer did business with—buying from them, selling to them, acting as their agent, or some combination of these—was central to his success and even, perhaps, identity.

Over time, storekeeping became more organized and differentiated. Grocers separated themselves from dry goods merchants, who separated themselves from haberdashers. Especially in the cities of the coast, they took fewer goods in barter or to resell. Still, even in the more refined establishments they retained some of the habits of the general merchants they evolved from. Mifflin and Massey might principally be called liquor and spice merchants, but they also sold cotton goods and "sundry other Articles, as usual." Newman Swallow sold wine and spirits and related goods such as beer and vinegar, but he also carried flour, salt, glassware, and hats. Only as the nineteenth century dawned did wine retailing become a frequently encountered specialty.

GOODS TO TRADE

A few storekeepers supplied themselves with wine by buying it directly from overseas exporters.[32] This option was not open to all retailers—only those who had reliable connections overseas and enduring operations in America. Importing retailers corresponded with exporters in the Wine Islands, Iberia, and at times even France and the Netherlands, accepting consignments from them and sending orders to them. Some channeled their requests through middlemen in London, Amsterdam, Paris, Lisbon, or Madrid, but they do not appear to have chosen this option often. A few aggressive retailers sent out vessels on their own initiative, hoping to barter outbound cargo for wine; in this case, they bore the costs of transport and assumed the risks of loss. In the competitive environment that materialized on both sides of the Atlantic after the Seven Years' War, European and Wine Island distributors encouraged such "adventures." Mifflin & Massey took such a step in 1762–63 when it consigned a cargo of lumber to Commyns Brothers & Powers of the Canaries; the storekeepers' ship returned with twenty-three pipes of Tenerife. Despite these transatlantic forays, by far the most significant source of wine for urban retailers was their local trading communities. Retailers usually dealt with a single supplier for each type of wine, depending on the importer's or wholesaler's connections with Europe and the Wine Islands. Seldom did they buy from merchants in other American towns.[33]

William West availed himself of all the options in the 1770s. At a store in Philadelphia's Front Street, he offered North American furs and skins and "A LARGE and neat Assortment" of India and European goods "suitable to the season." Prominent among the latter was wine he imported directly. He acquired Madeira from Donaldson & Searle between 1769 and 1777, placing orders with the exporters and accepting consignments from them. He detailed his customers' wishes to the suppliers, making sure they understood what he could sell in the Philadelphia market. He expected the firm to provide quality liquor, timely execution of orders, and full service. When he was disappointed, he let them know. On one occasion, he ordered a hogshead of wine; finding that it "proved ordinary" upon drinking it two years later, he returned it, asked for a replacement, and ordered an additional pipe. Correspondence with the Madeirans was the extent of his adventuring, though. He was a regular customer of the Philadelphia importer Reese Meredith for Madeira, and of one of Meredith's competitors for Canary and Sherry. He never procured wine from merchants based in other American cities.[34]

Retailers like West seldom kept large inventories of wine, so they frequently ran low—a situation that contributed to reliance upon each other. When importers and wholesalers could not quickly replace retailers' stocks, they turned to their fellow retailers. It was important to have a network of friends and colleagues to call on when that happened. The trading among competitors is perhaps the most surprising aspect of early American wine retailing, for it goes against the grain of "modern" practice. After 1760, retailers may have traded more wine among themselves than they bought from wholesalers and retailers. When West did not import from Madeira or buy from Philadelphia importers and wholesalers, he bought from storekeeper John Mitchell. In reverse, Mifflin & Massey's store accounts are full of sales to competitors. They sold wine to Charles Williams in 1761 and Andrew Doz the next year. Similarly, in the 1770s, the linen draper Thomas Amory of Boston turned to shopkeeper William Barrell for Madeira, even as he looked to the importers John and Jonathan Amory, close relations, for wine from the Azores. Whom one went to and helped was often shaped by blood connection, ethnic affiliation, and shared religion, but acquaintance could suffice to wrest some wine from peers. Transactions took place on a quid pro quo basis that bound the parties together. In an age when commerce was always precarious, helping others increased the likelihood that they would one day reciprocate. Sharing was a mark of cohesion in a community of traders. Information about who had a surfeit of wine was critical, and so information sharing formed a big part of network reciprocity. Exchanges were governed by informal rules about what goods to exchange, how much to mark up the drink and, generally, how not to offend one another. Ultimately, trading among retailers weakened the hold importers and wholesalers had over them.[35]

Public auction or vendue of wine was an important variation on the trade among retailers. Auctions for imported goods such as wine or spirits were a regular feature of a city's commercial schedule. Every city in America of any size had them. Venues varied: on or alongside a vessel, at a warehouse or countinghouse, in front of the house of the owner of the goods, at "The Merchants Hall," at a coffeehouse or tavern, or at a dedicated vendue house. Wherever they were held, urban retailers attended them; those with excess sold commodities in bulk, and those in need bought in lots of varying size. Before or at the time of sale, buyers could taste samples of wine. They could tender cash, bills, or sometimes barter goods. In St. Johns, Newfoundland, fish and oil were regularly "taken in exchange" at wine vendues. Mifflin & Massey bought at auction, paying the Philadelphia vendue master for a pipe of Vidonia, a pipe of Fayal, and a hogshead of red in 1761. Between May 1761 and September 1763, the firm acquired nineteen pipes in total, and all but a quarter-cask came from the vendue. Auctions were fast and provided "Great Bargains!" as advertisers never failed to remind would-be buyers. Many storekeepers preferred their comparative anonymity and simplicity—and their low prices. The auctioneer could assist the work of the retailers in many subtle and not-so-subtle ways, so staying in his good graces was good for business. Storekeepers saw that he was given presents, treated with food and drink, and allowed liberal credit for his own purchases when he called on them.[36]

Because most stores were not well capitalized, storekeepers maintained small inventories of merchandise. This was particularly true for wine and spirits; few enterprisers, even those heavily engaged in wine sales, maintained large stocks. Interestingly, inventories actually declined by half over the century, measured at the time of retailers' deaths. The relatively few retailers who stocked wine before 1765 left probated estates of £1,275 sterling, on average; the greater number of wine retailers after that time left £542. The values of wine and wine paraphernalia in the estates also fell, but their share of the inventories rose.[37] Because there were more small retailers who sold wine later on, the reduction in probate inventories over the century overstates the reduction in the inventory required for any level of wine sales. But there is a good reason to believe retailers became more efficient at managing their stocks: the price of wine rose dramatically after the imperial reforms of the early 1760s increased import duties on wine from Madeira and the Azores, putting pressure on retailers to reduce reserves. Reducing inventories reduced the capital they had invested in wine; this could result in substantial savings.[38] How could they reduce their wine inventories? Three things seem to have been at work. The number of shipments from wine-producing places like Madeira to American cities increased after the middle of the eighteenth century; since they were resupplied more often, retailers needed to keep less in reserve. They also realized the efficiencies of the trading among networks of retailers. Because they could buy from peers, each retailer could reduce the amount of wine he needed to keep. The network itself could be said to hold the inventory, and this reduced the quantity of inventory required per gallon or pipe of sales.[39] Moreover, retailers became more adept at calculating how much they needed to buy. They came to know what their customers wanted and catered to those tastes, reducing the need to hold inventory as a buffer against uncertain demand.

CUSTOMERS TO SERVE

Retailers sold wine locally, much as they procured it locally. Mifflin & Massey, for example, sold forty-two pipes of wine they acquired between May 1761 and September 1763 to twenty-four individuals and firms. All but three customers lived in Philadelphia. They acquired in relatively small lots: only six took more than a pipe, and most bought quarter-casks (about twenty-eight gallons). One of the few customers who bought more than a pipe was John Clow Sr. & Jr., a retailing firm in Sussex County, Delaware. Unless a customer ordered a specific wine, storekeepers kept only a few types of wine and sold them until they were exhausted. Those types then disappeared from their shelves until they acquired more; they seldom reordered wine before current stocks were sold. They also sold or rented the bottles and corks, decanters and glasses a customer might need for drinking. Not only did they know their customers' palates, they knew their aspirations.[40] Most sales were for cash or barter goods. As competition among retailers heated up in the 1750s and 1760s, and specie became scarcer, retailers began allowing store credit and granting longer periods for repayment. Still, credit sales never outstripped those for barter goods or ready money, and the latter was always preferred.[41]

The increased sophistication in business that coincided with the ending of the Seven Years' War affected wine retailers' approaches to their customers. They began offering a fuller set of services, becoming more attentive to consumers' needs, schedules, and desires. They called on prospective customers, taking care to know their prospect's circle and history. They tempted customers with samples, accepted returns, and offered advice on wine management and connoisseurship. They sold wine-related paraphernalia to accompany the drink. Finally, they became more flexible about payment options—offering credit, and not just on traditional terms but also for longer periods. Overall, they became more solicitous in their relations with customers. When a buyer complained about some wine he or she had bought, for instance, the seller would lavish attention on him or her— first with kind words, then perhaps with a humorous anecdote and an apology to defuse the tension, and ultimately with a promise to correct the matter. When a buyer defaulted in payment for wine, the retailer would complain discreetly to an intermediary rather than broadcasting the problem to the community. The customer was always right . . . even if not. Part of the increased attention to customers sprang from an awareness of mutuality, and part from the threat of competition. Whatever the spur, it was not uncommon for a customer in the second half of the century to request: "Do everything needful for me as you can and you may depend on my amply satisfying you, notwithstanding anything that can happen hereafter."[42] Solicitousness and leniency, linked to full service, became the order of the day.

Wine retailers also started using advertising. Philadelphia's George Meade, for instance, introduced wine into his portfolio of offerings in the 1760s. Within several months of opening his new Philadelphia store on Walnut Street Wharf in 1775, he began advertising Madeira, Tenerife, Port, rum, and spirits in large and small containers, from pipes down to bottles. By the early 1790s, now operating from larger quarters at the corner of Walnut and Third streets, Meade had honed the language that would draw customers to his store: he offered clients not just "Madeira" but "choice five years old bill Madeira wine," not just "Tenerife" but "Tenerife wines four and five years old, of a superior quality," not just "Sherry," but "old Sherry wine of the first quality." He meant to have "a constant supply of all these articles." Elaborate, informative, seductive blurbs like Meade's—reful-

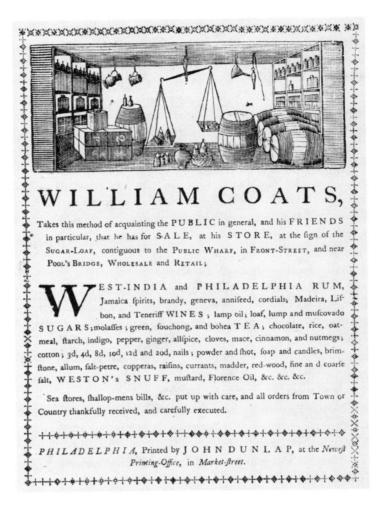

WILLIAM COATS,

Takes this method of acquainting the PUBLIC in general, and his FRIENDS in particular, that he has for SALE, at his STORE, at the fign of the SUGAR-LOAF, contiguous to the PUBLIC WHARF, in FRONT-STREET, and near POOL's BRIDGE, WHOLESALE and RETAIL;

WEST-INDIA and PHILADELPHIA RUM, Jamaica fpirits, brandy, geneva, annifeed, cordials; Madeira, Lifbon, and Teneriff WINES ; lamp oil; loaf, lump and mufcovado SUGARS; molaffes ; green, fouchong, and bohea TEA; chocolate, rice, oatmeal, ftarch, indigo, pepper, ginger, allfpice, cloves, mace, cinnamon, and nutmegs; cotton; 3d, 4d, 8d, 10d, 12d and 20d, nails ; powder and fhot, foap and candles, brimftone, allum, falt-petre, copperas, raifins, currants, madder, red-wood, fine an d coarfe falt, WESTON's SNUFF, muftard, Florence Oil, &c. &c. &c.

Sea ftores, fhallop-mens bills, &c. put up with care, and all orders from Town or Country thankfully received, and carefully executed.

PHILADELPHIA, Printed by JOHN DUNLAP, at the *Newelt Printing-Office*, in *Market-ftreet*.

Figure 8.2. Shop interior depicted on William Coats's
trade card, Philadelphia, 1760s.
Source: Courtesy of The Library Company of Philadelphia.

gent with references to type, grade, age, color, smoothness, and taste—became de rigueur in selling wine—discursive analogues to the more attractive and customer-friendly material spaces retailers were so busily constructing.[43]

Besides newspapers, wine merchants could advertise with their personalized business cards. Showing off the objects in his store was important enough to storekeeper William Coats that he emblazoned them on his trade card, reproduced here as figure 8.2. Coats kept a store during the 1760s "at the Sign of the

Sugar-Loaf" on Front Street in Philadelphia's Northern Liberties, selling sea provisions, "West-India and Philadelphia Rum, Jamaica spirits, brandy, geneva, aniseed, cordials; Madeira, Lisbon, and Teneriff WINES," sugar, spices, lamp oil, and necessities. Coats's card offered his customers a catalog of the tools of his trade, with the implied message of what he would do for them—something a storekeeper would not have bothered to do fifty years earlier. A wine pipe dominates the left-hand corner of Coats's card, with a bottle and glass atop it, ready to fortify the flagging spirits of an uncertain customer. On the right, a sugar cask stands upright, while four others lie on their sides, awaiting those who might need in quantity. Behind, fifteen wooden boxlike shelves display gin, case bottles, and other goods. Opposing them is a case with wine bottles and other commodities. Funnels and pitchers hang from the ceiling, in case smaller portions were to be needed or tests demanded. The room is packed yet orderly. This was a full-service enterprise that customers could go to for small and large needs.[44]

SPECIALTY WINE RETAILING

The emergence of wine retailing as a specialized business was part of the elaboration of distribution networks that connected the Atlantic world between 1640 and 1815. Specialization came relatively late to Anglo-America, and probably to Brazil as well, at least compared to England and Portugal. Yet it came earlier than has been allowed by American historians, who have tended to place it in the first decade of the nineteenth century, and it was central to the presence of European commodities throughout the American interior.[45]

Specialized wine retailers first were heralded in newspaper advertisements, city directories, and tax lists in the 1750s and became prominent in the 1770s. In Philadelphia, the first printed mention of a "wine store" or "wine shop" as a distinct establishment occurred in 1753; earlier notices listed wines among "goods too tedious to mention," although the tedium seldom stopped the retailer from listing as many as possible. The *Pennsylvania Gazette* of 1753 describes Samuel Grisley as the owner of a "wine store, below the Jersey market, where there is a green lamp before the door," where he sold "old choice Madeira wine, by the quarter cask, gallon and quart" and old Malmsey, Lisbon, and white wines by the bottle. Eleven years later, the paper noted that Francis Street ran a "wine store" in Water Street. The term *wine merchant* did not appear before 1772, although that is surely what Grisley and Street had been. At least three more wine specialists worked in Philadelphia at the outbreak of war—Benjamin Franklin's son-in-law Richard Bache, Thomas Batt, and John Mitchell.[46] During and after the Revolution, wine storekeepers, wine cellar men, vintners, and wine coopers proliferated.

Of the 514 traders listed in Francis White's 1785 *Directory* of Philadelphia, 5 were described as "wine merchant," "wine seller," or "liquor merchant," and another 11 were described as "distiller" (who, according to newspaper advertisements, regularly retailed wine and spirits). Clement Biddle noted 6 "wine merchants," "wine shops," and "wine stores" in his 1791 directory, and the highly reliable street-by-street-listing provided by Edmund Hogan four years later named 12 "wine merchants," the same number that appeared in the 1811 *Census Directory*. By 1814, there were at least 43 specialist retailers supplying drink to Philadelphians, as well as 47 distillers.[47] Specialization was not peculiar to Philadelphia: it swept Boston,[48] New York,[49] and Charleston,[50] as well—indeed, everywhere a density of stores served a population of drinkers. It was an option for retailers everywhere by the time of the Revolution.

A few retailers, such as Charleston's Newman Swallow, Philadelphia's John Wister, and Boston's Isaac Smith moved into specialty trading almost immediately after launching into business, even if they did not call themselves "wine merchants" or their shops "wine stores."[51] Most, however, found their way into specialization only gradually. An example was Charles Nicoll of New York. Born in 1738, Nicoll was one of two owners of a New York–based privateer, the *Oliver Cromwell*, during the Seven Years' War. With some of the *Cromwell*'s prize money, he commenced a trade selling prize rum and sugar to fellow New Yorkers as early as 1759 from a store on a wharf on the lower east side of Manhattan. As prize profits began to dwindle at the close of war, he regularized his sugar and rum interests, since he knew Caribbean waters well and his contacts there were extensive as a result of his privateering, and at the same time pushed into wine, since it rounded out a North American–West Indian sugar-trading voyage.[52]

After 1766, Nicoll specialized in wine and spirits to the exclusion of other goods until his death in 1779, with and without partners, despite obstacles raised by the war. His customers bought 6,500 gallons of wine and spirits, paying £4,300 New York currency. Wine dominated their purchases; spirits—rum, spirits, brandy, geneva, and porter—comprised only 13 percent of the quantity they took. They favored wines from Madeira, the Azores, the Canaries, Lisbon, Porto, Malaga, and France. Nearly three-quarters (73 percent) of Nicoll's sales were Madeira; one-thirtieth (3 percent) was Port. As Nicoll's reputation grew, he also provided wine-related paraphernalia and services to clients, which gave him an edge over nonspecialists. Customers could taste and compare a dozen varieties and grades at Nicoll's store. They could get bad wine "improved" on the spot. They could get wine in small and large quantities, as little as one bottle or as much as thirteen pipes. They could find the latest in fashionable glassware and wine tools: wine and cordial glasses in various sizes and with various decorations, wine decanters, wine cisterns, wine coolers, corkscrews, table mats, and the like. They could buy or rent washed bottles, procure corks, and have bottles corked and sealed. They could get gesso and brandy for refining and fortifying wine. They could even avail themselves of Nicoll's cartage service: the store would retrieve containers from customers' residences or stores, fill them, and return them improved and filled. The size and sophistication of the market had evolved to the point where a man could make a living providing specialist goods and services such as these.[53]

JOHN WISTER OF PHILADELPHIA, WINE BROKER

In addition to the importer-wholesalers who connected North Americans to wine suppliers around the Atlantic, tavern keepers, distillers, and coopers who sold wine as a principal occupation or an ancillary one, and retailers who operated stores where customers could learn about wine and buy it, there was a small cadre of wine traders who can best be characterized as "brokers" who traded wine among the others who had excess and those who needed it to sell to consumers. The existence of brokers is not surprising when people who would otherwise have considered themselves competitors trade with each other. It is a form of specialization that could arise only in an organized and differentiated market.

Of those whose business records have survived, the clearest example of a wine broker was John Wister. Wister was born in 1708, the seventh of the nine children of Hans Caspar Wüster and Anna Catharina Müller of Hilspach, six miles from Heidelberg, the capital of the Rhenish Palatinate, where his father was a forester in the service of its elector. Wister probably apprenticed as a woodsman in the Black Forest. After his father's death in 1726, he left for Philadelphia, following his oldest brother, Caspar, who had moved there the preceding decade. During his first four years, John worked for his brother, most likely as a charcoal maker, acquired a house on Market Street, and married Salome Zimmerman, from a family that had left Germany before Wister. He married twice more: to Anna Catharina Rübenkam, a native of Hessen-Rheinfels, who had migrated to Philadelphia with her parents, and to Anna Thoman, a native of Switzerland, who had lived as a nun in the commune at Ephrata. Anna Catharina bore Wister four children. In 1761, without their consent, their daughter Catharina married a Welsh soldier-turned-merchant, Samuel Miles. Vehemently opposed at first to the non-German match, Wister eventually forgave them and made Miles his partner in 1767. He signed the Philadelphia merchants' nonimportation agreement of 1769, but played no visible role in the American revolutionary conflict. He was a Moravian and an intimate of Count Zinzendorf, but not a religious zealot. He was a founder of the second oldest fire company in the city, a friend of "the hermits of the Wissahickon," a dispenser of funds to needy Palatines, a distributor of bread to the poor, and a supporter of the Pennsylvania Hospital. He died a rich man at his country house in Germantown in 1789.[54]

Wister commenced trading wine as soon as he acquired an undistinguished three-story brick house on the north side of Market Street in 1731. For nearly three decades he worked alone, although a cousin also worked out of the house, perhaps in some contractual relationship. Then, in the early 1760s, Wister began to form alliances. First, he linked himself to Owen Jones, the father of the woman who married his eldest son, Daniel, but that alliance lasted only a few months. Next, he established a partnership with his son-in-law Samuel Miles, whose family was already living in Wister's house. Finally, after the usual apprenticeship, John's youngest son, William, joined them in 1771. Throughout these ownership changes, the firm sold, "wholesale & retail," "West India, New England, and Philadelphia Rum, and Brandy by the Hogshead, Madeira and Tenerife Wines by the Pipe and Quarter Cask, Lisbon and Malaga Wines in Quarter Casks, Muscovado and White Sugars in Barrels, Sweet Oil, Also Tea and Coffee." Soon after William acquired a share of the firm and took over its management, John removed himself from active involvement; the following year, he left it entirely, Samuel and William continuing operations as "Miles & Wister." Wine trading persisted during the war, but, with peace, they reconfigured the firm and moved away from wine.[55]

Wister bought wine from many purveyors, many of whom were outside the usual group of importers and wholesalers, and often in quantities that seem small given the size of his business. Accounts from Wister's earliest years in business (1731–44) show him buying from shippers, importers, wholesalers, and retailers alike. He bought eighty-seven pipes of wine, ten pipes per year on average, between 1736 and 1744. He bought large quantities of Madeira from the importer Isaac Norris Sr. in the 1730s, a pipe of "wine" from Dorothy Aspden (the widow of the storekeeper Mathias Aspden) in 1736, a pipe from the sea captain Nathaniel Dowse in 1737, four pipes of Vidonia from Welsh importer Evan Morgan in 1739 and a cask of red from him the next year, twelve and a half gallons of Madeira from the agent of the Madeira exporter Dr. Richard Hill (Charles Willing) in 1740, and seven chests of wine from the storekeepers Alexander Stedman and Peter Robertson in 1741. In all, twenty-two suppliers sold Wister wine; among them were importers such as Morgan, Stedman, and Willing, but a larger number were retailer-wholesalers such as John Dillwyn, Thomas Lloyd, and James Thompson. Wister apparently preferred nonimporting traders: half his stock came from them. He bought in small lots: only one of his purchases during this time was greater than ten pipes, and it was only fourteen pipes; most purchases (twenty-eight of thirty-one) were fewer than five pipes. It was uncommon for Wister to specify the type of wine he bought; he recorded only Madeira, Vidonia, red, and unspecified "wine." Surprisingly, since wine dealers usually also sold spirits, he acquired little rum. He rarely imported himself.[56]

Business increased as Wister entered his third decade in trade. Between 1749 and 1754, he bought 415 pipes of wine, almost seven times as much per year as previously. Most lots (44 of 71) were still small, 5 pipes or fewer; only 14 lots contained more than 10 pipes, although they constituted 58 percent of the quantity. The range of wines and suppliers widened. He bought Madeira, Lisbon, Fayal, Bordeaux, and "wine" from fifty-eight sellers over the six years. He moved even farther away from relying on preexisting relationships with city distributors than he had in the 1730s and 1740s: only four of his fifty-eight suppliers were holdovers from previous years, and the most frequently he bought from any supplier was on four occasions. He continued favoring American rather than European distributors, although he avoided the largest ones, and preferred dealing with retailers rather than importers and wholesalers. One gets the sense Wister was a buyer of last resort for some sellers who were selling out at low prices.

Wister cultivated a network of customers, using his German origin and facility with languages to build ongoing commercial relationships with tavern keepers and other retailers. He sold to them in bulk. Originally most of his customers lived in Philadelphia, and he pursued their custom as they moved out into the Lancaster and York backcountry that Palatine migrants favored. All but 20 of Wister's 156 customers in 1747 and 1748 were of German or Dutch origin. Of those whose residence can be ascertained (for four-fifths it can), only one-fourth (24 percent) lived in his own city and county; nearly one-third (32 percent) lived in Lancaster County and one-tenth in Berks County, areas where Wister's German ethnicity stood him in good stead. The remainder were scattered throughout Montgomery, Washington, York, Bucks, Chester, and Dauphin counties, mirroring the European settlements in Pennsylvania at midcentury. Three buyers lived in Maryland and New Jersey. The call from each customer could be quite sizeable, for they included many tavern keepers and retailers. His two biggest customers were the tavern-keeping Gross brothers, George in Lancaster Borough and Christian in York Town. Also significant was Henry Keppele, an immigrant German who rented from Wister two buildings next to Wister's Market Street residence and kept a tavern in one of them. (Wister's other tenant in 1752 was Benjamin Franklin.) Between 1748 and 1755, Wister sold Keppele twenty-seven pipes of wine and spirits valued at £642 currency. Most was recorded as "wine" (89 percent of the quantity and 93 percent of the value), but the price suggests Madeira. The rest was rum. Generally, Wister sold Keppele a pipe or two at a time, although on occasion the bill was for a hogshead or quarter-cask. In 1755, he also began to supply Keppele with sugar and molasses, which the tavern keeper used for mixed drinks.[57]

There was one significant exception to Wister's avoidance of importers. He always favored Madeira in purchases—or, rather, his customers did—but Rhenish wine was preferred by some of the non-English population of greater Philadelphia, and Wister used his German background to get it for them. Since demand for wine was high in Germany, Rhenish was often difficult to procure for Philadelphians. Wister tried to import it himself on only three occasions. Instead, he directed Philadelphia importers to the German and Dutch distributors he knew in the Greater Rhine/Neckar/Amsterdam area who had stocks of Rhenish wines or at least information about them. His letters and accounts shed little light on why he did it this way. He may have wanted the wine but not in the normal quantity shipped; he may not have wanted to use his capital in a venture that risked the loss of cargo or vessel; he may have been using his connections in Europe on behalf of a business acquaintance from whom he would receive cash, credit, or another quid pro quo; or some of his agents in Europe may have asked him to introduce them to wine importers in Philadelphia. Whatever the scenario— and these are not mutually exclusive—Wister combined his international and local networks to supply himself and support other members of a transatlantic exchange group.

Ostensibly, Wister's business changed little between the 1730s and the 1760s. He continued to buy from whoever had what he wanted at the best price. In 1758–60, he had fewer customers (only sixty), in part due to wartime operations in the Pennsylvania backcountry, but the customers he had were German; one-fourth lived in Philadelphia City and County, one-fourth in Lancaster County, one-tenth in Berks, and the rest in Chester, Montgomery, Northampton, York, and Bucks counties. Drawing on family and ethnic networks, he developed a small customer base in other cities; he supplied his nephew Caspar Wistar, a distiller, with wine to sell at Caspar's New York City still house, for example. In 1759, he sold 184 pipes; over one-third (39 percent of quantity and 34 percent of value) was rum and Jamaica spirit, the rest wine. Madeira was preeminent among the wines (28 percent of quantity and 39 percent of value), followed by Tenerife (20 percent and 19 percent).

But other aspects of Wister's trading did alter. He became more adept in managing inventory—calibrating the demand of his customers—and stocking a complex array of goods. This was easier for him than for others, because he did not move from place to place as many retailers were fond of doing. From the start, he had a well-equipped house, with three brick outbuildings to use for storage. Moreover, he became savvier in marketing and more adept at drawing and maintaining customers. Like the importers and retailers, he offered connoisseurship training: tutorials on how to taste wine and tell good wine from bad. He offered samples. He visited the counties where customers lived when they did not come to him. He supplied mixtures tailored to individuals' tastes. He provided bottles and casks in various sizes. About the only marketing tool Wister did not adopt was newspaper advertising. In short, he offered his customers knowledge, assistance, and price—the result of savvy buying and marketing.

RURAL WINE RETAILING

In western Pennsylvania, in new towns on the Ohio River, and in remote outposts in the center of the continent, European Americans drank imported liquor. The population of North America was more than seven-tenths rural throughout this period, and the rural population was growing more rapidly than the urban. Enterprisers from the coastal cities sought the custom of people on the frontier, integrating them into Atlantic networks and creating "a steady commercialization of economic life."[58] Coastal wholesalers and retailers supplied backcountry middlemen, stocked rural stores, carted wine and spirits inland, provided rural customers with credit, and accepted their produce for resale on the coast and across the sea. Sometimes they even established stores in order to sell to patrons. They did these things by creating and maintaining connections that integrated backcountry people into transoceanic conversations and networks.[59] A group of middlemen—opportunistic, creative, and sometimes a little bit shady—constructed another set of links in the decentralized and self-organized economy of a widening Atlantic world.[60]

Chief among the goods in rural stores was wine, for European Americans everywhere wanted a drink that they or their forebears had known at home. Rural consumers went to three types of suppliers for wine and spirits before the last third of the eighteenth century. Most commonly, they patronized the taverns and inns that sprang up wherever white people settled. There, they could drink liquor or buy it by the gallon and quart to take home. A few very substantial backcountry drinkers bought wine and spirits from exporters working at the point of production; this was, not surprisingly, less common inland than on the coast. Less prominent men and women who desired larger quantities than were sold in taverns bought from importers and wholesalers in the eastern seaports. These traders supplied planters from Maryland through Florida, even those far inland.

After 1763, frontier consumers began to find wine and spirits in general stores as well; retailers were following the settlers into the interior and bringing drink with them.

Many of the rural retailers hailed from the country, but most of the best-documented examples come from the ledgers and account books of the urban merchants who sold to them. Most urban suppliers who focused on the country sold to retailers in the "near" backcountry of the city they inhabited; this is, for example, what John Wister did. Country people controlled the retail operations from there, linking their neighbor-customers to coastal and in some cases British and European suppliers. A few of the largest country retailers mimicked their urban suppliers by reselling goods to networks of dependencies, friends and relations in their own hinterlands. These were most often enterprisers who managed a number of businesses; one such merchant was George Frey, who was the largest grain miller in Pennsylvania, ran a tavern and a store in Middletown, and maintained a network of retailers throughout eastern and central Pennsylvania that looked to him for wine and liquor supplies.[61] A smaller number of suppliers also provisioned the "deep" backcountry, west to Detroit and Kaskaskia, north to Nova Scotia, and south to Florida. Even as they attempted this, specialty storekeepers began to appear on the scene, in most places a generation or so after they appeared on the East Coast.[62]

In rural districts, where crossroads communities, plantations, and farms were often a great distance from one another, combining retailing, crop marketing, and money management kept storekeeping general. "The store was the primary" and at times only "mercantile operation in the backcountry," so it "functioned in some capacity as a central place" and "had numerous activities to perform." Given "the shortage of cash and the lack of banking institutions" in rural areas, the store also served as a financial clearinghouse. Some of the ancillary services provided were more critical there than in the cities, as there were fewer alternatives nearby. Stores had a plethora of items; given the isolation of inland communities, it was important to customers that they did.[63]

Distributing wine through country stores was similar in many ways to the urban version, especially in the creation and intense management of business networks. There were a few differences: the longer distances created problems that elicited considerable inventiveness from the retailers. Randle and John Mitchell, for example, created a network of chain stores—the first ones that were not staffed principally by family members. Retailers with a primarily urban clientele sold wine throughout the year, but for those who dealt heavily with buyers in the country, sales in the summer were slower, rural buyers making most of their purchases in September when they brought their harvest to market and stocked

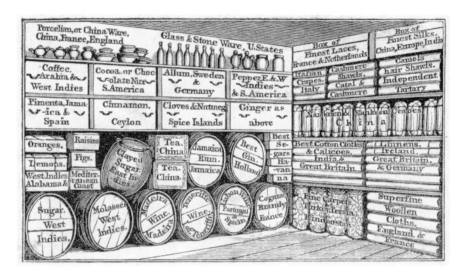

Figure 8.3. *Country Store, Exhibiting the Productions of Various Countries*,
by an unknown artist, before 1826.
Source: Emma Willard, *Geography for Beginners; or, The Instructer's [sic] Assistant*
(Hartford, 1826). Courtesy of Rare Books Division, The New York Public Library,
Astor, Lenox and Tilden Foundations.

up on winter provisions. Also, country storekeepers had to accept barter goods, because that was often all the buyers had; city storekeepers could more often insist on cash.

The transactions of two of the best-documented country stores—one southern, one northern—show the operations of rural wine retailing. These examples were the work of urban merchants who bought or established stores in the backcountry, following customers—Kershaw of Charleston and Baynton, Wharton & Morgan of Philadelphia.

Joseph Kershaw, his brother Ely Kershaw, William Ancrum, John Chesnut, and Aaron Loocock acquired three preexisting retail outposts in rural South Carolina in the late 1750s and early 1760s. Joseph managed the store at Pine Tree Hill (now Camden) in the central part of the state; the other two stores were at Rocky Mount and Chatham. Kershaw's store sold a wide array of necessities—food, drink, clothing, tools, and seed.[64]

From their base in Philadelphia, Baynton, Wharton & Morgan's ambitions ran as far as the banks of the Mississippi. The point of entry for their "grand speculations" was hardly grand, though: a simple, wooden general store in the shadow of Fort Pitt, in what is now Pittsburgh. The firm built this structure—the first shingle-sided house in town—in 1765 upon the arrival of George Morgan, the firm's youngest partner.[65] From it, Baynton, Wharton & Morgan supplied everyday necessities like clothing and drink to soldiers and the community that grew up around them; in addition, they managed a trade with Indians, exchanging liquor, jewelry, and weapons for furs and skins. They kept the Fort Pitt store open for five years while they established three satellite operations: near Fort Kaskaskia, on the Mississippi River about 125 miles north of its confluence with the Ohio; near Fort Chartres, about 25 miles farther north; and in the shadow of the Cahokia Court House, yet another 40 miles farther north in what is now East St. Louis. In the end Baynton, Wharton & Morgan's inland business failed, frustrated by partners "too much entertain'd with the Golden Dreams of Tagus" and ill equipped to deal with the realities of frontier life.[66] But in 1765 neither success nor failure was clear.[67]

Rural retailing was personal, handled face-to-face, storekeeper to buyer. Most stores were small, run by a man, perhaps his wife, and a servant or clerk. At the Kershaw store there does not appear to have been a clerk, although family members may have lent a hand from time to time. If Kershaw was not there, there were no sales. Baynton, Wharton and Morgan's Fort Pitt operations were larger, employing at least two clerks, one of whom was a slave, but their customers were by and large known to the staff, residents of the area or frequent visitors. Among the ninety-six customers in the first year for which accounts survive and for whom residence and occupation is discoverable, one finds sixteen army officers, twelve carpenters, coopers, and sawyers (hardly surprising in a community that could not fell and hew timber fast enough to meet construction needs), six Indian leaders and tribes, two Frenchmen, and one widow-shopkeeper. Morgan and his clerks knew all but a handful of them because they lived within fifty miles of the store and much of the business was repeat. Some thirty-one of the ninety-six customers purchased wine or spirits in 97 transactions at the Fort Pitt store; nine returned for wine and twenty-two for rum. Most customers frequented the store several times each month; the less frequent exceptions being the peripatetic George Croghan, three itinerant Detroit traders who shuttled between that settlement and Fort Pitt, and the representatives of the Indian tribes. At Pine Tree Hill a decade later, in March and April 1775, eighty-one buyers purchased wine and spirits 173 times; twelve of them were regular wine buyers and seventy-seven were regular rum buyers.

Rural retailing was slow paced and small scaled. Kershaw's day book reflects the routine. In six weeks of March and April 1775, a fairly busy time of the year, he opened his store on thirty-four days and sold to 218 customers. Most were men; only 4 percent were women. He sold 1,674 individual items. On an average day, twenty men and women bought 49 items. The average buyer returned three times to buy eight items over the six weeks.[68] The situation was similar at Fort Pitt: the average purchase of wine and spirits by Baynton, Wharton & Morgan's customers was just over a gallon; the largest lot was thirty-six gallons and the smallest a pint.

Customers' tastes in drinks were basic. The extremely detailed day book kept by Kershaw shows that drink and sundries loomed equally large in the store's sales, but they were dwarfed by cloth, which comprised one-third of his business. Wine and spirits made up one-eighth of Kershaw's sales; rum comprised the largest share, followed by wine. Several types of spirits were recorded—West Indian rum, New England rum, and Jamaican spirit—but not many. A small amount of gin and brandy passed over the counter in subsequent years. Wine was noted only as "wine." Baynton, Wharton & Morgan's customers found a similarly limited range. In 1765, for instance, George Morgan and his clerks sold 409 gallons of liquor for £268 sterling. Rum was the favored drink, comprising 82 percent of total volume. Wine comprised some 14 percent: the expensive Madeira 12 percent and the cheaper Lisbon, 2 percent, both of which were sent by partner Thomas Wharton from Philadelphia. The firm maintained a separate "Rum Account" in the accounts, but not a "Wine Account." There was a difference in station between wine customers and spirits customers. Some twenty-nine customers bought some liquor in 1765–66. Six bought only wine, including Dr. Potts and the minister to the Second Regiment, who bought Madeira, and a trio of officers, who took Madeira and Lisbon. Two groups (one of unnamed packhorse men) bought both wine and spirits. The remaining twenty-one customers bought only spirits, mainly rum, including three Delawares who took rum "for the Use of the Crown," Indian negotiator George Croghan, the blacksmith James Berry, and an "Adventure to the Illinois." Imported wine was the drink of officers, doctors, ministers, and wealthy men; artisans and soldiers bought rum.

JOHN MITCHELL OF PHILADELPHIA, RETAILING INNOVATOR

John Mitchell first brought wine to the backcountry during the economically charged prerevolutionary period, in the same years when the Wisters were specialized wine brokers. The Wisters, alongside the importers and other retailers, were aggressively courting rural tavern keepers and storekeepers around Philadelphia—traveling to visit them and playing host when they came to town, and expanding the range of services they offered along with the wine. In an extraordinary leap of imagination, Mitchell realized there were potential rural entrepreneurs whom he could help go into business in exchange not only for the right to sell them wine and other products, but also for a fraction of the profits of the enterprise. He and his brother set up a franchise store operation with resident storekeepers in each town. In each store the storekeeper was a partner in the store or an appointed employee; they were not family members. These stores are the first recorded franchise stores in America. In Britain, some retailers had established "ostensibly independent but mutually supportive" subsidiary stores in nearby villages and staffed them with family members. But nothing like the Mitchells' franchise system existed before the nineteenth century.[69]

The son of one Philadelphia merchant and the brother of another, John Mitchell first appeared on the scene in 1754, when he was listed as having income of £28 Pennsylvania currency and owning property on Walnut and Fifth streets. By 1762, he was working in concert with his brother Randle in the West India trade: in Dominica and Martinique, which were then occupied by the British, he acted as supercargo of their joint concerns, negotiating the sale of grain and the purchase of sugar, molasses, rum, and spirit; in Philadelphia, he worked in his brother's various concerns—a dry goods warehouse and a sugar refinery. By 1768, he had begun to branch out, selling European and East Indian goods on his own at a Front Street store just south of the London Coffee House; two years later, he formed a partnership with the trader John Murray, while continuing to work with Randle.[70]

Until 1773, John and Randle sold wet and dry goods and other commodities to people living to the west and north of the city. At the store on Front Street, the brothers sold wine, spirits, cloth, clothing, tea, sugar, coffee, gammon, biscuit, and other comestibles. Desiring to broaden their sales, they looked beyond the city. To create customers for themselves, they established franchise stores in Allentown, Reading, and Trappe before 1772 and in Caernarvon and Middletown in 1773—all places "well known for their good situation and considerable trade." Originally set up in March 1773, the Middletown store was typical of the system: John and Randle each owned a third, as did John Williams, the resident storekeeper. The Mitchells were to supply Williams "with all sorts of good wares & merchandises necessary from the said store at their own proper cost and on their credit and the said JW was to have (for his trouble and attendance on the sale of the goods and the recovery of the debts and every other thing . . .) one third part of the issue and profits arising from the Trade and Business carried on at said store, or to suffer one third part of the losses arising thereon." Since the Mitchells did a heavy business in liquor, wine and rum flowed freely.[71] In addition to the franchise stores, the Mitchells struck exclusive supply relationships with stores owned by other retailers. In Lancaster, they formed a partnership with the merchant Charles Hamilton and the tavern keeper George Moore in 1773, when Hamilton and Moore had "removed from" a house "they lately lived in" and opened a store with "a large and neat assortment of goods, suitable to the season." There, with the help of their Philadelphia suppliers, they maintained "a large and general" stock. They would, they assured would-be customers, keep a ready supply of wine, rum, molasses, coarse and fine salt, "boulting cloths, for merchant and country work," saddle goods, and German and English steel.[72]

The Mitchells steeped themselves in "the art and mistery of shopkeeping." They stocked the stores with what was to the customers the "correct" complement of goods. They paid close attention to the quantity, quality, and price of goods sent to each store—"the best that can be got" for the most reasonable price. Certain goods were a must. As a clerk in the Reading store noted, "sugar, tea, coffee & some other tryfling things" were the things "that brings a store customers"; if the store had "good sugar, tea & coffee," then it would "have the Town custom." Moreover, whenever the customers' friends came to town and wanted anything, the customers "always will recommend . . . that store where they get their things." One of the Mitchells' exclusive customers, a storekeeper in York, wholeheartedly agreed: the "welfare of my general sales dependes much on that artickel [sugar] being good and well liked by the people." Wine was also "necessary"; to maintain its viability, no country store eschewed Madeira and rum. Repeat custom depended upon both, in sufficient plenty, of sufficient quality, and at decent prices.[73]

The brothers kept a "Book of Goods" in which they recorded the commodities they sent to each store. Of wine and spirits supplied between March and August 1773, for instance, they sent forty-seven pipes of rum, four of Tenerife, and one each of brandy and cordial. Much of this they pulled out of their cellar in Philadelphia which, at the same time, they were filling with lots of Canary and Lisbon bought from their principal supplier, the importers Merediths & Clymer. Of the fifty-three pipes they shipped, thirty-one went to three of their stores: Allentown, Caernarvon, and Reading. The remainder went by wagon and boat to the retailers with whom the brothers had forged the supply contracts, chiefly Hamilton & Moore in Lancaster and Wright & Murray in Southampton. The storekeepers wanted wine and rum, and they wanted it quickly: they managed their stocks by laying up wine and spirits before the onset of winter made transport difficult, and then by selling them until they were exhausted. The "ballance of liquors are fallen," "our rum is almost all gone," or "I am completely out of wine" was a constant refrain of agents and storekeepers in the field writing back to Philadelphia.[74]

An advantage of franchise retailing was that when one store fell short, it could call on a sister store rather than appealing all the way back to the brothers in the city. Caernarvon could more readily draw upon Reading than restock itself from Philadelphia. When "there was a great demand for" wine bottles at the Reading store and Mitchell experienced difficulty procuring a shipment from Caspar Wistar's factory in New Jersey, the storekeepers went to Henry Stiegel's glasshouse in nearby Manheim and purchased a hogshead of them. Similarly, Mitchell turned to storeowners such as Charles Hamilton in Lancaster, John Wright in Southampton, and John Wilkins in Carlisle when his stocks fell low. When "in great need for some" cloth and Mitchell could not send any, his clerk went to a Lancaster storekeeper.[75]

The Mitchells kept their stores fully staffed and closely watched. Each store had at least one, usually two, resident storekeepers plus a clerk. Young, single male clerks, like Peter Anspach, could be moved from place to place as need arose. John Mitchell visited each store at least twice a year. He ordered resident storekeepers to visit other stores not in the system and company customers who resided in distant parts of the counties, not just to collect debts but also to gather orders and "drum up business." The brothers also kept close watch over what arrived at and left the Philadelphia store for these rural outlets. John Mitchell personally examined the wine and rum containers, for instance, and informed the storekeepers "whether they are full or not before they leave town," so that they could learn whether the cartmen and boatmen were defrauding them.[76]

Real benefits accrued to a network of stores. But it also incurred new costs, principally heavy investment in infrastructure and inventory, and sizeable and numerous debts neither quickly nor easily collected.[77] The costs accumulated on Randle in late 1773; in addition to overextending himself with multiple stores and illiberal credit, sales did not meet expectations. He declared bankruptcy and began extricating himself from debt by selling off the brothers' "goods on hand" and renting their stores. John regrouped by reestablishing himself as a specialized wine and spirits trader. He placed an ad in the *Pennsylvania Gazette* announcing his "Wine, Spirit, Rum and Sugar Store." Much like Wister decades before, although this time acknowledging the specialty, John provided twelve kinds of wine—"new or old," "dry or sweet," "genuine," "excellent," or "of the best quality," in any desired quantity—plus three kinds of porter, two kinds of ale, two kinds of rum, Hollands geneva, and French brandy. He continued to supply his former store partners in the country in much the same way as he had before. But while he provided the range of products expected in a general store, his principal interest lay in their liquor sales.[78] The reimposition of nonimportation, the outbreak of fighting, the closure of ports, and the disruption of shipping frustrated the operation. He moved away from retailing liquor in 1775 toward guns and hardware. By 1776, that was all he did.[79]

An important benefit of Mitchell's backcountry network was the commercial information exchanged through it. In Philadelphia, at the center, it was critical for the owners to know what happened to their investments. The storekeeper on the periphery needed to be able to satisfy customers' particular demands. Not infrequently, John Reynolds in Reading asked John Mitchell in Philadelphia to buy specific goods from specific retailers. When Reynolds ordered a pipe of the "best Tenerife Wine," he directed Mitchell's attention to particular stores. "Perhaps your Brother may have the Wine, as we had the last from him." "Look out for the best & cheapest to be had in the City," the Reading storekeeper enjoined; "see if there is any good to be sold at the Coffee House."[80]

The network also provided feedback, particularly about the quality of the goods. Working out of the Reading store, Murray and Connelly informed the brothers in 1772 that the Fayal they had sent turned out "but middling" and requested directions on "how to fine it & bring it to be a little stronger and sweeter." Three months later, Murray and Connelly received some rum from Philadelphia, found it wanting, and had "a Man . . . who is a Judge [of such things] . . . try the Rum," who reported it to be "very new & weak" and "wasted." Charles Hamilton wrote to the Mitchells in 1774 to discuss some wine and spirits sent from Philadelphia to Lancaster for a tavern keeper; the latter found "they won't do." As Hamilton explained, the liquors "are strong and good but have when mixed in water a twang not much better than Philadelphia Rum. I have never tasted anything on rum or spirits equal to it and can compare it to nothing more like than the taste of isinglass warm from a still. I would have been glad you had inspected the spirits & tried them in water. They are in the tavern keeper's sellar and have been trying to get the bad taste off by putting some things into them as they cannot be used else." Clearly, the drink was unsatisfactory, and the brothers were expected to fix it.[81]

The Mitchells' correspondence disseminated principles of connoisseurship, as did Madeira exporters' and other Philadelphia merchants.' The art of fining and improving wine was complicated and formed the subject of numerous exchanges. Once, Hamilton was vexed by a hogshead of spirits Mitchell had sent him, for it possessed a "still burned taste." Hamilton and his buyer had added tea leaves but that only blackened the color without improving the taste. They were at a loss what else to do. Mitchell responded with tips gleaned from his suppliers and friends in Philadelphia.[82]

Exchanges like these conveyed messages, explicit and implied, about country taste, the level of demand, and the prices people would tolerate. Thomas Hartley of York wrote about the arrival of some Sherry and the likelihood of a market for Madeira in 1775. He had no doubt that Sherry would

> suit the latitude of York, instead of Madeira which is too expensive for such Oeconomists and Patriots as the Inhabitants of this place. I am almost certain that the wine you sent Baltzer Spengler will be agreeable. The wine in the Taverns of this town called Madeira is too strong and wants age and the low price it is sold at will not enable the tavernkeepers to procure better. Unless the ordinary people get a better Taste which will induce the tavernkeepers to change their present wine merchants, I fear we shall not be able to introduce much of your Madeira among them. But be assured that I shall make it my particular study to forward your interests in this country. I have tasted the Porter which you sent to [Robert] White and am sorry to tell you I do not like it, it is ill corked and the quality not of the best. . . . What formerly I had from you was excellent and praised by all.

When Hamilton later wrote the brothers ordering ten hogsheads of Philadelphia rum, he explained that drinkers in Lancaster wanted rum that was "strong and brandy colored." Likewise, when Wilson & Falconar wrote in 1774, the firm reported it had "never sold any of" the Sherry that Mitchell had shipped; such wine, the Philadelphia retailer learned, "does not suit" Bucks County tastes. He shipped no more.[83]

John Mitchell tried to formalize part of his informal network. The franchise store operation evolved out of his and his brother's earlier business retailing wine, spirits, cloth, clothing, tea, sugar, coffee, gammon, biscuit, and other comestibles to Philadelphia consumers and distributing them to taverns and stores in Philadelphia's near hinterland. When it ended, he returned to selling wine and spirits to those same people, the people who made up his network of suppliers, customers, neighbors, and friends. But while it lasted, he created a more formal network of people bound to each other by written contracts and organized by designated roles. The innovation was a powerful one, although one that would not be entirely successful until a couple of generations later. It brought capital and expertise from the metropolis to the backcountry while also taking advantage of country people's personal relationships with their customers. It made use of the distributor's networks of suppliers and knowledge of who had wine to sell as well as the retailers' networks of customers and knowledge of their neighbors' financial and personal situations. When it worked well it assured the storekeeper of the right goods to sell and the town-based distributor of outlets for his products. Perhaps most important, in this period when long-distance distribution was being regularized and institutionalized, the model could be repeated in town after town. It did require intensive management, but the scope for the exercise of management skills was broadened considerably beyond the handful of outlets that could be directly overseen by a small number of partners.

Storekeepers and tavern keepers were some of the most important agents in the early Anglo-American economy.[84] They used their premises to create and extend the economic, social, and political networks that constituted their communities. The rituals of enterprise and hospitality were enacted in their premises. At stores like Swallow's and the Mitchells,' consumers found wine, spirits, and an array of necessary and luxury goods. At taverns like West's and Smith's, they found drink, food, and lodging for themselves and provisioning and stabling for their horses. The sites formed a physical envelope for selling, negotiating, and buying, and for observing what was being bought and sold by others. They were home to conversations among traders, citizens, and friends—between retailers and customers, and among customers.

Taverns were the community's common parlors; they brought people together for drinking, eating, and lodging, and tavern keepers made most of their money from this socializing. The central room was the ground-floor "bar" or "public" room where patrons introduced themselves to each other, massaged relationships, and cemented friendships. Tavern keepers encouraged merchants and retailers to use the spaces for lubricating trade, and they became salesrooms for commodities and negotiation rooms for deals: prizes, properties, structures, and slaves were sold and bought; insurance contracts, legal trusts, and freight terms were hammered out; goods and estates were auctioned; portraits were painted; hair and beards were cut. Taverns also offered space for political activities. The combination of sociability with hospitality was not new in the eighteenth century, and savvy tavern keepers combined them with an eye toward drawing neighbors and strangers into the bar and keeping them coming back.

Stores effectively functioned as the public's open countinghouse and were no less open to social connections. They brought people together for shopping, at once both a solitary and a social act. Retailers were constantly looking for ways to offer more goods, provide more services, and ultimately draw more patrons. They sold lottery and theater tickets, collected contributions to subscriptions and charities, and provided shipping news. Some retailers rented out part of their floor space to fellow retailers to offer a wider variety of merchandise. Others offered specialty services in wine and spirits. They peddled consumption advice—for instance, on how to maintain and serve a wine after it was purchased—alongside the physical products.

Tavern keepers and storekeepers made sure their premises were centers for information dissemination: they had newspapers lying about; they tacked broad-sides and announcements to the walls; they compiled and made available price lists, pattern books, and shipping lists; they encouraged stagecoaches to leave from their stoops. Storekeepers and tavern keepers profited from those who came to acquire business information and trade and, over time, these activities became more important to their profitability.[85]

Both taverns and stores functioned as "point[s] of intersection among a number of different networks."[86] In this regard, the retailers played a critical role in the evolution of communities. Savvy proprietors built spaces where patrons could be comfortable enacting and communicating their business connections. The communities people created in stores or taverns were tangible—individuals buying and drinking together in a physical space—and imagined—in the sense that the networks were relationships, not objects, and so depended on participants' thoughts and mentalities. The retailer, thus, was a kind of impresario, a manager of a store- or tavern-theater in which, if he did the job well, many people had their hour upon the stage—and paid to do so. The fee was a glass or a cask of wine, or some other commodity.

Stores and taverns were "vital institutional factor[s] in the formation" and elaboration of networks. "Connecting so many dynamic networks in so many ways," they "acted as a kind of structural foundation for a great deal of creative" commercial, communal, and social activity. Their spaces formed a physical "public sphere"; the networks using them became "publics," independent of established institutions and at times critical of them; the roles performed in them created actual economic spheres of decided material consequence and mental "public spheres" of interest and discourse.[87]

The development of North American distribution is an example of self-organization. By the turn of the nineteenth century, there were organized and systematic ways to bring products from Europe and the West Indies, and the manufactures of the cities of the Atlantic coast to consumers throughout European North America. There was an American distribution system—complementing the Atlantic distribution system—that had not existed 125 years earlier. Retailers almost casually offered goods from China, India, Morocco, Spain, Portugal, France, Holland, Germany, and Sweden, in addition to England, Scotland, and Ireland. The stores and their contents bound Americans to the outside world—to the next county, the next colony or state, the next continent, and the next empire.[88] Storekeepers made connections, built and managed networks, exchanged goods and information with foreigners and inland communities, learned about new and old markets, unique or traditional tastes, and peculiar or widespread problems, and linked the American West to port cities of the coast and markets on the other side of the Atlantic.

At any given moment, the change was almost imperceptible, but cumulatively there had been a transition from a world where moving products, people, and information around the Atlantic rim and into the interior of North America was difficult, slow, and expensive to a world where the same activities were relatively easy, rapid, and cheap. Perhaps most dramatic, the conquering of distance had become ordinary in people's minds, whereas 150 years earlier each instance was practically a miracle. Fleets of ships traversed the oceans, ready to take goods and people back and forth. In the port cities, exporters and importers set themselves up to deliver goods to the ships or receive goods from them and expedite them on their way. In the field, interlocking networks of taverns, shops, and traders of all kinds were ready to deliver the goods to consumers, often taking as payment barter items to be routed back along the trading paths in the opposite direction.

This momentous change arose from the activities of multitudes of individuals: Richard Hill, who removed to Madeira to avoid the opprobrium of bankruptcy; his son Henry, who returned to Philadelphia to represent the firm and take his place in society; John Wister, who made a living buying wine remainders and surpluses to resell to the German-speaking tavern keepers and storekeepers of Philadelphia's hinterland; Newman Swallow and Joseph Kershaw, who managed stores that sold wine to consumers alongside other "goods too tedious to mention"; and Daniel Smith and George Frey, who ran taverns that nourished their communities. None of these people took it upon himself to create an American distribution system, let alone an Atlantic one. The more perceptive among them may have reflected on the changes they saw in their lifetimes, but they would not have claimed that they had much to do with bringing them about. But collectively they did, each taking advantage of the opportunities he saw and building on the structures, patterns, and institutions laid down by his predecessors.

Part III

CONSUMING WINE

"Articles of Nourishment Both Mundane and Useful": Wine Consumption in an Emerging Atlantic Economy

In 1744, Virginia, Maryland, and Pennsylvania established a joint commission to arbitrate disputed land claims with the Iroquois. The Scotsman William Black, who served as secretary to Virginia's commissioners, left a diary of the Virginia delegation's trip to Philadelphia on commission business. Liquor flowed from the first day of their journey northward, when "the sailors, for their trouble, got a Bottle of Rum." On arriving in Annapolis, the Virginians were "Conducted to the first Tavern in Town" and welcomed in a private room "with a Bowl of Punch and a Glass of Wine." The following day, Maryland's governor, as "Compleat" a gentleman as ever there was, invited them to his home: he received them "in the hall," where, "in the intervals of the Discourse," they were entertained "with some Glasses of Punch"; in the dining room, a meal "show'd a face of Plenty and Neatness, more than Luxury or Profuseness"; back in the hall, "the Glass was pushed briskly round, sparkling with the Choicest Wines, of which the Table was replenished with [a] Variety of Sorts." The ensuing Monday, the commissioners attended a private ball in the colony's Council Room, adjacent to which were tables laden with "several sorts of Wines, Punch, and Sweet Meats" for those avoiding a "Dancing Match" and desiring "a cheerful Glass."[1]

After five lubricous days, the party pressed on. It stopped from time to time at public houses along the way, supping on bread, cheese, wine, punch, and cider. Three more days brought it to the outskirts of Philadelphia. There, the secretary of Pennsylvania and a handful of the colony's and city's leading men welcomed the party al fresco "with a Bowl of fine Lemon Punch big enough to have Swimm'd half a dozen of young Geese." Each having quaffed at least four glasses, they crossed over the Schuylkill River and presented themselves at the home of Governor Thomas, who met them at his gate "with great Civility," led them into his hall, and presented them "with a Glass of Wine." Exhausted, Black retired to his room at the home of the secretary, but, before he could call it a day, his host "forced" on him yet another "Glass of Wine."

Black rambled about Philadelphia on his first full day there, looking at "the Shipping," examining a privateer, and inspecting the wharfs. Several eminent townsmen welcomed him at one of their homes with a "few glasses of Wine." Afterward, he moved on to a coffeehouse and then the Governor's Club (its members were gentlemen who met "e'ery Night at a certain Tavern" to spend "a few Hours in the Pleasures of Conversation and a Cheerful Glass"). The day closed with "a very Genteel Supper," after which "several sorts of Wine and fine Lemon Punch [were] set out [on] the Table, of which every one might take of what he best lik'd, and what Quantity he Pleas'd." Although he spent most of the next day recovering, Black attended that evening a "very Grand" entertainment at the home of the governor, who provided "a very fine Collation" and, after dinner, a table "furnished with . . . great plenty of the Choicest Wines." True to custom, "the Glass went briskly round," "sometimes with sparkling Champaign, and sometimes Rich Madeira, Claret, or whatever the Drinker pleas'd." On occasion, Black broke the routine of business by taking tea and Madeira with ladies he fancied or spending the evening with an old friend who was "free" of "a Glass of Good Wine." Toward the end of Black's stay, he returned the hospitality extended the commission by hosting "an Entertainment" for the Philadelphians, renting a private room at the Three Tuns Tavern and offering them "a very Grand Table." On this, after dining, he set "all the sorts of Wine the Tavern cou'd afford, and that in great Abundance."

Black's, a diplomatic journey of white male officials, is perhaps an extreme example, but eighteenth-century Americans drank imported wine and spirits in truly awesome quantities. Drink was part of everyday routine and ritual observance at home and in government buildings, mercantile chambers, and counting houses, in the public and club rooms of taverns, on the banks of rivers and along county boundaries. People drank among friends and strangers, men and women, whites, reds, and blacks, elites and middling people. They drank to do "some Business" like that of the commission as well as to lubricate "a little chit chat" at a dinner party, "a Party of Pleasure," or a ball. They attributed meanings of health, wealth, and refinement to the core acts of quenching thirst, providing hospitality, and getting drunk. As the availability of imported drinks expanded, people came to view them less as extraordinary and more as staple "articles of nourishment" necessary for good "domestic management." Liquor sustained cooking, dining, and hospitality, and also housekeeping and doctoring.[2]

Historians have invested considerable analysis on two aspects of early American drinking: drinking by elite white men—and its place in the business they conducted, the politics they debated, and even the revolution they staged—and the taverns and public spaces where people drank—debating the nature of the resulting "bourgeois public sphere." In fact, drinking alcohol, particularly in domestic and quasi-domestic spaces, was far more ordinary and ubiquitous than we—the survivors of later temperance movements—usually imagine. While it is not necessary or even warranted to regard early Americans as always drunk, it is not distorting to see them as never far from drink.[3] The reexamination of drinking is part of understanding the first "Consumer Revolution," when "rising incomes and growing supplies of cheap goods combined to create 'a major watershed' in Anglo-American life: the emergence of a consumption economy and a consumption culture."[4] The proliferation of goods resulted in a common "language of goods" and a standardization of demand that upset preexisting social structures. The flood of "amenities and luxuries" effected "an exceptionally rapid expansion of consumer choice, an increasing standardization of consumer behavior, and a pervasive Anglicization of the American market." As a result, the poor "made 'necessaries' of goods that were their fathers' decencies, their grandfathers' luxuries."[5] Evidence about Americans' consumption of imported wine deepens our understanding of how people caught up in the Consumer Revolution adopted goods and used them in their social projects, and how they attributed significations to them—significations that were often homely and mundane.[6]

At the same time, it calls into question the placement of early modern drinking within a "public sphere" where ideas were articulated, negotiated, and distributed, and participants perhaps ventured as equals. Scholars have focused particular attention on the tavern and its role in fomenting political and social discourse. This line of inquiry leads to the beliefs that, in the run-up to the American Revolution, drinkers favored public coffeehouses and taverns, and the meanings of drink and drinking that arose in public settings dominated discourse. If anything, the reverse was true: the home was, by far, the most common venue for drinking. People first learned about alcohol around the hearth. Much of the physical and social environment of drinking outside the home—"sodalities that exclusively cultivated their own welfare," such as tavern companies, coffeehouse fellowships, salons, and clubs—copied the physical space and hospitality of an imaginary moneyed household.[7]

Thinking about drinking as centered in the home gets us closer to what it meant to early Americans. To do so requires taking the material aspects of drinking seriously, especially the spaces consumers drank in and the accoutrements of wine consumption, which were themselves physical objects and goods that could be purchased, displayed, and wielded. For too long scholars of material culture have been cordoned off in their own "museum world," separated from historians investigating the economic, social, and psychological import of actions and things. A stance that may be termed "consequential materiality" reconnects people's behaviors and ideas to the production, distribution, and use of goods in their lives. A consequential materialist perspective asks how changes in the quantity and variety of imported wines, as well as the ways they were acquired and used, affected the economic and social institutions organized around them. Investigating the material artifacts of wine consumption helps us to understand the world they fashioned. It embeds the relationships between people's consumption and their identities in the physicality of their lives.[8] And it asks how people manipulated the boundaries between domestic spaces and public ones—in part by the use of material objects—thus shedding light on the public sphere as well as the private.

This chapter and the next two attempt a broader understanding of early American drinking: where people drank, with whom they drank, what they drank, why they drank what they did, and what they thought they were doing when they were drinking. Because the geographic evidence is plentiful, these chapters restrict their focus to drinking within English-speaking America. On the other hand, because the evidence on types of drink is scanty, we cannot restrict the discussion to Madeira. It is almost impossible to talk about the different uses of Madeira, Lisbon, Claret, and Canary, and often tricky to distinguish between wine and spirits, as drink is frequently described only as "liquor." This chapter sets the stage by examining the concrete and material basis of drinking. It first examines the uses of alcohol in the home and then the quasi-domestic—or quasi-public—spaces where drinking was part of rituals of sociability. It also discusses what we know about the ways women and nonwhites drank, to the extent these were different from those of white men. The next two chapters examine the sociocultural dimensions of why people drank, and what they made of what they were doing.

DRINKING AT HOME

Women were usually responsible for procuring household drink and maintaining it, although the extent of control differed with geography. Households most frequently acquired their wine by purchase, although sometimes as gift, hospitality, or inheritance.[9] In the early seventeenth-century English world, the mistress of a house was to have the knowledge and skill to manage wine; she was charged with stocking a cellar, monitoring its upkeep, mixing and improving the liquor, and handling its distribution. Gervase Markham, always a keen observer, thought it "necessarie" in 1623 that the "Hous wife be skilled in the selection, presentation and curing of all sorts of wine," since wines were "usual charges under her hands." If they were mishandled, the husband would experience "much losse." Other experts agreed. After midcentury, however, a regendering set in: conventional wisdom and prescriptive literature became more scientific, and wine management more dependent on knowledge of chemistry and technology. New instruments like the thermometer and hydrometer were required for cellaring, and new formulas involving chemicals for improving were introduced. According to prevailing understanding, men were more comfortable with science and equipment, so the task of stocking a cellar and caring for liquor was reassigned to them.[10]

In this regard, adherence to metropolitan norms in the English-speaking colonies and states was casual at best. In most of the American households whose records have survived, the woman managed the purchase and care of alcohol used in family cooking, dining, and doctoring: tasting and selecting it, buying it, carrying it from the tavern or store, checking on its flavor, and, if need be, "improving" it. Wine remained largely in her more domestic sphere, given its utility in chores, healthfulness in diet, and success in doctoring, rather than in a man's chemically and technologically improving the drink, promoting his occupation, and burnishing his family's repute through accessories. Boston storekeeper Robert Gibbs regularly passed wine over his counter to the wives of his customers during the 1660s. Philadelphia wives received Madeira from the proprietor of the Three Tuns Tavern in the 1720s. In the accounts for the Pine Tree Hill store in central South Carolina some fifty years later, Joseph Kershaw sold and delivered much of the wine to account holders' wives, even if no woman had a named account. Daughters, granddaughters, and other female relatives in the late eighteenth century, such as Landon Carter's daughter at Sabine Hall, Anne Tasker Carter of Nomini Hall, Martha Washington's granddaughter at Mount Vernon, and Philip Kiesecker's daughter in Schaefferstown, supervised the acquisition and distribution of alcohol. Some widows who were neither storekeepers nor tavern keepers continued to order wine directly from their dead husband's correspondents, to buy it in local taverns and stores, and to record it in their own household accounts.[11]

Some elite urban men in America did adopt the new managerial role assigned them in Britain. The merchant Robert Pringle of Charleston procured wine in 1746 and 1747, recording what he bought for household use. The first recorded month of expenditures was typical for him. On May 9, he obtained 288 empty bottles at auction and then filled them with some Claret and rum he had in his cellar. On May 12, he bought a cask of Madeira from a fellow importer and three gallons more from another importer. Three days later, he acquired about 60 gallons of Claret. In all, between May 3, 1746, and April 30, 1747, he personally bought 127 gallons of Madeira and French wine, 58 gallons rum, and 38 gallons beer. In less than a year he bought 223 gallons of liquor—at 4 ¼ gallons per week, a rather stupendous amount! His purchases indicate roughly what wines and spirits urban consumers of his social rank brought into their homes in the middle decades of the eighteenth century. Pringle brought not just "wine" but Madeira, Spanish (Sack), and French (Claret and white), as well as rum, brandy, and beer. He bought wine from importers and sea captains. He bottled it fairly quickly, placed it in a subterranean cellar, and drank it as the occasion arose. He imported rum in casks in company with his business partner, taking it out of their store, charging it to his personal account, and bottling it himself, or bought it in bottles from Charleston dealers. Whatever the drink, Pringle's "husbandry" remained fairly constant; he made one or two purchases of alcohol each month, except that immediately following his wife's death. But in America this remained uncommon. While husbands often held the keys to the cellar and took an interest in its contents, wives usually procured the alcohol and managed the cellar.[12]

Probate inventories shed some light on who kept wine in the home and what they stocked. They register people's effects at the time of their deaths, so they may be skewed toward the wine stocks of older people, on average. But they show how, as wine became expensive, its customers were the wealthier members of society. At the same time, they reinforce the picture of increasing varieties of drinks and increasing distinctions among drinkers that comes from other evidence.[13] Consider the alcohol left by decedents in five jurisdictions—Suffolk and Hampshire counties in Massachusetts, New York County in New York, all of South Carolina (although in 1803–7 just Charleston County), and Jamaica—at several periods during the long eighteenth century (tables 9.1 and 9.2).[14] In general, the percentage of estates possessing alcoholic beverages grew over the course of the century, as did the number of types of drink, with urban estates consistently owning greater variety. Most of the drinks householders favored were locally produced cider and imported or locally distilled rum, but, over the century, an increasing number of households favored wine—a trend consistent with the increasing availability of a range of wines evidenced by firm, store, and tavern records.[15]

Drinkers' economic positions influenced their liquor consumption. (The converse—how wine marked class and, within the category of wine, which types—is explored in the next chapter.) Consumers' probated estates show how consumption of wine and spirits was correlated with wealth (table 9.1). Early in the eighteenth century, people who left Madeira in their estates were no wealthier than other drinkers—in fact, in some cases, they were less wealthy. In Suffolk County,

Table 9.1. Wealth at death and value of wine in probate inventories (in pounds sterling), 1700–1807

Years	Area	Number of inventories	Average value of estate[a]			Average value of	
			All decedents	Wine holders	Madeira holders	Wine[b]	Madeira[c]
1700–1705	Jamaica	295	760	711	1,072	98	187
1703–1707	Hampshire County, MA	39	129	0	0	0	0
1703–1707	Suffolk County, MA	172	336	209	199	10	9
1703–1712	New York County, NY[d]	48	972	230	230	64	64
1713–1716	Jamaica	301	777	673	293	5	2
1732–1736	Jamaica	509	1,636	3,215	4,215	64	131
1732–1741	South Carolina	409	721	1,041	616	13	6
1765–1774	Suffolk County, MA	947	406	1,346	1,827	31	32
1765–1774	South Carolina	1,599	1,131	5,182	5,220	19	32
1790–1799	New York County, NY	182	1,116	2,196	4,490	309	585
1803–1807	Charleston County, SC	503	2,027	7,092	6,428	185	277
1803–1807	Hampshire County, MA	336	408	1,444	0	5	0
1803–1807	Suffolk County, MA	445	1,502	4,806	5,107	54	82
1807	Jamaica	60	8,411	15,283	13,506	173	82

Sources: Suffolk County and Hampshire County Probate Inventories, 1703–7, 1765–74, 1803–7, Massachusetts State Archives, Boston; New York County Inventories, 1703–12, 1790–99, New York City Municipal Archives; Albany County Inventories, 1703–12, 1790–99, New York State Archives, Albany; South Carolina Inventories, 1732–41, 1765–74, Charleston County Inventories, 1803–7, South Carolina Department of Archives and History, Columbia; Jamaica Inventories, 1700–1705, 1713–16, 1732–36, 1807, Jamaica Archives, Spanishtown.
a. Madeira holders are included in wine holders, and wine holders in all decedents.
b. In estates with wine.
c. In estates with Madeira wine.
d. These estates included only Madeira wine.

for instance, an average decedent left an estate worth £336 sterling in 1707, an average wine-holding decedent left an estate worth only £209, and an average Madeira-holding decedent left even less—£199. At some point, perhaps as early as the 1730s, if Jamaica and South Carolina estates are representative, that changed. In the decade between the wars, 1765–74, the average Suffolk decedent left an estate worth £406, while the average wine holder left over three times that amount (£1,346), and the average Madeira holder left over four times that amount (£1,827). By the beginning of the nineteenth century, the average Suffolk County decedent left an estate worth £1,502, while the average wine holder left three times that amount (£4,806), and the average Madeira-holder three and a half times that amount (£5,107). By the later period (1790–1807), in Suffolk and New York counties, decedents possessing Madeira were wealthier than decedents who held any wine, who in turn were wealthier than all decedents. In Charleston County and Jamaica, somewhat surprisingly, decedents with wine were wealthier than decedents as a whole, although the refinement an expensive Madeira conveyed did not correlate with greater estate.

Wine and, in particular, Madeira become more expensive over the course of the eighteenth century compared to overall price indices and the prices of other alcoholic beverages. At the end of the previous century, imported wines like Madeira and Canary were not more expensive than imported spirits and, in many taverns and stores, not markedly more expensive than imported ale, porter, or beer, although domestically made beer and cider were always cheaper than anything else.[16] Thereafter, liquor prices diverged. In the decades leading up to 1750, Madeira commanded a premium over West India rum in the Philadelphia market of £2 to £5 sterling per 110 gallons. But, through 1815, the price of Madeira rose dramatically (2.7 percent per year), whereas the price of rum fell (0.2 percent per year). By 1774, Madeira fetched a premium of more than £20 over the rum price of £12 sterling per 110 gallons. After the Revolution, Madeira's price maintained its prewar levels through 1792, after which, prompted by the imposition of new federal duties disproportionately targeting Madeira, it almost tripled, from £38 in 1792 to £102 in 1815. The price of West India rum, in contrast, only doubled, while Pennsylvania rye whisky fell by two-thirds and Holland gin by three-quarters. Tavern prices mirrored market prices. As a result, only people with money could afford Madeira.[17]

 Buying and drinking wine sent a number of signals by 1775. Among them was that a wine drinker had money, and a Madeira drinker even more.[18] The signals were similar everywhere, thus unifying an emerging social elite, distinguishing those who could afford to drink wine from those who could not. George Washington gave Madeira and French to his friends; poorer planters did so less often or gave less expensive types such as Lisbon and Canary. Drinkers who were poorer yet favored spirits. As a result, decedents kept alcoholic beverages like rum and cider more frequently than wine throughout the century (Table 9.2). Wine seems not to have been kept by probated rural Hampshire County householders in the early eighteenth century, and in only a handful of probated households in the early nineteenth century.

This is decidedly odd, but whether it reflects drinking or recording habits is uncertain. More Suffolk County estates held wine at the end of the period, although they preferred other alcoholic beverages throughout: in 1703–7, almost 4 percent of inventories had wine in them, but the total percentage of alcoholic

Table 9.2. Summary of wines and other alcoholic beverages in probate inventories, 1700–1807

Years	Area	Number of inventories	Percentage of inventories containing				Number of varieties enumerated	
			Just wine	Just other alcoholic beverages	Both wine and other beverages	Total	Wine	Other alcoholic beverages
1700–1705	Jamaica	295	1.0	6.4	3.4	10.8	6	6
1703–1707	Hampshire County, MA	39	0.0	10.3	0.0	10.3	0	2
1703–1707	Suffolk County, MA	172	0.6	8.1	2.9	11.6	4	6
1703–1712	New York County, NY	48	2.1	12.5	4.2	18.8	1	7
1713–1716	Jamaica	301	0.7	4.7	1.0	6.4	3	9
1732–1736	Jamaica	509	2.4	4.9	2.6	9.9	13	16
1732–1741	South Carolina	409	0.5	5.1	1.0	6.6	6	6
1765–1774	Suffolk County, MA	947	0.7	9.3	1.3	11.3	15	17
1765–1774	South Carolina	1,599	2.1	6.3	5.0	13.4	23	31
1790–1799	New York County, NY	182	1.1	5.5	3.8	10.4	13	15
1803–1807	Charleston County, SC	503	3.0	5.4	3.8	12.2	14	20
1803–1807	Hampshire County, MA	336	0.0	21.1	0.9	22.0	6	9
1803–1807	Suffolk County, MA	445	2.2	7.9	3.6	13.7	14	28
1807	Jamaica	60	0.0	25.0	18.3	43.3	6	10

Sources: See source note for table 9.1

drinks in inventories was over 11 percent; by the beginning of the next century, almost 6 percent had wine in them, while the total percentage of alcoholic drinks was over 13 percent. The difference was somewhat more pronounced in Hampshire County, where no wine was found in inventories at the beginning of the eighteenth century, and in less than 1 percent of inventories a century later. New York County was an anomaly: the percentage of estates with alcoholic beverages declined over the century, although the variety of types increased. The century-long dominance of cider, beer, and spirits, especially rum, spurred on by the plentiful supply of molasses and Americans' push into distilling, is clear.

The varieties of wine and other alcoholic beverages owned by householders increased over time in each jurisdiction. In the two northern metropolitan counties (Suffolk and New York), estates possessed three to thirteen times the number of varieties of wine at the end of the century than earlier. A slightly smaller increase—four to two times—occurred in the number of varieties of other alcoholic drinks. In Hampshire County, the pattern is similar, but the number of varieties is lower, both early and late. This is what one might expect, given the rural region's insignificant role in wine trading and its lower population density. Increases in alcoholic variety may have occurred earlier in Caribbean households than in North American, but in the latter a significant jump took place in the first two-thirds of the eighteenth century.[19]

Anglo-Americans reinterpreted the ways their metropolitan cousins used wine; sometimes the reinterpretation was creative, other times forced. Americans, for instance, did not drink Port or French wines to any great extent. Their absence is, at first glance, somewhat surprising for a periphery that was supposedly keen to emulate metropolitan style. British contemporaries, such as William Eddis, found the "quick importation of fashions from the mother country . . . really astonishing" in 1771, for "a new fashion" was "adopted earlier by the polished and affluent American than by many opulent persons in the great metropolis."[20] Perhaps, historians surmise, "cultural evolution in England and America" was "a single integrated process," and an Anglicization emulative of English behavior and goods shaped North American culture.[21] If this was so, one would expect to find Port or Claret in probated estates, for Port was the principal wine drunk in Britain, and Claret had a wide, passionate following among its aristocracy. Neither appears in American inventories to any great extent. This was both a response to economic realities and a misreading of European values and cues. Britain's wars with France, consuming nearly half of the eighteenth century, impeded the flow of continental wines to America and raised the cost of those that overcame naval interruptions and colonial prohibitions through increased insurance and duty. In peacetime and war, the Navigation Acts and related commercial laws imposed heavier American duties on mainland Portuguese wines like Port than wine from Madeira and the Azores. The post-1763 "equalizing" requirement decreed that mainland Portuguese wines flow through England, thereby imposing the costs of overland or coastwise transport in addition to the cost of Atlantic transport.

In addition—or as a result—a taste for drier European wines, such as Claret, never gained wide currency in the English-speaking colonies and states, even among elites. Some drinkers, like Thomas Jefferson, who had traveled extensively in France, preferred it, but they were few. Americans favored the richer, more full-bodied Wine Island wines. In the 1600s, people who drank wine drank Canary, Fayal, and Madeira when they could get it. In the 1700s, when the War of Spanish Succession blocked Canary, drinkers in search of an inexpensive wine shifted to Fayal wine from the Azores; at the same time, colonists assigned to Madeira the role that Port had played in the metropolis, especially after Madeira's price began to rise. Only during and after the American Revolution did French and mainland Spanish wines find significant favor in the United States and what was left of British America.

HOUSEKEEPING AND FAMILY DOCTORING WITH WINE

Early Americans used wine for a host of nonnutritional purposes that surprise people today. White wine was frequently used in housekeeping. It was regarded as a potent cleaning agent for glasses, dishes, and floors as it cut grease and removed soap, streaks, and film. It got rid of spots effectively. A compound of wine and salt would clean copper pots of tarnish. Manuals offering "useful advice on female accomplishments . . . and efficacious means of preserving beauty, health and loveliness" told women to use wine to create a cosmetic cream that kept hands gentle and prevented dryness. The Paste of Palermo, with its pint of spirits of wine, prevented hands from chapping, "smooths their skin, and restores their softness." A wash of white wine gave "luster to the face," while a spoonful of white brandy in the *Crème de l'Enclos*, a face mask, created a "wash, for the removal of tan" and freckles. Distilled wine could make candlesticks more prone to light and hats and boots easier to clean. Wine also served as a fumigant, forming the base of a solution for destroying bedbugs.[22]

At its most hyperbolic, wine could cleanse the house of an occupant, providing an unhappy housewife a medium in which to dissolve ratsbane to rid herself of an abusive husband.[23] Most ministrations were not so lethal, of course. Wine figured prominently in family medicine, although the amount varied "with the sophistication of the practitioner"—the less one knew, the more one used. Using wine to heal was at least as old as Christianity, and folk practitioners and elite householders alike took to heart St. Paul's aphorism to "take no longer water, but use a little wine for thy stomach's sake and thine other infirmities." They "firmly believed that alcoholic beverages were a positive good—beneficial to health as well as conforming to the mind and body." Mores opposed inebriation, not drinking. Only at the end of the eighteenth century did temperance concerns turn minds away from the use of wine and other forms of alcohol and caution against their presence in the home. Indeed, domestic wine drinking did not suffer serious opprobrium before the 1820s, and doctoring with wine was never repudiated. Medicos whose forebears had debated the merits of alcohol as a cure for disease or a substitute for water never completely dismissed wine.[24]

Regarding it as a stimulant, folk practitioners prescribed wine as a cure for headache, melancholy, hysteria, labor, gout, and scurvy, to name only a few afflictions. When the Philadelphia housewife Elizabeth Drinker mentioned liquor in her diary, she almost always brought it up in the context of treating family members, sometimes to prevent sickness, other times to cure it. In June 1802, for instance, she "put up two quarts of strawberries in two bottles, filled them up with brandy, and added a quantity of pounded loaf-Sugar" for her sickly, aging husband, who took "it with water for drink at meals." The following month, she "put Blackberries into Brandy" and made jelly of those berries that were unripe, both concoctions highly "recommended" as cures for a "disorder" afflicting her husband. Liquor was part of a healing application, and she introduced spirits and wine to preparations much as she would an ingredient for a jelly or cake. For her own ailments, the Maine midwife Martha Ballard approached matters similarly. She took "some hott Brandy tody" to induce a sweat and placed hot flannels soaked in "warm Brandy" on her head when she felt "very unwell," much as she would later put rum and salt on a burn. Drinker and Ballard were traditionalists, working within a framework of folk medicine whose practitioners tended to prefer the stronger ardent spirits and "to use more alcohol than did trained physicians." They followed popular pharmacopoeia and cure books (such as Samuel Stearns's *American Herbal*), used easily obtained patent medicines (which were until the late nineteenth century as much a part of the world of alcohol as of medicine), and devised their own remedies.[25]

Better read and more aggressive in incorporating new and innovative treatments, the Philadelphia householder Elizabeth Coates and the Virginia planter Landon Carter took their cues from fashionable London and Edinburgh medical publications. Carter's commentary on doctoring with wine is extensive and revealing. Owner of a large number of slaves, Carter forced wine-enhanced medications on his laborers. In 1757, he administered "3 spoon fulls Syrrop of Diacodiane in a glass of Madeira wine" to a slave with smallpox. This was state-of-the-art practice; in Britain and Europe, wine and wine with sugar were common solvents for drugs. Later on, Carter gave another slave "a weak vomit" and wine whey infused with chamomile flowers for her "severely Hysterical symptoms"; during recovery, he prescribed some wine and water in order "to strengthen her," and a placebo of wine, water, and brown sugar to induce calmness. Carter relied on emetic wine to induce bile discharge when his "indoors family" fell sick. In Europe, he used it to treat apoplexy but, at home, he prescribed it for almost anything. It "brought off," he bragged, "much curdled sower Phlegm," as well as raising low spirits, reducing pains in the neck, inducing vomiting, and checking bilious discharge. In 1774, when he was troubled by "a most violent return" of the colic, caused, he feared, by "eating Pease on some cheese," or else by drinking a glass of Madeira, he self-prescribed "medicated wine," three glasses of which gave him "4 or 5 motions, and for a while . . . established great ease." To further facilitate recovery, he added sweet Mountain wine to "a gentle meal of chicken and . . . poached eggs." Carter showed some restraint—he did not follow the advice of experts in animal husbandry who counseled the administration of red Port wine and Jesuit's bark to horses afflicted with bilious colic. But in most other instances he followed their cues.[26]

COOKING AND DINING WITH WINE

In any middling or elite household Americans drank wine with their food. Mealtime drinks constituted the most common and extensive use of wine throughout the period. Wine and wine-laced preparations complemented dishes at midday and evening meals, and sometimes at breakfast and intervening collations, surviving recipes and cookbooks suggest. Since the latter were not printed in Anglo-America before the 1790s, cooks consulted British texts, like Alice Smith's *Art of Cookery* (1758) and Elizabeth Raffald's *Experienced English Housewife* (1769). The "receipt" books kept by Mount Vernon's Martha Washington, her granddaughter Nelly Custis, Salem's Susan Berry, and Charleston's Harriott Pinckney Horry closely follow British cooking in both technique and recipe; indeed, their books were little more than handwritten transcriptions of recipes published in English books and newspapers. Wine was central to this "Anglicized" cuisine. Horry's Charleston "receipt book" from 1770 offered instructions for adding "a little Madeira wine" to a sausage stuffing and a pint of wine to a fish sauce. Her beef "à la mode" used wine as a flavoring. Wine was a common ingredient in stews and fricassees as well as desserts: a half to a full pint of wine was required for orange, yam, and little puddings, and three spoonfuls of Sherry for carrot pudding. Benjamin Franklin thought cooking with wine important enough to return to it frequently in the almanac he published for fifty years, and Amelia Simmons's *American Cookery*—the first cookbook to be written and published in

America for Americans—continued to accord wine a central culinary role when
it appeared in 1796. No larder, these books tell us, would have been well stocked
without wine. Beef, meat pies, custards, rice and fruit puddings, trifles, cakes: for
making these, the resourceful American housewife was to keep imported wine,
cordial, and brandy in her pantry, as well as making her own.[27]

The act of dining, too, would have been strangely incomplete to the affluent
and middling without a glass of wine filled from a bottle or decanter that sat on a
table or sideboard. Dining and drinking at home was an important way a southern planter defined himself as genteel and hospitable, and his family as refined,
accounts left by William Byrd II, Landon Carter, Philip Fithian, and George
Washington suggest.[28] Early in the eighteenth century, Byrd made heavy use of
wine at Westover, his plantation on the banks of the James River, where he filled
his cellar with wine, cider, and beer. His favorite breakfast and evening beverage
was milk, which he sometimes gave up for mulled wine, homemade wine, or
chocolate. When company was present, he always served wine. He preferred Bordeaux and Burgundy, taking his cue from Londoners, who had been passionate
for Claret when he had lived there in the years before the outbreak of the War
of the Spanish Succession, but he also stocked Madeira, Rhenish, and Canary.[29]
A half century later, Landon Carter deployed wine in much the same way at
Sabine Hall. He had "his own pleasures": smoking his pipe, riding, studying and
writing, conversing with friends and visitors, entertaining, "having an occasional
dram with other leading men of the county." During the twenty-six years in
which he kept a daily diary, Carter partook of more kinds of wine than Byrd had,
including Madeira, Claret, Mountain, and red. He most commonly drank wine
after a meal, not with it, as Byrd did, allowing himself "one bottle after dinner,
and now and then two on any extraordinary occasion." By 1768, he concluded his
family was overindulgent, calculating its annual consumption to be one hundred
gallons of wine, and pulled back. All the same, he and his daughter continued
"using it generally every day" at meals.[30]

After a meal, dinner guests regaled themselves "with a variety of wines, in crystal decanters," "fruits, comfits, and other delicacies all . . . placed on a bare table
of the finest mahogany." Such was "the luxury of the English" colonists, as was
their toasting of healths "more than once" in Madeira, Constantia, Champagne,
and Claret before moving on to "tea, punch, and other liquors." Travel writers
dwelled on the luxuriousness of the wine table. Yet dining and entertaining with
wine were not restricted to the wealthy or elite. Throughout Anglo-America, children were given wine "in the morning as soon as they rise." Improvers of manners sought to teach the social skills that accompanied wine to those unfortunate
enough not to have grown up with them. "Persons of Mean Births and Education,

who have unaccountably plung'd themselves into Wealth and Power" had much need of learning exactly what wine should be bought, how it should be kept, and what should be drunk and when. Amelia Simmons was not writing for the benefit of women like Martha Washington when she published her recipe book, full of instructions on how to use and serve wine, "calculated for the improvement of the rising generation of females": not so much for "the Lady of Fashion and Fortune" but for those "reduced to the necessity of going into families in the line of domestics, or of taking refuge with their friends or relations, and doing those things which are really essential to the perfecting them as good wives and useful members of society." Susannah Carter showed the "frugal housewife" how to make her own wine if she had no means with which to buy imported wine, and to display whatever she had on "her Table to the genteelest Advantage." Wine was a marker of gentility, and cultivating its etiquette part of gaining access to the hospitality of refined people.[31]

WINE HOSPITALITY

A rather remarkable scene painted above the mantel of a house built for a Southbridge, Massachusetts, judge shows the link between domicile and wine, between wine drinking and hospitality (plate 11). The picture depicts a country gentleman in the third quarter of the eighteenth century, probably the proprietor, wearing an officer's kit and tricorned hat and holding a glass of wine or punch in his hand. He stands behind a table, on which sits a full punchbowl, before a gambrelled home (possibly the tavern he owns, although for a rural tavern it is unusually massive); in the distance rocks a three-masted oceangoing ship (odd, since the judge had no known connection to the sea, which lay sixty miles to the east). Whatever the other messages being sent, the judge stands in entreaty, as if beckoning the viewer to enter his house and offering wine as a lure. In all its naiveté, the mantel highlights the myriad of familiar, almost intimate ways in which wine was used. Most notably, it hints at the extension of the household not just to relatives and servants but also to acquaintances and strangers.[32]

Offering wine was a time-honored way of receiving and entertaining guests, and was done at almost any family, social, and business occasion. When their ship was wrecked off Florida in 1696, the Englishman Jonathan Dickinson and his companions were given "a cup of Spanish wine" by St. Augustine's Spanish governor soon after they arrived and were sent to warm themselves in his kitchen. Dickinson accepted the wine as a mark of "the people's great kindness" and as a medicine. Likewise, on his arrival into New York the following year, Benjamin Bullivant was treated by Governor Fletcher "with a glasse of wine" and a tour of the fort.[33] From Philadelphia, the president of the Second Continental

Congress, Henry Laurens, much impressed by the fact that his son gave "good Madeira Wine to his guests . . . in the Garden" of his Charleston home, asked him to "lay in a pipe or two" for himself before Christmas, so he could set the same tone upon return. The planter William Byrd II used wine to convey generosity and kindness in the early decades of the eighteenth century. In 1718, he, a sea captain, and two others "took part of a bottle" at his home and "drank to the prosperity" of a voyage to Madeira in which they were part owners. He gave two bottles of wine as presents to Abraham Salle's son. He and a cousin drank some French the day Byrd's son Parke was born, and the following day they drank another bottle, Byrd having to broach an additional pipe to do so. When two friends stayed at Westover one night, they drank a bottle of wine and "were merry"—so, too, at the New Year's celebration. He offered "burnt Claret and cake" to those who attended the funeral of the son whose birth he had previously toasted. Byrd's neighbors, fellow planters, and Williamsburg contacts drank in his home, and he in theirs. While visiting some neighbors, Byrd and his wife were treated to "a bottle of good wine," of which the host was "very generous." When others were ungenerous, Byrd noted that in his diary, too: while visiting his brother-in-law's father, he remarked upon the "very moderate" supply; each day, they had "a bottle of good wine first and then a bottle of bad." He considered this inhospitable.[34]

"After the Ladies retired" from the table after entertaining guests in a Virginia household, the men regaled themselves with "a Bottle of Wine, & a Bowl of Toddy for Companions." Another group of planters frequently "sat after Dinner till Sunset" and "drank three Bottles of Medaira, [and] two Bowls of [rum] Toddy!" One entrée in 1794 "was accompanied" by Madeira and Claret, which they kept drinking "right through dessert," as well as "cider, weak or strong beer, . . . [and] white wine." After a full meal, drinking continued. Towards the end of dessert, "any ladies who are at the dinner leave the table and withdraw by themselves, leaving the men free to drink as much as they please, because then bottles go the round continuously, each man pouring for himself. Toasts are drunk, cigars are lighted, diners run to the corners of the room hunting night tables and vases which will enable them to hold a greater amount of liquor." The dinner was "prolonged in this manner far into the night," although eventually the table was "deserted because of boredom, fatigue or drunkenness."[35]

These scenes, memorialized by Moreau de St. Mery, were replicated across America—indeed, around the Atlantic—and were deliciously captured in George Roupell's *Mr. Peter Manigault and His Friends* (figure 9.1). The genteel hospitality and the mastery of libidinous excess expected of host and guest are articulated in this ink-and-wash sketch of the 1760s. Seven men are seated around

Figure 9.1. *Mr. Peter Manigault and His Friends*, by George Roupell, c. 1760.
Source: Courtesy of Winterthur Museum, Winterthur, Delaware.

a mahogany table, the tablecloth and napkins having been removed. All are giving or receiving toasts. Their mood is relaxed yet controlled—it is certainly not Bacchic. Enough drink is available. One detects, as well, a sufficiency of paraphernalia: wine bottles made of dark glass, one resting on a stand, a decanter, tall-stemmed goblets made of clear unengraved glass sitting on the table, a glass lying before the host (its stem probably shattered in the toast).[36]

Visiting notables like Moreau de St. Mery were served "good" wine by powerful people. They visited the affluent and were showered with kindness, because they were themselves people of status, and they were witnessing "great events" or visiting those who had. Some scholars believe this was different from an older English conception of hospitality, which held that it was a "duty of the host to receive all comers, regardless of social status or acquaintance." The earlier form of hospitality was "a household activity, emanating from the *domus* and concerned with the dispensing of those goods best afforded by it—food, drink and accommodation," as well as "a Christian practice sanctioned and enjoined by the Scrip-

Figure 9.2. *Sir John Denham and His Worthy Tenant,*
by Thomas Berwick, 1790s.
Source: [Arnaud Berquin], *The Looking-Glass for the Mind* (New
York, 1800), 105. Courtesy of The Library Company of Philadelphia.

tures on all godly men." Early modern pundits thought this set of norms to have
been severely compromised by the eighteenth century which, in their particular
representation, was a fallen state of conspicuous consumption and display. No
longer was it necessary to win reputation "by open generosity, by the feeding of
the many," and "regular communal interaction within the great house." Rather,
"the delectation of the few" now mattered. The host could engage in "new forms
of expenditure, on buildings, clothes and banquets" and in pursuing urban pleasures.[37]

Women participated in hospitality rituals as well. They drank at the dining
and tea tables. In many households they played visible roles as hostesses, offering
drink and managing the outfitting of the table and sideboard.[38] One is hardly
surprised that elite women like Lucy Carter and Nelly Custis were constantly in
attendance at or assisted their patriarchs' parties. Yet their presence and behavior were mimicked by many women, not just the aristocracy. The cover of a late
eighteenth-century instruction manual depicts a less-exalted female performing the same role (figure 9.2). Here, standing next to a sideboard, a landowner's
daughter offers a glass of wine to a "worthy tenant" who has come to pay his rent.

The arrangement is stylized; a nearly contemporary engraving for *The History of Mother Twaddle* (1809) shows a girl serving wine to a giant in the same pose. A farmer's daughter was not very high in the social hierarchy of America at this time, but the girl shows her proper manners by her act of noblesse oblige. The message of the manual cover is that even middling and poor girls can learn how to be hospitable, and one way to do so was by serving wine. These lessons were part of the explosive print culture of the early Republic. Characters in "a tale of truth" such as *Charlotte Temple* (1801), the most popular American novel of the period, or *Margaretta* (1807) entreated their charges "to take some refreshment" in wine. Advice to young newlyweds counseled wives that "a little generous wine will sometimes dissolve the strong humors, and dilute the narrow principles" of miserly and spendthrift husbands. Conduct of life books like *The Parlour Companion* of 1810 intimated that "wine was best for drawing out the fire" of hot foods too quickly consumed, counseling hostesses that "a glass of Sherry" should be brought from the sideboard for that purpose immediately. Etiquette manuals, when they finally emerged as a significant genre in the early Republic, instructed hostesses and their guests on how to handle wine. "The mistress . . . should acquaint her company with what is to come" during a meal, and in particular should tell them "what wine or other liquors is on the side board." It was, however, "the part of the master to ask or invite" "any of the company seem[ing] backward in asking for wine" to drink, "or he will be thought to grudge his liquor." According to *A Treatise on Politeness and Delicacy of Manners*, published in Baltimore in 1811, it would have been "unseemly in ladies" of this company "to call for wine"; that duty fell on "the gentleman present," who should ask them "whether it is agreeable to drink a glass of wine and what kind of the wine present they prefer." After dinner, since sitting and drinking with the men would also be "unseemly," women retired . . . but only after two or three glasses. It was "extremely rude," one 1815 novelist pointed out, for a hostess to neglect "to order a drink" for a guest.[39]

Women also drank alcohol as part of tea-table sociability. We have come to think that, at afternoon tea, women drank tea. Elizabeth Drinker made no mention of drinking liquor in her daily Philadelphia diary; her nearly continual refrain from 1758 through 1807 was "drank tea." But if she meant "drank only tea" she would have been atypical. The service of tea—a late-afternoon ritual presided over by the women of the household—was usually amplified with wine and cordials. As early as 1683, the writer on manners Steven Blankaart declared to a generation of men and women aspiring to appear genteel that brandy, "Anise Water, *Lavas* Water, Orange Water, Lemon Water, Gilded Water [all cordials], [and] Gin" were suitable "if used in moderation, during dinner, or after dinner, or after drinking tea." Mrs. Winthrop invited Samuel Sewall to a "Meeting at her House" in 1709, and for tea offered him wine, ale, and tea. In England and America, tea was a private drink, unlike coffee, which was usually consumed in inns, taverns, and coffeehouses. Tea was drunk at home as a complement to breakfast, a mid-morning tonic, or a late-afternoon diversion when men were present. It was regularly consumed alongside alcohol, as William Black discovered in Philadelphia. By the time of the Revolution, the ritual had reached its apogee. The marquis de Barbé-Marbois reported on it while serving as secretary to the French legation in Philadelphia in the 1780s. Family members would "seat themselves at a spotless mahogany table, and the eldest daughter of the household or one of the youngest married women makes the tea and gives a cup to each person in the company"; in summer, they added wine or fruit to the offering. Elsewhere, the routine and menu were similar. Although Drinker may have drunk no liquor at tea, many others did. "The tippling of drams" was so widespread that, by the 1800s, a movement was afoot to ban drams from the parlor, even at the risk of making its denizens "peevish and quarrelsome."[40]

Wine was increasingly costly and in some cases rare, and it was developing a language and style of use all its own, revealing gentility and knowing. All the same, it was a relatively cheap luxury: a young family or a tradesman who could not afford a grand home might afford an elite wine and decanter. "The middling sort could scarcely be expected to aspire to traditional liberality or magnificence; their charity had to be conversant with small and limited things." Wine was so delimited. Moreover, hospitality in familiar spaces was common and serving wine resonated with older hospitality norms. Host and guest behaved as if they were neighbors and friends. By greeting a visitor at the gate, inviting him or her into the house, and offering wine, as had the governors greeting Black in Maryland and Pennsylvania, a host implied reciprocity of relation and mutuality of obligation and aspiration first imprinted in domestic relationships. Drinking "a few Glasses of what was very Good" wine, taking "a few Glasses of Madera" or any "Cheerfull Glass" of wine, and passing "a few hours in Conversation" over it: these pleasantries fell to all who visited the homes of relatives, friends, and business contacts.[41]

"A KINDNESS WHICH THEY NEVER FORGET": DRINKING IN QUASI-DOMESTIC SPACES

Most scholars have preferred to investigate drinking in taverns and public houses, where it played a role in creating a discursive "public sphere," into which all entered shorn of rank, and where logic and persuasion, not authority, status, and credential, held sway.[42] This conception of social interactions is highly stylized, even for the coffeehouses and taverns so lauded by historians. But, in any case, much drinking outside the home did not take place in the public rooms of taverns. And, instead of re-creating the open-to-all bonhomie of the tavern, people who consumed alcohol outside the home often tried to re-create the intimacy, familiarity, and generosity of the imagined moneyed household. It is more useful to think of this drinking as quasi-private, rather than quasi-public. Quasi-domestic drinking mirrored the ordinariness of household use, with its overtones of being fed and cared for. Wine and spirits were used by churches, colleges, and hospitals as part of their domestic authority, in loco parentis, providing many of the elements of nurturance. Complicating this appropriated power, many times these institutions had an interest in seeing the drinkers mentally alert, physically sound, and willing to work—an agenda that could be satisfied with a cheap liquid source of carbohydrates, calories, and sugar. An especially strong signifier of home, wine imparted to administrators, their charges and, by extension, their institutions attributes of comfort and companionship and, at the same time, connection and control. It was a natural part of work, domestic life, and play to a degree that it has not been since the first significant wave of temperance struck the United States in the 1820s.

"THE FERMENTED BLOOD OF THE GRAPE"

The church was the greatest reification of family in any community, and wine had always been part of the Christian sacrament of the Eucharist, so church services and events were awash in wine. To commemorate "God's love of his people" with his gift of "the fermented blood of the grape," most early American Protestants used imported fortified European wine.[43] Catholics also allowed wine, although only by the celebrant.[44] Lone among Christians in eschewing ceremonial use were Quakers, who regarded themselves as neither Protestant nor Catholic.[45] Nor did Jews allow themselves to drink wine in services, but they did use raisin wine for ceremonial purposes.[46]

Liturgical debates over whether it was proper to use "real wine" rather than unfermented juice did not heat up until the 1830s temperance movement. Before that, American clerics generally agreed that, since "sacramental signs" were "supposed to be 'natural,' that is, unmistakable and able to be specified unambiguously," the wine "had to be [the] fermented juice of the grape." Neither unfermented nor soured nor diluted wine would suffice. This consensus was easier in Anglo-America than in Europe because there were fewer Catholics holding up wine as Christ's own blood whom the Protestant clergy felt the need to differentiate themselves from.[47] The use of "real wine" to celebrate Communion was an accepted fact of Protestant religious life in North America.[48]

Figure 9.3. A *Parish Feast, Humbly Inscrib'd to the Church-Wardens, Vestrymen, Questmen, and Parish Officers, by Sr. Guzzledown Tearefowl*, by an unknown artist, 1740. This engraving details the self-interest of church officers who meet and dine with silver and crystal—that is, who eat and drink lavishly. On one goblet is inscribed "Prosperity to the Church."
Source: Courtesy of The British Museum—Department of Prints and Drawings, London. © Copyright the Trustees of The British Museum.

The sacrament was usually celebrated once a month.[49] In Protestant congregations, officers used collection money to "furnish the table" with imported wine and local bread. At Boston's Anglican King's Chapel in the 1720s, the sexton spent about £1 a month to purchase "Bread & Wine" for the congregation; by the 1750s, his outlay had risen to only £4 (not very much, given the congregation's size). Similar levels of outlay prevailed in Boston's Third Congregational Church, which had more communicants and members.[50] Reformed and evangelical groups followed along: the Dutch Reformed in New York, the Moravians in Pennsylvania, and the Salzburger Moravians in North Carolina all spent roughly the same on imported wine.[51] The management of Communion funds occasionally led to charges of misappropriation and overindulgence. Observers commented on drunken ministers, and artists satirized the use of church property for personal drinking (figure 9.3). But clerical high jinks never created significant animus against the clergy in America.[52]

Regardless of denominational beliefs, wine flowed abundantly to the church family after the service and outside the building.[53] Both Samuel Sewall, a good New England Congregational minister, and Matthew Patten, a New Hampshire farmer who faithfully attended his local Congregational church, nonchalantly reported quaffing liquor in the churchyard after service. Churchyard drinking was so casual in Virginia, in fact, that the House of Burgesses outlawed it in 1710, but to no avail.[54] Church ordinations and elections concluded with entertainments embellished with wine. Boston's "Old South" Church spent £17 so that its minister could provide wine to a regional governing committee that met at his home in 1755; it paid Dr. Sewall for wine, tea, coffee, sugar, biscuit, and tobacco to celebrate the installation of another minister in 1766—one-third of all costs were wine related. Families brought wine and cake to church weddings and funerals. Deacons provided a minister with money for wine upon his election to a pulpit, and they gave his family wine during his and his wife's interments. Inasmuch as funerals were "society events," the bill for wine at them could be quite steep. At the 1678 burial of David Porter in Hartford, the expense of wine, spirits, and cider consumed by those who retrieved his body, looked into his demise at the inquest, and mourned his passing was more than that of his shroud and coffin. The dead or the heir could impress those left behind with ringing bells, a surfeit of pallbearers, a quality coffin and covering . . . and a profusion of drinks after the burial.[55]

"eating pies & drinking wine"

Given the ubiquity of alcohol and the spirits of the young, it is hardly surprising that college students were afloat in it, much as today. The tutors and students at Harvard stored casks of wine, brandy, and cider in their rooms and broached them at their pleasure. Henry Flynt, who kept a daily diary recording sixty years of tutoring there, was nothing less than a small-time drinks middleman. Consider the year 1718. In June, Flynt bought forty-eight empty bottles from fellow tutor Thomas Robie, paying for them in cider; later that month, he filled them with wine he got from his sister. Several months later, Flynt, Robie, and another tutor bought 24 gallons of Madeira; later Flynt bought 110 gallons more. In October, they bought a barrel of cider. Of course, they could draw on the common barrel kept at the refectory, but they preferred having their private reserve. Toward the end of the year, the tutors turned to brandy and, again, Flynt served as banker. The college officers happily quaffed vats of wine, spirits, cider, and beer.

Nor was drinking restricted to officers. Affluent boys arrived with wine or bought it while in residence and, as one of the most eminent medical men of the age remarked, "a stock of Wine the property of an undergraduate could not from the nature of Things remain a stock long." In 1721, Flynt dispensed liquor to his charges, especially a nephew who lived in his house "under his eye." That year, he twice bought wine from a storekeeper and sweet wine and cider from a tavern keeper, and what he did not drink himself he resold to students. The college expressed concern that "Scholars" might "unnecessarily frequent Taverns" and required them, before going "into any Tavern, or Victualling House in Cambridge, to eat and drink there," to obtain "Leave from the President or one of the Tutors." It also imposed fines on those "guilty of Drunkenness." But it worried more that they might go into debt doing so, and so forbade students to acquire wine and spirits "without paying immediately for the same, or without a Note under the Hand of one of the Tutors." Whatever the standing rules, enforcement was lax. There were many opportunities for what John Adams remembered nostalgically as "the free use of Cider and the very moderate Use of wine and ardent Spirits."[56]

Harvard may not have been typical in its permissiveness. Other colleges interpreted more strictly their role in loco parentis, soon after that doctrine was codified in the 1760s. Yet students everywhere drank, and a clash was inevitable. At reputedly "dour" Princeton, for instance, a group of young men had "a fine feast" one Sunday afternoon in 1786, "eating pies & drinking wine." Soon after, two other scholars made numerous trips to town for cakes and beer. When the junior class passed its midterm exams that year, eleven students had "an elegant supper" and too much to drink at a tavern. While Princetonians who drank did so away from campus and were punished for it, the records suggest that drinking there was just as prevalent as in Cambridge, and the restrictions ineffective. Wine, cider, drinking, drunkenness, and control over one's own drunken behavior were viewed as marks of manliness and rites of passage. They could not be easily expunged.[57]

A NECESSARY "COUNTER-POISON"

It was only natural that wine became central to the work of hospitals since wine occupied such a prominent place in the early modern materia medica. Charitable hospitals first arose in Anglo-America in the middle decades of the eighteenth century. Known for implementing experimental and practical medical techniques, their staffs prescribed wine for a wide range of conditions and cures. Philadelphia's Pennsylvania Hospital, established in 1751 by Benjamin Franklin, was the first of these new foundations. Like its British analogues, it stocked large amounts of wine and made it available to attending physicians and surgeons, who administered it to patients for all kinds of preventative and recuperative purposes. Franklin's hospital was not alone in such practice. The New York Hospital (founded in 1771), the Philadelphia Dispensary (1786), and the Boston Dispensary (1796) all did the same. The institutions kept meticulous accounts of their wine, a reflection of its importance to the prescription and dispensation of drugs, the large amounts stocked, and the possibilities for misappropriation.[58]

Physicians used wine as an essential additive to medical compounds and a principal cure for many diseases. Wine also formed a basic part of a hospital's "right course of diet." It bolstered recuperation and was thought to counteract "the ill Quality and Malignity of the Air, which is always impure in Hospitals." Dr. John Crawford's notes reveal the current enlightened thinking. Born in northern Ireland and employed in hospitals in the East Indies from 1763 to 1778, the West Indies from 1779 to 1793, and Demerara until his death in 1813, Crawford observed and implemented many uses of wine. On transferring to Barbados, where he took charge of the Naval Hospital, he introduced a plan he had known in Bengal. The plan had four types of diet—Full, Middle, Low, and Milk—and wine was central to each. "The common drink of those on [the] Full and Middle diet is toast and water, hardy water, or wine and water, two ounces of Madeira to each pint, or as the Surgeon might deem necessary." Those on the Low and Milk diets could have "barley water with or without wine, as their cases may require." Wine was further incorporated into the Low diet's midday dinner, which added two spoonfuls of Madeira and half an ounce of sugar to a pint of mutton broth. Wine should be given "with due limitation," it was accepted, but was preferable to ardent spirits, which were to be avoided. Especially when there was little animal meat and much farinaceous food at hand, wine was considered an "essential article of nourishment." Hospital doctors agreed that wine was a necessary "Cordial and Counter-poison."[59]

QUASI-DOMESTIC HOSPITALITY

Drinkers also generalized the tradition of providing hospitality in the home, incorporating domestic approaches and attitudes into otherwise official, commercial, and communal situations. Thinking of drinking as extending outward from the home, rather than the coffeehouse or tavern, better explains the ease and affect with which William Black and his fellow commissioners negotiated the multitude of persons they encountered on their journey to Philadelphia. Sometimes the quasi-domestic welcome was literally domestic: Maryland's governor received Black and his colleagues "in the hall" "with some Glasses of Punch," and then took them into his dining room for a meal. Drinking on such occasions was quasi-domestic in the sense that it was restricted to members of a certain group. It was withdrawn from the gaze of the public and hence from unsolicited publicity, as was drinking in one's own home. Even when this type of consumption took place in a public house, it usually transpired in the private spaces within it, such as a tavern's upper room. The norms of household behavior prevailed; the environment bore household affect; the aim in engaging such affect was to establish a basis for acquaintance, friendship, even intimacy. Such a disposition made drinkers as "light as air," more pliable and easier to work with. It made them seem accessible to one another, granting to all the informal freedom of continued acquaintance. Perhaps it also made close and confidential relations more likely to ensue.

Official and commercial events often required exaggerated displays of hospitality that conflated social and business motives, although not social and business ranks. On Black's diplomatic mission, the work of the salon and treaty room was fused; the success of the latter was lubricated with the support of the former. Militia musters, elections, and governmental meetings would have been less fruitful without bottle hospitality. On being presented to his county's militia as its commander in 1710, William Byrd II entertained the officers in his home, setting out a hogshead of wine for his soldiers in a nearby churchyard. The next day, he dined at Colonel Randolph's with several officers, while "all the people" were entertained with a hogshead of wine punch he had brought along for the purpose. Class distinctions were reflected in the settings for drinking: officers were treated in a quasi-domestic sphere; ordinary soldiers were feted in a public space—if not exactly open to all, still open to many.[60]

Gentlemen standing for election were expected to treat the voters to liquor. As a candidate for one of the two seats of Frederick County in Virginia's House of Burgesses, young George Washington supplied thirty-four gallons of wine (six of which were "best Madeira" obtained from the son of a local tavern keeper), sixty-six gallons of rum or rum punch, a gallon of brandy, and forty-five gallons of cider and beer to voters and hangers-on at the July poll. Notwithstanding the outlay of over a quart and a half per voter, his "only fear" was that his people "spent with too sparing a hand"! Liquor procured votes and encouraged loyalty. William Black commented on this aspect of the "Entertainments or Barbecues" required if one wanted "to be sent a Representative": "If a Man makes" the voters "Drunk twice or thrice a Year, this Injury is a Kindness which they never forget, and, he is sure of their hearts and their hands." Furthermore, lawmakers could seemingly make no law without liquor. While they did not acknowledge crafting legislation over drink, they frequently arrived in a stupor and afterward stumbled to taverns where they continued to discuss the day's business and strategize on winning the favor or thwarting the desire of the governor and his councilors in the assembly. Byrd's diary records numerous examples. After being sworn in as member of the colony's executive Council, he "drank too much French wine and played at cards" at its president's home. Indeed, any visit to the president went hand in hand with a bottle of Claret, and Byrd thought nothing of finding the president and another "almost drunk" when he called. When his duties brought him back to Williamsburg, he frequently retired after sessions to the home of another councilor, went "into the vault, and drank a glass of Rhenish." In the city on Council business in 1711, he and several lawmakers "went to dine with the governor because it was Saint George's Day" and there got "very merry . . . in drinking the healths and in making the Commissary drink them."[61]

Drinking by legislators and officials at events where business and pleasure merged was ordinary, even if drunkenness was frowned on. Pennsylvania's leaders met at an inn with some of Philadelphia's "principal gentlemen" to celebrate the king's 1734 birthday and downed forty-nine quarts of wine, fifteen quarts of wine punch, twenty-one mugs of cider, and twenty mugs of beer; two days later, they met and drank twenty-one quarts of wine, seven quarts of beer, and four quarts of cider. Ten years later they facilitated the diplomatic work of William Black's commission with "cheerful glass" after glass in their homes, taverns, and chambers. The governor gave the commission a "hearty welcome" of wine, first at his gate, then in his hall, and finally in his dining room, more or less mandating a reciprocal encounter. In none of these spaces were rank or authority repudiated or ignored, as they might have been in the "bourgeois public sphere." Drinking and its attendant rituals, in fact, both "strengthened the reciprocal networks of patronage and dependence that fostered elite authority and popular deference" within a stratified society and generally reinforced cohesion among the parties. The hierarchies of the family and the unwritten code organizing its members were the norm, even if those hierarchies were intimate and permeable.[62]

Being hospitable with wine extended well beyond the powerful and affluent and their great events. Mundane occurrences, such as raising barns, opening mills, and launching boats became wine-rich events for the extended family. For services rendered, wine was regarded as an appropriate expression of gratitude. Early in the eighteenth century, it was quite common to drink a bottle of Madeira with one's neighbors after running property lines, as Samuel Sewall did, or to provide it to friends who helped raise a barn. Farmers thanked (if not paid) those who had come to their aid by giving them liquor: Joshua Hempstead used alcohol to lubricate the raising of a new house and church, and Matthew Patten did the same for the clearing of a swamp. For rural consumers, the thanks were more often in spirits than wine, but the gesture and sentiment were similar.[63]

A "TRADITIONAL AID" TO LABOR

Wine and spirits also served a number of functions in the labor market. These functions lack a specifically domestic character, although they do not represent the open commons of the tavern, either. One of liquor's principal uses in the workplace was as an aid to actual labor. Black opens his 1744 itinerary by giving some sailors a bottle of rum "for their trouble." Shipowners likewise topped up their hands' rations with wine or rum as a way of keeping them content and willing to work more, sometimes giving them more than maritime and naval custom dictated. On land, church committees gave builders who were working on the churches wine or spirits for their toil in addition to wages. Farmers used rum to encourage hired hands to clear swamps and erect barns and fences. Distributing liquor to workers was so common, in fact, that they regarded it as one of their perquisites. "The practical part of hard labour," a reader of the *Pennsylvania Gazette* was told, rendered "liquor absolutely necessary." "A man's business" often obliged him "to go into the water," to expose himself to the rain, or to wet his clothes with sweat; at such times, "a small quantity" of wine allowed the worker "to cool himself." Rum was the principal work-time aid and wage complement. Some employers preferred "substitutes" for what they regarded as "detestable liquor" or "liquid fire": locally distilled fruit brandy, "sweet milk and water, butter-milk, and water, strong beer and water, cider and water, wine and water, vinegar and water, and melasses and water." But most considered spirits and wine "a traditional aid" to arduous endeavor and "an important supplement for low wages."[64]

Nowhere were the perquisites more engrained than in the militia, navy, and army, where liquor was seen as central to the viability of any mission. Officers viewed wine as a necessary aid to work, despite those who thought it invited disorder. One sergeant in Boston's militia drank too much wine on a 1638 training day and was slapped in irons and forced to wear a red "D" badge denouncing his "Drunkenness." In punishing his excess, the court admitted the commonality of the behavior and hoped to make an example of the misbehaving sergeant. Yet it did nothing to ban the dispensing of drink on training days. Alcohol and fighting were thought to be inextricably linked: "before battle, to heighten their belligerency and steady their nerves," after it, "to celebrate a victory . . . being elated with success," or on any occasion when it seemed wise for officers "to ingratiate themselves with the troops." The militias' approach was mirrored by the empire's on a larger scale. When a permanent English navy was formed in 1655, commanders issued wine as part of rations. Throughout the eighteenth century, His Majesty's navy annually contracted for a supply of Madeira, to be procured at the island, and from time to time some red Port. By the time of the American Revolution, British and American naval commanders allowed each sailor a pint of wine or a half-pint of brandy each day, while generals sanctioned more than one-third of a pint of liquor each day for the men of the army. General George Washington firmly believed that "the benefits arising from the moderate use of . . . liquor, have been experienced in All Armies, and are not to be disputed."[65]

Spirits and wine also functioned as wages, especially when specie ran low, as it often did. Phyn & Ellice in cash-poor Schenectady paid their bateaux-men in rum when they sent them to Niagara and Ontario in the 1760s, for instance, and Daniel Campbell paid his bateaux-men in the same currency ten years later, in addition to what they consumed on the trip. James Burd paid the craftsmen building his new house in Lancaster County in pipes of Madeira wine. A New Hampshire farmer paid Matthew Patten a half-pint of rum for Patten's survey of the farmer's land. In turn, Patten sent a bottle of rum to his tailor as payment. Even the usually temperate Martha Ballard took brandy as payment, for she could use it to cook and doctor. Buyers of goods and services paid in liquor when specie was scarce or when laborers valued the drink more than wages because of its high resale value. Spirits and wine were prime means of payment, the exchange rate determined by the prevailing wholesale market price of the drink. There was some risk in getting liquid wages—leakage, evaporation, adulteration, and the like—but at the same time the possibility of profit upon resale. And, in a pinch, you could always drink it.[66]

In some places, liquor came to function as a principal barter currency, not just in the workplace but beyond. Like Patten, laborers used the drink they received as wages to pay their debts. Joshua Hempstead did so when he paid Goodman Ricks half in rum and half in salt for some goods Hempstead had purchased from him in 1716. Four years later, he sent a barrel of rum he had received as pay from a sea captain to a New London storekeeper as payment for hats and yarn. Likewise, when he bought a plot of land, Hempstead paid for it in rum, which he had previously received as payment from the New London storekeeper for goods Hempstead had sold him. Wherever commercial exchanges took place without cash, spirits and wine could function as current money. Whether wine or rum were dominant depended on the strength of the community's ties to the Atlantic and Caribbean trades, its inland trade (the fur and skin trades revolved around rum and brandy), and regional industry (New England and the Philadelphia area were large distilling centers). Hence, Hempstead's New London, its economy tied to the Caribbean, saw more rum than wine in its marketplace, whereas Nicoll's New York saw more wine than rum.[67]

A FRATERNITY OF ELITE WHITE MEN?

The historians' established representation of drinking is public, masculine, white, luxurious, and borderline excessive. Pringle in his store, Manigault in his dining room, and Black on the road are the colonies' canonical drinkers. Patten in a swamp, Sewell before a barn, Adams in a salon, and Princetonians on a spree are snapshots of this activity. This chapter has argued for the importance of drinking at home, and this raises further questions: What did women drink—and when, where, and with whom? What about black people and Indians? Everyone could drink: how did the ways they did so reflect their differences? A paradox shaped private drinking in the evolving English Atlantic world: imported liquor was inclusive, because everyone drank it; imported liquor was exclusive, because people did not drink it the same way. Conditions and perceptions in Anglo-America structured this paradox and provided the backdrop for contemporary discourse and practice.

"SOME OTHERWISE DISCREET WOMEN"

Alcohol was no respecter of sex, but sex was some respecter of alcohol.[68] Women bought wine and cordials in taverns and stores, accepted them from friends and suitors, and concocted homemade versions. Much preparing and drinking took place under their watch in the home, including their own tippling. They drank cordials and wine at tea and dinner, at weddings and funerals, and at church. They read about women drinking, perused images showing them drinking. That they were full participants in the drink culture of the age is attested to by reports of women tippling too much.

Indications of the ordinariness of female drinking are found on the pages of popular English novels and magazines that early American booksellers and printers reprinted and early Americans readers devoured.[69] The heroine in Smollett's *Roderick Random* (1748), like many, drank a glass of cordial "to recruit her spirits," after which she "thoroughly revived" herself with "a little mulled wine." In *Tom Jones* (1749), Fielding set out "A *Dialogue*" between a landlady and a chambermaid that was "proper to be read by all Innkeepers, and their Servants." It recounts the story of "two young Women in Riding-habits" who arrived at an inn: "one of the most beautiful Creatures in the World" and her maid. When asked by the landlady if she desired white wine, the lady requested Sherry. Thereafter, when she arrived at another "fair-promising Inn" prostrate with fatigue and ordered water, her companion "very judiciously" changed the request to wine. "Drink another glass of wine" was Squire Western's advice to Tom and the young lady in the last pages of the book. In the English literature that American women read, many females drank knowingly, even enthusiastically. Fielding's heroine in *Amelia* (1752) thought nothing of ordering "a Bottle of Wine" for supper, and she dumped a suitor for not procuring her some. Of course, some women were duped into drinking wine so as to be more easily seduced, as in the pages of *Pamela* (1740) and *Peregrine Pickle* (1751). Drinking could get out of hand, too, as it did with the middle-aged widow Mrs. Ellison, "no Flincher at the Bottle," who, when "a little warmed with wine" at dinner, indulged "some Freedoms in her Discourse towards" a sergeant. Mrs. Ellison provided a useful contrast, handy for making a point about moderation and morality.[70]

When Americans, encouraged by high literacy and a boom in publishing after independence, entered the novel-writing arena in 1789, the same matter-of-factness attached to female drinking. Some protagonists might be under threat from wine's seductive capacity, but many, having first been undone by it, subsequently use wine to undermine the unscrupulous men who pursued them. In nearly all cases, female familiarity with wine was complete, and its use natural. Martha Read's beggar Monima used "a glass of refreshing cordial" in 1802 to restore her relatives and sent wine to refresh her friends, while Sarah Wood's Amelia did not think it an affront to her virtue to restore her own spirits with wine the same year. Discomfort arose only later amid temperance agitation. It was a "superabundance of aliment" that was to be abjured—not drinking per se, which most advisors on manners considered a pleasure.[71]

Equally indicative of the commonness of female drinking was its appearance in painting and engraving. In England, by the end of the eighteenth century, both the queen and a supporter of "the rights of women" were depicted as middle- or lower-class housewives clutching their glass or bottle of wine (figure 9.4). Over half of the characters in George Woodward's farcical *Apologies for Tippling* (1804) were female (figure 9.5). The print was hugely popular in America. The first lady, seated in a chair, does not bother with niceties, but upends a bottle of wine into her mouth. A second "can't think what makes" her "so dry," it being "very unusual," and treats herself to a nip in the morning. A plump matron "firmly believe[s]" her wine to be "the best Doctor in [the] world." "I feel myself always so agreeable after a glass of shrub," slurs a fourth, more emaciated crone. It was the "oil in rum that always agrees" with the stomach of a rather coarse member of the demimonde. A more stylish counterpart also found time for a tipple and, much like any connoisseur, studies a small glass containing "a very fine wholesome Cordial." "A little brandy in one's Tea can do nobody any harm," pronounces the last woman of the series as she pours it from a bottle into a cup.[72] In satire, female drinking cut a wide socioeconomic swath and revealed a broad range of behavior.[73]

Real-life accounts confirm artistic renderings. Diaries reveal that women frequented taverns as guests and regulars. There were probably more women in taverns than account books reveal; the charges for a wife's purchases were often recorded to her husband's account since he was bound by law to pay her debts. Criminal files also show women occasionally drinking in taverns. Their drinking was almost never the subject of the prosecution—more often it was sexual prof-

Figure 9.4. *The Rights of Women,*
by George M. Woodward, 1792.
Source: George M. Woodward, *Elements of Bacchus;*
or, Toasts and Sentiments (London, 1792), facing
p. 31, plate 16. Courtesy of Print Collection, Miriam
and Ira D. Wallach Division of Art, Prints and
Photographs, The New York Public Library, Astor,
Lenox and Tilden Foundations.

ligacy—but their presence is telling nevertheless.[74] That young girls wanted to
drink alcohol—and did so—is suggested by the antics of General Riedesel's two
daughters, who drank the dregs left by a celebration of the queen of England's
birthday that was held amid the flurry of the American Revolutionary War. Their
mother disapproved, yet she did not repudiate other "appropriate" consumptions:
when the Riedesels "were in want of water," for instance, she allowed her daughters to drink wine. Of a lower class, tavern keepers' daughters and barmaids, who
served liquor to others, enjoyed many a nip. Female shoppers were also at risk, for

Plate 1. View of the island from afar, by John Greenwood, 1783.
Source: From Private Collection.

Plate 2. A view of Funchal, by William Hodges, 1784.
Source: © 2008 by The Kelton Foundation, Santa Monica, California.

Plate 3. *The Fortaleza São Lourenço (Governor's Castle)*,
by Edward Hawke Locker, 1804. Source: This item is reproduced by permission
of The Huntington Library, San Marino, California.

Plate 4. *The Jesuit College*, by Edward Hawke Locker, 1804. Source: This item
is reproduced by permission of The Huntington Library, San Marino, California.

Plate 5. View of the harbor and Loo Rock, by John Greenwood, 1783.
Source: From Private Collection.

Plate 6. *Borrachas*, or wine transporters, with a goat
skin full of wine, by an unknown artist, before 1821. Source: William Combe,
A *History of Madeira* (London, 1821), facing p. 89. Courtesy of Special
Collections Library, University of Michigan, Ann Arbor.

Plate 7. *Borrachas* with oxen, sleigh, and a pipe of wine, by an unknown artist, before 1821. Source: William Combe, *A History of Madeira* (London, 1821), facing p. 87. Courtesy of Special Collections Library, University of Michigan, Ann Arbor.

Plate 8. Wine press on Madeira, by Thomas Picken, before 1843.
Source: W. S. P. Springett, *Recollections of Madeira* (London, 1843).
Courtesy of the Cleveland Public Library.

Plate 9. *Alexander Gordon of Letterfourie* (1715–1797),
by an unknown artist, n.d. Source: Private Collection.

Plate 10. *Sea Captains Carousing in Surinam*, by John Greenwood, c. 1755–1769.
Source: Courtesy of the St. Louis Art Museum, St. Louis, Missouri.

Plate 11. Moses Marcy house overmantel panel painting, by an unknown artist, c. 1754–1775. Source: Courtesy of Old Sturbridge Village, Sturbridge, Massachusetts.

Plate 12. *The Toast*, by an unknown artist, c. 1810–1815.
Source: Courtesy of John P. Nugent Collection, Newburgh, Indiana.

Plate 13. *A Country Wedding,* by John Lewis Krimmel, 1814. Source: Courtesy of the Pennsylvania Academy of the Fine Arts, Philadelphia. Gift of Paul Beck Jr.

Plate 14. Wine bottle, with an "RW" seal, manufactured at Caspar Wistar's Wistarburgh Glassworks, near Salem, New Jersey, for his son Richard Wistar, c. 1745–1755. Source: Courtesy of Collection The Corning Museum of Glass, Corning, NY. Gift of Elizabeth Wistar.

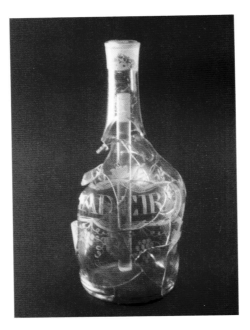

Plate 15. Thomas Jefferson's Madeira decanter, 1775–1800.
Source: Courtesy of Thomas Jefferson Foundation, Inc., Monticello.

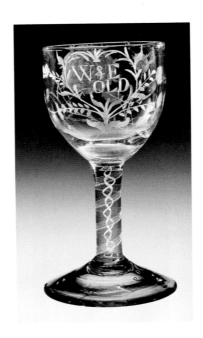

Plate 16. Wine goblet, made and engraved by Henry
William Stiegel for his daughter's marriage to William Old, at
his American Flint Glass Manufactory, Manheim, Pennsylvania, 1773–1774.
Source: Courtesy of Collection The Corning Museum of Glass, Corning, NY.
Gift in part of Roland C. and Sarah Katheryn Luther, Roland C.
Luther III, Edwin C. Luther III, and Ann Luther Dexter.

Figure 9.5. *Apologies for Tippling*, by George M. Woodward, 1804.
Source: Courtesy of The Library Company of Philadelphia.

such were the prevalence of douceurs that "Maid-Servants and the lowest class of Women" often learned "the first Rudiments of Gin-Drinking" and tippling wine when searching for provisions and supplies at chandler shops.[75] Lovers, too, found wine indispensable. Women gladly received gifts of sweet wine and cordials from men, as did Mary Cartwright when she accepted two bottles of Hungary water from Robert Pringle. Women memorialized wine's role in courtship in prenuptial cutwork showing a couple grasping a wine-filled goblet in testimony to their commitment and union (figure 9.6). Given its gendered connotations in myth and religion and its disinhibiting power, wine was tailor-made for lovemaking and mating. *Advice to the Fair Sex* of Philadelphia went so far in 1803 as to argue that its making and drinking, which Christ had done at Cana, were "innocent mirth" and "not inconsistent with religion."[76]

Women's choice of alcohol differed from men's. Both sexes drank wine but, sadly, there is little discussion by women of whether they favored one wine over another. There is some intimation that women preferred "cordials" and "made wines." Women were consistently said to have bought the former and they pre-

Figure 9.6. Courtship cutwork, by an unknown artist, 1810.
Source: Courtesy of Winterthur Museum, Winterthur, Delaware.

pared both, whereas men were said to favor ardent spirits and beer. The difference lay in the proof, one suspects: cordials and made wines were distilled spirits whose alcohol content ranged from 50 to 110 proof, whereas ardent spirits ranged from 80 to 190 proof.

Cordials also had a different valence, one that sprang from domestic management of food and medicine, and this feminized them. Cordials were often made at home, sweetened—they were very sweet—and aromatized—mixed with fruits, spices, herbs, or nuts. They were thought to be stimulating, reviving, invigorating, restoring, and comforting because of the additives, in contrast to ardent spirits, which were "made with fire" (that is, distilled) and so uncontrollable. Seventeenth-century men steeped in physic peddled them as medical draughts to invigorate the heart and comfort and exhilarate the body. In reality, they were hardly medicinal; they were just a weaker form of spirits, a point frequently made by more enlightened medicos. Cordials were "fit to be kept in private Families, as a present and certain Relief, for sudden Qualms, Faintness, Sickness, or low Spirits," all of which women were more prone to than men; but, doctors warned, they were "never to be taken but in Case of Necessity."[77]

By the early eighteenth century, cordials had been appropriated by women as their drink, one that stood in notional (if false) opposition to male spirits. They had acquired many of the attributes given to women in the period—sincere, genuine, warm, and hearty. It is at this time that cordials and made wine became irrationally reverenced. While nowhere near the fetishization that men lavished on imported wines and wine cellars, the change was nonetheless significant. Instruction manuals and cookbooks for women and girls began describing how to prepare them. At roughly the same time, glass manufacturers began making small bottles and glasses for women to store and drink them in, and medicinal drug makers began selling these bottles, and their contents, throughout the Atlantic community. Unlike male wine fetishes, cordials and their bottles never became a mark of gentility; rather, they served as signs of dissolution.

Although they could drink relatively unobserved by the men who kept the records and, as keepers of the larder, whenever they pleased, women apparently drank more moderately than men. Women were described and painted in altogether different postures from men. Behavior at a cordial- and wine-covered tea table was more controlled and hierarchical than in an often disorderly and democratic club. At tea, for the most part, women met acquaintances (their guests or their hosts), for almost exclusively social encounters, often with both sexes, and had one-on-one or small-group conversations. Few women were reported as losing their composure at tea. Despite this, as the rage for tea advanced over the course of the eighteenth century, immoderate drinking by women became a public issue. While they did not become "beastly" or "inhumanly" drunk, women "tippled" drams, and the result was nearly the same as with cordial drinking—loss of control and, at times, consciousness. Byrd clucked in private disapproval in the 1710s when his neighbors' wives drank heavily, but he did not do so often, nor did any of his contemporaries. By the 1730s, the problem had grown great enough for the printer of the *Pennsylvania Gazette* to report the "sudden death" of a woman from "the violent Effect of strong Drink." The cause was the not uncommon "practice of some otherwise discreet Women" drinking "two or three drams" of rum "in a Morning." Such a habit took "away their Sense of Shame and of Duty," their "Fear of Censure," and their ability "to support their Rank and Credit in the World." Habitual moderation was one of the virtues that made women "amiable or valuable to men"; and while drunkenness was "far more frequent among . . . Men than among" women, it was regarded as more de-stabilizing to women, because they were both citizens and mothers. In time, "the tippling of drams," "one of the evil consequences of the habit of tea-drinking," flowed well beyond the parlor: "hysterical women," noted the foremost authority on "diet and regimen" in 1812, were finding apothecaries' drams, either "mixtures and draughts" or "plain brandy," and homemade wine as soothing as and cheaper than tea, and they were drinking it in solitude. Had female familiarity with wine not been so widespread, the doctor's concern would not have had much reso-nance.[78]

In one final respect, women's drinking is said to have differed from men's: agenda. One might conclude from comparing pictorial representations and news-paper reports of men drinking with the comparatively few discussions of women drinking that drinking was less instrumental for women: women gathered and drank to socialize, whereas men did so to realize ulterior motives, such as trans-acting business, furthering a political scheme or agenda, or advancing a career. Such inference is problematic. On the one hand, men often gathered merely to socialize with friends. On the other hand, women could have had agendas when they were invited or accepted invitations to tea. Some could have tried as hostesses to advance their own, their husband's, and their family's position by impressing guests with their house, glassware, furniture, and wit, much as their husbands were doing in their clubs' meeting rooms. Nothing need ever have been said—the visitation alone or the presence of expensive metropolitan drink or glassware may have been enough. Given the pitfalls of analytic modes that interpret life as always in pursuit of ulterior motives, it is better to view female and male drinking as remarkably similar in purposes, from the pleasant feeling of tipsiness through easy sociality with friends to instrumental furthering of other agendas.

THE COLOR OF WINE

It is harder to get a clear view of the drinking behavior of people of color than of that of women, because it was exceptional for whites to write about nonwhite drinking, or at least describe it objectively and in detail. Still, some clues have survived. Blacks consumed liquor in many of the same ways that whites did. Free blacks and, depending on the community, some slaves obtained "strong liquors" at public taverns, punch shops, tippling houses, and dram shops. If they enjoyed liberty to travel away from their plantations and had money to spend, slaves fre-quented drinking establishments on trips to markets in search of food, clothing, tobacco, and housewares. They "were not just surreptitiously served at a back entrance; rather, they entered the houses" by the front door and fraternized with whites. John Hook kept two ledgers at his Bedford County (North Carolina) store in the 1770s, and in the four years before the outbreak of war 10 percent of the customers were slaves, and the chief purchases were liquor. This happened in the Caribbean and in southern and northern North American cities. New York's Geneva Club, infamous for its pickpockets and thieves, met in a public house and included free blacks and slaves among its members in the colonial period, while across town slaves frequented Hughes' Tavern, where they were said to have hatched the slave conspiracy of 1741.[79]

Free blacks and slaves bought alcohol not only from tavern keepers but also from masters, overseers, neighbors, and "plain folk" (meaning plain white folk). According to the most thorough account of eighteenth-century American slave life, "alcohol was a significant medium of interracial exchange." Masters and overseers sold and gave their slaves a variety of drinks above and beyond rations. It was not unusual for slaves to buy it at slave-run shops and taverns in the slave quarters. This seems to have been the setup at Drax Hall, Jamaica, where most of the wine bottle fragments discovered were found in an excavation of an eighteenth-century slave quarters. Landon Carter's slave Nassau bought liquor from a local Virginia farmer; his Ginny obtained it from a neighboring overseer. Other slaves procured it from the county's "night shops." The more trusted slaves often provided Carter with wine and rum—testimony that a fully functioning market for liquor served blacks as well as whites.[80]

Slaves also received alcohol as dietary supplements and gifts. Apart from medical treatment, drink most commonly came to them in the form of daily rations and harvest bonuses. Several plantations' accounts suggest they received rum or whisky as "reward for hard work," sometimes as a supplement to the daily diet of fish, vegetables, and roots, but more often at the end of a yearly work cycle. Rose Price's slave gangs at Worthy Park in Jamaica consumed about eight puncheons of rum each year as part of their rations. Less routine but no less significant were gifts not directly tied to plantation agriculture. At one of Price's Jamaican coffee estates, slaves in the "first class" gang were given Christmas "gifts," including two bottles of rum, while those of the "third class" received only one bottle. Thomas Thistlewood gave his slaves Lincoln, Dick, and Abba "each a bottle off rum" and Cudgoe and Solon a bottle to share "between them" on Christmas Day 1774; two more bottles went to Leon and Pompey, two more to Chubb and Strop, two more to Jenny, Damsel, and Bess, and two more to the "rest of [the] women." He did not limit his gifts to holidays. Thistlewood gave liquor to slaves after having sex with them, and to others for special reasons: for giving birth to a boy he sent Flora a bottle of rum; for entertaining "Company at the Burial" of her son he offered Abba some rum; for catching a runaway he gave another slave a bottle of rum; "at laying the first stone" of a building he provided the masons with the same; "for catching Pompey stealing canes" the watchman earned "a drink & 2 bitts"; and for building a slave's coffin and digging her grave he gave slave carpenters each a bottle of rum.[81]

Black people seem to have drunk little wine. The retail establishments open to them were either second-tier urban establishments or rural venues and so had limited variety, and probably little wine. British West Indian plantations had easy access to a cheap, if not free, supply of spirits, inasmuch as they produced rum there. The same was true for farming areas in the Chesapeake that produced whisky and cider and for distilling centers in New England and the mid-Atlantic region that produced rum. Also, blacks enjoyed less income and, as wine became expensive compared to spirits over the eighteenth century, wine became out of reach. Furthermore, to the extent that slaves were drinking to escape, they could get a greater "kick" from spirits, rum having at least twice the alcoholic content of wine. While it was not uncommon for blacks to drink liquor, drinking wine remained unusual for them in Anglo-America.[82]

Where the story of blacks' acquisition of alcohol most markedly diverges from that of whites' is in the allegation of theft. Theft was about the only means by which slaves procured wine, as opposed to spirits, which they found in plantation taverns and stores in plenty. Blacks were most frequently recorded as drinking wine after whites alleged it had been stolen from them. William Byrd II reported that his slaves stole wine and beer from his cellar at Westover in 1711 after a servant left the cellar door unlocked. A slave woman was called before New London's court for "stealing Mr. Durfey's wine." In 1757, Thistlewood's Tolby got drunk on "raw wines" he supposedly filched in western Jamaica; although for an unspecified reason Thistlewood meted out no punishment, he later flogged his Jimmy, who got drunk and burned a hole in the piazza floor. Carter's Nassau often got "excessively" and "inhumanly" drunk on liquor he supposedly purloined, and on one occasion he drank most of the mulled wine prepared to treat his master's gout. The slaves Carter noted drinking were usually household slaves who enjoyed easy access to the cellar. Over outnumbered southern planters, there loomed as well the specter of slaves robbing them on a more massive scale. At its most extreme, it manifested itself in outright looting, as when a Georgia plantation was sacked in 1765, its "wine room" broken open and "a quantity" of Madeira and rum taken by "some Negroes" belonging to traders. Unknown slaves, of course, probably made off with wine sometimes, but in most instances it was household slaves who allegedly did the job. Whether they actually did steal the wine can never be known. The record is, as we know, hopelessly biased.[83]

However procured, black people drank for many of the same reasons that white people did. Liquor provided some nourishment, supplementing an impoverished diet. It made a day's work easier. It was an ingredient of sociability. One suspects hosting and hospitality prevailed in free black homes and among slave families and communities in British America, although there is no record of it.[84] Yet it is also likely that slaves had reasons for drinking that whites never experienced. In a curious comment, at once insightful and patronizing, Richard Bickell noted that alcohol "drowns[,] for a short time," slaves' "reflections that they are despised and burthened." For some, drinking alcohol may have even been an act of defiance, disrupting the master's routine and creating confusion in the household. Ultimately, however, what it meant to blacks to drink, and to drink wine rather than the more easily obtainable rum, will probably never be known. But it could not mean exactly the same thing to them as it did to whites.[85]

Black people were seldom reported to be in control of liquor's effects. White people noticed blacks drinking when the results were deleterious: "inhuman" and "bestial" behavior, the loss of control and sometimes even consciousness, and destruction of property were what they reported. Not coincidentally, the 1741 New York "slave conspiracy" was whispered to have been hatched in a tavern. Presumably, blacks enacted the same behaviors, from abstinence through moderation to drunkenness, that white people did; but the descriptions were written by whites who felt outnumbered and taken advantage of. What they detailed was loss of control, not moderate deportment—which, of course, confirmed in their minds their abilities to master their own urges.[86]

Indians drank wine even less frequently than blacks, although contemporaries noted that Henry Hudson gave them wine upon their first encounter with the Dutch in 1609: "they were all merrie"; the experience "was strange to them . . . for they could not tell how to take it."[87] The evidence is that the North American Indians produced no alcohol before the Europeans arrived, despite the fact that grapevines lined the banks of the rivers and streams. As white settlements advanced into the continent, the Indians took to drink. Some Indians may have had to overcome cultural hurdles, such as the perception that red wine was blood—"All Americans have at first a loathing for our wines," noticed a Quebec priest in 1662–63—although the early Dutch and French encounters do not provide much substantiation to such hesitation. Spirits were more common among the Indians than wine, but what they drank depended on where they acquired it and whom they obtained it from. In New France wine consumption was comparatively prevalent. The immigrant fur-trading population was accustomed to drinking wine back home and the religious community needed it for Communion; the Indians consumed it alongside French brandy throughout the colonial period. In English-speaking America, they consumed less wine and more rum, brandy, and whisky. Over the course of the eighteenth century, as wines, which had to be imported, grew more expensive relative to spirits, many of which were domestically made, spirits came to dominate among Indian consumers. By the time of the Revolution, it was rare for Indian chiefs or government officials to express concern over the presence of wine; what they abjured were spirits.[88]

Most of the wine the Indians did acquire came in the course of exchange with the Europeans for furs and skins. Tavern keepers, storekeepers, and traders also sold wine to the "savages," and traders and military men gave it to them. Wine, like brandy or rum, could serve as payment for goods or be given in advance to secure hunters' services. Early mariners and traders like Christopher Newport of Virginia, who supplied Powhatan with Sack, carried extensive supplies of wine to woo the natives, buy their goods, and procure food supplies; the Europeans also drank it themselves. Later on, importers, wholesalers, and retailers Baynton, Wharton & Morgan of prerevolutionary Philadelphia supplied Indians in western Pennsylvania with Madeira.[89]

Among Lake Superior traders toward the end of the eighteenth century, "the trading ceremonies at the beginning and end of the year and on the repayment of debts usually featured gifts of alcohol." Moreover, "the food on which the trader depended, such as wild rice, game, and maple sugar, was in large part obtained with liquor." As a result, wine and spirits participated in the food associations between Europeans and Indians as most barter goods did not. "Generosity with food was expected of all people, and those who were generous were considered to be fulfilling their obligations towards other members of the society." Wine and spirits "were incorporated into the food sphere of exchange and treated as objects to be shared or traded for other objects of food." Wine was seen as a way to feed, and so "a symbol of the close social relationship that both aboriginal people and traders were seeking to establish."[90] Liquor, more than any other good, served as an indicator of goodwill. "Objects in this category could be given away or traded one for the other. Such transactions created a trader-aboriginal society in which trust was possible." Not surprisingly, then, as the eighteenth century progressed, wine was given to Indians in the course of diplomacy in a ritual context of gift or toast. It was used to create or maintain alliances, finalize peace treaties, and mark important meetings and decisions, although the quantities suggest the Indians often had a lot left over for everyday consumption. The practice of giving gifts of wine became a diplomatic necessity for the British during the Seven Years' War, and it persisted into the nineteenth century.[91]

Among white people's reports of Indians drinking, drunkenness and lack of control were prominent narratives. These references appear in the reports of missionaries and traders, and the passage of laws forbidding sales of spirits and wine to Indians after 1635: "having once acquired a taste" for wines, the Indians were reported to "seek them with such passion that some strip themselves of everything, and reduce their families to beggary, while others sell even their own children, in order to obtain the means of gratifying this furious craving." They were, some French thought, "only too eager for . . . drinks—both men and women experiencing a singular pleasure, not in drinking, but in becoming drunk." Not all reports were so pessimistic: the conquerors realized that some could "drink merely out of human respect, without having any great craving for liquor," and "the act of taking a few drinks of brandy or of wine . . . while eating in the house" of a trader was not uncommon. Nonetheless, they believed the state of affairs needed to be managed. Indians, they felt, could not control their liquor consumption, and the intent of most white legislation was to exclude Indians from taverns and, in some places, stores as well, or at least to bar them from purchasing liquor.[92]

Although tavern life has received more attention from scholars, the principal locus of drinking in eighteenth-century America was the home. Women were principals in managing the household's acquisition, storing, and dispensing of wine and other drinks. They even "manufactured" drinks, by making cordials and other alcoholic concoctions. Because it was home-based, drinking participated in the homely arts and virtues—feeding the hungry, ministering to the sick and infirm, and providing hospitality to the displaced. Alcohol was a principal ingredient of most people's diets, so people away from home—or, more accurately, people in temporary *alternative* homes such as hospitals and colleges—were provided it or provided it for themselves as a way to be "at home." It was an important part of religious, military, and civic rituals and performances. Its homelike character permeated many nonhome venues, especially when hospitality was offered.

At the same time, just as the Consumer Revolution was making goods like wine available to more people, elite consumers were eager to highlight how the ways they drank were special—economically, socially, culturally, and politically. They showed themselves as a group apart by what they drank—wine, which was expensive—and the gendered, racialized, and economically stratified circumstances in which they drank it. That there was more than one public meant that there was more than one reality perceived by consumers.[93]

In addition, wine and other alcoholic beverages were always perceived as dangerous because of their ability to make people drunk. Elite white men presented their own drunkenness as robust and manly, but they frowned on women who got drunk as dissolute, and blacks and Indians who got drunk as barbaric. All of these categories showed how carefully wine had to be managed and controlled. Of course, all of the groups continued to find ways to make themselves "merry."

"Power to Give Sudden Refreshment" and Respect: Health, Refinement, and the Consumption of Wine

As wine and spirits became increasingly available in Anglo-America after the middle decades of the seventeenth century, many varieties replaced a few. Some drinks remained "common"; others became luxuries, linked to persons, places, and events that signified refinement and wealth. As wine grew ordinary, certain groups in society sought to refine its use, taste, and status. They singled out certain varieties of wine as especially praiseworthy, created "wine" as a subject of discourse, established an etiquette of wine display and consumption, and created rituals around its use. Few of the shifts were mere extensions of European culture; contrary to "trickle-down" theories of culture, they were products of the interactions among metropolitans, provincials, and creoles. Wine distributors contributed to the creation of refined wine-drinking culture, but it was mainly the work of consumers who shared their experiences and discourse with others along the links and nodes of their networks.[1]

The Atlantic-wide drink culture that emerged was simultaneously inclusive and exclusive. This may seem paradoxical. Yet, these features were consonant with a self-consciously enlightened age and the large, porous oceanic community in which they occurred. Wine consumption expressed similarities and included drinkers who recognized a shared set of signs and understandings, even as it created differences and opportunities to exclude others. The practices and manners associated with wine will be addressed in the following chapter. This chapter examines wine discourse through the lens of the two debates that figured most prominently in the process of differentiation and exclusion: scientific, medical, and health colloquies over the benefits of wine prescription and usage, and social debates over the gentility of drinking.

Both debates were new. The European settlements of North America were still tenuous for much of the seventeenth century. As food products, wine and spirits were principally regarded as mechanisms promoting well-being; the exceptions were their use in religious ceremonies and the sense of sociability they engendered. Toward the end of that century, as the economic success of the European colonies became more secure and new emigrants flooded in, alcoholic beverages joined the conversations people were beginning to have about how to live what they perceived to be their increasingly commercialized lives. In Anglo-America, as well as in Britain, these conversations revolved mainly around health and opulence. Wine became part of the debates about bodily constitution and the right way to behave in the world.

"THE HAVEN OF HEALTH"

The effects of wine and spirits on the functioning of both body and mind are visible to others. From time immemorial, drinkers and medical practitioners have chronicled the effects of consuming them, and whether they were problematic. However, wine and spirits were not subjected to empirical investigation before the late seventeenth century, when "experts" with scientific, medical, and dietary perspectives entered into conversation with one another and the drinkers themselves.

"A MATTER OF DIET, OR ALIMENT"

Before the late seventeenth century, the particular physiological effects of drinking alcohol were generally agreed upon, even if only dimly understood. Wine delivered more nutrients than any other alcoholic beverage, perhaps more than any other drink. It was seen as an "aliment," or nourishment. The fortified wines that Anglo-Americans imported and retailed had the most carbohydrates: 100 grams of aqua vitae (brandy), gin, rum, or whisky contained only a trace of carbohydrates, and 100 grams of beer, 3.8 grams of carbohydrates. But 100 grams of table wine contained 4.2 grams and 100 grams of a fortified wine such as Madeira, 7.7 grams. Consequently, wine, and Madeira in particular, was a significant source of energy for seventeenth- and eighteenth-century drinkers. Madeira also had a higher level of potassium than table wine, spirits, or beer. Drinking wines with high amounts of potassium replaced the potassium in people who were depleted by illnesses like diarrhea and cholera. In an age when bacterial afflictions were pandemic, potassium-rich wines were especially valuable.[2]

Some of the best testimony for the nutritional value of wine was naval. During the Age of Sail, wine served as an aliment to mariners and passengers alike. In the 1630s, voyagers to Maryland were advised to bring Claret, Sack, and "burnt [reduced] wine" with them for shipboard use. Margaret Winthrop, on traveling to join her husband in Massachusetts, was told to carry Sack for the mariners' health, and probably also their good humor.[3] Ships' drinking water became polluted through the introduction of foreign substances, sometimes saltwater, or storage in "foul wine casks, which turned it sour, and occasioned a violent dysentery." The alternatives were to strain the bad water with a filtering stone, boil it, and drink it the next day, or to drink liquor. The latter was easier.[4] In 1656, a New York ordinance stipulated that "for the preservation of health . . . on a long voyage," "everyone on board ship should be bound to drink his ration of wine every day" and not be allowed "to save it or sell it." English seamen patrolling American shores were allowed wine as part of their rations—unofficially after 1655, officially after 1731—although their principal drink was rum. At the end of the eighteenth century, British sailors received one pint of rum or wine per day, as did American seamen, until Congress halved the amount in 1794 and restricted it to rum and whisky. Commissioned officers in particular drank wine on board, consuming it as their principal beverage. This is, again, a reflection of the class differences in drinking; officers usually came from a higher social station than their men, and certainly received higher wages; besides, the cabin and gun rooms fed not only their charges but also their guests. Officers' stores could be very large. Before he left New England on one transatlantic mission early in the nineteenth century, the American commander Edward Preble laid in a half pipe and six demijohns of good Madeira, 120 bottles of old Port, and four cases of Claret, plus eight gallons of Cognac, two cases of gin, a case of cherry brandy, and a variety of liquors, cider, porter, and beer! Alcohol was a staple for men on the high seas.[5]

Wine also boosted diet landside. As an influential medical treatise summed up the matter on the eve of English colonization, wine "adds unto an empty stomache fulnes, and from a stomack fil'd, it takes the dulnes." Or, as the literary boulevardier Thomas Love Peacock later quipped—"when you are thirsty," you use alcohol to quench thirst, and "when you are not thirsty," you use it "to prevent" thirst.[6]

"As a matter of diet, or aliment," wine was much "better than water," for water was often foul in America. Whether it was polluted or pathogenic is not completely knowable until archaeologists more fully investigate the matter. What is clear is that contemporaries perceived the water as bad. At least from the early 1600s, experts like Richard Short and laymen like John Winthrop described the dangers posed by water, and considered alternatives. The dangers were diachronic. As late as 1820, New York's water was so "poor and brackish" that inhabitants had to mix it "with some French brandy or gin to make it safe to drink."[7]

Foul water was everywhere, "impregnated with foreign materials." Humans and animals defecated and died in rivers and lakes that settlers also used for washing their bodies and clothes and dumping manufacturing byproducts. Large rivers diluted pollutants found in dead flesh and industrial waste, but most settlers did not draw upon such sources for drinking water. They went instead to seemingly purer springs and streams, but they did not disperse bacteria and parasites quickly.[8] The same was true of wells and the sewers that leeched into them, in which decomposing flesh led to giardiasis or E. coli poisoning.[9]

Water might also induce lead poisoning. As late as 1815, lead pipes brought water to towns and lead cisterns stored it. "By these arts, a large proportion" of the population was "daily and hourly consuming a quantity of the most virulent and insidious poison." The danger of lead was broadcast by a few individuals and groups throughout the eighteenth century and several jurisdictions outlawed lead containers, but few laws were enforced and few warnings heeded. Even if the quantity of "noxious matter" was minute, it was often enough to keep men and women drinking wine.[10]

"BACCHUS TURN'D DOCTOR"

The populace at large believed both wine and spirits moderately consumed to be good for the body, as matters of sound personal nutrition and pragmatic domestic management. Those with access to liquor drank it, regarding it as a valuable and necessary component of diet. Most professionals agreed, at least at first. However, experimental scientists around the Atlantic began to question the received wisdom in the last third of the seventeenth century. The debates they waged on the place and use of wine and spirits in everyday life created new meanings for wine and its consumption.

Medical ideas about the use of wine and spirits were increasingly complicated, and often contested, as anatomists, chemists, and physicists interested in physiology and pathology revised and extended their knowledge through trial and error. The "experimentalists" disagreed with "traditionalists," and later with others of their own ilk, on how best to treat the sick, including whether to administer liquor. This interest belonged not to an identifiable branch of therapeutic science but sprang from general inquiries into physiology and pathology which, in the last third of the seventeenth century, took a mechanistic and interventionist turn. Reconfiguring alcoholic cures, questioning the efficacy of certain liquors, and positing alternatives to them were ways to overturn received wisdom. Quite a few practitioners distinguished between wine and spirits, usually regarding wine as beneficial, or at least benign, in contrast to spirits, which might be deleterious. At the same time, the phenomenon reflected the commercialization of the medical marketplace in the eighteenth century. Entrepreneurs and doctors commodified wine, hawking it to medicine takers and wine drinkers as nourishment and physic. The promotion of wine tapped into two traditions for preventing and curing disease: using wine as a secondary agent in which a drug was dissolved or as a primary agent that was itself the cure.

Vinum Medicatum

The more common approach was to view wine as a diluent or solvent of unpalatable drugs, a wound cleanser, and a pain reliever. A *Vinum Medicatum* for "the aid of sick People" was a wine "wherein Medicines have been infused"; the wine eased the ingestion of the unpleasant-tasting nostrum.[11] Practitioners agreed on this point from the 1640s to the 1810s. Yet there was continued elaboration of it in usage, and out of the refinements there emerged some distinctions between wines and spirits, even if little differentiation among wines.

Any compendium detailing the composition of drugs and prescriptions—from the first London College of Physicians' *Pharmacopoeia Londinensis* of 1618 through Anthony Thompson's *London Dispensatory* of 1815 and its various American counterparts—included recipes for taking and compounding drugs with wine. Nicholas Culpeper's 1649 translation of the *Pharmacopoeia Londinensis*, for instance, printed a recipe for *Aqua Mirabilis*, a prophylactic against stomach disorders and apoplexy and a restorer of lost speech. As did many "receipts," it included wine and brandy in its formula of things to be combined: "Cloves, Galanga, Cubebs, Mace, Cardamoms, Nutmegs, Ginger, of each one drachm, juyce of Chelondine, half a pound, *Aqua-vitae*, a pound, White Wine[,] three pints (or three pound which you please)[.]" Preparations like these remained standard among British and American elite and folk practitioners for over a century. When the Massachusetts Medical Society's *Pharmacopeia* was published in 1808, it contained prescriptions nearly identical to those found in British and European publications, although it presented the information in English (not Latin), added native American drugs to the materia medica, and deleted useless remedies. Prescription after prescription specified wine.[12]

Pharmacopoeia reflected prevailing elite ideas, publicizing the prescriptions of educated men. Once or twice removed, they also informed popular behavior. The popular press repeated the prescriptions of the books. The *New-Hampshire Gazette* brought to the attention of readers a "most excellent medicine" for plague. They were to boil sage and rice in three pints of Muscadine wine, "strain it and set it on the fire, and put in it long pepper, ginger, and nutmeg, of each the third part of an ounce, beat together to a fine powder; let it boil a little, then put in it 2 ounces of treacle, 1 ounce of mithridate, and a quarter of a pint of Angelica water; dissolve the treacle and mithridate in the Angelica water before you put them in." Two spoonfuls a day, readers were assured, would ward off the plague as well as smallpox, measles, surfeits, and fevers. Almanac readers in Virginia were offered a cure for dropsy in which wine was the diluent: those in search of relief from the accumulation of watery fluid in "the serious cavities" or connective tissues were to dissolve a pint of juice expressed from artichoke stem leaves in a pint of Madeira, and take up to six spoonfuls in the morning and evening. Likewise, they were told that coughs, "asthmatick complaints," and incipient consumptions would all be cured by a concoction of two quarts of Madeira and two ounces each of gumolibanum, Balsam of Gilead, and tolu, or, if these were not available, a thrice-daily dose of gum ammoniac, dissolved in pennyroyal tea, four spoonfuls of honey, and a half-pint decoction of wood lice, white wine, and saffron. Almanac and newspaper nostrums drew upon professional compendia. Elite and popular opinion embraced the notion that wine was a useful addition to medicines.[13]

Doctors routinely used wine to clean and treat wounds. They sometimes rubbed or washed wounds with wine to remove filth and "other extraneous things." They cleaned lacerated wounds incurred in a fall from a horse, clearing them of "dirt, sand, gravel, or whatever may be got into the same, with a sponge wrung out of wine"; and they bathed gunshot wounds with water, allowed them to bleed for a time, and then rebathed them with spirit of wine. After such preparatory cleansing, doctors applied wine dressings, such as an arm compress "dipt in warm wine" or a leg compress "dipt in wine or brandy," or they washed gangrenous skin with linen soaked in spirits.[14]

Akin to wine's time-honored use as a cleanser was its application as an anesthetic. The sick were commonly given wine to render their experience less traumatic, especially those afflicted by wasting diseases. Wine was sometimes used "to quiet the commotion" of surgical pain, although more ardent spirits achieved this more effectively. Wine was even given in advance, as a "stimulant," to help prevent surgical shock—wrongly, as it turned out. Using wine to heal wounds and lessen pain is one of the messages of William Hogarth's popular 1732 engraving *A Midnight Modern Conversation*, although it is easy to miss amid the iconographical riot. Here, in figure 10.1, one sees a drunken man with two knots in his wig (the mark of a doctor) pouring a bottle of wine on the wounded head of an officer, who has fallen down onto the floor in a stupor. This is not mere satire.[15] For centuries, it was common practice, when inflicted with wounds from iron instruments, for soldiers to suck out the blood, spit wine, wine and oil, or "Samaritan Balsam" into the wounds, and then cover and bind them. Through the late eighteenth century, wine served these dual cleansing and pain-relieving

Figure 10.1. A *Midnight Modern Conversation*, by William Hogarth, 1732.
Source: Courtesy of The British Museum—Department of Prints and
Drawings. © Copyright the Trustees of The British Museum.

functions. When a general's wife took care of a fallen major during the American
Revolution, she did what others recommended. Finding that the officer, through
"whose cheeks a small musket ball had passed, shattering his teeth and grazing
his tongue," could take only "a little broth, or something liquid," she gave him
a bottle of Rhenish, "in hopes that the acidity of the wine would cleanse" the
wound and dull the pain. It did both handsomely, and he "became cured" by
keeping the wine "continually in his mouth."[16]

    For similar reasons, wine was viewed as useful before, during, and after child-
birth. It ameliorated the mother's heartburn and vomiting while she was carrying the child. About "the only painkiller" and fortifier midwives administered to
induce labor was wine; during labor, mulled wine or an ardent spirit fortified the
woman "if she seemed weak." It was not uncommon for physicians to prescribe
"a glass of wine and a bit of chicken" to "hysteric women" after delivery. Whether
or not the mother was hysterical, it was helpful to give her "a little thin gruel, with

a spoonful or two of wine." (In contrast, midwives were pointedly advised to keep clear of "brandy, spirits, gin, and all kinds of cordials.") The pregnant and sick were probably the most frequent users of wine as a painkiller.[17]

The medical community theorized about why wine was useful. Between 1600 and the findings of Pasteur and Lister in the 1860s, the most common explanation for infection from wounds was that exposed tissue and blood made contact with noxious miasmas in the air, allowing infectious organisms to generate in the wound. As an influential surgical manual observed in 1701, "air is a mighty hindrance of their cure": the "nitrous, clammy and . . . arsenical Qualities or Particles of the Air" passed "to the Bottom of the Wound," doing harm. Wine counteracted air's effects. It flushed the wound of extraordinary matter, both invasive and airborne, and even resisted the "Malignity of the Air," which was "always impure in Hospitals." According to an older school of thought, wine was a red, hot (ardent) fluid, which counteracted too much cold, dry, black bile, and kept the humors in balance. "Hot" wine contracted the tissue and blood vessels, and so controlled bleeding and arrested the secretion of pus. Doctors of this school ordered wine baths and applied wine compresses to effect "agglutination" and "consolidation"—that is, the clumping of blood corpuscles and the adhesion of wound surfaces. Following time-honored Galenic logic, they felt the need to "conserve the equal temperament" of the afflicted and unafflicted parts. "Strong liquors . . . of a heating nature," William Buchan advised readers of his popular *Domestic Medicine* of 1772, "congeal the blood and . . . solder up the wound." By this time experimental scientists were chipping away at the twin edifices of spontaneous generation and humoral theory, but by 1815 no consensus emerged about the care of wounds.[18]

Contemporaries did not knowingly use wine to antisepticise wounds—that came only after Lister—but many thought there was a connection between wine and antisepsis, and some doctors attempted to counter the decomposition of tissues, as in ulceration, suppuration, or gangrene, with wine. Those who felt all sepsis was bad—there was not yet universal agreement—also believed it was related to vegetable putrefaction, and prescribed vegetable preservatives such as wine as "antiseptics," in much the way that cooks washed rotting fruit in vinegar. Wine resisted putrefaction "powerfully," even as it also "corroborates and quickens [agglutination], [and] hinders Excessive Suppuration and the Dissolution of the Nerves."[19]

"A Great Restorative to a Weak Constitution"

George Washington's first posthumous depiction (figure 10.2) highlights the persistence of wine remedies into the nineteenth century. Curious with one so

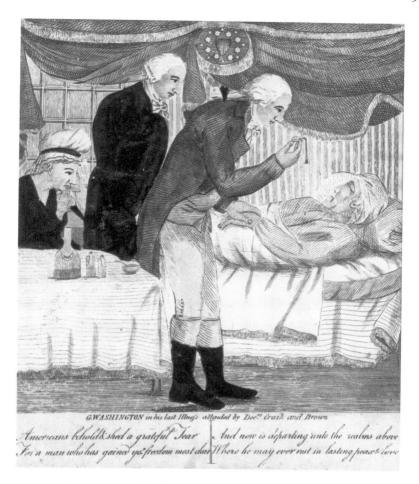

Figure 10.2. G. *Washington in His Last Illness*, engraved by
Edward Pember and Samuel Luzader, 1800.
Source: Courtesy of Winterthur Museum, Winterthur, Delaware.

august, the president is shown lying prostrate on his bed, doctors at the ready, a
bottle of wine on his side table. It is one of the few images showing early Americans with a bottle of alcohol. But whether the wine was there primarily to assist
or to cure is unclear. Whether to use wine to effect a cure was still problematic in
Washington's day, the subject of contest for nearly two centuries.

At the founding of England's first American colonies, medical and popular
opinion converged: wine was benign, and it might even cure disease. Writers saw
many beneficial and few harmful effects from drinking it. It was "medicinable,"

the doctor Tobias Whitaker reminded physicians in 1638 — something to nourish, "corroborate, correct putrefaction, open obstructions, [and] exhilarate the spirits." "What more" was "wanting or needful for the preservation or restauration of life and health"?[20] In a popular treatise first published in 1693, William Salmon of London detailed applications for Port, Tent, Alicante, Canary, Malaga, and Sherry, and he maintained his support into the next century, prescribing wine (but not spirits) for many ailments. Rhenish and Canary warmed and strengthened the stomach, increased the appetite, prevented dropsy, soothed colic, expelled wind, and killed worms, for instance. Port, he implied, was not as palatable, despite its being full-bodied and aiding digestion.[21]

The use of wine to cure came under attack in the fourth quarter of the seventeenth century. Salmon and the practitioners who shared his opinions found their views questioned by doctors who focused on behavior (diet, health, and hygiene) and disease. The consumption of alcohol, the critics argued, destroyed physical well-being and encouraged receptivity to certain diseases. They believed people could avoid smallpox by eschewing wine, among other things, and propagated the notion that wine induced gout. The new thinking was part of "a general desire to discard the past and adopt new ideas" in the natural and medical sciences. Traditional thinking was still dominated by Galenic teaching that human health depended upon humoral balance. Adhering instead to the contemporary ideas and methods of Francis Bacon and René Descartes, the new scientists turned to clinical observation for explanations. William Harvey, one of the most famous of the experimentalists, opined that once "physicians definitely knew the micro-structures and micro-mechanisms of aliment and the body," "they could intervene and advise with radically improved effectiveness." However, the new experimental method did not produce a definitive conclusion about the efficacy of wine in medicine. The points of view, which shaped practice for over a century, fell into three camps.[22]

One group of scientists and clinicians clung to the idea that wine was beneficial. This was Salmon redivivus, although this group subscribed to a philosophy of greater personal and social control than had seventeenth-century advocates. Drunk in moderate amounts, wine "fortifies the Stomach, and other parts of the Body, helps Digestion, increases the Spirits, heats the Imagination, helps the Memory, gives vigour to the Blood, and works by Urine." But when drunk excessively, it "heats too much, corrupts the Liquors of the Body, intoxicates, and causes many pernicious Diseases, as Fevers, Apoplexies, Palsie, Lethargy and the like." The key was moderation. Wine used appropriately agreed "at all times, with any Age and Constitution," preserving "the Health of the Body." Peter Shaw defended the "Juice of the Grape" in 1724: drunk "in moderate quantities," wine had "power to give sudden refreshment, to warm the stomach, [and to] gently stimulate its fibres." A pint of Canary battled malignant fever; warm Canary cured smallpox; any wine remedied venereal disease and hysteria. Similarly, Lancaster County's Edward Shippen Sr., who supplied Pennsylvania troops with Madeira during the Seven Years' War, claimed that wine was "accounted not only by physicians but by other experienced persons" the "most wholesome liquor . . . in the world." Sack and Canary were "accounted a great Restorative to a weak Constitution." "Weak punch and wine & water, vinegar & water, small beer, sour milk & water" were "better at lessening the effects of heat upon the body than spirits," as they "keep up a due perspiration, abate internal heat, and resist putrefaction."[23]

Writers who believed wine was useful in combating disease discussed the relative value of drinks in the second third of the eighteenth century. Shippen's neighbors in Lancaster found Lisbon more efficacious than Madeira, and Madeira more than Fayal or Sherry in battling common complaints at the end of the American Revolution. At the same time, Dr. John Crawford, who would eventually manage military hospitals in Barbados and Demerara and settle in Maryland, acknowledged "the recruiting powers of wine . . . particularly salutary." He preferred red wine to "every kind of medicine" for "disease incident to the liver." At hospitals in the West Indies, he allowed Madeira, Claret, and Rhenish "in the quantity suited to the several cases." By the time Crawford was doctoring, a consensus was emerging that different wines were appropriate for different ailments and patients. Unfortunately, there is little commentary on which wine did what. As the author of the period's most influential military medical treatise noted, "wine is the best of all cordials in the decline of fevers," as it was of scurvy and dysentery, too, "and is a much better restorative than rum, or any other spirits, however mixed or prepared; it is likewise an excellent means to prevent infection." Madeira wine above all other wines "should be preserved for the use of the sick."[24]

One of the most notable of those who attempted to explain wine's curative properties was the Scot John Brown, who espoused the controversial new ideas that tissues existed in a state of excitement, and disease represented increased or decreased excitability. Brown hypothesized that there were only two basic diseases—*sthenic* (strong) and *asthenic* (weak)—and that they could be cured respectively with sedatives such as opium, to counter overexcited tissue, and stimulants such as wine, to move underexcited tissue. Spirits were less than helpful. Fruit and grain liquors were forbidden. Not just any wine was allowed, though; doctors who followed Brown detailed specific wines for specific maladies. The fanatical American student of the Brunonian method Dr. David Hosack advised a sufferer whose digestive organs were debilitated to take "a beefsteak and a glass of wine and water" for breakfast and "a bit of old cheese and crackers" after dinner, in addition to a half-pint of Madeira or Port each day. To another, he prescribed drinking "water & a few glasses of Madeira" with dinner.[25]

A second group of students of diet, health, and hygiene argued that wine was a bane to the human constitution. Spurred on by attention to social and familial problems and their causes in the early eighteenth century, which famously fixed its gaze on "Mother Gin" in the 1730s, a string of investigators concluded that wine produced more diseases than it cured or eased. George Cheyne, the formerly obese Scot whose life's mission was to reorder English national foodways with a milk-and-seed diet even as he struggled to corral his own weight—at one point he weighed nearly 450 pounds—eschewed wine and grain-based liquors, pushing water instead. Cheyne believed water preserved the appetite and promoted digestion. The lapsed iatro-mathematician understood he was up against history and habit: wine was "as common as Water" when he first published in 1724. "The better Sort scarce ever dilute their Food with any other Liquor." Cheyne warned them that they did so at their peril. Wine inflamed their blood "into Gout, Stone, and Rheumatism, raging Fevers, Pleurisies, Small Pox, or Measles"; it "enraged" their passions, causing "Quarrels, Murder, and Blasphemy"; it dried up "their Juices"; and it "scorch'd and shrivel'd" their "Solids." Cheyne stressed the especially "bad Consequences of the common Use of [undiluted] strong-bodied Wines," such as Madeira, Port, and Sherry, although he grudgingly allowed "the consumption of "light wines of middling Strength, or strong Wines diluted with Water." Only "Luxury and Concupiscence" made wine necessary, and these were poor justifications.[26]

Within a half century, Cheyne's teachings had been absorbed into the theory and practice of countless professionals. While Buchan, Benjamin Rush, and Brown were arguing for comfort with it, Cheyne's followers regarded wine as "the greatest bane of all." They barely acknowledged the hierarchy of drink, setting wine among the worst. Wine, like strong liquor, "harden[s] everything" in "natural digestion." "The most perfect cures," therefore, consisted in "total abstinence." Wines "oppress our spirits, blunt our senses, destroy the strength of our stomach and the balsamic quality of the blood, thicken the juices, throw the humours into an excessive motion, excite to venery, stimulate and contract the solids, which being not duly repaired cease to perform their functions." Wines encourage a "superfluity of phlegm," which in turn weakens the brain and overburdens "the animal spirits," causing the drinker to grow "stupid, weak, forgetful, [and] liable to catarrhs, and other more dangerous distempers" and the "instruments of digestion [to] grow weaker." "Strong drinks" were always unsuitable. So were fermented drinks like wine and beer, even though they produced bad effects "in a less degree." Their consumption was "a foolish liveliness."[27]

A third medical-scientific group staked out middle ground: wine was not bad per se; its effects depended on the age of the patient, the foods it was taken with and when, and for which diseases it was applied. A highly vocal opponent of Galenic humoral pathology, which still held sway over many practitioners, the Scots medical professor William Cullen believed that disease originated in disturbances in the nervous system. He condemned purgatives and laxatives and advocated stimulating and sedating tonics, among which he put some wines. "Ripe and perfect wine," rather than new wine, he wrote in his *Materia Medica*, was "fit to strengthen the stomach," "promote a regular digestion," and "stimulate the whole system." Wine was an excellent stimulant, but he warned that in the amount usually required to do its work, it was an "intoxicating and a powerful sedative." As a general rule, "simple water" was more advisable.[28]

Cullen had immense influence throughout the Atlantic world. In the United States, one of his students, Benjamin Rush, was the most respected expositor of the professor's precepts. When Rush became the professor of the theory and practice of medicine at the newly established College of Philadelphia, he advised correspondents, readers, students, and patients to forgo alcohol, except in very particular circumstances. When influenza struck the city in 1790, Rush prescribed warm wine punch and wine whey as a "constant drink" when a patient's cry was weak, rather than bleeding. But he seldom advocated anything stronger than watered-down wine.[29]

Like some of the advocates of wine, those who believed it depended on the patient and the disease tried to distinguish liquors' effects. In a 1771 letter to Benjamin Franklin that he revised and republished as a separate essay after the Revolution, Rush detailed the generally execrable effects of "spirituous liquors": stomach sickness, universal dropsy, obstruction of the liver, motions, palsy, and gout. Spirits destroyed "more lives than the sword": they corroded personal property and undermined moral probity. Spirits might have some benefits—in especially cold or warm weather, and during hard labor—but none surpassed those of wholesome substitutes like wine. Wine did not induce gout as spirits did, and had the additional advantages of being cheaper and less intoxicating.[30] In 1784, in a fit of excess precision, Rush embedded wine in a visual hierarchy of drink he called the "Moral and Physical Thermometer" (figure 10.3). The device ranked drinks on a scale between +70 and −70. Water topped the measure at +70 in terms of encouraging "Health, Wealth, Serenity of mind, Reputation, long life,

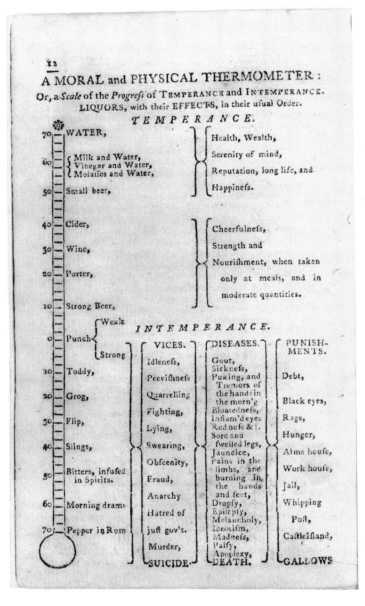

Figure 10.3. "A Moral and Physical Thermometer,"
by Benjamin Rush, 1784–1790.
Source: Benjamin Rush, *An Inquiry into the Effects of Spirituous
Liquors upon the Human Body* (Boston, 1790), 12. Courtesy of
The Library Company of Philadelphia.

and Happiness," succeeded by small beer, cider, wine (at 30), porter, strong beer, and finally punch (at 0), which, when made with spirits, stood at the threshold of intemperance. Wine provided "Cheerfulness, Strength and Nourishment" in moderation, as did cider, porter, and strong beer. All were preferable to drinks made with spirits (below 0). The worst were morning drams (–60) and pepper in rum (–70), which foretold suicide, death from disease, and the gallows.

Because of the lack of closure to the debate among the professionals, uncertainty over the curative properties of wine persisted through the first quarter of the nineteenth century. Old, often ancient precepts continued to guide clinicians and patients, even after experimentalists had undone much of the structure of Galenic medicine.[31] People continued to believe wine would cure their diseases and make them healthy, and practitioners prescribed accordingly.[32] For many of them, far removed from the medical debates in Britain and Europe, the "middle way" seemed the easiest and safest approach. If there was a norm in America, it was an often ambivalent, highly particularistic combination of abstinence and consumption.

"Drink Wine and Have the Gowt," or Drink None and "Have the Gowt as Well"

The contradictions of the findings of the experimentalists, and the perpetuation of traditions were at work in the search for a cure for gout—recurrent attacks of acute arthritis. Was wine part of the cause of gout, or part of the cure? If it was part of the cure, which ones should be prescribed? Doctors and drinkers had no comprehension of gout's chemistry. Only in subsequent centuries was it discovered that gout results from a buildup of uric acid. Instead, contemporaries variously thought that wine caused gout, exacerbated it, eased it, cured it, or had nothing at all to do with it. Opinion was divided between those eschewing it and those allowing it.[33]

The belief that gout and wine had something to do with each other was old. "Drink wine and have the gowt," quipped Thomas Cogan, or drink none and "have the gowt as well." In the second half of the seventeenth century, experimental scientists and doctors began investigating the connection. Thomas Sydenham systematically detailed wine's effects in his "Treatise of the Gout and Dropsy," a good example of the new experimental scientific method and its faith in detailed firsthand observation. Sydenham argued that the disease could be acquired or inherited. It could be acquired by absorbing "tartarous, urinous or other salts . . . present in wines and strong liquors." Even if it was inherited, it was "enrag'd by Luxury," including indulgence in wine and spirits. In either case, one should avoid wine. On this Sydenham was adamant, and his argument set the terms of debate for the ensuing century.[34] A hundred years later, William Cadogan's *Dissertation on the Gout, and All Chronic Diseases* (1771) developed the "enrag'd by Luxury" argument. Cadogan argued that gout arose from the "abuse of our constitutions: indolence, intemperance, or vexation" ("anxiety" in today's language). For the first time, a medical expert avowed that gout was not hereditary and not incurable. "It could be averted, remedied, or at least relieved by adoption of a temperate regime." Such a regimen, pace Sydenham, embraced the use of wine, along with vinegar, pickles, mustard, and bread.[35]

Despite Sydenham's and Cadogan's arguments, many doctors persisted in believing that wine could cure a sufferer of gout, or at least minimize the pain he or she experienced. It is hard to recapture this position, as it was more referred to by opponents than articulated by exponents; but one suspects it was as old, if not older, than Sydenham's position. One to laud wine was the Galenically enriched Robert James, author of the widely distributed *Medicinal Dictionary* (1745). Wine, with its "large Quantity of Tartar," "excellently" conveyed "morbific Matter through the Kidneys." Tartarous wines' evacuating properties, the handbook informed readers, would help relieve gout's symptoms. James's tome appeared in the middle of the eighteenth century, but it summarized a century of thinking. Benjamin Rush embraced the position that wine would not harm the gouty as part of his campaign to distinguish the effects of wine and spirits. Lecturers at the College of Physicians in Philadelphia continued to tout wine's benefits well after the establishment of federal government. The beliefs were popular as well as scientific. Newspaper advertisements boasted that "Old and Strong MADEIRA . . . often removed the most violent fits of the Gout." A "small wilderness Root . . . steeped in Madira Wine," a friend informed Benjamin Franklin, would "carry off any fit of the Gout in a very few Hours time," in "a couple of Glasses."[36]

The end result was a kind of "therapeutic nihilism," which left practitioners and patients able to think whatever they wished. Confusion reigned as much in 1815 as in 1615. Some held to the old belief that wine caused gout. Others adhered to the equally long-standing idea that "punch cures the gout," or at least would not adversely affect the constitution. Sufferers in America, as elsewhere the Atlantic, thus had a number of options. The Virginia planter Robert "King" Carter "left off drinking red wine" out of the belief that it was "a great propagator" of gout, although he still drank white wine and ale. Carter's fellow planter William Byrd II favored Madeira when the gout was upon him. A friend of both men sought a cure in Port, while another friend drank no wine at all. The decisions facing Carter, Byrd, and their peers in the 1710s, 1720s, and 1730s were much what they had been a century before, and what they would be a century later.[37]

"TABLES OF THE OPULENT"

In seventeenth-century British America, wine was not an elite beverage. A quart of Madeira wine frequently cost the same or slightly less than a quart of Caribbean rum and only slightly more than a quart of English beer. Similarly, pipes of wine were valued less than or equal to similarly sized hogsheads of rum and barrels of beer in early probated estates. Early assemblies passed laws curtailing the payment of wine to laborers and the sale of wine to sailors and Indians, which reflected the breadth of nonelite consumption in the seventeenth century.[38]

Over the course of the eighteenth century, however, wine became a drink of "the opulent," signifying the possession of wealth and property. An exposition of the social meanings of wine emerged; it was similar to the discourse on health in that people distinguished among alcoholic drinks. Homemade fermented beverages and spirits implied less wealth, imported wines more, and certain wines the most. Prices of wine in local markets and values of wine in probated estates rose markedly. Madeira became more expensive vis-à-vis manufactured spirits like West Indian rum as well as imported Canary and Lisbon. The luxury price and status of Madeira were not lost on contemporaries. William Smith Jr. noted in 1757 that New York's "richer sort" kept "very plentiful tables" groaning with rare and choice Madeira. From the Seven Years' War onward, "the tables of the opulent" in the West and East Indies "seldom exhibited then, any other wine" but Madeira. The "Extravagant Disposition" of Virginia's planters, "many of them" with "very great estates," was evidenced by their preference for Madeira. With it, they lived "very well, haveing all the necessaries on their Estates in great plenty."[39] While Madeira attained the heights of luxuriousness, other drinks gained reputations for being cheaper alternatives.[40]

From the middle decades of the eighteenth century, northerners and southerners used drinks to make class distinctions. "People of Fortune" in New Hampshire drank "very good" wine and old imported rum, observed the traveler James Birket in 1751, whereas "the lower sort" drank common wine, new and locally distilled rum, cider, and beer. In Maryland, men likewise drank "according to their circumstances." Gentlemen "brew small Beer with English Malt; strong Beer they have from England; as also French wine and Brandy with which they make Punch; or with Rum from the Charibbee Islands, or Spirits of their own distilling, from Apples, Peaches, etc. Madeira wine is the most common and the most noble of all their Strong Drinks." In contrast, "the Poor brew their beer with Melasses and Bran, or Indian Corn dried in a Stove." The same year, a recently settled Salzburger wrote his community's governing directors (who had hoped to make money from importing Rhenish) that "most of the people who came into" North Carolina were "poor and had to worry about food and clothing rather than about wine."[41] In South Carolina, wine became so "excessive dear" that people could not "afford to drink" good wines like Madeira. They were forced, one irate importer grumbled, "to use wines . . . from the Canaries at a much cheaper price." In response, the merchants imported Sherry, which was cheaper than Madeira, but it did not bear "a good stamp" and had to be sold to "the lower class of People" who would buy it only if packed in small casks.[42]

The 1764 import duty on Madeira—an attempt by the mother country to tap America's wealth—made it more expensive and solidified its reputation for sumptuousness. Ironically, so too did the fitful nonimportation attempts of the late 1760s and the wartime ban on Portuguese wine. Near the end of the conflict, the marquis de Chastellux recapitulated what others had long said: Madeira was "an article of luxury."[43]

Americans continued to connect certain wines to wealth after the war. Commercial conversations appropriated Madeira pragmatically, considering the ways Madeira's expense and standing with the wealthy affected luxury merchandizing. When, for instance, the Virginia wine merchant and planter William Lee tried to resurrect a clientele after the Revolution, he encountered one obstacle after another, for the gentry were "the only people that drink wine" in his state. His plan was to widen the variety of wines and move into spirits and thereby increase total sales, but he was not optimistic. Other suppliers were more sanguine, believing "a country rising fast to wealth & consequently to luxury" like America would favor more expensive drinks; Madeira exporters expected the States would "call for much" of the wine, since "luxuries of exotic refinement" were "pouring fast" "into the lap" of Americans.[44]

Social colloquies used wine metonymically: the rich were known by their wines, as by their horses and houses. A playwright could use Madeira as a sign of a character's assets in 1784: he "doth shine in gold and silver, and drinketh wine from Madeira and France, and doth ride in a chariot." Americans visiting Britain a few years later saw Madeira in a similar way: a gentleman was required not only to "powder his hair," "receive his company, ride the county," and mix with the best sort but also to drink a glass of Madeira after dinner. The use of wine for display prevailed as much in the States as in Britain and Europe. Aspiring style-conscious southern "bucks" did "not take up with" tea, even when with the ladies, but quaffed Madeira and, if not Madeira, Port or Sherry. Being wealthy, living well, and drinking "good wine" was a hallmark of gentility in the early years of the new Republic.[45]

A "PASSION FOR SUPERIORITY"

Money and manners advanced in parallel. The historian Gordon Wood has described the components of eighteenth-century "quality" as the "cultivated, man-made criteria having to do with manners, taste, and character" that proclaimed to all "the fundamental classical characteristic" of gentility: "being free and independent . . . in a world of dependencies, learned in a world only partially literate, and leisured in a world of laborers."[46] In this world, "what one consumed helped define one's status," but possessions alone were insufficient to denote quality; rather, consumers had to know how to perform with them: how to talk about them, use them, and conduct themselves with them. "Not the mere possession, but the due application of wealth merits praise." As the desire for gentility swept over the upper and middling sorts of the North Atlantic basin, and as their ability to buy expensive goods increased, the choice of rare, costly wines — worthy of discussion and served with appropriate language, skill, deportment, and ritual — became an important sign of a drinker's refinement.[47] So much had the drinking of wine become a mark of politesse by the 1780s that, in writing to his wife from the States, the comte de Ségur groaned about "the quantity of Madeira . . . one must drink" with American men "all day long . . . out of politeness," much as one had to drink tea "with the ladies out of gallantry."[48]

By the middle third of the eighteenth century, a proper Bostonian was to be "genial; generous to needy people of all classes; and a drinking man without equal," one who could consume great quantities of wines and talk about them intelligently. When the wealthy but arriviste merchant John Swanwick launched himself on the Philadelphia social scene, he provided a lavish entertainment featuring aged sterling wines that became the talk of the town for their cost, profusion, and richness. In one issue of the 1750 *Boston Weekly News-Letter*, a writer asked his readers, without risking any incomprehension: "who can keep a genteel House without a cask of wine in his cellar? How very *unpolite* to invite a friend to Dine, and be wanting in wine or punch. So very *sickish*" to serve "any thing of our own Country make." The style of living that incorporated wine drinking and the manners accompanying it became such a part of the idea of a gentleman that wine could stand for refinement itself.[49] The Princeton-educated Philip Fithian developed an appreciation for such associations. While tutor to the children of Robert Carter III at Carter's seventy-thousand-acre plantation along the Potomac, Fithian attended a ball in 1774 and pronounced its dinner "as elegant as could be well expected." On offer were "several sorts of Wine, good Lemon Punch, Toddy, Cyder, Porter & c."; they were knowingly chosen, stored, enhanced, and served, well matched to the food. Months later, he attended "an elegant Supper," made refined by its "good Porter & Madeira."[50]

Remarkably, offering wine as a display of refinement crossed racial lines. Dr. Alexander Hamilton saw in an "Indian King" whom he encountered in Rhode Island the profile of a gentleman. The Indian had thirty thousand acres "of very fine levell land round this house," with tenants, horses, and cattle. He lived in 1744 "after the English mode" and his queen dressed "like an English woman" in "high modish" "silks, hoops, stays and dresses." He educated his children to the belles lettres. He was, in short, "a very complaisant mannerly man." Confirming this, the king treated Hamilton "with a glass of good wine," as would any gentleman. That he did so was ironic, for a myriad of laws still prohibited retailers from dispensing alcohol to Indians. But this Indian, in the day's racialized morphology, was more civil than savage, and his genteel appearance and behavior trumped the niceties of legal categorization.[51]

People in the less developed parts of the continent also deployed wine in projecting actual or assumed social identities and performing refined roles. Offering wine was understood to show discernment, assuring the guest that the host was different from his rude surroundings. In 1788, along the banks of Ohio's wild yet "delightful" Muskingum River, one guest was overwhelmed by a profusion of imported drink offered by his host: excellent wine, brandy, spirits, and beer that made the table "as elegant" as the host's neighbors', perhaps "as any in Boston." A traveler through Canada a few years later had no trouble interpreting the offer of "a good deal of Port & Madeira" as "a point of politeness" and recognized a lower, if still palpable, level of refinement when a host served raspberry rum and grog "in wine decanters and glass tumblers."[52]

Summing up a century when the process of differentiation through refinement had gained ground, John Adams observed that "no one principle . . . predominates in human nature so much, in every stage of life" as a "passion for superiority."[53] Indeed, wine and devices like it became more important in America than in Britain, for Americans did not have external markers of aristocratic ascendancy. With the emphasis on knowledgeable discussion and correct use, the possibilities for failure and the opportunities to distance oneself from the failed and unrefined were enormous. As early as 1708, Ebenezer Cook compared the behavior of a common planter, who inhabited a "smoaky Seat," ate corn pone, mush, and hominy, drank "sider on the fret" before the meal, and guzzled rum from a runlet after it, with that of a genteel planter, who lived "in an antient Cedar-House" and regaled Cook with "good Punch," "Wild Fowl and Fish delicious Meats," and pampered him with "*Madera* strong in flowing Bowles" — indeed, "a purple Flood of gen'rous Wine." Cook recognized the differences, but did not despise the unrefined because of them. Not so young Fithian, who dined with a hapless tobacco inspector sixty-six years later. The inspector, it seems, was "rather Dull" and "unacquainted with company," "for when he would . . . drink" to the health of his hosts in a toast, he "held the glass of Porter fast with both his Hands, and then gave an insignificant nod to each one at the Table, in Hast, & with fear, & then drank like an Ox." Great errors, it seems. Even one so young as Fithian knew that not only was the drink the wrong one for the toast (it should have been Madeira), but also that the way the inspector held the glass was uncouth and the phrasing of his toast lacking in all "manner."[54]

A RHETORIC FOR WINE

Wine was nearly perfect for conveying gentility, since it was a decidedly flexible signifier. As a sign of wealth and refinement, it was nearly universal throughout the Atlantic world; it showed, in a word, one's "cosmopolitanism." Its flexibility involved contemporaries in quibbling over how it defined true gentility, for these traits could never characterize an entire population. British Americans drew on three sets of tools to reinforce the performance begun by placing the glass, bottle, or decanter on the table. A spoken and behavioral language of discrimination was elaborated during the eighteenth century, mirroring the increasing variety of wine and other drinks available; the refined drinker could show a fine appreciation by using the language correctly. A panoply of skills was devised—choosing the wine, caring for it, and deploying it appropriately on the sideboard or table and in one's hand—that allowed the wine drinker to demonstrate a number of skills in front of others. Other capabilities were "backstage" skills, providing a pretext for conversations about the care of wine: a refined person could demonstrate mastery of techniques as well as the fact that he or she was wealthy enough to need them. Perhaps most important, "correct" deportment was established, letting drinkers show that they understood how drinking interacted with the mores of their community. Collectively, language, skills, and deportment provided an expanded rhetoric that wine consumers deployed to show they belonged in the polite company of refined and cosmopolitan people.

Language

Over the eighteenth century, drinkers came to admire a table "replenished by a variety of sorts" of "choicest wines." They valued a host who brought "forward, in succession, a variety of *old wines*," each one "having a character a little better than that which preceded" it, and all having "some remarkable history connected with them." The details of the wine before them were "an important part of social conversation." Gracious host and refined guest showed each other their appreciation for the nuances of their situation by talking about wine; distinguishing good wine from indifferent showed the knowledge that made it appropriate for both to be admitted into elevated circles. Conversely, an inability to talk about what was on the table, like "a table ill-served and attended," reflected badly "on the conduct of the master or mistress" or on the quality of the guest. Such discourse, sharpened by voracious devouring of newspapers, connoisseurship compendia, and self-help books, was central to "Domestic Management; or, The Art of Conducting a Family" by the time James Madison became president, even if it was also satirized because easily imitated and sometimes thin.[55]

A language of distinction among wines followed the proliferation of varietals and types of wine available. By 1807, four varieties of Madeira were elevated by producers and distributors to "noble" status and used to make unblended wine. Each variety, marked by its level of sweetness, was ripe for comment. Detailed explanations, often long, arose when a distributor tried to sell a particular variety or when a consumer overrode a trader's recommendation and insisted on another. What happened with Madeira happened with other wines as well. At least five books in English, seven in French, four in Portuguese, and three in Spanish appeared between 1790 and 1815 to lead readers through the specifics of European viticulture and viniculture, familiarizing them with the numerous varieties.[56]

Beyond varietals, a language developed to identify sensory traits that producers, distributors, and consumers valued. Early description of wine was metaphorical and barely operational; either it was related to one of the five senses or it was hopelessly vague. Confounding clarity, no two authors agreed. Andrew Boorde, an author popular in the seventeenth-century colonies, advised readers of his 1598 *Breviarie of Health* to choose wine carefully, by appearance and smell: "it must be fine, fayre, and clene to the eye; it must be fragraunt and redolent, having a good odour and flavour in the nose; it must sprynckle in the cup"; it "must be colde and pleasaunt in the mouthe; and it must be strong and subtyll of substaunce." Ten years later, another writer popular with Americans announced that "five qualities there are wine's praise advancing: strong, beautiful, grand, cool, and dancing." Such impressionistically defined characteristics were not meant to be precise or exact; rather, they were intended to be "a series of elaborately plausible compliments paid to wine." "Of all the analogies out there, there might be one that best expands our minds, opens our horizons, delights our imaginations." Given the seventeenth century's fixation on Galenic properties and sense impressions, the terms may have been deployed to induce an effect rather than to describe the product. Such compliments were vague, difficult for consumers to ascertain, and disputable.[57]

By the early eighteenth century, the highly sensual language was becoming literal, standardized, and usable. The most influential writers in this tradition were Jacques Savary des Bruslons and, after he died, his brother Philémon Louis Savary, who oversaw publication of their monumental *Dictionnaire universel de commerce* in the 1720s. The dictionary, translated into English and expanded by Malachy Postlethwayt in 1751, became the most influential commercial compendium of the age, finding a place in most American merchants' and gentlemen's libraries. Its articles on wine isolated four sensory categories to which drinkers should attend: color, taste, smoothness, and body. The categories became those of subsequent writers. Consumers and distributors alike found in it a lexicon that helped them derive a discriminating rhetoric.[58]

"Color" denoted the hue or tint of the wine. Encyclopedias placed detailed descriptions of "the coloring matter of wine" alongside those on "ingredients in different wines" and "adulteration of wine." Color was a distinctive marker, an index of the kind or class of the wine that even the least adept drinker could appreciate. "Taste" was less precise. It denoted the flavor of the wine, generally regarded as either sweet or acid. "Smoothness" (what the Savarys labeled "flavor") was sometimes thought to be subordinate to taste. A smooth wine was soft or pleasing; that generally meant free from acidity or sharpness—that is to say, more or less sweet. "Body" referred to the strength or weight of the wine, as opposed to its weakness or thinness. With fortified wines, it also connoted alcoholic strength.[59]

In discussing the four sensual traits, distributors and consumers elaborated the terminology. Color became not just red and white but also pale, straw, pink, amber, and ruby. Taste was not just sweet and dry, but also honeyed, flowery, peppery, and herbal.[60] Moreover, categories were mixed together in discussion. When Madeira distributors fortified wine in response to customers' demands, taste and color were linked. In the West Indies, sweeter, darker wines were appreciated. Consumers to the north asked for dryer, lighter wines: South Carolinians preferred extremely pale white wine that was moderately fortified; Philadelphians requested golden wine; New Yorkers wanted an amber, slightly reddish mix; Bostonians preferred both pale and dark varieties. Finally, further increasing connoisseurs' opportunities to display understanding was the instability of the traits themselves. As Europe's leading enologist put it in the 1810s, "the quality and taste are continually varying."[61]

This discourse arose first in commercial conversations, as sellers and buyers analyzed the drink and drinking. Consumers read the letters and advertisements of their suppliers, as we have seen, looking for detailed descriptions of variety types, traits, and maintenance techniques. They then passed on the language of differentiation and discrimination they gleaned to other drinkers in their households. The tutor Philip Fithian, for instance, learned many of his distinctions from his employer, who bought the wine. Mrs. Mary Brewton Motte Alston of Charleston taught the language of wine to her grandson. She often sent him to the attic to retrieve the day's wine. "After having the decanters filled, she would always taste" the wine "to be certain" the young boy "had not made a mistake"; she would lecture him on particular traits, and "he would always follow her example." In this way, he learned "at a very early age" how to "discriminate between the various kinds of wine, their ages, etc." In a word, wrote one American expert on etiquette, "when invited to dine or sup at the house of any well-bred man, observe how he doth the honours of the table"—for one "cannot please without" being master of them all.[62]

Toward the end of the eighteenth century, aesthetes joined the fray, publishing accounts and manuals to guide the increasingly large group of drinkers who wanted to show their refinement. John Croft's 1788 *Treatise on the Wines of Portugal* was the best of the genre. Writing of Madeira, he mixed technical and sensory details:

> Perhaps sound, old mellow Madeira may be preferred to any other sort of Wine as a good stomachic. There are two sorts which grow in the island. . . . The genuine, natural, and best sort, is of the colour of oil, and tinges in the glass, affording a hue or shade of a light blue, and has a kernelly taste like a walnut. The commoner sort is made of the ordinary grape, and they tinge it in the Wine-press with the *uva roxa*, or red grape, which they cultivate on the island for that purpose, and it makes the wine of a foxy or deep colour. As the caprice of fashion has reigned in England of later years in respect to Wines, as well as other articles of luxury, sometimes they required them of one colour, and at other time of another.

Toward the end of the book, Croft advised readers on "the best time to bottle" wine and "the proper time to begin to drink." Similarly, in 1793, Duncan McBride published his *General Instructions for the Choice of Wines and Spirituous Liquors*, in which he listed "those Wines which are best to be used at the Tables of the Opulent." He described in detail Madeira, red and white Port, white Lisbon and Carcavelos, Canary, Sack, and Vidonia. He adumbrated traits precisely, giving the wherewithal for distinguishing one drink from another. Finally, he detailed information on how wines were "counterfeited, prepared, and mixed," so as to clarify for the consumer "the jumble of different wines, ardent spirits, and various infusions"; confusing them could not help but be "prejudicial to the constitution," not to mention to the adroit drinker's social persona.[63]

Skill

Displays of skill in dealing with wine also demonstrated a person's familiarity with it, and the appropriateness of his or her presence in polite society. With their control over the hall, drawing room, or dining room, hosts were in the most advantageous situation to demonstrate their abilities to perform wine-related activities with certainty and precision. Some skills reflected the great vinicultural innovations, such as fining and forcing wine, "improving" it, packing and storing it, and aging it. Others, such as setting the table with appropriate glassware and paraphernalia, and deploying them correctly, reflected the increasing availability of affordable furnishings. Making the effort to concern oneself with these aspects of wine was itself part of the project of aligning oneself with those in the know and with the means to do something about it.

Many of the skills were conveyed by distributors to their customers and then refashioned. American and British consumers eagerly jousted over this terrain; in selecting a fining method, they contradicted or improved upon distributors' approaches. Madeira's exporters firmly believed, for instance, that a "gentleman" should fine in one of several approved ways, so as not to harm the product. Accordingly, they spilled much ink describing the merits and demerits of blood, milk, and egg whites as fining agents. They also spent a lot of time training visitors how to use fining utensils and how to detect a properly fined wine. To a gentleman "who knows what genuine Madeira wine is," it would have been "as ridiculous to talk of a particular shade of paleness" as it would have been to "to talk to a Jockey of the particular color of a horse" when his animal was already "possesst of every point of excellence." Distributors taught buyers that a knowing connoisseur cared about the taste, not the color, how to achieve a desirable taste, and the significance to attach to it. After such epistolary and hands-on tutelage, "even the most ignorant" would "be able to discriminate" as any genteel connoisseur.[64]

Suggestions on when to ship and land imported wines, methods of handling them, ideas on how to care for them in the cellar, when to rack, fine, bottle, and bin, when to drink, how to detect leaded wine, and how to improve the wine were also found in self-help manuals and popular compendia. Specialized works described how to care for wine. Such books were not new. From *A Booke of Secrets* (1596) through *The Art and Mystery of Vintners and Wine-Coopers* (1682), earlier writers had broached the subject.[65] But subsequent writing on skill with wine surpassed all that came before. British and American experts deluged interested readers with new types of advice.[66]

André Jullien wrote the manual that influenced elite wine-drinking Americans most. Widely read in America in both French and English, it was the culmination of earlier attempts by others to reduce the subject to a science. No one would write about wine in the same way after it appeared in 1813. Jullien told cellar owners how to keep their rooms "in a fit state to receive wines that require age, and the means of improving those . . . inconvenient for that purpose." True connoisseurs should know about "the taste and character of the different vintages, the signs which indicate their being kept a long or short period," "their consequent loss," and "the diseases and alterations to which they are subject." They should fully understand the "many precautions to be taken" in cask and bottle maintenance, paying attention to the age that wines acquired in wood, their "limpidity at the time of bottling," the duration and timing of bottling, the choice of bottles and corks, and proper binning. Since they would be "obliged to mix the common wines, to render their taste palatable," they must thoroughly master the art of admixture. They should "guard against and prevent alterations and degenerations." Jullien demanded that consumers do what distributors had learned to do the previous century: fortify and blend a wine that suited the drinker and the event, and keep it in a fit state for drinking.[67]

Elite drinking became characterized by an elaborate series of steps that communicated a code of superiority: the greetings, movements, drink choices, conversation topics, and toasts were all highly worked out. Contemporary paintings tell us that there was even a distinction between the size of the host's glass and the guest's (the host's was larger). Each step had to complement the others; painstaking efforts were exerted to arrange them in their proper sequence. When properly combined, refinement should be obvious. Receiving and dining rooms, not surprisingly, were critical stages for the display of wine skill, and an extensive hortatory literature emerged in the late eighteenth century to manage them. This body of instruction told householders, for instance, that, on formal occasions, the bottle was not to be placed on the table for each guest to pour at will. Rather, a servant was to pour it from a sideboard, neatly—"not to wipe the Mouth" of the bottle with his or her hand. Each person had his or her own glass, which was to be changed after each drink. In less elite situations, "Young Housekeepers" were to exhibit all the skills of a butler, much as they were beforehand to concoct "made wines," fabrication being the option of those who could not afford the real thing.[68]

As glassware became commonplace, holding glasses the right way also separated the connoisseur from the rest. The first treatise on painting to describe ways to depict holding a glass was published in Dutch in 1707 and translated into English in 1738. In it, the blind Low Countries painter-turned-theorist Gérard de Lairesse illustrated "the different grace[s] in taking hold of a glass." Each handling

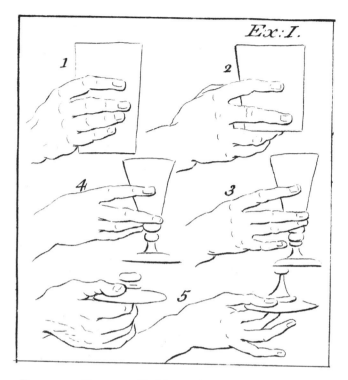

Figure 10.4. Five ways of holding a glass of wine, engraved by
John Carwitham, before 1738.
Source: Gérard de Lairesse, *A Treatise on the Art of Painting, in
All Its Branches* (London, 1738), 34, plate 12. Courtesy of Art &
Architecture Collection, Miriam and Ira D. Wallach Division of
Art, Prints and Photographs, The New York Public Library, Astor,
Lenox and Tilden Foundations.

was keyed to a social class. Moving for the most part from lower-class to high, but
from the top of the page to the bottom: "the one takes it [a tumbler] with a full
fist," as did Fithian's tobacco inspector; the second takes a tumbler "lower with
some manners"; the fourth "is a lady's woman, who, fearful of spilling, holds a
stemmed wine glass handily, yet less agreeably" than the third, "a princess" holding the goblet "with the tips of her three fingers, drawing warily and agreeably the
little finger from it"; finally, "a prince holds it handily and cautiously below on
the foot." Informed by similar principles, the young George Washington and his
cousin Lawrence mercilessly laughed at a friend at midcentury "for holding the
wine glass in the full hand." Directly through books like Lairesse's treatise and

indirectly through lore derived from it, lessons on the right way to signal class and refinement with correct handling of wine paraphernalia found their way into the deportment landscape of Anglo-American gentlemen like Washington and aspiring gentlemen like Fithian.[69]

Deportment

Carrying oneself well as a wine drinker and handling wine's effects were other ways of extending the rhetoric of wine to denote wealth and refinement. The etiquette literature that taught the skills of preparing drinks also addressed deportment while under the influence of alcohol. The seventeenth-century authors were principally concerned with drunkenness. Henry Peacham, author of *The Compleat Gentleman*, first published in 1622 and frequently reprinted, read and quoted throughout the English-speaking world, treated the matter as one of the "qualities" of "Minde or Body" "required of a Noble Gentleman." Peacham dressed in a genteel garb the Christian stand against "excessive drinking" in a chapter called "Reputation and Carriage." From one's carriage and address, "the height of our Judgements (even our Selves) is taken"; the "principall meanes to perceive it is Temperance and . . . Moderation of the minde." Temperance was a "bridle" against passion; one must "avoid excessive drinking," or one would not be "fit for anythinge." Yet Peacham did not demand abstinence; he allowed wine to be "moderately taken," as did the doctors of his day.[70]

Many early commentators distinguished ordinary drunkenness from "bestial drunkenness," and more or less tolerated the ordinary variety. "Bestial drunkenness" was the state of intoxication when one lost one's senses, particularly the abilities to stand steadily and speak coherently. In *The Art of Living in London* (1642), Peacham elaborated: "Above all things beware of beastly drunkennesse," for it led to inhuman "challenges and quarrels" and caused "the death of many." Men when drunk were "apt to say or doe any thing, . . . to lose their hats, clothes or rapiers, [and] not to know what they have said" and how much money they possessed or lost.[71]

As the decades passed, Peacham's criterion remained the standard. It did so in large measure because it spoke to an audience standing at a particular juncture of a commercial and social transformation in Anglo-American life. From the Restoration, as the first Consumer Revolution matured and luxuries spread among buyers, men and women became "confused over who precisely ought to make up" the genteel classes. Only kings and aristocrats could lay claim to gentility before 1600 and landholding families—the "gentry"—by 1700, but new tests were devised thereafter. The new tests included "manner," which, unlike lineage or property, could be imitated. Manners were applied to the *ars bibendi*.

In the top right margin, handwritten: *diff. in wine + other drinks*

In discussions of the components of "quality" from the late seventeenth century onward, moderation in drinking was valorized. Anarchic drinking, "that Swinish Sin," merited considerable disapproval.[72]

Early Americans wrestled with what it meant to be a moderate, "unbeastly" drinker. The Virginia planter William Byrd II "repeated and obsessively reviewed . . . the expected behaviors of an eighteenth-century gentleman" in his diary. His journal was "a form of reassurance and a record of mastery," and he rarely let pass a chance to comment on those whose mastery lapsed when drinking too much. He chastised the master of the Williamsburg grammar school in 1709, for example, "reminding a man with genteel pretensions that gentlemen might be 'merry' but never 'drunk.'" Not surprisingly, Byrd almost always described himself as merry and seldom drunk, his own behavior adhering to "a common standard of social behavior." Byrd, who had read Peacham, constantly "strove to meet that standard."[73]

Each generation that followed looked to the handling of drink and of drunkenness as mirrors of composure and gentility. Yet determining the line that separated genteel from disreputable was not uncomplicated. It could depend on the company: drunkenness might be tolerated in Annapolis's Tuesday Club, since it was viewed only by friends, men of similar station. Or it could depend on the venue: drinking excessively in one's home, in the private reaches of one's club, or in an elite tavern might be similarly overlooked. It could even depend on the drink itself. Ardent drinks like gin and whisky more readily contributed to loss of control. They were more often considered "deleterious to the health, morals, and 'economy of the community'" than wine.[74]

Late in the seventeenth century, pundits began advising drinkers on how to physically handle drinks, not just how to avoid drunkenness. Guides instructed young men and women to drink with a certain élan. In 1663, *Youths Behaviour* advised the young to "sop not in wine," "make not much noise with thy teeth" when drinking, "fill not thy glass in such a manner that the wine runs over," and "drink not too leisurely nor too hastily." First promulgated in France in 1595, these rules were translated into English only during the early days of the Restoration. They had valence for a people undergoing economic and social change, and they enjoyed remarkable longevity. George Washington copied them into his 1745 commonplace book. Similar guides detailed other "Ways of Deportment" for "Persons of Quality" and expanded the impermissible. Do not drink alone. Do not call for a drink "before the persons of quality have drank." Do not receive a drink "on that side next the person of honour"; "those . . . accurately bred receive it generally on the other." Do not call out loud to the servant for wine, but speak in a low voice or use gestures. Do not toast oneself. In making a toast, "drink it gravely . . . and deliberately . . . at once, with our eyes in the glass (not staring about the room) and be sure our mouth be not full." "Gurgling it down too fast" would "nauseate the whole Table" and be "more fit for a Jugler, than a Gentleman." When "the person of honour drinks the health to you," one must "be uncovered, inclining forward, till he has drank, and not pledge him without precise order." Politesse and the knowledge on which it was based emerged as intrinsic parts of the emerging consumer system.[75]

Wine rules were satirized even as they were revered, because they were copyable. *Chesterfield Travestie; or, School for Modern Manners*, which was published in Philadelphia in 1812, enjoined its readers: "When you are drinking a glass of wine, roll your eyes about the room over the brim of the glass, like a felon, brought up by Habeas-Corpus, to a judge's chamber"—and, "after you have taken a large draught, bring forth a loud sigh, as if your breath was escaping from your body." Of course, as is often the case with parody, those interested in wine drinking could learn what (not) to do from this.[76]

Pictorial representation was another important transatlantic medium for disseminating the rhetoric of wine. It flourished in every society that touched the Atlantic, although with more relish in Protestant areas.[77] Less self-consciously didactic than etiquette manuals, paintings and engravings offered feasts of display—of exemplary deportment, lapses from it, the bearing appropriate for particular classes, sexes, and races, and for restricted situations and groups—with all the opportunities for mistakes, revelations, and irony. Artists drew on the equation of wines with luxury and refinement, and the understanding that some wines were more luxurious than others. Viewers "read" good wines as "visual signs that announced exalted class," along with "Georgian houses, export ceramics, silk fabrics, Chippendale furniture, chased silver, flower and fruit gardens, polite behavior, ample food, and even body fat."[78] Consumers purchased artworks that guided them through the deployment of wine as a prop in their social dramas: removing the cloth, displaying the bottle, passing the decanter, toasting one's neighbor, and maintaining one's composure. Art "spoke" to them in the language of correct deportment even as it showed the appropriate accessories. Viewers could also find out how not to act: the inept, the buffoon, the drunkard, and the inappropriate mingler with other classes and sexes were all targets for ridicule in depictions of drinking.[79]

Physical bearing was especially revealing to contemporaries. Byrd's mastery of genteel restraint is recapitulated in George Roupell's ink-and-wash drawing of *Mr. Peter Manigault and His Friends* (figure 9.1). A wonderfully stylized presentation of masculine refinement, it is also a study in composure, actual and hoped for. Eight men sit around a table give and receive toasts: they are relaxed—certainly not beastly, or even Bacchic. Control is their watchword. A gentleman sits unless giving a toast, behaves in certain ways while toasting, holds the glass, bottle, and decanter just so: the viewer is instructed on all.

The composure projected by Roupell's scene is shattered by another painting composed at roughly the same time, which by subversion makes a similar statement about the subtleties between drunken and appropriate deportment. In a large oil painting entitled *Captains Carousing in Surinam* (circa 1755–69) (plate 10), John Greenwood describes an imaginary event among real friends (the men were never all in Surinam at the same time) that satirizes various drinking postures and, while eschewing didacticism, points to a correct way of acting. Greenwood caricatured a group of Rhode Island overseas traders "on a spree" in the West Indies: Jonas Wanton has fallen into a drunken stupor, Godfrey Malbone is dancing, Captain Nicholas Powers vomits into his pocket, Captain Nicholas Cook holds a large pipe, and Captain Ezekiel Hopkins raises a glass of wine. The painting was likely executed for a club that met in a Newport tavern. While it reveals almost nothing about Surinam—or Newport—it says a lot about deportment. Drinking among colleagues and friends, it suggests, was often private or, as here, semiprivate, in a tavern's club room. The faraway place shows them beyond the home community's easy gaze. The men drink only with other men, and men of their acquaintance, in an atmosphere of camaraderie and friendship. Finally, they show a mixture of inclinations to drink. Near chaos is depicted: one drinker wears his nightshirt; another is seriously ill from overindulgence, and on the verge of catching fire; another is asleep, dead drunk; still another cheats at cards. Yet in the middle stands Captain Hopkins, fully erect and sober, correctly holding a glass of wine and sending an important message about maintaining one's calm in a melee, properly using glassware, and using wine as a bond of friendship, not discord. One could still maintain one's composure when, all about him, his fellows were not.

Representations of material objects were also important in communicating expected behaviors and performances as the first Consumer Revolution raged on. Display and performance were important in establishing and cementing social relations, and performances needed not only actors but also props and sets. British Americans of middling and elite ranks purchased British and Dutch paintings and engravings, such as those by Hogarth and De Hooch, that taught them what to do with drink-related objects. They displayed them in their homes and taverns, alongside landscape scenes and heads of British royalty.[80] Such images "served not only as a guide" for behavior but also "as a focus of conversation in which particularities" such as the relative status of the drinkers, the corrosiveness of luxury, and appropriate ways to behave "could easily be 'read into' the simple iconic images." These images, of course, might have been regarded "as objects of solitary contemplation," but more likely they "functioned actively" in public and political life, inasmuch as they presupposed "social exchange."[81]

Anglo-American consumers also acquired homegrown American art depicting drinking. Perhaps the most revealing representations were those crafted for the sitters themselves, because they show real people as they wished to be seen. Skill with wine paraphernalia, knowledge of wine ritual, and proper bearing and demeanor could all be deployed in pictures as signs of wealth and refinement. The oil-on-wood overmantel panel at the Moses Marcy House, painted during the Seven Years' War and reproduced as plate 11, shows a country gentleman wearing an officer's kit and a tricorned hat and holding a glass of wine or wine punch. On occasion, the subject might be more intimate, as it was in the 1760s when Giles Cooke of Maryland commissioned a family portrait. In this anonymous work, the planter, his wife, and two daughters sit around a table. The scene is remarkably stark, typical of the almost Methodistic tone of much early American portraiture. Yet what it shows is revealing: the table is set with wine, glassware, and a bowl of cherries. Cooke, in a portrait that was to be seen by relatives, neighbors, and strangers, decided to combine Spartan simplicity with highly comfortable and well-made if not lavishly excessive and probably imported clothing and furnishing, imported alcohol, wine drinking in the home, women drinking or at least in the vicinity of drink and, above all, control (he has drink, but does not drink it). Through this portrait, Cooke gave himself, his family, and subsequent generations a picture of middling domestic respectability in which wine and consumption were physically and morally central to genteel life.[82]

Images of American drinking were neither extensively produced nor widely disseminated before the fourth quarter of the eighteenth century, when independence unleashed a freer press upon the public. *The Merry Fellow's Companion; or, American Jest Book* (1797) opened with a picture of a wineglass and bottle on a table around which men are sitting and animatedly discussing some matter, in a pose several steps more reserved than Greenwood's debauch. Other works took up the subject of wine hospitality and the behavior of the host. The frontispiece of *The Book of Nouns* (1802), by depicting a wineglass and bottles, encouraged readers to think about the absolute minimum number of paraphernalia one needed for drinking. Arnaud Berquin's children's book, *The Looking-Glass for the Mind* (1804), re-creates an extension of hospitality (figure 9.2) in which a dutiful landowner's daughter, standing in front of a sideboard laden with two decanters, two bottles, and a glass, offers some wine to a tenant paying his rent, while her less generous brothers sneer at the farmer's rude dress behind his back. This illustration is particularly apposite, because of its double entendre: the

reader would easily understand the tenant's lack of refinement from his clothes
and posture, but he or she would also have recognized or been directed to the
fact that the daughter's response—pretending not to notice the tenant's rough-
ness and exhibiting a comfort with wine, paraphernalia, and hospitality—was
"polite." Unlike her brothers, the girl does not denigrate the honest, robust man
of the soil; not for her is the sniggering condescension of an effete elite. She was
a true Anglo-American wine connoisseur, even if in her teens, and even if a girl.

class

THE RITUAL OF TOASTING

As wine became symbolically charged, rituals emerged to make use of it, and
they, too, were incorporated into exhibitions of wealth and refinement and the
rhetoric of wine. Consumers elaborated the rituals in the ways they displayed,
served, and drank wine, creating complex dramas of choosing the wine, matching
it to food, opening the bottle, allowing the wine to breathe, decanting it (choosing the decanter, presenting it, and using it to pour), and serving it (choosing the
glass and pouring the wine), not to mention buying, storing, and caring for the
beverage. How to execute these steps was discussed in private conversations and
widely disseminated publications. Carrying them out well displayed familiarity
and comfort with the objects and symbols of genteel living, distinguishing the
refined from the coarse, unsophisticated, and nouveaux riches.[83]

American drinkers were particularly enamored of the toast, a ritual in which
language, skill, and deportment came together. Highly gendered—it was almost
invariably given by a man, although in Scotland women joined in—the toast
was volleyed by drinkers of all classes. They could easily be bawdy. But it was the
elegant toast that garnered the most attention. An elegant, refined toast required
appropriate surroundings, proper sequencing of drinks and speeches, witty phrasing, eloquent delivery, and correct handling of glassware. A man could show himself genteel by displaying sufficient appreciation for his surroundings and companions, and matching his toasting performance to them. The toast, in effect,
became an important ritual for distinguishing himself from the common and
aligning himself with the refined. It became yet another prop in the performance
of superiority.[84]

Toasts and toasting reinforced the reigning economic, political, gender, and
social relations. Not only did the toasters declare their allegiances publicly but
their stylized performances excluded others and enacted both respect and deference. In much the way that formal meals function today, toasts reiterated and
sometimes celebrated "degrees of hierarchy, inclusion and exclusion, boundaries
and transactions across the boundaries." Toasting "distinguishes order, bounds it,
and separates it from disorder," "us[ing] economy in the means of expression by

allowing only a limited number of structures." Toasts bound participants to each other, institutionalized and legitimized their ties, and declared their common allegiance to abstract or absent "higher" goals or institutions. They demanded participation of all assembled, and structured the experience by enacting their relationships in a standardized form. Thus, they not merely externalized experience but also codified it and reaffirmed its hierarchies and boundaries. As oral performances, toasts were contingent. Contingency created anxiety about the relationships among participants, which had to be reiterated each time they met, and allowed ambivalence into the expressions of allegiance.[85]

Toasts apparently arose in England in the late sixteenth century out of a reawakened "inclination to live together in company" that was borrowed from the Dutch. They flourished throughout the English-speaking world during the remarkable efflorescence of sociability that characterized late Stuart and Georgian society.[86] They arrived in the colonies with the founders. The Baron de Lahontan, for one, could not but remark with astonishment upon the "huge bumpers" that were used to celebrate a guest in 1694. Even though Samuel Sewall worried about the effects of the ritual, he was not immune to its charms, happily toasting the queen's 1714 birthday with round after round of wine in a South End tavern. The custom must have spread quickly, for Sewall's contemporary Cotton Mather had decried it as "common" the year before. Francis Goelet spent much of his time in New England at midcentury drinking a glass of wine as a greeting, making toasts with "wine & arrack punch galore" and then "singing, roareing & c. until morning, when one could scarce see one another."[87]

The toast was a highly elaborated affair at the time of its greatest popularity. While visiting General Washington's headquarters in 1780, the marquis de Chastellux found himself quite amazed. The formal midday dinner was *à la anglaise*, consisting of two principal courses and dessert, at which "the cloth was taken off, and apples and a great quantity of nuts" and wine were provided, which "General Washington usually continues eating for two hours, toasting and conversing all the time." The toast was more fervently deployed in the evening. After the cloth was removed, "good Bordeaux and Madeira were placed on the table," and Chastellux found he "could not refuse" a glass of wine "when offered." "Less accustomed to drink than another," he accommodated himself "very well to the English 'toast'": into very small glasses,

> you pour yourself out the quantity of wine you choose, without being pressed to take more, and the "toast" is only a sort of refrain punctuating the conversation, as a reminder that each individual is part of the company and that the whole forms but one society. I observed that there was more solemnity in the toasts at dinner: there were several ceremonious ones; the others were sug-

gested by the General and given out by his aides-de-camp, who performed the honors of the table at dinner, for one of them is seated each day at the head of the table, near the General, to serve all the dishes and distribute the bottles. The toasts in the evening, however, were proposed by Colonel Hamilton, as they occurred to him, without order or formality. After supper the guests are generally asked to propose a "sentiment," that is to say, a lady to whom they are attached by some sentiment, either of love or friendship, or perhaps from preference only.[88]

Perhaps because he was a foreigner adjusting himself to new conventions, Chastellux captured many of the salient aspects of toasting as it prevailed at the end of the eighteenth century. The ritual drew on the multiple significations of drink, first of all the sense of exclusionary sociability. The drinkers collectively affirmed their allegiances to each other, to the subject of the toast, and to the values or goals that united them. They did this in ways that were relatively formal, stylized, and hierarchical. Affirming relations to each other tapped reservoirs of social skill: it affirmed they were "each . . . part of the company and . . . the whole forms but one society," while declaring, by precedence and degree of effusiveness, the required deferences and distances between people. Even when the manifest content of the toast was antimonarchical, republican, or otherwise subversive, the action affirmed the order of the drinkers' social universe. Everyone could do this, but not everyone could do it well. One had to have nerve, wit, poise, social resources, and the right paraphernalia.

Chastellux identified two attitudes in American toasting: sentimental and ceremonial, or, to adopt more modern terms, emotional and political. Sentimental-emotional toasts were probably the most common, because there were so many unofficial opportunities to toast. Those that Byrd of Virginia and Hamilton of Maryland recorded earlier in the century were examples. They were expressions of private sentiments by friends, usually sitting around a table. They often articulated a common theme or referred to a common experience, such as sharing a glass or bowl, apparently a distinctively American custom. By the time Chastellux was writing, this behavior was ordinary, if alarming to visitors. The comte d'Estaing sniffed that the Americans thought little of "drinking to the health of ten persons with each drop one swallows, . . . and drinking from the same enormous goblet from which many have just wet their uninviting lips." The comte de Ségur, no novice when it came to drinking, was similarly shocked: "the moment a toast was given," there ensued the "vile custom . . . of circulating an immense bowl of punch round the table, out of which each guest was successively compelled to drink."[89]

Sentimental-emotional performances were memorialized in artwork. In the

1810s, an unknown painter caught upper-middling toasters in the act: seven gentlemen, all with long clay pipes, are gathered in a small room in a private home, perhaps a study, around a table draped in red cloth; atop the table sits a Delft punch bowl, a glass decanter, a ladle, and an open snuffbox (plate 12). Thus well equipped, the men are drinking from stemmed glasses. Two stand: one is ladling punch, and the other begins to utter a toast, although few seem to be focused on the witticism. The display shows the men as they wished to be represented: properly dressed, posed with appropriate accoutrements and libations, and engaged in orderly conviviality. More homely are the commoners John Lewis Krimmel sketched in his 1814 oil painting *A Country Wedding* (plate 13). Krimmel's folk are ready to toast the newlyweds in much the same way, although perhaps with less tone than the unknown painter's eastern gentlemen.[90]

Ceremonial-political toasts were public expressions of honor, respect, and affiliation; the words told the listener whom the toaster honored and respected, and intimated he was affiliated with them. Usually the subject of the toast was not those around the table, and the tone was decorous and polite if not philosophical; it was almost never bawdy. A "craze" for such toasts took hold in America in the middle of the eighteenth century, and it accelerated with the Revolution. As it did so, the ritual became more elaborate and rigid than it had been earlier in the century, when expressions were simpler, compositions more impromptu, and the time the toasts given and the glassware used during the meal less regulated. By the end of the century, complex paeans to official and semiofficial objects worthy of notice were constructed, uttered with varying degrees of formality, and managed with designated glassware from a sideboard or table stripped of its cloth.[91]

An elaborate example of ceremonial-political toasting was noted in the *Pennsylvania Gazette* in 1755. On the feast day of their patron, Philadelphia's Free Masons processed from their headquarters in a tavern to a church, where they attended service, and back again. After their meal, fourteen "toasts were drank in the Masonic Manner, under repeated discharges of Cannon, planted in the Square" before the inn:

- The King and the Craft.
- The Grand Master of England.
- Our Brother Francis, Emperor of Germany.
- The Grand Master of Pennsylvania.
- Our Brother, his Honour the Governor of Pennsylvania.
- Our Brother, His Excellency John Tinker, Esq., Governor of Providence, Returning him Thanks for his kind Visit.
- The Grand Master of Scotland.

- The Grand Master of Ireland.
- The several Provincial Grand Masters of North America and the West India Islands.
- All charitable Masons.
- All true and faithful Masons, wheresoever dispersed or distressed, throughout the Globe.
- The Arts and Sciences.
- General Braddock, and Success to His Majesty's Forces.
- Prosperity to Pennsylvania, and a happy Union to His Majesty's Colonies.

Only the first (to the king), the penultimate (to the general who was directing the war in the West), and the last (to the security of the Union) were purely political. The toasts to the emperor and the two governors were mixed, for they were also Masons. The other toasts were directed to lodge members and masters throughout the world, and to the Masons' Enlightenment project of promoting art, science, prosperity, and happiness. The overall cry was one of solidarity, progress, and prosperity under the benevolent rule of the king and his peer, the emperor, their brother.[92]

Newspapers recorded ceremonial-political toasts given on noteworthy occasions and, in particular, their order, confirming the importance of the ritual and spreading it by educating the uninitiated. When New York's new governor Charles Hardy came ashore in America in 1755, he arrived at the fort and, "after drinking the usual Healths," "received the Congratulations of the Clergy, and other Gentlemen of Distinction." After dining, he walked to the Commons, where again, with rounds of toasting, "the Joy of the People was witnessed by the Consumption of several Bottles of good Old Madeira." Colonists everywhere celebrated the accession of George III in 1760 with toasts. When the news was announced in Philadelphia, the governor gave "an elegant Entertainment," "where His Majesty's and all the Royal Family's Healths were drank." At "another elegant Entertainment" several blocks away, "Gentlemen of the City" drank loyal healths "together with [toasts to] His Prussian Majesty, Prince Ferdinand, Prince Henry, and all the brave and gallant generals, admirals, officers, seamen and soldiers, in His Majesty's Service." Whatever the public occasion, newspapers noted who was being feted and whether complimentary toasts were returned. Almost always, they informed their readers that toasting was concluded with "that decorum necessary on such occasions." The first toast was often "an indispensable Bumper" and could not be refused, but later toasts could be drunk in portions "as moderately as each Gentleman inclined," for a mark of gentility was control over drink.[93]

The Stamp Act crisis of 1765–66 considerably complicated the ways Americans expressed their allegiances, ceremonial and political, and this alteration was reflected in toasts. Opposition to new regulations and feelings of abandonment competed with imperial identity and loyalty to the king. At first, Americans tried to resolve these contradictions by lauding the land—showing respect for the "King of Pennsylvania" and the "King of America"—and representing the opponent of the legislation as a standard-bearer for Britannia's lost virtue. Throughout Anglo-America, direct action against stamp officials was toasted with both "Long Life and Prosperity to His Majesty the King George the Third" *and* "Destruction to the Stamp Act."[94]

Bostonians celebrated the act's repeal the following March with ringing bells, discharging cannon, hoisting "the colors of all the ships" and, of course, toasting with wine. But for the most part subsequent ceremonial-political toasts were different, for they redrew the lines of fellowship and community, excluding Britons. Under the boughs of the Liberty Tree, the Sons of Liberty drank patriotic toasts, uttered "other decent expressions of joy," and erected a magnificent fireworks pyramid on the Common. Not to be upstaged, John Hancock, whose brig had brought the news of the repeal, hosted "a grand and elegant entertainment" for "the genteel part of the town" and "treated the populace with a pipe of Madeira." Many pipes, overflowing bowls, refilled glasses, and countless toasts to "the Prosperity of America" and "the Course of Liberty" were the order of the day at an "elegant entertainment." Loyal toasts to Britain persisted, but, with the passage of time, they were eclipsed by loyal toasts to America.[95]

Central to the health and refinement that toasts announced was an underlying message of order and naturalness. The eighteenth century was a time of self-conscious exposition seeking the "true," "natural," and "foundational." The conversations about the health consequences and social meanings of wine constituted part of the quest. Because so much evidence bore on the effects of alcohol on the body, but so little of it was systematic or comparative, intelligent if casual observers could disagree about what the effects were. The efflorescence of health theories is testimony to the seeking and the confusion. In the event, most home-remedy providers—mothers, grandmothers, and midwives prominent among them—seem to have fallen back on received wisdom.

At the same time people used drinks as social differentiators. It was easy to use alcohol for conspicuous consumption because observers knew the relative prices of the beverages and the cost of the equipment. But once the elaboration of meaning had begun, mere expenditure of money no longer sufficed. Especially in Anglo-America, people required signals "that collectively were the index of the social self: social graces, eating skills, proper carriage, body control, knowledge of the arts, informed taste in fashion, carved furniture, and powdered wigs. As agents in an interpretive system, the signs . . . presented were not merely bystanders in a picture, for these things had the cultural power to personify, to endow a sitter with the social, civic, or personal attributes he or she sought. And all forms of visual display in eighteenth-century British North America . . . were bearers of identity and class definition."[96]

Elaborated displays such as toasting solidified the social order by asserting who could participate in them, in what order, and with what drinks and props; who were one's fellows and what superordinate allegiances united them; who and what deserved respect as part of the display. An individual could display health and refinement by the way he or she performed, accessorized, and contextualized the ritual. As Philip Fithian and most drinkers knew, toasting depended on nuance of demeanor, emotion, gesture, and selection. It confirmed that there was an order, and reaffirmed the toasters' place in it. If one learned anything from toasting, it was the centrality of self-control and social control to refinement.

ARS BIBENDI: "THE FASHIONABLE ORNAMENTS OF LIFE"

The range and subtlety of meanings that wine and spirits could convey grew as they became increasingly available and varied during the early modern era. Physically and metaphorically, Americans began incorporating alcohol in performances in which they acted out their economic, social, and political identities, even as they enjoyed "the pleasures of the bottle." Drinkers took possession of wine, the venues in which it was drunk, and the paraphernalia for drinking it as props that displayed their wealth and refinement, and they expressed their solidarity with or distance from others. To do so, they built on the ways of thinking and acting with wine that they had inherited from British and other Atlantic cultures and from their own past, and they thereby constructed communities uniting people across geographical boundaries.[1]

In using objects to convey meanings, drinkers had to deal with their materiality. Wine's liquidity forced consumers to rely on containers of several sorts for receiving, storing, and consuming it. Such "fashionable ornaments of life," from storage cellars to drinking glasses, give us some of the best surviving evidence of the ways consumers used wine and what they thought they were doing—bringing "the pleasures of the bottle" to themselves and others, and elevating themselves in a world they desired.[2] Two analytical approaches important for interpreting objects offer insights into such usage and thinking. One tradition regards drinking as dramaturgical behavior, and the objects drinkers use as "props" in carrying out their performances.[3] Another tradition posits drinking paraphernalia—the props—as "boundary objects," things whose meanings are sufficiently common across geographical, political, and temporal boundaries that they communicate effectively among otherwise diverse people and cultures.[4] These approaches taken together illuminate American drinkers' pleasurable and instrumental ex-

periences, and the ways they bound people together and kept them apart. The
meanings so shared allowed drinkers to use cellars, bottles, decanters, and glasses
to communicate particular things about themselves and their attitudes toward
the world, but, like all communication, the meanings were contingent, temporary, and ambiguous, and so could also lead to misunderstandings, confusion,
and disputes.

Contemporaries understood that, by using the right accoutrements and demonstrating their correct use, they could establish themselves as refined or common, as they wished, and that the objects would communicate to newcomers
and strangers as well as to neighbors. Baltasar Gratian observed in his eighteenth-
century handbook for aspiring gentlemen that "the manner is that which is
always most obvious and visible. It is the outside, the mark, the sign, and the
specification, as it were, of the thing. By that external, we come to the knowledge
of the internal. [A stranger makes] himself known to us in some measure by his
air and his figure." The material and visual signs were "as significant as the verbal"
for eighteenth-century Americans, as "the former was believed to be the 'outer'
sense that led most directly to the verbal 'inner' realm where common sense,
fantasy, and memory joined external perceptions in understanding."[5]

CELLARS

Evidence of a connoisseur's integrity often lay deep underground in a basement or high above in an attic. Innovations in wine storage were adopted by
distributors in the middle decades of the seventeenth century, and thereafter
appropriated by consumers as useful props in their performances of wealth and
refinement. Cellars were not only symbolic; they stored the wine, and provided a
place where it could be aged, resuscitated, and improved. The functional aspects
of cellars were a requirement for the performance aspects. Building or renting
a private cellar announced that one bought wine in sufficient quantity to need
that much storage, and intimated that the owner used the space to engage in the
"mysteries" of aging, resuscitating, and improving wine. Acquiring one was "the
beginning of a long process . . . of establishing themselves as experts."[6]

The practice of storing wine in subterranean "caves" emerged in England
during the middle decades of the seventeenth century. In 1663, Samuel Pepys
visited what may have been one of the first underground cellars and saw bottles
standing on shelves; several months later, he described a space that had been
arched to ease the movement of barrels. Riding the wave of wine consumerism,
Pepys built his own cellar at a time when London importers, wholesalers, vintners, and coopers began boasting of caves. Cellars made an advantage of their

Figure 11.1. *Charity in the Cellar,* by William Hogarth, painted 1735 (engraved 1837).
Source: Courtesy of The British Museum—Department of Prints and
Drawings. © Copyright the Trustees of The British Museum.

relatively low, constant temperature, their damp, and their lack of light—ideal
conditions for most European wines—and they afforded greater security from
theft. William Hogarth depicted one such cellar in the 1735 engraving entitled
Charity in the Cellar (figure 11.1): small and dark, it was nonetheless secure and
outfitted with a plethora of bottles, bowls, braziers, funnels, and other storage,
bottling, and service items.[7]

The incorporation of cellars into American wine-drinking culture lagged behind that of England; when Governor Richard Bellomont introduced a cave into
his New York home at the end of the seventeenth century, he was thought to
be introducing a novelty.[8] Soon, though, cellars caught the fancy of those who
could afford them. They were especially favored by southerners. The Virginia
planter Robert Beverley, who was also trying to produce an American wine,

erected "caves and a wine press" at his Beverley Park plantation in Tidewater before 1715. Beverley's sometime friend Robert "King" Carter built an extensive half-basement cellar in his Lancaster County manor house in the 1720s. It incorporated two large chambers flanking a central passage room, each with its own closet at the gable ends of the house. The cellar's smaller, western closet had wall sockets for shelves, individual bins for glass bottles, and timber stops on the floors to prevent casks from rolling about. It housed Carter's substantial personal stock, which he consumed at his table and in the bedroom. More common in its simplicity was the storeroom of another planter, who cut a cave beneath his York River dwelling. Only five feet below grade, it measured twenty-seven feet in length and eleven in width, and possessed wooden floors and walls; it encased the planter's entire collection of wine and glassware.[9] Northern drinkers and tavern keepers also incorporated cellars into their dwellings, although usually on the more intimate scale of the York River bibbler. In the larger cities, the houses and offices of liquor merchants almost always contained cellars, storage being central to their work. Sale advertisements for merchants' offices and residences mentioned "a commodious cellar under the whole" and "a large vault" under the street and running along the front of the house, if they existed. Even in the Ohio River Valley, traders often maintained "a cellar in the bank" of a river or creek near where they moored their boats. They needed such "conveniency" for climate control, security ("keep[ing] the beer and other matters in"), and status (impressing visitors who wanted wines properly maintained). Country traders in America, like their urban counterparts, knew how to use cellars as props in their economic and social projects.[10]

A distinctly American contribution to storage was the warm attic cellar. The fashion was first forged in the colonies of the Lower South and the Caribbean basin, where distributors and consumers adhered to principles articulated by Madeira's exporters. A native of Carolina, Colonel Bleek was in 1731 the first to build a vault over an oven for the sole purpose of keeping his Madeira, knowing as he did that such wine "must be put into the warmest places" to prevent it from souring. Seventy years later, Charlestonians were building both warm attic and cool subterranean cellars to house their burgeoning wine collections. Colonel William Alston's grandson Jacob Motte Alston—the same boy who received tasting lessons from his grandmother—was frequently sent to "the wine rooms" in Alston's attic to "bring down the kinds of wine" the lady wished. The rooms he visited comprised two garrets, each about eight feet by sixteen feet, with louvered windows and doors. There Colonel Alston inscribed accounts of his inventory by chalking notations on its walls and doors, as he did on April 23, 1792, when "39 dozn botles of Madeira Wine [were] drawn off" in advance of his hosting a

Columbus Centennial commission dinner. Alston's friend the lawyer John Rutledge built a similar attic cellar across town. Before the end of the eighteenth
century, other Charleston-area rice planters were doing the same. By that time,
the fashion for attic caves had spread as far south as Savannah and as far north
as Richmond. One especially aggressive Richmond-area planter placed the new
and old stock he imported in an attic he installed directly above his office so that
he could check on its amelioration with ease.[11] Madeira's exporters and importers encouraged cellar building, lecturing their customers on appropriate levels
of warming after acquisition. "Heat and dryness are in all cases of great benefit,
and cold and damp of great detriment to wine," wrote one. "You will therefore be
particularly careful to put your wine into a dry and warm place, both while it is in
the cask and afterwards while in bottles, and if it is kept warm, it will continue to
improve as fast in the bottle as it would in the cask. And at the same time be free
from loss by the soakage of the wood and free from all risk of leakage." "Nothing
is more pernicious than a cold raw damp cellar," he added. "If possible keep your
wine always in a place where Fahrenheit's Thermometer is never under 70 degrees and never above 90 degrees of heat."[12]

A wine cellar was a particular type of prop, a concealed prop.[13] Some props are
revealed, used directly in front of an audience, whose members are expected to
understand their meanings; others are concealed. Revealed props, such as pictures and sideboards, can be observed by anyone in range, regardless of whether
the "performer" is present. There are distinctions among revealed props. Some
revealed objects are fixed permanently on display, like grapes in a frieze or chandelier. Promoting their owners' ongoing projects with no further input from the
owners, they announce their meanings to all who see them. They are positioned
in advance and, unlike their owner's conversation or deportment on a particular occasion, cannot be brought into play without prior consideration. For this
reason, they are often taken to signify the owner's stable beliefs or actions, thus
vouching for the sincerity of the performance. Other revealed objects, such as
the glassware around a dining table, for instance, or the corkscrew in a tavern's
club room, are displayed only for particular occasions, yet brought out so regularly that viewers expect them. In contrast, concealed objects are usually out of
sight, deployed only when the owner thinks it serves his or her interest to do so.
The revelation can be an even more powerful device, perhaps. Because they are
usually concealed, observers may infer that their existence or use is not meant to
be observed, and therefore is more reflective of the sincerity of owners' performances than objects usually on display. Hence, owners sometimes reveal them—
perhaps "accidentally"—at the right time. They are similar to "the ungovernable

aspects of expressive behavior"—"the expressions one gives off"—that observers use as "a check on the truth of what is conveyed by the governable aspects," such as "verbal assertions" and revealed objects.[14]

Cellars themselves are usually unseen by guests and other outsiders to the household, so they are concealed, but often their existence is known. Apart from the practical keeping and improving functions, owning a cellar implied economic and social independence (the owner could stock wine free of the vagaries of supply and transport), displayed the financial ability to stock a collection and provide a place for it, and demonstrated a regard for the guests to whom the wine would be served. It intimated that the wines might be valuable and hard to obtain—hence the need to safeguard them. It also polished a reputation as someone "in the know": it was a physical manifestation of an owner's interest and skill in the factors affecting wine service; acquiring a cellar was a major step toward solidifying the right to be called a connoisseur.

Cellars became part of an enlightened, gendered cultural production. Managing cellars and handling wine in them in the eighteenth century were performed by wealthier, better-educated men. The practice of binning, which Robert Carter and Colonel Alston were following, was first introduced at about the same time as cellaring. Distributors and consumers began storing their wines by laying new-fashion cylindrical bottles on their sides in shallow divisions called "bins" that were inserted into cellar walls. Bins were brick below ground and wooden above. Binning allowed more wine to fit into a cellar; it also kept the corks wet, which expanded them, sealing the bottles, thus extending the lives of the wine.[15] For advice on binning, consumers turned first to "experts" in related aspects of viniculture who possessed experimental and methodical knowledge. Perhaps the most useful hints came from the English gardening writer Philip Miller who, in his popular 1731 treatise *The Gardener's Dictionary*, advised laying bottles "slopewise" on a three-inch sand or sawdust floor "and not setting them upright, which lets in air." Miller's treatise exerted enormous influence on Americans, as to a lesser extent did mid-eighteenth-century dictionaries and encyclopedias. It was because Landon Carter was following Miller that the planter tied and waxed his corks with rosin and left the bottles "buried four inches in dry sand."

Using and recounting advice like Miller's or an encyclopedist's—there were few if any homegrown American compendia before 1815—became part of the performance of skill; it distinguished a refined gentleman from a mere poseur. A gentleman should have not only the means to install cellars and bins but also the leisure and knowledge to know where to look for advice, experiment with alternatives, and maintain them properly—setting the bottles in a certain way, storing their wines at the right age and temperature, leaving them for a certain length of time, and so on. He would possess, as well, the language to discuss his display of skill.

It was not much of a reach for connoisseurs who obsessed over cellars and bins to demand bin labels in their quest to display wealth and refinement. Such markers were first introduced toward the end of the eighteenth century. Before that, owners identified the contents of bins by writing above the bins in paint, chalk, or ink. Colonel Alston did so. Other owners wrote on paper scraps tacked to the bin. They found all these methods unsatisfactory, for the marks could be easily erased. They abandoned writing on wood or paper in favor of durable, moveable labels made of pottery, lead, slate, or wood. Through a hole pierced in its top, the label could be fixed above or below the bin opening.

In time, the often-expensive labels became a field of competition for connoisseurs. Bin owners could buy labels in a variety of materials—from gold and silver to stone or wood—and shapes—circle, semicircle, coat hanger, rectangle, and square—and calligraphic styles. Seeing a market opportunity, manufacturers expanded their label lines and allowed customers to order them to taste. By the 1790s, manufacturers were mass-marketing them, differentiating them for specific classes of customers. Wedgwood offered plain labels to American consumers at 2d. each, and named labels—Madeira, Malmsey, Port, Lisbon, Claret, Hermitage, Hock, Rum, Brandy, Arrack, Shrub, and Holland—at double that price. If desired, he would inscribe a purchaser's name above that of the alcohol, further linking buyer, class, and commodity.[16]

Cellars and their appurtenances gave rise to a whole family of opportunities to uncover the props. Because cellars were major improvements whose construction could have been observed, and which would have been advertised if the house or office were sold, the existence of the cellar space was known to many of the owners' intended audience. The act of excusing oneself to go to the cellar to bring up the wine, or asking one's servant to do so, would also have announced its existence. Bringing down the wine with an accompanying bin label announcing varietal and year—as Colonel William Alston often did—would have intimated that the cellar housed several types of wine, and reflected on the host's discrimination in selecting an appropriate one. These could be accomplished with more or less fanfare in the course of entertaining guests. More intimately, a host could take the audience into the cellar itself to view the bins, labels, and bottles, as Governor Bellomont, Robert "King" Carter, and President Jefferson loved to do. The implication was that the guest was especially esteemed or privileged to be admitted into the private space, and that whatever the guest saw there was a deep

Figure 11.2. Eighteenth-century English ceramic
wine bin labels.
Source: Courtesy of V&A Images/Victoria and
Albert Museum, London.

reflection of the host, because not usually seen. One expects it was reserved for discussions that allowed both host and guest to display their mastery of wine.

GLASSWARE

Some of the greatest advances in consumers' options for extending the pleasure of drinking wine and displaying wealth and refinement were made with glassware. This was enabled by the improvement of glassmaking technology in the period. Distributors and consumers innovated with glass storing, serving, and drinking paraphernalia, extending the field of connoisseurship beyond the act of consuming alcohol. Drinking, by its very nature a fleeting experience, was given greater permanence by the glassware. "Consuming" glassware, therefore, was a behavior with more external and long-term consequences than consuming liquor but, of course, complementary. Glassware lived on after the wine it contained, and so choosing it could be taken to be "serious" evidence about the drinker.[17]

Prior to the middle decades of the seventeenth century, Anglophone consumers used glaze- and neck-less earthenware jugs to store and serve alcoholic drinks. These were modifications of classical amphorae and often manufactures of European principalities. By the founding of Virginia and Massachusetts Bay, the standard jug contained between one-half pint and two pints; it was globular, with a neck and a handle, made from clay, glazed with white tin oxide, and imprinted with the name and date of the wine in blue underglazing.[18]

Early seventeenth-century English and Anglo-American drinkers who owned bottles and cups possessed Italian and, to a lesser extent, German manufactures. But foreign glass had its problems. Despite the fineness and elegance of its execution and decoration, it was extremely fragile, as were its English imitations. It was accordingly scarce.[19] Glassware did not become common in England until George Ravenscroft, who had worked in Venice as a trader, perfected the Venetian method of adding lead oxide to the melt in the 1670s. The glass he produced was much less fine than the Venetians'; it was heavy and dark, with a black or blue-gray hue. Yet its more robust composition made it longer-lived and easier to manipulate into bolder forms. From a factory in central London and a second workshop at Henley-on-Thames, Ravenscroft made a type of crystalline glass that looked like rock crystal, soon called "flint glass."[20]

After Ravenscroft, English glassmaking became profitable, and English glassware spread abroad. Ravenscroft's and his imitators' bottles and glasses eclipsed foreign versions in metropolitan and colonial markets. They were so successful that glassware manufacture was not commercially viable in Anglo-America until

Casper Wistar, the brother of the wine specialist John Wister, concluded his first successful blast in 1738 (plate 14). Even then, Americans could not compete effectively with the greater volume and cheaper price of British glass. Long after the peace of 1783, British manufacturers produced the bulk of bottle and drinking glass used by Americans, even though Germans and Bohemians increasingly provided competition.[21]

Improvements in glass and reductions in price increased the range and variety of glassware available to consumers, widening the range of those who could drink with glass and, at the same time, allowing differentiated meanings. Glassware became at once a common necessity and a fashionable commodity. Fashion items are objects whose significations depend on their type, variety, or design, or the way they are deployed in social intercourse, independent of functional use. For an object to be a fashion item, it has to be available in a range of forms and affordable enough that consumers can discard, or at least disregard, the versions they already own. Fashions in glass allowed consumers to embellish their performances with ancillary significations of discernment and refinement that could be remote from pragmatic considerations. Possessing and deploying glass paraphernalia also announced a consumer's allegiance to a taste community. The owners could exhibit "good taste" to men and women in their group by their possession and use of bottles, decanters, and glasses with particular styles, designs, decorations, and colors. They could also manifest an attentiveness to changes in social norms, particularly changes in elite tastes. Glass props fuelled a continual reinvention of the "up-to-date," compared to the "old-fashioned," because a type or form previously fashionable could be replaced with a new one. When marrying Colonel George Washington, Martha Dandridge Custis was not content with using the previous generation's glassware, nor was her husband, and they ordered crates á la mode from London. Characteristic of a man of his means, Henry Hill changed his glassware on at least three occasions between 1772 and 1798, as new engraved emblems became modish. When glasses with engraved stars on them became stylish in Europe, for instance, he chose starred glassware. Deploying a new item displayed the owner's skill in discerning nuances of significations and responding appropriately, in addition to his or her means to do so. Fashionable serving and drinking glasses greatly increased the scope for performing not only wealth but also refinement in eighteenth-century America.

Drinkers also used drinking objects to make their own and others' drinking recognizable and coherent. In essence, wine props both sent messages and created cultural communities: one could not only call attention to oneself with glass but also establish bonds among people. Wine props were particularly useful, because they functioned as "boundary objects"—pliable enough "to adapt to local needs and the constraints of the several parties employing them, yet robust enough to maintain a common identity across sites. They are weakly structured in common use, and become strongly structured in individual-site use. These objects may be abstract or concrete. They have different meanings in different social worlds but their structure is common enough to more than one world to make them recognizable, a means of translation." Boundary objects helped solve "the problem of common representation in diverse intersecting worlds."[22]

Glass wine-related items were well suited for transgressing physical boundaries and creating cultural communities of pleasure and taste. They were plentiful. They were various, with different functions, shapes, and sizes, while adhering to "fairly vague" ideal types. Variations catered to divergent desires and budgets. Glassware gave Atlantic connoisseurs a common material language, while providing the flexibility for people in dispersed localities to "reinterpret their concerns to fit their own programmatic goals." The Madeira island distributor Thomas Murdoch passed out and sold small cordial wineglasses to visitors and customers who called on him, arguing that the art of using a glass was a cosmopolitan and—in the true sense of that word—boundaryless skill. His drinkers, scattered throughout the empire—from John Caufield in Calcutta, John Taylor in Dacca, Ebenezer Robertson in Calcutta, James Shoolbred in Charleston, Charles Vaughan in Boston, and his numerous customers in London—were to drink Newton & Gordon's Madeira and other heavily fortified wines from the same glass, in the same manner. Glasses provided "a means of communicating and cooperating symbolically" in multiple political, economic, and social arenas around the globe. Buyers in far-flung places communicated enough with others around the world to acquire glass objects and replicate their meanings, but they were independent enough to adapt them to local vernacular tastes and needs.[23]

The effect of glassware transgressing boundaries was "to develop and maintain coherence" in the rapidly changing, highly diverse Atlantic world, even as viewers and users reinterpreted the objects to fit their own situations. There was consensus about the core of what they signified, and that agreement formed the basis of a common wine and drinking culture in Anglo-America and around the ocean. English glassware was used throughout the Portuguese world, for instance, in much the same way that Portuguese wine was used throughout the English-speaking world. Glassware helped travelers from Boston to Funchal to Rio to Kingston to London make sense of the different physical and social worlds they entered or simply passed through, because the travelers recognized and understood the objects. Wine paraphernalia promoted recognition and thereby created a material community, if only fleetingly. In 1791, in the rather rude wilds of Canada, Patrick Campbell's obliging host brought out his glassware. Although

not well schooled in the arts of wine connoisseurship, as was a knowing Philadelphia buck, he sensed a call for refinement and poured the gentlemen's drink
into clear glass wine decanters, and without spilling it, even if all he could pour
was raspberry rum and grog. All men recognized the elegance conveyed.[24] Moreover, a toast with a wineglass was similar around the Atlantic. None of the many
Frenchmen flooding America in the 1780s and 1790s had any difficulty interpreting it, whether or not they understood the language. Europe's wine exporters
and America's wine importers and retailers were active in developing and maintaining the coherence by making sure their customers understood wines, cellars,
bins, and labels "correctly." Glass props embodied a common display culture in
which connoisseurs oceanwide recognized and communicated with each other
and, in the process, created a transimperial wine-drinking community.

BOTTLES

The earliest signs of a revolution in wine paraphernalia appeared in the styling
and manufacturing of storage containers used by consumers, particularly bottles.
Buyers soon recognized glass bottles' improvements over earthen containers.
"Glass-bottles are preferr'd to Stone-bottles," the author of *Vinetum Britannicum*
wrote in 1676, for a number of good reasons: earthenware leaked, was rough in
the mouth, difficult to see through, less easily uncorked, and more apt to allow
wine to taint. Conversely, to paraphrase Benjamin Franklin, glass hurt not wine.
Glass bottles did not degrade. Their contents were not exposed to oxygen, thus
reducing evaporation and contamination. Nor were their contents liable to de-
compose when in contact with glass, or to damage by light, because the glass was
colored black or dark green.[25]

The earliest glass bottles used by Anglo-Americans looked much like the
earthen jugs they replaced: they had more or less globular or spherical shapes
(a "shaft-and-globe" design"), with long, parallel necks and rings or rims below
their lips, under which strings were tied to anchor corks to the bottles; they were
pale green in hue; and they were fairly light in weight. Appearance evolved as
bottles came into greater use. By the turn of the eighteenth century, the body
was dramatically accentuated, producing an almost bulbous shape; the neck was
tapered and much shorter; and the glass was nearly black. Quart bottles were the
norm, and they remained so.[26]

During the early decades of the eighteenth century, as retailers and consumers
began cellaring wine, they discovered it improved with age. Over a period of
years, the wine fared better in bottles stored on their sides, because the corks did
not dry out as quickly as when standing upright. Since it was easier to handle and
store cylindrical bottles on their sides, drinkers began requesting such containers

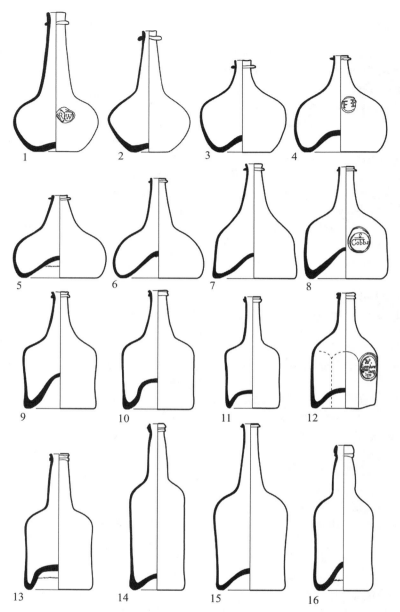

Figure 11.3. Evolution of wine bottle shapes, c. 1650–1820.
Legend: 1—before 1652; 2—c. 1655–65; 3—c. 1675–90; 4—c. 1690–1710;
5—1685–1715; 6—1710–30; 7—1725–35; 8—1730–45; 9—1740–60;
10—1750–70; 11—1750–65; 12—1770; 13—1750–70; 14—1750–70;
15—1770–1800; 16—1790–1820.
Source: Based on Ivor Noël Hume, "The Glass Wine Bottle in
Colonial Virginia," *Journal of Glass Studies* 3 (1961): 99–101.
Drawn by Lorene Sterner.

and manufacturers reconfigured the vessels. The body became mallet shaped, wider than before and at times wider than high, with straight sides that had been rolled on a flat steel surface; the already tapered neck was elongated. This bottle was the norm by the 1720s. The shape continued evolving and, by 1740, a more or less uniform design had appeared: the bottle was narrower and taller, the sides being straightened to the point that the mallet became cylindrical. Thus English glassmakers had developed the prototype for the nineteenth-century machine-made bottle that still predominates today.[27]

Cylindrically shaped wine bottles found a growing market in the early decades of the eighteenth century. In the Anglo-Iberian wine trade, wine was bottled near the point of consumption by retailers and consumers. Most Portuguese and Spanish exporters to America shipped wine in barrels and sent the bottles separately, unlike the French, who shipped wine in bottles packed in straw-filled boxes or casks. Wealthy planters in Anglo-America were transferring wine to cylindrical bottles themselves by the beginning of the eighteenth century. Indeed, they are the second-most numerous artifacts found in archaeological excavations.[28]

As the risk of transporting bottles decreased and the merits of bottled wine became better known, American consumers found it easier to find bottles from London and Bristol in America. The diffusion of English glassware coincided roughly with the first American manufacture of bottles: from the 1750s, newspapers advertised American bottles not intended for medicine or snuff. By the 1780s, at least three American manufacturers were producing wine bottles and glasses, even as British, German, and Bohemian makers increased their exports. Still, while bottles became more prevalent, they never constituted the norm before 1815: most people continued to buy wine in generic, all-purpose ceramic jugs. As table 11.1 shows, the presence of bottles in probated estates rose, while remaining unusual: whereas less than 1 percent of the 856 estates surveyed in the first quarter of the eighteenth century had bottles, some 7 percent of the 1,430 estates had them a century later. In 1815, bottles were still uncommon, even if more readily available. They could still effectively serve as markers of wealth.[29]

Refinement was an elusive quest for consumers and manufacturers. Bottles may have signaled gentility, but some bottles were more genteel than others. Bottle owners often marked their bottles with seals to distinguish them from other consumers' bottles in the vintner's shop or publican's house. Toward the end of the production process, when the glass was hot and adhesive, a small disc of glass could be affixed to the bottle and on this disc embossed the initials, name, or coat of arms of the bottle's owner. In England, bottle seals were in use as early as the 1650s, and English colonists adopted them almost immediately. Seals found near Jamestown are identical to several sealed British bottles unequivocally dated to

Table 11.1. Wine-related storage items in probated estates

Items	First quarter, eighteenth century[a]	Second quarter, eighteenth century[b]	Third quarter, eighteenth century[c]	Fourth quarter, eighteenth century[d]	First quarter, nineteenth century[e]
Bottles (full and empty)	2	38	243	1	105
Cases (of full and empty bottles)					11
Demijohns			2	7	74
Jars					26
Jugs			8		61
Total inventories registered	856	918	2,546	215	1,430

Sources: See source note for table 9.1

a. Jamaica, 1700–1705 and 1713–16; Hampshire and Suffolk counties, MA, 1703–7; Albany and New York counties, NY, 1703–12.

b. Jamaica, 1732–36; South Carolina, 1732–41.

c. Hampshire and Suffolk counties, MA, 1765–74; South Carolina, 1765–74.

d. Albany and New York counties NY, 1790–99.

e. Jamaica, 1807; Hampshire and Suffolk counties, MA, 1803–7; Charleston and Kershaw counties, SC, 1803–7.

before 1653.[30] Most commonly, a seal denoted ownership by a gentleman, merchant, or innkeeper, as it did for Mareen Duvall, whose Maryland plantation's excavation revealed some thirty-two seals, fourteen of which bore his initials, four more those of the planter who married his widow, eight more those of his neighbors, and seven more those of area merchants.[31]

Similar enough to be recognized across geographies and languages, seals served an obvious exclusionary function. They announced that the wine and their owners were special. Seals signaled the owner's means to buy labels and bottles, and might imply that he or she had a supplier, cellar, or bins. People of middling wealth, who increasingly had a taste for wine but no coats of arms, found it useful to be able to identify their own bottles, and perhaps also to introduce the possibility that they, too, kept a cellar. Those who bought wine in small amounts brought their bottles to retailers, tavern keepers, and vintners to be filled, or rented bottles from the same men. Merchants charged extra for bottles, so it was cheaper for consumers to provide their own, although if monogrammed bottles broke, one hardly saved much. Seals also provided a measure of security.

Since there was often doubt about the volume of others' bottles, using one's own container removed uncertainty and minimized unfair dealings. Seals also provided a mark of warranty that the wine had not been tampered with, as Benjamin Franklin was told in 1767 "that they may be delivered to thee in safety." Such protection was critical when the quality and quantity of contents were hard to discern before purchase and were often interfered with after leaving the hands of the producer and exporter. In the most extreme, and much like monogrammed silver, crockery, and linen, seals constituted a disincentive against theft and resale by third parties.[32]

Exporters and distributors realized that they could use bottle seals to promote their wares. This was especially important to a distributor if he was providing personal blends or rare wines to the consumer, for many of the same reasons that he branded his name on a cask. Late in the eighteenth century exporters began putting seals on bottles to identify their own house's exports. "Leacock" and "Newton Gordon [&] Murdoch" of Madeira did this. Trade- or brand marks featuring the name of the exporter were first advertised in American newspapers in 1815, although exporters had been experimenting with branding for decades by ordering bottles for their own private use embossed with the firm's seal or initials, and having correspondents advertise the arrival of their wines by name. Seals were bespoke for this purpose. Bottles were displayed on both sideboard and table to guests as revealed props, and those that were not yet brought out could be viewed in the cellar, if entry was allowed. Brands announced to an interested person that the host knew the wine and the house supplying the wine, key components of connoisseurship.[33]

DECANTERS

After glasses and bottles, decanters were the wine-drinking objects Americans most commonly placed on their tables, not only to pour the wine but also to effect the manner of a connoisseur. Usually made of clear glass and stoppered, decanters had their origins in the square silver or glass serving bottles of ancient Rome and the small, bulbous, flat-handled, short- and narrow-necked earthen jugs of sixteenth- and seventeenth-century northern Europe. Almost as soon as Ravenscroft demonstrated the ability to make clear, durable flint glass in England in the 1670s, manufacturers there turned their attention to this timeless container form. They first produced decanters for upper-class drinkers, but, as the eighteenth century advanced, they sold to the middling sort. Silver and ceramic decanters continued to be produced through the early 1800s, the latter continuing to be the most common dispensing item among less affluent and rural folk; but glass decanters, early defined as "bottle[s] of clear Flint Glass for holding the wine, etc., to be poured off into a Drinking Glass," dominated wine service after 1700.[34]

Decanters were made for passing—they invited interactions among drinkers and so became the sine qua non of group sociability. Ravenscroft had this use in mind. His "decanter jugs" had narrow necks broadening out to the rim, sizable shoulders, cylindrical bodies and handles. Some he decorated with trailed glass, molded ribs, or pincered glass with a lattice effect supplied with hollow, loose-fitting, pear-shaped stoppers. Variations proliferated. Other glassmakers began marketing decanters of their own designs that, with globular bodies and narrow necks, strongly resembled the "shaft-and-globe" bottles of the day. The shaft-and-globe decanter type predominated in the first fifty years of the eighteenth century. It was memorialized in the drawings that Dr. Alexander Hamilton sketched on the pages of his Tuesday Club's minutes.

Over the years, several fashionable permutations superseded the shaft-and-globe arrangement, and consumers saw them as refined markers of ever-changing fashion. Between 1745 and 1775, cylindrical bodies, rounded shoulders, and curving necks on mallet-and-shoulder decanters became popular; their bodies were generally twice the height of the necks, and the rims were plain. By the end of the American Revolution, however, the shoulders had nearly disappeared, having been replaced by tapered sides. Then, by the century's end, two new variants captured the imaginations of wine drinkers. One had its neck rims further turned out and had additional neck rings. Another had slanted sides that rose at an angle from an expanded base to a long neck. This was the celebrated "Rodney," launched soon after the admiral defeated the French at the Battle of St. Vincent in 1780. Being "plastic enough to adapt to local needs," the Rodney fit snugly on the surface of a dining or writing table and stayed put when a ship rode through choppy seas; in time, it graced tables that had no need for stability, situated as they were in the interiors of Atlantic-facing states.[35]

Whatever the design, decanters preserved and served the wine—and also displayed it and reflected on those who drank it. Its presentation possibilities were striking. Better than a bottle, a decanter of clear glass exhibited a wine's chief visual trait—its color. Wine's translucency, when refracted through crystal in candlelight, added to the luster of the object, the drink, the event, and the owner. One of the century's more notable enophiles, Benjamin Franklin singled out this very feature when praising his London landlady on her 1769 birthday:

> Time hurts not Glass. This Wine must be preserv'd
> And at my Table serv'd:
> There thro' the Chrystal Vase it shines.[36]

Shaft and Globe
c. 1680-1740

Cruciform
c. 1705-1720

Shoulder
c. 1710-1740

Mallet
c. 1750

Taper
c. 1780

Indian Club
c. 1810

Classic
c. 1810

Pillar-cut
c. 1825

Figure 11.4. Evolution of wine decanter shapes, c. 1680–1825.
Source: Based on Robin Butler and Gillian Walkling, *The Book of Wine
Antiques* (Woodbridge, 1993), 142–43. Drawn by Lorene Sterner.

Decanters showed guests that the hosts had the means to buy them, and allowed the hosts to show their skill in using them: what wine a particular decanter should hold, what place it should have at table, what direction it should move around the table, and the like.

In addition, the decanter was a highly manipulable, easily changeable *objet de vertu* that could exhibit ever-shifting facets of taste. Its plasticity was valuable to status performance in the same way that the bin label's was. To articulate ever more genteel forms, glassmakers introduced engraving in the middle decades of the eighteenth century. From the 1750s in Great Britain and the 1760s in North America, manufacturers engraved decanters with the names of the wine they contained, the name being set within a cartouche on their bodies. The first specialized decanters to be advertised in North America appeared in 1760 when the *New-York Gazette* announced the availability of "new fashioned, engraved, also flowered and letter'd" and "square and round Decanters of different sizes." As early as 1761, readers of the *Boston Gazette* learned they could buy "best engrav'd flower'd wine . . . decanters" in their city. New York consumers could go to one retailer's shop in 1763 for "gallon, three quarts, and quart Champaign decanters, cut and ground Madeira, Port, Claret, and Mountain ditto." In 1764, Philadelphia-area shopkeepers advertised the "best quart and pint decanters labelled Madeira." Indeed, from 1760, connoisseurs living in any large port city could acquire decanters engraved with a number of names—Ale, Beer, Burgundy, Champagne, Greek, Lisbon, Madeira, Old Hock, Red, Red Port, Rhenish, Sherry, White Port, and White—as well as with the name of their clubs or societies. The one decanter belonging to Jefferson to have survived was inscribed with "Madeira" (plate 15).[37]

Decanters dripped both wealth and politesse. They implied a penchant for group socializing—that mode of association so valorized by the age. Displaying multiple decanters suggested a level of wealth that was not the lot of those who had only one. Probate inventories testified to the status of decanter owners. As table 11.2 hints, few early eighteenth-century decedents left estates with decanters or decanter stands (coasters placed underneath decanters to protect table tops): between 1703 and 1712, no estate contained one. The numbers grew slowly: in the second quarter of the century, 11 of the 918 probated estates had them; in the third, 97 of 2,546; in the fourth, 29 of 215; by the first quarter of the nineteenth century, 70 of 1,430. Fifty different estates in South Carolina contained "Madeira," "Bishop," "Punch," "Wine," and unnamed decanters in the decade preceding the Revolution. By the 1790s, New Yorkers possessed the full range of types: large, small, pint, quart, plain (probably in contrast to engraved), glass, wine, and undifferentiated (merely designated "decanter"), plus decanter stands. Estates from the first decade of the nineteenth century exhibited a similar range in size, decoration, and material, although decanters were then listed as often in pairs as singly. Many of these estates possessed a dozen or so small pint decanters, indicating an increase in the practice of providing a decanter at each place setting.

Table 11.2. Wine-related serving and drinking items in probated estates

Items	First quarter, eighteenth century	Second quarter, eighteenth century	Third quarter, eighteenth century	Fourth quarter, eighteenth century	First quarter, nineteenth century
Coasters				1	43
Cups	1				4
Decanters		11	97	29	70
Glasses: ale, beer, cider, and porter	1		11	1	1
Glasses, cordial			1		4
Glasses, drinking	1	4	20	1	3
Glasses, punch			3		
Glasses, wine	6	18	190	27	134
Glassware		7	1	1	28
Goblets			1	1	8
Rummers					8
Stands: bottle, decanter, dram, liquor, and wine			65	1	38
Tumblers, inc. wine tumblers		6	44		57
Total inventories registered	856	918	2,546	215	1,430

Sources: See source note for table 9.1 and explanatory notes for table 11.1.

Consumers who could not afford a different decanter for every drink could project some refinement by using decanter labels or, as they were sometimes called, decanter tags or tickets. The earliest decanter labels were cast in gold and silver and were expensive. Since not all who wanted decanters could afford silver or gold, cheaper ivory and mother-of-pearl alternatives were introduced. They were cut into small geometrical shapes, usually rectangles but sometimes crescents; less common shapes bore heraldic, cartouche, and asymmetrical forms. Labels were sold individually and in sets of three, six, or twelve. The most typical was suspended around the neck by a chain, and could be removed and set upon another decanter. As the eighteenth century wore on, shapes and designs became more elaborate and refined, including fruiting vines, shells, and occasionally lion pelts. One particularly interesting early nineteenth-century label bore the shape of a ring that was slipped over the top of the bottle or decanter, and narrated on its band the mid-1790s itinerary of the ship that had brought the Madeira in its hold.[38]

Decanter labels, much like bottle labels, were also tailor-made for the ongoing social performances of a widening, increasingly affluent middle class. Middling consumers did not have to own as many engraved decanters as the number of wines they served; a decanter and a dozen or so tickets would suffice. They did not have to buy a new ticket if the decanter broke. Nor did they have to discard the decanter if the fashion for a certain wine faded. In an age when paper labels were not yet fixed to bottles as a matter of course, decanter labels projected a cosmopolitan style showing off the foreign origin of the drink. While they did not display as much wealth as individually etched decanters did, they distinguished their owners from those who drank whatever came to hand and who might not even know the difference. The labels, along with other service-related objects, helped consumers construct an image—and reality—of men and women of "true luxury" and "knowing discernment."

GLASSES

Glasses were the most common form of wine paraphernalia in the Anglophone world after 1680. They were bespoke boundary objects and nearly perfect fashion items. The material's malleability meant they could be produced in a wealth of styles and with wide variation in decorative motif, responding to local tastes when manufacturing became local. Its cheapness (Ravenscroft's legacy) meant that most people could own at least one or two, and its startling clarity meant a connoisseur could discern the color and density of the wine inside. In the ensuing century, manufacturers marketed a voluptuous range of wineglasses through which consumers could reveal their wealth, taste, and awareness of fashion, even if they did nothing but let them sit on their sideboards. Wineglasses helped create a cultural community that a member would recognize anywhere.

The first English glasses were copies of Venetian ones, but the designs gradually moved away from Italian models. Ravenscroft's initial creation, the heavy baluster glass, was a bold, pure, and unadorned form marked by a short, urn-shaped knop or stem to facilitate the drinker's grasp. Over time, manufacturers lightened it by placing air bubbles or "tears" in the stem and sometimes in the base of the bowl, presenting lighter, often fussier balusters, and varying the bowls with added waisted funnel, bell, bucket, tulip, ogee, double ogee, and pan-top shapes alongside the traditionally rounded funnel shape.[39] Designs evolved more slowly after 1750, but manufacturers continued to innovate to satisfy the rapidly growing demand of consumers who wanted low cost and maximum display. Some glassmakers produced a "Silesian-stem" wineglass that had a multi-sided stem that tapered from the bowl toward the foot. Others maintained the straight stem and lightened it by inserting a series of small bubbles into it, which they then twisted and stretched to form multiple helixes of air. In the late 1750s and 1760s, manufacturers worked opaque white or colored glass into the stem, twisting them the same way that they had bubbles. Some glasses had a single series of twists, others a double series; yet other glasses had air and color spiraled in tandem; and in still others, a number of colors (like red, white, and blue) were intertwined.[40]

Glassmakers and with them consumers also attended to the glass's external decoration: wheel engraving, stipple engraving, enameling, and gilding provided the variety that wine drinkers favored. Such decoration added "elegance" and, as any good retailer knew, "elegance adds to the rapidity of the sale."[41] Wheel engraving first became popular in the 1730s, when bands, flowers, vines, fruits, or grains were etched around the rim of the glass (figure 11.6a). Some manufacturers began catering to customers' political proclivities by releasing Williamite or Jacobite glasses, depending on their sympathies. The latter bore symbols of the Scottish Pretender: portraits of Bonnie Prince Charlie in Highland attire, thistles, roses, rosebuds, oak leaves, and stars, words such as *Amen* and *Fiat* (mottoes of his followers), and verses of the Stuart national anthem (figure 11.6b–c). Others produced glasses with portraits of military heroes—Admiral Vernon and Lord Nelson were favorites—or scenes of overseas shipping, wishing Godspeed to the launch of a privateer or commemorating a wartime seizure of an enemy vessel. In the 1770s, glassmakers began cutting the stem into small, diamond, hexagonal, or shield facets and cutting the bowl and foot similarly. In the last quarter of the century, they decorated the bowl with cut motifs, such as bands of stars, classical frond swags, and cartouches of shields.

Each decade stamped its own fashion onto stemware. In 1745, glasses were cut; by 1757, they were engraved and flowered; in 1767, they were pointed. In 1768, some glasses were fluted; in 1770, others ribbed; by 1787, still others molded. One of the most colorful trends to stir the imaginations of drinkers was enameling. William and Mary Beilby of Newcastle, especially, became famous for vines, fruits, fruits, landscapes, and coats of arms that they painted in a variety of colors on the bowls of their glasses. Equally au courant was the gilding of James Giles and William Absolom and the stipple engraving of David Wolff and Jacobus Van Den Blijk. By 1800, drinkers in Britain and the States could personalize and decorate their stemware to taste, or at least find so many variants that almost any taste could be satisfied.[42]

Americans did not manufacture wineglasses with the same gusto that they

Figure 11.5. Evolution of wineglass shapes, 1676–1820.

Legend: 1—Anglicized Venetian, 1676–90; 2—Anglicized Venetian, 1676–95;
3—Heavy Baluster, 1685–1720; 4-Flat—Faced Silesian Baluster, 1705–20; 5—Heavy
Knopped Baluster, 1720–35; 6—Light Baluster, 1720–60; 7—Plain, with Tears,
1700–40; 8—Plain, without Tears, 1720–1820; 9—Incised Twist, 1735–50; 10—Air
Twist, 1735–60; 11—Mercury Twist, 1740–60; 12—Opaque White Twist, 1750–80;

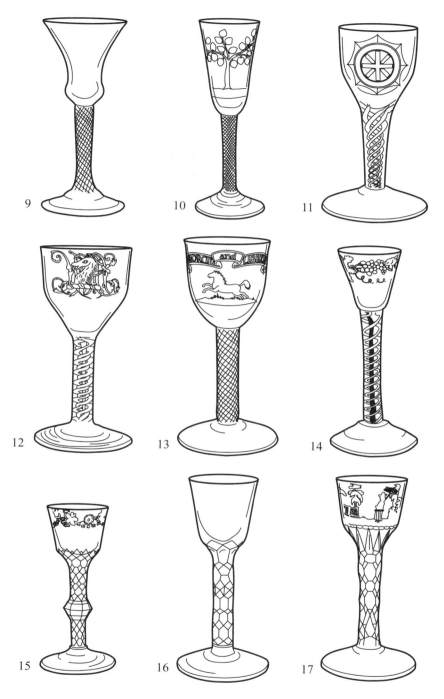

13—Mixed Twist, 1760–75; 14—Color Twist, 1760–80; 15—Early Facet, 1745–60;
16—Late Facet, 1780–1800; 17—Cut, 1780–1820.
Source: Based on G. Bernard Hughes, *English, Scottish and Irish Table Glass from the Sixteenth Century to 1820* (New York, 1956), chaps. 4–9. Drawn by Lorene Sterner.

Figure 11.6a–c. Ale, "Amen," and "Fiat" glasses.
Source: Courtesy of (a) Bristol's Museums, Galleries & Archives;
(b) Philadelphia Museum of Art: The George H. Lorimer Collection, 1953;
and (c) Bristol's Museums, Galleries & Archives.

did bottle and window glass; indeed, they did not produce wineglasses on any scale until the 1810s. Henry William Stiegel, who operated a factory in Manheim, Pennsylvania, between 1763 and 1774, manufactured some. In 1769 alone, he sold 223 "fine" wineglasses, 5,648 plain wineglasses, 24 wine-water glasses, 77 bulbed glasses, 29 large glasses, 3 glasses, 2 Freemason glasses, 48 fine beer glasses, and 32 beer glasses. But Stiegel was unusual, and his tenure was brief. German immigrant Casper Wistar and his son Richard, the first commercially successful American manufacturers, produced panes and bottles at the United Glass Company in southern New Jersey between 1739 and 1776, but very few wineglasses. There is no record of John Elliott producing anything more specific than basic "wineglasses" at his Philadelphia Glass Works, and these were a sideline for him. After the Revolution, John Frederick Amelung's glassworks in Maryland made wineglasses and engraved tumblers, but the output was small. As important as they were in the history of American glassmaking, none of the early manufacturers produced wineglasses in any variety, except perhaps Stiegel.[43]

After 1740, the lag between metropolitan advances in glassmaking and their

availability on the periphery was reduced.[44] Retailers in eastern cities hawked
new styles within a year or so of their introduction in England. The "newest fashion" was what sold, with fashion extending to the shape of the bowl, construction
of the stem, and decoration overall. In the 1730s, only "drinking glasses" and
"double flint wine glasses" were advertised in the *Pennsylvania Gazette* as being
for sale in Philadelphia. In the following decade, imported single and double flint
glasses, white flint wineglasses, dram glasses, drinking glasses, and tumblers regularly appeared. Advertisers sometimes noted the manufacturer, but for the most
part they thought it sufficient to name only the city of origin, such as London or
Bristol. Styles proliferated, and by 1750 buyers in larger towns could find "a compleat assortment of flint glass ware, consisting of decanters, Spanish wineglasses,
Britannia ditto, olive and diamond ditto, globe and olive egg bowl ditto, bell bowl
ditto, twist stem ditto, & c." Even when French, German, and Dutch manufacturers were able to compete freely in the glassware market after the American
Revolution, English glasses still dominated.[45]

Americans favored decorated wine ware. In 1761, Philadelphians learned that
they could buy "worm'd and engrav'd" wine and ale glasses. Their city's John
Gibson sold "beautiful enamelled wine glasses, with cut stems" three years later.
Imported "flowered wine glasses, with many other sorts" were available in nearby
Chester County in 1775, and imported "plain and labelled goblets, and white
glass beakers," wine glasses, cider glasses, pint, half-pint, gill, and half-gill tumblers, and proof bottles showed up a few months later in Philadelphia, despite the
nonimportation and nonconsumption restrictions imposed on wine by the Continental Association. Although retailers' stocks were depleted during the war,
soon after its end Philadelphians' choices were extensive, both "plain and gilt."[46]
Americans also favored personalized glassware. Secret societies were among the
earliest to have their own glasses. Freemasons had them, their glasses first appearing in 1754. Individuals could also acquire glasses engraved with their initials or
coats of arms. One of the best examples of personalization is a wine goblet that
Stiegel engraved on the side of the bowl with the initials "W & E OLD" for his
daughter Elizabeth's marriage to William Old in 1773 (plate 16).[47]

Glasses came in a variety of sizes, and the range may have implied different
uses. Between 1667 and 1672, for instance, John Greene, a partner in the London glass-selling firm of Measey & Greene, specified to Venetian suppliers his
need of differently sized glasses for Claret, Sack, and beer. Ravenscroft produced
similarly named glasses, as well as brandy and covered "drinking or 'sullibub'"
glasses when he commenced production in 1683.[48] After the 1730s, when engraving turned fashionable, retailers advertised glasses engraved with apples and
apple leaves, grape bunches, vine leaves and tendrils, and barley and hops ears.

Whether these depictions designated contents—cider, wine, and ale or beer, respectively—is unclear, although it seems plausible. Yet they also appeared in ads for large and small glasses alike, so it is doubtful drinkers adhered to consistent usage; nothing independently confirms the supposition. Most English manufacturers made three sizes of wineglass at midcentury: large, intermediate, and small. American consumers' orders and glass-sellers' invoices confirm that the same state of affairs prevailed in American households before 1740: three sizes prevailed, and glasses for drinking particular wines were unusual.[49]

In the 1740s, glass manufacturers began fostering glass's role as a fashion item by introducing glasses "designed" for specific drinks. They were aided in this effort by wine exporters—who believed their product would be perceived as more refined if it required a special glass—glass importers—who were happy to sell more varieties of glassware—and consumers—who were attentive to competitive fashion. Dram glasses—small glasses for drinking cordials and spirituous liquors—made their first appearance in Salem, Boston, Hartford, New York, and Philadelphia newspaper advertisements in 1746. Glasses for ale were first advertised in 1761, for punch in 1766, for the mixed drink sling and the cordial orange water in 1771, for grog in 1781, for Port in 1787, and for porter in 1797. Other glasses received distinct names keyed to their shapes and sometimes drinks. Tall, cylindrical, decorated, and colored "broad mouth'd large drinking" glasses with knobbed or "prunted" stems called "rummers" (or *röemers* after similar Dutch and German vessels) were introduced as early as 1765. Small, thin flutes called "ratafias" were sold in the same decade to hold a cordial flavored with fruit kernels, which some consumers believed tasted best in just such a glass. Retailers advertised taller flutes in 1777. An aptly named "guzzler," shaped like a tumbler and capable of being gripped with two hands, was designed for hearty drinks like beer and cider and launched in 1785.[50]

For all its rising luxury status, Madeira enjoyed no special glass association in America or Britain. There is an invoice for "4 goblets labell'd Madeira" sold by Joseph Stansbury of Philadelphia in 1773, but this may simply indicate vessels engraved with the word "Madeira" at a purchaser's behest. Apart from this slip, no record has surfaced of manufacturers or retailers offering a Madeira glass before 1820. This is odd, since Madeira glasses had already been produced. In 1799, a firm in Madeira ordered and received from a London wholesaler at least six dozen glasses for holding Madeira. These may simply have been the small, specialized cordial glasses that had been around for a century, or a variant of the newer Port and Sherry glasses of the 1780s; alternatively, they may have been custom-made. What is most striking is that Madeirans learned of them from drinkers in India, where the wine was increasingly in vogue. In Bengal, as early as 1788, some twenty-two "Madeira glasses" were listed in one Briton's probated estate, and there are similar mentions in other estates each year thereafter, a telling example of the transimperial flow of goods and practices around the Anglophone world. Toward the end of the eighteenth century, the use of wine-specific glasses in India was communicated back to Madeira's exporters, who wrote to England for them and began training American visitors to drink with them.[51]

By 1815, probate inventories in America show increasing distinctions being made among glasses. Before 1775, the principal distinctions were among glasses for wine, cider, and beer. Of the 4,320 decedents' estates surveyed in 1700–74 and shown in table 11.2, 114 contained "wine glasses" and 50 "tumblers," while 25 had "drinking glasses" and another dozen ale, beer, cider, and porter glasses. Only a few bore other designations: 3 estates had "punch glasses"; 1 listed a "cup," 1 a "cordial glass," and 1 a "goblet." Eight listed "glassware." By the first quarter of the succeeding century, the variety had grown. Of the 1,430 estates surveyed, 134 had wineglasses (some marked "Mountain" or "Claret") and 57 tumblers (including "wine tumblers"), while 8 had "goblets," 8 "rummers," 4 "cups," 4 "cordial glasses," 3 "drinking glasses," and 1 "ale, beer, cider, or porter glass." Twenty-eight listed just "glassware," a less striking category before. All the same, it was unusual to find the array that a Charleston importer advertised as coming from London in 1803: quart and pint decanters (fluted and hooped); three types of half-pint goblets; five types of wineglasses (fluted and engraved diamond lace, Adelphi, London border and stars, Van Dyke, and stem engraved); neatly cut and plain cordial glasses; beer glasses; half-pint tumblers; and water carafes.[52] Not until the advent of steam-powered cutting toward the beginning of nineteenth century did extensive decorated glass "sets" or "services" become prevalent as they became affordable.[53]

Ultimately, the voluptuous range of multivalent glass sizes, types, and decorations helped communicate cosmopolitanism—connections to an increasingly elaborated, seemingly geographically boundless world. When an American hosted a Frenchman by serving Portuguese wine from English glasses, he sent a message that he and his guests belonged to the same refined world: same drink, same glass, same decanter, same toast, and same taste, even if certain particularities differed. Such was the message sent in 1803, when the brief French occupation of Louisiana came to a close. An array of small and large cut wineglasses made in Europe were raised in New Orleans in four toasts at the official banquet marking the territory's transfer to the States: the first toast, to the United States and Jefferson, was drunk with Madeira; the second, to Spain and Charles IV, with Malaga and Canary; the third, to France and Napoleon, with pink and white Champagne; and the last, to the "eternal happiness of Louisiana," with a wine of each drinker's choosing. In the cultures of the attendees' European origin and influence, the glasses, the wines, and the toasts constituted shared customs and meanings that structured a boundless community. By 1803, glassware, like the wine it contained, provided a beautiful and clear, if brittle, lens through which to refract an Atlantic wine culture and the spirit of universal cosmopolitanism.[54]

Four years on, several crates arrived at a mansion overlooking the Hudson River that States Dyckman was building north of Manhattan. The politician and landowner received the carved wood and gilt-metal eight-light chandelier representing Mercury, the god of commerce, holding a wine flask, which he had ordered from London, and he placed it in his front sitting room, along with new glass- and chinaware. Both with this costly, fashionable, and practical object, placed at the center of his house, in the center of the room designed for tippling and toasting, and with the newly purchased gilt glasses, also procured in London, Dyckman sent a message that he was wealthy and refined, a drinker and a connoisseur, individually astute and socially gregarious—in short, a cosmopolite. Whether he was talking to a relative, guest, or servant—indeed, whether or not he was even present—his chandelier, the glasses below it, and their alcoholic contents broadcast important messages, as did his cellar below, even as they performed less exalted, utilitarian services.

Drinkers throughout the early nineteenth-century Atlantic world would have understood the highly sensible and intricately wrought chandelier, the glasses, and the cellar, because they, too, used wine referents as metonyms signifying wealth and refinement, decorating their homes with emblems of wine and drinking, and furnishing their cellars and tables with wine paraphernalia. They did not need them to enjoy the liquor, of course. But by the dawn of the new century, connoisseurs had a range of storage and service props to choose among to exhibit their discernment. The need for proper words, mastery of skills, and correct behavior while drinking spilled over into the selection and use of ornamentation. The raison d'être of the market for wine—wine consumption—had changed the culture and meanings attached to common objects.[55]

Coda

⸺ •◆• ⸺

"The Pleasures of the Bottle"

Bottles and pipes lay on their sides in Dyckman's cellar and kitchen; coolers, corkscrews, monteiths, coasters, decanters, and glasses stood on his sideboard and table; and wines of a great variety passed his and his guests' lips, while high above the god of commerce hovered as if ready to pour wine down upon them. These material objects *en ensemble* conveyed various, often subtle messages. They provide mute witness to the proliferation of wine in the home, where sociability and nourishment were intertwined for the women and men who drank from Dyckman's cut glasses. They provide glimpses of discourses on science, medicine, and health, and the appropriations people made of objects to further their points in debates over refinement and gentility.

Drinking was also fun. Before the semiotic and discursive uses of wine, there was "the Gratification of Sense," as Rev. Matthew Heynes put it in 1701, "the Enjoyment of a Diverting and Use-full Good-fellowship" that is so evident in artwork painted and engraved in the ensuing 115 years. The "pleasure of sense" (in George Berkeley's apt phrase) experienced when drinking wine was seldom directly revealed in the largely nonconfessional records that have come down to us.[1] But it is easy to infer the personal experiences behind the assertions that wine made "the sage frolic, and the serious smile," causing them to be as "light as air," because, as Benjamin Franklin observed, "spirits rise" "as wine flows in." Wine gives "great pleasure," for "it animates a man, and enables him to bring out" what had hitherto been "repressed." Writers on both sides of the Atlantic agreed that alcohol elevated and exhilarated drinkers' spirits, and proceeded to explicate the consequences of risen spirits in detail. "Wine can clear the vapors of despair." "By making all our Spirits Debonair," it threw "off the Lees, the Sedement of Care." A "Fully flowing Bumper" disperses feelings of disappointment and despondency and drowns "all remembrance of Grief."[2]

Drinkers before 1815 needed neither doctors and dieticians nor social pundits and innovative enterprisers to understand the effects of alcohol, and appreciate "the pleasures of the bottle": the enjoyment, delight, gratification—and intoxication—that wine offered. Then, as now, a glass or a pint stimulated and relaxed people. William Shakespeare observed that wine "provokes, and unprovokes, makes him stand to, and not stand to"—"much drink may be said to be an equivocator"—and William Congreve noticed it made men "light as a Grasshopper." Medical minds such as Tobias Whitaker saw that wine "exhilarate[d] the spirits" and revived "sad souls." Most who described its effects wrote in a generalized Galenic vein, and their understanding of individual stimulation and group sociability was grounded in a discourse that considered wine as both a promoter and a marker of health. But whatever the particular discourse, people drank for pleasure, saw drinking as enjoyable, and offered drink to gratify others. While capable of being co-opted for a variety of agendas, drinking offered personal pleasure as much as anything else.[3]

As a refreshment that "invigorate[d] the mind," and, indeed, altered it, wine needed justification. A principal justification was that it induced loquacity: "wine (transparent thing!) no secret can retain." In some circles, looseness of tongue was deemed virtuous in the seventeenth century, because of its association with honesty: "Oh! That second Bottle is the Sincerest, Wisest, and most Impartial, Downright Friend we have; tells us truth of ourselves, and forces us to speak Truths of Others; banishes Flattery from our Tongues, and distrust from our Hearts; sets us above the mean Policy of Court Prudence; which makes us lie to one another all Day, for fear of being betrayed by one another at Night. And . . . the errantest Villain breathing, is honest as long as that Bottle lives." The association between garrulity and truth persisted—as strong in eighteenth-century America as in seventeenth-century England. George Washington reported that the French officers "dos'd themselves pretty plentifully" with wine when he met them in the backwoods of western Pennsylvania in 1753. This "soon banish'd the restraint which at first appear'd in their Conversation & gave license to their Tongues to reveal their Sentiments more freely." Echoing earlier ideas about drink while asserting the primacy of his species, the Virginia lawyer St. George Tucker penned a doggerel asserting wine to be "the essence of truth":

> I have heard from my youth,
> That in wine there is truth:
> And let him who the maxim disputes
> Just put by his glass,
> And go feed upon grass,
> And drink puddle water with brutes.[4]

Another justification of wine-induced loquacity focused not on honesty but on the eloquence in declamation and conversation it produced. Those engaging in toasting (although perhaps not all sober onlookers) agreed with the ancient philosophers who asked "what man is not eloquent in's drink?" At least when drunk in moderation, wine was held to "actuate and quicken" wit. The American poet Francis Hopkinson acknowledged the ubiquity of this view when asking in 1792:

> Who cannot make his likeness fit,
> Must take a glass to help his wit,
> Because, 'tis said, Madeira wine
> Will sharpen wit, or make it shine,
> Just like a shaving in a blaze, or
> A hone or strap, will shet a razor.[5]

Emergent in the eighteenth century was an emphasis on pleasures of the imagination that flowed from the bottle, wine's creative and intellective effects. Taking a page out of Rabelais's *Gargantua* ("When I drink, I think; and when I think, I drink") and understanding that one might "mistake words for thoughts," men of letters began to valorize control over words and conversations while drinking, as well as alcohol-induced intellection. They began by stating the obvious: "Wine throws a Man out of himself, and infuses Qualities into the Mind which she is a Stranger to in her sober Moments." The "Person you converse with, after the third Bottle, is not the same Man who at first sat down at Table with you." The new qualities could be bad, of course, but they could also be eloquent and wise. Wine furnished "fancy with wings," and "Without it we ne'er should have had/ Philosophers, poets or kings." Drinking did "not *improve* our Faculties," Franklin observed in his hair-splitting way, "but it enables us to *use* them." Perhaps this line of thought was best caught by Georg Lichtenberg, who, in his end-of-the-eighteenth-century *Reflections*, noted that "in certain studies there is no harm in doing one's thinking and writing while slightly drunk, and then revising one's work in cold blood": "the stimulus of wine" was seen as "favorable to the play of invention, and to fluency of expression."[6]

Underscoring wine's pleasurability was a widening of wine sociability over the course of the eighteenth century, with a new emphasis on group drinking. Drinking wine was already established as a social phenomenon. Drinkers should drink with others (if in public, other men), it was felt, not alone. Thus, Shakespeare's Brutus offers Cassius "a bowl of wine" with the promise to "bury all unkindness." "A friend, and a Bottle" was all John Oldham's "design" in 1680, knowing full well that one "that's top-full of Wine" had "no room for Treason" (something very much on English minds that season). As the seventeenth century turned, observers increasingly called on wine as a source of "sudden friendship." Wine became part of a "sign system" for displaying genteel behavior within a group. Drinkers began appreciating their consumption as a mechanism for engendering sociability, and a mark of it. Enjoying the pleasure of "A Friend" became one of the "good reasons why" people "should drink" wine. Two bottles markedly "brighten'd the chain of friendship"; with "some wine and cold provisions," men formed "good company." Characters in Frederick Reynolds's *Management* (1799) and James Kenney's *Turn Out!* (1812)—two plays with wide American audiences—crowned their friendship with bottles of Madeira, as did real-life actors on America's revolutionary stage—Benjamin Franklin, George Washington, John Adams, and Thomas Jefferson.[7]

Wine drinkers were bombarded with messages about its sociability in popular engravings. Adorning the cover of a cheap American novel published in Philadelphia in 1800, "Two Wealthy Farmers" sit around a table and a bottle of wine (figure Coda.1). Some fifteen years later, four smiling blades do the same in a London publication, gathering before a spread of fruit and a decanter of wine in the wee hours of the morning; the center of their attention is a gentleman who, with a hand on the decanter and sporting a tiepin shaped like a wine bottle, serenades them on the benefits of drinking five bottles apiece (figure Coda.2). Such images, and a mountain of similar evidence, show that early modern men and women thought that sharing drink was part of a good time with others.

Wine and wine drinking were so closely associated with pleasurable socializing that they were appropriated to provide the gloss of friendship and sociality on political and commercial occasions.[8] Such was the case in 1724, when the governor of Pennsylvania, Sir William Keith, and Colonel French of Newcastle proposed—over "some excellent Madera" at a tavern on Third Street—that Benjamin Franklin set up a press in Philadelphia and take on printing "the public business." Business was conducted over wine in the formal environment of an official's hall, the relaxed surroundings of a tavern, and the frolic and mayhem of outdoor streets and gardens.[9] Wine sealed commercial agreements and signaled the resolution of legal disputes.[10] It bound communal ties and mended broken ones. As a symbol, it transcended public and private arenas and popular and elite differences, and accentuated people's interdependence.[11]

Wine also became an important complement to the work of associations that arose in the late seventeenth century and flourished in the eighteenth. Clubs, societies, salons, cafes, literary, scientific, and artistic academies, and reading, debating, and lecture groups emerged in the decades after the Restoration, in part because they provided alternatives to traditional family, church, town, and court

Figure Coda.1. *The Two Wealthy Farmers*, by an unknown artist, c. 1800.
Source: *The Two Wealthy Farmers* (Philadelphia, 1800), cover. Courtesy of
The Historical Society of Pennsylvania, Philadelphia.

institutions. As they gained prominence, "sociability" itself acquired connotations of both intra- and interassociational exchange. Drinking wine encouraged
members of associations to live and work happily and harmoniously together.[12]
The pretext of associational meetings was instruction, conversation, and debate,
but what lubricated nearly all of them was the delight of drinking, whose highly
ritualized acme was the toast. This is what Dr. Alexander Hamilton tried to convey in his account of Annapolis's Tuesday Club, when remarking that "the spirit
of wine and brandy, of rum, whisky and such liquors . . . very often" gave "a philip"
to members' spirits. Alcohol was "always used in those assemblies called Clubs"
when toasting; "when it first arises to the Alembic of the head," he explained
in bastardized Galenic language, "it surprisingly produces good humor, makes
the dumb to talk, the morose good natured and merry, the mistuned musical, the
enimy a friend." Particularly important to such associational drinking were the
"democratical tendencies" of such groups. When it whet wit and imparted "a
pleasant flavor to discourse," wine drinking brought men together—such as land-

Figure Coda.2. *Irish Hospitality*, by Isaac Cruickshank, 1815.
Source: Courtesy of The British Museum — Department of Prints and
Drawings. © Copyright the Trustees of The British Museum.

lord and tenant — who for reasons of blood or rank might not ordinarily have
shared the same stage.[13]

It is doubtful that drinking together eroded the orders of society, however, as
recent scholars have suggested. In France, where the word *sociability* was coined,
it connoted "egalitarian interaction among individuals with different corporate
standing." While it was "a mode of exchange" that was "free of the ritualistic constraints of corporate hierarchy," there was little that was radical or democratic in
either the sites or the practices of sociability. It was the same in England. Charles
Darby could lampoon clubs for their inattention to hierarchies, indeed for their
encouragement of faux leveling, and incur no wrath in 1680: "Cups reconcile
Degrees, and Natures too;/He Noblest is, who can in Drink out-do." Almost a
century later, the comte d'Estaing, recoiling at the high degree of familiarity
expressed when Americans drank together, could comment quite smugly on the
nonhierarchical nature of group drinking: "One becomes accustomed to using
a knife as a spoon, doing without napkins, drinking to the health of ten persons
with each drop one swallows, quenching one's thirst, . . . keeping the most somber
table in the world, eating nothing more for the next three hours, and drinking
from the same enormous goblet from which many have just wet their uninviting
lips." But for all the freedom of club and association ways, d'Estaing realized,

little changed outside their doors and after their meetings. Men and women, to take another example, might drink sociably together, as they did in Boston's Sans-Souci Club and Orchestra, but gender equality did not result.[14]

Gifts of wine also drew on the sociable and pleasurable connotations of wine and drinking. Just as one could drink wine with others to gratify oneself and them, one could also give wine to them and achieve much the same effect, both near and far. Indeed, such presents, when spanning great distances, increasingly celebrated a global interdependence of people and combined elements of work and play, exchange and enjoyment, and public and private. Gifts of alcohol, especially gifts of wine, served as emblems of patronage-clientage and a more disinterested pleasure. By 1678, New Yorkers were in the habit of sending a bottle or two of wine, some glasses, and a loaf of sugar as gifts to friends. Charleston men sent bottles of good wine to women they courted in the 1740s. The ambitious Philadelphia merchant Daniel Roberdeau, who wanted "to present a particular friend of note in London" with a mark of his esteem in 1764, wrote to a Portuguese wine firm for "a quarter cask of Madeira . . . without any regard to price" and the very best the island afforded, much as the Jewish merchants Aaron Lopez and Jacob Rodriguez Rivera gave presents of Port to Frederick Smyth and Daniel Horsmanden in 1773 when the latter—two judges—visited Lopez and Rivera's Newport. Drawing on wine his family had kept in its cellars for years, Thomas Jefferson shipped his former science professor at the College of William and Mary thirty-six bottles of Madeira in 1775. War did nothing to dampen the flow of such civilities. General Chastellux sent General Washington a cask of Claret as a token of his esteem, which the latter added to his growing store of wine presents. The giving of wine went on and on. Throughout it, "pleasure in the gift," as Jacques Godbout clarifies, was "in fact crucial to the gift." "It is not an added ingredient. It is tied to freedom, it is proof that there is no constraint, it is confirmation of a social bond." A gift of wine was always more than mere mercantile or social exchange, marked by the creation of debt, equivalent repayment, and introduction of counterdebt. Pleasure ensued for both donor and recipient. By the end of the eighteenth century, because of the remarkable improvements in transport, "presents of wine" had become the "usual thing to send" to those across the seas to whom "you wished to show a mark of gratitude" or respect, but whom, for reasons of geography, you did not know all that well.[15]

Giving wine whose status had been burnished as a luxury—something one could do by the late eighteenth century—was a premier mark of Atlantic cosmopolitanism. It showed the recipient that he or she was an object worthy of respect and deserving of (and, by implication, able to experience and appreciate) pleasure. It displayed the giver as a person of discernment, means, and bonhomie.

With respect to the wider world of Atlantic commerce and society, giving wine in part built, deployed, or maintained exchange networks. When Henry Hill in Philadelphia sensed a connection was possible or a market was opening, he sent a bottle of wine to a backcountry storekeeper. When Robert Lenox in New York feared a customer was in danger of bolting to another distributor, he sent some Madeira. When Richard Brush in Boston sought to procure the help of a London firm in pursuing a transatlantic insurance claim, he, too, sent a bottle. Wine gifts extended and perpetuated exchange relationships. Giving wine, paradoxically, established rank and hierarchy even as it affirmed social bonds and solidarity. "It helped to order and give meaning to experience by setting" the gifts and the parties apart. Hill could afford to give the gift, for instance, while the storekeeper could not. Wine gifts communicated to recipients like him "what they should expect" of givers like Hill, Lenox, and Brush: attentiveness, civility, and the desire to please and, of course, be pleased in return. In this way, they reinforced commercial and social expectations.[16]

When George Washington learned that his niece had given over fifty-six bottles of Madeira as presents one year, he ordered a halt to such munificence; in future, she was to give them only to "particular and intimate acquaintances," "some of the most respectable foreigners," and "persons of some distinction." The duty upon wine made Madeira "one of the most expensive liquors"—its price could be 25 percent higher than that for the same amount of Claret. But Washington did not stop giving or drinking. He urged his niece to offer his friends and guests Claret, not Madeira, "*unless* it be on extraordinary occasions," when pleasing the guest surpassed pleasing the host.[17]

Washington's wine giving was an act of hospitality and a mark of refinement, much as the alcohol was also a mechanism for health and well-being—indeed, it lay near to him when he was on his deathbed as medicine, painkiller, or both. It was also part of his everyday life, worked into its fabric, both painful and pleasurable. He was eager to see that Mount Vernon was "more than usually well stocked with ["remarkably fine"] Madeira," and, while his "manner of living" was "plain," or so he said, "a glass of wine and a bit of mutton are always ready." It was said he was "a reserved man [but he] became pleasant, free and sociable at dinner" with a glass of wine in his hand. Enjoyment and contentment were the guiding lights of his drinking, by himself and with visitors, and they made his home, he informed his aging mother, "a well-resorted tavern."[18]

Conclusion

"IF BACCHUS, NOT NEPTUN, WERE GOD OF THE SEA"

Oceans of Wine would have been a different book had it taken the popular perspective that social and economic transformations of the early modern Atlantic world can be understood in terms of geography, climate, technology, and state policy. In such a frame, wine production, distribution, and consumption are determined by soil, climate, and insect regimes, the Atlantic trade winds and currents, the transit times of ships and the storage conditions in their holds, the prodigious distances across trackless seas and rudimentary routes to inland markets in the Americas, the alliances between England and Portugal and their wars with France and Spain, and the Byzantine complex of laws governing colonies. Here, natural and agricultural opportunities drew settlers where they made a living sending cod, fur, grain, rice, and sugar back to consumers in Europe. And, here again, the climates of the Western Hemisphere, the oceanic winds and currents, and the soil of the Wine Islands created an opportunity for growers in Madeira to supply wine to immigrants and settlers across the Atlantic craving provisions and manufactures. Moreover, trade agreements between England and Portugal, as well as the imperatives of Portuguese overseas commerce, made Anglo-America and British India attractive destinations for Madeira's produce. A book that analyzed the period from 1640 to 1815 thus could be most informative; it would certainly be shorter.

But *Oceans of Wine* is not that book. Its presupposition—and the approach to history it embodies—is that geography, climate, technology, and state policy constituted the critical context in which growers at the Achada or Bello Monte, distributors in Funchal, Philadelphia, and Cincinnati, and drinkers on Barbados plantations and in Boston townhouses lived, worked, and consumed. But this context offers only partial insight into the participants' lives, labors, behaviors, and attitudes: it does not show how people responded to the opportunities, challenges, and constraints they faced in the workaday world; it does not uncover the intricate webs of cooperation and conflict they spun in their dealings with each other; it does not reveal the elaborate and evolving institutions they built, wittingly and unwittingly; and it is silent on the meanings they elaborated and reelaborated in dialogue with others as they built and reinforced their projects. It leaves out, in short, the principal concern of *Oceans of Wine*: the connections among real people—wine producers, distributors, and consumers—and the institutions they developed and managed over a 175-year period.[1]

The contacts and links between individual participants enhanced organizational sophistication in each locale of activity, while encouraging and developing interactions between these disparate sites. It all began as a way for the islanders to cope with the evaluation of their principal crop, sugar. Early in the seventeenth century, under pressure from Brazilian and, later, Caribbean competition, Madeirans began converting land from sugarcane cultivation to grapevine agriculture. By midcentury, soon after the Braganzas reclaimed the Portuguese Crown, exports of wine were outstripping exports of sugar. The alliance between the English and Portuguese monarchs opened Madeira's trade to England's subjects, when in 1663 Parliament passed the Navigation Act allowing wine from Madeira and the Azores to pass to the Anglo-American colonies free of Crown duty. In response, traders from England began taking up residence on the island in the last half of the seventeenth century, bringing ambition and some capital with them. But their principal asset was Atlantic-wide networks of family, ethnic relations, coreligionists, and friends on whom they drew for their customers. The evolution of the Atlantic distribution of Madeira wine over the eighteenth century was the result. Originally, wine suppliers on the island sold to ship captains and others en route between Europe and the New World, but then found they could sell wine for personal consumption as well as resale to their contacts in the destination ports. These customers offered the Madeira vintners a steadier and larger, albeit more discriminating, market. Thus began ongoing conversations between consumers and the Madeira exporters that would transform the trade. The exporters worked more closely with their suppliers of grapes, encouraging them to plant more vines and offer more varieties, while they themselves created blends to satisfy the particularities of taste in various destinations. In European America, agricultural experimenters had failed to create their own wine industry, but the shipments arriving in wooden barrels and casks from Madeira, as well as Bordeaux, Lisbon, Oporto, the Azores, Jerez, and the Canaries, provided drinkers with wine at affordable prices, and profits for the tavern keepers who served them. Meanwhile, with glass prices falling, new styles of bottles and decanters and innovations like Ravenscroft's flint glasses encouraged greater differentiation among drinks and drinkers.

Shipping and exporting accelerated between the 1720s and the 1810s, with exports reaching an all-time high during the Napoleonic Wars. Meanwhile, throughout the eighteenth century, new expatriates were arriving in Madeira to staff the exporters' trading houses. They came in especially large numbers during the 1740s and after the Seven Years' War, many of them Americans escaping hard times at home as well as Scots who had supported the Pretender. Their conversations and interactions with Anglo-American importers brought new insights and spawned innovation. Exporters learned, for example, that American consumers preferred wine that had been heated and agitated in the holds of ships—the longer the voyage, the better—thus prompting them to send their wine from Madeira as far as India and even China before shipping it to Charleston and Philadelphia, an expensive and time-consuming proposition resolved through innovation technology whereby Madeira merchants developed capability of fortifying, heating, and agitating the wine before it left their warehouses. Trade and shipping embargoes during the American Revolution blocked wine imports into the rebellious colonies and resulted in growing inventories of wine in the exporters' warehouses. But this also gave the "stock" a chance to mature, and, when shipments resumed after the war, consumers found they preferred the aged wine and requested more of it. So by the early nineteenth century, innovation, experimentation, and even happenstance had turned Madeira from the mediocre table wine it had been a century before into a refined manufactured product.

The merchants working with each other on either side of the Atlantic also developed innovative business methods. More local competition motivated Madeira exporters to build networks of loyal and reliable customers, while the Seven Years' War introduced new clienteles in India and the Americas. To meet these demands, the Madeira firms adopted more regular and consistent business methods, developed enduring relationships with the customers, and cultivated their networks more assiduously. They sent partners to visit markets, where they established resident agents to manage customer relationships more closely, a task made all the more challenging by the rise of variegated retail environments in those markets. They instructed their buyers on "improving" the wine and tailoring it to particular tastes, and they differentiated the grades of wine for drinkers with fatter wallets who wanted to distinguish themselves. Marketing changes, technological innovations, and inventories of aged wine required capital, to get which the exporters increased the size of their partnerships, and this, of course, required more structured organizational forms and formal accounting methods.

Wine importing in the seventeenth century was largely episodic and opportunistic, but by the eighteenth century, a few traders in the British American port cities employed more systematic import-export strategies. They invested in American produce—furs, fish, grain, tobacco, rice, and sugar—for export to Britain and Europe while importing manufactured goods and certain foodstuffs. They cultivated counterpart networks in the ports and capitals of Europe, which secured good prices for American commodities and provided products that were in demand in places like Boston, Philadelphia, Charleston, and Kingston. Wine was one of the important commodities on the westbound leg of the trade. The importers constructed networks to build supplier and customer bases, just like the Madeira exporters. They cultivated tavern-and storekeepers who stocked wine, invited them to sample the product, and explained the fine points of preparing, serving, and drinking it, and they provided credit. They also visited customers in their places of business, as did the Madeira exporters.

A vigorous market emerged among wholesalers and retailers for trading wine. Although some tavern-and storekeepers only bought wine to sell to drinkers, a group of merchants, middlemen, and retailers began trading wine with each other, and a number of them also supplied taverns and stores in their city's hinterland. Some, too, maintained taverns or stores there, where they served their own customers. These retailer-traders used the trading network to replenish their stocks, while their sales restocked the inventories of competitor-colleagues. Specialized brokers emerged and, although they imported from time to time, their stock in trade was knowing who had wine and who needed it. These brokers maintained connections with retailers in case they needed wine or had excesses to sell; they also kept abreast of current wine prices, changes in supply from the wine-growing regions, and new trends in drinking habits.

Until the Seven Years' War, most people bought their wine in taverns, either drinking it there or taking it home, but changes afoot in consumption patterns even before the war accelerated after it, probably due to mid-eighteenth-century improvements in glassmaking technology. The availability of sturdy and inexpensive glass containers encouraged more stores to sell wine. The last two-thirds of the eighteenth century saw an expansion and elaboration of retailing, as more and more stores stocked their selves with an increasing variety of goods. Storekeepers saw opportunities in differentiating themselves from their competitors—tapping into their existing networks and creating new ones for their wine trade. They expanded their backcountry market, introduced glass windows into their storefronts and display cases inside, and began specializing in particular products. These specialty stores could present to the best advantage the goods themselves, as well as the storekeeper's expertise.

Wine and spirits became central to domestic hospitality offered by the men and women who patronized American stores and taverns. During the seventeenth century, alcohol was used in the home for cooking, dining, socializing, doctoring, and cleaning. Over the course of the eighteenth century, wine grew commonplace, and people refined its use, taste, and status, creating a discourse for the beverage and an ever more complex procedure for drinking it. For Americans, the wines that came from Europe and the conversations and practices about their consumption internationalized diet and behavior. Scientists, doctors, and pundits debated its healthfulness at least from the 1720s, while drinkers and aesthetes drew upon the developing scientific and health literature to focus on gentility, making certain wines and their uses markers of refinement. A specialized language developed to describe wine, physical deportment in displaying and toasting with it, use of a proliferating array of paraphernalia—cellars, bins, screws, decanters, coasters, mats, and properly sized glasses. By 1750, wine and its accoutrements marked wealth and knowledge, joined connoisseurship and class. And with declining prices of bottles and glasses, refinement became accessible to those who could not have afforded it a century before. Even so, not everyone could drink the best Malvasia or London Particular grades, nor in the appropriate manner. Wine by the time of President Madison had become a greater marker of wealth than in John Winthrop's America.

Oceans of Wine captures these developments in a unified study of production, distribution, and consumption that features ever-increasing organization and integration, while, not surprisingly, raising a number of questions. Was, for instance, the Madeira complex and market for wine driven by demand or supply—by citizen or state? Did the individual matter more in building commercial life, or was it the apparatus of government—not only the laws and their enforcement but also less directly via immigration and settlement schemes—that caused populations to spread and flourish? Questions like these about the period 1640–1815 and its place in history address the ultimate source of early modern Atlantic dynamism, and although this work privileges the role of the individual, it certainly acknowledges the importance of the state in terms of context. Moreover, such a dichotomy, while having vexed early modern historians for decades, may actually be miscast and ultimately inapposite; who would argue for a single, ultimate source of vitality in political or economic life that can be identified once and for all? Consumer demand and state power are, of course, extremely important. But so, too, are unintended or unanticipated population bursts and declines, and site-specific practices in information exchange, financing, trade, and shipping, as well as local tastes and whims. In a self-organized system such as evolved in the early modern Atlantic economy, components—big and small, official and unofficial—fed on each other all the time, reinforcing, restricting, directing, and modifying themselves. Historians need to consider the relationships between the components rather than constructing chimerical hierarchies. The most interesting questions ask how the components fit together, and how individuals react to, take advantage of, or are stymied by their relationships as citizens and subjects of the early Atlantic world of wine.

But what of these relationships? Looking at them reveals key traits common to the larger Atlantic community. First of all, connections and experiences were inherently decentralized, with the peripheries of the wine trade often as important as the centers, or more so. Decision making and implementation occurred closer to the action than previously acknowledged. Government officials and policy makers in London, Lisbon, Philadelphia, and Bahia impinged only indirectly on the Hills, Searles, Guiomars, Teles Menezeses, Freys, and Allens of this story, and similarly these traders had limited influence on local scenes and players further out on the margins of the wine-trade network. Conversation and personal contact shaped relationships among agents; and they all had the power of choosing to participate in a transaction, a relationship, or a network, or of declining to do so if it did not meet their needs. In an empire, a trade, even a firm, management had to be flexible, critical information had to be shared, control had to be dispersed, and authority had to be delegated, ad hoc, throughout the communities, groups, and individuals positioned across the network and to the farthest reaches of the Atlantic world.

The dispersed actors, of course, were not isolated; they belonged to networks that they had constructed or inherited and that provided linkages and integration across economic sectors and imperial geographies. Most significant was the work of distributors, to whom I pay considerable attention. In order to exchange goods, merchants built interimperial networks from their family, neighborhood, and friendship connections, their oceanic travels, and their opportunistic alliances and joint ventures whose genesis could often be traced to nothing more than proximity, serendipity, or happenstance. Their strategies allowed them to marshal dispersed resources and mitigate the swings in supply and demand, accommodate the fickleness of consumers, and cope with the unreliability of distributors. Their commercial, informational, and social networks operated on two levels: externally, they provided connections to the broad constituency of members and wide range of markets; internally, they comprised groups and markets unto themselves. Networks allowed members to preserve and archive information specific to any one place, while drawing on a deep well of information about consumers' tastes, the successes and failures of other merchants, the prosecution or overlooking of infractions of commercial laws, and the like, accumulated from throughout the dispersed catchment area of the wine business.

Networks were where groups resolved conflicts, where uncooperative, shoddy, or failing suppliers were dealt with, where hostile competitors were confronted, and where political and economic adversity and reversals were faced. Networks offered collective solutions to market failures resulting from the information and transaction costs of long-distance trade and premodern technology. Rather than states or polities taking the lead in such circumstances, responses grew out of the contacts among agents working and living within the contexts shaped by exogenous conditions (geography, climate, technology, and state policy) in situ, so to speak, where the business of wine operated.[2]

This highly networked world was also "self-organized." This dimension emphasizes the creative and opportunistic responses of individuals to the world they lived in, and the structures, organizations, institutions, and ideas they developed and inhabited in concert with others that helped them loosen constraints and seize opportunities. Their trade routes, forts, and towns, their business and social organizations, their credit and product-sharing arrangements, their ideas and worldviews emerged as they navigated the ocean of wine. Over the course of the period, they refined and differentiated their product, developed maritime, financial, and storage institutions, increased the scale and complexity of their trading organizations, enhanced their capital base—and, as a result, Madeira wine became increasingly incorporated into an elaborate dance of sociability and status. These events need not have happened the way they did; they were not foreordained by state policy, agricultural productivity, or wind direction. Preconditions mattered less than individual actions and initiatives, often taken at the spur of the moment or in response to an immediate exigency. As a result, the emerging communities and institutions exhibited unpredictability, spontaneity, and personality even as they produced a surprisingly well-ordered system.

These traits were integral to the Madeira wine complex but not unique to it. The trade is in many ways representative of how Atlantic trades were organized and how institutions grew up around them in the years between 1640 and 1815. With the exceptions of the traffic in slaves, sugar and its byproducts, tobacco, and fur, few trades have been studied in sufficient detail to be conclusive, yet archival material documenting other commodities such as medicines, spices, ceramics, iron wares, and cloth goods certainly suggests strongly that they generated markets, trades, and "complexes" that were decentralized and interdependent across empires. Here, too, producers, traders, and consumers built and used conversational and discursive networks to buy, to sell, and in a myriad other ways to make sense of what they were doing. The evolution of the Atlantic economy and society thus can usefully be thought of as a self-organizing system. The characteristics of the Madeira system are replicated wherever the behavior of traders themselves, rather than the dictates of a monopoly agent, whether state or private, initiated changes in the features of a trade. Each trade, of course, will respond to circumstances specific to the commodity. The state may play a lesser or greater role, and the weight of metropolitan/peripheral influences may shift somewhat. Nevertheless, and absent extensive comparisons between Madeira and other commodities that would have obstructed the flow of present narrative, and with detailed analysis of these other markets still to be completed, the general outline that has emerged from the study of Madeira shows every sign of holding true elsewhere.[3]

A study of connections raises one final question: Were the peoples of the early modern "Trans-Atlantick region" connected? Were they integrated by trade and unified by common commercial and social ideals hammered out while consuming the same commodities in similar public spaces around the ocean rim?[4]

At first glance, the early modern Atlantic world appears a Babel. The peoples of the states and regions facing the ocean were divided by language, customs, culture, and ideas, their public spaces were arenas of dispute, and the important links that could have been forged between them constantly were lost in translation. Local environments, events, and personalities distorted what people heard and made communication difficult if not impossible. The ideas of England's "Country" political writers swirled about the heads and coffeehouses of America's revolutionaries, but to the horror of the authors back across the Atlantic the colonists refracted the ideas through the lens of recent actions of the Ministry and Parliament, their own historical experiences, and readings of old and current texts, and drew very different conclusions.[5] José Alonso Ortiz, the Spanish translator of Adam Smith's *The Wealth of Nations*, added to the text subjects he thought the Scottish economist "forgot" to discuss. The German bourgeoisie embraced the ideals of the American Revolution and lauded Americans for championing such precepts, but since their idea of liberty was economic and religious, rather than political, the Germans drew on American ideas only to support civic and legal equality for the bourgeoisie vis-à-vis the nobility. Every reader interprets his or her own text.[6]

A contrasting "bridge rather than a barrier" scenario, however, holds that commercially integrated areas were tied together by similar institutions, styles, laws, and ideas. The British sugar complex offers the most prominent example. The "sweet malefactor" cultivated in England's Caribbean colonies by slave labor wrenched from Africa and production technology derived from Brazil was financed and distributed by metropolitan bankers and merchants and consumed throughout Europe and America. When distilled into rum, sugar molasses tied Native Americans into the Atlantic commercial world. Sugar bound together the lives of people around the ocean between 1650 and 1800, transforming their diets and their tastes.

Cohesion derived from more than commodities. Collaboration among Atlantic peoples, for example, resulted in 1772 in the founding of Kew Gardens as a royal horticultural laboratory that through the 1780s and 1790s linked imperial agricultural improvement projects throughout the British Empire, bringing a farrago of plants and animals to the outskirts of London, where they were cultivated, nurtured, and doctored, tested for their dietary and commercial possibilities. They were then exported to English-speaking territories in Europe, Africa, Asia, and America, accompanied by gardeners and experts in animal husbandry who advised, observed, and reported back. Such a project could not succeed, however, without exchange; scientific knowledge about the properties of the flora and fauna grew, and links of all sorts—dietary and agronomic, even aromatic and visual—developed among the participants, much as was the case with sugar.[7]

Bridge, then, or barrier? The 175 years between 1640 and 1815 stand halfway between the establishment of connections between the Atlantic rim's four continents and today. During this time, people at continental remove from each other necessarily lived and worked with substantial degrees of independence, separated by distances and the vagaries of the era's still-evolving transportation and communications technologies. Social and political control were subject to misunderstanding and delay, and so to interpretation and modification. But these people's worlds were not isolated, unconnected, or autarkic. In fact, commodities, institutions, and habits organized them into something that it makes sense to call an "Atlantic world," which integrated lives and projects across geographical and political boundaries. The stories of Madeira elucidate these interconnections: within the emerging and evolving interimperial transatlantic markets for it; between the men and women who built and managed the markets; and among the consumers who quenched their thirsts with the beverage while giving meaning and cultural forms to its consumption in the years between the restoration of the Portuguese Crown and the fall of Napoleon. To understand this period requires attention to the communion and commonality created by these disparate yet linked activities, for they defined the period and gave meaning to the entire Atlantic region and the lives of the people within it.

What legacy did economic and social connections bequeath? An epochal leap forward in organization transformed the eighteenth-century Atlantic world. The complexity of transoceanic trade surpassed intra-European, Baltic, and Mediterranean trade because distances were greater, increasing travel times. Meanwhile, communications lagged, financial investments took longer to realize returns, and shipping risks multiplied. Maintaining cultural continuity across the Atlantic created additional challenges, felt more acutely by the migrating settlers than the friends and kin they left behind. But the productivity of the Americas justified persevering in the face of crippling problems and fueled the desire to find ways to mitigate them by inventors, merchants, and enterprising folk of all sorts.[8] Some improvements were technological. Most important among these were larger and faster ships, but other such changes were also introduced, as in the betterment of food and wine and their packaging, and these are increasingly studied by scholars.[9] Organizational changes, however, have been less appreciated, even though they are no less important. Madeira's exporters built networks that incorporated the islanders who produced the unfermented grape juice, or must, the continental Europeans who supplied barrels and bottles, and the Americans who had commodities to trade for wine and who drank it. The exporters started by selling wine to ship captains in Funchal before making a transition that involved consigning wine to agents residing nearer the customers, then to establishing partners in the consuming countries who managed sales and delivery. Importers, wholesalers, and retailers in Anglo-America began by selling wine in their cities but then expanded to riding a circuit beyond the cities, where they found new markets and clienteles before setting up their own stores in the near backcountry and farther hinterland. As their customer base expanded, the merchants became keen supporters and patrons of the services provided by the entrepreneurs who built canals and roads to the west and supplied regular post and packet services inland and across the Atlantic. Traders on both sides of the ocean overcame the difficulty of making secure payments by availing themselves of the services of a new group of metropolis-based financiers who worked on commission services and extended credit.

Better-integrated trade organization translated into more vigorous wine distribution and marketing that reached more consumers and increased the variety of products available to them: exporters in Madeira began shipping wine of different grades and vintages; importers in Anglo-America polled their customers to make sure they were importing the optimal selections of wines for the market they served; retailers and tavern keepers expanded from the basic choices of wine, cider, or rum, each in only one variety, that had previously been the norm. Retailers upgraded their premises and display techniques and, by the end of the eighteenth century, some had begun dealing only in wine and the accoutrements connected to its consumption. By 1815, Philadelphia had nearly a hundred such specialist retailers who stocked a variety of wines, an array of mixers, and appropriate paraphernalia. Their clientele could sample the wares, take advantage of competitive deals, and even treat themselves to tutorials in drink connoisseurship. Remarkably, Cincinnati, still a backcountry town, had almost a dozen such operations.

Coordinating longer voyages that were transporting heavier cargos, stationing partners and agents in foreign ports, maintaining variegated inventories of products, and constructing ever more elaborate premises for marketing and consumption required larger, more intricate and complex enterprises. But difficulties of administration and control accompanied such complexity, pressuring partners to innovate in the ways they organized their firms. Some, such as Newton & Gordon, introduced an additional intermediate layer of supra-agents in America, between the next level of agents and their distributors and customers, who managed and coordinated the outreach to America. Similarly motivated, the Searles had a partner in residence at every center of consumer activity for their wine. Meanwhile, in retailing, Randle and John Mitchell transformed their retailing activities with the invention of a system of franchise stores that extended their custom and managed their accounts. The Mitchells' stores divided labor and ownership between the Mitchells and the storekeeper, thus establishing a new combination of roles. Like nearly all the other trends, the Mitchells' initiative accelerated rapidly after the Seven Years' War.

Larger enterprises and more complicated organizations required more capital. Participating in the wine business took more resources by 1815 than it had a century before. Prior to the 1740s, Madeira enterprises were usually partnerships between two kin-related merchants, both of whom resided on the island. By the last third of the century, successful export firms had taken on more partners, many of whom were neither related nor Madeira residents, but who could provide the infusions of capital required to maintain inventories and market products. The capitalization of midsized firms tripled, while that of large-sized firms grew ten- to twentyfold. A similar scenario unfolded in America: as the eighteenth century advanced, it became necessary for importers, wholesalers, and even some retailers to secure more partners with different backgrounds and contacts in order to access larger amounts of capital. By 1815, even country storekeepers and tavern keepers had silent partners who helped defray start-up costs and sustain operations.

This increase in firm and market organization broadened consumer choice. By 1800, drinkers selected from a wide variety of beverages, and by their choices distinguished themselves and displayed their attitudes toward health, their social solidarity, their refinement and cosmopolitanism, or their plainspokenness and patriotism. Thomas Allen's regular tavern patrons after the American Revolution could pick from twice as many wines as had been on offer in the colonial era, with quality and price increasingly differentiating their selections. Patrons also confronted a bewildering and often contradictory menu of prescriptions for using wine to treat physical and mental ailments. Meanwhile, proponents of home-brewed drinks wanted consumers to believe that their libations provided satisfactory alternatives to imported wine as markers of wealth and refinement, while proponents of the republican experiment chided wine drinkers for indulging in a foreign luxury product that they considered deleterious to the nation's independence. Still, American men and women favored imported wines, particularly high-priced grades, connecting consumption of these products to the reality of their gentility and refinement or their aspirations to such, ordered "correct" varietals and in time "approved" brands, like "Hill's," which they drank from the variously sized wineglasses they had purchased and that were engraved with "something emblematical of their patriotic principles," such as American eagles, or indicative of their status and success, like engraved coats of arms or initials.[10]

The Atlantic wine market continued to evolve through the nineteenth century and was marked by the age's overarching application of mechanical power in production and the globalization of markets. But the organizational mechanisms that had earlier transformed the industry also directed these nineteenth-century reconfigurations: interimperial economic and social activity, decentralized authority and action, networked business systems built on epistolary and oral conversation, and new commercial enterprises evolving by trial and error through the actions of individuals in contested spaces. Industrialization and globalization were complex phenomena that brought together for the first time an infinitely complex array of forces, structures, and people. Nevertheless, they were built on the achievements of the earlier era, using approaches, methods, and organizations they had inherited from the eighteenth century. The decentralized network of organizational forms honed in the long eighteenth century set the stage for the use of mechanized power and global markets that so profoundly shaped the contours of nineteenth-century economic development.[11]

Incremental technological improvement can thus be seen as leading to industrialization in the sense that individual behaviors leading to technical innovation were a *prerequisite* of "industrial revolution." Not the only one, of course. Asian and medieval European economies exhibited innovation, but neither harnessed mechanical power as eighteenth-and early nineteenth-century Europe did. Steam power set the latter apart and was the sine qua non of the Industrial Revolution.

The economist Gavin Wright has noted that "technological change is fundamentally a form of learning," and this was especially true of nineteenth-century change. The components of Britain's and America's industrial transformations, from their three big introductions—steam power, cheap metal, and clockwork organization—to a host of smaller inventions, were disseminated along network corridors. The "technological networks' infrastructure of knowledge, experience, procedures, and suppliers"—built on information and exchange systems favored and improved by the enterprising innovators in the wine trade decades earlier—increased "the expected payoff (and/or lower expected costs) of investment in certain technical areas while discouraging others."[12] Through the nineteenth century, the scale of the infrastructure grew as knowledge was codified and made more accessible through professional publications, employee training, study groups, and study abroad.[13] "Collective invention settings" offer good examples. During the development of the Cornish pumping steam engine between the 1810s and the 1850s, a group of mine "captains" published "a monthly journal reporting the salient technical characteristics, the operating procedures and the performance of each engine." The journal reveals how incremental innovations emerged, with firms gradually making "pertinent technical information . . . publicly available" so that others could employ the "common pool of technological knowledge to improve the technology in question further."[14] Such sharing created communities of practice—networks—that were "major sources of innovation and change." They acted as "facilitators of innovation, because members who innovate [were] able to share their ideas with other members, assist them and even obtain resources to develop their innovations."[15]

The globalization of trade in the nineteenth century also built on networked approaches and self-organized systems inherited from the eighteenth century. As exemplified by the Madeira wine trade, the worlds of Britons, Americans, and other citizens of Atlantic-facing states had already been "Atlanticized" by 1815 through substantial cross-oceanic, transimperial trading, if not fully globalized. In the nineteenth century, the application of steam power to transportation, especially ships, vastly increased speed and reliability. Beginning in the 1820s and 1830s, Britain's system of regulations, prohibitions, and duties—whose complexity and opacity had anyway inhibited rather than assisted in tapping the commercial riches of the empire—began to be disassembled, and trade barriers started to fall all around the Atlantic rim. The ensuing "First Era of Globalization" saw an increasing volume and variety of a trade in goods and services across borders, as well as freer international flows of people and capital.[16] Supply networks—of the type the Madeira wine traders created—proliferated. Companies that manufactured cotton textiles, for instance, networked themselves across continents and oceans to "suppliers of raw materials and to transportation and distribution services," as well as to "networks for the research and development" of newer, more fashionable, yet usable fabrics.[17] Global supply chains increased the need for trade credit, regular and reliable transportation, and networks of partners, agents, correspondents, and friends who could serve burgeoning numbers of dispersed customers. European migrations to North America also grew in volume and scope, and the interior of the continent became settled along lines that by the mid-1800s drew on well-established modes of organization. More than a million men, women, and children arrived from Ireland alone. Their patterns of settlement and the economic niches they occupied show how they used the four powerful, sometimes overlapping networks available to them: families, brokers, shipping companies, and assistance societies. Emigrants then wrote back to the communities they had left, encouraging relatives and friends to join them. They were links in a chain migration phenomenon bringing laborers to North America that was forged from personal and networked connections.[18]

Both industrial production and globalized trade required increased capital, as shown by developments in the glassmaking industry. Caspar Wistar, whose glassware lined the shelves of his brother's Philadelphia wine store, founded and financed a New Jersey glassworks in the 1730s with profits from land speculation and in partnership with four glassmakers he had brought over from Germany. The capital required was small—several thousand pounds sterling—with Wistar providing two-thirds and the others the rest. But when Amory Houghton Sr., a wealthy Massachusetts merchant, embarked on a similar glass manufacturing venture a century later, circumstances had changed. After unsuccessful attempts in Cambridge and Somerville, Massachusetts, and Brooklyn, New York, Houghton relocated to Corning, New York, in 1868 and established the Corning Flint Glass Company, a limited liability company capitalized at $125,000. Subsequently, Houghton had to increase his companies' stocks on several occasions, in part because of mounting research and development costs and of technology upgrading. With capital requirements growing too great to be met by the traditional partnership form, Houghton, like his contemporaries in other industries, adopted a corporate model to broaden the networks of partners and investors, who were now dispersed occupationally and geographically and would have little or no prior acquaintance with the owners. With Houghton's company, this innovation resulted from trial-and-error experimentation, but from the perspective of the economy as a whole, this organizational innovation followed the trajectory of financial changes that had preceded it in the previous century, similar forms being adopted by eighteenth-century chartered monopoly companies.[19]

New ideas about mechanical power and expanded long-distance trade in the nineteenth century were the results of seeds sown in fertile soil. Businesspeople in a very different world before 1815 had tilled that soil, and the networks, organizations, institutions, and traditions they fertilized it with enriched subsequent growth. Even today, business pundits are rediscovering the modes of organization these eighteenth-century entrepreneurs used—conversations, informal and indirect exchanges, networks, local autonomy, and informal empires. Now, these organizational strategies are essential; modern businesses must adapt quickly to sudden changes in the economy. But the market has been evolving rapidly for the last five hundred years.

ACKNOWLEDGMENTS

"Workers in history have peculiar obsessions," sighed an exasperated William Clements on being told that the library he had founded at the University of Michigan was acquiring a collection of manuscripts documenting the British army's supply of Charleston and Savannah during the American Revolution: "[O]nce in a hundred years, a man may come who wants to know the capacity of Revolutionary soldiers" for liquor, and posterity "may be enlightened."[1] Clements was not hopeful. But luckily others were . . . and are. Like the librarian who made the prescient and successful case for acquiring seemingly mundane material, other scholars, archivists, and friends have nurtured and continued to encourage the compulsive interests of those excavating the past. This book on wine could not have been written without them.

Individuals on three continents cooperated in the most generous manner to help me acquire the information I needed, by granting access to their manuscripts, opening their homes and offices, sharing materials in their personal possession, entertaining me splendidly for weeks on end, and subsequently answering incessant, often vague questions about the worlds their ancestors built and inhabited. Among those to whom I am particularly indebted are Adam and Christina Blandy, Madeira; Richard Blandy, Madeira; David Cossart, Suffolk; John Cossart, Madeira; Jacques A. Faro da Silva, Madeira; George and Joanna Gordon, Banffshire; Sir Richard and Lady Hanbury-Tenison, Gwent; William Leacock and Luisa Prado de Almada Cardoso, Madeira; John P. Nugent, Indiana; David Ogilvy Fairlie, Fife; Oliver Russell, Banffshire; James Symington, Oporto; H. James Welsh, Madeira; Alexander Zino, Madeira.

I am appreciative, as well, of the archivists, librarians, curators, and staffs managing materials deposited in more public repositories. They are so numerous that

I cannot name them all; their collections are detailed in the "List of Unpublished Sources" and in the endnotes. I especially came to respect the expertise of museum curators adept at linking material culture to early modern history. The greatest tribute I can offer these often underpraised, undervalued men and women is utilization of their documents and objects, the bedrock of the book itself.

If archival material were not treasure enough, I have been blessed with stimulating, generous colleagues who have provided assistance, advice, and encouragement. John McCusker, of Trinity University, read the entire manuscript. He has been a source of information, insight, and inspiration throughout my career; I cannot conceive of the field of Atlantic economic history without him in it. Paul Duguid, of the University of California at Berkeley, a sociologist by training but a far better historian than many practitioners of the craft, and Dena Goodman, of the University of Michigan at Ann Arbor, who can inhabit a writer's argument often better than the author himself, read a large portion of the manuscript at a critical moment in its creation; their contributions will be obvious to all who have benefited from their acumen and feedback. John Carson, who makes Michigan one of the most engaging history departments in the country, and Roderick McDonald, whose Boswellian bite reaffirms one's faith in pure intellection, generously read, commented on, and corrected earlier versions of several chapters.

These five form the tip of a mountain. I have benefited greatly from the stimulation and support of other colleagues, first at Harvard and, after 1997, at Michigan. Earliest among them was Oscar Handlin, whose wise counsel—"Write the book on wine, David—it will be brief!"—I only partially followed. Bernard Bailyn continues to blaze new trails for Atlantic history, and continues to pester me with questions remarkable for their provocative understatement. Knowing well what it is like to see a long project through to the end, he never failed to offer the support that was needed, and at just the right time. At Michigan, I encountered a wholly different breed of historian, yet one that warmly welcomed a newcomer. Apart from those already mentioned, I have benefited immensely from discussions with Mamadou Diouf (now at Columbia), Maya Jasanoff (now at Harvard), Martha Jones, Susan Juster, Mary Kelley, Victor Lieberman, Michael Macdonald, Jacob Price, Rebecca Scott, and Carroll Smith-Rosenberg. Among this cohort I must also include my graduate students, for they have humored my "peculiar [commodity] obsessions" and patiently endured occasional lapses into inattentiveness while I was writing. I have found a candor, interdisciplinarity, and kindness at Michigan that are peerless. In many subtle ways, this book bears its imprint.

One of the great joys of conducting Atlantic history research is its wide geographic scope, and I have been lucky to move around the Atlantic to archives and sites featured in the narrative and meet, learn from, and work with an intriguing array of scholars: David Armitage, José Barosa, Daniel Baugh, Rosalind Beiler, Norman Bennett, Huw Bowen, Cary Carson, Peter Coclanis, Luca Codignola, David Conroy, Nancy Cox, François Crouzet, Louis Cullen, William Donovan, Maria de Lourdes de Freitas Ferraz, Junia Furtado, Diogo Filipe Baptista Gaspar, Agustin Guímera Ravina, Amy Henderson, Carter Hudgins, Hugh Johnson, Andrew Mackillop, Dennis Maika, Gloria Main, Peter Mancall, Peter Marshall, Conçeicão Andrade Martins, Silvia Marzagalli, Kenneth Maxwell, Tony Molho, Philip Morgan, Leos Müller, R. C. Nash, Giorgio Perissonotto, Carla Rahn Phillips, Steven Pincus, Jorge Martins Ribeiro, James Robertson, Stuart Schwartz, Holly Snyder, Ian Steele, John Styles, Peter Thompson, Thomas Truxes, Richard Unger, Janny Venema, David Voorhees, José Vouillamoz, Timothy Walker, Lorena Walsh, Martha Zierden. And last but not least, Alberto Vieira of Funchal, who has single-handedly revivified Madeira's past and opened it up to others. All these experts have kindly answered questions, and for this I am grateful.

Information about wine production, distribution, and consumption is found in an array of sources, and I have had the good fortune to be helped by remarkably capable research assistants. The following have ferreted out information in Britain, Portugal, the Caribbean, and the United States: Jonathan Allsop, Catherine Cangany, Michelle Craig McDonald, Elsa Dias, Jonathan Eacott, Paula Alexandra Grazina Gonçalves, Jeffrey Kaja, Daniel Livesay, Amanda Moniz, Shannette Richards, Kesia Weise.

Even with such assistance, historical investigation and reconstruction can be lonely work. Friends around the Atlantic—many of whom are also scholars and so know the importance of well-timed diversion—have made the tasks more enjoyable than perhaps they should be. In Brazil: Inez Schacter. In England: Greg Barrow, Colette Bowe, Mark Cooke, Kenneth Morgan, Admiral Sir John Julian and Lady Oswald, Hugh Poole-Warren, Teresa Silva de Lopes, Jane Standley, Lord (Hugh) Thomas of Swynnerton. In France: Pierre Gervais, Hubert Vicente, François Weil. In Italy: Guidobaldo da Montefeltro. In the Netherlands: Gepke Gingst. In Nicaragua: Gary Stahl. In Portugal: Benedita Camâra, Alice Perestrelo de Vasconcelos, Viscountess Charters, Leonor Freire da Costa, Undersecretary Jorge M. Pedreira, Dr. Jorge Marcos Rita. In Turkey: Ahmet Semih Görk Pasha. In the United States: Brian Casey, Blake Crews, Barbara DeWolfe, Lil Fenn, Salvatore Fiumaro, Alison Games, Chris Golembeski, Nina Hauser, Wim Klooster, John Marksbury, Cathy Matson, Andrew O'Shaugnessy, Michael Paschke, Mark Peterson, Grant Schneider, Charles Steinman, Pat Strobel, Stuart Tabakin, Griselda Warr.

Wide-ranging Atlantic research cannot be undertaken without foundations and institutions possessing a breadth of vision willing to go against the grain of nationalistic interests and subsidize the work. This highly transnational project received generous financial support from the following organizations and programs, and I am extremely grateful to each of them: the American Philosophical Society (Philadelphia), Harvard University, the David Rockefeller Center for Iberian- and Latin-American Studies (Harvard University), the Fundaçao Luso-Americana (Lisbon), the Rackham Graduate School (the University of Michigan), the Charles Warren Center for Studies in American History (Harvard University), the Library Company of Philadelphia, the Pennsylvania Historical and Museum Commission (Harrisburg), the John Carter Brown Library (Brown University), the Mellon Foundation (New York), the Howard Foundation (Providence), the Henry Francis du Pont Winterthur Museum and Library (Wilmington), the American Antiquarian Society (Worcester).

My editor, Chris Rogers, moved me through the final phases of a not-uncomplicated project with an unsinkable, sustaining belief in it. His infusion of energy, optimism, and enterprise was invaluable. The readers that he found provided appropriate and usable suggestions, allowing me to tame what was admittedly a rather unruly draft and to improve it beyond all recognition. I cannot thank them enough, and I hope they forgive my not taking all of their suggestions, although this would have assuredly been a much better book had I been able to do so. My warmest personal thanks go, as well, to Robin DuBlanc, pitiless scrutineer, whose copyediting can only be recorded, never measured.

All these many years, the respectable if earthy Geyser Hancock — ever vigilant and expectant — has inquired — and not always unobtrusively — what I have been doing in the study. One has a beach house to be at the beach, and not holed up in a small eighteenth-century borning room, no? This book is my answer. Insufficient as it surely is, I hope he will not digest it with the same toothy voracity he did my first tome. Lex Kelso, who shares this sanctuary, deserves the greatest place in these acknowledgements. His combination of independence and warmth, as well as of distance and intrusion, nurtured the project in ways he cannot comprehend. Without his careful but engaged and respectful inquisition, often laborious but never grudging, I should never have attained mastery over the many subjects detailed herein, and without his continuous integrated triage I should never have finished the book when I did. He provided this assistance with the skill of a virtuoso and the consideration of a saint.

As for he to whom the book is dedicated, thanks or acknowledgement shall never suffice.

Truro, Massachusetts
January 1, 2009

A NOTE ON CONVENTIONS

Letters, spelling, and punctuation have been preserved in the quotation of original passages.

All dates before the Gregorian calendar was introduced in 1752 are given in the Old Style, yet the year is reckoned as beginning on January 1.

All numbers in the text are rounded; in the endnotes, they are as exact as possible. The reader should beware, however, the perils of false precision in comparatively data-poor periods before 1900.

While gender-inclusive language—"he or she" and "men and women"—is preferable, its usage in the present volume is abandoned, except when specifically accurate. There were several women involved in Madeira's production and distribution out of the thousands of enterprisers studied herein, and they are discussed. Yet they were nonetheless rare, and so for convenience and smoother prose, I adopt "he" and "men." In consumption, women were fully engaged, and the prose generally accounts for them.

CURRENCY

In this book, monetary values are converted to and stated in English pounds sterling, unless otherwise noted. This reduction allows for easier comparison, and it would not be foreign to the people described herein, for the pound was an important point of reference and comparison for anyone connected to transatlantic commodities. The reality, though, was extremely complex.

PORTUGUESE CURRENCY

By law, the currency of Madeira was that of Portugal: the islanders used the money of account prevailing on the mainland. The system was simple, based as it was on the unit of the *real* (plural: *réis*). An islander in the eighteenth century talked about and wrote the price of goods and services in terms of the *real*, *réis*, and *milréis* (1,000 *réis*). He or she wrote 1 *milréis* as "1$000," and 10,000 *milréis* as 10:000$000. (The modern dollar sign is used here to reproduce the older Portuguese *cifrão*.) In principle, the *real* was also the unit for real money used in payments involving physical coin, but its system was anything but simple: there were a variety of coins that were subjected over the course of the eighteenth century to several devaluations—the silver *cruzado*, *tostão*, and half-*tostão*, and the gold *moeda*, *cruzado*, before 1720 *dobrão*, after 1722 *dobrão* of eight *escudos* and *dobrão* of four *escudos* (called the *Johannes* or *Jo*, and "the universal gold coin in the Atlantic world" after the discovery of gold in Brazil during the 1690s). Even so, except for the *tostões* and *Jo*, Portuguese coin did not enjoy wide circulation on the island. Instead, inhabitants used Spanish coin: the gold *doblón*, *pistole* (of 32 *reales*), and *escudo* (of 16 *reales*); and the silver *peso de plata antigua* (called the "piece of eight" for its 8 *reales*, but also known as the dollar, *piastre*, or *cob*), the *peseta de vellon* (or *pistareen*, of 4 *reales*), and the *real de vellon* (1 *reale*).[1] The analysis in the present study recapitulates heavily the monies of account, although individual on-the-spot transactions central to the trade always involved one or several coinage systems.

Indeed, the Madeira wine complex participated in—and contributed to—the circulation of money throughout the larger Atlantic marketplace. During the eighteenth century, Spanish and to a lesser extent Portuguese silver (mined in South America) functioned as the Madeirans' principal currency—the *peso* ("the 'universal money' of the Atlantic world") and the *peseta*, alongside the *tostão* and half-*tostão*—so much so that in 1801 the Portuguese Crown ordered that a Spanish dollar pass current at 5 *pesetas* or at 1 *milréis*. Gold coin was seldom seen in Funchal. While Madeira was a stopping point for slave traders, the gold that these men acquired in Africa seldom made it back to the island, and certainly not in coin. Portuguese copper circulated in fairly limited amounts. Silver was the norm, yet at times even it was scarce. Enterprising Madeirans did obtain sterling from English naval forces calling on them for refreshment and from Anglo-American middlemen and consumers; yet the volume was never great, since Americans were more likely to pay in Spanish than English coin and most disbursements were handled by strangers working "on account," making subsequent payment in London or the other financial centers of Europe.[2]

The use of multiple currencies, while common as early as 1700, was first seriously targeted by critics only in the 1760s, when commercial frustrations with it grew intolerable. First, it created confusion in calculations and negotiations. Moving between the Portuguese and Spanish systems of accounting and exchange was often treacherous. The piece of eight as a money of account, for instance, did not bear the same value as a piece of eight in hand, even though it bore the same name. Compounding this predicament was the fact that merchants "accepted payment of . . . accounts in coin at an inflated value."[3] Second, critics alleged, reliance on other currencies destabilized Portuguese currency even further. Not only was Portuguese currency devalued several times—as in 1718, 1720, 1722, and 1747—but Spanish currency, to which the Portuguese was closely tied, was also devalued, first in 1642 and again in 1772. Merchants in Madeira were constantly afraid of devaluation.[4] Complicating any further disturbance was the reality that Spanish and Portuguese coins were worth less in Madeira than on the mainland. (Latin Americans and Anglo-Americans experienced the same predicament, vis-à-vis their respective capitals, as well.)[5] To these problems was added a third: the reliance on multiple currencies contributed to a decentering of wine export-ers' financial worlds. Since the seventeenth century, the Madeirans had drawn upon London, their largest customer base lying in Anglo-America, and to a lesser extent Paris and Amsterdam. Over the course of the eighteenth century, they drew upon Lisbon with greater frequency, and, after 1789, upon Philadelphia. With so many centers, the transfer of funds (ever arduous and fraught with risk) became even more of a management challenge. Finally, in an environment in which many currencies of many countries were accepted and in an empire and marketplace so vast that thorough scrutiny was well nigh impossible, fraud and counterfeiting were rampant. Coins used on the island, as throughout the Atlan-tic world, were frequently "clipped" by shaving, filing, or cutting metal from the edges. Their value was thus debased, often without the awareness of either buyer or seller. Merchants could not rely upon the apparent face value of the coin. While such concerns might have encouraged traders to embrace the use of paper money, the temporary and long-term costs of paper outweighed the perceived benefits.[6]

Given all that roiled the monetary system, enterprisers in the Atlantic wine trade constantly struggled to improve it. Overall, money was generally scarce on the island, since in "the trade of . . . Madeira with Lisbon the balance" was against the former: "all the Portuguese money naturally" went to the capital. One of the more intriguing initiatives to cope with this situation was begun by the island's nonnative exporters. Frustrated at the overall specie scarcity, some began mint-ing their own currency: *boyeiros escritos*, either printed or of copper, in 40, 50, 60, 80, and 100 *réis* units. With these chits, they would pay their employees and suppliers (who, after a certain period, could redeem them for specie).[7]

The Leacocks developed the most elaborate scheme (other firms devised them as well) in 1801 when the island was suffering from "a very great inconveniency for want of copper coin & half bits." Such coins were "almost extinct," even though a few years previous "a large sum was sent from Lisbon in copper & small silver coins for the use of the island." The principal loss they suffered came from their "not being often able to sell . . . effects for want of a small coin for change," especially in the sale of flax from their shop. It would, they felt, "be of great advantage & utility to have a quantity of copper medals made at Birmingham which would answer the purposes of a coin & . . . circulate & pass current in the island"; even if they did not achieve wide usage, they felt the chits would suffice for their wine suppliers and store customers. They sent detailed instructions and drawings to England for five differently sized and valued coins: three hundred were to be made the value and size of 1 farthing; five hundred, 2 farthings; six hundred, 4 farthings; four hundred, 8 farthings; and six hundred, 10 farthings. Actual values inscribed on each were to be 5, 10, 20, 30, or 40 *réis*; on one side of every coin was to be stamped and engraved the words, encircled and centered:

Payable by J. & W. Leacock in Madeira
Value 5 Reis
1800

On the reverse side was to appear a Bacchus astride a pipe of wine, encircled with vine leaves and grapes, and underneath him the phrase "Prosperity to Madeira."[8] Continually replenished, the chits passed as current money on the island for more than a century.

BRITISH AND ANGLO-AMERICAN CURRENCIES

A shifting, uncertain, and confusing supply of currency and fears about the value of what was at hand were not unique to Madeira. They plagued the entire Atlantic marketplace.

Men and women throughout the English-speaking Atlantic community accounted for their transactions in pounds, shillings, pennies, and farthings. Moreover, English-speaking producers, traders, and consumers had recourse to a variety of coins. The coin of the realm was minted in England: a gold guinea (worth a pound and a shilling), a silver pound sterling (worth 20 shillings), a silver crown (worth 5 shillings), a silver shilling ("s."—worth 12 pennies), a copper penny ("d."), and a brass farthing.

But while different in their monies of account and real monies, Britons and Anglo-Americans experienced many of the same difficulties as the Iberians and Madeirans. As in Portuguese Madeira and Brazil, the coin of Britain's empire was Spanish, not that of the metropolis to which they addressed allegiance. Furthermore, each colony, imitating the metropolitan model, had its own current money, and the value of that money was always some fraction of the metropolitan value.

Depending on the terms of trade of the colony in question, that value fluctuated from month to month and year to year, it being frequently published in most eastern port newspapers during the eighteenth century. Columns devoted to the "current price" of money were some of the most avidly read portions of any publication.

The acquisition of independence by the thirteen colonies only complicated currency calculations in the English Atlantic world. Some states adopted the dollar and cents system early on, but other states continued to adhere to the older metropolitan and colonial system and newspapers quoted current prices for both pounds and state and federal dollars. Furthermore, even if one's state had converted to what became the new American scheme, a merchant could continue to accept and account in British monies. Many did. Only by the second decade of the nineteenth century were most adhering to the new federal system.

Abbreviations Used in the Notes

AAS	American Antiquarian Society, Worcester, Massachusetts
ABS	American Bible Society, New York, New York
ADF	Arquivo Distrital do Funchal, Funchal
AHM	*Arquivo Histórico da Madeira*
AHR	*American Historical Review*
AHU	Arquivo Histórico Ultramarino, Lisbon
AN-Fr	Archives Nationales, Paris
AN-TdT	Arquivo Nacional da Torre do Tombo, Lisbon
APS	American Philosophical Society
APS, *Trans.*	*Transactions of the American Philosophical Society*
ARM	Arquivo Regional da Madeira, Funchal
BCM	Ballindalloch Castle Muniments, Ballindalloch, Scotland
Beekman Papers	Philip L. White, ed., *The Beekman Mercantile Papers, 1749–1799*, 3 vols. (New York, 1956)
BL	British Library, London
BNL	Biblioteca Nacional, Lisbon
Bolton Letters, vol. 1	André L. Simon, ed., *The Bolton Letters: The Letters of an English Merchant in Madeira, 1695–1714*, vol. 1 (London, 1928)
Bolton Letters, vol. 2	Graham Blandy, ed., *The Bolton Letters, 1700–1714*, vol. 2 (Funchal, 1960)
Carter Diary	Jack Greene, ed., *The Diary of Colonel Landon Carter of Sabine Hill, 1752–1778*, 2 vols. (Richmond, 1987)
CGP-Guildhall	Cossart, Gordon Papers, Guildhall Library, London
CGP-MWC	Cossart, Gordon Papers, Madeira Wine Company, Funchal
CGP-PC	Cossart, Gordon Papers, private collection, Stanstead, Suffolk, England
CPP	College of Physicians of Philadelphia Library
EM	*Elucidário madeirense*, 2nd ed., 3 vols. (Funchal, 1946)

"Endeavour" Journal	J. C. Beaglehole, ed., *The "Endeavour" Journal of Joseph Banks, 1768–1771*, vol. 1 (Sydney, 1962)
Franklin Papers	Leonard W. Labaree et al., eds., *The Papers of Benjamin Franklin*, 38 vols. (New Haven, 1959–2006)
GD	General Deposit, National Archives of Scotland, Edinburgh
Guildhall	Guildhall Library, Manuscripts Collection, London
HBS	Harvard Business School, Special Collections, Boston
Hill-EWS	Lamar, Hill, Bisset & Co. Papers, Edward Wanton Smith Collection, 4 folders, 1762–1802, Historical Society of Pennsylvania, Philadelphia
Hill-Haverford	Hill Family Papers, Howland Collection, Haverford College Library, Haverford, Pennsylvania
Hill-JJS(A)	Hill Family Papers, John Jay Smith Collection "A," 13 vols., 1698–1797, Library Company of Philadelphia
Hill-JJS(B)	Hill Family Papers, John Jay Smith Collection "B," 1 box and various account books, 1698–1797, Library Company of Philadelphia
Hill—SAGS	Hill Family Papers, Sarah A .G. Smith Collection, 7 folders, Historical Society of Pennsylvania, Philadelphia
HSP	Historical Society of Pennsylvania, Philadelphia
IOL	India Office Library, British Library, London
IRO	Island Record Office, Spanishtown, Jamaica
JCBL	John Carter Brown Library, Brown University, Providence, Rhode Island
JDPL	James Duncan Phillips Library, Essex Institute, Peabody Essex Museum, Salem, Massachusetts
JLP	Jacob Leisler Papers, New York University, New York, New York
JEH	*Journal of Economic History*
JIH	*Journal of Interdisciplinary History*
Laurens Papers	David R. Chesnutt et al., eds., *The Papers of Henry Laurens*, 16 vols. (Columbia, SC, 1968–2002)
LCP	Library Company of Philadelphia
Leacock Papers	Leacock Papers, private collection, Funchal
Letterfourie Papers	Gordon of Letterfourie Papers, private collection, Preshome, Scotland
LC	Library of Congress, Washington, DC
MHS	Massachusetts Historical Society
MNE	Ministério dos Negócios Estrangeiros, Lisbon
MSA	Massachusetts State Archives, Boston
MWC	Madeira Wine Company Archives, Funchal
NA-Sc	National Archives of Scotland, Edinburgh
NA-UK	National Archives of the United Kingdom, Kew, Richmond, Surrey, England

NA-US	National Archives, Washington, DC
NGL	Newton & Gordon Letter Books, private collection, Suffolk, England
NLI	National Library of Ireland, Dublin
NLS	National Library of Scotland, Edinburgh
NOSL	Naval Office Shipping Lists, National Archives of the United Kingdom, Kew, Richmond, Surrey, England
NYHS	New York Historical Society, New York, New York
NYPL	New York Public Library, New York, New York
NYSL	New York State Library, Albany
PMHB	*Pennsylvania Magazine of History and Biography*
PSA	Pennsylvania State Archives, Harrisburg
RS, *Phil. Trans.*	*Philosophical Transactions of the Royal Society of London*
SCDAH	South Carolina Department of Archives and History, Columbia
SCHS	South Carolina Historical Society, Charleston
SP	State Papers, National Archives of the United Kingdom, Kew, Richmond, Surrey, England
SPNEA	Society for the Preservation of New England Antiquities, Boston
VHS	Virginia Historical Society, Richmond
VMHB	*Virginia Magazine of History and Biography*
Washington Papers	W. W. Abbot and Dorothy Twohig, eds., *The Papers of George Washington*, 5 ser., 57 vols. (Charlottesville, 1976–)
WMQ	*William and Mary Quarterly*

NOTES

INTRODUCTION

1. *Collected Novellas* (New York, 1990), 259.
2. It was an extraordinary find . . . and one that kept recurring. For a detailed listing of most sources discovered and analyzed, see the List of Unpublished Sources.
3. A perception reminiscent of the introduction's title quote, taken from Daniel Defoe, *A Plan of the English Commerce* (London, 1728), vii, x.
4. Sadly, the dearth of surviving evidence of flows to Portuguese America does not allow much comparison between Brazil and the comparatively better documented English colonies to its north.
5. The best commodity histories combine sectors, yet they do so incompletely. Sidney W. Mintz looks only at production and consumption in *Sweetness and Power* (New York, 1985). Comparable omissions mar Jeffrey M. Paige, *Coffee and Power: Revolution and the Rise of Democracy in Central America* (Cambridge, 1997); Jordan Goodman, *Tobacco in History: The Cultures of Dependence* (London, 1993).
6. Linkage among sectors has not always been the case in the study of wine. Until recently, monographs on Portuguese, French, and Spanish wines have fit into the segmented, incomplete tradition of inquiry. Alan Francis and Harold Fisher provide good if partial general histories of Portuguese wine trading and shipping, Francis surveying the entire subject, Fisher focusing on Lisbon and Oporto, and both skirting production and consumption. Harold Fisher, *The Portugal Trade: A Study of Anglo-Portuguese Commerce, 1700–1770* (London, 1971); Alan Francis, *The Wine Trade* (New York, 1972). Port wine has received the greatest attention. Early scholars studied shipping and trading. A. Guerra Tenreiro, *Douro: Esboços para a sua história económica*, 2 vols. (Oporto, 1943–44); Virginia Rau, "O movimento da Barra do Douro durante o seculo xviii: Uma interpretação," *Boletim cultural/Camara municipal do Porto* 21 (1958): 5–27. In the past two decades, the rigorous social-scientific investigations of a handful of Portuguese, English, and American scholars have finally blown away the fog of mythology that has enveloped Port history. Even so, they remain fixated on growers

420

and traders. Conceição Andrade Martins, *Memória do vinho do Porto* (Lisbon, 1990); Norman R. Bennett, "The Golden Age of the Port Wine System, 1781–1807," *International History Review* 12 (1990): 221–48; Francisco Ribeiro da Silva, ""Do Douro ao Porto: O protagonismo do vinho na época moderna," *Douro—Estudos & documentos* 1 (1996): 93–118; Paul Duguid, "Lavradores, exportadores, comissários, e eapitalistas: Os componentes da região do vinho do Porto," *O Douro* 1 (1996): 201–24; António Barros Cardoso, *Baco & Hermes: O Porto e o comércio interno e externo dos vinho do Douro (1700–1756)*, 2 vols. (Porto, 2003). Growing, selling, shipping, and trading have been central to the narratives of other Portuguese wines. T. Bentley Duncan, *Atlantic Islands: Madeira, the Azores and the Cape Verdes in Seventeenth-Century Commerce and Navigation* (Chicago, 1972).

The history of France's wines is even better developed, yet it, too, focuses almost exclusively on region, cultivators, and production, evincing little concern for distribution and less for consumption. Recently, Thomas Brennan broke this mold. Théophile Malvezin, *Histoire du commerce de Bordeaux depuis les origines jusqu'a nos jours*, 4 vols. (Bordeaux, 1892); François-Georges Pariset, ed., *Bordeaux au XVIIIe siècle*, vol. 5 (Bordeaux, 1968); John G. Clark, *La Rochelle and the Atlantic Economy in the Eighteenth Century* (Baltimore, 1981); Thomas Brennan, *Public Drinking and Popular Culture in Eighteenth-Century Paris* (Princeton, 1988), and *Burgundy to Champagne: The Wine Trade in Early Modern France* (Baltimore, 1997); Louis M. Cullen, *The Brandy Trade under the Ancien Régime: Regional Specialisation in the Charente* (Cambridge, 1998).

7. Popular historians of everyday goods—bananas, cod, nutmeg, salt, and tea, to name a few—have appreciated better than academics the reciprocity of relationships among metropolitans and provincials, and between people and objects. Scholars criticize these "commodity parables" as long on explanation and short on evidence and analysis: often they are written by journalists and literary scholars largely unaccustomed to the grit of archival research, and grounded in myth and anecdote. But because they are vividly narrated, they have widened the audience for history and whetted readers' *and* scholars' interest in more evidenced and nuanced accounts of the production, trade, and consumption of goods. Henry Petroski, *The Pencil* (New York, 1990); Mark Kurlansky, *Cod* (New York, 1997); Giles Morton, *Nathaniel's Nutmeg* (New York, 1999); Virginia S. Jenkins, *Bananas* (Washington, DC, 2000); Joseph A. Amato, *Dust: A History of the Small and Invisible* (Berkeley, 2000); Michael Pollan, *The Botany of Desire* (New York, 2001); Giovanni Rebora, *Culture of the Fork* (New York, 2001); Mark Kurlansky, *Salt: A World History* (New York, 2002), and *The Big Oyster* (New York, 2006); Alan MacFarlane and Gerry Martin, *Glass: A World History* (Chicago, 2002); Roy Moxham, *Tea: Addiction, Exploitation, and Empire* (New York, 2003); Alan MacFarlane and Iris MacFarlane, *The Empire of Tea* (New York, 2004); Henry Petroski, *The Toothpick* (New York, 2007). In the wake of such investigation, "thing theory" is developing. Bill Brown, ed., *Things* (Chicago, 2004); Lorraine Daston, ed., *Things That Talk* (Cambridge, MA, 2004).

8. Arjun Appadurai, "Introduction: Commodities and the Politics of Value," in *The Social Life of Things*, ed. Appadurai (Cambridge, 1986), 33.

9. John Brewer, *Party Ideology and Popular Politics at the Accession of George III* (Cambridge, 1976); Ned C. Landsman, *Scotland and Its First American Colony, 1683–1765* (Princeton, 1985); Ian Steele, *The English Atlantic, 1675–1740: An Exploration of Communication and Community* (New York, 1986); John Brewer, *The Sinews of Power: War, Money and the English State, 1688–1783* (Cambridge, 1989); Linda Colley, *Britons: Forging the Nation, 1707–1837* (New Haven, 1992); David Hancock, *Citizens of the World: London Merchants and the Integration of the British Atlantic Community, 1735–1785* (New York, 1995); Peter Linebaugh and Marcus Rediker, *The Many-Headed Hydra: Sailors, Slaves, Commoners, and the Hidden History of the Revolutionary Atlantic* (Boston, 2000); Eliga H. Gould, *The Persistence of Empire: British Political Culture in the Age of the American Revolution* (Chapel Hill, 2000); David Armitage, *The Ideological Origins of the British Empire* (Cambridge, 2000).

10. David Hancock, "The British Atlantic World: Coordination, Complexity, and the Emergence of an Atlantic Market Economy, 1651–1815," *Itinerario* 23 (1999): 107–27. The idea is not dissimilar to what David Armitage later dubbed "circum-Atlantic history": "Three Concepts of Atlantic History," in Armitage and Michael Braddick, eds., *The British Atlantic World, 1500–1800* (London, 2002), 16–18.

11. On the interimperial flow of people and other goods, legal and illegal, see Virginia Harrington, *The New York Merchant on the Eve of the Revolution* (New York, 1935), 249–50; Geoffrey L. Rossano, "Down to the Bay: New York Shippers and the Central American Logwood Trade, 1748–1761," *New York History* 70 (1989): 229–50; Cathy Matson, *Merchants and Empire: Trading in Colonial New York* (Baltimore, 1998), 299; Marianne S. Wokeck, *Trade in Strangers* (University Park, 1999), 109–12; Neil Kamil, *Fortress of the Soul: Violence, Metaphysics, and Material Life in the Huguenots' New World, 1517–1751* (Baltimore, 2005); Wim Klooster, "The History of Interimperial Smuggling in the Americas, 1600–1800," in *Soundings in Atlantic History,* ed. Bernard Bailyn (Cambridge, MA, 2009); Michael Jarvis, *At the Crossroads of the Atlantic: Maritime Revolution and the Transformation of Bermuda, 1612–1815* (Chapel Hill, forthcoming), chap. 2. In *The Marketplace of Revolution: How Consumer Politics Shaped American Independence* (New York, 2004), Timothy Breen makes a strong case for consumption creating community. Similarly, the circulation of texts and ideas throughout the oceanic marketplace contributed to a common, coherent association with others outside one's empire. Terence Hutchison, *Before Adam Smith: The Emergence of Political Economy, 1662–1776* (Oxford, 1988), 128, 132, 224–25, 289, 304, 317–18, 328–29; Paul B. Cheney, "The History and Science of Commerce in the Century of Enlightenment, 1713–1789" (PhD diss., Columbia University, 2002); Istvan Hont, *Jealousy of Trade: International Competition and the Nation-State in Historical Perspective* (Cambridge, MA, 2005).

12. Except in matters relating to financial brokerage, where London was always the *primum mobile,* and, even then, there was wide use of bills of exchange drawn on Lisbon and, after 1783, Philadelphia.

13. Jack P. Greene, *Negotiated Authorities: Essays in Colonial Political and Constitutional History* (Charlottesville, 1994), 16, 23–24. In agreement are Mary S. Bilder, *The Transatlantic Constitution: Colonial Legal Culture and the Empire* (Cambridge,

MA, 2004); Daniel Hulsebosch, *Constituting Empire: New York and the Transformation of Constitutionalism in the Atlantic World, 1664–1830* (Chapel Hill, 2005); J. H. Elliott, *Empires of the Atlantic World: Britain and Spain in America, 1492–1830* (New Haven, 2006). Fred Cooper has described twentieth-century empires in Africa as having "long arms" (intellectual and political agendas) and "weak fingers" (the ability to implement and influence). *Colonialism in Question: Theory, Knowledge, History* (Berkeley, 2005), 197.

14. The father of the modern study of entrepreneurs, Joseph Schumpeter, argued that entrepreneurs were the principal drivers of economic growth, introducing products, developing markets, and devising forms of organization. But he was vague on what constituted innovation. *The Theory of Economic Development* (London, 1912). Cf. Thomas McCraw, "Schumpeter Ascending," *American Scholar* 60 (1991): 371–92; Oliver Williamson, *Markets and Hierarchies* (New York, 1975), 7, 14, 15, 17, 24–34, 47–49; W. Long, "The Meaning of Entrepreneurship," *American Journal of Small Business* 8 (1983): 47–59.

15. Thomas Doerflinger, *A Vigorous Spirit of Enterprise: Merchants and Economic Development in Revolutionary Philadelphia* (Chapel Hill, 1985); Hancock, *Citizens*.

16. Typical is the work of the sociologist Michael Mann, who sees the state as the conjunction of central control and geographical extent. The state is "inherently centralized over a delimited territory over which it has authoritative power. . . . the state elite's resources radiate authoritatively outwards from a centre but stop at defined territorial boundaries." "The Autonomous Power of the State: Its Origins, Mechanisms and Results," in *States in History*, ed. John A. Hall (Oxford, 1986), 122–23. This concept has been an organizing principle of historical analysis of the early modern era. For example, see John Brewer, "The Eighteenth-Century British State: Contexts and Issues," in *An Imperial State at War: Britain from 1689 to 1815*, ed. Lawrence Stone (London, 1994), 65. The "nation-oriented criteria of governments" create problems for enterprises with global ambitions. John Fayerweather, "The Internationalization of Business," *Annals of the American Academy of Political and Social Science* 403 (1972): 1.

17. Brewer, *Sinews of Power*, xi, xv–xvi, 252; John J. McCusker and Russell R. Menard, *The Economy of British America, 1607–1789* (Chapel Hill, 1985), 71–90, 331–50. See also Phyllis Deanne, *The State and the Economic System* (Oxford, 1989); Daniel Baugh, "Maritime Strength and Atlantic Commerce: The Uses of 'A Grand Marine Empire,'" in Stone, *An Imperial State at War*, 188–94; Peter Miller, *Defining the Common Good* (Cambridge, 1994); Chris Bayly, "The First Age of Global Imperialism, c. 1760–1830," *Journal of Imperial and Commonwealth History* 26 (1998): 28–47. For the earlier Marxist perspective, see Karl Polanyi, *The Great Transformation* (New York, 1944); Immanuel Wallerstein, *The Modern World-System II* (San Diego, 1988).

18. For a similar lack of centralization in other areas of Portuguese trade and governance, see António Manuel Hespanha, *As Vésperas do Leviathan: Instituições e poder político Portugal — Séc. XVII* (Coimbra, 1994); Christopher Ebert, *Between Empires: Brazilian Sugar in the Early Atlantic Economy, 1550–1630*. (Leiden, 2008).

19. The question of the primacy of structure over action — or vice versa — prompted much of the theorizing of Pierre Bourdieu. For his "reconciliation" of holism and individu-

alism, see *Distinction* (Paris, 1979), and *An Outline of the Theory of Practice* (Paris, 1972).

20. Richard Hill reproduced the approaches in reverse, going east toward Europe rather than west toward America. Yet, like Hill's, much of individuals' reproduction of social forms alters them in the process.

21. Friedrich A. von Hayek, "The Use of Knowledge in Society," *American Economic Review* 35 (1945): 519–30.

22. Douglass North, *Institutions, Institutional Change and Economic Performance* (Cambridge, 1990), 80–81.

23. Scholarship reconstituting historical networks is growing. Good examples are given in the notes to chapter 5. The sociologist Michel Callon maps material/semiotic relationships in society. His most famous essay describes the stages in which marine biologists, working to restock a bay with scallops, created a network in which members agreed to build and defend the effort. "Some Elements of a Sociology of Translation: Domestication of the Scallops and the Fishermen of St Brieuc Bay," in *Power, Action and Belief: A New Sociology of Knowledge*, ed. John Law (London, 1986). The sociologist Bruno Latour adopts a more heterodox view: the work of scientists was not a product of scientific principle or experiment but of scientists' beliefs, traditions, and practices; network members include not only sellers and buyers but also commodities, ledgers, monies, even attire. *Science in Action: How to Follow Scientists and Engineers through Society* (Cambridge, MA, 1987). In a nuanced analysis of intelligence gathering in late eighteenth- and early nineteenth-century British India, Christopher Bayly anatomized an informational actor network, detailing the multiplicity of inputs and the highly decentralized structure that helped Britain to achieve mastery over the subcontinent. *Empire and Information: Intelligence Gathering and Social Communication in India, 1780–1870* (Cambridge, 1996).

24. Mark Granovetter, "The Strength of Weak Ties," *American Journal of Sociology* 78 (1973): 1360–380, and "The Strength of Weak Ties: A Network Theory Revisited," in Peter Marsden and Nan Lin, eds., *Social Structure and Network Analysis* (Beverley Hills, 1982), 105–30. Granovetter's original article is one of the most cited in sociological literature.

25. D. J. Watts and S. H. Strogatz, "Collective Dynamics of 'Small-World' Networks," *Nature* (1998): 393, 440–42. Watts summarizes the findings in *Six Degrees: The Science of a Connected Age* (New York, 2003), 38–42, 83–91. It gave rise to the phrase—and later play and movie—*Six Degrees of Separation*.

26. Joel M. Podolny and Karen L. Page, "Network Forms of Organization," *Annual Review of Sociology* 24 (1998): 59.

27. William R. Ashby, "Principles of the Self-Organizing Dynamic System," *Journal of General Psychology* 37 (1947): 125–28, and *Design for a Brain: The Origin of Adaptive Behavior*, 2nd ed. (New York, 1960).

28. There is actually a fourth state, the plasma state, that is seldom observed because it exists only at extremely high temperatures and pressures.

29. As an analytical matter, emergent phenomena need not and often do not look like constituent parts—the human body is not an organic molecule writ large, for instance,

and a market is not a goal-seeking actor in the way that an entrepreneur may be. Understanding phenomena as emergent removes the constraint of having to apply the same historical constructs to all levels of analysis. Understanding a customer network requires analyzing an individual's goals and resources—particularly relationships and information—whereas the global market of which he is a part requires different, more impersonal categories, such as aggregate quantity, reliability of suppliers, and categories of intermediaries. Nevertheless, this approach imposes an obligation to explain the relationships among levels (something that is often not done). John H. Holland, "The Global Economy as an Adaptive Process," in *The Economy as an Evolving Complex System*, ed. Philip W. Anderson et al. (Redwood City, 1987), 5:117–18; Paul R. Krugman, *The Self-Organizing Economy* (New York, 1996), 3, vi, 36. See also Murray Gell-Mann, "What Is Complexity?" *Complexity* 1 (1995): 16–19; José A. Scheinkman and Michael Woodford, "Self-Organized Criticality and Economic Fluctuations," *American Economic Review: Papers and Proceedings* 84 (1994): 417–21; P. Per Bak and Kan Chen, "Self-Organizing Criticality," *Scientific American* 264 (1991): 46–53.

30. John Thomas, *The Rise of the Staffordshire Potteries* (New York, 1971); Chris Evans and Göran Rydén, *Baltic Iron in the Atlantic World in the Eighteenth Century* (Leiden, 2007).

31. Madeira has been the subject of an overview in English by Noel Cossart and detailed investigations in Portuguese by Alberto Vieira and others. However, a problem of Madeira studies has been their national insularity: Portuguese writers generally write as if foreigners played an insignificant role in the history of their wine; returning the favor, English-language historians seldom take into account the more numerous Portuguese exporters. Noel Cossart, *Madeira: The Island Vineyard* (London, 1984); Alain Huetz de Lemps, *Le vin de Madère* (Grenoble, 1989); Alberto Vieira, *O vinho da Madeira* (Funchal, 1983), and *Breviário da vinha e do vinho na Madeira* (Ponta Delgada, Açores, 1991).

32. The market leveled off after the 1810s, given the island's naturally limited supply and the rising competition from other wine-producing areas in Europe; the industry declined in the 1850s and 1860s as oidium and phylloxera devastated the vines and rootstock.

33. Theodore Hook, *Maxwell* (New York, 1831), 2:63, recording an 1813 visit.

34. Susan M. Stabile, *Memory's Daughters* (Ithaca, 2004), 9.

35. Andrew Sherratt, "Alcohol and Its Alternatives: Symbol and Substance in Preindustrial Cultures," in *Consuming Habits: Drugs in History and Anthropology*, ed. Sherratt (London, 1995), 11.

CHAPTER 1. THE TRIUMPH OF BACCHUS

1. Theodore Hook, *Maxwell* (New York, 1831), 2:63. Hook's visit is recorded in his letter to John Elliot, June 28, 1813, in *Gentleman's Magazine*, April 1896, 340.

2. *Admiralty Distance Tables*, 3rd ed. (London, 1951), 4:203.

3. Christopher Jeaffreson, *A Young Squire of the Seventeenth Century* (London, 1878), 1:172; Jeremiah Seller and Charles Price, *The Fifth Part of the General English Pilot*

(London, 1701), 7–8; Jedidiah Morse, *The American Universal Geography, Part II*, 2nd ed. (Boston, 1796), 1:635–36; John Pinkerton, *Modern Geography* (London, 1802), 2:767.

4. If they did not stop at the island, ships bound to the Canaries, the west coast of Africa, the Cape of Good Hope, or India generally passed to its east and, if bound to the Americas, to its west. A northern route via the Grand Banks of Newfoundland could be taken instead of the southern route to the Americas, but this was inadvisable, except in the autumn when it was free of ice. The Rennell Current flows southward from Cape Finisterre in Spain along the coast of Portugal; after skirting Cape St. Vincent and Gibraltar, it again flows southward; off the African coast, it continues as the Canary Current. On currents, see Admiralty Office, *Admiralty Weather Manual* (London, 1938), 204; Arthur Strahler, *Physical Geography* (New York, 1951); D. E. Pedgley, *A Course in Elementary Meteorology* (London, 1962); R. G. Barry and R. J. Chorley, *Atmosphere, Weather and Climate* (London, 1968); Hydrographic Office, *The African Pilot*, 13th ed. (Taunton, 1982), 1:31–54, 2:15–17, 183–96.

   William Bourne was one of the first to describe the clockwise circulation pattern of North Atlantic shipping in 1578, but he ascribed it to the currents. *A Booke Called the Treasure for Travelers* (London, 1578). His explanation persisted for a century. Edmond Halley delivered what became the locus classicus on winds in 1686: "An Historical Account of the Trade Winds, and Monsoons, Observable in the Seas Between and Near the Tropicks, with an Attempt to Assign the Phisical Cause of the Said Winds," RS, *Phil. Trans.* 16 (1686–87): 153–68. For later accounts, see William Falconar, *An Universal Dictionary of the Marine* (London, 1769); Albert Smyth, ed., *The Writings of Benjamin Franklin*, vol. 9 (New York, 1906), 372–413; Thomas Pownall, *Hydraulic and Nautical Observations on the Currents in the Atlantic Ocean* (London, 1787); James Rennell, *Observations on a Current That Often Prevails to the Westward of Scilly* (London, 1793). Not until the 1870s were circulation patterns seen to be caused by temperature changes. David W. Waters, *The Art of Navigation in England in Elizabethan and Early Stuart Times* (London, 1958), 20–21, 147–48, 201–6, 261–87, 311–12; Margaret Deacon, *Scientists and the Sea, 1650–1900: A Study of Marine Science* (London, 1971), 201–3.

5. Because return voyages from India, Africa, and the Canaries ran against the aforementioned winds, it was advisable to avoid Madeira and head for South America, and there pick up the Gulf Stream. William Dampier, *A New Voyage Round the World* (London, 1998), 271.

6. Zarco and Teixeira may have only rediscovered the island. Legend reports that Robert Machim of Bristol, his wife, and crew were blown off course and stranded on the island in 1344; Machim's wife died there and he erected a tomb on which he inscribed their saga. While Machim may not have survived, his crew made it to the Barbary Coast, where they were enslaved. There they made the acquaintance of another slave, Bartolomeu Perestrelo, whose daughter would marry Columbus and who eventually returned to Portugal. Perestrelo convinced King Duarte I to back an expedition to Madeira. Historians generally describe this expedition as occurring in 1419–20, although earlier dates are supportable. While there is no evidence to support

the idea of Phoenician visits, an Italian portolan chart from 1351 depicts the island and suggests pre-1350 exploration. Duncan confirms a 1425 expedition. T. Bentley Duncan, *Atlantic Islands: Madeira, the Azores and the Cape Verdes in Seventeenth-Century Commerce and Navigation* (Chicago, 1972), 7–8. Cf. Frederique Verrier, ed., *Voyages en Afrique noire* (Paris, 1994), 31–37, 174–75; Hans Sloane, *A Voyage to the Islands Madeira, Barbados, Nieves, S. Christophers, and Jamaica* (London, 1707), 1:9, citing Samuel Purchas's 1625 edition of Richard Hakluyt's 1601 translation of António Galvano's 1563 *Tratado*; Herman Moll, *Atlas Geographus; or, A Compleat System of Geography (Ancient and Modern) for Africa* (London, 1714), 4:691; Thomas Astley, "Supplement," in *A New General Collection of Voyages and Travels* (London, 1745), 1:558.

7. Jean Mocquet, *Travels and Voyages*, trans. Nathaniel Pullen (London, 1696), 18; Giacinto da Vetralla to Secretary of Propaganda, October 20, 1651, in Louis Jadin, *L'ancien Congo et l'Angola, 1639–55* (Brussels, 1975), 3:1,364; Moll, *Atlas*, 4:694; Jean-Bernard Bossu, *Travels in the Interior of North America, 1751–1762*, trans. Seymour Feiler (Norman, 1962), 12; Lord Adam Gordon, "Journal of an Officer . . . 1764–1765," in *Travels in the American Colonies*, ed. Newton D. Mereness (New York, 1916), 370; Robert Stewart to George Washington, March 10, 1768, in *Washington Papers*, Colonial Series, vol. 8 (1993), 75; George Forster, *A Voyage Round the World* (London, 1777), 1:9–10; "Log and Journal of the Ship *United States* on a Voyage to China in 1784," *PMHB* 55 (1931): 235–36; "A Description of the Island of Madeira," *Boston Magazine* (1784): 510, 551–4, 601–5; George Staunton, *An Authentic Account of an Embassy from the King of Great Britain to the Emperor of China* (London, 1979), 1:63; Robert Arbuthnot to ——, May 9, 1801, MS 5,208, fols. 26–27, NLS.

8. Louis Moreri, *Great Historical, Geographical and Poetical Dictionary*, ed. Jean Le Clerc et al., 6th ed. (London, 1694); Jeaffreson, *Young Squire*, 174; Sloane, *Voyage*, 9; William Gourlay, *Observations on the Natural History, Climate, and Diseases of Madeira, during a Period of Eighteen Years* (London, 1811), 6.

9. Moreri, *Dictionary*, s.v. "Madera"; Antoine Jean de Laval, *Voyage de la Louisiane* (Paris, 1728), 30; Anon., "A Description of the Island of Madeira," in Francisco Manoel de Mello, *An Historical Account of the Discovery of the Island of Madera*, abr. and trans. Francisco Alcoforado (London, 1750), 50, 31–32; *A Description of the Island of Madeira, with an Account of the Manners and Customs of Its Inhabitants* (London, 1783), 5–6; Robert Arbuthnot to ——, May 9, 1801, fol. 27; Richard Owen Cambridge, *The Works* (London, 1803), 120 ("The Scribleriad"); Duncan, *Atlantic Islands*, 29.

10. Sloane, *Voyage*, 9; Astley, "Supplement," 556; Moreri, *Dictionary*, s.v. "Madera"; Laval, *Voyage*, 29; *"Endeavour" Journal*, 165.

11. Gordon, "Journal," 371; Nicolau Caetano de Bettencourt Pita, *Account of the Island of Madeira* (London, 1812), 43–44; Gourlay, *Observations*, 6–10. Pita's account replicates nearly in full an anonymous work published eleven years earlier; he could not have written and published the earlier account in London, as he was only thirteen years old, and it is more likely he incorporated large chunks of it into his larger essay and then published it upon the completion of a medical degree at the University of Edinburgh.

12. Moreri, *Dictionary*, s.v. "Madera"; Astley, "Supplement," 558; Mocquet, *Travels*, 17; *Encyclopedia Britannica*, 3rd ed. (Edinburgh, 1797), 10:403.

13. Sloane, *Voyage*, 9; John Ovington, *A Voyage to Surat in the Year 1689* (Oxford, 1929), 11.

14. D. Fenning and J. Collyer, *A New System of Geography;: or, A General Description of the World* (London, 1771), 2:479.

15. Pita, *Account*, 33–34. Cf. Staunton, *Authentic Account*, 63.

16. Anon., *Description*, 47–48.

17. Astley, "Supplement," 560, paraphrasing Ovington, *Voyage*, 12; Thomas Heberden, "Observations on the Weather in Madeira," RS, *Phil. Trans.* 47 (1753): 357–59, 48 (1754): 617–19; Henry Hill, Notebook, 1763–64, Hill—SAGS; Gordon, "Journal," 371; *"Endeavour" Journal*, 162; Staunton, *Authentic Account*, 63; Gourlay, *Observations*, 32; Pita, *Account*, 33–34, 43; Robert Steele, *A Tour through Part of the Atlantic* (London, 1810), 24; Hydrographic Office, *African Pilot, Part I*, 2nd ed. (London, 1873), 65.

18. Sloane, *Voyage*, 9; Thomas Howe, "Observations on the Road of Funchal and the Isle of Madeira," in *The Annexed Sketch of the South Side of Madeira and the Desertas* (n.p., 1762), 3; Morse, *American Universal Geography*, 1:636; Gourlay, *Observations*, 31–8; Hydrographic Office, *African Pilot, Part I*, 69. See also Newton & Gordon to Alexander Gordon, February 19, 1769, NGL; Daniel Henry Smith to James Gordon, August 13, 1774, Loose Papers, Letterfourie Papers; Newton, Gordon & Johnston to Thomas Gordon, vol. 9, fol. 85, Newton, Gordon & Murdoch to Thomas Gordon, February 10, 1792, vol. 14, fol. 114, NGL; Leacock & Sons to William Leacock, June 21, 1794, Leacock & Sons, 1791–94 Letter Book, fol. 240, Leacock Papers.

19. Catalogue of Plants Brought from Madeira by J. Reed, 1690, Sloane MSS 2346/197–99, BL; "Description," 63; J. Britten, "R. Brown's List of Madeira Plants," *Journal of Botany* 42 (1904): 1–8, 39–46, 175–82, 197–200; D. T. Moore, "Some Aspects of the work of Robert Brown and the Investigator Naturalists in Madeira during August 1801," *Archives of Natural History* 28 (2002): 383–94; *"Endeavour" Journal*, 163; Gourlay, *Observations*, 11, 20, 27, 40.

20. Sloane, *Voyage*, 9; Ovington, *Voyage*, 132; Astley, "Supplement," 557; "Description," 61–63; Gourlay, *Observations*, 23. Madeira had its share of exotic fauna, too; it became famous for its waxbills, chaffinches, goldfinches, yellow finches, and canaries. It had no snakes and few frogs, toads, spiders, and beetles—pests infesting "most parts of Europe." Cadamosto, "Primeira Viagem," in *The Voyages of Cadamosto*, trans. and ed. G. R. Crone (London, 1937), 10; Sloane, *Voyage*, 11–12, 14; Anon., *Description*, 18; Astley, "Supplement," 562; Forster, *Voyage*, 1:26; Alfred Spencer, ed., *Memoirs of William Hickey*, 3rd ed. (London, 1919), 3:2; Morse, *American Universal Geography*, 1:636; "Account of a Voyage to the Western Coast of Africa, Performed by His Majesty's Sloop *Favourite* in the Year 1805," in *A Collection of Modern and Contemporary Voyages and Travels* (London, 1807), 6:10; Gourlay, *Observations*, 25.

21. According to official governmental censuses and more casual accounts. In 1455, Madeira's companion Porto Santo had 5 percent of the total inhabitants of both places; in 1797, it had 1 percent.

22. Contemporary reports by visitors are not always reliable. Lacroix stated the population in 1625 to be 25,000, closely approximating government figures. Shattocke, Jeaffreson, and Sloane gave 80,000 for 1675–1704, but the number was probably half that. Similarly, Howe in 1762 set the population at 100,000, and some repeated that number, while others raised it to 120,000, more than twice the actual total: James Gordon, 1763; Alexander Gordon, 1764; and Thomas Cheap, 1765. Stewart and botanists aboard Cook's *Endeavour* wrongly repeated 80,000. Early figures were repeated decades later, with little regard for more recent censuses and statistics: Anon., *Description*, 23. At least four official censuses were taken in the last four decades of the eighteenth century: 1767–69, 1779, 1781, and 1797; one may have been taken in 1743. A growth of 1 percent—the 1455–1851 average—was far below the rates achieved in all British American colonies (2.6 percent) and British North American colonies in particular (3 percent). McCusker and Menard, *Economy of British America*, 217. See source note to figure 1.5.

23. José Manuel Azevedo e Silva, *A Madeira e a construção do mundo atlântico* (Funchal, 1995), 2:646–47.

24. In 1768, for instance, there were 2,193 births and 5,243 deaths. *Encyclopedia Britannica*, 10:402. But this was a year in which there were serious outbreaks of measles and smallpox, when between fourteen and twenty people died each day. João António de Sá Pereira to Francisco Xavier de Mendonça Furtado, August 18, 1768, caixa ii, no. 340, AHU; Newton & Gordon to Francis Newton, July 17, 1768, vol. 4, fol. 229, NGL. The only other plausible explanation is a fall in marriages, a rise in marriage ages, or a fall in the size of families—all trends noticed by contemporaries. Still, even with infant mortality at 59 percent, the life expectancy of a child who survived birth was thirty-nine years, "near double" that of a child born and surviving in London. The natural growth rate was 2 percent; the crescimento natural was 1.4 percent. Thomas Heberden, "Of the Increase and Mortality of the Inhabitants of the Island of Madeira," RS, *Phil. Trans.* 57 (1768): 461–63; Richard Price to Benjamin Franklin, April 3, 1769, in *The Correspondence of Richard Price*, ed. W. B. Peach et al. (Durham, 1983), 1:58, 71–73; Gourlay, *Observations*, 28.

25. Maria de Lourdes de Freitas Ferraz, *Dinamismo sócio-económico do Funchal na segunda metade do século XVIII* (Lisbon, 1994), 90–91; Heberden, "Of the Increase and Mortality," 461; *EM*, vol. 1.

26. On the merchant contracts, see Alexandre de Gusmão, *Condiçoens com que se arremaata o assento do transporte dos Cazaes desta Corte, e das Ilhas para o Brazil* (Lisbon, 1747); caixa xix, nos. 117–18, AHU; João Gorjão, *O contracto dos tabacos* (Lisbon, 1833), 8; William Donovan, "The Politics of Immigration to Eighteenth-Century Brazil: Azorean Migrants to Santa Catarina," *Itinerario* 16 (1992): 47. Pre-1750 migrations deserve greater study. Cf. *EM*, 1:391–92; Virginia Rau, *Dados sobre a emigração madeirense para o Brasil no século XVIII* (Coimbra, 1965); Charles R. Boxer, *The Portuguese Seaborne Empire, 1415–1825* (London, 1969), 168–72; David Higgs, "Portuguese Migration Before 1800," in *Portuguese Migration in Global Perspective*, ed. Higgs (Toronto, 1990), 7–28; Maria de Lourdes de Freitas Ferraz, *Emigração madeirense para o Brasil no século XVIII* (Lisbon, 1989); Nicolas Sanchez Albornoz, "Los

migraciones anteriores al siglo XIX," in *Europa, Asia y Africa en America Latina yel Caribe*, ed. Birgitta Leander (Mexico City, 1989), 82–83; José Mattoso, ed., *História de Portugal* (Lisbon, 1993), 3:235–38.

27. For concern over out-migration in 1753, see caixa i, nos. 8–9, AHU; in 1758, see the *alvará* of July 4, 1758, which obliged the use of a passport, caixa i, nos. 154–57, AHU; in 1779, see João António de Sá Pereira to Martinho de Mello e Castro, November 20, 1779, caixa iii, nos. 526, 548–50, AHU; Antonio Delgado da Silva, comp., *Collecção da legislação portugueza* (Lisbon, 1830), 1:626–27. The best review of migration is Alberto Vieira, "Emigration from the Portuguese Islands in the Second Half of the Nineteenth Century: The Case of Madeira," in Higgs, *Portuguese Migration*, 43–50. Cf. Maria Licína Fernandes dos Santos, *Os madeirenses na colonização do Brasil* (Funchal, 1999); Walter Piazza, *Emigração açórico madeirense* (Funchal, 1999).

28. Ovington, *Voyage*, 13; Arbuthnot Letters, fols. 52–53, NLS; Pita, *Account*, 84, 120; Álvaro Rodrigues de Azevedo, *As saudades da terra* (Funchal, 1873), 746–51.

29. Nicole de la Croix, *Geographie moderne et universelle*, rev. ed. (Paris, 1800), 2:426; Pita, *Account*, 81–83. For the number of slaves in Madeira's population, see Albert Vieira, *Os escravos no arquipélago da Madeira, séculos XV A XVII* (Funchal, 1991), 143, table 32, but cf. 122–23, tables 24–25, and 174, table 42. Originally, Madeirans enslaved Canary Islanders to build *levadas* and work fields, but they eventually turned to black Africans. Sidney M. Greenfield, "Madeira and the Beginnings of New World Sugar Cane Cultivation and Plantation Slavery: A Study in Institution Building," *Annals of the New York Academy of Sciences* 292 (1977): 541–43.

30. Unfortunately, censuses did not isolate black slaves, nor did they distinguish free blacks bearing Portuguese names from other residents, since neither race nor color was a category of sufficient importance to Madeiran officials to merit mention. Accordingly, any estimate of the black population is speculative. September 24, 1663, E 3/86/155, IOL; "Escravos importados de 1718 a 21," *AHM* 6 (1939): 47–48; João José Abreu de Sousa, *O movimento do Porto do Funchal e a conjuntura da Madeira de 1727 a 1810: Alguns aspectos* (Funchal, 1989), 173–77; Maria de Lourdes de Freitas Ferraz, "A cidade do Funchal na 2.a metade do século XVIII—Freguesias urbanas," in *Actas do II colóquio internacional de história da Madeira* (Funchal, 1989), 267–68.

31. Newton & Gordon to Thomas Dongan, May 8, 1755, vol. 1, fol. 154, to Thomas Dongan, September 11, 1761, vol. 2, fol. 351, to Johnston & Jolly, May 29, 1765, vol. 3, fols. 409, 416, to Bean & Cuthbert, July 30, 1767, vol. 4, fol. 115, NGL; John Leacock to William Waddell, April 23, 1763, May 13, 1765, Leacock & Spence Letter Book, fols. 45, 65, 99, 185, 246, Leacock Papers; Fergusson & Murdoch to Neil Jamieson, June 4–August 4, 1765, Jamieson Papers, LC; Last Will of Dr. Richard Hill, August 15, 1761, vol. 8, fol. 5, Hill-JJS(A).

32. On abolition, see António Delgado da Silva, *Collecção de legislação portugueza desde a ultima compilação das Ordenaçãoes* (Lisbon, 1829–30), 1:811 (1761 *alvará*), 2:350, 500 (1768 *carta regia* and 1773 *alvará*); Francisco Moreira de Mattos to Francisco Xavier de Mendonca Furtado, November 20, 1767, caixa ii, no. 287, AHU; Newton & Gordon to Francis Newton, April 4, 1768, vol. 4, fol. 201, to Thomson & Whyt-

law, August 30, 1771, vol. 4, fol. 609, NGL. For continued presence in households, see Inventory, 1769, fol. 8, Inventory, August 29, 1771, Inventory, June 30, 1774, 1815, CGP-MWC. Of the treatment of blacks, little is known. See John Atkins, *A Voyage to Guinea, Brasil, and the West Indies* (London, 1735), 26; Fenning and Collyer, *New System of Geography*, 2:480; Morse, *American Universal Geography*, 1:635.

33. On the rights of strangers under international law, see Hugo Grotius, *De jure belli ac pacis* (Jena, 1673), bk. 2, chap. 2; Emmerich de Vattel, *Le droit des gens* (Leiden, 1758), bk. 1, chap. 19, sec. 213, bk. 2, chap. 8, secs. 99–115, 171–77; Polly J. Price, "Natural Law and Birthright Citizenship in Calvin's Case (1608)," *Yale Journal of Law and the Humanities* 9 (1997): 73–145. Discussion of the consul appears in chapter 6. Tamar Herzog has found much the same: local communities making distinctions between native and stranger without referencing legal codes. As a result, provincial decisions were largely ad hoc and contextual. *Defining Nations: Immigrants and Citizens in Early Modern Spain and Spanish America* (New Haven, 2003).

34. Trade between the countries had a long and profitable history. Since the reign of John I of England (1199–1216), the two had traded. Under a 1576 treaty, the Portuguese gave the English freedom to trade with Madeira and the Azores and, in return, the English allowed the Portuguese to trade with England and Ireland. For the pre-1642 relationship and the Latin version of the 1576 treaty, see Violet M. Shillington and Annie B. W. Chapman, *The Commercial Relations of England and Portugal* (London, 1907), 311, 144, 147, 151–53; Guernsey Jones, "Beginnings of the Oldest European Alliance: England and Portugal, 1640–1661," *Annual Report of the American Historical Association . . . for 1916* 1 (1919): 407–18. Trade relations suffered during Spain's occupation of Portugal between 1580 and 1640. Hoping to legitimize his right to the Crown, João IV sought to renew prior privileges Portugal had granted to England. His 1642 Treaty of Peace and Commerce codified "perpetual friendship": each country's nationals resident in the other country were to pay "only such customs and tolls as according to the ordinances of each place are at that time rated," and to have freedom of movement; their commerce was to be subject to the same laws and customs that applied to citizens, and to be guaranteed just treatment. Lewis Hertslet, comp., *A Complete Collection of the Treaties and Conventions* (London, 1840), 2:1–8; Shillington and Chapman, *Commercial Relations*, 177–204; Edgar Prestage, *The Diplomatic Relations of Portugal with France, England and Holland from 1640 to 1668* (Watford, 1925); Clyde L. Grose, "The Anglo-Portuguese Marriage of 1662," *Hispanic American Historical Review* 10 (1930): 313. Hardly was the ink dry than the agreements fell apart. João sided with Charles in the English civil war and, after Charles was beheaded, João continued to aid the Stuarts. The Commonwealth openly and aggressively retaliated, and a skirmishing war raged for several years. The two countries stopped fighting in 1653, and concluded treaty negotiations in 1654. The treaty that emerged represented "the zenith of the English ascendancy over Portugal." It allowed English merchants to trade to Portuguese settlements in India, Africa, and Brazil; in place of the more general stipulations of 1642, it set out detailed statements of English privilege; and it stipulated that the English were "to be favorably valued according to the rules of

the custom-house, and the ancient laws of the realm," and that, when fixed prices for valuation had to be changed, the changes should be negotiated with the English. Hertslet, *Complete Collection*, 2:8–20; Shillington and Chapman, *Commercial Relations*, 177–204.

35. Azevedo e Silva, *A Madeira*, 2:642–45.

36. Ibid., 1:404, 406; Duncan, *Atlantic Islands*, 54; Livros dos cobrancas de direitos por entradas (e saídas), no. 307 (1682), Alfândega do Funchal, and Livros dos direitos por saídas, no. 326 (1815), Provedoria e Junta da Real Fazenda do Funchal, AN-TdT.

37. Livros dos cobrancas e direitos, no. 307 (1682), Alfândega do Funchal, and Livros dos saídas, nos. 273 (1775), 326 (1815), Provedoria e Junta da Real Fazenda do Funchal, AN-TdT; Fenning and Collyer, *New System of Geography*, 2:480; Azevedo e Silva, *A Madeira*, 1:404–6.

38. Livros dos saídas, nos. 8 (1770), 273 (1775), 292 (1800), Provedoria e Junta da Real Fazenda do Funchal, AN-TdT; Pinkerton, *Modern Geography*, 2:767. Mention of ancillary foreigners can be found in English Factory Records, blue chest, bundle 1, packet 1, Blandy's Head Office, Funchal. There was a shortage of professionals to care for foreigners, except in medicine; there were fourteen registered surgeons (four foreign) in 1604–94, and 15 bloodletters in 1642–93. Azevedo e Silva, *A Madeira*, 2:726; A. Bandeira de Figueiredo, *Introdução a historia medica da Madeira* (Porto, 1963). Portuguese physicians and surgeons outnumbered foreign practitioners in 1650–1750. Azevedo e Silva, *A Madeira*, 2:758–62. The supply may have diminished after 1750. João António de Sá Pereira to Francisco Xavier de Mendonca Furtado, August 18, 1768, caixa ii, no. 340, AHU. After Thomas Heberden's death in 1769, medical care was provided by John Willison, George Drummond, Gregorio da Casta Faria, William Gourlay, Abraham Gordon, Joseph Adams, and W. R. Craufurd. English Factory Records, Blandy's Head Office, Funchal; Newton & Gordon to Parminter & Montgomery, April 4, 1768, vol. 4, fol. 200, NGL; Gourlay, *Observations*, dedication. Services improved by the turn of the next century. Caixa viii, nos. 1,715–17, AHU.

39. Newton & Gordon to Parminter & Montgomery, April 4, 1768, vol. 4, fol. 200, NGL; Thomas Cheap to Governor James Grant, August 30, 1765, bundle 244, BCM; Daniel Henry Smith to James Gordon, April 7, 1775, Letterfourie Papers; Francis Masson to Joseph Banks, May 27, 1773, Masson Letters, Natural History Museum, London; Cropley Rose to John Rawley, February 1780, Cropley Rose Letter Book, HSP; Benjamin Smith Barton to Benjamin Rush, July 2, 1787, Rush Papers, vol. 28, fol. 4, LCP; Spencer, *Memoirs*, 4; Francis Newton to Newton, Gordon & Murdoch, November 29, 1797, Loose Letters, CGP-MWC; Richard Lamar Bisset, Journal, April 11, 1801, item 2882, box 32, Independence Park Research Library, Philadelphia; Edward Jenner to John Eden, March 25, 1809, Dreer Collection, Physicians, Surgeons & Chemists Box, vol. 2, HSP; Jane Wallas to Miss Innes, February 24, 1818, Wallas Papers, GD 113/5/92/3, NA-Sc.

40. Robert Lamar Bisset to Henry Hill, December 19, 1791, folder 7, Hill-SAGS.

41. Francis Newton to Newton, Gordon & Johnston, February 1, 1790, vol. 12, fol. 218, NGL; *Pennsylvania Gazette*, May 7, 1800; *A Collection of Modern and Contemporary Voyages*, 5:8; A Lady of the State of New York, *The Fortunate Discovery* (New York,

1798), 76–81. The prince's trip to Madeira was aborted because it was feared the war with France might endanger his life.

42. Gourlay, *Observations*, v. The argument for Madeira as a health resort was buttressed by extended transatlantic medical debate, which was simply a reiteration of a point held by many doctors that, when drunk in moderation, Madeira was a painkiller or curative for many sicknesses. The most candid report was that of Joseph Adams, a physician on Madeira, who thought the situation "could not but be preferred by medical people for the winter residence of asthmatic, consumptive, or scrofulous constitutions." The "equal temperature" of the climate, the paucity of paved roads and wheeled carriages (lessening dust clouds), and the absence of artificial heating (diminishing particles raised by open fires) created conditions for an effective asylum. *A Short Account of the Climate of Madeira, with Instructions to Those Who Resort Thither for the Recovery of Their Health* (London, 1801), 4–9, 19. See also his "Observations on Pulmonary Consumption, and on the Utility of the Climate of Madeira, for Physical Patients," *Medical and Physical Journal* (April 1801): 10–20.

43. Robert Lamar Bisset to Henry Hill, December 19, 1791, vol. 10, fol. 212, Hill-JJS(A); Gourlay, *Observations*, v, 67. On the deadly tolls exacted by such cures, see Thomas Lamar to Ralph Inman, September 5, 1757, folder 1, box 1, Hill-SAGS; Robert Bisset to Henry Hill, July 28, 1764, vol. 6, fol. 162, Henry Hill to Robert Bisset, October 29, 1785, vol. 9, fol. 192, Dr. Abraham Gordon to Robert Bisset, June 27, 1788, Lamar & Bisset to Henry Hill, August 31, 1788, vol. 10, fols. 39, 43, Hill-JJS(A); Daniel Henry Smith to James and Alexander Gordon, July 15, 1774, Letterfourie Papers. For instances of untimely deaths in Madeira, consult the following gravestones in Funchal's old English burial ground: Christopher Mills, d. 1771; Charles Coye Brewster of London, d. 1786; Margaret Forbes of Callendar, d. 1798; Helen Charlotte Knight of Leacastle, d. 1801; and William Smart of London, d. 1802. On merchant resentment of invalids, see Newton, Gordon & Johnston to Francis Newton, February 1, 1790, vol. 12, fol. 218, Newton, Gordon & Murdoch to Francis Newton, December 6, 1792, fol. 455, to Thomas Gordon, December 15, 1794, vol. 16, fol. 193, to Thomas Gordon, March 5, 1798, fol. 260, and to Francis Newton, January 25, 1802, vol. 23, fol. 40, NGL; Leacock & Leacock to William Leacock, May 29, 1801, Leacocks Letter Book, fol. 258, Leacock Papers; March 23, 1805, Condell, Innes Letter Book, James Symington Papers, Oporto.

44. On the lack of newspapers, see *EM*, 2:191. The Society of Patriotism, Agriculture, Science, and Arts was founded in 1790, but nothing came of it. Caixa v, no. 887, AHU. Artistic associations did not appear until the next century. On the creation of the Aula de desenho e pintura in Funchal in 1809, see "Criação e funcionamento da Aula de desenho e pintura do Funchal," *AHM* (1931): 34–47. See also Steele, *Tour*, 30–3; John A. Dix, *A Winter in Madeira* (New York, 1850), 91.

45. On the confraternities, see Azevedo e Silva, *A Madeira*, 2:935.

46. Ovington, *Voyage*, 19–20. On the question of the maintenance of "a purity of blood" and how it affected the New Christian Jews, see generally Boxer, *Portuguese Seaborne Empire*, 266–69. Similarly, the Jesuits on the island, who allowed "Native Africans" to officiate as priests in other places, such as the Azores, were "totally averse" to "ad-

mitting . . . into Sacred Orders" anyone whose ancestors were Jewish or Muslim. On Pombal's ending of persecutions of New Christians, see J. Lucio d'Azevedo, *Historia dos Christãos Portugueses* (Lisbon, 1921), 346–58.

47. On the dullness of the place for single men, see Prince, "Journal," MHS; Francis Newton to David Campbell, December 6, 1748, vol. 1, fol. 7, NGL; John Barrow, *A Voyage to Cochinchina, in the Years 1792 and 1793* (London, 1806), 15.

48. Stewart to Washington, March 10, 1768, in *Washington Papers*, Colonial Series, vol. 8 (1993), 75–76; *An Account of a Voyage to India, China & c.* (London, 1806), 8.

49. Thomas Newton to Francis Newton, October 31, 1758, Thomas Newton Letter Book, fol. 44, CGP-MWC; Newton & Gordon to Parminter & Co., December 1759, vol. 2, fol. 106, NGL; Extract from Disbursements Book of Bachelors Hall Society, 1763–70, Cossart Scrap Book, CGP-PC; William Johnston to Thomas Gordon, June 11, 1785, Orders, vol. 9, fol. 33, NGL; William Johnston, *Plan of the Road of Funchal* (London, c. 1791). The property originally stretched from the Caminho da torrinha on the west to the line that was to become the funicular connecting the city to the Monte on the east; on the north it was bounded by the Levada de Santa Luzeia, and on the south by barren land.

50. Newton & Gordon to Francis Newton, July 28, 1764, vol. 3, fol. 322, to Samuel Bean, April 12, 1767, vol. 4, fol. 88, to Francis Newton, November 7, 1767, fols. 135, 302, vol. 5, fols. 246, 314, 417, vol. 8, fol. 347, and vol. 12, fol. 320, plus February 27, 1774, June 28, 1785, May 22, 1790, NGL; Newton & Gordon Wastebook and Ledger for "1764–1770," fols. 2, 9, 26, 27, 30, CGP-MWC; Account Current with James and Alexander Gordon, 1760, and Sundries Account, 1764, box 1, bundle 1759–66, Account with Scott, Pringle & Cheap, box 3, 1764–65, and Note, box 4, bundle 1766–67, CGP-Guildhall; Inventory, June 30, 1787, folder 4, Hill-EWS; John Leacock Sr. to William Leacock, June 20, 1798, Leacock Papers; Power of Attorney, October 3, 1783, vol. 9, fol. 18, Hill-JJS(A).

51. Marriages between foreigners were not uncommon. Because there was no Protestant church in the eighteenth century, Protestant marriages are difficult to document. Before 1782, the Englishman John Foster, for instance, married Catherine Clericeau, a daughter of the French Madeira merchant Nicolas Clericeau and a cousin of another French Madeira merchant, Jean Fayou, but the only record of it occurs in consular correspondence. Correspondence consulaire Madère, vol. 3: 1773–92, fol. 98, Affaires étrangères B/I/765, AN-Fr. There are better records for Catholic marriages. In the parishes of the Sé and São Pedro, the following marriages among foreigners were celebrated: 1758, Irish and Irish; 1759, English and French; 1760, Irish and American: 1761, Azorean and Bermudan; 1762, American (Barbados) and American (South Carolina); 1777, Irish and Irish; 1787, Scottish and American; 1799, Irish and Irish. Freitas Ferraz, *Dinamismo*, 63–64, 68–69.

52. Gordon, "Journal," 373; Hallbrook Gaskell, "Diary and Log of a Journey from Kilkenny to Liverpool and Thence to Philadelphia," 1789–91, *sub* May 2, 1789, MS Division, NYPL; Staunton, *Authentic Account*, 71; *Encyclopedia Britannica*, 10:402; Arbuthnot Letters, fol. 34, NLS.

53. The English merchants who married Portuguese women included Robert Cock,

Joseph Gillis, James David Webster Gordon, James Moore, and George Day Welsh. Nicolas de la Tuelliere, the French consul in 1775, also married the Portuguese Mlle. Monteiro de Guzman. Correspondence consulaire Madère, vol. 2, fol. 86, Affaires étrangères B/II/764, AN-Fr. Freitas Ferraz has reported on the marriages between non-Madeirans and foreigners in two central Funchal parishes. *Dinamismo*, 63–69. What she does not report, however, is the number of marriages between Madeirans and foreigners. The letters of foreigners and genealogical gleanings underscore their infrequency. Oddly enough, such marriages were not uncommon before 1550. Luis de Albuquerque and Alberto Vieira, *The Archipelago of Madeira in the XV-Century* (Funchal, 1987), 41. On English-speaking women marrying Portuguese men, see Ovington, *Voyage*, 19.

54. For an early exception to noncooperation, see Maria Julia de Oliveira e Silva, *Fidalgos-Mercadores no século xviii: Duarte Sodré Pereira* (Lisbon, 1992), 270, 326.

55. Arbuthnot Letters, fols. 52, 58, NLS. English consuls usually spoke Portuguese. William Norris to Thomas Norris, February 18, 1698, in Thomas Heywood, ed., *The Norris Papers* (Manchester, 1847), 44; Thomas Cheap to Earl of Rochefort, June 3, 1771, SP 89/71/130, NA-UK. Other instances of Britons and Americans speaking and writing Portuguese include James Gordon (A State of the Case, 1758, Letterfourie Papers), Joseph Gillis (Robert Bisset and Joseph Gillis to Henry Hill, February 28, 1770, folder 5, Hill-SAGS), John Marsden Pintard (Pintard to Elias Boudinot, January 15, 1783, ABS), James Searle (Searle to Boudinot, March 25, 1783, Connarroe Collection, vol. 1, fol. 85, HSP), Marien Lamar (Robert Lamar Bisset to Henry Hill, December 9, 1791, vol. 10, fol. 203, Hill-JJS(A)), and Lewis Searle Pintard (John Marsden Pintard, *To Timothy Pickering, Esq., Secretary of State* [New York, 1800], 12).

56. Newton & Gordon to Francis Newton, November 23, 1771, vol. 4, fol. 623, NGL. Governors came to recognize the importance of the British and British Americans to the economy of the island. They increasingly interceded in legal process on behalf of "strangers." Robert Bisset to Henry Hill, May 15, 1770, vol. 7, fol. 262, Hill-JJS(A). While dealings with one another increased, mutual suspicions persisted. Even by 1815, a very keen unwillingness of "strangers" to aid "natives" was evident. This reluctance operated on both the inter- and intrafirm levels. One example was the low number of firms with both British or American and Portuguese partners. The only known firms to have both in them include Amsinck, Connor & Passos; Bettencourt & Donaldson; Blackburn, Jenkins, Sanches & Co.; Carvalhal, Allen, Araujo & Co.; Da Cunha & Welsh; Dee & Goddard; De Vasconcelos & Brun; three partnerships formed by Pantaleao Fernandes; Jean Fayou & John Foster; Gonçalves & Denyer; Halloran, Da Costa Campos & Gordon; Pacheco & Pope; Theodore & Haddock.

57. On Masonic lodges, see António Egídio Fernandes Loja, *A luta do poder contra a maçonaria* (Lisbon, 1986), 245–315, 485–504. For a more general discussion of Freemasonry in Madeira, with good lists of members, see A. H. de Oliveira Marquês, *História da Maçonaria em Portugal* (Lisbon, 1990), 1:37–39, 45–49, 67–69, 130–43, 167–68. Among the 194 Masons who frequented the Funchal lodge in 1785–92 were eighteen foreigners. Madeira's Masons were persecuted in 1768–79, and again in 1792 out of fear of a link between island Masons and French revolutionaries. José

Viega Torres, "Promesso social," *Revista crítica de ciencias socias* 4 (1999): 109–35. Foreigners did not discuss their Masonry much, yet see Daniel Henry Smith to James Gordon, June 1–4, 1774, Letterfourie Papers.

58. Duncan, *Atlantic Islands*, 7–8; Regimento sobre a imposicao do vinho, 1461, 1545, and in *AHM* 15 (1972): 11–13; Hans Staden, *The Captivity of Hans Staden of Hesse, in A.D. 1547–1555, among the Wild Tribes of Eastern Brazil* (London, 1874), 16; Duarte Lopes, *Aanmerkelijke en geheugnis-waardige scheeps-togt . . . anno 1578* (Leiden, 1706).

59. Charles Sorel, *Le berger extravagant* (Paris, 1627), trans. as *The Extravagant Shepherd* (London, 1654), 160; Louis Jadin, *L'Ancien Congo et l'Angola, 1639–1655: D'après les archives romaines, portugaises, néerlandaises et espagnoles* (Brussels, 1975), *sub* 1651; Sloane, *Voyage*, 10; Noel Deerr, *The History of Sugar* (London, 1949), 1:100–105; Duncan, *Atlantic Islands*, 31; Barbara L. Solow, "Capitalism and Slavery in the Exceedingly Long Run," *JIH* 17 (1987): 719, 730.

60. For discussion of the export of wine and evolution of the pipe, see chapter 5. Cf. A. J. Biddle, *The Land of the Wine* (London, 1901), 2:194; Alberto Vieira to David Hancock, August 1998, containing MS table of exports.

61. Francis Newton to George Spence, December 6, 1748, vol. 1, fol. 10, January 30, 1754, vol. 1, fol. 82, October 23, 1754, vol. 1, fol. 126, NGL; Spence & Leacock to Parminter & Montgomery, April 23, 1763, to John Dale, September 15, 1764, Spence, Leacock & Spence Letter Book, fols. 47, 180; Robert Bisset to Henry Hill, November 25, 1769, folder 3, Hill-SAGS; Newton & Gordon to Francis Newton, September 14, 1770, vol. 4, fol. 514, June 9, 1777, vol. 6, fol. 239, NGL. H. E. S. Fisher, *The Portugal Trade: A Study of Anglo-Portuguese Commerce, 1700–1770* (London, 1971), 64–68, provides an excellent discussion of the Anglo-Portuguese textile trade, but ignores Madeira's participation in it. On the advantages brought by retail trading, see also Alexander Gordon to James Gordon, February 14, 1761, Letterfourie Papers; John Leacock to William Leacock, August 20, 1800, Leacock Papers.

62. Ovington, *Voyage*, 10–11, as paraphrased in Astley, "Supplement," 559; Parkinson, Reworking of Banks' Journal, typescript, 5, Royal Geographical Society, London; *EM*, 2:59, 61.

63. Mateus Fernandes, "Planta do Funchal" (1570), Biblioteca Nacional, Rio de Janeiro, reproduced in António Aragão, *Para a história do Funchal* (Funchal, 1979), plate 2; Azevedo e Silva, *A Madeira*, 1:147; *AHM* 3 (1933): 161–63. On the area of the town c. 1650–1700, see Sir John Narborough et al., *An Account o f Several Late Voyages and Discoveries to the South and North* (London, 1694), 3; Shattocke, "A Description," c. 1675, Eg. 2395, fol. 649, BL.

64. Barrow, *Voyage*, 7. Other accounts, however, suggest the town had doubled in length to three miles by the 1790s. Morse, *American Universal Geography*, 1:635.

65. Azevedo e Silva, *A Madeira*, 2:661, 669; Phérotée de Lacroix, *Relation universelle de l'Afrique, ancienne et moderne* (Lyons, 1688), 3:711; Shattocke, "Description," fol. 649; Sloane, *Voyage*, 9, 12; Stewart to Washington, March 10, 1768, *Washington Papers*, Colonial Series, vol. 8 (1993), 75; Mappa geral, 1797, caixa vi, no. 996, AHU; Pita, *Account*, 81, 100; João José Abreu de Sousa, "A população da freguesia da Sé em 1700,"

Das artes e da história da Madeira 7 (1968): 10–17; Barrow, *Voyage*, 7; *EM*, 3:104. In 1797, Funchal's three urban parishes contained 11,934, and its four rural parishes 6,958. Caixa vi, no. 996, AHU. Early nineteenth-century commentators like Pita give a larger population: 30,000 for 1812. Pita, *Account*, 100. But these are gross overestimates.

66. Francis Rogers, "The Diary," in *Three Sea Journals of Stuart Times*, ed. Bruce S. Ingram (London, 1936), 221; Gordon, "Journal," 372. Customs posts were created in 1477, and a structure to house the Funchal post was ordered to be built in 1486. Albuquerque and Vieira, *Archipelago*, 58. Designs and illustrations of the Alfândega Nova built in 1515–16 appear in Aragão, *Para a história*, ills. 23–24.

67. Rogers, "Diary," 221.

68. Rui Carita, *Introduçao à arquitectura militar na Madeira: A Fortaleza-Palácio de São Lourenço* (Funchal, 1991).

69. Mocquet, *Travels*, 17; Azevedo e Silva, *A Madeira*, 1:147; Shattocke, "Description," fol. 649; Jeaffreson, *Young Squire*, 173; Sloane, *Voyage*, 12; Laval, *Voyage*, 32; *Etat present de Portugal en l'année MDCCLXVI* (Lausanne, 1775), 94; Captain Skinner's *Plan of the Town of Funchal*, engraved in London in 1775; caixa xvii, no. 4,847 (1782), caixa xvi, no. 4,610 (1819), AHU.

70. On the governor and his command of the military, see Howe, "Observations," 2–3; Rigobert Bonne and Nicolas Desmarest, *Atlas encyclopédique* (Paris, 1788), map 102a; Forster, *Voyage*, 1:15. During the French and Napoleonic wars, the government increased regulars to 300 in 1793, 1,300 in 1796, and 2,898 in 1807. After 1815, military units returned to pre-1796 levels. Morse, *American Universal Geography*, 1:636; Diogo Pereira Forjaz Coutinho to Luis Pinto de Sousa Coutinho, July 16, 1797, caixa v, no. 976, AHU; caixa vii, no. 1,604 (1805), caixa viii, no. 1,685 (1806), caixa xvi, no. 4,611 (1807), and caixa xvii, nos. 4,610, 4,612 (1819), AHU. See also Paulo Miguel Rodrigues, *A política e as questões militares na Madeira o período das guerras napoleónicas* (Funchal, 1999), 435–47.

71. Luís Caetano de Lima, *Gèografía historíco de todos os estados soberanos de Europa* (Lisbon, 1734), 1:345; Forster, *Voyage*, 1:14–15; Wyndham Beawes, *A Civil, Commerical, Political, and Literary History of Spain and Portugal* (London, 1793), 2:174; SP 89/20/70–9, NA-UK; Mocquet, *Travels*, 15; Arbuthnot Letters, fols. 26–28, NLS; Newton & Gordon to Francis Newton, November 9, 1775, to John Montgomery, November 15, 1775, vol. 6, fols. 11, 14, NGL.

72. Azevedo e Silva, *A Madeira*, 1:612. At the Funchal Alfândega, there was a factor, a scribe for ship entrances (*entradas*), a scribe for ship clearances (*saídas*), four inspectors, the inspectors' four scribes, a receiver, a scribe of the *quinto* tax, the captain of the port (*alcaide do mar*), and the waterfront supervisor (*patrão-mor da ribeira*, also known as captain of the long-boat), plus a bevy of lesser officers, a doorman, and at least eight guards.

73. Colleção pombalina, MS 455, fol. 106 (November 10, 1772), fols. 150–55, BNL; Alberto Vieira, *Breviario*, 2nd ed. (Funchal, 1991), 49–53.

74. João Domazio Gorjao, *O contracto dos tabacos* (Lisbon, 1833); Dauril Alden and Warren Dean, eds., *Essays concerning the Socioeconomic History of Brazil and Portuguese*

India (Gainesville, 1977), 35, 41; Stuart Schwartz, *Sugar Plantations in the Formation of Brazilian Society: Bahia, 1550–1835* (Cambridge, 1985), 181, 185, 417; Robert Bisset to Henry Hill, July 20, 1763, January 1770, Hill Papers, vol. 6, fol. 61, Hill-JJS(A); Newton, Gordon & Murdoch to Tulloh, Brodie & Connell, April 20, 1802, to Chase, Chinnery & McDowall, May 3, 1802, to Joseph S. Lewis, November 28, 1807, vol. 23, fols. 233, 266, vol. 29, fol. 442, NGL.

75. Jeaffreson, *Young Squire*, 176; *EM*, vol. 1; Benedita Camara to David Hancock, July 16, 18, 2007.

76. Cheap to Pownall, July 1, 1765, CO 388/95, NA-UK.

77. On blocks theoretically raised in Portugal by natural law, and the ad hoc nature of local adjudication, see note 33, above. Cf. obstructions to property ownership by aliens residing in England. Daniel Statt, "The City of London and the Controversy over Immigration, 1660–1722," *Historical Journal* 33 (1990): 46; William Blackstone, *Commentaries on the Laws of England* (Chicago, 1979), 1:355–63; William S. Holdsworth, *A History of English Law* (Boston, 1926), 9:72–99; Clive Parry, *Nationality and Citizenship Laws of the Commonwealth and of the Republic of Ireland* (London, 1957), 40–65.

78. Great Britain Board of Trade, *Journal of the Commissioners for Trade and Plantations* (London, 1925), 4:28; John Marsden Pintard to Elias Boudinot, August 24, 1783, Boudinot Correspondence, ABS; John Leacock Jr. to William Leacock, January 18, 1800, Leacock & Leacock Letter Book 1799–1802, fol. 107, Leacock Papers. Lawsuits were "very troublesome," for "a determination" in Madeira was "only a determination that the same thing, however clear & obnoxious, must by tried in Portugal," unless of course a bribe was paid. Newton & Gordon to Parminter & Montgomery, August 20, 1768, vol. 4, fol. 236, NGL.

79. Spence, Leacock & Spence to William Bell, May 1, 1765, in Spence, Leacock & Spence 1762–65 Letter Book, Leacock Papers.

80. On the inequities of criminal justice, see James Moore, Petition, 1780, SP 89/92/413–520, NA-UK. Penal laws were seldom "enforced as they ought" to have been, and death, which was required for murder, was seldom inflicted on the natives if it was murder; a native had his relatives simply raise, through "friendly interruption," a defense of the protection of the honor of a woman, and all charges were dropped as a matter of course—even if no woman had been involved. Incarceration laws were invoked at the slightest pretense, and one could be easily imprisoned without cause. Foreigners and their properties were frequently abused.

81. On the slow handling of commercial suits, see Petition of Susanna Barrett, c. 1749, SP 89/49/1, 4, 7, 164, NA-UK. Bankruptcy law operated in much the same way as debt law. Bankrupts were not secure in their persons and were not exonerated from all retrospective demands. Appendix H, 1788, FO 63/11, NA-UK. The affairs of John Searle & Co., which had, by 1789, been "many years in the utmost confusion," underscore the point of insecurity. Government could be first claimant; when Searle owed "more than all his property can pay," the claims of the government were preferred over "those of residents." Newton, Gordon & Johnston to James Bell, September 26, 1789, vol. 12, fol. 142, NGL.

82. *Journal of the Commissioners for Trade and Plantations, 1718–1722*, 28; Newton & Gordon to Parminter & Montgomery, August 20, 1768, vol. 4, fol. 236, NGL. On Madeirans being forced to go to Lisbon and lengthy processual delays there, see Newton & Gordon to Parminter & Montgomery, August 14, 1771, May 25, 1776, NGL.

83. 600$000 was the rough equivalent of £173 sterling in 1775, which was the same as £16,195 sterling in 2006, using the retail price index. On Portuguese and British currency, see "Note on Conventions," at the end of the present volume. In the pages that follow, Portuguese, Portuguese colonial, and British colonial money is usually converted into British money for ease of comparison. Cf. the "troublesome lawsuit" the Hills confronted when a native landowner sued them over the right "of taking water out of the Nuns' caneland." The governor and chief judge sided with Lamar, Hill & Bisset, and the case was decided in its favor. Robert Bisset to Henry Hill, May 15, 1770, vol. 7, fol. 262, Hill-JJS(A).

84. *Bolton Letters*, vol. 2, *sub* March 31, 1705; Cheap to Pownall, July 1, 1765, CO 388/95, NA-UK. On the conservador, whose choice had to be approved by the island government, see A. R. Walford, *The British Factory in Lisbon and Its Closing Stages Ensuing upon the Treaty of 1810* (Lisbon, 1940), 41–43.

85. John Leacock Jr. to William Leacock, January 18, 1800, Leacock & Sons 1799–1802 Letter Book, fol. 107, Leacock Papers.

86. Azevedo e Silva, *A Madeira*, 2:807–8.

87. Albuquerque and Vieira, *Archipelago*, 59–60; *EM*, 1:257. In the 1770s, a general *junta* was established to sit in judgment over divisional *câmaras*; composed of the governor and thirteen procuradors elected by the chambers and councils, it ensured equal assessment of taxes.

88. Newton & Gordon to Francis Newton, July 17, 1768, May 8, 1790, vol. 4, fol. 229, vol. 12, fol. 316, NGL; Decrees and Certificates, caixa iii, nos. 518 (August 5, 1779), 531–36, 537 (November 20, 1779), 541 (November 20, 1779), 538 (November 27, 1779), 547, AHU. By the end of the eighteenth century, the Council had adopted a system whereby the rights to gather taxes were auctioned off in Funchal every other year. Alberto Vieira et al., "O munícipio do Funchal (1550–1650)," in *Actas I colóquio internacional de história da Madeira* (Funchal, 1990), 2:1,010; Vieira, *Breviario*, 53.

89. Lacroix, *Relation*, 711; Forster, *Voyage*, 1:11, 15; Carta do Sargento Mór e mappa geral, 1797, caixa vi, no. 996, AHU; Steele, *Tour*, 22; Azevedo e Silva, *A Madeira*, 1:128, 2:583, 959–61; "Relação de toda a despeza que Sua Magestade manda fazer em cada no na ilha da Madeira do rendimento que n'ella tem a Fazenda real," 1739, caixa i, no. 2, AHU; Parkinson, Re-working of Banks' Journal, 6; Rogers, "Diary," 221; Ovington, *Voyage*, 22.

90. Shattocke, "Description," fol. 649; Jeaffreson, *Young Squire*, 174–76; Rui Carita, *O Colégio dos Jesuítas do Funchal*, 2 vols. (Funchal, 1987); "Alguns documentos do mosteiro de Santa Clara do Funchal," *AHM* 4 (1935): 171–73.

91. Ovington, *Voyage*, 20–1; Atkins, *Voyage*, 26; Lima, *Geografia*, 345; Forster, *Voyage*, 1:15–16; Abel A. da Silva, "Seminario do Funchal," *Das artes e da história da Madeira* 6 (1964): 2, 6. Other manifestations of Catholic power were almshouses and hospitals,

the most prominent being the Hospital de São Lazaro, aiding lepers and, by 1700, smallpox victims and "such as have smarted for their feminine pleasures." Santa Casa da Misericórdia do Funchal, vol. 425-A, fol. 79v, ARM; "O hospital velho do Funchal," *AHM* 7 (1949): 115–18; José Pereira da Costa, "Notas sobre o hospital e a Misericórdia do Funchal," *AHM* 14 (1964–66): 122–23; Azevedo e Silva, *A Madeira*, 2:763, 773–74; Moll, *Atlas*, 4:695; Laval, *Voyage*, 31; Lima, *Geografia*, 345; Anon., *Description*, 67; *"Endeavour" Journal*, 163–64.

92. Ovington, *Voyage*, 20; Atkins, *Voyage*, 26; Lima, *Geografia*, 345; Forster, *Voyage*, 1:15–16; Pita, *Account*, 104. Pombal issued a decree on September 1, 1759, mandating the deportation of all Jesuits from Portugal and its dependencies. Correa de Sá to ——, November 6, 1767, caixa ii, nos. 284–85, Diogo Forjaz Pereira Coutinho to Martinho de Mello e Castro, December 6, 1789, caixa v, no. 864, AHU; Staunton, *Authentic Account*, 72; Steele, *Tour*, 28–29.

93. Many of the earliest converted vineyards were owned by religious orders. For a list of vine land rented out by the Santa Clara nuns in 1644, see Alberto Vieira, "A vinha o vinho," in *Os vinhos licorosos e a historia*, ed. Vieira (Funchal, 1998), 101–2. For later rentals by another convent, see Maria Eduarda Gomes, *O convento da encarnção* (Funchal, 1995).

94. Ovington, *Voyage*, 22. Cathedral canons only occasionally approved the burial of a Protestant in their cemetery. On the grant of a cemetery, see SP 89/54/1–9, NA-UK; Graham Blandy, ed., *Copy of Record* (Funchal, n.d.), 2. The first to be buried was the wife of the tavern keeper Henry Shapcote in 1770. Headstones indicate that non-British Protestants found rest there, too.

95. William W. Manross, ed., *The Fulham Papers in the Lambeth Palace Library* (Oxford, 1965), 239; Gaskell, "Diary and Log," *sub* May 5–7, 1789. Under Portuguese law, the English could not build a church that looked like a church; as a result, their building resembled more a hall or library. Blandy, *Copy*, 7; James W. Purves, *An Island Story: The Scots in Madeira* (Edinburgh, 1940); James M. Boxam, *The Church of England in Madeira* (London, 1857); H. A. Newell, *The English Church in Madeira* (Oxford, 1931). The situation of the Protestants was similar to that of the Moors and Jews, who had no mosques and synagogues, and received unequal treatment in marriage. Ovington, *Voyage*, 19–20.

96. Staunton, *Authentic Account*, 73. For an instance of early "oppressions," see Extract of a Letter from John Bisse[t], February 15, 1721, SP 89/90/39, and related papers, SP 89/29/83, 91, 99, 101, 103, 105, NA-UK.

97. Forster, *Voyage*, 1:11; Pita, *Account*, 105; "Log and Journal of the Ship *United States*," 238; Barrow, *Voyage*, 6. William Bolton's house was probably one of the few in 1700 with sash windows. *Bolton Letters*, 1:175.

98. Abreu de Sousa, "A população da Freguesia," 15; Mappa geral, 1803, caixa vii, no. 1,585, AHU. On the professionals and artisans in 1770–83, see Fatima Freitas Gomes, "Offi-cias e ofícios mecânicos no Funchal (séculos XVIII a princípios do século XIX)," in *Actas . . . II*, 212. On shops, see "Account of a Voyage to the Western Coast of Africa," 6:7; Account of Voyage from Dublin to Madeira, MS 14,165, Grattan Papers, NLI.

99. *"Endeavour" Journal*, 163.

100. Good illustrations and plans of the buildings and houses appear in Aragão, *Para a história*.
101. Gordon, "Journal," 372; Pita, *Account*, 104; "A Description," 55–56.
102. The now-demolished house lay next to the present-day building containing the Madeira Wine Company offices, on the corner of the Rua de São Francisco and Avenida Arriaga. March's house is described in some detail by Edward Wells, an American who stayed there in 1836–37. March (1791–1863), a New Hampshire native, worked as a clerk for another house for several years. On his early activities, see: Inventory Book, vol. 3, 1790–97, entries for 1798 and 1801, CGP-MWC; Newton, Gordon & Murdoch to Partners, May 13, 1806, vol. 27, fol. 355, NGL. In 1816, he became the American consul. Edward Wells, "A Trip to Madeira, 1836–1837," in *Madeira Fragments*, ed. Graham Blandy (Funchal, 1971), 8–10. An early nineteenth-century description of "a secondary house" appears in Theodore Hook's 1831 novel *Maxwell*, 2:61–64. "An English merchant's residence" is described in William Wilde, *Narrative of a Voyage to Madeira, Tenerife, and along the Shores of the Mediterranean* (Dublin, 1844), 60. For furnishings of similar houses, see the Newton & Gordon Inventory Books, 1770–1815, CGP-MWC.
103. Wells, "A Trip to Madeira," 8–10.
104. Technically, a *quinta* was the residence of a large rural property, and a *solar* was a manor house; in fact, there were few distinctions. José de Sainz-Trueva, "O Solar Nossa Senhora da Piedade," *Atlantico* 20 (1989): 302n2, lists known *quintas* and *solares* and their owners: Charles Murray, Bello Monte, 1779–88; Thomas Loughnan, 1773–79; Francis Theodore, 1773; Albuquerque e Camara, 1783; Page; Hill, Achada, 1754–90s; James Murdoch, Vale Formosa; Charles Alder, 1789; John Leacock, Vigia, Sao João Parish, 1788; Thomas Cheap, Pico dos Firios. For an account of the *quintas* at Monte, see Daniel Henry Smith to James and Alexander Gordon, May 29, 1775, Letterfourie Papers. On Hill's Achada, see Will, August 15, 1761, vol. 7, fol. 5, List, 1762–67, August 30, 1763, July 28, 1764, April 14, 1766, January 31, 1775, Hill-SAGS.
105. Sloane, Papers, from a Letter of 1704, Add. MSS 3,324, fols. 240–43, BL; Rogers, "Diary," 222; Gordon, "Journal," 372; *Encyclopedia Britannica*, 10:402.
106. "Description," 52–53; Letters from 1759, 1761, 1763, 1766, in Newton & Gordon, Letterfourie, and Leacock collections for accounts of shipwrecks off Funchal, esp. Robert Bisset to Henry Hill, October 22, 1763, vol. 6, fol. 75, Hill-JJS(A); Cropley Rose to John Fernandes, December 29, 1779, Cropley Rose Letter Book, HSP; *New-Haven Gazette*, April 17, 1788, 3.
107. Sloane, *Voyage*, 11–12; Pita, *Account*, 100; Howe, "Observations," 2–3; R. Bougard, *Le petit flambeau de la Mer; ou, Le veritable guide des pilotes cotiers* (Havre de Grace, 1789), 378–80; Barrow, *Voyage*, 5.
108. To handle unruly surf, Madeirans devised a special boat between 1650 and 1720: its oars were "shaped like oars, but much larger, and, towards the middle," there were "additional pieces of wood" in which were bored holes "to fix them upon two pegs . . . for the greater convenience in rowing." They fixed a joist or underledge on "the outside near the bottom" to prevent overturning. Atkins, *Voyage*, 27; Maria Riddell, *Voyages to the Madeira and Leeward Caribbean Isles* (Edinburgh, 1792), 2.

109. Gordon, "Journal," 371; João António de Sá Pereira to Francisco Xavier de Mendonca Furtado, August 30, 1768, caixa ii, no. 345, AHU; "Information," June 25, 1756, reproduced as document 6 in Maria da Paz A. Nunes Perestrelo de França, "Da administração pombalina no arquipélago da Madeira" (Ph.D. diss., University of Lisbon, 1965); Gordon, "Journal," 371; João António de Sá Pereira to Francisco Xavier de Mendonca Furtado, August 30, 1768, caixa ii, no. 345, AHU; Robert Bisset to Henry Hill, January 31, 1775, folder 5, Hill-SAGS.
110. Gaskell, "Diary and Log."
111. Santos Simões, ed., *Isabella de França: Journal of a Visit to Madeira and Portugal* (Funchal, 1969), 81; *EM*, 1:124. The hoist was demolished in 1939.
112. *Livros dos direitos por entrada*, nos. 146–56, 232 (1727–75, 1815), Provedoria e Junta da Real Fazenda do Funchal, Alfândega do Funchal, AN-TdT.

CHAPTER 2. THE CULTURE OF THE VINE

1. Henry F. Link, *Travels in Portugal, and through France and Spain* (London, 1801), 368. Its importance, Link concluded, did not translate into high-quality product: the wine was "generally very bad" in Portugal, paling in comparison to that of Spain, and "moderate wine drinkers" of Portugal were served "bad or at least very moderate" wine.
2. David Hancock, "Commerce and Conversation in the Eighteenth-Century Atlantic World: The Invention of Madeira Wine, 1651–1815," *Journal of Interdisciplinary History* 29 (1998): 203–4. The concept is discussed at greater length in chapter 5.
3. *Cincinnati Western Spy*, 1815, passim.
4. Total yield figures survive for only twenty-two harvests; they are buried in merchant correspondences. Hancock, "Commerce and Conversation," 203–4. In principle it should have been possible to reconstruct the amount of wine produced on the island or the acreage under cultivation each year from the parish-by-parish documents recording the collection of the *dízimo, impoziçao sobre o vinho, real d'agua,* and *subsidio literario* taxes. But most parish records do not begin until the early nineteenth century, and no series covers an entire year for all parishes. Only the *subsidio literario* gives estate-by-estate levels, but even then records survive only from the last quarter of the eighteenth century.
5. Nitrogen feeds the leaves and, with chlorophyll, converts the salts into compound chemical substances. Phosphorus protects the vines against infertile flowers and gaps and irregular clusters in the bunches, hardens the vines, and increases their productivity. Potash promotes the production and ripening of quality fruit and increases resistance to certain diseases.
6. Ovington, *Voyage*, 12; Moll, *Atlas*, 4:691–92; Fenning and Collyer, *New System of Geography*, 1:479; Thomas Gordon to Francis Newton, July 12, 1774, vol. 5, fol. 374, NGL; Staunton, *Authentic Account*, 1:68; Pita, *Account*, 43–44; Gourlay, *Observations*, 14–15. Francisco Albequerque, "Mapas en que se aprestam . . ." (unpublished MS, 1997), 106, which reports on the low-altitude, bluff-clinging Fajóa dos Padres estate in Quinta Grande parish, slightly west of Câmara de Lobos. This estate exem-

plifies the riches of the island's soil. In a sample taken from it, 64 percent is a sandy-gravelly sediment, 29 percent clay, 3 percent *humidade*, and the rest organic material. Its soil is classifiable as arenaceous clay. Its chemicals include nitrogen, phosphor pentoxide, potassium oxide, calcium oxide, magnesium oxide, ferric oxide, and aluminum oxide. Its pH is 6.0, just below the 6.5–7.0 level considered ideal for vines; as a result, it requires some liming to raise its alkalinity. This slightly acidic soil facilitates a greater binding to the plant than to the soil.

7. Government wine production records are extremely exiguous. For the upper/lower distinction, see the seventeenth-century decisions of the Camara, setting thresholds for purchasing prices, in Vereações, passim, ARM, and, later on, John Leacock to William Leacock, September 18, 1799, Leacock Letters 1799–1802, fol. 71, Leacock Papers. On the color of wines produced in the southwestern area of the island, see Thomas Gordon to Francis Newton, March 12, 1768, vol. 4, fol. 188, NGL. On what was normally produced in the north, see Newton & Gordon to George and John Riddell, November 12, 1761, vol. 2, fol. 380, to N. P. Smith, November 23, 1771, vol. 4, fol. 618, to Pierce Butler, October 18, 1800, vol. 21, fol. 70, NGL; John Leacock to William Leacock, June 4, 1793, Leacock & Sons 1791–94 Letter Book, fol. 203, Leacock Papers. For the census of 1787, see caixa v, no. 977, AHU. The north also led in the production of wheat; in 1787, north-side wheat was nearly double south-side. A similar 1786 census appears in Papéis vários, MSS 219, no. 29, BNL. In that year, when output totaled 18,993 pipes, producers in northern parishes produced 13,265 pipes, whereas southerners produced only 5,728 parishes. In 1817 was reported a census that may have been of the 1813 harvest: south-side vineyards produced 30 percent, and north-side 70 percent, totaling 22,269 pipes. Paulo Dias de Almeida's Description of the Islands, Inventario, vol. 2, AHU.

8. Scott, Pringle & Co. to East India Company, July 23, 1786, E 1/79/47, IOL; Newton & Gordon to Thomas, Stephen & Rose Fuller, February 28, 1774, vol. 5, fol. 311, Newton, Gordon, Murdoch & Scott to Pierce Butler, October 18, 1800, vol. 21, fol. 70, NGL; Reflexões, 1784–86, Papéis vários, MSS 219, no. 29, BNL.

9. Vieira, "A vinha," 92; Dispatch of the Governor, July 7, 1759, MS 174, box 1, AHU.

10. This and the following paragraph are based on Ovington, *Voyage*, 13; Arbuthnot Letters, fols. 52–53, NLS; Pita, *Account*, 84, 120. The rents of lands formerly owned by the Jesuits are detailed in Azevedo, *As saudades*, 746–51.

11. João José Abreu de Sousa, *O Convento de Santa Clara do Funchal* (Funchal, 1991), 109; Jorge Valdemar Guerra, "A colonia na Madeira: Um testemunho do século XVIII," *Islenha* 9 (1991): 93–123, esp. 99–100; Alberto Vieira, "O contrato de colonia," *Diário de notícias*, July 30, 1988; Benedita Câmara, "The Portuguese Civil Code and the *Colonia* Tenancy-Contract in Madeira, 1867–1967" (unpublished MS 2002), 3–9. Colonia contracts are found in Livro da venda de dereitos de agua do Convento de Santa Clara, 11:518–30, Livro do tombo divino do ano de 1750 do Convento de Santa Clara, vol. 13 (1750–59), fols. 149–51, 161–70, as well as Contrato, 1747, J/E7/43 (1745), and Contrato, 1793, J/B8/Cx. 10/120, Documentos patrimoniais dos Ornelas Vasconcelos, Arquivo da Familia Ornelas Vasconcelos, ARM. Some of those recorded in wills are described in Vieira, "A vinha," 111–13.

12. For analogous institutional developments in Porto, see Paul Duguid, "Lavradores, exportadores, comissários, e capitalistas: Os componentes da região do vinho do Porto," *O Douro* (1996): 201–24, and, in Burgundy, see Thomas Brennan, *Burgundy to Champagne: The Wine Trade in Early Modern France* (Baltimore, 1997), xix–xxi, 38, 43, 52, 66–75, 160–77.

13. Henry Vizetelly, *Facts about Portugal and Madeira* (London, 1880), 159; Anon., *Description*, 24.

14. Aaron Hill, *The Works*, 2nd ed. (London, 1754), 2:138–39; Richard Bisset to Henry Hill, June 26, 1785, vol. 9, fol. 142, Hill-JJS(A).

15. Link, *Travels*, 372.

16. Ibid., 370.

17. Leonard Mascall, *The Country-man's New Art of Planting and Grafting* (London, 1656); Newton & Gordon to Henry Holland, March 25, 1764, vol. 3, fol. 282, NGL; *"Endeavour" Journal*, 1:161–62; Agostinho Ignacio da Costa Quintella, *Tratado para a cultura das vinha em Portugal* (Lisbon, 1800), 48–54; Link, *Travels*, 373; Pita, *Account*, 64.

18. Sloane, *Voyage*, 10; Ovington, *Voyage*, 12; *Bolton Letters*, vol. 2; Atkins, *Voyage*, 24; Staunton, *Authentic Account*, 1:69; Newton & Gordon to Thomas Gordon, July 25, 1794, vol. 16, fol. 25, NGL. See also Barrow, *Voyage*; "Inventories" Books, vols. 1794–97 and 1798–1800, CGP-MWC; Pita, *Account*, 66. New varieties could be acquired through London partners and correspondents. Richard Lamar Bisset to Henry Hill, December 19, 1791, Hill-SAGS.

19. Diogo Pereira Fojarz Coutinho to Corregedor, May 16, 1783, Governo civil, no. 521, fols. 52–72v, ARM; Francisco Moreira de Mattos to João António de Sá Pereira, February 1, 1768, caixa ii, no. 288, AHU.

20. Newton & Gordon to Michael White, January 24, 1768, vol. 4, fol. 169, to Bond & Ryland, October 5, 1768, vol. 4, fol. 255, to Theodore Stone, November 23, 1769, vol. 4, fol. 404, Thomas Gordon to Francis Newton, May 9, 1772, vol. 5, fol. 37, for Listrão, Newton & Gordon to Edward Wood, January 24, 1784, vol. 8, fol. 172, for Sercial, Thomas Murdoch to Francis Newton, May 4, 1792, vol. 14, fol. 180, Newton, Gordon & Murdoch to Harriet Horry, February 17, 1802, vol. 23, fol. 102, NGL. Robert Stewart to George Washington, March 10, 1768, in *Washington Papers*, Colonial Series, vol. 8 (1993), 75–76; Gourlay, *Observations*, 14–15. Gourlay lived in Madeira from 1783 and wrote his treatise in 1808. It is the most authoritative contemporary summation of eighteenth-century Madeira vinicultural practice.

21. Gourlay thought that twenty-three varieties were too many, and that the number should be reduced to Bual, Tinta Negro Mole, and Verdelho. Pita, who plagiarized much of Gourlay, specifically mentioned only thirteen, but he added Tinta Negro Mole and recommended reducing the number to it, Bastardo, Verdelho, and Bual. Gourlay, *Observations*, 14–15; Pita, *Account*, 66. On the various *castas*, both *tintas* and *brانças*, see EM, 3:384; Richard Mayson, *Portugal's Wines and Wine-Makers: Port, Madeira and Regional Wines* (San Francisco, 1992), 212–14.

22. Gourlay, *Observations*, 19; Robert Bisset to Henry Hill, June 1, 1765, vol. 6, fol. 242, Hill-JJS(A); Lamar, Hill, Bisset & Co. to Henry Hill, May 3, 1787, folder 5, Hill-SAGS;

Lamar, Hill, Bisset to Henry Hill, July 11, 1787, vol. 10, fol. 20, Hill-JJS(A); Richard Lamar Bisset to Henry Hill, September 5, 1798, folder 7, Hill-SAGS; Thomas Murdoch to John Gibbes, May 29, 1802, vol. 23, fol. 312, to Joseph S. Lewis, April 18, 1804, vol. 25, fol. 387, NGL; William Leacock to John Leacock, August 17, 1807, Leacock & Leacock Letter Book 1807–10, Leacock Papers.

23. On Malvasia, see Frederic De Peyster, ed., *The Life and Administration of Richard, Earl of Bellomont* (New York, 1879), vii; Astley, "Supplement," 561; William Johnston to Thomas Gordon, September 8, 1784, vol. 8, fol. 319, to Francis Newton, May 10, 21, 1786, vol. 9, fols. 199, 214, NGL; Lamar, Hill & Bisset to Henry Hill, April 12, 1787, vol. 12, fol. 9, Hill-JJS(A); Gourlay, *Observations*, 19. Green or "raw" Malmsey—a "medium between" "our fine dry wine . . . & the real [red] Malmsey"—had a "bastard sweetness." It was "not at all times to be met with." It was "a whimsical wine, and . . . sometimes difficult to fine down." On green Malmsey, see William Johnston to Charles Chambers, December 15, 1787, vol. 10, fol. 93, Thomas Murdoch to Mr. Ward, November 6, 1789, vol. 12, fol. 161, NGL. There was occasionally a type called "dry Malmsey," which had "the flavor of sweet malmsey but not its richness." It was "not a common liquor . . . & only to be met with early in the year." Consumers in certain places, like Montserrat, were "much in the custom of drinking it." Newton & Gordon to Bond & Ryland, June 15, 1776, vol. 6, fol. 102, NGL; John Leacock Sr. to William Leacock, February 19, 1796, Leacock & Sons Letter Book 1794–97, fol. 84, Leacock Papers.

24. On Tinta, see *Bolton Letters*, 2:35, 45; *Beekman Papers*, 1:281, 380; Nowlan & Burges to Duckett & Jebb, January 6, 1760, Nowlan & Burges Letter Book, 1759–62, fol. 84, Nowlan & Leacock to Richard Sheffield, January 19, 1779, Nowlan & Leacock Letters, 1774–81, fol. 240, John Leacock to Michael Nowlan, November 15, 1786, Leacock Letters, 1784–89 & 1792–98, fol. 363, Leacock Papers; Richard Lamar Bisset to Henry Hill, December 19, 1791, vol. 10, fol. 212, Hill-JJS(A); Gourlay, *Observations*, 19.

25. "Description," 58; Gourlay, *Observations*, 14. Cf. Quintella, *Tratado*, 42–47.

26. "Description," 58; Barrow, *Voyage*, 22.

27. "Description," 61. Forster, *Voyage*, 1:22–23; Hill, *Works*, 2:125–26, details the construction of trellises on Madeira in the 1740s. Vizetelly, *Facts*, 157, 175–76. According to Vizetelly, wine from tree-trained vines was "only fit for distillation into brandy," since "good wine only comes from grapes grown near the surface" on trellises.

28. "Description," 58–59; Barrow, *Voyage*, 22–23; Forster, *Voyage*, 1:21–24; Anon., *Description*, 25; Riddell, *Voyages*, 9–10; Gaskell, "Diary and Log," *sub* April 11, 1789; *Encyclopedia Britannica*, 10:403; Pita, *Account*, 61–65. Compare trellising in the Douro Valley. Link, *Travels*, 371.

29. Forster, *Voyage*, 1:21; *Encyclopedia Britannica*, 10:403, Pita, *Account*, 63, repeating Forster; Vizetelly, *Facts*, 178; José R. F. Cabral to Rodrigo de Sousa Coutinho, August 18, 1798, caixa v, no. 1,019, AHU.

30. A succinct account of the calendar appears in S.J., *The Vineyard* (London, 1727), 103–12.

31. Link, *Travels*, 371–72.

32. Pita, *Account*, 44. Cf. Quintella, *Tratado*, 42–47; Link, *Travels*, 372.

33. Alan R. Toogood, *Grapes* (Toronto, 1993); Bolton Letter Book, May 20, 1706, May 30, 1709, MS Division, University of Kansas Library, Lawrence; Thomas Gordon to Alexander Gordon, February 19, 1769, vol. 4, fol. 296, NGL; Robert Duff to James Duff, January 15, 1786, Letterfourie Papers. For a summation of the traditional Portuguese approach to pruning, see Quintella, *Tratado*, 37–42. Cf. other contemporary comments: Peter Collinson, 1730, in Marion Tinling, ed., *The Correspondence of the Three William Byrds of Westover, Virginia, 1684–1776* (Charlottesville, 1977), 1:423–26; Hill, *Works*, 1:126–27; Link, *Travels*, 371.

34. Memo, 1793, Condell, Innes Letter Book, fol. 24, Symington Papers; Quintella, *Tratado*, 42–7; Lionel Frumkin, *The Science and Technique of Wine* (Cambridge, 1974), 9; Hill, *Works*, 2:133.

35. Gourlay, *Observations*, 15; Pita, *Account*, 65, 68. Cf. S.J., *Vineyard*, 108; Hill, *Works*, 2:133; José Veríssimo Alvares da Silva, "Memória sobre a cultura das vinhas, e sobre os vinhos," in *Memorias de agricultura premiadas . . . 1787, e 1788* (Lisbon, 1788), 1:34–40. On cultivation in the Douro Valley, see John Croft, *A Treatise on the Wines of Portugal*, 2nd ed. (York, 1788), 8–9, 13–14, 16; Link, *Travels*, 368–83. In Spain, see Donald R. Abbott, "The Spanish and the Sherry Trade" (PhD diss., University of California, San Diego, 1990), 113–19. For French agricultural practice, see Roger Dion, *Histoire de la vigne et du vin en France des origines au XIXe siècle* (Paris, 1977), 424–648; J. B. Gough, "Winecraft and Chemistry in 18th-Century France: Chaptal and the Invention of Chaptalization," *Technology and Culture* 39 (1998): 74–104.

36. On wind and hail: John Leacock Sr. to William Leacock, June 21, 1794, Leacock & Sons Letter Book 1791–94, fol. 240, and William Leacock to John Leacock Jr., August 17, 1807, Leacock & Leacock Letter Book 1807–10, Leacock Papers; Thomas Murdoch to Thomas Gordon, October 14, 1795, vol. 16, fol. 415, NGL. On fog: Newton & Gordon to Parminter & Montgomery, July 27, 1760, vol. 2, fol. 204, NGL; Robert Bisset to Henry Hill, May 11, 1765, vol. 6, fol. 238, Robert Bisset to Henry Hill, July 20, 1773, vol. 8, fol. 144, Hill-JJS(A); William Johnston to Thomas Gordon, June 28, 1783, vol. 8, fol. 91, NGL. On heat: September 26, 1702, August 28, 1704, October 16, 1706, Bolton Letter Book; Daniel Henry Smith to James Gordon, August 13, 1774, September 20, 1777, Letterfourie Papers; Newton & Gordon to Francis Newton, April 25, 1779, vol. 6, fol. 459, NGL; William Leacock to John Leacock Jr., August 17, 1807, Leacock & Leacock Letter Book 1807–10, Leacock Papers; Thomas Murdoch to Thomas Gordon, October 15, 1791, vol. 13, fol. 423, NGL.

37. September 26, 1702, May 14, 24, 1707, Bolton Letter Book; Francis Newton to George Spence, October 27, 1753, July 19, 1756, vol. 1, fols. 77, 218, Newton & Gordon to Henry Holland, December 21, 1765, vol. 3, fol. 453, Thomas Gordon to Francis Newton, November 23, 1771, vol. 4, fol. 623, NGL; Scott, Pringle, Cheap & Co. to East India Company Directors, March 31, 1772, E 1/56/39, IOL; Daniel Henry Smith to James Gordon, September 20, 1777, Letterfourie Papers; Lamar, Hill, Bisset & Co. to Henry Hill, October 9, 1784, October 26, 1784, vol. 9, fol. 88, Hill-JJS(A); William Johnston to Thomas Gordon, October 27, 1784, vol. 8, fol. 341, to Thomas Gordon, August 27, 1785, vol. 9, fol. 79, to Francis Newton, September 29, 1790, vol. 13, fol. 44,

NGL; John Leacock Sr. to William Leacock, October 26, 1796, March 10, 1797, Leacock & Sons Letter Book 1794–97, fols. 163, 21, Leacock Papers; Newton & Gordon to Francis Newton, September 25, 1794, to Thomas Gordon, October 21, 1803, vol. 16, fol. 101, vol. 25, fol. 187, NGL; Diary, October 15, 1803, Condell, Innes Letter Book, fols. 43–47, Symington Papers.

38. Oidium, a powdery mildew native to North America, first ravaged the vine's green parts in the 1850s. A fine, translucent cobweb-like growth, it spread rapidly over a plant, and then, by the wind, from plant to plant. The disease considerably reduced both fruit set and overall yield; wines produced from infected vines bore peculiar flavors. Just as the islanders were recovering from this plague, a far more serious one struck in the 1860s: phylloxera, a small yellow root-feeding aphid, another import from America, which feasted on roots and decimated what remained of the vines. Noel Cossart, *Madeira: The Island Vineyard* (London, 1984), 86–91, 121–24.

39. Newton & Gordon to Kearny & Gilbert, February 8, 1759, vol. 2, fol. 9, to Francis Newton, July 30, 1770, vol. 4, fol. 506, NGL; Robert Bisset to Henry Hill, July 11, 1771, folder 5, Hill-SAGS; Newton & Gordon to Francis Newton, July 12, 1774, vol. 5, fol. 374, to Thomas Gordon, January 31, 1790, vol. 12, fol. 313, NGL. For an early description of a decline in vine fertility, see Ovington, *Voyage*, 11–12, who notes that grape yield declined from sixtyfold around 1450 to twenty-five-fold in 1689. Moll, *Atlas*, 692, repeats him. The lifespans of individual vines are unknown; no one mentioned them. Neither was the density per acre nor the rate of replacement ever commented upon.

40. *"Endeavour" Journal*, 1:161–62; Robert Bisset to Henry Hill, June 25, 1772, vol. 8, fol. 118, Joseph Gillis to Henry Hill, June 26, 1785, vol. 9, fol. 144, Hill-JJS(A).

41. Caixa ii, nos. 289–93, esp. 291 (1737), 311 (1768), 345 (1768), 346 (1768), AHU; Michael Nowlan to James Archbold, November 15, 1756, Nowlan & Burges Letter Book, 1756–59, fol. 20, Leacock Papers; Daniel Henry Smith to James Gordon, January 25, August 14, September 8, October 2, 1775, Letterfourie Papers.

42. Richard Miles & John Miles to I. Hobhouse & Tyndall, April 10, 1723, Jefferies MSS, vol. xiii, fol. 45, Bristol City Library, Bristol; William Johnston to Francis Newton, September 9, 1786, vol. 9, fol. 269, NGL; John Leacock Sr., to William Leacock, September 15, 1792, Leacock & Sons Letter Book, fol. 154, Leacock Papers. On different harvests for different grapes, the times being set by the cultivator, which prevailed in the 1600s and early 1700s, see September 26, October 7, 1702, Bolton Letters, University of Kansas Special Collections.

43. The impetus for the Funchal inquiry came from British ministers like Lord Shelburne, Sir Edward Hawke, the Duke of Grafton, and General Conway, who in 1767 complained to the Portuguese ambassador António de Mello about merchant adulterations; Mello wrote to Sá Pereira. On 1768, see caixa ii, nos. 289–93, 310–12, 346, AHU; Newton & Gordon to Francis Newton, January 6, 1768, vol. 4, fol. 157, NGL. On 1775, see Daniel Henry Smith to Gordon Brothers, September 8, October 2, 1775, September 18, 1776, —— 1776, to James Gordon, October 8, 1784, and Robert Duff's Journal, September 28, 1787, Letterfourie Papers; Newton & Gordon to Francis Newton, September 11, 1775, vol. 5, fol. 549, to Francis Newton, Novem-

ber 9, 1775, vol. 6, fol. 11, to Thomas Gordon, September 8, 1784, vol. 8, fol. 319, to Thomas Gordon, September 1, 1785, vol. 9, fol. 83, NGL.

44. For 1784 and 1785, see Bylaws of the Harvest, September 4, 1784, Governo civil, no. 70, fols. 29v–33, Further Regulations, September 13, 1785, Governo civil, no. 70, fol. 35v (containing August 12, 1785 order), ADF. That these harvest rules be implemented was a consistent worry for wine exporters. Newton & Gordon to Thomas Gordon, September 8, 1784, vol. 8, fol. 319, September 1, 1785, vol. 9, fol. 83, NGL; John Leacock Sr. to William Leacock, October 8, 1784, Leacock Letters 1784–89, fols. 39–41, Leacock Papers. Merchants, too, prevailed "on the countrymen not to hasten the vintages," but they were not always successful. John Leacock Sr. to Michael Nowlan, October 8, 1784, Leacock Letters 1784–89, Leacock Papers; Newton & Gordon to Francis Newton, August 26, September 9, 1786, vol. 9, fols. 265, 269, NGL; Vieira, *Breviario*, 92–93. Governor Diogo Pereira Fojarz Coutinho continued the prohibition on the movement and mixture of north wines. Governo civil, no. 70, fols. 35–43 (September 13, containing August 12, 1785 and August 16, 1786 orders), ADF. The regulations were revised in 1819 and still in use in 1839. Registo geral da Câmara do Funchal, vol. 14, fols. 14–15v, ADF.

45. William Freeman to Richard Pickford, Matthew Da Gama, and Obadiah Allen, December 12, 1678, March 20, August 27, 1679, April 19, 1680, March 10, October 26, 1681, January 10, March 6, November 25, 1682, in David Hancock, ed., *The Letters of William Freeman, London Merchant, 1678–1685* (London, 2002), 52, 76–79, 115–17, 153, 201–2, 236; *Bolton Letters*, 2:23; Francis Newton to George Spence, December 6, 1748, vol. 10, fol. 10, NGL; Michael Nowlan to Gedley Clare Burges, September 13, 1760, Nowlan & Burges Letter Book, 1759–62, fols. 172–74, Leacock Papers; Thomas Gordon to Francis Newton, December 28, 1769, vol. 4, fol. 406, NGL; Daniel Henry Smith to James Gordon, February 26, 1774, Letterfourie Papers; William Johnston to Thomas Gordon, January 23, 1788, vol. 10, fols. 129–45, NGL; John Leacock Sr. to William Leacock, September 21, 1791, Leacock & Sons Letter Book 1791–94, fol. 32, Leacock Papers; Thomas Murdoch to Francis Newton, February 5, 1792, vol. 13, fol. 91, NGL; John Leacock Sr. to William Leacock, February 8, 1795, Leacock & Sons Letter Book 1794–97, fol. 19, Leacock Papers.

46. John Leacock Sr. to William Leacock, February 8, 1795, Leacock & Sons Letter Book 1794–97, fol. 19, Leacock Papers.

47. Robert Bisset to Henry Hill, July 20, 1763, March 28, 1764, vol. 6, fols. 61, 140, Hill-JJS(A).

48. Alexander Gordon to James Gordon, September 7, 1761, Letterfourie Papers; Thomas Gordon to Johnston & Jolly, September 26, 1768, vol. 4, fol. 248, Thomas Murdoch to Thomas Gordon, September 2, 1792, vol. 14, fol. 325, NGL. On *vinho a bica*, see Croft, *Treatise*, 8. On differences between *vinho a bica in mosto* and *vinho in limpo*, see J. W. Thudicum, *A Treatise on the Origin, Nature, and Varieties of Wine* (London, 1872), 692; Vizetelly, *Facts*, 189.

49. Robert Bisset to Henry Hill, November 18, 1772, vol. 8, fol. 135, Hill-JJS(A); Francis Newton to George Spence, June 6, 1749, vol. 1, fol. 26, NGL; Thomas Newton to Alexander Grant, January 12, 1752, Thomas Newton Letter Book 1752–60, fol. 86, CGP-

MWC; Michael Nowlan to Simmons & Clibbon, December 16, 1760, Nowlan & Burges Letter Book, 1759–62, fols. 196–98, Leacock Papers; Henry Hill to Dr. Richard Hill, January 18, 1762, Richard Bisset to Henry Hill, August 30, 1763, folder 3, Hill-SAGS; Robert Bisset to Henry Hill, July 20, 1763, March 28, 1764, vol. 6, fols. 61, 140, Hill-JJS(A); Thomas Gordon to Francis Newton, March 17, 1769, vol. 4, fol. 314, NGL; Robert Bisset to Henry Hill, March 19, 1771, vol. 8, fol. 86, Hill-JJS(A); Alexander Gordon to James Gordon, December 14, 1760, Daniel Henry Smith to Alexander Gordon, January 7, 1775, Daniel Henry Smith to James Gordon, January 21, 1774, Letterfourie Papers; Richard Lamar Bisset to Henry Hill, December 25, 1785, folder 6, Hill-SAGS.

50. Atkins, *Voyage*, 24; "Description," 64; John Hawkesworth, *An Account of the Voyages* (London, 1773), 2:7; *"Endeavour" Journal*, 1:162; Thomas Gordon to Johnston & Jolly, March 12, 1768, to Francis Newton, January 28, 1772, vol. 4, fols. 187, 639, NGL; Barrow, *Voyage*, 22–23. For carriers, see Newton & Gordon's *Borrador* books, CGP-MWC.

51. Cf. Newton & Gordon Journal, 1758–65, Newton, Gordon, Murdoch & Scott Journal, 1815, CGP-MWC.

52. Newton & Gordon Journal, 1758–65, CGP-MWC; Alexander Gordon to James Gordon, March 21, 1762, Letterfourie Papers.

53. Newton & Gordon to Andrew Ramsay, April 20, 1760, vol. 2, fol. 141, NGL; Thomas Cheap to John Pownall, July 1, 1765, CO 388/95, NA-UK; John Leacock Sr. to William Leacock, October 8, 1784, Leacock Letters 1784–89, fols. 39–41, Leacock Papers; William Johnston to Francis Newton, October 30, 1785, vol. 9, fol. 92, NGL.

54. Robert Bisset to Henry Hill, October 22, 1763, vol. 6, fol. 75, Hill-JJS(A); Thomas Gordon to Francis Newton, January 27, 1770, vol. 4, fol. 436, NGL; "Wine Book," 1772–88, CGP-MWC; Daniel Henry Smith to Alexander Gordon, January 7, 1775, Letterfourie Papers; John Leacock to William Leacock, July 15, 1796, Leacock Letter Book 1794–97, fol. 121, Leacock Papers.

55. John Leacock Sr. to Michael Nowlan, November 15, 1786, Leacock Letters 1784–89, fol. 363, Leacock Papers; William Johnston to Thomas Gordon, September 24, 1787, vol. 10, fol. 59, Thomas Murdoch to Thomas Gordon, September 2, 1792, vol. 14, fol. 324, to Thomas Gordon, August 19, 1797, vol. 18, fol. 52, NGL.

56. John Leacock Sr. to William Leacock, May 14, 1793, Leacock & Sons Letter Book 1791–94, fol. 201, October 3, 1794, Leacock & Sons Letter Book 1794–97, fol. 2, John Leacock Jr. to William Leacock, October 18, 1799, Leacock Letters 1799–1802, fol. 80, Leacock Papers.

57. Book of Wine Purchases, 1759–73, CGP-MWC.

58. Newton & Gordon to Francis Newton, January 27, 1770, vol. 4, fol. 436, NGL.

59. Francis Newton to George Spence, December 6, 1748, vol. 1, fol. 10, Newton & Gordon to Francis Newton, December 28, 1769, vol. 4, fol. 425, NGL.

60. Newton & Gordon to Francis Newton, December 28, 1769, vol. 4, fol. 426, to Thomas Gordon, January 23, 1788, vol. 10, fols. 129–45, NGL; Thomas Cheap to John Pownall, July 1, 1765, CO 388/95, NA-UK.

61. Livro do vinho recebido nas lojas, 1772–80, using both *caldo* and *almudado* mea-

sures, CGP-MWC; Thomas Murdoch to Thomas Gordon, September 2, 1792, vol. 14, fol. 324, NGL. *Vinho o caldo* is used here to denote a wine that was measured out in *caldeiros*. In contemporary usage, *caldo* denoted a broth, pottage, or gruel, *calda* a solution of sugar in hot water or a syrup, and *caldas* the residues of alcohol distillation. A *caldeiro* was a bucket or a pail and a *caldeiram* "a kettle, pan, or cauldron, or vessel" used to boil liquids in. On Madeira, a *caldeiro* was a jar made of reddish-yellow clay; it was a regular piece of equipment in an exporter's office and lodge. A. J., *A Compleat Account of the Portuguese Language* (London, 1701); Inventory, June 30, 1774, CGP-MWC. According to Madeira exporters' accounts, an *almude* in Funchal was about 13 percent larger than a *caldeiro*. Michael Nowlan to Gedley Clare Burges, July 16, 1761, Leacock Papers; March 2, 1763, Letterfourie Papers; Newton & Gordon Journal, 1764–74, vol. 2, fol. 657, and Newton, Gordon & Johnston Ledger, 1782–90, fol. 516, CGP-MWC; Leacock & Sons 1791–1800 Ledger, Leacock Papers. Typically, *vinho o caldo* was must juice, unclarified and untreated, while *vinho almudado* was fermented, racked, and treated. *Almudado* prices could occasionally be for must, although must that was placed in larger barrels. Joseph Gillis to Henry Hill, September 20, 1783, vol. 9, fols. 14–16, Hill-JJS(A); Thomas Murdoch to Thomas Gordon, September 2, 1792, vol. 14, fol. 325, August 19, 1797, vol. 18, fol. 52, NGL.

62. *Bolton Letters*, 2:17; John Leacock to William Waddell, November 16, 1764, to William Hunter, January 31, 1765, Spence, Leacock & Spence Letter Book, 1762–65, fols. 185, 205, Leacock Papers; Newton & Gordon to Johnston & Jolly, May 18, 1764, to Kearny & Gilbert, January 23, 1765, vol. 3, fols. 304, 361, NGL; Robert Bisset to Henry Hill, January 7, 1770, vol. 7, fol. 246, January 9, 1771, vol. 8, fol. 76, Hill-JJS(A); Thomas Gordon to N. P. Smith, November 23, 1771, vol. 4, fol. 618, William Johnston to Francis Newton, November 17, 1783, vol. 8, fol. 139, Thomas Murdoch to Thomas Gordon, September 2, 1792, vol. 14, fol. 324, NGL.

63. Newton & Gordon Journals, CGP-MWC; Leacock & Leacock Journals, Leacock Papers. Fixed *vereadores'* price floors and ceilings—which historically did not deviate much from the trend exhibited by growers' actual asking prices—confirm this rise: on average, 8$033 for 1640–99, 12$854 for 1696–1715, 14$161 for 1700–34, 24$171 for 1741–56, 41$662 for 1760–83, 66$228 for 1784–1801, 91$800 for 1802–9, and finally 133$600 for 1810–15. Alberto Vieira, unpublished MS, table, based on Vereações, ADF, supplemented with Vereações prices for other years.

64. William Johnston to Thomas Gordon, January 23, 1788, vol. 10, fols. 129–45, Thomas Murdoch to Francis Newton, vol. 12, fol. 23, to Thomas Gordon, March 25, 1789, vol. 16, fols. 101, 105–9, NGL; John Leacock Sr. to William Leacock, September 15, 1792, fol. 154, September 21, 1794, fol. 250, Leacock & Sons Letter Book 1791–94, Leacock Papers; Thomas Murdoch to Thomas Gordon, September 15, 1795, vol. 16, fol. 409, September 15, 1798, March 11, 1799, vol. 19, fols. 96, 209, Thomas Gordon to ———, 1815, vol. 37, fol. 22, NGL; John Leacock Sr. to William Leacock, September 23, 1796, January 13, 1797, Leacock & Sons Letter Book 1794–97, fols. 147, 182, Leacock Papers.

65. Thomas Murdoch to Thomas Gordon, September 15, 1795, vol. 16, fol. 409, to Francis Newton, January 1810, vol. 32, fol. 168, NGL.

CHAPTER 3. THE ENLIVENING GRAPE

1. Ovington, *Voyage*, 11; *Bolton Letters*, vols. 1–2; Newton & Spence to Aspinwall & Doughty, June 9, 1754, vol. 1, fol. 108, to George & John Riddell, March 9, 1756, vol. 1, fol. 196, NGL; Spence, Leacock & Spence to Charles Ogilvie, March 31, 1764, fol. 105, Spence, Leacock & Spence Letter Book 1762–65, Leacock Papers.
2. The concept of conversation is explored at greater length in chapter 5.
3. Thomas Williams et al., *The Complete Dictionary of Arts and Sciences* (London, 1765), vol. 2, s.v. "wine." "Body" denoted strength; "colour"—"appearance of bodies to the eye only; hue; die" or "tint of the painter"; "flavour"—"sweetness to the smell; odour; fragrance." Samuel Johnson, *Dictionary of the English Language* (London, 1755).
4. Gourlay, *Observations*, 14–20; Pita, *Account*, 67–71, which repeats Gourlay's material nearly word-for-word; Vizetelly, *Facts*, 159; *"Endeavour" Journal*, 161. Cf. Alberto Vieira, *História do vinho de Madeira: Documentos e textos* (Funchal, 1993), 424. The most commonly used press is described in Vicente Coelho Seabra Silva e Telles, "Memória sobre a cultura das videiras, ea manufactura dos vinhos," in *Memorias de agricultura, premiadas . . . 1790* (1791), 2:446–48, sec. 6. For presses used in making wine and cider in Europe, see: John Worlidge, *Vinetum Britannicum; or, A Treatise of Cider* (London, 1678), frontispiece; Jacob Vanier, *Praedium Rusticum*, bk. 10 (Toulouse, 1730), frontispiece, x; Noël Antoine Pluche, *Spectacle de la nature*, 6th ed. (Paris, 1732; London, 1743), 2:240–43; Philip Miller, *The Gardener's Dictionary*, 6th ed. (London, 1752), s.v. "wine press"; Denis Diderot and Jean le Rond d'Alembert, eds., *Encyclopédie; ou, Dictionnaire raissoné des sciences, des arts et des métiers* (Paris, 1765), 1:plate 2.
5. *"Endeavour" Journal*, 161; Hawkesworth, *Account of the Voyages*, 2:5–6; Silva e Telles, "Memória," 386–91, 410–11; Barrow, *Voyage*, 22. For a definition of "must," see Caspar Neumann, *The Chemical Works*, ed. William Lewis (London, 1759), 442; Williams, *Complete Dictionary*, vol. 2, s.v. "wine."
6. Miller, *Gardener's Dictionary*, s.v. "wines"; Diderot and d'Alembert, *Encyclopédie*, 17:283; John MacCulloch, *Remarks on the Art of Making Wine* (London, 1816), 85–86, 123–25.
7. Gourlay, *Observations*, 18. To test the density of fermenting juice and measure alcoholic strength, Europeans used a variety of instruments. The most common tool was the hydrometer, invented by Robert Boyle in the 1670s and improved by John Clarke in the 1730s. Later improvements were introduced. Robin Butler and Gillian Walkling, *The Book of Wine Antiques* (London, 1986), 53–56; Peter Mathias, *The Brewing Industry in England, 1700–1830* (Cambridge, 1959), 67–73; Cullen, *Brandy Trade*, 66–68, 81, 88. Madeirans favored Clarke's version after 1750. John Leacock Sr. to William Leacock, February 8, 1795, Leacock & Sons Letter Book 1794–97, fol. 19, John Leacock Jr. to William Leacock, May 29, June 27, 1799, Leacock Letters 1799–1802, fols. 35, 53, Leacock Papers; Thomas Murdoch to Tunno & Cox, March 25, 1798, vol. 18, fol. 290, to George Bridges, April 30, 1802, vol. 23, fol. 262, NGL.
8. S.J., *Vineyard*, 36. For customer complaints about continued fermentation after ex-

port, see Directors to Presidency of Madras, December 29, 1756, E 4/861/663–65, IOL.

9. Gourlay, *Observations*, 19. On gesso, see Walter Charleton, *Of the Mysterie of Vintners* (London, 1669), 203; Abbott, "Spanish and the Sherry Trade," 58. On lime, see Atkins, *Voyage*, 24–25; Miller, *Gardener's Dictionary*, s.v. "wines"; Alvares da Silva, "Memória," 58. Lime was more problematic than gesso, as it absorbed and destroyed "vegetable oils, which give wines all their odour and flavour" and left "a hot, and burnt taste." Hill, *Works*, 2:103.

10. Charleton, *Mysterie*, 202–3; Ovington, *Voyage*, 12; S.J., *Vineyard*, 36; Hill, *Works*, 2:102–3; Inventory, 1762–67, folder 3, Hill-EWS; James Hardy, *A Candid Examination* (London, 1778), 111; John Leacock Sr. to Richard Sheffield, January 19, 1779, Nowlan & Leacock Letters 1774–81, fol. 240, Leacock Papers; Alvares da Silva, "Memória," 58–71; Thomas Murdoch to Offley, Sealy & Son, June 26, 1805, vol. 27, fol. 19, NGL.

11. Pita, *Account*, 71.

12. One firm ordered the following instruments during the 1780s: a "large siphon or crane for drawing off from butts"; a "very good common crane for drawing off from common pipes"; and "four large crane-necked racking cocks of the properest metal not to prejudice wine." Newton, Gordon & Johnson to Thomas Gordon, April 7, 1783, vol. 8, fol. 29, NGL; Francis Newton to Newton, Gordon & Johnson, January 19, 1791, box 1791/92, bundle 6, CGP-Guildhall.

13. *Bolton Letters*, vol. 1, *sub* January 2, 1696, 2:33, 39, 60; Henry Hill to Dr. Richard Hill, January 18, 1762, folder 3, Hill-SAGS; Scott, Pringle & Cheap to Richard Derby, April 3, 1767, Derby Papers, 10/5, JDPL; Newton & Gordon to Francis Newton, November 3, 1768, vol. 4, fol. 268, to Samuel Thompson, December 2, 1772, vol. 5, fol. 138, December 6, vol. 5, fol. 276, to Francis Newton, October 18, 1783, vol. 8, fol. 132, to Thomas Gordon, November 29, 1785, vol. 9, fol. 120, November 9, 1789, vol. 9, fol. 293, to Francis Newton, May 24, 1783, vol. 8, fol. 67, to Lester & Murraugh, August 5, 1794, vol. 16, fol. 32, NGL; Alvares da Silva, "Memória," 74–75, s.v. "trasfego." On subsequent racking, see Newton & Gordon to Thomas Gordon, November 20, 1789, vol. 12, fol. 177, NGL; John Leacock Sr. to William Leacock, January 14, 1799, Leacock Letters 1799–1802, fol. 5, Leacock Papers.

14. Manuscript Book, c. 1600, fols. 26v, 27, 30r–v, Sloane MS 3692, BL; Gervase Markham, *Countrey Contentments; or, The English Huswife*, 2nd ed. (London, 1623), 147–49; "The Book of Contents of All Manner of Wynes," fols. 2v, 3, 3v, Add. MSS 22525, BL; Charleton, *Mysterie*, 160–65; *The Art and Mystery of Vintners and Wine-Coopers, Containing Approved Directions for the Conserving and Curing All Manner and Sorts of Wines* (London, 1682); Walter Charleton, *The Vintner's Mystery Display'd* (London, 1700); Jonathan Swift, *The Account Books*, ed. Paul and Dorothy Thompson (Newark, 1984), 191; S.J., *Vineyard*, 69; Williams, *Complete Dictionary*, vol. 2, s.v. "wine"; James Jenks, *The Complete Cook* (London, 1768), 322; Frances N. Mason, ed., *John Norton & Sons, Merchants of London and Virginia* (Richmond, 1937), 191; John Adams to William MacCreery, September 25, 1778, in Gregg L. Lint et al., eds., *Papers of John Adams* (Cambridge, MA, 1989), 7:75; Alvares da Silva, "Memória," 71–74; C. Kauffman, *The Dictionary of Merchandise and Nomenclature* (Philadelphia,

1805), 364; Gourlay, *Observations*, 19. Additives came and went with the decade. The influential *Complete Dictionary of Arts and Sciences* informed its readers in 1765 as to "the usual method of fining down wines, so as to render them expeditiously bright, clear and fit for use." The isinglass method, readers learned, was "best suited to the white wines"; for red wines, coopers commonly used "the whites of eggs beat up to a froth." Williams, *Complete Dictionary*, vol. 2, s.v. "wine."

15. Philip Miller listed the possibilities in 1752: isinglass, egg whites, alabaster powder, calcined flints, white marble, roch alum, new milk, and an alum and sulphur mixture. *Gardener's Dictionary*, s.v. "wines." See also Williams, *Complete Dictionary*, vol. 2, s.v. "wine"; Thomas Gordon to Alexander Munro, August 10, 1776, vol. 10, fol. 113, NGL; Robert Duff to James Duff, December 14–20, 1785, Letterfourie Papers; Memo, September 28, 1787, Scrapbook, CGP-PC; Thomas Murdoch to William Mitchell, June 4, 1792, vol. 14, fol. 224, NGL; *Encyclopedia Britannica*, 18:872. Like Duff, Thomas Murdoch also reviewed several of the possibilities, but dismissed most with "considerable objection." He approved only "the whites of eight or ten new laid eggs or, if the yolks also are put in, then half the number." Thomas Murdoch to Francis Newton, May 4, 1792, vol. 14, fol. 180, to Henry Heskith, October 15, 1799, vol. 20, fol. 67, NGL.

16. Gourlay, *Observations*, 19; Pita, *Account*, 67.

17. Richard Lamar Bisset to Henry Hill, September 11, 1786, folder 6, Hill-SAGS.

18. On blending, see Maynard A. Amerine et al., *The Technology of Wine Making*, 4th ed. (Westport, 1980); Maynard A. Amerine and Edward B. Roessler, *Wines: Their Sensory Evaluation* (San Francisco, 1976), 90–91; Frumkin, *Science and Technique of Wine*, 35–38. For blending of Madeira, see Cossart, *Madeira*, 76–107, which only discusses modern blending. The date for Port wine's blending is unclear, but three categories of wine for sale in Porto may suggest a penchant for blending in the second half of that century: "sufficient wines"; "insufficient wines"; *cobertura* wines that were used "to redeem insufficient wines." Gaspar M. Pereira et al., *Vintage Port* (Porto, 1999), 34, 96; George Robertson, *Port*, 4th ed. (London, 1992), 87–105; Paul Duguid and Teresa Silva de Lopes, "Ambiguous Company: Institutions and Organizations in the Port Wine Trade, 1814–1834, *Scandinavian Journal of Economic History* 47 (1999): 87; Conceição Andrade Martins, *Memória da vinho do Porto* (Lisbon, 1990), 291–92. For blending of Jerez, see Abbott, "Spanish and the Sherry Trade," 55, 114–15; of French, see Marcel Lachiver, *Vin, vigne et vignerons en région parisienne du XVIIe au XIX siècle* (Pontoise, 1982), 105–10; René Pijassou, *Un grand vignoble de qualité: Le Médoc* (Paris, 1978), 497, 500.

19. Robert Bisset to Henry Hill, February 10, March 28, 1764, vol. 6, fols. 139, 140, Hill-JJS(A); Thomas Murdoch to Thomas Gordon, January 28, 1789, vol. 11, fol. 218, NGL.

20. Alexander Gordon to Moses Henry, February 27, 1770, Alexander Gordon Letter Book 1765–75, fols. 181–82, Letterfourie Papers; Newton & Gordon to Francis Newton, October 30, 1785, vol. 9, fol. 92, NGL.

21. James Gordon to Alexander Gordon, May 22, 1769, February 27, 1770, James Gordon Letter Book 1765–75, fols. 132, 181, Letterfourie Papers; Thomas Murdoch to Thomas

Gordon, August 5, 1793, vol. 15, fol. 207, NGL; John Leacock Sr. to William Leacock, May 10, July 15, 1796, Leacock & Sons Letter Book 1794–97, fols. 109, 121,
Leacock Papers. The same took place in late eighteenth-century France, where "the
proportions for mixing wine vary, not following alone the quality of the wine added
but also according to the taste of the consumer. . . . the wines are treated in another
way for Paris and the interior of France." André Jullien, *Manuel du sommelier* (Paris,
1813), 75.

22. Miller, *Gardener's Dictionary*, s.v. "wines"; Neumann, *Chemical Works*, 445.

23. Neumann, *Chemical Works*, 445; *Encyclopedia Britannica*, 18:869–70; Kauffman,
Dictionary of Merchandise, 362.

24. Miller, *Gardener's Dictionary*, s.v. "wines"; Nowlan & Leacock to Richard Sheffield,
January 19, 1779, Nowlan & Leacock Letters 1779–81, fol. 240, Leacock Papers;
Sloane, *Voyage*, 10.

25. Letter and Proclamation of Governor José Correia de Sá, February 1, 1768, caixa ii,
nos. 289–90, caixa iv, nos. 822, 823, 825, 826, AHU.

26. Francis Newton to George Spence, September 4, 1755, vol. 1, fol. 173, NGL; *Bolton
Letters*, 2:35, 45; Cadwalader Colden to Amos Garrat, August 13, 1714, *Collections of
the New-York Historical Society for the Year 1917* 1 (1918): 20–21; S.J., *Vineyard*, 72. For
later instances of adding other wine for color, see *Beekman Papers*, 1:281, 376, 380;
Nowlan & Burges to Duckett & Jebb, January 6, 1760, Nowlan & Burges Letter Book,
1759–62, fol. 84, Nowlan & Leacock to Richard Sheffield, January 19, 1779, Nowlan
& Leacock Letters 1774–81, fol. 240, John Leacock to Michael Nowlan, November 15,
1786, Leacock Letters 1784–89 & 1792–98, fol. 363, Leacock Papers; Richard Lamar
Bisset to Henry Hill, December 19, 1791, vol. 10, fol. 212, Hill-JJS(A); Gourlay, *Observations*, 19.

27. Thomas Gordon to Captain John Diffell, January 17, 1776, vol. 6, fol. 38, William
Johnston to Francis Newton, January 22, 1786, vol. 9, fol. 133, Newton & Gordon to
John Woodbridge, January 12, 1756, vol. 1, fol. 189, to Duncan Davidson, March 31,
1772, to Serocold & Jackson, January 29, 1773, to Thomas, Stephen & Rose Fuller,
February 28, 1774, vol. 5, fols. 8, 170, 311, to Francis Newton, December 6, 1792, to
Samuel Vaughan, March 2, 1802, vol. 23, fol. 115, NGL.

28. James Hart, *Klinikh; or, The Diet of the Diseased* (London, 1633), 192; Michael R.
Best, "The Mystery of Vintners," *Agricultural History* 50 (1976): 365–68.

29. Miller, *Gardener's Dictionary*, s.v. "wines"; Thomas Lamar to Henry Hill, August 5, 1774,
vol. 8, fol. 149, Hill-JJS(A); James Murphy, *Travels in Portugal* (London, 1795), 14.

30. Newton & Gordon to John Drayton, April 19, 1771, vol. 4, fol. 561, NGL; John Leacock Jr. to William Leacock, November 1, 1801, Leacock Letters 1799–1802, fol. 210,
Leacock Papers. Adding sugar served several purposes: "In addition to helping bring
into balance what would otherwise have been unacceptably sour wines," sugar augmented "the alcoholic content of wines both as a means better to preserve them and
to increase the yield of brandy that could be extracted from them; it could also replace
toxic lead compounds used in the preservation of wines." Gough, "Winecraft," 76.

31. A general account of alteration and adulteration appears in John Beckmann, *A History of Inventions, Discoveries, and Origins* (London, 1846), 1:245–58. The first sig-

nificant case against adulteration was made by Defoe, Addison, and Steele when they exposed "the Affair of our Vintners" in the pages of the *Guardian, Review, Spectator,* and *Tatler* in 1710–12. They championed the cause of those who specialized in "true Natural" Portuguese wine, "neat, and unmix'd, without Acts and Adulterations" and who laid bare the practices of competing "Chymical Operators" fond of adulteration. Joseph Addison, February 7–9, 1709/10, *The Tatler*, no. 131, ed. George A. Aitken (London, 1899), 3:92–97; Daniel Defoe, *A Review of the State of the British Nation,* September 18, 20, 1711; Donald F. Bond, ed., *The Spectator*, vol. 3 (Oxford, 1965), no. 362, 353–57 (April 25, 1712: Steele); John C. Stephens, ed., *The Guardian* (Louisville, 1982), 522–24 (September 14, 1713: Addison), 737–39, 746 (September 25, 1713: Steele). For later criticism, see Stephen F. Geoffroy, *A Treatise of the Fossil, Vegetable, and Animal Substances, That Are Made Use of in Physick,* trans. G. Douglas (London, 1736), 243; Sir Edward Barry, *Observations Historical, Critical and Medical on the Wines of the Ancients* (London, 1775), 441; Hardy, *Candid Examination,* 81–83, 84–132; *Pennsylvania Ledger,* February 21, 1778; George Wallis, ed., *The Works of Thomas Sydenham, M.D* (London, 1788), 2:226–27; John Croft, *A Treatise on the Wines of Portugal,* 2nd ed. (York, 1780); Duncan McBride, *General Instructions for the Choice of Wines and Spirituous Liquors* (London, 1793), 23; John Wright, *An Essay on Wines, Especially on Port Wine* (London, 1795); *Encyclopedia Britannica,* 18:870; A. F. M. Willich, *Lectures on Diet and Regimen* (Boston, 1800), 280–85; Kauffman, *Dictionary of Merchandise,* 362; Richard Wedeen, *Poison in the Pot: The Legacy of Lead* (Carbondale, 1984), chap. 2.

32. E. S., *Britaines Busse; or, A Computation* (London, 1615), 7; William Vaughan, *Directions for Health, Natural and Artificiall,* 7th ed. (London, 1633), 29, a reworking of his *Natural and Artificiall Directions for Health* (London, 1600); *England's Happiness Improved* (London, 1697), 36; Link, *Travels,* 373–74; MacCulloch, *Remarks,* 123–24; Friedrich C. Accum, *A Treatise on Adulterations of Food, and Culinary Poisons* (London, 1820), 126–28; Thomas Murdoch to Evans, Offley & Sealy, June 5, 1795, vol. 15, fol. 138, to Tunno & Cox, March 28,1798, vol. 18, fol. 290, NGL; John Leacock Sr. to William Leacock, February 8, 1795, Leacock Papers. By the end of the eighteenth century, correct assessment of brandy by the hydrometer was essential. Today, the alcohol in vintage Madeira more than fifteen years of age is 19–21 percent of its volume; three-year Madeira is 17.5 percent. John J. McCusker, *Rum and the American Revolution: The Rum Trade and the Balance of Payments of the Thirteen Continental Colonies* (New York, 1989), 816. For other fortified wines, see Alan D. Francis, *The Wine Trade* (London, 1972); Warner Allen, *Sherry and Port* (London, 1952); George Robertson, *Port,* 4th ed. (London, 1978); Julian Jeffs, *Sherry,* 4th ed. (London, 1992). The "habit of adding brandy" prevailed in France by the early nineteenth century, when it was deemed "necessary" for the "common rough wines" of Languedoc, Roussillon, and Quercy. Jullien, *Manuel,* 76–77.

33. Vaughan, *Directions,* 29; Charleton, *Mysterie,* 183; *England's Happiness Improved,* 36; Violet Barbour, *Capitalism in Amsterdam in the 17th Century* (Ann Arbor, 1950), 92, 96; C. Anne Wilson, "Burnt Wine and Cordial Waters: The Early Days of Distilling," *Folk Life* 13 (1975): 58, 63; Neumann, *Chemical Works,* 445; Tim Unwin, *Wine*

and the Vine: An Historical Geography of Viticulture and the Wine Trade (London, 1991), 236–40. Blandy has argued that Madeirans fortified their wines as early as 1700–1710. Unfortunately, there is no evidence for their mixing the two, only for their producing a brandy from unused must and their exporting brandy and wine in the same ship. *Bolton Letters*, vol. 2, *sub* April 7, 1702; Bolton, Darrell & Morgan to Robert Heysham, January 20, 1704/5, no. 94, Bolton MSS, University of Kansas Library Special Collections. As to Port, Martins has argued that Oporto vintners brandied their wine as early as 1678. Again, there is no evidence to support this. It is more likely the practice arose in the 1720s, for there is evidence brandy was added by 1724. Martins, *Memória da vinho do Porto*, 288; Burnett to Newcastle, August 6, 1724, SP 89/31, NA-UK; Vicencio Alarte, *Agricultura das vinhas* (Coimbra, 1733), 149–52 (appropriating Silvestre Gomes de Morais, "Agricultura das vinhas," 1723); Pratt to Hitchcock, September 12, 1734, C/110/19–20, Castres to Stone, July 1, 1742, SP 89/ 42, NA-UK; *Novas instruccoens da feitoria ingleza: A respeito dos vinhos do Douro* (Porto, 1754), 2, 4–5; Fisher, *Portugal Trade*, 82–83.

34. *Poor Richard, 1743* (Philadelphia, 1743), in *Franklin Papers*, 2:367; "Description," 65; Miller, *Gardener's Dictionary*, s.v. "wines"; Francis Newton to Thomas Newton, August 4, 1753, to George Spence, October 27, 1753, vol. 1, fols. 62, 77, NGL; Beekman to Searle, 1761, *Beekman Papers*; Philip C. Yorke, ed., *The Diary of John Baker* (London, 1931), 151; Edward Antill, "An Essay on the Cultivation of the Vine," APS, *Trans.* 1 (1769): 246; Philip Mazzei to Giovanni Fabbroni, September 20, 1774, in *Philip Mazzei: Selected Writings and Correspondence*, ed. Margherita Marchione (Prato, 1983), 1:63; *Carter Diary*, 2:1134; John Leacock Jr. to William Leacock, May 29, June 27, 1799, Leacock Letters 1799–1802, fols. 35, 53, Leacock Papers.

35. Hill, Lamar & Hill to Samuel Galloway, March 5, 1754, Galloway Correspondence 1739–54, box 1, folder 1, Galloway Papers, NYPL. For modern discussion of fortification, see Amerine et al., *Technology*, 275–79; Roger Dion, *Histoire de la vigne et du vin au France* (Paris, 1959), 540–607; Lachiver, *Vin*, 105–10.

36. Michael Nowlan to Gedley Clare Burges, February 25, 1762, Nowlan & Burges Letter Book, Leacock Papers; Henry Hill to Richard Hill, January 18, 1762, folder 3, Hill-SAGS; Robert Bisset to Henry Hill, February 10, 1764, vol. 6, fol. 139, Hill-JJS(A); John Leacock to William Bell, May 1, 1765, Spence, Leacock & Spence Letter Book, fol. 239, Leacock Papers; James Gordon to Alexander Gordon, March 14, 1768, Letterfourie Papers; Newton & Gordon to Kearny & Gilbert, January 25, 1768, vol. 4, fol. 171, NGL; James Gordon to Alexander Gordon, May 22, 1769, John Gordon to John Rankine, October 18, 1774, fol. 492, Letter Book 1765–74, Letterfourie Papers; John Leacock to Michael Nowlan, June 2, 1779, fol. 267, Leacock Papers.

37. Hancock, "Commerce and Conversation"; John Leacock to William Leacock, October 10, 1794, Leacock & Sons Letter Book 1794–97, fol. 5, April 3, 1789, Leacock Letters 1789–91, fols. 71–75, Leacock Papers; Thomas Murdoch to Thomas Gordon, January 28, 1789, vol. 11, fol. 218, June 15, August 19, 1789, vol. 12, fols. 86, 121, NGL; Lamar, Hill, Bisset to Henry Hill, April 22, 1790, vol. 10, fol. 133, Hill-JJS(A); Johan Archenholz, *A Picture of England* (Dublin, 1791), 203; Thomas Murdoch to Evans, Offley & Sealy, June 5, 1793, vol. 15, fol. 138, March 22, 1794, vol. 15, fol. 366, to

Thomas Gordon, March 8, 1794, vol. 15, fol. 363, to Thomas Gordon, September 25, 1794, vol. 16, fols. 105–9, Thomas Murdoch to Thomas Gordon, August 19, 1797, vol. 18, fol. 52, James David Webster Gordon to Robert Lenox, September 30, 1803, vol. 25, fol. 173, NGL; John Leacock Sr. to William Leacock, May 29, June 27, 1799, Leacock & Sons Letter Book, 1799–1802, fols. 35, 52–58, Leacock Papers.

38. For Caribbean, southern, and Pennsylvania markets, see Isaac Norris Letter Book, December 7, 1717, HSP; Walter B. Edgar, ed., *The Letter Book of Robert Pringle* (Columbia, 1972), 2:611; Henry Laurens to Corsley Rogers & Son, May 16, 1755, in *Laurens Papers*, 1:248; Thomas Newton to Newton & Gordon, November 26, 1759, Thomas Newton Letter Book, CGP-MWC; Spence, Leacock & Spence to John Erskine, June 26, 1762, Leacock Papers; Newton & Gordon to Captain John Diffell, January 17, 1776, vol. 6, fol. 38, NGL; Baynton & Wharton to Thomas Newton, October 2, 1763, box 2, Tunno & Cox Order, February 2, 1795, box 41, bundle 1, Recapitulation, June 30, 1814, box 84, Thomas Murdoch to firm, March 31, 1815, box 86, CGP-Guildhall; Thomas Murdoch to Pierce Butler, October 18, 1800, vol. 21, fol. 70, NGL. For wine preferred in New Jersey, New York, and New England, see Anne B. Cunningham, ed., *Letters and Diary of John Rowe* (Boston, 1903), 389; Thomas Newton to Newton & Gordon, November 26, 1759, Thomas Newton Letter Book, CGP-MWC; Baynton & Wharton to Thomas Newton, October 2, 1763, box 2, CGP-Guildhall; Dorothy C. Barck, ed., *Letter Book of John Watts, Merchant and Councillor of New York* (New York, 1928), 63, 192, 214; John and William Gordon to Robert Lenox, October 11, 1805, vol. 27, fol. 123, NGL. Cf. wines for the London market: John Leacock Sr. to William Leacock, October 13, 1795, May 10, 1796, fols. 51, 1794–97 Leacock & Sons Letter Book, Leacock Papers. Hancock, "Commerce and Conversation," explains this in greater detail.

39. John Leacock to Michael Nowlan, April 25, 1785, fol. 136, Leacock Letters 1784–89, Leacock Papers.

40. Thomas Murdoch to Thomas Gordon, March 25, 1789, September 10, 1789, vol. 12, fols. 23, 136, NGL; John Leacock to William Leacock, March 8, 1790, Leacock Letters 1789–91, fol. 255, Leacock Papers.

41. John Montgomery & Co. to Newton & Gordon, December 8, 1775, box 1776/77, bundle 16, CGP-Guildhall. Most of the Lisbon houses got their brandy from Oporto, but some, like Montgomery & Co., "burned" their own.

42. John Leacock Sr. to William Leacock, December 5, 1792, May 14, July 2, 1793, Leacock & Sons Letter Book 1791–94, fols. 177, 201, 208, Leacock Papers; Thomas Murdoch to Thomas Gordon, January 20, 1794, to Evans, Offley & Sealy, March 22, 1794, vol. 15, fols. 246, 366, NGL; John Leacock Sr. to William Leacock, October 10, 1794, February 8, 1795, Leacock & Sons Letter Book 1794–97, fols. 5, 19, Leacock Papers; Thomas Murdoch to Thomas Gordon, December 15, 1794, March 27, 1795, vol. 16, fols. 193, 250, to Thomas Gordon, June 27, 1799, vol. 19, fol. 337, NGL.

43. Aaron Hill to William Popple, November 30, 1740, in Hill, *Works,* 2:103. For similar techniques introduced in France, see S.J., *Vineyard,* 111–12.

44. John Leacock Sr. to William Leacock, April 3, 1789, Leacock & Sons Letter Book 1789–91, fols. 71–75, Leacock Papers; Thomas Murdoch to Simpson & Davison, Sep-

tember 10, 1789, vol. 12, fol. 130, Newton & Gordon to Robert McHardy, October 21, 1800, vol. 21, fol. 78, NGL; Gourlay, *Observations*, 20; Pita, *Account*, 71–73.

45. Cato was the first to write about the effects of agitation. Marcus Porcius Cato, *On Agriculture*, trans. W. D. Hooper and Harrison B. Ash (Cambridge, MA, 1934), 43.

46. Thomas Murdoch to Henry Heskith, October 15, 1799, vol. 20, fol. 67, NGL.

47. Stephen Hales, *Vegetable Staticks* (London, 1727), 183–84. For less scientific accounts of island practice, see Gourlay, *Observations*, 19–20.

48. Cato, *On Agriculture*, 43; Cato, *On Farming*, trans. Ernest Brehaut (New York, 1966), 48, 101; Junius Moderatus Columella, *On Agriculture*, ed. Harrison Ash (Cambridge, MA, 1941), 75 (I.vi.19; x–xii); Pliny the Elder, *The Natural History*, ed. J. Bostock and H. T. Riley (London, 1855), 3:247–54 (bk. 14, chaps. 10–15). Men in the Middle Ages ignored the practice, which did not receive serious discussion until the second half of the eighteenth century. Miller, *Gardener's Dictionary*, s.v. "vitis"; Barry, *Observations*, 1–10, 48–58, 67–84, 442–43; Hardy, *Candid Examination*, 93.

49. Gough, "Winecraft," 94, citing Maupin's *Expériences sur la bonification de tous le vins* (Paris, 1770); Charlton, *Mysterie*, 205; S.J., *Vineyard*, 63–64; Miller, *Gardener's Dictionary*, s.v. "wines," detailing Alsatian heating in the expanded edition of 1752.

50. Sloane, *Voyage*, o; Ovington, *Voyage*, 11–12.

51. Wood is an exceptionally good insulating material. Its thermal conductivity varies between 0.14 and 0.16. Therefore, in a wooden ship, the temperature of the hold would remain for some time at the ambient temperature of the loading port, once the hatches were battened down. As most wooden ships had little or no ventilation once close-fitted hatch boards were on, the temperature in the hold would change only gradually, especially if the deck was well caulked. Of course, despite the insulation, there would be some transfer of heat through the boards over the course of the voyage. Yet this could be minimized by the color of the hull, the course being steered, and the state of the sea. Most ships' hulls in the 1700s were painted black or a dark color. Under such conditions, it is quite likely that the temperature in a tight ship's hold (due to the wooden and paint insulation and the buildup of vapor from cargo) might rise 10 to 20 degrees Fahrenheit above the ambient outside temperature when in the tropics. The temperature of the sea in the tropics would not lower the temperature of the hold, although some lowering would occur in temperate latitudes. The distance traveled also promoted amelioration. A ship going round-trip from London to Calcutta via the Cape and Bombay covered 22,000 miles, while a ship going between London and Kingston covered only 7,800. While the temperature differences between Kingston and Calcutta are not great, the threefold increase in tropical travel time greatly softened the drink. I am grateful to Captain Simon T. Waite, master of the *Cutty Sark*, Maritime Trust, Greenwich, for much of this information.

52. Francis Newton to George Spence, July 16, 1754, vol. 1, fol. 112, NGL; Nowlan & Burges to Charles Brennan, June 15, 1760, Nowlan & Burges Letter Book, 1759–61, fol. 148, Leacock Papers; Warren Johnson Journal, January 12, 1761, in *The Papers of Sir William Johnson* (Albany, 1962), 13:198; Robert Bisset to Henry Hill, June 1, 1765, vol. 6, fol. 242, Hill-JJS(A); Tench Tilghman to Newton, Gordon & Johnston, May 27, 1784, Donaldson & Stotts to Newton, Gordon & Johnston, May 27, 1785, box

1784/85, CGP-Guildhall; William Johnston to Nathaniel Beckford, April 15, 1785, vol. 8, fol. 420, NGL; Invoice Book 1782–90, entry no. 132 (April 22, 1789), CGP-MWC.

53. William Gooch to Edmund Gibson, bishop of London, January 14, 1734/35, in *VMHB* 32 (1924): 328; John Watts to Scott, Pringle, Cheap & Co., February 11, 1765, in Barck, *Letter Book of John Watts*, 331; Scott, Pringle & Cheap to James Grant, January 14, 1768, bundle 244, BCM; James Gordon to Alexander Gordon, January 1771, James Gordon Letter Book 1765–75, fol. 240, Letterfourie Papers; William Johnston to James Nasmyth, April 5, 1776, vol. 6, fol. 61, NGL.

54. Newton & Gordon to Crawfurd & Johnston, May 15, 1784, vol. 8, fol. 237, to John Taylor, May 8, 1798, vol. 18, fol. 367, NGL; Earl of Mornington to Lord Grenville, November 28, 1797, in Historical Manuscripts Commission, *Report on the Manuscripts of J. B. Fortescue, Esq.* (London, 1899), 3:400.

55. Barry, *Observations*, 48–53; Inventory of William Bampfield, June 3–9, 1773, South Carolina Probate Inventories, vol. R-7, fol. 375, SCDAH. Experiments in 1775–94 are recounted in Daniel Henry Smith to James & Alexander Gordon, December 1775, Letterfourie Papers; Thomas Gordon to Francis Newton, October 24, November 17, 1783, vol. 8, fol. 124, April 14, 1785, vol. 8, fol. 139, Thomas Murdoch to Thomas Gordon, November 20, 1789, vol. 12, fol. 177, to Francis Newton, September 1, 1792, vol. 14, fol. 322, NGL; Croft, *Treatise*, 24–25; Wright, *Essay*, 23–24.

56. An *estufa* was in some cases merely a small room heated by wood burnt in a cast-iron stove. When boilers were involved, they incorporated James Watt's 1769 improvement of Thomas Newcomen's 1712 engine. Most firms already had such engines, for they used them to pump water out of wells and streams and into countinghouses in order to clean wine pipes with scalding water. The normally powerful British Factory played no role in the adoption of *estufas*. On Fernandes and the first *estufas*, see "Representação of the Commerciantes, both National and Foreign," February 8, 1803, caixa vii, no. 1,431, AHU; Cossart, *Madeira*, 100; Vieira, unpublished MS, 80 and n139, citing João da Camara Leme, *Os três sistemas de tratamento de vinho* (Funchal, 1900), 6.

57. Quality firms were always reluctant to place their best wines in an *estufa*. Newton, Gordon & Murdoch to Robert Lenox, September 30, 1803, vol. 25, fol. 173, NGL; Diary, March 23, 1803, Condell, Innes Letter Book, Symington Papers.

58. Daniel Henry Smith to James & Alexander Gordon, December 1775, Letterfourie Papers; John Leacock Sr. to William Leacock, January 18, 1799, Leacock Letters 1799–1802, fol. 7, Leacock Papers. On *estufas* and the results, see Thomas Murdoch to John Campbell, April 14, 1798, vol. 18, fol. 316, to Thomas Gordon, June 27, October 15, 25, 1799, vol. 19, fol. 337, vol. 20, fols. 52, 81, to Henry Heskith, October 15, 1799, vol. 20, fol. 67, to Edmund Middleton, April 20, 1801, vol. 22, fol. 367, to Robert Lenox, February 2, 1802, vol. 23, fol. 81, NGL; John Leacock Jr. to William Leacock, January 18, April 29, June 27, 1799, January 18, August 28, October 28, 1800, January 23, 1801, Leacock & Sons Letter Book 1799–1802, fols. 6–9, 27, 52–58, 107, 192–94, 223, Leacock Papers; *Account* (1801); Gourlay, *Observations*, 19–20.

59. Thomas Murdoch to Robert McHardy, October 21, 1800, vol. 21, fol. 78, NGL.

60. John Leacock Sr. to John Parker, March 21, 1798, and John Leacock Jr. to William Leacock, January 18, June 27, 1799, and August 28, 1800, Leacock & Sons Letter Book 1799–1802, fols. 6–9, 52–58, 192–94, Leacock Papers.

61. Patrick E. McGovern et al., eds., *The Origins and Ancient History of Wine* (Amsterdam, 1995), 128–30, 180; Thomas Venner, *Via Recta ad Vitam Longam* (London, 1620), 30–31, although Venner admitted that not all new wines "breede obstructions"; William Vaughan, *Directions for Health* (London, 1617), 52; Nowlan & Burges to Samuel Hall, April 10, 1760, Nowlan & Burges Letter Book, 1759–62, Leacock Papers; Thomas Murdoch to Thomas Winter, March 28, 1788, vol. 10, fols. 201–2, NGL. On aging, see Gough, "Winecraft," 80; Bertrand B. Giulian, *Corkscrews of the Eighteenth Century: Artistry in Iron and Steel* (Yardley, 1995), 13–19; Helen McKearin, "Notes on Stopping, Bottling and Binning," *Journal of Glass Studies* 13 (1971): 120–27; William E. Pittman, "Morphological Variability in Late Seventeenth-Century and Early Eighteenth-Century Wine Bottles" (master's thesis, College of William and Mary, 1990), 6–49; Brennan, *Burgundy to Champagne*, 96.

62. *Bolton Letters*, 1:26, 2:32–39; Diderot and d'Alembert, *Encyclopédie*, 17:283–301, s.v. "vin."

63. Francis Newton to Thomas Newton, August 4, 1753, vol. 1, fol. 62, to George Spence, June 9, 1756, vol. 1, fol. 208, NGL; Michael Nowlan to Smith & Brewton, January 10, 1758, Nowlan & Burges Letter Book, 1756–59, fol. 57, Leacock Papers; Alexander Gordon to James Gordon, August 26, 1761, Letterfourie Papers; John Leacock to William Waddell, April 23, 1763, Spence, Leacock & Spence Letter Book 1762–65, fol. 45, Leacock Papers; Francis Newton to Alexander Gordon, January 24, 1768, vol. 4, fol. 170, to George Scott, fol. 282, to Philip Pinnock, February 17, 1770, fol. 449, NGL.

64. On aging by producers, see: Moll, *Atlas*, 4:692; Jonathan Swift to John Gay, March 19, 1730, in Harold Williams, ed., *The Correspondence of Jonathan Swift* (Oxford, 1963), 3:381; Warren Johnson Journal, May 1761, in *Papers of Sir William Johnson*, 12:212; Thomas Jefferson to William Small, May 7, 1775, in Julian P. Boyd, ed., *The Papers of Thomas Jefferson* (Princeton, 1950), 1:165. On the taste for old wine in America and the practice of aging it there, see Robert Carter to John Hyde, May 26, 1729, to Micajah Perry, July 2, 1729, Robert Carter Letter Book, fols. 62, 77, VHS; Carter L. Hudgins, "The 'King's' Realm: An Archaeological and Historical Analysis of Robert Carter's Corotoman" (master's thesis, Wake Forest University, c. 1981), 37, 40, 110–11, 204–8; Governor Samuel Ogle to Charles Lord Baltimore, January 10, 1731, *Maryland Historical Magazine* 3 (1908): 131; Mabel L. Webber, ed., "Journal of Robert Pringle, 1746–1747," *South Carolina Historical and Genealogical Magazine* 26 (1925): *sub* February 29, 1747; Harriott H. Ravenel, *Eliza Pinckney* (New York, 1896), 48; *Papers of Sir William Johnson*, 3:563; James Beekman to Evan & Francis Malbone, November 6, 1762, to Eleazer Trevett, May 11, 1763, in *Beekman Papers*, 1:422, 437; *South-Carolina Gazette*, October 24, 1761; *Pennsylvania Gazette*, September 8, November 10, 1763, June 13, 1765.

65. A precedent for intentionally aging wine may have been established by Canary Islanders in the previous decade. Cologan kept "upwards of 2,000 pipes of wine"

in his Tenerife cellars "purely to have them old and well prepared, being the only method to bring them into repute." Cologan to English East India Company Directors, November 12, 1765, Copybook D, Archivo Zárate-Cologan, La Orotava, Canary Islands, cited in Agustín Guimerá Ravina, "Las islas del vino (Madeira, Azores y Canarias) y la América inglesa durante el siglo XVIII: Una aproximación a su estudio," *Actas I colóquio internacional de história de Madeira* (Funchal, 1990), 2:930. Similarly, Porto merchants were beginning to sell aged three-year-old wine in the 1760s. Holdsworth, Olive & Newman to Baynton, Wharton & Morgan, February 15, 1766, Baynton, Wharton, & Morgan Papers, PSA; Link, *Travels*, 374; Daniel Henry Smith to James Gordon, April 16–24, 1776, Letterfourie Papers; Joseph Gillis to Henry Hill, April 4–May 6, 1783, vol. 9, fol. 2, Hill-JJS(A).

66. Francis Newton to George Spence, June 9, 1756, vol. 1, fol. 208, to Mackenzie & Edington, September 3, 1756, vol. 1, fol. 222, NGL; John Leacock to Michael Nowlan, March 26, 1785, Leacock, Spence & Leacock Letter Book 1784–89, fol. 116, Leacock Papers; Thomas Murdoch to Thomas Gordon, November 20, 1789, vol. 12, fol. 177; Staunton, *Authentic Account*, 69; Inventory, June 30, 1774, Invoice Book 4 (1770–74), no. 186 (May 11, 1774), Invoice Book 5 (1774–82), nos. 54–5 (August 11–12, 1776), 72 (May 1, 1777), 76 (June 6, 1777), Inventory, June 30, 1782, CGP-MWC.

67. John Watts to Scott, Pringle, Cheap & Co., January 13, 1764, in Barck, *Letter Book of John Watts*, 214.

68. On the "exceeding inferior" vintages of 1772 and 1773, see Robert Bisset to Henry Hill, June 25, 1774, vol. 8, fol. 118, Hill-JJS(A).

69. William Johnston to Francis Newton, October 11, 1784, vol. 8, fols. 328–29, NGL.

70. *Salem Gazette*, October 4, 1785; William Johnston to Thomas Gordon, March 25, 1787, vol. 9, fol. 380, November 24, 1791, vol. 14, fol. 15, NGL; John Leacock Sr. to William Leacock, August 16, 1791, Leacock & Sons Letter Book, fol. 2, Leacock Papers; Richard Lamar Bisset to Henry Hill, December 19, 1791, vol. 10, fol. 212; Francis Newton to Newton, Gordon & Murdoch, November 30, 1793, Loose Letters, CGP-MWC.

71. Thomas Murdoch to Thomas Gordon, July 3, 1793, vol. 15, fol. 183, August 5, 1793, fol. 207, William Johnston to Thomas Gordon, March 25, 1787, vol. 10, fol. 380, Thomas Murdoch to Thomas Gordon, August 5, 1793, vol. 15, fol. 207, NGL; June 1800, Leacock & Sons Ledger, 1791–1800, Leacock Papers; Inventory, June 30, 1802, folder 4, Hill-EWS; Inventory, June 30, 1805, Inventory Book (VI), 1805–7, Inventory Book VII, 1808, CGP-MWC. On imitations, see Thomas Lamar to Henry Hill, August 5, 1774, vol. 8, fol. 149, Hill-JJS(A); William Ballantyne to Editors, *The Times*, December 24, 1807, 4.

72. Francis Newton to Waddell Cunningham, April 30, 1753, vol. 1, fol. 31, NGL.

73. On measures, generally, see Alexander Henderson, *The History of Ancient and Modern Wines* (London, 1824), 385–90; McCusker, *Rum and the American Revolution*, 811–25; Ronald E. Zupko, *A Dictionary of English Weights and Measures* (Madison, 1968), 128–29; Duncan, *Atlantic Islands*, 259–66; Joel Serrão, *Dicionario de história de Portugal*, vol. 5 (Porto, 1985), s.v. "Pesos e medidas." On Portuguese receptacles generally, see Alvares da Silva, "Memória," 49–54; Silva e Telles, "Memória," 438–43.

74. On the pipe in Great Britain and her colonies, see 5 Anne, c. 27, s. 17; 6 Anne, c. 19, s. 1, c. 27, s. 22 (1706), 7 Anne, c. 7, s. 29, in Danby Pickering, ed., *The Statutes at Large* (Cambridge, 1764), 11:265; Henry Crouch, *A Complete View of the British Customs*, 5th ed. (London, 1755), 851; James Lightbody, *The Gauger and Measurer's Companion* (London, 1694), 108. On the confusion over the wine gallon at the end of the seventeenth century, and its resolution after 1700, see McCusker, *Rum and the American Revolution*, 812.

    For colonial measures, see Thomas Cooper, ed., *The Statutes at Large of South Carolina* (Columbia, 1837), 2:55–7; *Charter to William Penn, and Laws of the Province of Pennsylvania* (Harrisburg, 1879), 116, 140; *Votes and Proceedings of the House of Representatives of the Province of Pennsylvania*, in Pennsylvania Archives, 8th ser., 1 (Harrisburg, 1931), 141–42, 145, 148, 153, 200, 217–19, 268–69, 313; James T. Mitchell and Henry Flanders, eds., *The Statutes at Large of Pennsylvania* (Harrisburg, 1896), vol. 2, chap. 138; Barbados Assembly, *Acts Passed in the Island of Barbados from 1643 to 1762* (London, 1764), 334–36; *The Public Acts in Force, Passed by the Legislature of Barbados* (London, 1801); *The Colonial Laws of New York* (Albany, 1894), 2:828–29; William W. Hening, ed., *The Statutes at Large of Virginia* (Richmond, 1819), 6:235–36. Antigua adhered to the British 126-gallon standard in 1764; for other reasons, the law was nullified by the Privy Council. In 1800, Antigua passed a law lowering its pipe to 110 gallons. Francis Newton to George Spence, December 6, 1748, vol. 1, fol. 10, Newton & Gordon to William Snaip, May 18, 1764, vol. 3, fol. 305, to William Kirkpatrick of St. Kitts, August 23, 1766, vol. 4, fol. 36, NGL; *The Laws of the Island of Antigua* (London, 1805), 2:353. Jamaica adhered to 126 gallons in 1771. *The Laws of Jamaica* (St. Jago de la Vega, 1792), 2:90. Slowly, colonies and states adopted English norms. U.S. Department of State, *Reports of the Secretary of State, upon Weights and Measures*, Senate document no. 109, 16th Cong., 2nd sess., vol. 4, General Set no. 45 (Washington, DC, 1821), 22–43.

75. For containers smaller than pipes, see Newton & Gordon to Johnston & Jolly, June 1, 1767, vol. 4, fols. 95–96, NGL. For containers larger than pipes, see ibid.; William Johnston to Charles Fergusson, May 24, 1783, vol. 8, fol. 65, to Thomas Gordon, September 30, 1789, vol. 12, fol. 151, NGL. The large India pipes at times created havoc with shipping—making the ship "too deep in the water" and greatly increasing "her motion." Alfred Spencer, ed., *Memoirs of William Hickey*, 3rd ed. (London, 1919), 3:4.

76. The different measures were reconcilable, and a skilled merchant knew how to manage them. Prices in Madeira were quoted per 110-gallon pipe, and ultimate values were adjusted for any deficit or overplus. Francis Newton to George Spence, December 6, 1748, vol. 1, fol. 10, NGL. On another level, however, full reconciliation was nearly impossible. That is, there were two ways to measure wine volume: measuring by pot (a one-, five- or ten-gallon copper pot), or gauging by rod. On the contemporary art and science of gauging, see Richard Collins, *The Country Gaugers Vade Mecum; or, Pocket-Companion* (London, 1677); Lightbody, *Gauger and Measurer's Companion*, 108; Malachy Postlethwayt, *Universal Dictionary*, vol. 1 (London, 1755), s.v. "gauging"; Crouch, *Complete View*, 851, 873; John Stevenson, *Seamen and Merchant's Expedi-*

tious Measurer (London, 1795); I. Sequeira Jr., *A New Merchant's Guide* (London, 1798), 107–20. Most Madeirans adopted pot measuring, whereas customs officials and many consumers around the Atlantic favored rod gauging. Again and again, distributors juxtaposed the pot and the rod and, each time, the pot proved accurate or excessive, the rod short. The discrepancies were never effectively reconciled before 1815. Francis Newton to George Spence, May 22, 1753, vol. 1, fol. 50; Michael Nowlan to Gedley Clare Burges, December 16, 1760, Nowlan & Burges Letter Book, 1759–62, fols. 191–93, Leacock Papers; Newton & Gordon to Johnston & Jolly, April 28, 1765, vol. 4, fol. 401, to William Kirkpatrick, August 23, 1766, vol. 4, fol. 36, to Bond & Ryland, April 9, 1770, vol. 4, fol. 464, Thomas Murdoch to Francis Newton, March 13, 1789, to Richard Dowding, February 10, 1790, vol. 12, fols. 3, 227, NGL; Richard Lamar Bisset to Henry Hill, vol. 10, fol. 203, Hill-JJS(A); Thomas Murdoch to Allen & Smith of London, December 5, 1792, vol. 14, fol. 447, NGL.

77. William Johnston to Thomas Gordon, May 20, 1784, vol. 8, fol. 247, Newton & Gordon to Johnston & Jolly, April 28, 1765, vol. 3, fol. 401, to Samuel Bean, April 12, 1767, vol. 4, fol. 88, William Johnston to Francis Newton, September 20, 1779, vol. 6, fol. 511, to Thomas Gordon, September 30, 1789, vol. 12, fol. 151, Thomas Murdoch to Thomas Gordon, March 6, 1790, vol. 12, fol. 257, NGL; John Leacock Sr. to William Leacock, February 18, 1792, Leacock & Sons Letter Book 1791–94, fol. 76, Leacock Papers.

78. It was an unusual exporter who possessed no cooper's tools and supplies. Inventory, June 30, 1774, CGP-MWC.

79. The shifts in global sources for barrel wood have not been studied, but portions of the story are found in Alexander Gordon to James Gordon, October 11, 1761, Letterfourie Papers; Newton & Gordon to Thomas Gerry Sr. and Jr., December 12, 1762, vol. 3, fol. 74, to Samuel & John Span, December 22, 1793, vol. 15, fol. 296, to Lester & Murragh, August 14, 1805, vol. 19, fol. 14, NGL; Charles Wolley, *A Two Years' Journey in New York and Part of Its Territories in America*, ed. Edward G. Bourne (Cleveland, 1902), 41–42; Christoph Van Graffenried, *Account of the Founding of New Bern* (Raleigh, 1920), 300–302. European oak had to be split to follow the tubes and then had to be bent so that all the tubes were parallel to the staves; American oak did not need such reworking. New York, New Hampshire, and Quebec staves were also tried, as were Brazilian and Honduran staves, but parts carved from these varieties were sappy or thin.

80. On staves from sources other than Hamburg and America, see Newton & Gordon to Richard Cargill, February 23, 1775, vol. 5, fol. 457, William Johnston to Francis Newton, September 20, 1779, vol. 6, fol. 511, Memo, September 2–4, 1795, vol. 16, fols. 404–5, James David Webster Gordon to Thomas Gordon, April 30, 1802, vol. 23, fol. 265, to Robert Maitland, August 14, 1805, to Robert Lenox, September 7, 1805, to Robert Maitland, January 5, 1806, vol. 27, fols. 27, 36, 239, NGL; Robert G. Albion, *Forests and Sea Power: The Timber Problem of the Royal Navy, 1652–1862* (Cambridge, MA, 1926); H. S. K. Kent, "The Anglo-Norwegian Timber Trade in the Eighteenth Century," *Economic History Review*, 2nd ser., 8 (1955): 62–74; Arthur R. M. Lower, *Great Britain's Woodyard: British America and the Timber Trade, 1763–1867* (Mon-

treal, 1973); Sven-Erik Åström, "Britain's Timber Imports from the Baltic, 1775–1830," *Scandinavian Economic History Review* 37 (1989): 57–71.

81. Some timber, like that from Hamburg, was especially rough and needed sawing. For any container, the outside of the staves and heads had to be planed, the containers tested for leaks, the bungholes drilled and cauterized, and wooden hoops substituted for the fitting iron hoops. The work of the coopers was critical at this juncture, and it was incumbent upon the exporters to see that it was properly performed. Little was left to artisanal interpretation. Exporters' requests for pipe packs left nothing to chance, detailing with a precision that seems unrealizable the kind and appearance of the wood, the dimensions of all the pieces in the pack, and the dressing, finishing, jointing, bending, and numbering of each piece. William Bolton & Co. to Robert & William Heysham, July 28, 1709, *Bolton Letters*, 2:57; Memo, September 2–4, 1795, vol. 16, fols. 404–5, NGL.

Obtaining hoops posed slightly different challenges from obtaining staves. The norm for Madeira pipes was ten hoops per 110-gallons pipe, and it did not change much, although in 1775–1800 exporters began to add more hoops to protect pipes sent to hot climates. With hoops, the choice lay between wood and iron. Islanders preferred wooden, which had to be young, free of worm, and split. The island's chestnut trees were an early source of quality hoops, but they were easily exhausted. After Madeiran chestnut prices had risen to unacceptable levels by the early 1760s, distributors turned to the Canaries, and later the Americas. Iron was traditionally regarded as unnecessary, except during a pipe's construction as an aid to the cooper. Two things changed opinion. Heat from the lengthening duration of "normal" stays in the Indies and, later, the warming of pipes in stoves caused the wood to crack and leak. Exposure of the ship and its contents to the timber-eating *teredo navalis* worm caused islanders to bow to consumer pressure and replace wooden hoops with iron ones in the 1780s. *Bolton Letters*, 1:93; Newton & Gordon to John & William Pasley, April 18, 1764, vol. 3, fol. 296, NGL; Daniel Henry Smith to James Gordon, March 16, 1776, May 6, 1777, Letterfourie Papers; William Johnston to Nathaniel Beckford, April 15, 1785, vol. 8, fol. 420, William Johnston to Thomas Winter, December 1, 1787, vol. 10, fols. 90–91, James David Webster Gordon to Edward Pytts Middleton, July 8, 1806, vol. 27, fol. 403, NGL.

82. On leakage, see John Leacock Jr. to William Leacock, September 14, 1799, Leacock Letters 1799–1802, fol. 69, Leacock Papers; James Gordon to Edward Pytts Middleton, July 8, 1806, vol. 27, fol. 403, NGL; *Bolton Letters*, 2:26.

83. Thomas Murdoch to Edmund Boehm, November 20, 1789, vol. 12, fol. 172, to Richard Dowding, February 10, 1790, vol. 12, fol. 227, Newton & Gordon to Samuel Thompson, December 2, 1772, vol. 5, fol. 138, NGL; John J. McCusker, *Essays on the Economic History of the Atlantic World* (London, 1997), 80; William Johnston to Francis Newton, April 12, 1788, vol. 10, fols. 239–40, NGL; John Leacock Jr. to William Leacock, November 1, 1800, Leacock Letters 1799–1802, fol. 210, Leacock Papers; Invoice Book no. 5 1774–82, fol. 35, CGP-MWC; Thomas Murdoch to Law, Bruce & Co., September 30, 1801, vol. 22, fol. 280, NGL.

84. Robert Bisset to Henry Hill, June 1, 1765, vol. 6, fol. 242, Hill-JJS(A); Inventory, June 30, 1774, CGP-MWC; Thomas Gordon to James Jenkins, November 5, 1773, vol. 5, fol. 268, William Johnston to Thomas Gordon, November 9, 1786, vol. 9, fol. 293, November 20, 21, 1789, vol. 12, fols. 177, 183, April 4, 1795, vol. 16, fol. 254, NGL; Inventory, June 30, 1792, Inventory, June 30, 1802, folder 4, Hill-SAGS; Inventory, June 30, 1795, CGP-MWC; John Leacock Jr. to William Leacock, June 10, 1800, Leacock Brothers Letter Book, fol. 167, Leacock Papers; Condell, Innes Letter Book, March 23, 1803, Symington Papers. Most pumps and boilers also supplied kitchen and household water.

85. Thomas Gordon to Edward Cairns, February 3, 1769, vol. 4, fol. 287, to Richard Cargill, June 28, 1773, vol. 5, fol. 234, February 23, 1775, vol. 5, fol. 467, William Johnston to Edward Greathead, April 14, 1785, vol. 8, fol. 410, January 21, 1786, vol. 9, fol. 127, to Thomas Winter, December 1, 1787, vol. 10, fols. 90–91, Thomas Murdoch to Thomas Gordon, June 15, 1789, vol. 12, fol. 86, to Evans, Offley & Sealy, September 23, 1797, vol. 18, fol. 80, NGL; Newton & Gordon Invoice Book 4, no. 170 (February 6, 1774), Inventory, June 30, 1774, CGP-MWC. Rather than a guard against worm during voyage, painting was probably more effective as a protection against the day when casks stood in damp cellars. Kenneth Kilby, *The Cooper and His Trade* (London, 1971), 17–18.

86. Robert Bisset to Henry Hill, August 30, 1763, box 1, folder 3, Hill-SAGS; Inventory, July 1, 1767, folder 3, noting Portuguese padlocks, English locks, and iron locks; Inventory, July 1, 1772, folder 4, Hill-EWS.

87. Perhaps more typical, because of its slower engagement with lodges, was Newton & Gordon. In the early 1760s, it acquired two lodges. By 1800, it had at least seventeen. Journal, vol. 2, fol. 201, *sub* January 1762, Inventory, June 30, November 30, 1800, CGP-MWC.

88. Inventory, June 30, 1795, CGP-MWC; Thomas Murdoch to Law, Bruce & Co., April 16, 1801, vol. 21, fol. 346, NGL. On the need for padlocks, see William Johnston to Thomas Gordon, June 11, 1785, vol. 9, fol. 35, NGL. On above-ground cellars making use of ambient heat, see Hill, *Works*, 2:135; Silva e Telles, "Memória," 443–45; Barrow, *Voyage*, 22; Amerine et al., *Technology*, 279–95, 321–30.

89. Thomas Gordon to Francis Newton, January 6, 1768, vol. 4, fol. 157, NGL.

CHAPTER 4. "A REVOLUTION IN THIS TRADE"

1. Natives and foreigners had to sail to Brazil in annual fleets. European commodities had to be channeled to Portuguese America through certain mainland Portuguese ports. Certain goods grown, produced, or manufactured in Portuguese America had to be channeled to European states through Portugal or its dependencies. José Ferreira, Visconde de Borges de Castro, comp., *Supplemento á collecção dos tratados, convenções, contratos e actos publicos*, (Lisbon, 1872), 9:50–51; Lewis Hertslet, comp., *A Complete Collection of the Treaties and Conventions* (London, 1840), 2:1–8 (1642), 8–20 (1654); José Justino de Andrade e Silva, comp., *Collecção chronológica de legis-*

lação portugueza (Lisbon, 1855), 7:3 (March 15, 1648), 25–26 (January 25, 1649); ibid. (Lisbon, 1856), 8:76 (May 20, 1662).

2. Marien Lamar to ——, December 1, 1807, Newton & Gordon Scrapbook, vol. 1, CGP-PC. For earlier uses of the phrase, see John Leacock Sr. to William Leacock, August 16, 1791, Leacock & Sons Letter Book 1791–94, fol. 2, and January 31, April 14, 1800, February 20, October 26, 1801, Leacock & Leacock Letter Book 1799–1802, fols. 107, 131, 227, 28, Leacock Papers.

3. Edward Littleton, *The Groans of the Plantations* (London, 1689), 28.

4. The data on vessel size are not all consistent: there are variations between countries and over time; and there is a lively debate about how to translate stated tonnages into a common measure. Still, the trend is clear—a steady increase in the size of oceangoing ships from Europe. For Iberian shipping, see Carla Rahn Phillips, "Galleons: Fast Sailing Ships of the Mediterranean and Atlantic, 1500–1650," in *Cogs, Caravels and Galleons: The Sailing Ship, 1000–1650* (London, 1994), 98–114; João da Gama Pimente Barata, ed., *Estudos de arqueologia naval*, 2 vols. (Lisbon, 1989); Eugénio Estanislau Barros, *Traçado e construção das naus portuguesas dos séculos XVI e XVII* (Lisbon, 1933). For British shipping, consult Ralph Davis, *The Rise of the English Shipping Industry in the Seventeenth and Eighteenth Centuries* (London, 1962), 298, 395–96; John J. McCusker Jr., "The Tonnage of Ships Engaged in British Colonial Trade during the Eighteenth Century," *Research in Economic History* 6 (1981): 73–105. Richard Unger provides good comparative data in "The Tonnage of Europe's Merchant Fleets, 1300–1800," *American Neptune* 52 (1992): 247–61.

5. It was not that no slave traders stopped at Madeira. Independent traders after 1712 were supposed to steer clear of West Africa, where the Royal African Company possessed a monopoly on sales. So they stopped at Madeira and took on wine, after which they could legitimately claim to customs officials that they had cleared for Madeira, which conveniently enough was not far off the African coast. Nigel Tattersfield, *The Forgotten Trade* (London, 1991), 17.

6. J. F. Jameson, ed., *Johnson's Wonder Working Providence, 1628–1651* (New York, 1910), 24; Samuel Taylor Coleridge, *The Rime of the Ancyent Marinere*, part II, stanza 9, in *Lyrical Ballads* (London, 1798), 13. On the problem of empty holds and its solution, see chapter 1, n.59; John and Charles Carter to Hayward & Chambers, November 10, 1733, John, Charles and Landon Carter Letter Book, 1732–82, Manuscripts Library, University of Virginia, Charlottesville. On the bulkiness of wine, see John J. McCusker to David Hancock, 1999, author's correspondence. The gain from filling a hold with cargo or ballast instead of leaving it empty is hard to determine precisely. A 198-measured-ton vessel could stow about 593 barrels of 111 gallons each. On HMS *Unicorn*, a barrel with dimensions of two feet, nine inches diameter by three feet height had a volume of 17.7 cubic feet (equaling 111 gallons). Of these 593 barrels, 93 would likely have been disallowed for dunnage or broken stowage. Captain Simon Waite to David Hancock, June 20, 2001.

7. Thomas Pinney, *A History of Wine in America: From the Beginnings to Prohibition* (Berkeley, 1989), 104; David Mishkin, "The American Colonial Wine Industry: An Economic Interpretation" (PhD diss., University of Illinois, Urbana, 1966), 242. Pin-

ney provides the best study of viticulture and viniculture in America in *History of Wine.*

8. Drayton and Percy as quoted in Pinney, *History of Wine*, 13.
9. Ibid., 14.
10. Ibid., 24, 29, 31–33.
11. Ibid., 40–54. See also George Fenwick Jones, ed., *Detailed Reports, on the Salzburger Emigrants Who Settled in America*, vol. 15 (Athens, GA, 1990).
12. Pinney, *History of Wine*, 59–60, 88–91, 94, 95–98; John Leacock Commonplace Book, 1768–81, APS; Joshua Steel to Earl of Shelburne, June 1, 1782, vol. 87, no. 36, Shelburne Papers, Clements Library, Ann Arbor.
13. The grape was discovered about 1740 by James Alexander, a gardener for Thomas Penn who was working in William Penn's old 1683 vineyard on the banks of the Schuylkill River. Dufour bought a vine of this type and brought it from Philadelphia to Kentucky and from there to the Second Vineyard around 1802. It is not clear exactly what happened between 1683 and 1740 to sustain the Alexander hybrid. A vinedresser could have grafted the tasty grape uppers onto hardy rootstock, but that was not yet common practice. A hybrid is the offspring of two varieties of different species, and the Alexander grape hybrid probably occurred naturally by cross-pollination. Dufour modeled the Kentucky Vineyard Society after the not-yet-failed Pennsylvania Vine Company established in the early 1790s by the Frenchman Pierre Legaux in Montgomery County along the Schuylkill River's east bank. Dufour bought the Alexander vines from Legaux. Along with the Alexander grape, Dufour cultivated a "Madeira" grape at the Second Vineyard, but it is not known exactly what this grape was or where it came from. Pinney, *History of Wine*, 84–5, 117–26; *National Register*, November 30, 1816, 222.
14. Spain's declaration of war against England in 1656 and its seizure of English ships and England's aggressive military response obstructed the flow of Spanish Sherry, Malaga, and Canary abroad; indirectly, it encouraged the import of Portuguese wines into overseas territories. Similarly, France's declaration of war against England in 1665 moved the English to block the flow of French wines into England and its dependencies, reduce French imports, and accentuate the importance of imported Spanish and Portuguese wines. French and Spanish wines also suffered with respect to the provisioning of the countries that rimmed the Atlantic. French wines were banned and blocked in English-speaking areas during William's and Anne's struggles with Louis XIV, and they subsequently failed to recover the market they had enjoyed. During the Wars of Spanish Succession and Austrian Succession, the flow of wines from France, Spain, and the Canaries was again impeded. In the former conflict, the export of French wines to Portugal was blocked by the renewal of the Anglo-Portuguese alliance. In both wars, as well as in the Seven Years' War, the supply of Canary to the English-speaking colonies was cut by an increasingly aggressive and successful British naval and privateering force around the Atlantic. In 1762 and 1763, British men-of-war were ordered to seize all Canary wine; unofficially, all ships were encouraged to seize and make prize of French and Spanish wines. L. M. E. Shaw, *The Anglo-Portuguese Alliance and the English Merchants in Portugal, 1654–1810* (Aldershot, 1998), 194;

E. Bradford Burns, *A History of Brazil*, 2nd ed. (New York, 1970), 146. The case for Portugal's neutrality and the reciprocity of its interests with those of England is made by J. J. da Cunha de Azeredo Coutinho, *Ensáio económico sobre o comércio de Portugál e suas colónias* (Lisbon, 1794), trans. as *A Political Essay on the Commerce of Portugal and Her Colonies, Particularly of Brasil in South America* (London, 1801), 181–84, 191–96.

15. Vieira, "A vinha," 107n34. Vieira has also transcribed the Branco letters in *O público e o privado na jistória da Madeira*, vol. 1, *Correspondencia particular do mercador Diogo Fernandes Branco (1649–1652)* (Funchal, 1996). The originals are kept at the Convent of Santa Clara, Funchal.

16. The entry and exit registers discussed in this and the following paragraph are Livros dos direitos por entradas (e saída), Livros 306–9 (1650, 1699), Cobrancas, Alfândega do Funchal, AN-TdT. The 1650 duties were 888 *réis* for common wine and 1$000 for Malvasia, although Vieira suggests 400 *réis* for common wine. Until now, T. Bentley Duncan had done the most work on Madeira's seventeenth century exports. *Atlantic Islands*, 42, 45–47. I have drawn on Duncan in certain places, especially his analysis of geographic distribution, but have chosen to ignore his estimates for 1682 and especially 1687, as they are somewhat speculative: he derives a figure for a year by multiplying the one surviving month of that year by twelve; records for which all months of the year have survived suggest month-to-month and year-to-year fluctuations were considerable.

Reliable sources of export data are infrequent for the seventeenth century. In places, they can be substituted with other countries' import data. Occasional imports of wine from Funchal into Rotterdam are instructive. See, for example, Inv. 241, no. 97/154 (November 2, 1646), and Inv. 87, no. 66/135 (August 11, 1647), Notariel akten, Oud notarieel archief, Gemeentarchief, Rotterdam.

17. Joaquim Ignacio de Freitas and Feliciano de Cunha França, comp., *Collecção chronológica de leis extravagantes, . . . [1603–1761]*, vol. 2 (Coimbra, 1819), *sub* Proviso, July 12, 1712.

18. An instance of growing engagement is that of London agent and absentee planter William Freeman: Hancock, *Letters of William Freeman*, 8–13, 86–90, 234–36, 250–51.

19. Duncan, *Atlantic Islands*, 42, 45–47.

20. The division among the colonies is somewhat imprecise, because the *entradas* in most instances list only initial stops of outbound vessels; many pipes described as bound for the Caribbean were not unloaded there but held on board and sent to North America.

21. David J. Hancock, "Guerre et commerce (1750–1815)," in *Guerre et économie dans l'espace atlantique du XVIe au XXe siècle*, ed. S. Marzagalli and B. Marnot (Bordeaux, 2006), 331–74; Thomas Newton to Adoniah Schuyler, January 22, 1756, Thomas Newton Letter Book, CGP-MWC. Protected, Madeira faced no legal threat from Canary, although in another sense, American privateers capturing Spanish vessels often offloaded Canary wine as "Madeira" in American ports. Thomas Newton to

Malcolm Campbell, October 14, 1756, Thomas Newton Letter Book, CGP-MWC; Newton & Gordon to John Provoost, June 17, 1762, to John Tweedy, June 27, 1762, NGL, vol. 3, fols. 2, 10; and Alexander Hamilton to George Spence, December 13, 1758, Book of Assorted Letters, Leacock Papers.

The NOSL for North America have survived in such spotty fashion to make confirmation of the trend with extant lists impossible. These lists and colonial manifest books offer contradictory clues: average annual wine imports into Virginia actually rose after 1748, but dropped below pre-1739 levels after 1753 and remained low through 1775; imports into New York showed no change from before 1749, but a considerable drop in 1754–62 and a doubling in 1763–75.

22. When departure records from Madeira survive, they record cargoes of between seventeen and fifty-six pipes to North America and an overall global destination average of fifty-one pipes.

23. In Thomas Allen's New London tavern, a fairly typical port operation, wine and wine-related drinks constituted 29.4 percent (Madeira itself 20.9 percent) of the value of all alcoholic beverages dispensed in 1771–72. Madeira was the single biggest specific drink purveyed. Spirits constituted 62.2 percent of sales, 30.7 percent of which was rum and grog, while porter and cider comprised the remainder. No beer was dispensed. The range of drinks included wine of at least three types, punch, sangria, sling, bishop, rum, grog, liquor, gin, brandy, spirit, toddy, cider, and porter. Day Book, 1771–72, Allen Papers, AAS.

The typical rural inventory that Alexander Schaeffer maintained at the King George Tavern in Schaefferstown, Pennsylvania, is also worth examining for overall preferences. In 1762–73, the only named wine he kept was Madeira; it and drinks using it constituted 24.1 percent of the quantity sold in 1764. The spirit he dispensed in greatest volume was rum (it and rum-based drinks comprised 17.7 percent of the quantity sold in 1764). More popular was cider (35 percent); beer ran just behind rum (16.8 percent). Patrons also drank *bunsch, gatsel, mimm* and *tram*. Larry M. Neff and Frederick S. Weiser, trans., *Records of Purchases at the King George Hotel, Schaefferstown, Lebanon County, Pennsylvania, 1762–1773* (Birdsboro, 1987). A similar situation prevailed at Manheim's King of Prussia Tavern. Account book, 1768–69, HSP.

24. In the present analysis, I have decided not to estimate quarters and years when data are missing, as do Duncan, Lydon, and Nash. There is no indication that their estimation provides more reliable material for conclusions. Duncan, *Atlantic Islands*, table 2, p. 47; James G. Lydon, "Fish for Gold; The Massachusetts Fish Trade with Iberia, 1700–1773," *New England Quarterly* 54 (1981): 539–82; R. C. Nash, "English Transatlantic Trade" (PhD diss., University of Cambridge, 1982), 55–56. Given how much has to be assumed and how thin the evidence is, it is not clear that the approaches produce any better results than the one adopted here.

25. In 1761, America was glutted with Spanish and Canary wine, but in 1762 that flow was stopped by Spain's entry into the war. Crown desire to impede the return of such importation at the end of the war expressed itself in orders to British men-of-war in 1763 to seize and take as prize all Spanish (including Canary) and Lisbon wine. The orders

were never rescinded, yet seldom enforced after 1764. Newton & Gordon to Johnston & Jolly, September 21, 1763, vol. 2, fol. 206, to Robert Hooper, February 1, 1764, vol. 3, fol. 262, NGL.

26. The Sugar Act (4 Geo. III, cap. 15) was to take effect on September 29, 1764. Pickering, *Statutes at Large*, 26:33–52. On its imposition of duties, see: R. C. Simmons and P. D. G. Thomas, eds., *Proceedings and Debates of the British Parliaments respecting North America*, (New York, 1982), 1:489–92; *Journal of the House of Commons*, 29:934. On the later, unsuccessful push to relax the rule requiring Portugal's wines be shipped first to England, see "Reply to 'A Portugal Merchant,'" April 1768, in William B. Willcox, ed., *Papers of Benjamin Franklin* (New Haven, 1972), 15:107–10.

27. Thomas Newton to Newton & Gordon, November 27, 1762, box 3, bundle 1764–65, CGP-Guildhall; vol. 3, fols. 158, 305, 315, 330, NGL; John Searle to Thomas Riche, August 25–26, 1763, Society Collection, HSP; Oliver M. Dickerson, *The Navigation Acts and the American Revolution* (Philadelphia, 1951), 175–76. On the effect of the Sugar Act and resulting high prices, see Newton & Gordon to George & John Riddell, June 3, 1765, vol. 3, fol. 413, NGL. Richard Derby, for instance, stopped all orders in 1766; Salem's drinkers, he wrote, were "adverse to Madeira" and were cutting their consumption on account of the price. Richard Derby to Chambers, Hiccox & Chambers, April 3, June 1, 1767, Derby Papers, JDPL; Robert Bisset to Henry Hill, July 28, 1764, vol. 6, fol. 164, Hill-JJS(A).

28. In response to Charles Townshend's duties on glass, paint, lead, tea, and paper, first imposed in 1767, twelve of Britain's thirteen mainland colonies formed nonimportation associations in 1768 and 1769. In the northern colonies, associations banned goods dutied by the Townshend Acts, goods from Britain or Europe, and those capable of being produced in the colonies. Wine was critical to the New England and middle colonies' transatlantic trades in fish and grain. Well-read minds quickly remembered with no small measure of self-interest that geographers considered Madeira part of Africa, so did not proscribe its wine. In the southern colonies, where trades seldom involved a direct exchange of wine for staples, wine was explicitly prohibited. Meetings there specifically banned "any wines," although none enumerated Madeira. Some distributors stored or returned prohibited goods and, when they did not, some local committees of inspection forced them to do so. In most southern localities, adherence to the ban was fitful, and the nonimporters' resolve eventually faltered. Everywhere, wine distributors resented the ban, even if they had initially voted for it; in some places, they had completely ignored it.

On the pacts, see Thomas Cushing to Dennys de Berdt, January 19, 1768 [1769], "Letters of Thomas Cushing, from 1767 to 1775," *Collections of the Massachusetts Historical Society*, 4th ser., 4 (1858): 352–53; Sparks MSS, vol. 62, *sub* March 10, 1769, Houghton Library, Harvard College, Cambridge, MA; *The Case of the Good Intent* (Annapolis, 1772), republished in *Maryland Historical Magazine* 3 (1908): 141–57; *Maryland Gazette*, June 29, 1769; *Boston Chronicle*, June 8, 1769; *Virginia Gazette*, June 15, 1769; Frances N. Mason, ed., *John Norton & Sons, Merchants of London and Virginia* (Richmond, 1937), 96; *South Carolina Gazette*, December 8, 1769, June 29, July 6, 13, 27, October 26, 1769; *South Carolina and American General Gazette*, July

13, 1769; *Georgia Gazette*, September 13, 20, 1769; Merchants of Boston, *Observations on Several Acts of Parliament* (Boston, 1769). For the response of Philadelphia importers, see Francis & Tilghman to Newton & Gordon, March 7, 1770, box 5, CGP-Guildhall; *Pennsylvania Gazette*, July 26, August 23, September 20, 1770. On wine smuggling, see CO 5/72/253–59, 264, NA-UK, and nos. 22 and 30, Customs House Papers, 1704–89, vol. 10 (1769–70), collection 157, HSP. For a general discussion, see Charles M. Andrews, "The Boston Merchants and the Non-importation Movement," *Publications of the Colonial Society of Massachusetts* 19 (1918): 201–21; Samuel Eliot Morison, "The Commerce of Boston on the Eve of the Revolution," *Proceedings of the American Antiquarian Society*, 2nd ser., 32 (1922): 24–51.

29. W. Ford and G. Hirt, eds., *The Journals of the Continental Congress, 1774–1789*, vol. 1 (Washington, DC, 1904), 41, 43, 51–52, 75–81. Apart from Madeira and Azores wines, the association excluded British East Indian tea, British West Indian molasses, brown sugar, syrup, pimento, and indigo. The best account of the September resolutions and the later association appears in Jack N. Rakove, *The Beginnings of National Politics: An Interpretive History of the Continental Congress* (Baltimore, 1979), 49–52; Edmund C. Burnett, *The Continental Congress* (New York, 1964), 46–59.

30. Portugal closed its ports in July 1776 and reopened them in March 1783. England rescinded the Prohibitory Act in 1778. Decreto do Rei D. José, July 4, 1776, Palácio da Ajuda, Lisbon; Walpole to Weymouth, July 6, 1776, SP 89/82/179, NA-UK; Newton & Gordon to Samuel Bean, April 22, 1776, vol. 6, fol. 74, NGL; Decreto da Rainha D. Maria I, February 15, 1783 (Lisbon, 1783), in Collecção de leis, SP no. 2230, AN-TdT; John Marsden Pintard to Elias Boudinot, August 24, 1783, in John Marsden Pintard/Elias Boudinot Folder, Boudinot Correspondence, ABS; Thomas Gordon to Francis Newton, May 29, 1775, vol. 5, fol. 515, to Samuel Bean, April 22, 1776, vol. 6, fol. 74, to Charles McEvers & Co., April 3, 1777, fol. 207, to Francis Newton, April 25, 1779, fol. 459, NGL; Papeís vários, c. 1780, MS 219, no. 29, BNL.

31. Loring & Winslow to five firms, March 1, 1777, Joshua Loring to Newton & Gordon, July 14, 1777, box 1776/1777, bundle 15, April 2, 1779, box 1778/79, unnumbered bundle, CGP-Guildhall; William Johnston to Francis Newton, March 13, 1777, to Wilkinson & Gordon, April 5, 1777, to Daniel Wier, April 30, 1777, to Joshua Loring, October 1777, vol. 6, fols. 200, 208, 217, 290, William Johnston to Francis Newton, April 25, 1779, vol. 6, fol. 459, NGL. Cf. Edward E. Curtis, *The Organization of the British Army in the American Revolution* (New Haven, 1926), chap. 4; Willard O. Mishoff, "Business in Philadelphia during the British Occupation, 1777–1778," *PMHB* 61 (1937): 165–81; Bernard Mason, "Entrepreneurial Activity in New York during the American Revolution," *Business History Review* 40 (1966): 194–95; Robert M. Dructor, "The New York Commercial Community: The Revolutionary Experience" (PhD diss., University of Pittsburgh, 1975), 86–88.

On wine supplied to the Americans, see W. Ford and G. Hirt, eds., *The Journals of the Continental Congress, 1774–1789*, vol. 14 (Washington, DC, 1909), 1,093; Charles H. Lincoln, ed., *Naval Records of the American Revolution, 1775–1788* (Washington, DC, 1906), 138, 140, 142–43, 147, 151, 158; Charles Davney to William Davies, August 4, 1781, Letters and Documents Received in the Governor's Office, 1776–

84, Library of Virginia, Richmond; John C. Fitzpatrick, ed., *George Washington's Accounts of Expenses, 1775–83*, December 19, 1775, George Washington Papers at the LC (online); George Washington to Admiralty Board, May 13, 1780, 18:352, to Thomas Mumford, September 15, 1780, 20:57, to Board of War, July 9, to John Hancock, July 14, to Chevalier de Chastellux, July 19, 1781, in John C. Fitzpatrick, ed., *The Writings of George Washington* (Washington, DC, 1937), 22:343, 380, 394–95.

32. John Leacock to Sargent, Chambers & Co., February 17, June 20, November 16, 1776, to Samuel Gardiner, Jr., May 26, 1782, Nowlan & Leacock Letter Book, fols. 48, 67, 90, 112, 120, Leacock Papers. On war's encouragement of a trade with neutrals, see Robert Bisset to Henry Hill, July 28, 1764, vol. 6, fol. 164, Hill-JJS(A). Comparable work has not been done on wartime smuggling through neutral colonies in the American revolutionary period, although see Vincent T. Harlow, *The Founding of the Second British Empire, 1763-1793*, 2 vols. (London, 1952–64); Richard Buel, *In Irons: Britain's Naval Supremacy and the American Revolutionary Economy* (New Haven, 1998).

33. The *saídas* before 1779 do not list destinations, and the *saídas* from 1784 have not survived. Comparison of *entradas* and *saídas* for the years 1779–82 reveals that the share of wine imported by British Americans was somewhat greater than the share of wine ships that brought the wine, a fact attributable to the unusually large military consignments during the war. Of the 421 departures in these four years, 16 percent went to the British West Indies and 13 percent to British North America. Notable is another complementary document. Government clerks reduced the *saídas* for 1777–82 and 1784–86 to a table; they broke destinations down among "Europe, Africa, Asia, America" for the earlier period and according to the nationality of the shippers for the later period; according to them, total exports for 1784 were 8,358 pipes. Between 1784 and 1793, exports to the United States grew from 789 to 1,924 pipes: "Donde se mostra o augmento deste commercio depois da independencia da America, e o progressivo que promette a sua maior povoacao e luxo," caixa dl, doc. 151, no. lix, MNE.

34. William Johnston to Thomas Gordon, March 10, 1783, vol. 8, fol. 13, Newton, Gordon & Murdoch to Thomas Gordon, July 3, 1793, vol. 15, fol. 185, NGL; John Leacock Sr., to John Rowe, June 30, 1783, Nowlan & Leacock Letter Book, 1781–84, Leacock Papers. See also John H. Coatsworth, "American Trade with European Colonies in the Caribbean and South America, 1790–1812," *WMQ*, 3rd ser., 24 (1967): 245, 247.

35. French data is presented in Edmond Buron, "Statistics on Franco-American Trade, 1778–1806," *Journal of Economic and Business History* 4 (1932): 578–79.

36. *American State Papers: Documents, Legislative and Executive, of the Congress of the United States, (Class IV): Commerce and Navigation*, vol. 1 (Washington, D.C., 1832). Compared to other wines, reexports of Madeira wine were high in 1790–91 (70 percent), 1791–92 (39 percent), and 1792–93 (21 percent). After 1793, reexports of Madeira wine averaged 4 percent of total wine exports; in 1793–1806, they averaged 26 percent of Madeira imports. The quantities listed in the *American State Papers* are identical to those listed by the Portuguese consul in Philadelphia: "Charts of Portuguese Goods Imported into America," in caixas dl–dli, Collecção de ministério do negócios etrangeiros, AN-TdT. Values of imports from Madeira into the United States in

U.S. dollars, 1795–1801, appear in Timothy Pitkin, *A Statistical View of the Commerce of the United States of America* (Hartford, 1816), 194. The quantities of "wines" (not specified by type), distilled spirits, and molasses imported by the United States from October 1800 to September 1815, as well as their ten-year-average values, are given by Pitkin, *View,* 254, and Adam Seybert, *Statistical Annals* (Philadelphia, 1818), 256, 258, 260, 267, 269, 271, 273. Apart from a few computation errors, Pitkin's and Seybert's numbers agree with the *American State Papers.*

37. Newton, Gordon & Johnston to James Kerr, April 29, 1784, vol. 8, fol. 225, NGL.

38. Dauril Alden, *Royal Government in Colonial Brazil* (Berkeley, 1968), 63–66, 71–82; Eduardo de Castro e Almeida, comp., *Inventário dos documentos relativos ao Brasil existentes no Arquivo de Marinha e Ultramar de Lisboa,* 8 vols. (Rio de Janeiro, 1913–36); José C. Curto, *Enslaving Spirits: The Portuguese Brazilian Alcohol Trade at Luanda and Its Hinterland, c. 1550–1830* (Leiden, 2004), 180, 190, 194, 212, 224, 228, who reconstructs exports of wine from Portugal to Angola and *gerebita* (*cachaça*) exports from Brazil to Angola. Much of the wine in Angola came via Brazil.

39. Trade to and from Brazil is poorly studied outside the parameters of the sugar and gold industries; import records are less good and less studied for the beginning of the period than for its end. But see the monumental work of Conceição Andrade Martins, the only scholar to quantify all mainland production and distribution: "Vinha, vinho e política vinícola em Portugal: Do Pombalismo à regeneração" (PhD diss., University of Évora, 1997), anexos 4.1.1, 4.4.5, 4.4.6, 5.1. It is not possible to compare Madeirans' export levels to those achieved by Lisbon wine exporters, as the 1755 earthquake and fire destroyed all prior *saída* records for Lisbon. Some data are found in Compton to Tyrawley, August 6, 1729, SP 89/30–41, NA-UK; Bernardo de Jesus Maria, *Arte, e diccionario do commercio* (Lisbon, 1784), 212–13; Matthias E. Sprengel and Georg Forster, *Neue Beitrage zur Bolter und Landerfunde* (Leipzig, 1791), 7:20.

40. Alvará, March 8, 1649, in *Instituiçam da Companhia Geral para o estado do Brazil* (Lisbon, 1649); Leonor Freire Costa, *O transporte no Atlântico e a Companhia Geral do comércio do Brasil (1580–1663)* (Lisbon, 2002); Gustavo de Freitas, *A Companhia Geral do comercio do Brasil (1649–1720)* (Lisbon, 1951). The best article on its founding is Charles R. Boxer, "Padre António Vieira, S.J., and the Institution of the Brazil Company in 1649," *Hispanic American Historical Review* 29 (1949): 487–89. For the later grants of monopoly privilege to towns and companies, see Andrade e Silva, *Collecção de legislação portugueza,* 1:376–91, 445, 446, 426–41, 2:368–70, 3:106–7; *Instituição da Companhia Geral,* September 1756, secs. 12–19, 24; Manuel Nunes Dias, *A Companhia Geral do grão pará e maranhão* (Lisbon, 1970); Susan Schneider, *O marquès de Pombal e o vinho do Porto: Dependência e subdesenvolvimento em Portugal no século XVIII* (Lisbon, 1980); Kenneth Maxwell, *Pombal: Paradox of the Enlightenment* (Cambridge, 1995), 58–63.

41. Schneider, *O marquès de Pombal,* 261; Jorge Borges de Macedo, *Problemas de historia da industria portuguesa no século XVIII* (Lisbon, 1963), 195; Paul Duguid, "All in the Details: Snapshots of the Port Trade in 1777 and 1786" (unpublished MS, 2001), tables 2 and 6.

42. Administração-Geral do Porto de Lisboa, *O Porto de Lisboa* (Lisbon, 1960), 58;

Catherine Lugar, "The Merchant Community of Salvador, Bahia, 1780–1830" (PhD diss., State University of New York, Stony Brook, 1980), 38, 78, 80; José Jobson de A. Arruda, *O Brasil no comércio colonial* (São Paulo, 1980), 520, graph 96, table 102; Corcino Medeiros dos Santos, *Relações comerciáis do Rio de Janeiro com Lisboa* (Rio de Janeiro, 1980), 191, table xix, pp. 203–4, and *O Rio de Janeiro e a conjuntura atlântica* (Rio de Janeiro, 1993), 87, 152. One of the few record of imports into Brazil in 1779–89 lists 358 pipes of *aguardente* but not wine coming from Lisbon, 43 pipes from the Wine Islands, and 28 pipes from Porto. Luiz de Vasconcelos, "Memorias publicas e economicas da cidade de Sao Sebastião do Rio de Janeiro, 1779–1789," *Revista trimensal do Instituto historico geographica e ethnographico do Brazil* 47, pt. 1 (1884), 46–51. According to a slightly different calculation, Portugal sent on average 9,664 pipes of wine each year in 1796, 1798, 1800, and 1805–13. Averages decreased after 1807 as mainland viniculture was disrupted by invasion. Administração-Geral do Porto de Lisboa, *O Porto de Lisboa*, 58.

43. Carta regia, August 11, 1650, July 3, 1652, Câmara municipal do Funchal, vol. 6, fols. 100, 169–70, ARM, cited in Vieira, *Público*, 30, 13n40; de Freitas and de Cunha França, comps., *Collecção chronológica*, sub Proviso, July 12, 1712, Lei, March 20, 1736; Lei, July 15, 1735, Arquivo Histórico Ultramarino, Rio de Janeiro; Vieira, "A vinha," 106; Sousa, *O movimento do porto do Funchal*, 169–70, 187; Livros dos direitos por saída, 1779–1807, Provedoria e Junta da Real Fazenda do Funchal, Alfândega do Funchal, AN-TdT. Ten percent of Dona Guiomar's overseas shipping involved Brazil, and most of these cargoes carried wine. Bernardete Barros, *Dona Guiomar de Sá Vilhena: Uma mulher do século XVIII* (Funchal, 2001), 129. It nonetheless was a comparatively small volume. Some Madeira was shipped to Brazil via England. Account, 1784–86, MS 219, no. 29, BNL. For mainland and Lisbon exports, see: Martins, "Vinha," anexos V.1, pp. 153–56 (national totals), V.4.1, pp. 172–83 (Lisbon totals). On Brazilian imports, see Vasconcelos, "Memorias," 25–51; Frederic Mauro, *Le Portugal et l'Atlantique au XVIIe siècle* (Paris, 1960); Dias, *A Companhia Geral*, 504–12; Arruda, *O Brasil*; Paulo Neuhaus, *Economia brasileira: Uma visão histórica* (Rio de Janeiro, 1980), 138–39; Lugar, "Merchant Community"; Medeiros dos Santos, *Relações*, and *O Rio de Janeiro*; David Birmingham, *A Concise History of Portugal* (Cambridge, 1993).

44. Dennis Kincaid, *British Social Life in India, 1608–1937*, 2nd ed. (London, 1973), 21, citing the 1615–18 diary of Sir Thomas Roe; Edward Grey, ed., *The Travels of Pietro Della Valle in India* (New Delhi, 1991), 1:21, describing burnt wine in 1623; John Fryer, *A New Account of East-India and Persia* (London, 1698), 93, noting Muslims drinking Sherry and brandy, although not Claret and Rhenish, which the Europeans there drank; *Bolton Letters*, 2.

45. E 3/98/280v, 281r, 322, and E 3/99/81, 193–94, 194, 221, 254, 329, IOL; Henry Love, *Vestiges of Old Madras* (London, 1913), 2:35nn2–3; *Records of Fort St. George: Diary and Consultation Book of 1714* (Madras, 1929), 89–90. The first island agent was Joseph Hayward, who had previously supplied a company ship with twenty-five pipes for the settlement at St. Helena and fifteen pipes for the fort at Bencoolen. Through the 1760s, the agency remained in the hands of the twelve successors to his firm, from Hayward & Rider (1721–23) to Chambers, Hiccox & Denyer (1777–85). An-

other agency was created in the 1760s when the directors appointed Scott, Pringle & Co. (1766–77); in 1777, they replaced the Scott firm with Fergusson, Murdoch & Co. (1777–84). Minutes, January 8, 1766, B 81/315, IOL. Agent houses always possessed London partners who were present or past members of the Court of Directors: William Rider in 1738–41, 1743–46, 1748–51, 1753–54, Charles Chambers Sr. in 1755–57, 1763–66, 1768, Charles Chambers Jr., in 1770, 1773, Thomas Cheap in 1777–78, 1780–83, Samuel Smith in 1783–86, and David Scott in 1788–91, 1793–96, 1798–1801. Charles Fergusson's brother-in-law George Dempster sat on the Direction in 1769 and 1772. James G. Parker, "The Directors of the East India Company" (PhD diss., University of Edinburgh, 1977). Other agents held substantial amounts of company stock: Samuel Hayward owned £500 of stock in the 1710s, for instance, and Charles Fergusson acquired £500 of stock in the 1760s. L/AG/14/5/2/322, L/AG/14/5/3/316, L/AG/14/5/16/292, 295, IOL.

46. *Fort William–India House Correspondence*, 1:2, 465.

47. Tonnages are discussed in Jaap R. Bruijn and Femme S. Gaastra, *Ships, Sailors and Spices: East India Companies and their Shipping in the 16th, 17th and 18th Centuries* (Amsterdam, 1993), 55, 76–77, 107, 117, 130–33, 142, 179. Between 1701 and 1760, the average tonnage for 929 outward sailings of English Company ships was 428 tons; by 1786, the average had risen to 783 tons. *Fort William–India House Correspondence*, 4:163–64, *sub* December 22, 1786. While French and Swedish Company ships generally sailed past the island, Portuguese, Danish, and Ostend Company vessels often stopped there for wine. Danish ships averaged 569 tons in the 1730s and 1740s, and 948 tons in the 1790s and 1800s, and Ostend ships between 406 and 433 tons in 1715–32. English Indiamen were usually the lightest.

48. James Gordon to James & Alexander Gordon, December 15, 1765, 1765–75 Letter Book, fol. 12, Letterfourie Papers; *Fort William–India House Correspondence*, 3:543 (December 19, 1763), 4:270 (November 26, 1764), 5:287 (February 16, 1767), 525 (February 2,1769), 259 (December 7, 1769), 6:178 (January 25, 1770). Cf. E 4/863/193–95/ no. 27, 307–9/no. 3, 431–32, 443–46, 674, IOL.

49. Joseph Gillis to Henry Hill, May 6, 1783, Hill-JJS(A), vol. 9, fol. 2, HSP; *Fort William–India House Correspondence*, 6:1 (January 17, 1770), 6:158 (March 25, 1772), 7:62 (March 30, 1774), 7:293(October 17, 1774). Examples of Portuguese and Lisbon involvement in the supply of wine to English East India are found in the letters of Mayne & Co. of Lisbon, 1771–92, which mainly supplied private trade buyers: Mayne & Co. Papers, Kinross House Muniments, GD 29, NA-Sc.

The private trade was divided between privilege traders and allowance traders. The privilege traders were the captains, officers, and crew working aboard Indiamen. By custom, they were allowed to buy and carry in total twenty pipes of wine to the subcontinent freight-free, individual amounts varying with rank. The ship itself was allowed to carry an additional five pipes for the captain to dispense or sell as need arose. Allowance traders were passengers granted permission by the captain to stow, for a fee, any number of pipes the space would allow. According to company tradition, privilege space comprised roughly 5 percent of all cargo space. Newton & Gordon to Johnston & Jolly, March 27, 1764, vol. 3, fol. 288, Newton & Gordon to Francis & Tilghman,

March 12, 1773, vol. 5, fol. 182, NGL; Robert Bissett to Henry Hill, January 20, 1764, vol. 6, fol. 106, Hill-JJS(A); Thomas Lamar to Henry Hill, February 8, 1766, box 1, folder 1, Hill-SAGS. Allowance space depended on the passengers and the voyage. Thomas Williamson, *The East India Vade-Mecum* (London, 1810), 2:118, notes how wine "always sold well at the annual auction" in India.

50. George Souza has kindly shared with me the results of his analysis of the 1732–99 *decretos* usually issued in response to petitions to transship goods.

51. Barros, *Dona Guiomar*, 105–13, 129.

52. Joseph Gillis to Henry Hill, May 6, 1783, vol. 9, fol. 2, Hill-JJS(A).

53. Markets to the east of India had long been supplied with wine (Bencoolen since 1714), but erratically. Only in the 1770s and 1780s did the eastern settlements begin to be regularly supplied, when the directors ordered four hundred pipes to be laden each year on average on noncompany "chartered ships." *Fort William–India House Correspondence*, 5:192 (March 17, 1769), 8:155–56 (October 25, 1776), 9:282 (December 22, 1785); Newton & Gordon to Charles McEvers & Co., February 8, 1775, vol. 5, fol. 460, and to Samuel Bean, April 22, 1776, vol. 6, fol. 74, NGL.

54. *Fort William–India House Correspondence*, 9:282 (December 22, 1785), 10:94–95 (April 12, 1786), 10:157, 163–64 (December 22, 1786), 10:312 (November 21, 1787); Newton & Gordon to Donaldson & Stotts, June 8, 1785, vol. 9, fol. 30, NGL. Inhabitants of other cities participated as well. Thomas Bayne Brown in Lisbon, executor of a Portuguese national, invested estate funds by shipping Madeira to Bengal in the early 1790s. Thomas Graham to George Graham, September 6, 1792, GD 29/2146/3, NA-Sc.

55. Newton, Gordon & Murdoch to Robert Lenox, September 16, 1799, vol. 19, fol. 414, NGL. On the Leacock scheme, see John Leacock to Cleland, White & Co., January 31, 1798, Leacock & Sons Letter Book 1794–1801, fol. 193, John Leacock to William Leacock, January 31, April 6, May 29, October 18, December 1, 1799, January 18, May 12, July 8, 1800, March 27, 1802, Leacock Letters 1799–1802, fols. 10, 17, 35, 80, 104, 107, 142, 178, 215, 219, 310, Leacock Papers. Williamson describes the postwar competition that sprang up after the war for America. *East India Vade-Mecum*, 2:118–20. Especially revealing of the non-Madeiran private traders trying to carve out a niche in the deregulated environment are the 1786–92 letters of William Barlow, a London wine merchant who shipped Claret, Champagne, and Port to India. William was a brother of Sir George Barlow, a governor there. MSS Eur. F 175–76, BL.

56. Williamson, *East-India Vade Mecum*, 2:116; William Milburn, *Oriental Commerce* (London, 1813), 1:5–7, listing the restrictions imposed on individuals loading Madeira "on the extra ships" and thence back to England; Newton, Gordon & Murdoch, June 7, 1793, vol. 15, fol. 151, to James Sheafe, October 4, 1794, vol. 16, fol. 128, to Thomas Gordon, June 13, 1795, vol. 16, fol. 289, to Dring, Gordon & Connell, October 11, 1798, vol. 19, fols. 104–5, to Thomas Gordon, vol. 20, fol. 81, NGL; John Leacock Jr. to William Leacock, October 18, 1799, December 8, 1800, fols. 80, 215, Leacock Letters 1799–1802, Leacock Papers.

57. The 1640 port book, E 351/910, NA-UK, is analyzed by A. M. Millard, comp., *Analyses of Port Books, Recording Merchandises Imported into the Port of London . . .*

for Certain Years between 1588 and 1640 (n.p., 1950–59), 6. Cf. Thomas Heywood, *Philocothonista; or, The Drunkard, Opened, Dissected, and Anatomized* (London, 1635), 5. For 1675–96 data, see Francis, *Wine Trade,* 317; John Houghton, *A Collection of Letters for the Improvement of Husbandry and Trade* (London, 1681–83), 1:178. Cf. George F. Steckley, "Trade at the Canary Islands in the Seventeenth Century" (PhD diss., University of Chicago, 1972), table 30, p. 236, who recalculates French, Portuguese, Spanish, Canary, Italian, and Rhenish imports and gives higher, more accurate numbers. His statistics are used here.

Advertisements suggest the relative insignificance of Madeira in seventeenth century. The first example of an ad hawking Madeira in London was placed by the merchant Peter Barachin, who sold Madeira for 6s., Rhenish for 5s. 6d., and Tenerife for 4s. in 1694. *London Gazette,* June 11, 1694. Advertisers then felt the need to state Madeira was "as good as" Canary wine, at a time when heated debates were raging over the merits of Port and Claret.

58. It is possible that mainland figures include those of imports from the Western Islands (the Azores). But there is no mention of the inclusion and one would think such an important source of Atlantic wine would merit its own separate entry.

59. Shakespeare, I *Henry IV,* I.ii.128, noting "a Cup of Madera" in 1596; John Harrington, "The Salerne School," in *The Englishman's Doctor* (London, 1607), 8; *Scottish Book of Rates* (1612), republished in C. Innes, ed., *The Ledger of Andrew Halyburton, 1492–1503* (Edinburgh, 1867).

60. Carl A. Hanson, *Economy and Society in Baroque Portugal, 1668–1703* (Minneapolis, 1981), 198; Alvará, October 17, 1768, Andrade e Silva, *Collecção de legislação portuguegueza,* 2:368–70; Account, 1784–86, MS 219, no. 29, BNL. For Lisbon's surviving port records for 1762–1815, see Livros 1978–2023, 2028, 2115, 2159, 2171, 2174, 2179, 2183, 2188, 2192, AN-TdT.

61. Administração-Geral do Porto de Lisboa, *O Porto de Lisboa,* 58, 62 (it is not clear whether this compilation includes wine); Macedo, *Problemas,* 187–200; Fernando A. Novais, *Portugal e Brazil* (São Paulo, 1983), 248–49.

62. Croft, *Treatise;* Mayson, *Portugal's Wines and Wine-Makers;* Schneider, *O marquès de Pombal,* 262. Data on the price of wine in Portugal in 1640–1815 is woefully incomplete. Hanson provides some seventeenth-century data. *Economy and Society,* 96. More study is needed. In Lisbon, local wines were cheaper, and not surprisingly preferred, while Douro wines were more expensive. The yearly average of eighty pipes is for 1779–1807 shipments to Lisbon; none were sent to Oporto.

63. The period 1763–75 did see a 125 percent rise in the number of ships bound for Europe over those leaving for Europe in 1727–39, but this still amounted only to ten departures per year.

64. The Madeira that went to France was usually Malvasia, which the French wanted for their Caribbean and India settlements. "Plan to Establish a Commerce between France and Madeira," January 22, 1765, B/I/684/224–24v, and Report, January 9, 1768, B/I/685/69r–71r, as well as B/I/765, vol. 3, Affaires etrangères, AN-Fr; Albert Silbert, "Un carrefour de l'Atlantique: Madere," *Economia e financas: Anais* 22 (1954): 435–36. France's consul in Madeira felt his presence was needed primarily to solve French

shippers' general trade problems quickly, not to facilitate wine business. Nicolas De la Tuelliere, "*Eclairissements* on the Island of Madeira in 1777," March 29, 1777, Affaires etrangères B/III/385, Correspondence consulaire— Madère, AN-Fr. On Madeira's "very little correspondence" with Spain, see: Spence, Leacock & Spence to David Loudon, August 14, 1764, Spence, Leacock & Spence Letter Book 1762–65, fol. 158, Leacock Papers.

65. On Dutch wine imports and reexports, see Onslow Burrish, *Batavia Illustrata; or, A View of the Policy, and Commerce, of the United Provinces* (London, 1728), 2:347– 48, 363–64, 378; Paul Wentworth to Newton, Gordon & Johnson, January 1, 1790, box 1790/91, bundle 6, CGP-Guildhall; Henriette De Bruyn Kops, "Liquid Silver: The Wine and Brandy Trade between Nantes and Rotterdam in the First Half of the Seventeenth Century" (PhD diss., Georgetown University, 2005).

66. On the possibilities of a rising market in the Baltic states and Russia, see William Murdoch to Francis Newton, June 7, 1793, vol. 15, fol. 151, to Thomas Gordon, May 6, 1799, vol. 19, fol. 285, to Thompson & Bonar, April 28, 1806, vol. 27, fol. 348, to Messrs. Tuite, April 27, 1807, vol. 29, fol. 24, NGL.

67. Nina Ellinger Bang and Knud Korst, eds., *Tabeller over Skibsfart og Varetransport gennem Øresund, 1661–1783* (Copenhagen, 1939), vol. 2, pt. 2a, pp. 3–5, pt. 2b, pp. 244–52. Published tables cease in 1783, although the toll was recorded well into the nineteenth century. My calculations assume that an *aum* (*ohm*) equaled thirty-nine gallons, and a *fade* (cask or vat) two pipes. Included under the rubric "vin" were rum, genever, arrack, brandy-wine or burnt-wine, wine vinegar, and citron. The Madeirans obtained fish more commonly from the North Sea—not the Baltic—ports of Sweden.

68. Barbara L. Solow, "Introduction" *Slavery and the Rise of the Atlantic System*, ed. Barbara L. Solow (Cambridge, 1991), 20.

CHAPTER 5. A "COMMERCE OF MINDS"

1. The term *merchant* here embraces all five functions. For the five-part breakdown, see Oliveira e Silva, *Fidalgos-Mercadores*, 81–94.

2. A list of 929 distributors for 1700–1815 is compiled from several sources. In the Livros dos entradas e saídas, one finds the names of the *consignatarios*, the men or women to whom dry goods, fish, flour, rice, and the like were consigned for either sale on the island or reexport to Lisbon, Portuguese Africa, Brazil, and Asia, and who also managed the export of wine. These references are not complete: the *entradas* cover only the years 1727–1807, and the *saídas*, although they are complete for 1721–23 and 1727–33, are incomplete for 1733–68. The problem of missing export records is surmountable, however. Since every wine exporter was involved in importing other goods, the problem is minor—all exporters are included—although some nonexport-ers may also be included, for not all (though very few) importers were exporters. More serious are other shortcomings: first, before 1727, *entradas* do not exist and *saídas* exist only for 1721–23; and, second, these records usually list only heads of mercantile firms or prominent members. Junior partners or sleeping senior partners in large firms are

usually not mentioned. The latter is less serious a problem for Portuguese firms, which were always small. Thus, the corps gleaned from the Funchal customs records needs to be augmented. This can be done with miscellaneous information entered into mercantile and governmental records from 1703 onward. Yet, even so augmented, the final tally of 929 is only a lower estimate. The women included three widows of distributors, plus Dona Guiomar Madalena de Sá Vilhena, one of the island's largest landowners and a contractor supplying India-bound ships with wine. In Portugal, women in the period could run their own business, although they were subject to the authority of their parents or husbands; it was more common, as a result, for widows to assist their husband's business or continue his work upon his demise. Barros, *Dona Guiomar*.

3. The Americans in 1768 included Marylanders James Jenkins, Thomas Patten, and Joseph Gillis, all of Lamar, Hill, Bisset & Co.; New Yorkers John Searle and James Ayres; and another Marylander, Henry Cock. The representation of Quakers and Huguenots was high, out of proportion to the general population.

4. Duncan *Atlantic Islands*, 56–57. It is unclear from Duncan whether "the total amount of export taxes paid" in 1620 is a sum for all exporters or only the top eighteen exporters; the former is assumed here. Unlike later years, the bulk of whose duties were levied on wine, the duties in 1620 were levied on both sugar and wine, making a calculation of wine pipes impossible.

5. Livros dos direitos por saída, nos. 307–8 (1807), Provedoria e Junta da Real Fazenda do Funchal, Alfândega do Funchal, AN-TdT.

6. Staunton, *Authentic Account*, 71; Pita, *Account*, 119.

7. Of those who merged, Henry, Robert, and Valentine Cock and George and Thomas Patten, all from Maryland, and James Jenkins from Philadelphia joined British firms and gave up national trading affiliations. George Day Welsh, a Pennsylvanian whose sea captain father had once plied the waters between the West Indies, Madeira, and the middle colonies, did the same. The three-generation house of Lamar, Hill, Bisset & Co. exemplified those firms that unraveled. It collapsed after the founders and their children died off and members of the third generation opted to diversify their activities and remain at home in Philadelphia. Typical of the imprudent were the concerns managed by John Searle III and John Colpoys, who escaped creditors in 1798 by fleeing to the Cape of Good Hope and Ireland respectively, and by Searle's cousin the American consul John Marsden Pintard, whose financial and commercial speculations forced him to flee back to Philadelphia and New York in 1799. Americans who remained in Madeira included John Leander Cathcart, Richard Foster, Marien Lamar, Lewis Searle Pintard, William Shaw, William Steinson, and George Day Welsh. Others, like John Howard March, arrived after 1807.

8. Livros dos direitos por saída, nos. 275 (1727), 293 (1768), 307–8 (1807), Provedoria e Junta da Real Fazenda do Funchal, Alfândega do Funchal, AN-TdT.

9. Michael Nowlan to Gedley Clare Burges, June 29, 1759, Nowlan & Burges Letter Book, 1756–59, fol. 3, Leacock Papers.

10. William Phelps is first listed as an island exporter in 1778. Some five years later, he took as partner James Morrissey, who had come out from Ireland in 1777. Phelps set up as a sole proprietor in 1786. Livros dos entradas, no. 155, *sub* September 12, 1778,

AN-TdT; Original Genealogy, in author's possession; Sir Bernard Burke, *A Genealogical and Heraldic History of the Landed Gentry of Great Britain*, 10th ed. (London, 1900), 1263–64; John Blunt, *Dursley and Its Neighborhood* (London, 1877), 91–92.

11. Walter and Robert Scot first appeared in Funchal's Customs House records in 1728 and 1729, respectively. Livros dos saídas, no. 252, fols. 53 (December 15, 1728), 69 (August 25, 1729), AN-TdT. After spending several years on his own, brother John took over the management of the house in 1736 or 1737 when Robert moved to London. CO 137/17 *sub* May 29, 1737, NA-UK; Kenneth G. Davies, ed., *Calendar of State Papers* (Colonial), vol. 43 (London, 1963), *sub* October 13, 1737; Edgar, *Letter Book of Robert Pringle*, 1:29n8, 158; Will of Robert Scot, dated April 11, 1769, proved June 1, 1771, PROB 11, NA-UK; Arthur H. Plaisted, *The Manor and Parish Records of Medmenham, Buckinghamshire* (London, 1925), 139–40.

12. Barrett's relatives are discussed in SP 89/49/1, 4, 7, 164, *Pope v. Barrett*, January 21, 1748/49, Chancery Proceedings, 1714–58 (Zincke, 1630), and *Pope v. Young*, 1768, Chancery Proceedings 1758–1800 (no. 2071), NA-UK. The Duffs' activities are documented throughout the Letterfourie Papers. John Leacock's schooling is detailed in the 1736 Admissions Register, fol. 241, Christ's Hospital Records, MS 12,818/8, Guildhall Library, London; his apprenticeship articles (March 9, 1741) are found in Book of Assorted Letters, Leacock Papers. Leacock's brother William was admitted to Christ's at the age of ten in 1740 and apprenticed to Antigua merchant Jacob Thibou in 1747. Peter Coldham, ed., *Child Apprentices in America from Christ's Hospital, London, 1617–1778* (Baltimore, 1990), 98.

13. On Vallette (1696–1752), see *Collections of the New York Historical Society for 1893* (New York, 1894), 261. His father and brother became planters in Jamaica. He eventually settled in New York, where he became involved in transporting servants from London, and in 1723 married Maria Jay. Isaac N.P. Stokes, ed., *The Iconography of Manhattan Island* (New York, 1922), 4:601. On Sarsfield, see Luis Peter Clode, "Algumas familias inglesas que passaram a esta ilha," *AHM* 7 (1949): 68–79; Patrick Sarsfield to Dominick Sarsfield, May 28, 1716, acc. no. 2,930, NLI; David Dickson, "An Economic History of the Cork Region in the Eighteenth Century" (PhD diss., University of Dublin, 1977), 515–16. On the Gordons, see Alistair and Henrietta Tayler, *Jacobites of the 1715* (Aberdeen, 1934), 108–9; [An Englishman,] *A Genuine and True Journal of the Escape of the Young Chevalier* (London, 1749).

14. What little is known of the Newtons before 1748 is documented in vol. 1 of the NGL. On Spencer, who was an executor of Anthony Pintard's estate in New York in 1740 and appears to have converted to Catholicism in Madeira, see *Zenger's New-York Weekly Journal*, January 7, 1740; *New-York Gazette, and Weekly Post-Boy*, October 1, 1750; Deposition of George Harrison, September 28, 1760, CO 5/20/82, Circular, May 20, 1760, and Letter, July 4, 1758, of George Spencer, WO 34/30/277–80, NA-UK.

15. For references to Catholicism, see Spencer material in n. 13.

16. Old Swinford Marriage Register, February 16, 1712, Worcestershire Record Office, Worcester, England; Broseley Birth Register, October 28, 1716, Shropshire County Record Office, Shrewsbury, England; Petition of Susanna Barrett, 1748, SP 89/49/4, NA-UK; *Beckford v. Perry* (1751), C 11/1667/15/1–2, NA-UK; Bachelors Hall Members

List, 1763, Scrapbook, CGP-PC; Thomas Gordon to Francis Newton, March 11, 1775, vol. 5, fol. 480, NGL. Notable bachelors after 1750 included William Casey, Andrew Donaldson, Joseph Gillis, and David Henry Smith.

17. John F. Padgett, "Organizational Genesis, Identity and Control: The Transformation of Banking in Renaissance Florence" (2000, unpublished MS), 12.

18. On Leacock, see Book of Assorted Letters, 1749–1808, John Leacock to Mary Knight, August 3, 1757, to Elias Locke, August 3, 1757, and Genealogy, Leacock Papers. His daughter married the Madeira trader Thomas Murdoch IV. Earlier, William Bolton Sr. married the daughter of Philip Barrett, and William Casey wed the niece of Henry Shapcote. On the Scots, see below. On Hill, see Hill Genealogy, vol. 13, fol. 26, Hill-JJS(A). On Phelps, see Phelps Family Tree, in author's possession; Ron Phelps to David Hancock, March 15, 1996. See also the marriage of Thomas Loughnan: St. Clement Danes Marriage Register, April 5, 1770, and St. Mary (Old Marylebone Rd.) Birth Register, May 28, 1781, Westminster City Archives, London; Will of Thomas Loughnan, June 20, 1789, PROB 11/1180, NA-UK. John Searle IV (1783–1837) married a daughter of the Irish Madeira trader David Taylor, Catherine Mary, in 1811. John Masterton married Anna Murdoch, the daughter of James Murdoch, and formed Murdoch, Masterton & Co. in 1800.

19. The British and Portuguese merchants and firms kept formal social relations to a minimum, as chapter 1 noted. Marriage to Portuguese women was the stuff of tradition, for the scion of the first English family resident there, John Drummond, married a Portuguese woman. His descendants, along with those of other intermarriages, were regarded as being as much Portuguese as English or Scottish by 1640 and easily moved between the competing national groups. William Drummond, *Genealogy of the House of Drummond* (Edinburgh, 1831), 94; Luiz Peter Clode, *Registo genealogico familias que passaram à Madeira* (Funchal, 1952), 110–11; Duncan, *Atlantic Islands*, 55. Given the ease of their assimilation, the numbers of intermarriages was significantly augmented only in the late eighteenth century when several key British merchants wed daughters of Portuguese merchants or landowners: Robert Cock, Joseph Gillis, James David Webster Gordon, James Jenkins, James Moore, and George Day Welsh. Such alliances often raised the opprobrium of the island's British establishment, especially when the liaison brought no land or title. Cropley Rose to John Saunders, July 22, 1780, Cropley Rose Letter Book, HSP; Journal of Robert Duff, April 9, July 5, 1788, Letterfourie Papers; Newton, Gordon & Johnston to Evans, Offley & Sealy, April 9, 1788, vol. 10, fol. 233, NGL. Still, intermarriages were rare, as the marriage registers for the parishes of the Sé, São Pedro, and Santa Luzeia demonstrate. The Sé's marriage registers for 1749–91 reveal that two other British merchants were probably Catholic and married Portuguese women: Thomas Magrath and William Reynolds. The Dutchman André Smits also married a Portuguese woman. In the same period, only two foreign women are known to have married a Portuguese man. *Indice dos registos de casamentos do Concelho do Funchal — Freguesia da Sé (1539–1911)* (Funchal, 2002); Genealogy, Welsh Papers, private collection, Funchal.

20. Henry Hill to Newton & Gordon, November 4, 1773, bundle 5 ("1771–1776"), box 1, CGP-Guildhall.

21. A superb example of family connections governing the firm is Searle & Co. John Searle II of New York took over John I's work as a sea captain in the North Atlantic trade until he settled in Madeira in 1748. At various times his brother James Searle and their cousins and nephews Edward Clark, John Marsden Pintard, and Lewis Searle Pintard worked in the house. The firm collapsed in 1794. Alfred V. Wittmeyer, *Registers of the Births, Marriages, and Deaths, of the "Eglise Francoise a la Nouvelle York," from 1688 to 1804* (New York, 1886), 183–254; Edward Clark to James Jarvis, March 4, 1780, James Jarvis Papers, Connecticut State Library, Hartford; *Collections of the New York-Historical Society for the Year 1893* (1894), 135–36, 230, 298, 367, 374–75, . . . *for the Year 1894* (1895), 112–13, and . . . *for the Year 1895* (1896), 73, 146, 179; Stannard Warne, comp., *A Collection of Historical Memorials relating to the Searle Families of Great Britain and America* (London, 1897); John E. Stillwell, *Historical and Genealogical Miscellany* 3 (1914), 55–57; *New York Genealogical and Biographical Register* 69 (1938): 157, 203. On James Searle (d. 1797), who became a delegate to the Continental Congress, see Henry Simpson, *The Lives of Eminent Philadelphians* (Philadelphia, 1859), 872–75; U.S. Congress, *Biographical Directory of the American Congress, 1774–1927* (Washington, DC, 1928), 1505. On the Pintards, see *Documents relating to the Colonial History of the State of New Jersey*, vol. 23 (Paterson, 1901), 410, vol. 30 (Somerville, 1918), 330, 338, 380, 390; Letters concerning John Marsden Pintard, 1796–98, 6:168, 10:101, 12:463, 23:92, Timothy Pickering Papers, MHS; *Letters from John Pintard to His Daughter Eliza Noel Pintard Davidson, 1816–1833* (New York, 1940), 1:ix–xxii; Walter Barrett, *The Old Merchants of New York City* (New York, 1863), 216–29; Edwin Salter, "Huguenot Settlers and Land Owners in Monmouth County, New Jersey," *New York Genealogical and Biographical Record* 20 (1889): 30–31; Charles W. Baird, *History of the Huguenot Emigration to America* (Baltimore, 1966), 232–34, 294–97.

22. Equally revealing is the makeup of the firm founded by James Gordon of Letterfourie and managed by him, his brother Alexander Gordon, and their nephews James, Robert, and William Duff of Pitchaish. Alistair and Henrietta Tayler, *The Book of the Duffs* (Edinburgh, 1914), 2:466–88, *Jacobites of the 1715* (Aberdeen, 1934), 108–9, and *Jacobites of Aberdeenshire and Banffshire in the Forty-Five* (Aberdeen, 1928), 144, 203–4; John Burke, *Landed Gentry*, 18th ed. (London, 1972), 384–85. According to one contemporary account, Prince Charles Edward gave Alexander Gordon a ring after the battle of Culloden in remembrance of his meritorious service. [Englishman], *Genuine and True Journal.*

23. On the Loughnans, Fergussons, Dempsters, and Fearnses, see George Spence to Francis Newton, October 26, 1753, vol. 1, fol. 77, NGL; Michael Nowlan to Gedley Clare Burges, June 24, 1756, Nowlan & Burges Letter Book, 1756–69, Leacock Papers; John Burke, *Genealogical and Heraldic History of the Landed Gentry* (London, 1847), 406–7; Sir Bernard Burke, *A Genealogical and Heraldic Dictionary of the Peerage and Baronetage* (London, 1959), 846–48; James Fergusson, ed., *Letters of George Dempster to Sir Adam Fergusson, 1756–1813* (London, 1934); Last Will of James Fearns, written March 13, 1797, proved June 13, 1797, PROB 11/292, NA-UK.

24. Francis Newton may have briefly served as a clerk in Reid & Stewart of London before

he joined Johnston's firm. Francis Newton to Andrew Henderson, October 15, 1748, to David Ross, November 12, 1748, to Andrew Newton, November 12, 1748, to Alexander Grant, December 6, 1748, and to George Spence, December 6, 1748, vol. 1, fols. 2, 4, 5, 10, to Thomas Newton, June 30, 1753, to George Spence, 1754, vol. 1, fols. 55, 99, to George Spence, January 15, 1756, to Alexander Johnston, February 7, 1758, vol. 1, fols. 189, 281, to Alexander Johnston, February 7, to John Provoost, May 13, 1758, end of vol. 1, NGL. On Johnston, who later joined in a slave-trading venture with another Madeira trader, Robert Scot, see Hancock, *Citizens*, 52–56. On Thomas Newton's subsequent activities, see Thomas Newton Letter Book, CGP-MWC.

25. Granovetter, "The Strength of Weak Ties," and "The Strength of Weak Ties: A Network Theory Revisited."

26. Beneficial to the firm was Cheap's work as director of the East India Company in 1777–78 and 1780–83. During the 1760s and 1770s, Robert Scot Sr. and John Scot Sr. died, and the partnership was reorganized with the addition of sons Robert Scot Jr. and Joseph Pringle and cousin David Scot. But toward the end of the century, on the death of John Pringle in 1791, the firm admitted Henry Veitch and Henry's brother Robert. Again, the firm looked beyond blood: the Veitches were the sons of one of Joseph Pringle's closest friends and neighbors in Berwickshire but had no familial tie to the three families. Much of the advantage the firm enjoyed in 1763–1836 can be traced not only to its control of the consulship for all but one of seventy-four years—Murray succeeded Cheap, Joseph Pringle succeeded Murray, and after a brief hiatus Veitch became consul—but also its blend of strong and weak ties among partners. On the extremely complicated connections among them, see Will of Robert Scot, dated April 11, 1769, proved June 1, 1771, PROB 11, NA-UK; Plaisted, *Manor and Parish Records of Medmenham*, 139–43; Burke, *Landed Gentry*, vol. 3 (1853), 267; Alexander Pringle, *The Records of the Pringles or Hoppringills of the Scottish Border* (Edinburgh, 1933), 171–79; T. Craig Brown, *The History of Selkirkshire* (Edinburgh, 1886), 2:299–313, 335–48; Burke, *Landed Gentry*, vol. 2 (London, 1846), 903; James W. Buchan and Henry Paton, eds., *A History of Peebleshire* (Glasgow, 1927), 3:438–43; William Wilson, *Folklores and Genealogies of Uppermost Nithesdale* (n.p., n.d.), 206–13; *Genealogical Fragments* (Berwick, 1855), 13–15; *The Court and City Register* (London, 1765), 109; Thomas Cheap to Secretary of State, June 3, 1771, SP 89/71/130, NA-UK; *Gentleman's Magazine* 64, supplement (1794), 1206; Will of Thomas Cheap, proved 15 April 1795, PROB 11/1259, NA-UK; Academia das ciênciàs de Lisboa, *Descriptive List of the State Papers, Portugal, 1661–1780, in the Public Record Office London* (Lisbon, 1983), 3:15, 25–26, 56, 71, 83–84, 87–88; Parker, "Directors of the East India Company," 197–99.

27. Joel M. Podolny and Karen L. Page, "Network Forms of Organization" *Annual Review of Sociology* 24 (1998): 59; Silvia Marzagalli, "The Establishment of a Transatlantic Trade Network: Bordeaux and the United States, 1783–1815" (unpublished MS, Harvard Atlantic Seminar, 2003), 2–3; David Hancock, "The Trouble with Networks," *Business History Review* 79 (2005): 467–91. The meaning of "network" is imprecise, having been applied to a multiplicity of operations and situations at various times. Robert G. Eccles and Nitin Nohria, *Beyond the Hype: Rediscovering the Essence of*

Management (Boston, 1992), 25–26. On the lack of a distinct overarching theory, see Amalya L. Oliver, "Networking Network Studies," *Organization Studies* 19 (1998): 1–31; Walter W. Powell and Laurel Smith-Doerr, "Networks and Economic Life," in *The Handbook of Economic Sociology*, ed. Neil J. Smelser and Richard Swedberg (Princeton, 1994), 368–402.

A "theory" of general networks is nonetheless emerging from a host of small-scale studies in a wide variety of disciplines: Duncan J. Watts, *Small Worlds: The Dynamics of Networks between Order and Randomness* (Princeton, 1999); John F. Padgett, "Multiple Networks and Multiple Discourses" (unpublished MS, Santa Fe Institute Program, 1998); Eric R. Wolf, "Kinship, Friendship, and Patron-Client Relations in Complex Societies," in *The Social Anthropology of Complex Societies*, ed. Michael Banton (London, 1966), 1–22.

28. The published scholarship that deploys network analysis is voluminous. Jacob R. Marcus, *Early American Jewry* (Philadelphia, 1951); Bernard Farber, *Guardians of Virtue* (New York, 1972); Jerome H. Wood Jr., *Conestoga Crossroads: Lancaster, Pennsylvania, 1730–1790* (Harrisburg, 1979), 93–112; Lorena S. Walsh, "Community Networks in the Early Chesapeake," in *Colonial Chesapeake Society*, ed. Lois G. Carr et al. (Chapel Hill, 1988), 200–41; Darrett Rutman and Anita Rutman, *A Place in Time: Middlesex County, Virginia, 1650–1750* (New York, 1984); Eli Faber, *A Time for Planting: The First Migration, 1654–1820* (Baltimore, 1992); Peter Bearman, *Relations into Rhetoric: Local Elite Social Structure in Norfolk, England, 1540–1640* (New Brunswick, 1993); John Padgett and Christopher Ansell, "Robust Action and the Rise of the Medici," *American Journal of Sociology* 98 (1993): 1259–1319; Rosalind Beiler, "Distributing Aid to Believers in Need: The Religious Foundations of Transatlantic Migration," *Pennsylvania History* 64, supplement (1997): 73–87; Leos Müller, *The Merchant Houses of Stockholm, c. 1640–1800: A Comparative Study of Early-Modern Entrepreneurial Behavior* (Uppsala, 1998); R. Darrell Meadows, "Engineering Exile: Social Networks and the French Atlantic Community, 1789–1809," *French Historical Studies* 23 (2000): 67–102.

Network analysis is especially good for the study of modern business: Yoram Ben-Porath, "The F-Connection: Families, Friends, and Firms and the Organization of Exchange," *Population and Development Review* 6 (1980): 1–30; Eccles and Nohria, *Beyond the Hype*, and *Networks and Organizations* (Boston, 1992); Thomas J. Peters, *Liberation Management* (New York, 1992); Gary Gereffi and Miguel Korzeniewicz, eds., *Commodity Chains and Global Capitalism* (Westport, 1994); Odd Jarl Borch and Michael B. Arthur, "Strategic Networks among Small Firms: Implications for Strategy Research Methodology," *Journal of Management Studies* 32 (1995): 419–40; Anna Grandori and Giuseppe Soda, "Inter-firm Networks: Antecedents, Mechanisms and Forms," *Organization Studies* 16 (1995): 183–214; Maxine Robertson et al., "The Role of Networks in the Diffusion of Technological Innovation," *Journal of Management Studies* 33 (1996): 333–59; Gisèle Umbhauer, "The Economics of Networks," and Ehud Zuscovitch, "Networks, Specialization and Trust," in *The Economics of Networks: Interaction and Behaviors*, ed. Patrick Cohendet (Berlin, 1998), 1–13, 244–45. Business and trade histories that incorporate such theory, apart from those already mentioned, include Mary B. Rose, *Firms, Networks and Business Values: The British and American Cotton Industries since 1750* (Cambridge, 2000); Silvia Marzagalli, *Les boulevards de la fraude: Le négoce maritime et le blocus continental, 1806–1813* (Villeneuve d'Ascq, 1999); Nuala Zahedieh, "Credit, Risk and Reputation in Late Seventeenth-Century Colonial Trade," *Research in Maritime History* 15 (1998): 53–74.

29. Vieira, *Público*, vol. 1; *Bolton Letters*, vols. 1–2; Oliveira e Silva, *Fidalgos-Mercadores*, 266–69, 235, 295.

30. Francis Newton to Johnston, Hunter, Ellworthy, and Lauder, November 1748–June 1749, vol. 1, fols. 3, 5, 17–19, 26, new 1a, new 2, NGL.

31. John Corrie to Thomas Gordon, January 7, 1771, box 5, bundle 1770–71, Cossart & Gordon Papers, and Christ's Hospital Admissions Registers, c. 1735–42, MS 12,818/8, fols. 229–55, MSS Section, Guildhall Library, London; Ursula Carlyle, Mercers Company, to David Hancock, August 22, 2001. Christ's alumni later tapped by Leacock included William Antrobus of Antigua, Richard Allnutt of London, and John Jackson of Antigua. Coldham, *Child Apprentices*, 91, 98, 100.

32. Thomas Newton to Anthony Sarly, January 22, 1756, to Malcolm Campbell, January 22, 1756, to Dr. Robert Knox, March 23, 1756, to Evan Cameron, June 3, 1756, to Malcolm Campbell, September 27, 1756, to Francis Newton, February 12, 1759, Thomas Newton Letter Book, fols. 1, 3, 7, 15, 19, 50, and Samuel & David Bean to Newton & Gordon, April 15, 1760, Loose Letters, CGP-MWC; Thomas Gordon to Francis Newton, April 8, May 15, 1769, vol. 4, fols. 326, 341, Newton & Gordon to Fisher & Berney, April 20, 1789, vol. 11, fol. 41, NGL. Similarly, William Alder had met the merchant A. Clow in Liverpool and, on setting up business in Madeira in 1790, tendered his "best services" based on the establishment of that acquaintance. William Alder to A. Clow & Co., April 26, 1790, Correspondence folder 1785–98, box 60D, Claude W. Unger Collection, HSP.

33. Henry Hill to Richard Hill Sr., December 11, 1742, Hill Family Papers, folder 2, Hill-Haverford. Hill's wife, Ann Meredith, was disowned by the faith for her attendance at plays and her appearance in "dress and address." They were married in an Anglican church.

34. Thomas Newton to Francis Newton, February 12, 1759, Thomas Newton Letter Book, CGP-MWC; Newton & Gordon to Francis Newton, April 8, 1769, vol. 4, fol. 326, NGL.

35. Thomas Newton to Francis Newton, November 26, 1759, Thomas Newton Letter Book, fol. 68r, CGP-MWC; Newton & Gordon to Francis Newton, May 15, 1769, vol. 4, fol. 341, to Nicholas Hoffman & Son, March 20, 1789, vol. 12, fol. 7, to Alexander Johnston, February 25, 1783, vol. 8, fol. 7, NGL; Leacock & Spence to Bethune & Prince, September 15, fol. 11, Leacock & Spence Letter Book, 1765–68, Leacock Papers; Marien Lamar to Henry Hill, July 27, 1771, folder 5, Hill-SAGS; Robert Arbuthnot to Mrs. Arbuthnot, May 11, 1801, fol. 29, NLS; John Howard March to Thomas March, February 5, 8, 1816, fol. 61, March Letter Book, University of New Mexico Library, Albuquerque.

36. Peter Mathias, "Risk, Credit and Kinship in Early Modern Enterprise," in *The Early*

Modern Atlantic Economy, ed. John McCusker and Kenneth Morgan (Cambridge, 2000), 15–35; Anne Wegener Sleeswijk, "Social Ties and Commercial Transactions of an Eighteenth-Century French Merchant," in *Entrepreneurs and Entrepreneurship in Early Modern Times*, ed. C. Lesger and L. Noordegraaf (The Hague, 1995), 205–6.

37. Ben-Porath, "F-Connection," 3–4.

38. Wolf, "Kinship," 7; Ben-Porath, "F-Connection," 12. "Social capital" is "a store of value" generated when individuals foster relationships among themselves, which in time may redound to the benefit of those involved. The relationships "create trust by fostering shared norms, improve contract enforcement by easing information flows, and enhance sanctions against deviant behavior by facilitating collective action." Sheilagh Ogilvie, "How Does Social Capital Affect Women?" *AHR* 109 (2004): 327. On the idea, also see James S. Coleman, "Social Capital in the Creation of Human Capital," *American Journal of Sociology* 94 (1989): S95–S120; Robert D. Putnam, *Making Democracy Work: Civic Traditions in Modern Italy* (Princeton, 1993); Nan Lin, *Social Capital: A Theory of Social Structure and Action* (New York, 2001).

39. Gillian Cookson, "Family Firms and Business Networks: Textile Engineering in Yorkshire, 1780–1830," *Business History* 39 (1997): 1–20; Granovetter, "The Strength of Weak Ties," 1360–1380, and "The Strength of Weak Ties: A Network Theory Revisited," 105–30.

40. Thomas Lamar to Henry Hill, February 8, 1766, folder 3, box 1, Hill-SAGS.

41. Newton & Gordon to Charles McEvers & Co., 8 February 1775, vol. 5, fol. 460, to Samuel Bean, April 22, 1776, vol. 6, fol. 74, NGL. The British merchants were fascinated by the dispute and read whatever pamphlets they could procure. Chief among those discussed by them was John Dickinson's *Letters from an American Farmer in Pennsylvania* (Philadelphia, 1768).

42. Thomas Lamar to Henry Hill, February 8, 1766, box 1, folder 3, Hill-SAGS. The American John Howard March similarly focused on his country. Of the correspondents he supplied in his first year in exporting, 1815–16, all but 13 percent resided in the United States. March Letter Book, vol. 1.

43. James Johnson to George Spence, March 24, 1759, Letter Book of Assorted Letters, Leacock Papers; Robert Bisset to Henry Hill, February 26, 1787, vol. 10, fol. 2, Hill-JJS(A).

44. Peter Burke provides the best modern historical explication of early modern "conversation" in *The Art of Conversation* (Cambridge, 1993), 91, although he narrows his focus to speech acts, which he believes were also ruled by "the spontaneity and informality of the exchanges" and "their 'non-business-likeness.'" One scholar who has paid attention to the connections between speech acts and literate discourse, as here, is Robin Lakoff, *Talking Power: The Politics of Language in Our Lives* (New York, 1990), 40–53. Earlier studies explored the characteristics of conversational behavior in modern society and, although their work is not historically grounded, some of their insights are relevant and incorporated in the pages that follow: H. Paul Grice, "Logic and Conversation," in *Syntax and Semantics 3: Speech Acts*, ed. P. Cole and J. Morgan (New York, 1975), 41–58; Susan K. Donaldson, "One Kind of Speech Act: How Do We Know When We're Conversing?" *Semiotica* 28 (1979): 259–99; Stephen Levin-

son, *Pragmatics* (Cambridge, 1983); John Wilson, *On the Boundaries of Conversation* (Oxford, 1989).

45. Hancock, "Commerce and Conversation," 203–4n9. The role of conversation in modern business has been examined by Jeffrey D. Ford and Laurie W. Ford, "The Role of Conversations in Producing Intentional Change in Organizations," *Academy of Management Review* 20 (1995): 541–70; John J. Quinn, "The Role of 'Good Conversation' in Strategic Control," *Journal of Management Studies* 13 (1996): 381–94; Mark Casson and Nigel Wadeson, "Communication Costs and the Boundaries of the Firm," *International Journal of the Economics of Business* 5 (1998): 5–27; Nigel Wadeson, "Two-Way Communication Costs and the Boundaries of the Firm," *International Journal of the Economics of Business* 6 (1999): 301–29.

46. Newton & Gordon to Francis Newton, August 1, 1778, vol. 6, fol. 422, to Inglis & Hall, March 23, 1769, vol. 4, fol. 320, to Francis Newton, April 14, 1768, April 10, 1770, vol. 4, fols. 201, 478, to Alexander Johnston, October 2, 1783, vol. 7, fol. 122, to Thomas Gordon, March 3, 1784, vol. 8, fol. 193, to Francis Newton, December 6, 1799, vol. 20, fol. 108, to Robert Lenox, December 12, 1803, vol. 25, fol. 239, to Joseph S. Lewis & Co., May 29, 1807, vol. 29, fol. 71, NGL; Lamar, Hill, Bisset & Co. to Henry Hill, August 14, 1788, vol. 19, fol. 42, Hill-JJS(A).

47. Newton & Gordon to Alexander Johnston, July 25, 1772, vol. 5, fol. 93, to Thomas Gordon, July 3, 1793, vol. 15, fol. 185, March 27, 1795, vol. 16, fol. 250, NGL.

48. Gedley Clare Burges to James Archbold, June 22, 1746, Nowlan & Burges Letters, 1755–74, fol. 14, Leacock Papers; Newton & Gordon to John Parminter, July 27, 1761, vol. 1, fol. 322, to Robert Lenox, September 17, 1799, vol. 20, fol. 1, NGL.

49. The relationship with John Rowe of Boston is revealing of networks providing information on markets, bankruptcies, laws, etc. Rowe provided Newton & Gordon with information about prices, markets for cargoes, and shipping regulations and vice versa. "Our Market is poorly supplied with provisions," Rowe wrote in 1762, and accordingly for their "government," he annexed prices current. In turn, he would be glad "to be advised the prices of our wines with you & you may depend on our embracing the first convenient opportunity of consigning you a few pipes." When he failed to repay Newton & Gordon in a timely fashion for wines consigned him a few years later, other merchants in America—Gregg, Cunningham & Co. of New York—supplied the firm with information about his finances and reasons for refusing to pay; eventually, it pressed the case for reclamation. Not until 1788, well after the death of Rowe, was the firm able to gain repayment from the widow. Richard Derby to Chambers, Hiccox & Denyer, December 2, 1768, box 10, folder 1, Derby Papers, JDPL; Newton & Gordon to John Rowe, September 17, 1762, vol. 3, fol. 45, April 4, 1767, to Thomas Newton, vol. 3, fol. 45, to John Rowe, April 14, 1768, July 23, 1771, vol. 4, fols. 79, 205, 597, to Francis Newton, May 28, 1774, vol. 5, fol. 361, and November 9, 1775, vol. 6, fol. 11, to Henry Hill, August 14, 1788, vol. 10, fol. 42, NGL. On Lenox, see Newton & Gordon to Robert Lenox, May 5, 1803, vol. 25, fol. 3, NGL. Cf. the case of Philadelphia defaulter Thomas Riche. Riche Letter Book, vol. 1, pt. 1, fol. 224, pt. 3, fol. 33, HSP.

50. William Shackleford Jr. to Richard Derby, February 27, 1756, box 10, folder 5, Richard

Derby to Joseph Choate, August 29, 1760, June 24, 1761, box 10, folder 1, Derby Papers, JDPL. On India, Newton & Gordon to Francis Newton, May 29, 1775, vol. 5, fol. 515, to Wilkinson & Gordon, April 5, 1777, vol. 6, fol. 208, NGL.

51. Francis Newton to George Spence, March 1759, vol. 1, fol. 17, NGL.

52. John Leacock to Parminter & Montgomery, May 31, 1768, Leacock Letters 1765–68, Leacock Papers; Newton & Gordon to Robert Lenox, February 2, 1802, vol. 23, fol. 78, NGL.; Thomas Lamar to Henry Hill, February 22, 1774, vol. 8, fol. 153, Hill-JJS(A). For an example of information being passed about bankrupts, see Kearny & Gilbert to Newton & Gordon, July 10, 1770; List of Bankrupts in London, Edinburgh and Glasgow, 1772, in Johnston & Jolly to Newton, Gordon & Johnston, 1772, Alexander Johnston & Son to Newton & Gordon, August 18, 1772, box 6, CGP-Guildhall.

53. *Bolton Letters*, vols. 1–2; Francis Newton to George Spence, December 6, 1748, June 6, 1749, vol. 1, fols. 10, 26, to Willing, Morris & Swanwick, September 12, 1792, vol. 14, fol. 356, to Mordecai Lewis, August 25, 1794, vol. 16, fol. 59, to Thomas Gordon, April 22, 1802, vol. 23, fol. 235, NGL; Lamar & Bisset to Henry Hill, February 2, 1787, vol. 10, fol. 2, Hill-JJS(A). On struggles over cooperation, see Grandori and Soda, "Inter-firm Networks," 1–3; Mark Granovetter, "Economic Action and Social Structure: The Problem of Embeddedness," *American Journal of Sociology* 91 (1985): 481–510.

54. Isaac Norris Sr. to Benjamin Bartlett, December 7, 1717, Isaac Norris Sr. Letters, 1716–20, vol. 8, HSP; Francis Newton to George Spence, March 23, 1756, vol. 1 fol. 199, NGL; John J. Smith, ed., *Letters of Doctor Richard Hill and His Children* (Philadelphia, 1854), 119–50.

55. Thomas Lamar to Henry Hill, February 8, 1766, box 1, folder 3, Hill-SAGS; Francis Newton to George Spence, June 9, 1756, December 6, 1756, February 17, 1757, NGL, vol. 1, fols. 208, 235, 248; Thomas Newton to Francis Newton, October 31, November 29, 1758, September 4, 1759, Thomas Newton Letter Book, fols. 44, 46, CGP-MWC; Thomas Newton to Newton & Gordon, July 10, 1762, box 8, bundle 1774–75, CGP-Guildhall; Newton & Gordon to Thomas Newton, June 9, September 3, 1763, May 15, 1765, June 3, 1765, vol. 3, fols. 154, 193, 407, 411, to Charles McEvers & Co., October 27, 1775, vol. 6, fol. 1, NGL; Thomas Cheap to James Grant, August 30, 1765, bundle 244, Macpherson-Grant Papers, BCM; David Henry Smith to James Gordon, July 25, 1774, Letterfourie Papers; John Howard March to Thomas March, May 25, August 23, 1816, to John Mutter, July 14, 1816, March Letter Book, fols. 183, 211.

56. Newton & Gordon to Alexander Johnston, June 19, 1761, vol. 2, fol. 309, NGL. Nearly every other firm of Newton & Gordon's size and scale and ambition maintained resident partners in London. Robert Scot had moved there in the late 1730s, and John Pringle joined him in the late 1750s. James Gordon of Letterfourie settled in 1760, as did Thomas Lamar in 1762, Charles Fergusson in 1763, Charles Chambers Jr. in 1764, Arthur Ahmuty by 1768, Thomas Cheap and John Pringle in 1773, and Charles Fergusson in 1774. E 1/46/249, 1/61/139, 1/51/128, 1/57/67, 224, IOL. Of the major firms, only the Leacock firm did not send a partner to London in the 1760s and 1770s; not until the 1790s did William Leacock move there; before that, their representative was a relative of Michael Nowlan, Elizabeth Deverell. E 1/79/172, IOL. Most firms did not keep partners there for a long period, and like the Leacocks opted for using agents:

Paul Amsinck & Son representing Edward William Allen & Co. (in 1786, Carval-hal, Allen & Araújo); Demersier & Rivaz for Joseph Selby; John Kingston for Arthur Ahmuty & Co.; and Lewis Tessier for Robert Linton.

57. Francis Newton to Waddell Cunningham, July 4, 1755, to John Provoost, August 2, 1758, Newton & Gordon to David Barclay, December 6, 1764, to John Provoost, July 23, 1766, March 28, 1767, to Mackintosh & Hannay, July 8, 1767, to Greg, Cunning-ham & Co., January 9, 1770, vol. 1, fols. 165, after 281, vol. 3, fol. 353, vol. 4, fols. 33, 76,105, 428, NGL.

58. Philip D. Curtin, *Cross-Cultural Trade in World History* (Cambridge, 1984), 4; E 1/76–77, IOL; Robert Bisset to Henry Hill, November 7, 1792, folder 7, Hill-SAGS.

59. Robert Bisset to Henry Hill, August 2, 1794, folder 7, Hill-SAGS; John Leacock Jr. to William Leacock, January 23, 1801, Leacock & Sons Letter Book, 1794–1801, Leacock Papers; Lewis Pintard Letter Book, 1795–99, passim, NYHS. Lenox (1759–1839) was the youngest of three brothers who had all emigrated from Kirkcudbrightshire, Scot-land, soon after the Revolution had ended. He married Rachel Carmer (1763–1843) of New Brunswick, New Jersey, in 1783. David settled in Philadelphia as a banker; James eventually returned to Scotland. On Robert, see: Newton, Gordon & Murdoch to Jeffrey & Russell, December 19, 1791, vol. 14, fol. 53, to Robert Lenox, April 19, 1795, vol. 16, fol. 263, to Colt, Baker, Day & Co., October 11, 1798, vol. 19, fol. 105, to Thomas Gordon, April 22, 1802, to William Cole, August 16, 1802, vol. 23, fols. 235, 392, NGL; Lenox Family Papers, 1718–1836, NYPL. Sadly, there is no evidence illu-minating why a house dismissed or switched agents—whether they were too passive, thievish, or unwilling to offer what other agents were offering, like additional business, easier insurance, or financial connections.

60. Robert Arbuthnot to his mother, May 11, 1801, Arbuthnot Letters, fol. 29, NLS; John Leacock Jr. to William Leacock, October 28, 1800, Leacock & Leacock Letter Book 1799–1802, fol. 206, Leacock Papers; Newton, Gordon & Johnston to Francis Newton, February 1, 1790, vol. 12, fol. 218, NGL.

61. A stroll around the English Burying Ground demonstrates that invalids ultimately did not find Madeira's climate a boon; indeed, given the pollen-laden air, it probably pre-cipitated their demise. Most died within months of their arrival. Newton & Gordon to Francis Newton, December 6, 1792, vol. 14, fol. 455, NGL. Cf. Newton & Gordon to Bond & Ryland, April 9, 1770, to Jeffrey & Russell, March 1, 1792, to Thomas Gordon, December 15, 1794, March 5, 1798, vol. 4, fol. 455, vol. 14, fol. 114, vol. 16, fol. 193, vol. 18, fol. 260, NGL.

62. Gordon Brothers to James Gordon, December 27, 1761, Letterfourie Papers; Newton & Gordon to Thomas Gordon, February 20, 1793, vol. 15, fol. 64, Thomas Murdoch to Francis Newton, February 1, 1790, vol. 12, fol. 218, NGL; John Leacock Jr. to William Leacock, October 18, 1799, October 28, 1800, May 28, 1801, Leacock & Leacock Let-ter Book 1799–1802, fols. 80, 206, 258, Leacock Papers.

63. On marketing in general, see Gereffi and Korzeniewicz, *Commodity Chains*; Pamela W. Laird, "Interactions in the Evolution of Advertising" (unpublished MS, 1999); Hancock, "Commerce and Conversation," 214–18.

64. Newton & Gordon to Samuel Vaughan, March 2, 1802, vol. 23, fol. 115, NGL. Cf. Cos-

sart, *Madeira*, 105–14; Malcolm Bell Jr., "The Romantic Wines of Madeira," *Georgia Historical Quarterly* 38 (1954): 322–36; André Simon and Elizabeth Craig, *Madeira: Wine, Cakes and Sauce* (London, 1933), 19–28.

65. Joseph Gillis to Henry Hill, September 20, 1783, vol. 9, fols. 14–16, Hill-JJS(A); Newton, Gordon & Murdoch to Robert Lenox, April 19, 1795, vol. 16, fol. 263, NGL; John Howard March to Thomas March, February 22, 1816, to John Jones, July 3, 1816, March Letter Book.

66. Newton & Gordon to Johnston & Jolly, February 18, 1767, to Thomas Gordon, December 10, 1783, NGL, vol. 4, fol. 67, vol. 8, fol. 150; John Leacock to William Leacock, November 2, 1794, Leacock & Sons Letter Book 1794–97, fol. 6, Leacock Papers. Cf. Bonnie H. Erikson, "The Relational Basis of Attitudes," in *Social Structures*, ed. Barry Wellman and S. D. Barkowitz (New York, 1988), 99–122.

67. Newton & Gordon to Richard Cargill, June 23, 1773, to Thomas Gordon, June 15, 1789, to Edmund Boehm, November 20, 1789, vol. 5, fol. 234, vol. 12, fols. 86, 172, to Law, Bruce & Co., September 30, 1801, vol. 22, fol. 280, NGL; Bill of Lading Book 1791–99, Leacock Papers. For a well-evidenced history of brands, free of the ahistorical approach that taints most discussions, see Paul Duguid, "Developing the Brand: The Case of Alcohol, 1800–1880," *Enterprise and Society* 4 (2003): 405–41. For an emerging awareness of brands among American wine distributors and consumers, see John Vaughan to Newton & Gordon, December 15, 1794, bundle 9, box 41, to March & Benson, March 23, 1814, June 6, 1814, box 86, CGP-Guildhall; John Howard March to Thomas March, March 22, 1816, March Letter Book, fol. 105; *Poulson's Daily American Advertiser*, October 10, 14, 1800, March 16, 1801, January 12, July 18, 19, September 4, 21, 1815.

68. William Johnston to Thomas Gordon, February 12, 1787, vol. 9, fol. 340, NGL.

CHAPTER 6. MERCHANTS INTO CAPITALISTS

1. The words *capital* and *capitalist* did not mean in the eighteenth century what they came to mean later on (especially as concerns the capitalist's ties to labor), and the treatment that follows adheres to earlier meanings. In the eighteenth century, "capital" denoted the "stock of a company, corporation, or individual with which they enter into business and on which profits or dividends are calculated." *Oxford English Dictionary* (online), s.v. "capital." For definitions before 1830, see Randle Cotgrave, *A Dictionarie of the French and English Tongues* (London, 1611), s.v. "capital"; Edmund Burke, *Reflections on the Revolution in France* (London, 1790), 51; Arthur Young, *Travels in France* (London, 1792), 529; Morse, *American Universal Geography*, 1:442; Jean Baechler, *The Origins of Capitalism* (New York, 1976), 20–28; François Crouzet, *The First Industrialists: The Problem of Origins* (Cambridge, 1985), 10; Richard Grassby, *The Idea of Capitalism before the Industrial Revolution* (New York, 1999).

2. Zuscovitch, "Networks," 243; Grandori and Soda, "Inter-firm Networks," 13.

3. John Searle III to Newton, Gordon & Johnston, December 9, 1789, box 1788/89, CGP-Guildhall; Newton & Gordon to Thomas Gordon, March 6, 1790, vol. 13, fol.

257, NGL; Richard Lamar Bisset to Henry Hill, September 17, 1791, vol. 10, fol. 146, Hill-JJS(A); Daniel Henry Smith to James Gordon, March 16, June 15, 1776, Gordon of Letterfourie Papers.

4. Savvy firms understood this need, and by the end of the century were sending Portu-guese representatives to London and New York—people "who understand the assort-ment of goods fit" for Madeira, and "have great advantage over us on this account." John Leacock Jr. to William Leacock, January 23, 1801, Leacock & Leacock Letter Book 1799–1802, fol. 223, Leacock Papers. On the importance of knowledge in cloth in London, see John Styles, "Product Innovation in Early Modern London," *Past and Present* 168 (2000): 124–70.

5. Newton & Gordon to Thomas Gordon, April 22, 1802, vol. 23, fol. 235, to Francis Newton, May 26, 1806, vol. 28, fol. 367, NGL.

6. John Howard March to Thomas March, November 1, 1816, March Letter Book, fols. 238, 242.

7. Jameson, *Johnson's Wonder Working Providence*, 247; Duncan, *Atlantic Islands*, 172.

8. Alexander Gordon to James Gordon, October 8, 1760, Chalmers & Co. to James Gordon, September 15, 1762, March 2, 1763, September 14, 1763, James Gordon to Alexander Gordon, July 8, 1766, Letterfourie Papers; Newton & Gordon to Thomas & Thomas Gerry, December 12, 1762, vol. 3, fol. 74, to Thomas Newton, October 18, 1763, vol. 3, fol. 223, to Robert Hooper & Co., November 4, 1763, vol. 3, fol. 234, to Johnston & Jolly, February 4, 1766, vol. 4, fol. 2, to John Rowe, April 14, 1768, vol. 4, fol. 205, to Francis Newton, December 6, 1769, vol. 4, fol. 420, to Newton & Gordon, February 24, 1785, vol. 8, fol. 31, to Donaldson & Stotts, August 20, 1785, vol. 9, fol. 66, to Jeffrey & Russell, December 19, 1791, vol. 14, fol. 53, to Charles Vaughan, January 6, 1793, vol. 15, fol. 13, NGL; Newton & Gordon to Thomas Gerry Sr. and Jr., Decem-ber 2, 1762, to William Brown, December 2, 1762, to Thomas Newton, October 18, 1763, to Robert Hooper, November 4, 1763, box 1, bundle 4, box 3, bundle 1764–65, CGP-Guildhall.

9. Alexander Gordon to James Gordon, October 8, 1760, Chambers, Torngren, Bel-lenden & Co. to James Gordon, September 15, 1762, March 2, September 14, 1763, Alexander Gordon to James Gordon, July 8, 1766, Letterfourie Papers; Orders from Gothenburg, 1764–65, box 3, CGP-Guildhall. Charles Murray supplied the Marquis of Carmarthen with a detailed report on the state of the island's fish trade in 1786. Memo, July 15, 1786, FO 63/7, NA-UK.

10. Richard Hill to Richard Hill Jr., March 4, 1741, folder 1, Hill-Haverford. On diversifi-cation, see Alfred D. Chandler Jr., *Strategy and Structure: Chapters in the History of the American Industrial Enterprise* (Cambridge, 1962), 14–15, 42–49, and *Scale and Scope: The Dynamics of Industrial Capitalism* (Cambridge, 1990), 8–9, 39–45.

11. Vieira, *Público*, vol. 1; Hancock, *Letters of William Freeman*; *Bolton Letters*, vol. 2; Francis Newton to George Spence, December 6, 1748, June 6, 1749, vol. 1, fols. 16, 26, NGL; Robert Bisset to Henry Hill, July 20, 1763, vol. 6, fol. 63, Hill-JJS(A); Robert Bisset to Henry Hill, August 30, 1763, folder 3, Richard Lamar Bisset to Henry Hill, December 25, 1785, folder 6, Hill-SAGS. A taster might be a foreigner, but that was rare. Thomas Gordon's nephew William Caulfield served as Newton, Gordon &

Johnston's taster in the 1780s. Newton, Gordon & Johnston to Thomas Gordon, July 22, 1786, vol. 9, fol. 254, NGL.

12. Robert Bisset to Henry Hill, July 31, 1763, vol. 6, fol. 64, Hill-JJS(A); James Gordon to Alexander Gordon, December 5, 1765, Letter Book 1765–75, fols. 5–6, Letterfourie Papers; John Leacock Sr. to William Leacock, August 16, 1791, fol. 2, Leacock & Sons Letter Book, 1791–94, Leacock Papers; Francis Newton to Newton & Gordon, March 28, 1770, box 5, CGP-Guildhall.

13. Francis Newton to Newton, Gordon & Johnston, January 19, 1791, box 1791/92, CGP-Guildhall; Newton, Gordon, & Murdoch to John Campbell, April 14, 1798, vol. 18, fol. 316, NGL; Lamar, Hill, Bisset & Co. or Searle & Co. to Samuel Galloway, August 20, 1764, folder 7, Galloway Papers, LC; Alexander Oliphant to James Duff, January 14, 1767, Oliphant & Co. Letter Book, fol. 18, GD 306/1/1, NA-Sc.

14. Newton & Gordon to John Rowe, September 13, 1762, to Thomas & Thomas Gerry, December 12, 1762, to Thomas Newton, April 22, 1763, vol. 3, fols. 42, 74, 130, NGL; Grandori and Soda, "Inter-firm Networks," 16–17. On joint ventures generally, see Farok J. Contractor and Peter Lorange, "Why Should Firms Cooperate?" in *Cooperative Strategies and Alliances*, ed. Contractor and Lorange (Oxford, 1988) 1–28, 57–68; Giovanni Balcet, *Le joint ventures multinazionali: Alleanze tra impresse, competizione e pore di mercato economia mondiale* (Milan, 1990); Carlo Turati, *Economia e organizzazione delle joint venture* (Milan, 1990).

15. Francis Newton to George Spence, April 1, 1749, vol. 1, fol. 15, NGL; Alexander Gordon to James Gordon, December 27, 1761, Letterfourie Papers. Compare the Searles' New York schemes as described in Thomas Newton to Francis Newton, December 26, 1758, February 19, 1759, Thomas Newton Letter Book, CGP-MWC.

16. Francis Newton to George Spence, March 7, 1757, vol. 1, fol. 248, NGL; Thomas Riche to John Searle, August 9, 1764, Thomas Riche Letter Book, vol. 1, HSP; Newton & Gordon to Thomas Gerry Jr., May 23, 1766, vol. 4, fol. 23, to Johnston & Jolly, February 18, 1767, to Hugh Moore, April 1, 1783, to Archibald Moncrief, November 25, 1791, and to Samuel Donaldson & Co., September 25, 1794, vol. 4, fol. 67, vol. 8, fol. 18, vol. 14, fol. 21, and vol. 16, fol. 96, Newton, Gordon & Johnston to Hugh Moore, April 1, 1783, vol. 8, fol. 18, NGL.

17. Kenneth J. Arrow, "The Organization of Economic Activity: Issues Pertinent to the Choice of Market versus Nonmarket Allocation," in *The Analysis and Evaluation of Public Expenditures: The PPB System* (Washington, DC, 1969), 1:62; T. K. Das and Bing-Sheng Teng, "Trust, Control, and Risk in Strategic Alliances: An Integrated Framework," *Organization Studies* 22 (2001): 1–2, 6–7; Borch and Arthur, "Strategic Networks," 7. See also Charles F. Sabel, "Studied Trust: Building New Forms of Cooperation in a Volatile Economy," in *Industrial Districts and Local Economic Regeneration*, ed. F. Pyke and W. Sengenberger (Geneva, 1992), 215–50. Sabel's concept of "studied trust" is applicable to the Madeiran case. More recent discussions of trust in a historical context include Luuc Kooijmans, "Faith and Trust: The Van der Meulen Family," in *Entrepreneurs and Entrepreneurship in Early Modern Times* (The Hague, 1995), 25–34; Mathias, "Risk, Credit and Kinship," 15–35; Francesca Trivellato, "Sep-

hardic Merchants in the Early Modern Atlantic and Beyond" (paper presented at the American Historical Association Annual Meeting, January 2006).

18. A more elaborate self-governance prevailed in the diamond trade. Lisa Bernstein, "Opting Out of the Legal System: Extralegal Contractual Relations in the Diamond Industry," *Journal of Legal Studies* 21 (1992): 115–57.

19. Francis Newton to George Spence, October 27, 1753, vol. 1, fol. 77, NGL; Invoice, May 7, 1774, box 8, CGP-Guildhall.

20. Daniel Henry Smith, Memoranda to London Partner on goods "For the [Funchal] Counting House," 1770s, Letterfourie Papers; John Leacock Sr. to William Leacock, August 12, 1796, Leacock & Sons Letter Book, fol. 135, Leacock Papers; John Howard March to Thomas March, November 25, 1815, September 23, 1816, fols. 13, 224, March Letter Book; *The Book of Trades; or, Library of the Useful Arts, Part I* (New York, 1807), 129. Separate "East India" books do not commence in the island firms' record keeping until 1813. Accounting manuals purchased and possessed included Daniel Dowling, *A Compleat System of Italian Book-keeping according to the Modern Method Practised by Merchants and Others* (Dublin 1765); William Perry, *The Man of Business, and Gentleman's Assistant* (Edinburgh, 1780); George Fisher, *The American Instructor* (Philadelphia, 1787); Thomas Dilworth, *The Young Book-keeper's Assistant* (Wilmington, 1798); Charles Hutton, *A Course of Book-keeping, According to the Method of Single Entry, with a Description of the Books, and Directions for Using Them* (Philadelphia, 1788, 1815).

21. A State of the Case, c. 1758, Letterfourie Papers. Adam Smith believed in the inferiority of Iberian record keeping as well, contrasting how different were "the conduct and character of merchants," which he related to their profits. *Wealth of Nations,* IV.vii.3.

22. Jesus Maria José, Book of Current Accounts, 1706–32, ARM.

23. Jorge Pedreira (unpublished ms, European University Institute conference, October 2001), and his draft book manuscript, January 2003; Tome José Pereira Araújo and Domingos Oliveira accounts, in CGP-Guildhall. The records of Porto exporters suggest much the same conclusion. The accounts of Ferreira, the largest Portuguese house in 1834, still kept records erratically and sloppily, often on scraps of paper. In contrast, Sobral & Pinto, which worked closely with the English house of Swann Knowsley, kept records in the standard northern European manner. Not all English firms in Oporto maintained pristine records, either, nor did all English firms in Funchal. Young firms, like Hunt, Roope & Sandeman, slowly started keeping pristine records only at the point that they assumed economic leadership in the community. I am indebted to Paul Duguid for some of this information.

24. Reusage of pipes was common. Pipes being used as rum containers are noted in the 1750s in Port of New York City Manifest Books, vol. 36, nos. 13, 45, New York State Archives, Albany; Thomas and John Lawrence to Baynton, Wharton & Morgan, June 4, 1764, Baynton, Wharton & Morgan Papers, PSA. On common business practices, see John Marsden Pintard to Elias Boudinot, January 15, 1783, Boudinot Correspondence, folder 40, ABS; Robert Bisset and Joseph Gillis to Marien Lamar, February 28, 1770,

folder 5, Robert Bisset to Henry Hill, August 2, 1796, folder 7, Hill-EWS; Richard Lamar Bisset to Lamar & Bisset, December 9, 1791, vol. 10, fol. 210, Hill-JJS(A).

25. *Book of Trades*, 129.

26. In 1761, the capital stock of a comparably sized competitor—Smith, Ayres & Co., a firm of four partners—was set at £3,000 sterling, each partner contributing at least £500. Newton & Gordon to John Parminter, July 27, 1761, vol. 2, fol. 322, NGL.

27. Nowlan & Leacock Ledger 1774–84, Leacock & Sons Ledger 1791–1800, Leacock Papers. No later figures survive. The total capital of Leacock & Spence for 1759–74 amounted to 4:000$000.

28. Newton & Gordon to Johnston & Jolly, vol. 4, fol. 90, to Francis Newton, November 27, 1773, vol. 5, fol. 279, to Thomas Gordon, April 26, 1785, vol. 8, fols. 438–45, to Francis Newton, November 10, 1798, vol. 19, fol. 142, NGL.

29. The firms inventories are found in Newton & Gordon—1753, 1759–63, 1765–66, 1771, 1774–75, 1778, 1782–83, 1790–91, 1805, 1807–15, in Inventory and Ledger Books, 1760–1815, CGP-MWC; Lamar, Hill, Bisset & Co.—1762, 1767, 1772, 1777, 1782, 1787, 1792, 1802, in folders 1–4, Hill-EWS; Leacock & Co.—1776–78, 1791, 1796, 1800–1803, 1805, 1807–8, 1810, 1815, in Nowlan & Leacock Ledger, 1774–84, Leacock & Sons Ledgers, 1790–1815, Leacock Papers. The 1753 Newton & Spence inventory is found in Journal, 1751–53, CGP-MWC. The currency translations done here employed the year-by-year exchange rates listed in John J. McCusker Jr., *Money and Exchange in Europe and America, 1600–1775: A Handbook* (Chapel Hill, 1978), 113, and for later years provided personally by McCusker. When a rate was not available, an average was used. The average rate of exchange between 1753 and 1775 was 65d. sterling per 1,000 *réis*; actual rates did not vary much from the average. In addition to these three firms' inventories, see inventories in the Letterfourie Papers: David Henry Smith to James and Alexander Gordon, May 11, 1775, noting December 31, 1774 inventory. On the difficulties of making up annual balances because the "accounts with the Country Men are so many" and the "accounts with the Hucksters never shut," see Francis Newton to George Spence, July 16, 1785, vol. 1, fol. 169, NGL.

30. Wine Inventory, 1802, folder 4, Lamar, Hill, Bisset & Co. Papers, Hill-EWS; Newton & Gordon Inventory Books, CGP-MWC; William Johnston to Thomas Gordon, March 25, 1787, vol. 9, fol. 380, NGL.

31. Clerks were also chosen for nonpatrilineal reasons. Thomas Gordon's father, for instance, found for Newton & Gordon a Dumfries boy who "writes a good hand" and wanted work as a clerk; he was "the son of the man who carries the halberds for the magistrates" in Gordon's native Dumfries Town, but was no relative of Gordon. Thomas Gordon to Newton & Gordon, April 29, 1766, Scrapbook, CGP-PC.

32. *Bolton Letters*, vol. 2; Livros dos entradas, 1721–23, 1727–28, AN-TdT.

33. Gedley Clare Burges to Michael Nowlan, February 28, 1756, Burges Letter Book, fols. 2–3, Leacock Papers; Newton & Gordon to John Parminter, July 27, 1767, vol. 2, fol. 322, NGL.

34. Newton & Gordon to Andrew Ramsay, April 20, 1760, to Thomas Newton, December 12, 1762, to William Thomson, April 22, 1763, to Johnston & Jolly, February 14, 1766, and to Kearny & Gilbert, July 28, 1766, vol. 2, fol. 141, vol. 3, fols. 81, 137, vol. 4,

fols. 5, 34, NGL. More than death forced restructuring. Madeira firms were always remarkably fluid and experienced a high level of change in their partners. Alexander Gordon to James Gordon, October 22, 1760, September 21, 1762, January 15, 1766, Letterfourie Papers; Newton & Gordon to Johnston & Jolly, February 14, 1766, vol. 4, fol. 5, NGL. It was not unusual for a merchant to have belonged to four or more distinct trading houses during his career.

35. I am indebted to Jorge M. Pedreira for some of the information on partnership law in Portugal.

36. G. B. Richardson, "The Organisation of Industry," *Economics Journal* 82 (1972): 883–96.

37. Francis Newton to Andrew Newton, November 12, 1748, to George Spence, May 22, 1753, vol. 1, fols. 4, 50, to Francis Newton, July 28, 1764, vol. 3, fol. 322, to Samuel Bean, April 12, 1767, vol. 4, fol. 88, to Francis Newton, November 7, 1767, February 20, 1769, vol. 4, fols. 135, 302, to William Smyth, June 28, 1785, vol. 9, fol. 47, to Thomas Gordon, May 22, 1790, vol. 12, fol. 320, NGL; 1764–70 Newton & Gordon Wastebook-Ledger, fols. 2, 9, 26, 27, 30, Journal, vol. 1 (1758–65), fols. 150, 201, CGP-MWC; Account Current with James and Alexander Gordon, 1760, and Sundries Account, 1764, box 1, bundle 1759–66, Account with Scot, Pringle & Cheap, box 3, 1764–65, Note, box 4, bundle 1766–67, CGP-Guildhall; Inventory, June 30, 1787, folder 4, Hill-EWS; John Leacock Sr. to William Leacock, June 20, 1798, Leacock Papers; Power of Attorney, October 3, 1783, vol. 9, fols. 18, 123, Robert Bisset to Henry Hill, December 25, 1763, vol. 6, fol. 100, Joseph Gillis to Henry Hill, October 31, 1770, vol. 8, fol. 32, Lamar, Hill, Bisset & Co. to Henry Hill, June 2, 1784, vol. 9, fol. 48, Hill-SAGS.

38. Newton & Gordon to Henry Hill, July 29, 1773, to Francis Newton, November 27, 1773, to Jacob Wilkinson, February 27, 1774, vol. 5, fols. 246, 279, 314, NGL; Thomas Cheap to Thomas Gordon, June 2, 1773, Samuel Johnston to Thomas Gordon, July 20, 1774, box 6, CGP-Guildhall.

39. Richard Hill to George Dillwyn, December 24, 1760, box 4, Hill Family Folder, Hill-EWS; Alexander Gordon to James Gordon, October 8, 1760, George Bellenden to James Gordon, March 2, 1763, Letterfourie Papers; Newton & Gordon to Johnston & Jolly, February 4, 1766, vol. 4, fol. 2, NGL; James & Alexander Gordon to George Bellenden & Co., July 8, 1766, Letterfourie Papers; Thomas Gordon to Francis Newton, December 6, 1769, February 13, 1770, vol. 4, fols. 420, 444, NGL; Joseph Gillis to Henry Hill, June 13, 1770, vol. 8, fol. 1, Hill-JJS(A).

40. April 20, 1816, March Letter Book, vol. 1, fol. 123, April 20, 1816; Power of Attorney, October 3, 1783, vol. 9, fol. 18, Hill-JJS(A).

41. Oliveira e Silva, *Fidalgos-Mercadores*, 270, 326; Newton, Gordon & Johnston to Thomas Gordon, September 14, 1785, vol. 9, fol. 84, NGL; Memorial of Thomas Blackburn to Lord Grenville, 1796, FO 63/22, NA-UK.

42. A factory had probably arisen in Lisbon by 1642; certainly one was there in 1654, when England's treaty with Portugal defined the rights of Englishmen, especially their right to a judge conservador. In 1717, Lisbon's Factory had ninety members; in 1722, Madeira's factory had thirteen. Shillington and Chapman, *Commercial Relations*, 182, 191; Bundle "1722," "Minutes" Chest, Blandy's Head Office, Funchal.

Some of the responsibilities of a consul general and a vice-consul were later set out in 8 Geo. I, cap. 17, ss. 1–6. Cf. *Bolton Letters*, 2:23. On fights over the question of whether Madeira should have an independent consul general—the Lisbon consul general and British ambassador to Portugal said no, while the Madeirans said yes—see Letters of Benjamin Hemmings et al., Add. MSS 61510, fols. 1–175, BL; John Methuen to ——, SP 89/18/227, Petition, November 1713, SP 89/89/71, February 29, 1715, March 10, 1716, SP 89/24/25, 52, NA-UK; John Oldmixon, *Memoirs of the Press, Historical and Political* (London, 1742), 26–34; Newton & Gordon to Johnston & Co., January 3, 1763, to Thomas Newton, April 22, 1763, vol. 3, fols. 85, 136, NGL.

43. France appointed a resident consul before 1668. Vereaçoes, August 28, 1668, ARM; Affaires etrangères, B/I-III/763–65 (1671–1793), AN-Fr; Silbert, "Carrefour de l'Atlantique," 389–442. For records of other Europeans' consuls, see Legatie in Portugal (1651), 1783–1804, Consulaat-Generaal te Lissabon (1773), 1780–1809, and Staten-Generaal—Liassen Portugal (ingehomen ordinaris brevén, 1641–1795), Algemeen Rijksarchief, The Hague; Danish Consular Archives, Archives of Foreign Affairs, TKVA, Portugal, 1–5, Rigsarkivet, Copenhagen. For records of American consuls, see Dispatches of the American Consul at Funchal, in vol. 1 (1793–1831), T 205/T1, NA-US.

44. In its narrowest sense, a factory was a collection of "factors"—mercantile agents or commission merchants who bought or sold for others. But almost from their inception, factories accepted as members those merchants who traded on their own account. The earliest recorded mention of a factory in Madeira appears in 1706, when the vice-consul and several merchants were imprisoned by the Portuguese. In 1708, Factory members collectively resolved to impose on themselves "a tax of 50 réis per pipe for defraying accidental charges &c." and then agreed not to load private cargo on British naval vessels, for navy commanders were demanding more than £4 per pipe in freight, which was a price without precedent. The first surviving account of the Madeira Factory's deliberations appears in 1722, when a group of merchants recorded their debate on the applicability of a new British law imposing duties on British firms. At this juncture, most English-speaking merchants were Factory members, although by the end of the century just as many English speakers were not. Throughout its life, membership averaged about twelve traders, representing eight or ten different firms. The Factory per se survived until 1812, when it dissolved itself as outdated and unnecessary. Benjamin Hemming to Sir Charles Hedges, Samuel Hutchinson, to John Milner, December 8, 15, 15, 1706, fols. 128, 124, 126, John Milner to Benjamin Hemming, fol. 127, Blenheim Papers, vol. 410, BL; *Bolton Letters*, 2:57; Blandy, *Copy of Record*, 1, 6–7; Bolton, Darrell & Morgan to William Bolton, June 16, 1706, November 5, 1707, September 25, 1708, Bolton Papers, Special Collections, Library, University of Kansas; *Journal of the Commissioners for Trade and Plantations, 1704–1708/9* (London, 1920), 535. An association that persisted in calling itself the "Factory" carried on price-fixing and relief-dispensing for thirty-six years following dissolution.

45. On Factory work generally, see Shillington and Chapman, *Commercial Relations*, 13–45; *Bolton Letters*, 2:"Intro." Cf. A. R. Walford, *The British Factory in Lisbon and*

Its Closing Stages Ensuing upon the Treaty of 1810 (Lisbon, 1940), on Lisbon's association; and John Delaforce, *The Factory House at Oporto* (London, 1990). On the
Factory at Madeira, see British National Stock Account, December 31, 1774, packet 1,
bundle 1, English Factory Records, Blandy's Head Office, Funchal; John Marsden
Pintard to Elias Boudinot, May 25, 1784, folder 41, Boudinot Correspondence, ABS;
Cossart, *Madeira*, 27–28, 35, 116. On annual "donations," which protected "against
any attacks of the Inquisition" by keeping foreigners on good terms with the government, as well as funded sick or shipwrecked seamen and pensioned "such of its own
body as shall have . . . declined in their circumstances," see Blandy, *Copy of Record*,
1–3; João Antonio de Sá Pereira to the Count of Oeiras, April 30, 1768, caixa ii, no. 318,
AHU; Staunton, *Authentic Account*, 73–74.

46. Newton & Gordon to Thomas Newton, December 26, 1760, December 1761, January
22, 1762, vol. 2, fols. 256, 393, 413, to Alexander Johnston & Co., January 21, 1761,
vol. 2, fol. 266, Francis Newton to Thomas Gordon, February 5, 1792, vol. 14, fol. 91,
NGL. On adherence and the consequences of opposition to price-fixing, see Francis
Newton to George Spence, September 4, 1755, vol. 1, fol. 173, Newton & Gordon to
Thomas Newton, February 11, 1763, vol. 3, fol. 96, to Moore & Johnston, July 27, 1777,
vol. 6, fol. 253, to Francis Newton, January 10, 1787, vol. 9, fol. 348, to Francis Newton,
December 24, 1789, vol. 12, fol. 201, NGL.

47. This and the following paragraph draw upon John Bisset to ——, February 15, 1721, SP
89/90/39, H. Frankland to William Pitt, January 14, 1761, SP 89/54/1, and Order from
the Portuguese King, January 3, 1761, SP 89/54/9, NA-UK; British National Stock
Account, 1774 & 1807, bundle 1, English Factory Records, Blandy's Head Office, Funchal; Newton & Gordon to Johnston & Jolly, October 23, 1763, vol. 3, fol. 230, NGL.

48. Newton & Gordon to Thomas Gordon, September 30, 1789, vol. 12, fol. 151, NGL;
Minutes, bundle 1, English Factory Records, Blandy's Head Office, Funchal; Blandy,
Copy of Record, 3; Francis Newton to Newton & Gordon, March 9, 1792, bundle 6,
box 1791/92, CGP-Guildhall.

49. For Colson, Smith & Robinson's refusal and eventual payment, see Minutes, November 6, 1806, bundle 1, packet 6, English Factory Records, Blandy's Head Office, Funchal; Blandy, *Copy of Record*, 3. A native — Manoel Henriques de Oliveira — vexed the
Factory throughout the 1780s and 1790s, as well, but the Factory had less sway over
the Portuguese. William Johnston to Thomas Gordon, September 14, 1785, vol. 9, fol.
84, Thomas Murdoch to Thomas Gordon, June 5, 1794, vol. 15, fol. 467, NGL; Francis
Newton to Thomas Gordon, March 9, 1792, box 1791/92, bundle 6, CGP-Guildhall.

50. In contrast to some of their product innovations that were contemporaneously recognized as novel.

CHAPTER 7. STRONG NETWORKS OF WEAK TIES

1. Walter C. Hartridge, ed., *The Letters of Robert Mackay to His Wife* (Athens, GA,
1949), 238.

2. The few surviving letter books and account books kept by merchants working in non-

English-speaking markets do not lend themselves to comparison to the mountain of material left by Anglo-American distributors. At this point the evidence that has surfaced does not suggest significant differences in distribution activities.

3. On the English-language background of the uses of "merchant," see Hancock, *Citizens*, 9–10. Cf. John Weever, *Ancient Funeral Monuments* (London, 1631), 341; *The Character and Qualifications of an Honest Loyal Merchant* (London, 1686), 1, 6; John Kersey, *Dictionarium Anglo-Britannicum*, 1708 (Menston, England, 1969), s.v. "merchant"; *Guardian*, September 25, 1713; Daniel Defoe, *Tour through the Whole Island of Great Britain* (London, 1724), 1:124, *The Complete English Tradesman* (London, 1726), 1:7–8; *A General Description of All Trades* (London, 1747), 140; R. Campbell, *The London Tradesman* (London, 1747), 284–85. Cf. Richard Grassby, *The Business Community of Seventeenth Century England* (Cambridge, 1995), 8–11; David H. Sacks, *The Widening Gate* (Berkeley, 1991), 125–26; Robert Brenner, *Merchants and Revolution* (Princeton, 1993); Perry Gauci, *The Politics of Trade* (Oxford, 2001), 8–9, 20–23, 34–35; Jacob M. Price, "What Did Merchants Do? Reflections on British Overseas Trade, 1660–1790," *Journal of Economic History* 49 (1989): 282; Peter Earle, *The Making of the English Middle Class: Business, Society and Family Life in London, 1660–1730* (Berkeley, 1989), 34.

On merchants in the Portuguese world, and a similar evolution in meaning, see David G. Smith, "The Mercantile Class of Portugal and Brazil in the Seventeenth Century: A Socio-Economic Study of the Merchants of Lisbon and Bahia, 1620–1690" (PhD diss., University of Texas, Austin, 1975), 16–18; A.J., *A Compleat Account of the Portugueze Language* (London, 1701); Notícia geral do comércio (c. 1767), Codex, fol. 3, in Biblioteca Nacional do Rio de Janeiro, Secção de manuscritos, cited in Lugar, "Merchant Community," 32–33; Jorge M. Pedreira, draft MS on Lisbon merchants.

4. Bernard Bailyn, *The New England Merchants in the Seventeenth Century* (Cambridge, MA, 1955), ix; Phyllis W. Hunter, *Purchasing Identity in the Atlantic World: Massachusetts Merchants, 1670–1780* (Ithaca, 2001), 3.

5. Nicasius de Sille to Maximilliaen van Beeckerke, May 23, 1654, in I. N. Phelps Stokes, *The Iconography of Manhattan Island, 1498–1909* (New York, 1922), 4:148–49. See also "Secretary van Tienhoven's Answer to the Remonstrance of New Netherland," November 29, 1650, in Edmund B. O'Callaghan, ed., *Documents Relative to the Colonial History of the State of New York* (Albany, 1856), 1:422–23.

6. Matson, *Merchants and Empire*, 3–4, 334n5; Robert M. Dructor, "The New York Commercial Community: The Revolutionary Experience" (PhD diss., University of Pittsburgh, 1975), 14, 32.

7. Leila Sellers, *Charleston Business on the Eve of the American Revolution* (Chapel Hill, 1934), 49; Stuart Stumpf, "The Merchants of Colonial Charleston, 1680–1756" (PhD diss., Michigan State University, 1971), abstract and 46–51, 69–73; Nuala Zahedieh, "The Merchants of Port Royal, Jamaica, and the Spanish Contraband Trade, 1655–1692," *WMQ*, 3rd ser., 3 (1986): 570–93.

8. "The Discontented Group," *Massachusetts Magazine*, February 1790, 68; Doerflinger, *Vigorous Spirit*, 57, 58, 62, 68; Gary B. Nash, "The Early Merchants of Philadelphia:

The Formation and Disintegration of a Founding Elite," in *The World of William Penn*, ed. Richard S. and Mary M. Dunn (Philadelphia, 1986), 338, 350; Dructor, "New York Commercial Community," 14–18, 21; Bruce M. Wilkenfeld, "The Social and Economic Structure of the City of New York, 1695–1796" (PhD diss., Columbia University, 1973), 11, 49, 53, 169.

9. For seventeenth-century merchants, see John Hull Letter Book, 1670–83, vol. 1, fols. 87, 117, 123–24, vol. 2, 437, 508, AAS; Jeffries Family MSS, vol. 1, fols. 54, 76, 78, 103, 106–10, MHS; Mereness, *Travels in the American Colonies*, 10–11.

10. For this analysis, a wholesaler of wine is an individual who handled large quantities (no less than quarter-casks), managed bulk sales, and referred to having imported the goods or brought them from the vessel; a retailer, on the other hand, generally listed small quantities, usually mentioned a shop, often insisted on cash, and sometimes thanked customers—something a wholesaler never did. Problems arise when wholesalers also retailed from stores. Fuller analysis appears in David Hancock, "Markets, Merchants and the Wider World of Boston Wine, 1700–1773," in *Entrepreneurs: The Boston Business Community, 1700–1850*, ed. Conrad E. Wright and Katheryn P. Viens, (Boston, 1997), 62–95.

11. *AHR* 9 (1904): 524; Governor Edmund Andros to Commissioners of Trade, March 1, 1678, in Peter R. Christoph and Florence A. Christoph, eds., *The Andros Papers, 1677–1678* (Syracuse, 1990); Peter R. Christoph, ed., *The Dongan Papers, 1683–1688*, part 2 (Syracuse, 1996), *sub* 1683; Bond, no. 1059, JLP; Kingsland Deposition, June 8, 1689, NYHS; Reinier Willemse Account, 1680, no. 1024, John Tatham, October 30, 1689, no. 1394, Stephen Van Cortlandt to Edward Randolph, December 22, 1688, no. 0996, JLP; Peter R. Christoph, ed., *The Leisler Papers, 1689–1691* (Syracuse, 2002), 473–523; Edmund B. O'Callaghan, ed., *Documentary History of the State of New York* (Albany, 1850): 2:1–250, and *Colonial History of the State of New York*, 3:572–96; John Miller, *A Description of the Province of the City of New York . . . 1695*, ed. John G. Shea (New York, 1862), 50–51, 108–12; Frederic De Peyster, ed., *The Life and Administration of Richard, Earl of Bellomont* (New York, 1879), 16–21, ii, xiii.

12. The customs ledgers record ships arriving with dutiable wine in January–June 1703, March–November 1704, April–November 1705, March–November 1707, June–October 1708, and March–April 1709. It is possible that the 1704, 1705, and 1707 records are complete, since Atlantic shipping slowed considerably during the winter. But 1703, 1708, and 1709 records are incomplete and 1706 is missing. Julius M. Bloch, Leo Hershkowitz, et al., eds., *An Account of Her Majesty's Revenue for the Province of New York, 1701–1709* (Ridgewood, 1966).

13. NOSL for New York, 1715–22, CO 5/1222–23, NA-UK.

14. NOSL for Boston and Salem record no entries in 1714 and 1715, one in 1716, two in 1717, nine in 1718, and eight in 1719. No ships or masters are recorded as entering the ports more than once; these NOSL do not record consignees' names. The thirty-six "important" exporters were the twenty-five who exported at least five pipes over the 5 ½ years, plus eleven who exported less than that but did so in more than one year.

15. The numbers of traders in New York and Massachusetts are not strictly comparable. The New York Manifest Books appear to have cataloged every importer for each ship

arrival. The Massachusetts NOSL record only one consignee per shipment; this is almost certainly a shorthand—few shippers could fill the entire hold of a ship. The quantities of wine should be comparable, however. On ways to increase the stock of wine through "smuggling"—shipping it as vinegar, declaring and paying duty on only a portion of a cargo of it, and, most notoriously, failing to declare and pay duty on any of it—problems for the British Empire from 1763 through 1781, see *Boston Gazette*, December 28, 1768.

16. In Massachusetts, the thirty "important" importers are the twenty who imported at least eighty pipes, plus nine who imported less than that, but did so in more than one year, plus Nathaniel Balstone, who imported sixty-five pipes in 1752, a more than 90 percent market share for that year. In New York, the fifty-six "important" importers are the twenty-four who imported at least eighty pipes, plus thirty-two who imported at least ten pipes, but did so in at least four years. The definition of "important" is somewhat arbitrary, used only to give the reader a sense of the data. A complementary analysis of the Massachusetts import data is given in Hancock, "Wider World," table 1, p. 69.

17. This difference, however, may be partially attributable to the way the data were recorded. Similar results are obtained by analyzing the New York NOSL, which for the purposes of cohort reconstruction are probably less complete a listing given the kind of information being recorded. The NOSL for 1763 and 1764 detail ninety-four separate enterprisers importing wine into the city. In these two years, 3,406 pipes of wine were imported; each importer averaged 36 pipes at a rate of 18 per year. Half and third shares were most popular. In these two years, the top ten importers took in only 36 percent of the total, with none of them taking more than 5.1 percent, usually in no more than two ships.

18. The results of the following analysis are set out and analyzed in greater detail in Hancock, "Wider World," 62–95; the following paragraphs draw upon its material. A database of vital statistics and social activities of 383 Massachusetts merchants in the NOSL was constructed, amplified with information found in the Thwing Index at the Massachusetts Historical Society and the various reference works and manuscript collections cited in the notes that follow. To the 383 were added 9 individuals and firms not directly engaged in shipping—Chase & Speakman, Nathaniel Cossin, Andrew Craigie, Samuel Fletcher, William Hunt, John Moore, Poole & Clarke, Edmund Quincy, and Jonathan Williams—who advertised in newspapers or whose business records have survived. For 105 of the 198 who worked and lived in Boston, some indication of primary activity was ascertained. Some 48 of the 105 were "merchants." *Boston News-Letter*, and *Boston Weekly Advertiser*, 1758 and 1765; Amory Letter Books, Amory Papers, LC; Edmund Quincy (1703–1788) Papers, MHS; Bossenger Foster Day Book, 1780–83, AAS.

19. Numbers are derived from Dructor, "New York Commercial Community," appendices A and C, as well as tables II-7, V-14, pp. 29, 171. Confusing in Dructor's discussion is an inconsistent distinction between "selling records" and "commodity dealers." When necessary, recourse should be made to the data in his appendices, rather than in his tables. Appendix F details wine shipped into New York City during the war: forty-

three vessels arrived from Madeira and other places with wine; usually, from eight to ten ships entered each year, with the exception of 1778, 1781, and 1782, when only one or two did. On the foreign merchants trading in New York, see *Daily Advertiser*, February 27, 1786, February 4, 1794; *Minerva, and Mercantile Evening Advertiser*, July 15, 1796; *New-York Gazette*, December 24, 1799; *Mercantile Advertiser*, 1800; *New-York Price Current*, August 27, 1803.

20. The same can be said of Philadelphia. The number of wine importers and wholesalers trading there rose. Philadelphia city and county merchants advertising wine in the newspapers grew from one in 1730 to twenty-five in 1764. *Pennsylvania Gazette*, August 29, 1729, October 14, 1731, August 22, 1734, June 5, July 3, 1735, December 2, 1736, 1764 (passim). After the Revolutionary War, the import and wholesale wine market continued to grow, although by what rate is unclear—because, inexplicably, merchants appear to have shied away from advertising with the gusto they had before the conflict. Some sense of growth is recorded in the "Registers of Duties Paid on Imported Goods" for 1781–87, 6 vols., RG 4, PSA, which lists 380 different individuals and firms plying a trade in the commodity, and most of these were importers and wholesalers. Finally, *Poulson's Daily American Advertiser* carried advertisements for thirteen wine importers and two wholesalers, and twelve importer-wholesalers in 1815, when just over three-quarters of wine advertisers were involved in importing and wholesaling. Almost 90 percent of the traders lived and worked within six blocks of the Delaware and four blocks of Market Street. Wine traders increased at a slower rate than did merchants in general. Included was the Portuguese importer Teles de Menezes who acted as the agent for Madeira exporter Dona Guiomar de Sá Vilhena in 1776–89. The size of Philadelphia's larger overseas trading community grew dramatically after the founding of the colony in 1680: from 8 merchants trading overseas in 1690, the group had soared to 230 by 1756, 335 by 1775, 514 by 1785, and 1,023 by 1814. Nash, "Early Merchants"; Constables Returns for 1775, Philadelphia City Archives; Doerflinger, *Vigorous Spirit*, 17, citing Francis White, *The Philadelphia Directory* (Philadelphia, 1785); *Kite's Philadelphia Directory for 1814* (Philadelphia, 1814).

21. The eighteen *Boston Gazette* advertisers are distinguishable from store- or shopkeepers as not mentioning a store or shop, and as advertising sales in large containers (like pipes). In all, the *Boston Directory* for 1807 listed 385 merchants, 125 storekeepers and shopkeepers, and 19 innkeepers and tavern keepers. *Boston Directory*, 40–41. Of the eighteen importers and wholesalers advertising in the newspapers, as opposed to being listed in the directory, thirteen worked upon the wharfs—seven on Long, and three on India. See also Gayle E. Sawtelle, "The Commercial Landscape of Boston in 1800: Documentary and Archaeological Perspectives on the Geography of Retail Shopkeeping," 2 vols. (PhD diss., Boston University, 1999), fig. 4.3.

22. *Columbian Centinel*, July 12, 1806, January 14, 1807; *Boston Gazette*, January 26, 1807; *Repertory*, April 14, December 4, 1807; cf. *Federal Gazette, and Philadelphia Evening Post*, December 11, 1793, where an insurance broker was combining such work with importing Madeira.

23. In 1782–85, 70 percent (238 of 342) of Newton & Gordon's consignees were private buyers; they took 29 percent of the wine. In 1797, 73 percent (35 of 46) of the Lea-

cocks' purchasers were buying for personal consumption; they took 23 percent of the volume. Similarly for the extended Hill firm; in 1762–67, 58 percent of all consignees were ordering it for personal consumption. There are no later statistics for the Hill firm. Newton & Gordon, Bills of Lading books, CGP-MWC; Leacock Bills of Lading Books, Leacock Papers; Lamar, Hill Inventories, folders 1–4, Hill-EWS. One might think the Revolution and the problems it raised with Americans' repayment of debts owed to European and Madeiran creditors might have induced a decline in direct sales, but just the opposite seems to have happened.

24. William Byrd, *The Secret Diary of William Byrd of Westover, 1709–1712*, ed. Louis B. Wright and Marion Tinling (Richmond, 1941), 5, 98; John Howard March to Thomas March, November 1815, March Letter Book; John & Charles Carter to Hayward & Chambers, November 10, 1733, John & Charles Letter Book, 1732–82, Alderman Library, University of Virginia, Charlottesville; Robert Pringle to Andrew Pringle, February 10, 1743, in Edgar, *Letter Book of Robert Pringle*, 2:501; Henry Laurens to John Knight, June 26, 1755, in *Laurens Papers*, 1:271; *Carter Diary*, 2:671–72, 824; John Wickham Commonplace Book, 1803–38, *sub* August 22, 1804, VHS.

25. John Cadwalader of Philadelphia received individual shipments from Lamar, Hill, Bisset & Co. and John Leacock, although when stocks ran low he also approached local Philadelphia merchants Meredith & Clymer, storekeepers George Meade, and tavern keepers: Charles Carroll to Lamar, Hill, & Bisset, October 10, 1772, December 30, 1785, March 14, 1786, March 23, 1789, April 9, 1792, April 15, 1795, October 15, 1798, April 21, 1802, to Wallace, Johnson & Muir, March 20, 1783, Charles Carroll of Carrollton Letter Book, 1771–1833, fols. 19v, 83, 98, 110, 122, 123, 130v, 136v, 62v, NYPL.

26. Thomas Hancock to Walter & Robert Scot, December 2, 1737, Thomas Hancock Letter Book, 1735–40, to Richard Hill, November 24, 1750, Thomas Hancock Letter Book, 1750–62, HBS; Invoice from Richard Hill to Thomas Hancock, March 5, 1747, Boston Public Library; John Hancock to Lamar, Hill & Bisset, January 20, November 12, 1767, Hancock Business Papers, HBS. After the Revolution, Lamar, Hill & Bisset resumed shipping two pipes per year to Hancock. Cf. *Laurens Papers*, 2:89, 111–12, 3:22, 151, 5:136–37, 167, 193, 643, 6:440, 7:196–97, 207, 268, 295–96, 295–96, 307, 11:303.

27. Isaac Norris Sr. to Miles & Richbell, May 22, December 22, 1703, February 22, 1703–4, Isaac Norris Sr. Letters, 1702–4, Norris of Fairhill Papers, HSP.

28. Bailyn, *New England Merchants*, 100. See also Doerflinger, *Vigorous Spirit*, 76–77. The best overviews are Price, "What Did Merchants Do?"; Hancock, *Citizens*. On daily operations in a London countinghouse, see Jacob M. Price, ed., "Directions for the Conduct of a Merchant's Counting-house, 1766," *Business History* 28 (1986): 132–50; Hancock, *Citizens*, chap. 3.

29. John van Cortlandt to Newton & Gordon, February 8, 1764, John van Cortlandt Letter Book A, 1762–69, fol. 84, NYPL. For a discussion of Van Cortlandt's general merchandising, see Harrington, *New York Merchant*, 11–12, 29, 59–60, 77–79, 88, 90–92, 148, 209–10. See also New York Manifest Books of Entries, 1743–1751, 1754–1760, NYSL.

30. John Van Cortlandt Ledger D, NYPL.

31. Isaac Norris Jr. to Pantaleão Fernandes, April 25, December 24, 1741, Norris Letters, HSP; Gerard Garret Beekman to John Channing, January 12, 1749, to William Beekman, June 6, 1752, *Beekman Papers*, 1:72, 143; Isaac Norris Sr. to Richard Miles, November 25, 1717, Norris Letters, HSP; Hewes & Anthony to Brown & Benson, February 10, 1787, March 19, 1788, Brown Papers, box 173, folder 7, box 173, folder 9, JCBL. On one merchant arriving in Madeira and securing a supplier because he and the exporter John Searle were both natives of New York, see James Jarvis to De-Neufville & Son, December 26, 1779, Jarvis Letters, Connecticut State Library, Hartford.

32. Abraham De Peyster Account Book, October 17, 1730, fol. 132, box 2, no. 4, and passim, NYHS.

33. William Trent Ledger A, 1724–31, Norris of Fairhill Papers, vol. 13, fols. 29, 74–75, 98, 123–24, HSP; Gerard Garret Beekman to Robert Shaw & William Snell, January 20, 1749, *Beekman Papers*, 1:74.

34. Isaac Norris Sr. to Richard Miles, May 29, 1707, Isaac Norris Sr. Letters, 1706–9, Norris of Fairhill Papers, vol. 7, fol. 70, HSP; William Trent Sr. Ledger, 1703–8, fols. 90, 107, HSP; Isaac Norris Sr. Ledger, 1709–40, Norris of Fairhill Papers, vol. 15, fols. 228–229, HSP.

35. Gerard G. Beekman to John Searle, June 3, 1764, to Eleazer Trevett, October 10, 1764, to Hill, Lamar & Hill, January 15, 1759, to David Barclay & Sons, 1758, *Beekman Papers*, 1:466, 474, 328, 337.

36. John Searle to Samuel Galloway, August 29, 1763, box 1, folder 5, Galloway Papers, NYPL; Peter Stuyvesant to Scot, Pringle & Scot, 1757, 1759, Peter Stuyvesant Letter Book, 1757, NYHS. On the use of captains to buy wines, see Gerard Garret Beekman to George Spencer, May 25, 1753, *Beekman Papers*, 1:176. On the use of supercargoes, see Isaac Norris Sr. to Miles & Richbell, and to Nicholas Braddock & Joseph Hammerton, December 1, 1705, April 4, 1706, Isaac Norris Sr. Letters, 1704–6, Norris of Fairhill Papers, vol. 6, fols. 117, 119, 151, HSP; Gerard Garret Beekman to George Spencer, July 1752, *Beekman Papers*, 1:145; John Codman to John Searle & Co., March 18, 1788, Codman & Smith Letter Book, 1785–89, John Codman III Papers, SPNEA. See also Mathias, "Risk, Credit and Kinship," 15–35; Zahedieh, "Credit, Risk and Reputation," 63–70; Mark Casson, *Entrepreneurship and Business Culture: Studies in the Economics of Trust* (Aldershot, 1995), and *The Economics of Business Culture: Game Theory, Transaction Costs, and Economic Performance* (Oxford, 1991); Zuscovitch, "Networks," 243–63.

37. Baynton, Wharton & Morgan Papers, PSA; William Lee Letter Books, 1783–86, VHS; box 13, folders 165–70, 174–75, 177, John Codman III Papers, SPNEA.

38. Isaac Norris Sr. to Benjamin Bartlett, December 7, 1717, Isaac Norris Letters, HSP; Lamar, Hill, Bisset & Co. to Samuel Galloway, March 8, 1763, Galloway Family Correspondence, vol. 6: 1762–64, Galloway-Maxcy-Markoe Family Papers, LC.

39. Brailsford Papers, C 9/177/28, C 9/293/50, C 110/152, NA-UK; Jefferies Letters, vol. 1, fols. 54, 76, 78, 103, 106–10, Jefferies Family MSS, MHS; W. H. Whitmore, ed., *A Volume relating to the Early History of Boston, Containing the Aspinwall Notarial Records from 1644 to 1651* (Boston, 1903), 75, 107–10, 158, 178, 180, 210, 212, 242–45,

248, 254, 260, 292–96, 349, 358, 363–64, 375, 397, 419; George F. Dow, ed., *Records and Files of the Quarterly Courts of Essex County, Massachusetts* (Salem, 1911), 2:203, 392–93; *Suffolk Deeds*, vol. 6 (Boston, 1892), 64, 87, 89, vol. 8 (Boston, 1896), 182, 195, 248, 429; "Cuthbert Potter's Journal," in Newton D. Mereness, *Travels in the American Colonies* (New York, 1916), 10–11.

40. Thomas & John Lampriere to Baynton, Wharton & Morgan, May 7, 1764, Baynton, Wharton & Morgan Papers, PSA; Thomas Wharton Ledger A, 1752–56, fols. 35, 104, HSP; Francis & Relfe Invoice Book, 1759–61, HSP.

41. Letters to and from Willing, Morris & Swanwick, 1783–85, Willing, Morris & Swanwick Papers, MG 134, PSA; *Dunlap's American Daily Advertiser*, May 1, 1793, 1; Andrew Clow Letters, 1784–90, boxes 1–2, Simon Gratz Collection, HSP; John Hamilton & Nathaniel Drew Ledger, 1805–7, fols. 41, 102, HSP; *Beekman Papers*, 3:1058, 1068, 1109; box 13, folders 165–70, 174–75, 177, John Codman III Papers, SPNEA. Confirming evidence is found in advertisements on the pages of the *Royal Gazette and Newfoundland Advertiser*, 1810–15, when forty-five different traders placed 140 different wine advertisements: "wine" and Port were each listed in 31 percent of the ads, Madeira 30 percent, Catalonia 17 percent, Sherry and Claret each 15 percent. Lesser wines included Lisbon, Tenerife, Spanish, Mountain, Benicarlo, Malaga, Marsala, Muscat, Vidonia, French, Champagne, Barsac, Vin de grave, Naples, and Sicily.

42. Jonathan Dickinson to Richard Miles & Co., November 26, 1718, Dickinson Letter Book, fol. 225, Tench Francis Invoice Book, 1759–61, HSP.

43. Gerard Garret Beekman to Thomas Marshall, January 7, 1754, to Cunningham & Schoals, October 21, 1754, to Eleazer Trevett, May 11, 1763, to James Clark, August 20, 1764, to Thomas Clifford, December 7, 1761, to Alexander Keith, February 16, 1785, *Beekman Papers*, 1:200, 230, 240, 244, 436–37, 472, 395, 3:1055–56.

44. Isaac Norris Sr. to Miles & Richbell, December 1, 1705, May 23, 1706, Isaac Norris Letter Book, fols. 117–19, Isaac Norris Sr. Letters, 1704–6, HSP; Abraham De Peyster Account Book, fols. 69–85, April 1, May 14–October 21, 1728, NYHS; John Searle to Samuel Galloway, May 19, 1764, box 1, folder 7, Galloway Papers, NYPL.

45. Gerard Garret Beekman to Townsend White, July 27, October 21, 1754, *Beekman Papers*, 1:218, 229.

46. Jonathan Dickinson to Richard Miles, November 17, 1716, Dickinson Letter Book, 1715–21, fol. 106, LCP; Peter Stuyvesant to Robert Tucker, April 14, 1757, March 14, 1758, Peter Stuyvesant, Copy Book of Letters, 1751–63, NYHS.

47. Gerard Garret Beekman to Townsend White, August 13, 1753, August 5, 1754, to John Channing, May 9, 1747, March 29, 1748, April 14, 1757, *Beekman Papers*, 1:184, 219, 45, 17–18.

48. *Boston Post-Boy*, July 23, 1764; *Pennsylvania Gazette*, April 10, 1766; *Boston Gazette*, November 7, 1768; *Pennsylvania Evening Post*, January 6, June 24, 1783; *Independent Gazetteer*, January 21, 1783, March 11, 1784; *Pennsylvania Packet*, July 29, 1783; *American Herald*, September 3, 1784; *Independent Journal*, April 20, 1785; *Columbian Herald*, March 7, 1785. James E. Vance Jr., *The Merchant's World: The Geography of Wholesaling* (Englewood Cliffs, 1970), 31.

49. Dennis J. Maika, "Commerce and Community: Manhattan Merchants in the Seven-

teenth Century" (PhD diss., New York University, 1995), 83, 91, 93, 96. On agents, see October 3, 1787, MS Houghton bMS Am 1649.9, HSP.

50. Account, November 10, 1708, William Trent Sr. Ledger, 1703–8, fols. 229–31, HSP. After expenses were deducted, the transaction was worth £197 6s. 3d. There was no prior transaction involving Paxton and Trent, although Paxton brought in brandy in December 1706, and earlier listings of wine in 1704 and 1705, although these were not imported by Paxton and Trent. Ibid., fols. 19d, 174, 181, 217.

51. Norris of Fairhill Papers, vol. 13, ledger A, 1724–31, fols. 75, 98, HSP.

52. Abraham De Peyster Account Book, 1723–33, box 2, no. 4, Frederick Ashton De Peyster Manuscripts, NYHS.

53. Philip Cuyler Letter Book, 1755–60, NYPL. On Cuyler, see Harrington, *New York Merchant*, 241.

54. Max Savelle, *George Morgan: Colony Builder* (New York, 1932), 7; Charles Carroll to Wallace, Johnson & Muir, March 20, 1783, Charles Carroll of Carrollton Letter Book, 1771–83, fol. 62v, NYPL; Ludlow & Gould to Elias Hasket Derby, April 26, 1787, Elias H. Derby Letters, box 11, fol. 6, JDPL; John Codman III to John Searle III & Co., April 6, 1789, Codman Papers, SPNEA.

55. Gerard Garret Beekman to John Channing, May 9, 1747, November 30, 1747, March 29, 1748, November 26, December 13, 1750, *Beekman Papers*, 1:18, 36, 45, 75, 135.

56. Gerard Garret Beekman to Townsend White, October 8, 15, 1753, January 17, 1755, November 6, 1762, May 3, 1763, to Ebenezer Flagg, n.d., to James Searle, March 15, 1760, to Solomon Townsend, April 27, 1761, to Eleazer Trevett, May 5, 1763, *Beekman Papers*, 1:189, 190, 244, 422, 436, 281, 356, 376, 436; Jonathan Dickinson to Richard Miles, Jonathan Dickinson Letter Book, 1715–21, fols. 101, 109, HSP.

57. Isaac Norris Sr. to Miles & Richbell, May 22, 1705, Isaac Norris Letters, HSP; Gerard Garret Beekman to John Searle, September 24, 1763, *Beekman Papers*, 1:446; Hewes & Anthony to Brown & Benson, March 19, 1788, box 173, folder 9, Brown Papers, JCBL.

58. Johnson, *Dictionary*, s.v. "counting-house"; *Pennsylvania Gazette*, July 22, 1762. For London countinghouses, see Hancock, *Citizens*, chap. 3.

59. With regional variations, one finds similar structures in other American port towns. On Charleston, see Martha Zierden, "A Trans-Atlantic Merchant's House in Charleston: Archaeological Exploration of Refinement and Subsistence in an Urban Setting," *Historical Archaeology* 33 (1999): 75; Richard N. Côté, "Fine Wine and Thoroughbreds: The Friendship of Thomas Jefferson and Col. William Alston," *Journal of the American Wine Society* 28 (Winter 1996): 112–14. The large double house (after 1791 occupied by William Alston) at 27 Lower King Street, built by Miles Brewton about 1769, had not only a cellar but also a large attic with three distinct spaces, one of which was used as a wine storage space. See also the three-story brick double house (45 feet by 50) at 116 Broad Street, built in 1763, in Martha Zierden and Kimberley Grimes, "Investigation of Elite Lifeways through the John Rutledge House" (Charleston Museum, 1989). 8 and 10 Bedon's Alley provided extra service and storage space for Scots merchant Adam Tunno, whose main house and office were a block to the east. The merchant James Cunningham had a countinghouse on the first floor and a residence

above at 5 Bedon's Alley, in 1740–45. Other houses included Isaac Mazyck's home (constructed c. 1783) at 86 Church Street, the John Deas Jr./Adam Tunno house (c. 1780–87) at 89 East Bay Street, with a stone cellar the importers used for storing their wine, and James Gordon's home (c. 1792) at 87 East Bay Street. Jonathon Poston, *The Buildings of Charleston* (Columbia, 1997), 54, 61, 76–77, 102–3.

60. William J. Murtagh, "The Philadelphia Row House," *Journal of the Society of Architectural Historians* 16 (December 1957): 12–13. For early eighteenth-century examples, see Philadelphia Wills and Inventories, bk. D, nos. 292 (John McComb Jr., 1723), 302 (Thomas Masters, 1723), 309 (Caleb Jacob, 1724). Cf. Elizabeth Spera, "Building for Business: The Impact of Commerce on the City Plan and Architecture of the City of Philadelphia, 1750–1800" (PhD diss., University of Pennsylvania, 1980), 90–93, 143–45, 165–67. Although she does not analyze the countinghouse/residence type closely, her commentary is helpful.

61. The shell of the house of Samuel Neave still stands at 272–74 South Second Street, on the northwest corner with Spruce. Insurance Policy Minutes, August 5, 1760, the Philadelphia Contributionship, the Contributionship Companies, Philadelphia; Report 1349, Historic American Buildings Survey: Pennsylvania, LC; George B. Tatum, *Penn's Great Town*, 2nd ed. (Philadelphia, 1961), 157, fig. 14; Richard J. Webster, *Philadelphia Preserved: Catalog of the Historic American Buildings Survey* (Philadelphia, 1976), 21. Other combined houses and offices occupied by Philadelphia merchants are recorded in Webster, *Philadelphia Preserved*, 26, 76–77, 93–94: 518–20 Front Street; 620 Arch Street (Historic American Buildings Survey: Pennsylvania, LC, 1483, 25 by 65 feet, demolished 1965); 628–30 Arch Street (1965); 113 North Water Street (1963); 525 Quarry Street (1960); 113–15 Summer Street (1968); 117 North Sixth Street (1959); 113 Spring Street (1973).

62. Charles Stedman (1713–84) and his older brother Alexander Stedman (1703–94) were natives of northern Scotland. Charles owned and captained ships trading between London and Rotterdam. Charles and Alexander settled in Philadelphia in the late 1730s and 1740s, respectively, Charles working as a captain and storekeeper from 1737, and Alexander as a storekeeper from 1746. They provided a large share of the German immigration shipping in the 1750s and 1760s, and probably began trading wine in the 1760s to offset their losses in the immigration trade. They were partners of Stiegel's Manheim iron- and glassworks. On Charles Stedman's house, now 244 South Third Street, see Historic American Buildings Survey, PA-1359, LC; Nicholas B. Wainwright, *Colonial Grandeur in Philadelphia: The House and Furniture of General John Cadwalader* (Philadelphia, 1964), 6, 10, 88–89; Webster, *Philadelphia Preserved*, 25; George B. Tatum, *Philadelphia Georgian: The City House of Samuel Powel and Some of Its Eighteenth-Century Neighbors* (Middletown, 1976), 4–6, 64; Mutual Assurance Company, *The Architectural Surveys* (Philadelphia, 1976), 27–29; Marianne Wokeck, *Trade in Strangers* (University Park, 1999), 70, 89. Charles Stedman put the house up for sale in 1766 and sold it to Samuel Powel in 1769. Charles remained loyal to Britain, serving in its army. Despite being captured twice, he stayed in Philadelphia, where he died in 1784 and was buried at Christ Church. Edward Hogan, *Prospect and Check on the Next Directory* (Philadelphia, 1795), 127.

63. Lamar & Bisset to Henry Hill, July 10, 1787, vol. 10, fol. 17, Hill-JJS(A).

64. Hill bought the Meade/Pemberton house for £3,700 Pennsylvania current money. On Hill's house, see Historic American Buildings Survey: Pennsylvania, LC, 1334; George Roberts, "Dr. Physick and His House," *Pennsylvania Magazine* 92 (1968): 67–86; Webster, *Philadelphia Preserved*, 15–16; Amy Henderson, "321 South Fourth Street" (master's thesis, University of Delaware, 1997). See also Henry Hill to Joseph Pemberton, January 16, 1782, Pemberton Papers, vol. 36, p. 62, fol. 7, HSP; Lamar & Bisset to Henry Hill, February 26, 1785, vol. 9, fol. 109, June 1, 1785, vol. 9, fol. 132, July 10, 1787, vol. 10, fol. 17, Hill-JJS(A); Robert Lamar Bisset to Henry Bill, May 1, 1787, box 1, Hill-EWS; Mary Lamar to Henry Hill, February 21, 1787, box 1, folder 1, Hill-SAGS; *Claypoole's American Daily Advertiser*, January 30, 1799; Richard Lamar Bisset, Journal, April 19, 1801, box 32, item 2882, Research Collection, Independence National Historical Park, Philadelphia.

65. *Pennsylvania Gazette*, January 20, June 25, 1747, March 6, July 19, 1753, December 9, 1756, February 15, December 6, 1759, December 3, 1767, October 5, 1774, July 2, 1783, October 19, 1796; *Pennsylvania Chronicle*, August 3, 1767; *Claypoole's American Daily Advertiser*, January 30, 1799, March 13, 1800; *New-York Gazette*, May 21, 1764; *Rivington's New-York Gazetteer*, December 16, 1773; *South-Carolina Gazette and General Advertiser*, October 26, 1784; *Independent Chronicle and the Universal Advertiser*, January 19, 1792; *Columbian Centinel*, July 5, 1794. Two large Southwark row houses had typical cellars. *Pennsylvania Gazette*, December 23, 1762. One advertisement describes a house at 78 Walnut Street with cellars laid with lime, floored with two-inch planks, and plastered; its two brick arched stables, with "excellent lofts over them," were also laid with lime and two-inch planks. Together, they held two hundred pipes. *Pennsylvania Gazette*, October 19, 1796; cf. March 3, 1747, September 27, 1750, April 5, 1753, June 6, 1754, March 18, 1755, June 1, 1757, February 25, 1762, April 12, June 21, 1764. A cellar was usually a subterranean structure, but "cellar" was often interchangeably used with "store." *Pennsylvania Gazette*, April 29, 1756.

66. Poston, *Buildings of Charleston*, 54, 61, 76–7, 102–3; Major Thomas Simons, merchant, Charleston, March 30, 1805, Charleston City, Probate Inventory, vol. 353, no. 10, SCDAH. Warehouses were increasingly necessary as merchants built up large inventories of aged wine and spirits. Knowledge of warehouses is thin, grounded in evidence dating almost entirely from the late eighteenth- and early nineteenth-century period. The impermanent nature of many early American building materials and the needs of modern transportation systems have led to their dismantling or destruction. A few have survived in Philadelphia, and these suggest that warehouses commonly possessed large brick constructions, multiple stories (two and a half or three), gambrel (sometimes gable) roofs, double doors on first and second floors, hoist tackles, rectangular plans, open stairs to upper floors, and longitudinal partitions. Webster, *Philadelphia Preserved*, 18, 33, 40–41, 63 (Penrose's warehouse, Southwark, 1797; a warehouse, 105 DeLancey Street, early 1800s; Beck's warehouse, 18–20 South Delaware Avenue, 1805; a warehouse, 329 South Water Street, 1810; Latour's warehouse, 508 South Water Street, 1817–18); *Pennsylvania Gazette*, October 26, 1749, November 3, 1763.

67. *Pennsylvania Gazette*, December 23, 1762, April 12, June 21, 1764, December 3, 1767, October 5, 1774.

68. Even the superb study by Bernard Herman pays little attention to business spaces, preferring to discuss the merchants' townhouses as private homes. *Town House* (Chapel Hill, 2005), 33–76. A possibly English watercolor was in the possession of Francis Randolph of New York as late as 1966, and is badly reproduced in Mary R. M. Goodwin, "The Colonial Store" (unpublished MS, Colonial Williamsburg Foundation, 1966), 223a. Cf. *The Sequel* (1733), a satirical print showing a merchant's or banker's inner and outer room, in Frederic G. Stephens and M. Dorothy George, eds., *Catalogue of Political and Personal Satires Preserved in the Department of Prints and Drawings in the British Museum* (London, 1978).

69. Insurance surveys say nothing about furnishings. Probate inventories do not say much more, perhaps because the space (or at least its contents) remained the property of surviving partners. Still, what they include is suggestive. The information that can be culled from inventories largely documents early nineteenth-century offices. Earlier offices remain dim, yet no reason has surfaced to suggest they changed dramatically from even earlier offices. For indications of floor plan and furnishing, see the Massachusetts colony and state probate inventories for Suffolk and Hampshire Counties at the Massachusetts State Archives, Boston: James Griffin, dry goods merchant, Boston, 1766; Samuel Wentworth, sugar and coffee merchant, Boston, August 14, 1767; Enoch Brown, cloth and wine merchant, Boston, 1784; Daniel Sargeant, merchant, Boston and Gloucester, July 14, September 15, 1806; Edward Alexander, wine and spirits merchant, Boston, November 24, 1806; Joseph Cutler, merchant, Boston, December 18–19, 1806. For Kingston and Port Royal, Jamaica, see Robert Ingram, of Port Royal, November 19, 1701, bk. 5, pp. 147–50; Samuel Ivers, July 14, 1807, bk. 109, p. 52; James Dryken, August 14, 1807, bk. 109, pp. 65–67; John Burrowes, September 25, 1807, bk. 109, pp. 116–18, IRO.

   The problem with most probates is that they list real estate, merchandise, and furniture, but do not always itemize goods and furnishings by room. Massachusetts and Jamaica inventory takers routinely differentiated rooms, but New Yorkers did not. Somewhat helpful are the following inventories at the New York City Municipal Archives—New York City Inventories, 1783–1844: Ephraim and Isaac Cock, merchants, April 25, 1796, C156; Joshua Green, merchant and shipowner, September 30, 1797, G111; Unnamed Partner of Nootnagel, Schwartz & Rogers, September 1, 1799, UN 22. Similarly, Charleston inventory takers only occasionally distinguished rooms: W. Laserrs, October 13, 1741, 10:QQ104; W. Scott, May 1, 1765, 11:W269; G. Bedon, January 4, 1769, 15:X428; D. Stoddard, February 10, 1770, 16:Y187; J. Chapman, February 13, 1770, 16:Y214; T. Gadsden, March 16, 1770, 16:Y255; T. Carher, June 22, 1771, 17:Z1; Robert & Stott, September 29, 1772, 18:Z270; N. Swallow, April 13, 1773, 19:Z326; J. Wilson, wine merchant, December 28, 1773, 19:Z444; J. Fowler, October 29, 1772, 18:C179; A. Michie, September 13, 1774, 20:AA30; Major T. Simons, March 30, 1805, 353/10; J. Callaghan, August 1, 1807, 438/46—all at SCDAH.

70. Herman, *Town House*, 35. John Walters Gibbs was a German who had moved to Charleston before the Revolution. He aided the British during their occupation of the

town, and for that reason was placed on the list of Loyalists whose estates were to be confiscated. *Royal Gazette*, March 20, 1782. In 1783, he petitioned for relief, and the petition was granted, whereupon he announced reentry into "commission business." The Assembly thought him "a Character beneath the attention or Resentment of this House"—more a victim of his own "buffoonery" than a turncoat. Robert Lambert, *South Carolina Loyalists in the American Revolution* (Columbia, 1987), 286–88. Gibbs sold wine, property, horses, and slaves for others, first from 11 Queen Street and later from 45 Church Street, where he died in 1789. In 1785, he seems to have joined with William Graham in Graham & Gibbs. *City Gazette and Daily Advertiser*, September 16, 1783; *South Carolina Gazette and General Advertiser*, December 20, 1783, January 17, 1784; *Charleston Evening Gazette*, October 1, 5, 1785; *Columbian Herald*, March 31, August 18, 1788; Probate Inventory, 1789, book B, fols. 191–94, SCDAH. Gibbs's 1789 countinghouse constituted 15 percent of the value of his probated estate. Cf. the similar house and office of general and wine merchant John Callaghan. Probate Inventory, August 1, 1807, vol. 438, n. 46, SCDAH.

71. Herman, *Town House*, 71, 5.
72. Major Thomas Simons, merchant, Charleston, March 30, 1805, vol. 353, n. 10, SCDAH. Cf. *Charleston Morning Post and Daily Advertiser*, January 21, 1786; *City Gazette and Daily Advertiser*, February 18, 24, 1792, December 30, 1794, February 16, 1795, January 4, March 21, 22, May 26, November 15, 19, 1800, March 12, 1803, July 3, July 30, 1804, January 7, 29, March 22, April 2, 3, June 15, 1805. Simons (1765–1805) was a member of one of the founding Huguenot families of Carolina and the son of the extremely wealthy planter Maurice Simons (1744–85). Inheriting his father's immense wealth when Maurice Simons died in a duel in 1785, he commenced trading at 2 Gaillard's Wharf in 1792, where, like his father, he performed factor and wholesale services. Besides two city lots, he owned at the time of his death a schooner, forty-seven slaves, a farm on the city's outskirts, a 477-acre plantation, and a share in another 200-acre plantation. Robert Simons, *Thomas Grange Simons III, His Forebears and Relations* (Charleston, 1954), 10, 26, 36, 77–84.
73. *American Weekly Mercury*, December 7, 1732; *Pennsylvania Gazette*, May 6, 1731, February 8, 1739, November 19, 1741. Peter was born in 1697, the son of Benjamin and Mary Baynton. His activities are recorded in Peter Baynton Letter and Account Book, 1721–26, HSP; Peter Baynton Ledger, 1728–31, Baynton, Wharton & Morgan Papers, PSA. He drowned on February 22, 1744, when a schooner on which he was sailing to Burlington sank in the Delaware; with him died a former apprentice who had married his niece. *Pennsylvania Gazette*, March 1, 1744. His business fell to his twenty-two-year-old son John (1722–73), who commenced trading from the Front Street countinghouse. Compare the father's 1728–31 business to the son's trade in 1754–60: in the later period, John, who had married the daughter of the wine merchant Peter Chevalier, sold more wine and spirits to at least fifty-one different individuals, almost all of whom were Philadelphians, including four women. John's wholesale and retail business favored wine: in 1754 and 1755, it constituted 63.8 percent of all sales, in contrast to rum, 33.6 percent, and spirits, 1.9 percent. John sold to bigger fry: those who bought wine took away roughly thirteen gallons from each transaction. If one

removes from this group the large-scale wholesalers and retailers who bought a pipe or more, the average falls between 1 and four gallons per transaction. John Baynton's Journal (incorrectly labeled "Peter Baynton's Journal" unless it was the journal of John's younger brother, Peter Jr.), 1754–60, HSP.

74. *Pennsylvania Gazette*, January 25, February 1, 1759.

75. John Baynton to Hill, Lamar & Hill, August 24, 1759, January 15, 1761, June 26, 1762, Baynton, Wharton & Morgan Papers, PSA; Baynton & Wharton to Lamar, Hill, Bisset & Co., August 4, December 8, 1759, fols. 156, 194, Baynton & Wharton Letter Book, 1758–60, HSP.

76. On the Baynton firms, see *Pennsylvania Gazette*, January 17, November 13, 1760, August 16, 1761, November 10, 1763, February 28, 1765, April 12, June 18, 1768, October 5, 1774; Baynton & Wharton Letter Book, 1758–60, 1761, HSP; Baynton, Wharton & Morgan to Henry Whyte, February 16, 1766, Baynton, Wharton & Morgan Papers, PSA; Savelle, *George Morgan*, 4–5.

77. Appadurai, "Commodities and the Politics of Value," 33.

CHAPTER 8. THE WET GOODS BUSINESS

1. In the present study, I group tavern keepers and their ilk (proprietors of inns, alehouses, coffeehouses, dramshops, grogshops, punch houses, porter houses, beer houses, and the like) among retailers. Whatever the distinctions, they all sold goods in small quantities to ultimate consumers. The differences between retailers and wholesalers were evident in England by 1640. They were reflected in the fees (called premiums) paid to have one's son trained as an apprentice. In the early seventeenth century, London wholesalers charged between £20 sterling and £100 to take on apprentices, although in desirable trades they could get from £200 to £300; over a century later, they ranged from £500 to £1,000 sterling in the City. Retailers always charged less, although their fees also rose in the period 1640–1815. Startup capital for overseas importers, exporters, and wholesalers in the 1600s ranged between £400 and £1,000 sterling, whereas that for shopkeepers seldom exceeded £20. The quantities they sold sometimes distinguished wholesalers from retailers. In prerevolutionary Pennsylvania, a trader who sold twenty gallons or more in a single transaction was considered a wholesaler, and below that a retailer. *Pennsylvania Gazette*, March 26, 1772. However, that which divided them was not always clear or critical. Richard Grassby, "Social Mobility and Business Enterprise in Seventeenth-Century England," in *Puritans and Revolutionaries: Essays in Seventeenth-Century History Presented to Christopher Hill*, ed. Donald Pennington and Keith Thomas (Oxford, 1978), 364–66, and *Business Community*, 64–72, 83; I. K. Ben-Amos, *Adolescence and Youth in Early-Modern England* (New Haven, 1994), 87–88.

2. Earle, *Making of the English Middle Class*, 44–45. J. A. Chartres makes a similar point: "Leeds: Regional Distributive Centre of Luxuries in the Later Eighteenth Century," *Northern History* 37 (2000): 117.

3. Apart from Chartres, only a few scholars have looked in any depth at the distribution of consumer goods. Hoh-Cheung Mui and Lorna Mui, *Shops and Shopkeeping in*

Eighteenth-Century England (London, 1988), 173–248; Margaret Spufford, *Small Books and Pleasant Histories* (Cambridge, 1981), and *The Great Reclothing of Rural England* (London, 1984); Peter Clark, *The English Alehouse: A Social History, 1200– 1830* (London, 1983).

4. A wine cooper concerned himself not only in "the finishing and refining all Sorts of Wine" and "restoring of Wines pricked, ropey, or otherwise decayed, to their origi-nal Flavour and Colour" but also "in the Direction of the different Branches of the Wine Trade"—packaging, selling, "even planting the Vine." *Pennsylvania Gazette*, March 28, 1765. On coopers and vintners mixing and doctoring wines and consumers buying from them: *South Carolina Gazette*, April 22, December 23, 1732, January 25, October 4, November 15, 1735; Byrd, *Secret Diary*, 54–57; *Pennsylvania Gazette*, March 4, 1729, May 11, 1738, May 15, 1740, June 20, October 23, 1755; *New York Gazette*, November 25, 1758; *Boston News Letter*, June 20, 1715, June 21, 1718, July 10, 1735, July 17, 1736; *New-England Weekly Journal*, July 6, 1730. For rare lists of vint-ners' goods, see Mary Previdge, Probate Inventory, March 26, 1703, liber 6, pp. 14–16, Richard Maydon, Probate Inventory, August 19, 1703, Walter Crumbie, Probate In-ventory, September 21, 1715, liber 10, pp. 183–84, IRO; Unknown Vintner, New York, New York, Probate Inventory, 1799, UN19, New York City Municipal Archives. On distillers selling wine, see *Pennsylvania Gazette*, June 30, 1748; *New-York Mercury*, May 22, 1758; *New-York Gazette*, February 27, 1764; *New-York Journal*, December 4, 1766, April 6, 20, 1775.

5. In the present study, I use the term *storekeeper* to comprehend proprietors of both stores and shops. Distinctions between a "store" and a "shop" (as between a "store-keeper" and a "shopkeeper") denoted little in England and its American settlements after the middle decades of the seventeenth century. The occupation of storekeeper probably originated in the English army or navy, for, by the early seventeenth century, a "storekeeper" was "an officer or official in charge of naval or military stores." By the 1640s, the term had broadened to denote either the keeper of defensive materials or the seller of consumer goods. From midcentury onwards it meant almost the same as "shopkeeper": one can be called a "storekeeper" if the operation was large, and a "shop-keeper" if it was small, but the distinction was never scrupulously adhered to; the work of either, it was widely thought, demanded "Little Skill, Art or Mystery," unlike that of the overseas merchant. Thomas Powell, *Tom of All Trades*, ed. Frederick J. Furnivall (1631; London, 1876), 32; John Chamberlayne, *Angliae Notitia: Present State of En-gland*, 21st ed. (London, 1704), 3:532; Samuel Johnson, *The Rambler* (London, 1751), no. 113, para. 8; John Charnock, *A History of Marine Architecture* (London, 1801), 2:238. Both stores and shopes were places where the public could find an array of goods to buy in small quantities. Contemporary descriptions and physical remains in Anglo-America do not suggest different uses, offerings, or sizes; news advertisements and probate inventories do not imply more expansive stocks for stores or more restric-tive inventories for shops; they were not subject to different laws, nor were they treated differently when laws were interpreted. The distinction between "large" stores and "small" shops found no wider adherence in America. *American Weekly Mercury*, July 27, 1721; *Boston Weekly News-Letter*, October 11, 1750; *New-York Mercury*, March 8,

1756; Andrew Burnaby, *Travels through the Middle Settlements in North-America, in the Years 1759 and 1760*, 3rd ed. (London, 1775), 47; *The Journal of Nicholas Cresswell, 1774–1777* (Port Washington, 1924), 17; *Independent Chronicle*, April 29, 1784; Morris Birkbeck, *Notes on a Journey in America* (London, 1818), 97. To muddy meanings further, the terms for storekeepers and shopkeepers were sometimes used synonymously with "merchant." As early as 1704, Sarah Kemble Knight noticed that "the title of merchant" was given "to every trader" in New Haven who rates "their goods according to the time and spetia they pay in." *The Journal of Madam Knight* (Boston, 1972), 22. The modern definition appears in Vance, *Merchant's World*, 25, summarizing Theodore N. Beckman and Nathanael H. Engle, *Wholesaling: Principles and Practice* (New York, 1937), 21–22. Not until the early 1800s did the sometime British distinction between a large store and a small shop creep into American parlance, and then it was employed mainly by foreigners. Thomas Ashe, *Travels in America, Performed in 1806* (Pittsburgh, 1808), 1:51–52, 340.

6. Thomas Walduck to James Petiver, 1710, in "T. Walduck's Letters from Barbados," *Journal of the Barbados Museum and Historical Society* 12 (1947): 35.

7. Records of taverns are thin for 1640–1750 and comparatively thick for 1750–1815. The following have been analyzed: James West and Gregory Marlow, Philadelphia, Account Book, 1690–1703, George Emlen, Philadelphia, Probate Inventory, 1710, HSP; Daniel Smith, Rehoboth, Massachusetts, Account Book, 1707–11, AAS; John Harris Jr., Harrisburg, Pennsylvania, Ledgers, 1748–91, PSA and HSP; Elijah Williams, Deerfield, Massachusetts, Tavern Ledger C, 1750s-60s, Henry N. Flynt Library, Old Deerfield, MA; William Manning, Billerica, Massachusetts, Account-book, 1753–78, HBS; Unknown, Upstate New York, Tavern Ledger, 1759–61, NYSL; Robert & Lydia Moulder, Chichester Township, Chester Co., Pennsylvania, Account Book, 1760–71, HSP; Lowrance, Rowan Co., NC, Tavern and Store Accounts, Duke University Library, Durham; Arnold Hudson, Lewes, Delaware, Day Book, 1765–66,; Joseph Ogden, Philadelphia, Accounts Receivable Ledger, 1769–71, HSP; James Southall, Williamsburg, VA, Accounts, 1768–76, Huntington Library, San Marino; Thomas Allen, New London, Letters and Day Books, 1769–85, AAS; Samuel Adams, Salem, Diary, 1786–92, NYPL. Other sources have been examined but not analyzed; they do not alter the conclusions. Brown's Tavern, Salem, Account Books, 4 vols., 1784–1817, JDPL; Dimmick's Tavern, Pocasset, Massachusetts, Account Book, 1781–1815, Falmouth Historical Society, Falmouth, Massachusetts; Flowers Account Book, 1789–1828, and Unknown, Hopewell, New York, Day Book, 1801–15, MSS Department, Rhees Library, University of Rochester; Brewer, Annapolis, Ledger, 1810, Maryland Hall of Records, Annapolis; Sarah Marriner, Lewes, Delaware, Day Book, 1812–13, Alexander McCalla Day Book, 1814, HSP; Graham, Elizabeth, New Jersey, Account Book, 1815–30, New Jersey Historical Society, Newark.

8. Sarah Martin, *The Comic Adventures of Old Mother Hubbard and Her Dog* (New York, 1807).

9. For Boston, see Samuel Drake, *Old Boston Taverns and Tavern Clubs* (Boston, 1917); Gayle Elizabeth Sawtelle, "The Commercial Landscape of Boston in 1800: Documentary and Archaeological Perspectives on the Geography of Retail Shopkeeping,"

2 vols. (PhD diss., Boston University, 1999), figs. 4.1, 4.3. For New York, see Nan A. Rothschild, *New York City Neighborhoods: The 18th Century* (San Diego, 1990), 66–67; Wilkenfeld, "Social and Economic Structure," 32, 169–70ff; Dructor, "New York Commercial Community," 23–24, 164–65, who does not include tavern keepers among his selling units but whose conclusions describe well the situation of tavern-keepers. For Philadelphia, see Peter Thompson, "A Social History of Philadelphia's Taverns, 1683–1800" (PhD diss., University of Pennsylvania, 1989)," 221–22. For Charleston, see John G. Leland, "Early Taverns in Charleston," *Preservation Progress* 16 (1971): 1, 6–7.

10. Jerome H. Wood Jr., *Conestoga Crossroads: Lancaster, Pennsylvania, 1730–1790* (Harrisburg, 1979), 11, 12, 97; Lancaster Borough Tax Lists, 1759, 1770, PSA; William H. Egle, ed., *Provincial Papers: Proprietary and State Tax Lists of the County of Lancaster for the Years 1771, 1772, 1773, 1779 and 1782* (Harrisburg, 1898), 602–17; Town List, including 54 in Borough, 1807, Tavern Lists, RG 24, PSA; Marri Lou Scribner Schaimann, *Taverns of Cumberland County, Pennsylvania, 1750–1840* (Lewisburg, 1994), xi; John R. McGrew, comp., *Index of Tavern Licenses Allowed by York County, Pennsylvania: 1749–1806* (York, PA, 1992), 5–6.

11. The numbers are drawn from an analysis of all advertisements placed by retailers in the 1786 and 1815 issues of the *Carlisle Gazette*, the 1786 and 1815 issues of the *Pittsburgh Gazette*, and the 1795 and 1815 issues of the Cincinnati *Western Spy*. See also Clarence E. Carter, ed., *The Territorial Papers of the United States*, vol. 3 (Washington, DC, 1934); Fortescue Cuming, *Sketches of a Tour to the Western Country* (Pittsburgh, 1810), 195; John Melish, *Travels through the United States of America* (Philadelphia, 1815), 1:233; Norris F. Schneider, *Taverns on Zane's Trace* (Zanesville, 1997), 2–6; John R. Grabb, *Taverns and Hotels in Chillicothe, Ohio, 1799–1850* (Chillicothe, 2001); W. A. Provine, "Lardner Clark, Nashville's First Merchant and Foremost Citizen," *Tennessee Historical Magazine* 3 (1917): 41; Rhea M. Knittle, *Early Ohio Taverns* (Ashland, 1937), 100–102, 15–16; Margaret Burr DesChamps, "Early Days in the Cumberland Country," *Tennessee Historical Quarterly* 6 (1947): 212.

12. Early on the colonists did not replicate metropolitan class distinctions. An inn in England "catered mainly to the gentry": a large operation, it sold wine, spirits, an array of other alcoholic and nonalcoholic beverages, and food, and provided accommodation. A tavern sometimes "sold wine to a fairly select clientele," but it did not offer an inn's "extensive accommodations." The alehouse was the most common institution in England, patronized by the bulk of the population; in it one could buy ale and beer, but not wine, for drinking on or off the premises. D. Foster, "Inns, Taverns, Alehouses, Coffeehouses, etc., in and around London" (typescript, Westminster City Archives, n.d.); André L. Simon, *The History of the Wine Trade in England* (London, 1909), 3:192, 196–97; Henry C. Shelley, *Inns and Taverns of Old London* (Boston, 1923); Mathias, *Brewing Industry*, chaps. 4–6; Robert W. Malcolmson, *Popular Recreations in English Society, 1700–1850* (Cambridge, 1973), 71–74; Clark, *English Alehouse*, 6–14; Wolfgang Schivelbusch, *Tastes of Paradise: A Social History of Spices, Stimulants and Intoxicants* (New York, 1992).

In America, however, the terms *inns, taverns, ordinaries,* and *public houses* were synonymous. Each was a place "where food and beverages could be consumed" and rooms rented in varying degrees of quality and range. John F. D. Smyth, *A Tour in the United States of America* (London, 1784), 1:49–50. But this is not to say that there were no distinctions; they were just less rigid. "No monolithic 'tavern'" served Americans, Peter Thompson reminds us, "only many public houses." Any space could serve as or contain a tavern, even a jail. Thompson, "Social History," 6, and *Rum Punch and Revolution: Taverngoing and Public Life in Eighteenth-Century Philadelphia* (Philadelphia, 1998), 289–90; Frances Manges, "Women Shopkeepers, Tavernkeepers, and Artisans in Colonial Philadelphia" (PhD diss., University of Pennsylvania, 1958), 71; Richard P. Gildrie, *The Profane, the Civil and the Godly: The Reformation of Manners in Orthodox New England, 1679–1749* (University Park, 1994), 63–83; Joe G. Taylor, *Eating, Drinking and Visiting in the South* (Baton Rouge, 1982), 12–13, 44–61.

13. Clarence S. Brigham, *Paul Revere's Engravings* (New York, 1969); James L. Chew, "An Account of the Old Houses of New London," *Records and Papers of the New London County Historical Society*, pt. 4, vol. 1 (1893): 75–96; Reginald Bolton, *Washington Heights* (New York, 1924), 64–78; James Grant Wilson, *The Memorial History of the City of New-York* (New York, 1892), 1:454; James W. Hosier, "Travelers' Comments on Virginia Taverns, Ordinaries and Other Accommodations from 1750 to 1812" (master's thesis, University of Richmond, 1964); Marion C. Link, "Exploring the Drowned City of Port Royal," *National Geographic* 17 (1980): 151–83. For rural designs, see Eric Ekholm and James Deetz, "Wellfleet Tavern," *Natural History* 80 (1971): 48–57; Thomas Edsall, *History of the Town of Kings Bridge* (New York, 1887), 17–18; Harold D. Eberlein and Cortlandt Van Dyke Hubbard, *Historic Houses of the Hudson Valley* (New York, 1942), 21–29, 45–7; Kathleen E. Johnson, *Van Cortlandt Manor* (Tarrytown, 1996), 35–41; Charles F. Hayes III, *The Orringh Stone Tavern and Three Seneca Sites of the Late Historic Period* (Rochester, 1965), 1–63; Evan J. Miller, "Historic Houses in Dauphin County," *Dauphin County Historical Review* 9 (1961): 20–21.

　　For contemporary American exteriors, see the Red House (Longfellow's "Wayside Inn"), built 1686, in Sudbury, Massachusetts, in *Appleton's Journal*, May 16, 1874, 609–11; Manning's, built 1647, a tavern from 1752, in Billerica, Massachusetts, in E. F. Bacheller, *Colonial Landmarks* (Lynn, 1896), 15–17; Old Blue Bell Tavern, Kingsbridge Road, and Fraunces Tavern, New York, in D. T. Valentine, *Manual of the Corporation of the City of New York for 1857* (New York, 1857); Blue Bell Tavern, Kingsbridge Road, in *Appleton's Journal*, December 13, 1874, 737–39; Black Horse Inn, the tip of Manhattan, in *Appleton's Journal*, November 7, 1874, 577–78; Indian King Tavern and City Tavern, Philadelphia, c. 1800, in William Birch, *The City of Philadelphia* (Philadelphia, 1800), plates 8 and 27; *Brother Sailors as You Pass Pray Call in & Take a Glass*, tavern painting, colonial or early Republic period, Peabody Essex Museum, Salem, MA; Phila Martha Adams, *Tavern by the Ferry Landing* (1814), Connecticut Historical Society, Hartford; tavern views in *A View of Dry Harbour* and *A Prospect of Rio Bona Harbour* (London, 1769). For contemporary American interiors, see *Pennsylvania Gazette*, July 1, December 2, 1731; Robert Graham, "The Taverns of Colonial Philadelphia," APS, *Trans.* 43 (1953): 321; *Tavern Kitchen* (early 1800s), reproduced in

Kym S. Rice, *Early American Taverns* (Chicago, 1993); Washington Allston, *Tavern Scene* (1811–18), Oberlin College, Oberlin, Ohio.

14. George Emlen, Probate Inventory, 1710, Philadelphia Will Book C, no. 191, p. 235, Collections of the Genealogical Society of Pennsylvania, vol. 90, HSP; Patent, 1687/88, *Pennsylvania Archives*, 3rd ser., 9 (1894): 357–58; Hannah B. Roach, comp., "A Philadelphia Business Directory for 1690," *Pennsylvania Genealogical Magazine* 23 (1963–64): 127; William B. Rawle, ed., "The First Tax List for Philadelphia County, A.D. 1693," *Pennsylvania Magazine* 8 (1889): 91; unknown book draft, chap. 10, Boggs Collection, box 3, HSP, citing Deed Book F, no. 10, pp. 217, 323, 350.

15. English analogues appear in Ronald Paulson, *Hogarth's Graphic Works*, rev. ed. (New Haven, 1970), 1:231–33, and 2:ill. 218. Cf. two later British engravings: *Settling the Affairs of the Nation* (London, 1775), depicting a comfortable, orderly interior, replete with plates, glasses, cans, and bottles on shelves, a barmaid, a large fireplace, and walls trimmed for the winter holidays; *The Dram Shop* by Thomas Rowlandson (London, 1815), showing a crowded, disorderly tavern interior, strewn with wine pipes of "Old Tom" and "Deady's Best Cordial," three drunk women, and three pickpocketing courtesans. Dutch sketches by seventeenth-century artists appear in Jessica Kross, "'If You Will Not Drink with Me, You Must Fight with Me': The Sociology of Drinking in the Middle Colonies," *Pennsylvania History* 64 (1997): 28–30.

16. George Emlen, Probate Inventory, 1710, Philadelphia Will Book C, no. 191, p. 235, Collections of the Genealogical Society of Pennsylvania, vol. 90, HSP.

17. Procurement of locally distilled rum and whisky was common in the course of doing business. Daniel B. Thorp, "Doing Business in the Backcountry: Retail Trade in Colonial Rowan County, North Carolina," *WMQ*, 3rd ser., 48 (1991): 387–408; William Manning Tavern Book, 1753–70, and Customer Accounts, 1770–78, HBS.

18. West and Marlow Account Book, HSP; Roach, "Philadelphia Business Directory," 126; Rawle, "First Tax List," 90.

19. Daniel Smith, Tavern Account Book, 1707–11, *sub* March 8, 17, June 20, 1709, September 1710, AAS. Cf. Richard L. Bowen, *Early Rehoboth* (Rehoboth, 1946), 2:115–17.

20. West & Marlow Account Book, 1690–1703, HSP; Daniel Smith, Tavern Account Book, 1707–11, AAS. On the Commons in Deerfield, Massachusetts, 20 percent of Elijah Williams's 1758 customers came from the town, and another 50 percent hailed from farmsteads just west of the Connecticut River, up to twenty miles from the town. Most customers deferred payment or exchanged goods and labor for liquor; less than 10 percent paid in cash. Those that paid in cash were "strangers"—one-time purchasers passing through the town. Weekly transactions entered into Williams's tavern day book for 1758 fluctuated between 3 and 118, and in 1759 between 0 and 58. All but three patrons were male. Deborah J. Binder, "Liquid Assets: Major Elijah Williams as a Taverner in Eighteenth Century Deerfield" (Research paper—Historic Deerfield Fellowship Program, August 1979), 15, 26–27, figs. 7–8. A largely local clientele of similarly situated people irregularly attending was the norm. At John Shewbart's London Tavern and Coffee House in Philadelphia, there were 245 customers between 1736 and 1743. All were men, all drinkers, most Philadelphians employed in the mari-

time trades and dispersed throughout the city. Only 28 percent came more than nine times, whereas 72 percent came nine times or fewer, and 34 percent came once. *London Coffee House and Tavern Journal*, 1736–43, Coates-Reynell Collection, HSP, as analyzed by Sharon V. Salinger, *Taverns and Drinking in Early America* (Baltimore, 2002), 59.

21. A comparison of the dealings of the founder of Harrisburg and his son, John Harris Sr. and Jr., reveals some of these changes. Harris Sr. had established a tavern next to his ferry house on the east bank of the Susquehanna River, 110 miles due west of Philadelphia, where the road from Philadelphia crossed the river and connected with the Great Road running astride the Appalachian crest. John Harris Sr. Receipt Book, 1749–69, John Harris Jr. Receipt Book, 1760–91, PSA; John Harris Jr. Ledger, 1761–75, fols. 18, 220, 226, HSP. The 1761–75 ledger contains accounts going back to 1751.

22. Constance V. Hershey, "The City Tavern: Historic Furnishings Plan" (Denver, National Park Service, 1974), 61–4; Nan Rothschild and Diana Rockman, "City Tavern, Country Tavern: An Analysis of Four Colonial Sites," *Historical Archaeology* 18 (1984): 112; Kym Rice, *Early American Taverns: For the Entertainment of Friends and Strangers* (New York, 1983), 31; Peter J. Thompson, "The 'Friendly Glass': Drink and Gentility in Colonial Philadelphia," *PMHB* 113 (1989): 549–73.

23. William Coit to Thomas Allen, January 21, 1772, Ebenezer Fitch to Thomas Allen, August 31, 1772, Comfort Sage to Thomas Allen, September 2, 1772, John Chenevard to Thomas Allen, October 15, November 3, 24, 1772, box 2, folder 2, Samuel Olcott to Thomas Allen, April 6, 13, May 10, 1773, John Chenevard to Thomas Allen, July 6, 27, August 4, October 11, 22, November 16, 1773, box 2, folder 3, Thomas Allen Papers, Allen Family Collection, AAS. Marked similarity to Allen's New London tavern operations is found in the tavern kept by George Frey of Middletown, Pennsylvania: Ledger Book B, 1766–73, *Inventarium* Book, and *Copier* Book A/*Factura* Book A, 1773–78, Frey Papers, private collection, Middletown, PA. Cf. Stephen J. Perkins, "Command You Me from Play Every Minute of the Day" (master's thesis, University of Delaware, 2001), 36; Thorp, "Doing Business"; Moulder Accounts, 1760–1817, HSP; *Pennsylvania Gazette*, June 19, 1766, August 11, November 17, 1768; Arnold Hudson Account Book, 1765–66, HSP.

24. Thorp, "Doing Business," 390–93, 401, 404–5, and *The Moravian Community in Colonial North Carolina: Pluralism on the Southern Frontier* (Knoxville, 1989), 123. On ancillary activities, see Patricia Gibbs, "Taverns in Tidewater Virginia, 1700–1774" (master's thesis, College of William and Mary, 1968), 132–34, 138; Anne Hedges, "Richmond Taverns in the Years 1775–1800" (master's thesis, University of Richmond, 1993), 76, 80–81; Thompson, "Social History," 187–90. On competition, see *Pennsylvania Gazette*, July 26, 1759; Tavern Copier Buch A/Factura Buch A, November 1773–78, Frey Papers, private collection, Middletown, PA; Ebenezer Fitch to Thomas Allen, 1786, box 4, folder 3, Allen Family Papers, AAS.

This great tavern rebuilding was evident in every American city. It manifested itself primarily in enhancing buildings and furnishings. Eugene P. McParland, "The Socio-Economic Importance of the Colonial Tavern in New York during the British Period, 1664–1776" (master's thesis, City University of New York, 1970), 68–70; Thompson,

"Social History," 418–31, 466–67, and *Rum Punch*, 68–73. For enhancement in Philadelphia, see Ogden Accounts Receivable Ledger, 1769–71, HSP; Survey, no. 1340, March 4, 1768, Contributionship Office, Philadelphia; *Pennsylvania Gazette*, July 7, 1768; *Pennsylvania Gazette*, March 10, June 2, November 24, 1768, March 9, 1769, October 25, 1770, January 17, May 30, July 18, 1771. For Charleston, see Probate Inventory, Benjamin Backhouse, September 21–22, 1767, of Catherine Backhouse, December 26, 1767, reel 6, fols. 176–80, 223–29, SCDAH; *South Carolina Gazette*, November 24, December 1, 1766, February 16, March 30, June 29, November 23, 1767. For Boston, see Probate Inventory, Seth King, January 2, 1804, 102:1–8, Suffolk County, MSA; *Massachusetts Mercury*, May 22, December 18, 1798; *Columbian Centinel*, October 11, 1797, February 28, March 10, April 21, 1798, June 29, December 11, 1799, September 27, 1800; *Boston Price-Current*, February 1, 1798; *Boston Gazette*, November 24, 1800, August 27, 1801, September 29, 1803.

The improvements were reflected in the values of tavern keepers' estates at their demise. The estates of Massachusetts, New York, South Carolina, and Jamaica tavern keepers averaged £392 sterling in 1701–39, after adjusting for differences in colonial currencies. The values of tavern keepers' estates in 1766–1807 averaged £1,049, nearly triple the 1701–39 value. At the same time, liquor's share of estates fell from 25 percent in the first half of the eighteenth century to about 2 percent in the first decade of the nineteenth. Even though the value of the liquor increased, the value of real property devoted to taverns increased much more. When adjusted for inflation, with 1700 as the base year, the average probated tavern keeper estate value rose from £466 sterling (for 1701–39) to £708 (1766–1807), representing only a 52 percent increase.

25. Mifflin & Massey Ledger, fols. 17, 79, 124, 167, 170, 178, 198, 288, HSP.

26. Inventory of Newman Swallow, April 13, 1773, bk. Z, fols. 326–32, Charleston City, SCDAH. Of particular interest are the lists of stocks and debtors. On Swallow's business, see *South-Carolina Gazette*, January 11, May 31, 1770, and April 11, 1771. For examples of other general retailers selling wine, see *New-York Gazette*, February 20 (Folliott), 27 (Dalzell), May 7 (Dalzell, and Gilliland), 1764; *Royal Gazette*, August 22, 1778 (Coupland & Tench), January 9 (Brander), August 28, 1779 (Hall & Birks).

27. Some retailers sold wine before the midcentury war, of course. It is just that they did so infrequently; it was never a major thrust of endeavor. In Philadelphia, Benjamin and Samuel Shoemaker had a small store on Water Street from which they sold beeswax, furs, skins, flour, rice, butter, pork, gammon, iron, staves, beer, rum, and Madeira. The Shoemakers, who were mainly in the business of arranging freight and passage, bought their wine from an erstwhile friend and dinner companion, Dr. Richard Hill of Madeira. Between August 1746 and October 1747, they imported thirty-nine pipes of wine from Hill and sold it in thirty-one lots to fifteen named individuals (all but one were Philadelphians), several unnamed buyers, and a Pennsylvania/Newfoundland captain whose ship they owned a share of. Just as revealing is the work of Joseph Ogden, who initially eschewed the distribution of wine and spirits for the sale of dry goods from a store he kept on Chestnut Street. Only after he expanded his operation into a combined store/tavern in 1752 did he begin to sell alcohol. Thereafter, a typical day saw the sale of rum (the bulk sold), wine, corks, bottles, plates, pots, tea, pease,

spices, molasses, and cloth. Shoemaker Ledger; HSP; Joseph Ogden Accounts Receivable Ledger, fols. 4–7, new 1–2, HSP; *Pennsylvania Gazette*, July 9, 1761, August 16, September 20, 1764. See also *Pennsylvania Gazette*, May 12, 1737 (John Valentine in Fishbourn's Store), March 12, 1751, October 3, 1751 (Thomas Archdall, and Randle Mitchell).

28. Philadelphia and Boston retailers in the post-1761 era having wine accounts include Tench Francis Ledger and Invoice Book, 1759–63, Mifflin & Massey Ledger A, 1760–63, John & Peter Chevalier Day Book, 1760–66, Benjamin Fuller Papers, 1762–99, 5 vols., and Daniel Roberdeau Letter Book, 1764–71, HSP; John and Jonathan Amory Papers, vol. 51, fol. 3, HBS; Thomas Amory Account Book, 1770–71, Philip Ammidon Letter Book, *sub* January 7, 20, February 4, 22, March 15, August 17, 1804, February 25, March 27, April 12, 1805, MHS.

29. For discussion of the probate inventory database for the present study, see chapter 9.

30. Looking for general retailers advertising wine as available in their stores and shops in Philadelphia newspapers, one discovers that, in 1734–38, eight different retailers advertised wine, as far south as Pine, as far north as Market, and between Water and Third. Four decades later, in 1774–78, fifty-three different enterprisers advertised it, and thirty of them worked between Cedar and Race streets and the Delaware River and Fifth Street. *Pennsylvania Gazette*, 1734–38, 1774–78. Roughly the same number prevailed in 1815, with fifty-six different retailers advertising wine. Those who retailed wine worked within a seven-square-block area; no retailer worked more than a twenty-five-minute walk from importers' and wholesalers' countinghouses and wharves.

31. *Pennsylvania Packet*, November 3, 10, 1781.

32. The network of inland British suppliers that kept London and smaller cities like Leeds provisioned with drink was similar. J. A. Chartres, "Food Consumption," in *London, 1500–1700: The Making of the Modern Metropolis*, ed. A. L. Beier and R. A. Finlay (London, 1986); J. A. Chartres, "The Marketing," and "Leeds," in *Chapters from the Agrarian History of England and Wales, 1500–1750*, ed. Joan Thirsk (Cambridge, 1990), 115–32.

33. Mifflin & Massey Ledger, fols. 17, 79, 124, 167, 170, 178, 198, 288, HSP.

34. William West Ledger, 1770–77, fols. 22, 29, 37, 39, 44, 52, 55, 60, 114, 116, 133, 143, 150, 198, William West Papers, HSP; *Pennsylvania Gazette*, September 18, 1766, November 29, 1770, March 17, 1773; *Federal Gazette*, October 25, 1791.

35. William West Ledger, 1770–77, fols. 22, 29, 37, 39, 44, 52, 55, 60, 114, 116, 133, 143, 150, 198, William West Papers, HSP; Mifflin & Massey Ledger, fols. 17, 79, 124, 167, 170, HSP; Receipt and Cash Book, Boston, 1770–71, Thomas Amory Account Book, vol. 1, MHS.

36. For vendue sales offloading wine, see Mifflin & Massey Ledger, fols. 17, 79, 124, 167, 170, HSP; *Pennsylvania Gazette*, September 20, June 2, 1764; *Virginia Gazette* (Rind), July 28, 1768, March 11, May 4, October 20, 1775; *Royal Gazette and Newfoundland Advertiser*, July 29, October 21, 1813, September 15, November 10, 1814, January 12, March 8, June 1, July 27, September 14, 27, 29, October 12, November 23, 28, 1815. A similar method was buying wine at the auction of someone deceased. *Pennsylvania Gazette*, October 11, 1764. Vice admiralty sales served as a different type of auction.

Virginia Gazette, April 11, 1755 For a brief discussion of auctions, see Fred M. Jones, *Middlemen in the Domestic Trade of the United States, 1800–1860* (Urbana, 1937), 33–43. On merchants dumping at vendue, see Price, "What Did Merchants Do?" 272. Cf. Ray B. Westerfield, *English History of American Auctions* (New Haven, 1920), 172–79, who felt dumping had little impact on the market before 1775. In fact, the impact depended heavily on the market dumped upon. Philadelphia and New York had a lively vendue scene, and British merchants frequently dumped unsold goods there. In the Chesapeake, however, the population was highly dispersed and towns widely scattered; it made little sense to dump there, although even there the popularity of vendues rose after 1783. Vendues gained in popularity in Philadelphia at midcentury. Manges, "Women Shopkeepers," 93.

37. Few inventories detailing individual retailers' stocks have been discovered, so cross-decade comparisons are difficult. For explanation of the probate data I have compiled, see chapter 9. The figures are in pounds sterling and have been adjusted for inflation. While real averages fell over the period 1700–1807, nominal values declined less dramatically: from £1,148 sterling to £974. A distinction emerges between proprietors who sold wine and those who did not. Before 1766, the retailer who sold wine possessed an estate nearly double that of retailers who did not; too, after 1765, the wine seller's probated estate fell more dramatically than the non–wine seller's—from £2,686 to £497.

38. Harold B. Gill, "The Retail Business in Colonial Virginia" (draft MS, Colonial Williamsburg Research Report, 1984), chap. 2, pp. 1–2, 10, 25; Agreement, November 1, 1765, and Inventories, 1768–74, John and Jonathan Amory Papers, vol. 51, fol. 3, HBS; *Boston New-Letter*, June 13, 1765, June 12, 1766, January 22, 1767.

39. It is a standard result in the economics and business literature that the quantity of inventories needed to avoid running out rises less than linearly with sales volume.

40. Mifflin & Massey Ledger, fols. 17, 79, 124, 167, 170, HSP; Backus Family Account Books, vol. 22, bk. 1798, HBS; Hewes & Anthony to Brown & Benson, August 12, 1788, box 173, folder 9, Brown Papers, JCBL.

41. This and the following paragraphs draw on information gleaned from the following accounts: Samuel Neave Ledger, 1752–56, Tench Francis Ledger and Invoice Book, 1759–63, Mifflin & Massey Ledger A, 1760–63, John & Peter Chevalier Day Book, 1760–66, Benjamin Fuller Papers, 1762–99, 5 vols., Daniel Roberdeau Letter Book, 1764–71, HSP. See also John and Jonathan Amory Papers, vol. 51, fol. 3, HBS; Thomas Amory Account Book, and Philip Ammidon Letter Book, *sub* January 7, 20, February 4, 22, March 15, August 17, 1804, February 25, March 27, April 12, 1805, MHS. Ammidon had a store at 30 India Street in 1803–5. *Boston Gazette*, January 10, 1803, July 5, December 20, 1804.

42. Thomas Willson to Thomas Allen, May 16, 1768, Thomas Allen Papers, AAS.

43. *Pennsylvania Chronicle*, April 13, 1767, December 20, 1773; *Pennsylvania Journal*, September 13, 1775; *Pennsylvania Evening Post*, December 19, 1775, January 21, 1779, November 12, 1781, March 22, 1782; *Pennsylvania Gazette*, March 20, 1782, January 29, September 17, 1783, January 14, April 28, September 1, 1784, August 17, 1785, August 2, 1786, February 17, 1790; *Federal Gazette*, April 8, 1790, October 25, Novem-

ber 2, 1791, January 20, 1792; *Pennsylvania Gazette*, October 19, 1796. Meade's new house and shop were insured by the Philadelphia Contributionship in 1782. Policy, no. 650, September 30, 1782. Meade's 1775 store was fairly new, built about 1760, and considerably bigger—forty by thirty feet, three stories, with brick partition walls "to the garret floor." It was "finished inside in a good plane manor" and "painted inside & out." It was actually a double house: the more important eastern division ran along Third, and contained the entry hall, countinghouse, kitchen, and piazza; the western division facing Walnut Street contained Meade's living quarters, which were marked by a highly ornamented door. Important to Meade's growing business was the large storage building behind it: forty-two by fifteen feet, and two stories high, with a smokehouse in part of it (although the insurance would have been voided had Meade decided to use it).

44. Coats's store stood near where Front Street crossed Pegg's Run. Despite the signboard, Coats was not exclusively a dealer in sugar. See also *Pennsylvania Gazette*, June 24, September 23, 1762, August 2, 1764.

45. Doerflinger, *Vigorous Spirit*, 77. Myron H. Luke places specialization by product and area in the first decade of the nineteenth century, later than the present analysis does. "Some Characteristics of the New York Business Community, 1800–1810," *New York History* 34 (1953): 400–401.

46. A few enterprisers, like John Wister, who is discussed hereafter, had specialized before 1753, but they were unusual. On Grisley, see *Pennsylvania Gazette*, September 13, 1753. Also suggestive is William Braventon's ad two years later stating that he was commencing work as a wine cooper and a vintner (occupations which in England commonly retailed wine), having resided in London and Portugal and "acquired much experience [there] in the art and mystery of the wine trade." *Pennsylvania Gazette*, June 26, 1755. On his contemporaries Denormandie & Peirce, see *Pennsylvania Gazette*, December 24, 1761. On Street, see *Pennsylvania Gazette*, July 26, 1764; *Pennsylvania Chronicle*, January 28, 1768. In 1772, an ambitious German immigrant described himself as a clerk who "would suit a wine merchant best, as in Europe he has been a considerable time in that trade, as well for himself as others, and consequently is a good judge of wines." *Pennsylvania Gazette*, March 26, 1772. For other wine specialists' advertisements in the 1770s, see *Pennsylvania Gazette*, May 12, 17, August 21, 25, 1773, May 11, 12, November 23, 1774, March 29, May 2, 1775; *Pennsylvania Journal*, January 4, March 29, April 5, 12, 1775.

47. Postwar establishments are recorded in *Pennsylvania Gazette*, January 14, April 28, September 1, 1784; Francis White, *The Philadelphia Directory* (Philadelphia, 1785), 12, 38, 50, 76, 77; *Pennsylvania Gazette*, August 17, November 2, 1785, August 2, 1786, February 17, 1790, November 2, 1791; *Federal Gazette*, May 19, August 13, 1790; Clement Biddle, *The Philadelphia Directory* (Philadelphia, 1791); *Federal Gazette*, January 26, 1792; *Dunlap's American Daily Advertiser*, May 1, 1793; *Pennsylvania Gazette*, October 19, 1796. The first federal census for Philadelphia City and County listed no "wine merchants" in Southwark Town, but nine lived in the rest of the city. Hogan, *Prospect*, listed twelve others. The third federal census of 1810 listed no "wine merchants" (the descriptor may have fallen out of fashion), but it mentioned three owners

of "wine stores." The *Philadelphia Directory* of 1811 listed seven wine merchants, store-keepers and shopkeepers, in addition to five proprietors of "liquor stores." Subsequent references appear in *Poulson's American Daily Advertiser,* October 13, 20, 1810; *Kite's Philadelphia Directory for 1814* (Philadelphia, 1814).

48. The earliest Boston ads were for John Hamock's specialty shop. *Massachusetts Gazette,* July 10, 17, 24, 1735, July 15, 29, 1736, June 9, 15, 23, 1737; *Boston Evening Post,* June 24, July 1, 1751, May 25, 1752, May 7, 1753, March 18, April 1, 1754, April 21, 1755, July 9, 1759; *Massachusetts Gazette,* February 7, 14, 21, June 19, 26, 1760, March 2, 9, August 9, 16, 1764; *Boston Gazette,* September 7, 1761, February 9, 1767; *Boston News-Letter,* February 5, 1767. An advertisement placed by the 1765 vendue master announced auction held at a "wine cellar" on King Street. *Boston Gazette,* November 28, 1765. There were also ads for Joshua Blanchard's wine cellar on Dock Square between 1769 and 1774, in *Boston News-Letter,* August 17, September 28, 1769, October 13, 20, 27, 1774, and *Boston Evening Post,* September 28, 1774. For post-Revolution specialists, see Boston Tax Taking and Rate Books, 1800, City Hall, Boston; *The Boston Directory* (Boston, 1800, 1803, 1805, 1807); for 1800 and 1807, *Boston Gazette, Columbian Centinel, Independent Chronicle,* and *Massachusetts Mercury;* and esp. *Columbian Centinel,* July 5, 12, September 10, 1806, January 17, 28, August 29, 1807, September 29, 1808, and *Boston Gazette,* July 27, 1807; *Boston Directory* (Boston, 1807). See also Sawtelle, "Commercial Landscape," 1:90.

49. *New-York Gazette,* February 18, 25, May 26, June 16, 1760; August 13, 1761. Cf. ads for coopers and vintners: *New-York Gazette,* June 28, 1764; *Rivington's New-York Gazetteer,* September 29, 1774. The records of the storekeeper Charles Nicoll have survived and they reveal much about highly focused business in the 1760s, 1770s, and 1780s. Moreover, directories from the 1780s note the presence of specialty operations. By 1807, at least ten shopkeepers maintained establishments primarily focused on the retail of liquor, but by then directories no longer regularly counted generalists. *Longworth's Almanac* (New York, 1807).

50. In Charleston, where the overseas merchant community was smaller, James Wilson and John O'Leary were known as "wine merchants." From Store no. 4, on Colonel Beale's Wharf, in 1771, Wilson offered "Madera, Port and Lisbon wine, by the pipe, quarter cask, or dozen; Frontenac and Claret, by the dozen; Holland Gin, in cases; Jamaica, West India, and Northward Rum, by the hogshead, quarter cask, or three gallons; Coniac brandy; fine Porter, in bottles; and English white wine vinegar, fit for Pickles"; and he promised to "dispose of [them] on reasonable terms, for cash, or short credit." At his death, his cellar contained six different kinds of wine, four kinds of rum, arrack, gin, brandy, "liquors," cider, porter, and beer. Wine constituted 74 percent of the total value of all drinks listed as remaining in his bayside store; of this, Madeira comprised 54 percent. It was common for one specializing in drink to stock wines, but not necessary. Although the shopkeeper John O'Leary possessed an impressive array of liquor three decades later—some 67 percent of his estate's total value ($2,629)—he had no wine. *South Carolina Gazette,* December 5, 1771; Probate Inventories, Charleston County, September 28, 1773, bk. Z, September 22, 1804, fol. 444, bk. D, fol. 276, SCDAH.

51. Others who specialized included the Philadelphians George Meade (see *Pennsylvania Chronicle*, April 13, 1767, December 20, 1773; *Pennsylvania Journal*, September 13, 1775; *Pennsylvania Evening Post*, December 19, 1775, January 21, 1779, November 12, 1781, March 22, 1782; *Pennsylvania Gazette*, January 29, 1783, January 14, 1784, August 17, 1785, February 17, 1790; *Federal Gazette*, October 25, 1791; *Pennsylvania Gazette*, October 19, 1796), and Hugh Moore (see Newton & Gordon to him, April 1, 1783, vol. 8, fols. 18–22, NGL).

52. Record Book of the Privateer *Oliver Cromwell*, 1758–67, Clements Library, Ann Arbor; Day Book, 1758–65, Letter Book, 1765–66, Charles Nicoll Papers, NYHS; *New-York Mercury*, March 26, Aril 2, 16, August 9, October 29, November 5, 1759; *New-York Journal; or, General Advertiser*, supplement, November 13, 1766. Dructor, "New York Commercial Community," 181–82. Charles Nicoll may have wed Elena Pinyard in New York in October 1759, although more likely he wed Bersheba Bozus. During the Stamp Act crisis, he joined the Sons of Liberty. His son Matthias married Sarah Taylor in 1777 in New York. Charles died there two years later and was buried in Trinity Churchyard.

53. Day Book, 1765–68, Account Book, 1768–75, Account Book and Day Book, 1773–75, Account Book, 1777–78, Day Book, 1779–80, Charles Nicoll Papers, NYHS.

54. On the Wister family and businesses, see Caspar Wistar to Ludwig Wuester, September 25, 1737, and to Baltasar Langhaer, December 9, 1736, Wistar Family Papers, HSP, cited in Rosalind J. Beiler to David J. Hancock, September 12, 2004; Rosalind J. Beiler, "The Transatlantic World of Caspar Wistar: From Germany to America in the Eighteenth Century" (PhD diss., University of Pennsylvania, 1994), "Caspar Wistar: German-American Entrepreneur and Cultural Broker," in *Human Tradition in Colonial America*, ed. Ian Steele and Nancy Rhoden (Wilmington, 1999), 161–79, "From the Rhine Valley to the Delaware Valley: The Eighteenth-Century Transatlantic Trade Channels of Caspar Wistar," in *In Search of Peace and Prosperity: New German Settlements in Eighteenth-Century Europe and America*, ed. Hartmuth Lehman (College Park, 2000), 172–88, and "Peterstal and Wistarburg: The Transfer and Adaptation of Business Strategies in Eighteenth-Century American Glass-making," *Business and Economic History* 26 (1997): 343–53; Harry M. and Margaret B. Tinkcom, *Historic Germantown* (Philadelphia, 1955), 56–58; Milton Rubincam, "The Wistar-Wister Family," *Pennsylvania History* 20 (1953): 142–64; John W. Jordan, ed., *Colonial Families of Philadelphia* (New York, 1911), 1:257–75; *American Historical Record* 2 (1873): 51–52.

55. *Pennsylvania Gazette*, March 13, 1760, February 25, December 30, 1762, June 2, 1763, February 16, 1764, March 12, 1767, September 29, 1768, June 21, 1770, April 11, September 5, 1771, April 16, 1772, January 6, April 21, September 15, 1773, May 5, 1779, ——, 1783.

56. This and the following paragraphs draw upon Wister's business records and complementary papers: Receipt Book, 1739–46, Wister Family Collection, Winterthur Library; Receipt Book, 1749–54, Ledger, 1747–72, HSP; Policy nos. 114–18, June 1–2, 1752, no. 967, November 6, 1764, Philadelphia Contributionship, Philadelphia; Isaac Norris Sr. Ledger, 1731–40, Norris of Fairhill Papers, vol. 14, fol. 111, John Reynell Day

Book, 1732–34, fols. 66–76, John Reynell Account Book, 1738–61, fols. 76, 92, Coates Family Papers, HSP; Frey Copier Buch A, November 1773–July 1778, fols. 27, 38, 40, 79, 85, 93, 113–14, 222, Frey Papers, private collection, Middletown, PA. On Henry Keppele, see *Pennsylvania Gazette*, October 26, 1749, November 8, 1750, March 20, 1760, May 21, 1761. By 1760, Wister and Keppele were jointly handling city business for Lancaster customers. For a business profile similar to Wister's, see the Samuel Miles Account Book, 1761–62, and for later business done by his son William Wister, and Samuel Miles, see Miles & Wister Receipt Book, 1771–81, 1783–87, Winterthur Library.

57. Johann Heinrich Keppele arrived from Germany in Philadelphia in 1738, several years after Wister. Starting as a butcher, he moved into commerce. He was in Philadelphia at least in 1748–55. He ran a store in Lancaster by 1756. During the 1760s, from at least 1764, he was keeping a store opposite the prison in Market Street. He bought the Three Crowns Tavern on the Lancaster Road in 1767 (he sold it four years later). Throughout his career, he was heavily engaged in managing consignments of immigrants. On Henry Keppele, whose career deserves closer study, see R. Thomas Mayhill, *Lancaster County, Pennsylvania Deed Abstracts and Revolutionary War Oaths of Allegiance*, rev. ed. (Knightstown, 1973), 187; *Pennsylvania Gazette*, March 20, 1760, May 21, 1761, July 12, August 23, 1764, June 20, 1765, January 24, 1771; A. G. Roeber, *Palatines, Liberty, and Property: German Lutherans in Colonial British America* (Baltimore, 1993), 123–24, 246–48; Wokeck, *Trade in Strangers*, 66, 71, 81.

58. Joyce Appleby, "Value and Society," in *Colonial British America: Essays in the New History of the Early Modern Era*, ed. Jack P. Greene and J. R. Pole (Baltimore, 1984), 309.

59. Two recent scholars have highlighted the import of network formation. Bradford J. Wood, *This Remote Part of the World: Regional Formation in Lower Cape Fear, North Carolina, 1725–1775* (Columbia, 2004), chap. 4, who highlights kinship, neighborhood, and commercial connections that bound towns in the region together; Kim M. Gruenwald, *River of Enterprise: The Commercial Origins of Regional Identity in the Ohio Valley, 1790–1850* (Bloomington, 2002), 62, who argues that "fostering the growth of a town's hinterland in the West depended on a merchant's ability to create connections between his customers and the wider world of capital and goods on the Atlantic seaboard."

60. Scholarship on the country store is not as up-to-date as it deserves to be. On rural retailing and inland distribution, see Jacob Burnet, *Notes on the Early Settlement of the North-Western Territory* (Cincinnati, 1847); Jeptha R. Simms, *The Frontiersman of New York* (Albany, 1882), 1:252–53; R. H. Fleming, "Phyn, Ellice and Company of Schenectady," *Contributions to Canadian Economics* 4 (1932): 7–39; Fred M. Jones, *Middlemen in the Domestic Trade of the United States, 1800–1860* (Urbana, 1937), 44–47; Nelson V. Russell, *The British Regime in Michigan and the Old North West, 1760–1796* (Northfield, 1939); Lewis G. Atherton, *The Southern Country Store, 1800–1860* (Baton Rouge, 1949); Gerald Carson, *The Old Country Store* (New York, 1954); Lawrence A. Johnson, *Over the Counter and on the Shelf* (Rutland, 1961), and *Storekeeping in America, 1620–1920* (Rutland, 1961); Lewis G. Atherton, *The Frontier*

Merchant in Middle America (Columbia, 1971), 45–58; Stevenson Fletcher, *Pennsylvania Agriculture and Country Life, 1640–1840* (Harrisburg, 1971), 277–79; Doris D. Fanelli, "William Polk's General Store in Saint George's Delaware," *Delaware History* 19 (1981): 212–28. Several recent scholars are working to remedy the situation. Willis L. Shirk Jr., "The Robert Barber, Jr. House: A Relic of Quaker Hegemony," *Journal of the Lancaster County Historical Society* 96 (1994): 79–98. Most thought-provoking is Ann Smart Martin, "Commercial Space as Consumption Arena: Retail Stores in Early Virginia," *Perspectives in Vernacular Architecture* 7 (2000): 201–18.

61. The details of Frey's life before storekeeping are recounted in David Hancock, "The Triumphs of Mercury: Connection and Control in the Emerging Atlantic Economy," in Bailyn, *Soundings*, 112–40.

62. I do not discuss itinerants because so little has been found about them. The avoidance should not be construed as suggesting unimportance. Their means were insufficient to support the transport of wine pipes or barrels or the cost of their purchase, but the few surviving lists of their goods indicate that a small cask or a few bottles were hawked. A detailed study of land-based peddling in America remains to be written. Most historians treat itinerants only in passing. David Jaffee, "Peddlers of Progress and the Transformation of the Rural North, 1760–1860," *Journal of American History* 78 (1991): 511–35; Thorp, "Doing Business," 400; Daniel H. Usner Jr., "The Frontier Exchange Economy of the Lower Mississippi Valley in the Eighteenth Century," *WMQ*, 3rd ser., 44 (1987): 165–92; Gill, "Retail Business in Colonial Virginia"; Glenn Weaver, "Some Aspects of Early Eighteenth Century Connecticut Trade," *Connecticut Historical Society Bulletin* 22 (1957): 25; Jones, *Middlemen*, 12, 47, 51, 56, 59, 61–63. Several scholars have looked more closely: William J. Gilmore, "Peddlers and the Dissemination of Printed Material in Northern New England, 1780–1840," in *Itinerancy in New England and New York*, ed. Peter Benes (Boston, 1986), 76–89; Richard R. Beeman, ed., "Trade and Travel in Post-revolutionary Virginia: A Diary of an Itinerant Peddler, 1808–1808," *VMHB* 84 (1976): 174–88; J. R. Dolan, *The Yankee Peddlers of Early America* (New York, 1964); Richardson Wright, *Hawkers and Walkers in Early America* (Philadelphia, 1927).

63. Charles J. Farmer, "Country Stores and Frontier Exchange Systems in Southside Virginia during the Eighteenth Century" (PhD diss., University of Maryland, 1984), 2:189–90. Farmer examined 3,066 customer accounts from stores in southside Virginia between 1750 and 1800.

64. Account book of Joseph Kershaw, 1774–75, State Historical Society of Wisconsin, Madison. Born in Yorkshire in 1727, Kershaw moved to Charleston as a young man and before 1758 worked as a clerk in the saddlery business of John Laurens & Co. In that year, he began managing a store at Pine Tree Hill for William Ancrum, Lambert Lance, & Aaron Loocock, a general merchandising firm. He married the Quaker Sarah Mathis in 1763 and changed the name of Pine Tree Hill to Camden five years later. After Lance's death in 1773, he joined the Chesnut, Kershaw, Ancrum & Loocock partnership, and presided over their Camden stores and interests. An ardent patriot, he was a member of the Provincial Congress and a commissioner responsible for explaining the cause of independence to backcountry settlers. He died in 1791.

Laurens Papers, 2:18n3, 4:180–81, 208n8, 7:418; Thomas J. Kirkland and Robert M. Kennedy, *Historic Camden*, part 1, *Colonial and Revolutionary* (Columbia, 1905), 375–81; Walter B. Edgar and N. Louise Bailey, eds., *Biographical Directory of the South Carolina House of Representatives* (Columbia, 1974), 1:374–77; Joseph Ernst and Roy Merrens, "Camden's Turrets Pierce the Skies," *WMQ*, 3rd ser., 30 (1773): 549–73; Rachel N. Klein, *Unification of a Slave State: The Rise of the Planter Class in the South Carolina Backcountry, 1760–1808* (Chapel Hill, 1990); Kenneth E. Lewis, *The American Frontier: An Archaeological Study of Settlement Pattern and Process* (Orlando, 1984); Michael Woods, "The Culture of Credit in Colonial Charleston," *South Carolina Historical Magazine* 99 (1998): 358–80.

65. Baynton, Wharton & Morgan's Fort Pitt Store Day Book, 1765–67(–72), Western Pennsylvania Historical Society, Pittsburgh; Lawrence S. Thurman, "An Account Book of Baynton, Wharton, and Morgan at Fort Pitt, 1765–1767," *Western Pennsylvania Historical Magazine* 29 (1946): 141–46; George Morgan Letter Book, 1767–68, fols. 7, 14–15, 17, 22, 26, 28, 31, 35, 37, George Morgan to Dr. John Morgan, June 8, 1770, Baynton, Wharton & Morgan Papers, PSA; Thomas Merton, "An Historic Mansion," *Pittsburgh Dispatch*, December 9, 1894; *History of Allegheny County* (Pittsburgh, 1889), 1:443–44; Zadock Cramer, *The Ohio and Mississippi Navigator*, 3rd ed. (Pittsburgh, 1802), 20; Ashe, *Travels*, 1:40. The first resident agent was John Irwin; he was replaced for mishandling store funds (especially maintaining his mistress, Elizabeth Guthrie) in 1767 by John Campbell. From 1772, Morgan's store was employed as a tavern by George Semple (1729–1804), who as early as 1764 had run a tavern in the area. Mark Welchley, *Pittsburgh, Pennsylvania, Gazette Genealogical Gleanings, 1786–1820*, vol. 1 (Aliquippa, 1987). Although the first store in what became Pittsburgh, it was not the first in the area. Indian trader John Fraser sold from a storehouse nearby in 1753, and from 1754 the Ohio Company agent William Trent sold from a log house he erected on Redstone Creek, thirty-seven miles from Fort Pitt. K. P. Bayley, ed., *The Ohio Company Papers* (Arcada, 1947), 20, 27–28.

66. An allusion to Ovid's *Metamporphoses*, 2:251, on delusions of wealth built upon river transport.

67. As soon as the firm was settled in Fort Pitt, it cast its eye toward the undeveloped Illinois Country. Fort Pitt became more a way station than a destination: a depot for a trade that looked back to Europe and forward into America to a degree it had not done before. A first attempt was made in 1765, when the firm consigned roughly £20,000 in Indian goods to Fort Pitt, where they were to be broken up and reshipped down the Ohio. It was this new venture that propelled the firm to construct the store. En route to Pittsburgh, the first attempt's convoys were ambushed by the Paxton Boys and similar dissident whites, and the goods almost completely destroyed. Undaunted, the firm commissioned George Croghan to visit the Illinois, and partner George Morgan to reside at Fort Pitt and supervise the movement of goods. The venture succeeded for a number of years. Four invoices from 1767 and 1768 mark its reach. With the store as entrepôt, the firm sent out four large convoys of goods to clerk Matthew Clarkson, who had left Fort Pitt to take up residence in a store the firm had erected near Fort Chartres. The bulk of its shipments were comprised of "merchandise"—dry goods

like cloth, iron goods, and some groceries. But wine and spirits formed a not insignificant part of the shipments, constituting almost 40 percent of the value shipped (wine
alone, 7 percent). In all, the firm sent out from Fort Pitt between April 1767 and July
1768: 2,420 gallons of rum, 30 gallons West India spirit, 580 gallons of shrub, and 450
gallons of wine (Madeira and Lisbon equally). Invoice for Fort Chartres deliveries, Invoices for Fort Pitt deliveries, August 9, August–November, November 9, 1775, Baynton, Wharton & Morgan Invoice Book, PSA. The Cahokia store was made famous
by the allegation that Pontiac was beaten and killed by Peoria Indians in 1769 upon
leaving the store. Howard H. Peckham, *Pontiac and the Indian Uprising* (Princeton,
1947), 310–11.

68. Similarly slow paced was Elijah Williams' Deerfield Store in 1744, when only ten
    people per month bought liquor. Binder, "Liquid Assets," 20.

69. Nancy Cox to David Hancock, February 2, 2005; Nancy Cox, *The Complete Trades-
    man: A Study of Retailing, 1550–1820* (Aldershot, 2000), 190–91. The importance of
    the model that inhered in the Mitchells' branch system cannot be stressed enough.
    Branches next apparently arose in central Massachusetts and eastern Connecticut:
    the Dwights of Springfield placed clerks in nearby towns from 1783, as did Elijah
    Backus of Norwich about the same time. One of Backus's sons-in-law established a
    store in Marietta, Ohio, in 1789 and branches in Zanesville and Waterford, Ohio. The
    branches in Ohio were seldom staffed by family members, but by arm's-length busi-
    ness acquaintances. In this sense, the Mitchells, working thus nearly two decades be-
    fore, blazed a trail. Margaret E. Martin, *Merchants and Trade of the Connecticut River
    Valley, 1750–1820* (Northampton, 1939), 16, 74–101, 110; Atherton, *Frontier Merchant*,
    45–58; Bruce Daniels, *The Connecticut Town* (Middletown, 1979), 147–48; Gruen-
    wald, *River of Enterprise*, 57–59, 97.

70. Sequestered John Mitchell Papers, 1762–81, PSA. It is not clear when or where
    Mitchell was born. He may have been the son of Abraham and Jane Mitchell. More
    likely, he was the son of the Scotsman Abraham Mitchell (1710–88) and Sarah Robins,
    who married in 1734 in Philadelphia. The most likely year of John's birth is 1741. At any
    rate, John had at least three, maybe four brothers, all of whom worked in Philadel-
    phia after 1751: Hugh, Randle, Alexander, and perhaps Abraham. John married Mary
    Davie and they had several children: Andrew, Mary, and perhaps James. Randle mar-
    ried Jane Macky, and they had a son, James. In 1759 and 1760, Randle was a partner of
    Abraham Usher in a firm that dealt in European and India goods. By 1762, John and
    Randle joined John Malcolm to manage the "South Sugar House." Hannah B. Roach,
    comp., *Colonial Philadelphians* (Philadelphia, 1999), 83, 86, 115; F. Edward Wright,
    ed., *Abstracts of Philadelphia County, Pennsylvania Wills, 1763–1784* (Philadelphia,
    1998), nos. 1594, 1674, and 1895, . . . , 1777–1790 (2004), nos. 2385, 2424, 2538, and
    2548, and . . . , 1790–1802 (1998) *sub* Andrew Caldwell; *Pennsylvania Gazette*, Janu-
    ary 1, May 30, 1751, January 2, September 20, 1753, February 1, 1759, October 4, 1759,
    September 18, 1760, March 4, 1762, April 21, November 24, 1763, August 9, 16, 1764,
    June 13, 1765, June 26, 1766, June 23, 30, 1768.

71. On plans to open a new store in Caernarvon, see John Taylor to John Mitchell,
    March 5, May 10, 31, June 7, 1773, John Mitchell Papers, PSA. On the dissolution of

the Allentown partnership, see January 7, 1774, ibid. The records of the Middletown store bought from George Frey and managed by John Williams have survived. The store was well financed. In 1773, Williams agreed with John and Randle Mitchell of Philadelphia to erect a store in Middletown. Williams carried the stuff found in most general stores: sugar, salt, augers, knives, jewelry, thread, tea, linen, coffee, tobacco, combs, fabrics, glass panes, and frying pans. John Williams Day Book and Ledger, March 1773—March 1774, APS. In the fairly typical month of April 1774, the store was open thirteen days. Then, he sold to 281 different items to 101 buyers, at a daily average rate of 22 different items to 8 purchasers. Taking into consideration their return, there were in fact only 60 different customers at Williams's Middletown store, and almost all of them lived in or around Middletown. The few nonlocal customers were storekeepers, like Matthew Hollenbaugh, who came from Lebanon in search of three double-flint half-pint tumblers, three single-flint half-pint tumblers, six wineglasses, two half-pint decanters, three gill glasses, two pint decanters, and seven gallon bottles. It was a short-lived operation: the Mitchells withdrew their support in 1773, Williams closed up shop, and the store was offered for sale in 1774. *Pennsylvania Gazette*, January 5, 1774.

72. *Pennsylvania Gazette*, April 14, 1773, February 2, 1774.

73. Peter Anspach to John Mitchell, June 27, 1774, Charles Hamilton to John Mitchell, September 23, 1774, John Mitchell Papers, PSA. Liquor was commonly found in rural stores. See Advertisements of S. & S. Salisbury, Worcester, Massachusetts, Greene & Lincoln, Worcester, and Daniel Waldo, Lancaster, Massachusetts, August 6, 20, November 11, 1778, *Massachusetts Spy*; Fanelli, "William Polk's General Store," 218. Still, not all rural stores stocked it. John Cameron Ledger, 1767–69, Wistar Family Papers, HSP.

74. Book of Goods, 1773, John Reynolds to John Mitchell, August 11, 1772, Harris Donaldson to John Mitchell, May 5, 1774, John Mitchell Papers, PSA.

75. John Taylor to John Mitchell, August 15, 16, 1773, George Irwin to John Mitchell, December 1, 1773, John Williams to John Mitchell, June 29, 1774, John Mitchell Papers, PSA.

76. Ibid.

77. Murray & Connelly to John Mitchell, November 8, 1772, February 2, 15, 1773, Charles Hamilton to John Mitchell, April 15, 1774, John Mitchell Papers, PSA.

78. *Pennsylvania Gazette*, November 26, 1774; Ledger, 1770–72, fols. 54, 60, John Mitchell Papers, PSA; John Williams Day Book, 1773–74, APS.

79. John Mitchell's subsequent career is harder to reconstitute. In March 1776, Mitchell offered his services to the Pennsylvania Committee of Safety and was appointed "Muster Master of the Naval Armaments and to the Artillery of Pennsylvania." During the war, Mitchell's firm supplied the American army and navy with provisions, while Mitchell personally served as colonel in the state militia, a commissary of its artillery troops, a muster master of the Pennsylvania navy from 1776, and a deputy quartermaster general in the Continental Army from 1778. British occupation forced him to vacate his store. When the British evacuated Philadelphia in June 1778, he returned there, lived in rented quarters, and served for two years as a liaison between

Congress and General Nathanael Greene. In 1781, he was granted the Masonic degree of inspector. Most likely, Mitchell left Pennsylvania in the wake of financial disaster (he told George Washington of having had "bad Success in Trade") and, helped by Masonic and army friends, he relocated in Charleston, South Carolina. He was a justice of the peace of the Charleston District by 1784 and a constable in 1785, when he was also a partner of one Donnom at 23 Bay Street. Between 1789 and 1791, he hounded George Washington for an appointment in the federal government, but to no avail. His papers were sequestered between 1796 and 1800 during proceedings over the insolvencies of Pennsylvania comptroller John Nicholson and fellow land speculators. A Col. John Mitchell, reputedly the deputy quartermaster general, died there in 1826, at the age of eighty-five. For subsequent activities, see *Pennsylvania Gazette*, May 2, April 18, October 10, 1771, April 16, October 28, November 11, 1772, March 31, November 10, 1773, April 20, 1774, October 13, November 24, 1784; *Pennsylvania Chronicle*, October 14, 1771, October 3, 1772; *Pennsylvania Evening Post*, July 30, 1776, January 17, July 4, August 1, 1778, Richard K. Showman, ed., *The Papers of General Nathanael Greene*, vol. 2 (Chapel Hill, 1980), 387–89, 460–61, vol. 3 (1983), 132, 273, 287, 303–11, 462, 470, 474, 477; *Washington Papers*, Presidential Series, vol. 2 (1987), 347–48, vol. 6 (1996), 101, vol. 7 (1998), 389; John Tobler, *The South-Carolina and Georgia Almanack* (Charleston, 1784), and . . . , 1785 (Charleston, 1785); *South-Carolina Gazette*, May 15, June 19, 1784; John Milligan, *The Charleston Directory* (Charleston, 1790), 26; *Charleston News and Courier*, January 27, 1826.

80. John Reynolds to John Mitchell, March 23, 1772, April 13, 1773, Peter Anspach to John Mitchell, April 10, May 8, 1774, John Mitchell Papers, PSA.

81. Murray & Connelly to John Mitchell, November 8, 1772, Februrary 2, 15, 1773, Charles Hamilton to John Mitchell, April 15, 1774, John Mitchell Papers, PSA.

82. Thomas Hartly to John Mitchell, February 1775, Charles Hamilton to John Mitchell, July 18, 1775 John Mitchell Papers, PSA.

83. Charles Hamilton to John Mitchell, November 1772, April 1774, June 9, 1774, Wilson & Falconar to John Mitchell, November 23, 1774, John Mitchell Papers, PSA.

84. "Agent" is not unproblematic, of course. The prevailing modern definition implies doing work for another individual; the common early modern definition denoted a "material cause or instrumentality whereby effects" were "produced," with or without the implication of "a rational employer or contriver" (*Oxford English Dictionary*, 2nd ed. [1989], s.v. "agent"). It is the latter sense that it is deployed here.

85. Cunningham, *Letters and Diary of John Rowe*, 67, 100; Drake, *Old Boston Taverns*, 73.

86. Woodruff Smith, *Consumption and the Making of Respectability, 1600–1800* (New York, 2002), 147.

87. Salinger, *Taverns*, 242; Jürgen Habermas, *The Structural Transformation of the Public Sphere*, trans. Frederick Lawrence (Cambridge, 1992); Smith, *Consumption*, 151; David S. Shields, *Civil Tongues and Polite Letters in British America* (Chapel Hill, 1997), xv–xvi.

88. Day Books 2 (1773–74) and 16 (1800–1801), and Ledgers D (1773–74) and K (1797–1805), Frey Papers, private collection, Middletown, PA. Cf. Account book of Joseph

Kershaw, 1774–75, State Historical Society of Wisconsin, Madison; Gruenwald, *River of Enterprise*, 50–53, 97–98.

CHAPTER 9. "ARTICLES OF NOURISHMENT BOTH MUNDANE AND USEFUL"

1. These and the following paragraphs draw upon William Black, "The Journal of William Black, 1744," *PMHB* 1 (1877): 117–32, 233–49, 404–19, 2 (1878): 40–49. Later, he was a merchant in Manchester, Virginia, and a planter near Richmond.
2. Jeremy Belknap, *History of New Hampshire* (Boston, 1792), 3:263.
3. Perhaps Black's Americans loved their liquor excessively and, by later standards, paid too "much homage to Bacchus." A "great drinking of Madeira Wine" was "the Custom" in New York in the 1740s, for instance, and Benjamin Franklin thought nothing of drinking two bottles of it at night in the 1780s. Benjamin Franklin, *The Autobiography and Other Writings*, ed. L. Jesse Lemisch (New York, 1961), 122; Franklin to William Strahan, February 16, 1784, in Smyth, *Writings*, 9:172. William Rorabaugh was the first historian to address head-on the matter of how much Americans drank in a groundbreaking study published in 1979, suggestively entitled *The Alcoholic Republic*. His analysis shaped all subsequent interpretations of drinking and the effect of independence on drinking behavior. W. J. Rorabaugh, *The Alcoholic Republic: An American Tradition* (New York, 1979), 7, 10, 11, 18–19, 232–33; M. E. Lender and J. K. Martin, *Drinking in America* (New York, 1982), 36; Andrew Barr, *Drink: A Social History of America* (New York, 1999); Cf. Dennis Kincaid, *British Social Life in India, 1608–1937*, 2nd ed. (London, 1973), 21.

   As a question of history, the matter is irresolvable. Statistical precision is impossible: before 1789, the data are thin and unconvincing. The evidence does not support a conclusion that Americans drank less when they were colonists than when independent. "Americans drank not only any place but also any time," and "on all occasions," before the Revolution and after. A lot of wine, spirits, and other alcoholic beverages were consumed from 1640 to 1775, and roughly the same amount per capita afterward, although the share in each category of drink shifted over time and the perception of overindulgence as a problem intensified. Given the data, nothing more can be claimed. Nor should it be: there is something problematic in tying a social and cultural institution like drinking and trouble with it to a mythical originating moment of rupture. So connecting induces a kind of "genesis amnesia" that whitewashes or ignores the particular and contingent circumstances, forces, and accidents in history and attributes change to revolutionary birth.
4. Warner Schlote, *British Overseas Trade from 1700 to the 1930s* (Oxford, 1952), 41–50; Maxine Berg, *The Age of Manufactures: Industry, Innovation, and Work in Britain, 1700–1820* (Oxford, 1985), 28–29, 38–40, 274–78; Brewer, *Sinews of Power*, 184–85; Neil McKendrick, "The Consumer Revolution of Eighteenth-Century England," in *The Birth of a Consumer Society*, ed. McKendrick et al. (Bloomington, 1982), 99–134; Christine Macleod, *Inventing the Industrial Revolution: The English Patent System, 1660–1800* (Cambridge, 1988); Mui and Mui, *Shops and Shopkeeping*.

5. Richard L. Bushman, "Shopping and Advertising in Colonial America," 233; Timothy H. Breen, "'Baubles of Britain,'" 452; Cary Carson, "The Consumer Revolution in Colonial British America: Why Demand?,"604–5, all in *Of Consuming Interests: The Style of Life in the Eighteenth Century.* ed. Cary Carson, Ronald Hoffman, and Peter J. Albert, ed. (Charlottesville, 1994).

6. One of the more important unasked questions concerns non–British-imperial imports into English-speaking America, like wine. Carole Shammas, "The Revolutionary Impact of the European Demand for Tropical Goods," in McCusker and Morgan, *Early Modern Atlantic Economy*, 165–72. Few commodity studies make sense of foreign foods and drinks. Apart from Shammas's discussion, see Mintz, *Sweetness*; and James Walvin, *Fruits of Empire: Exotic Produce and British Taste, 1660–1800* (New York, 1997).

7. The idea of the public sphere was introduced by Jürgen Habermas, in *Strukturwandel der Öffentlichkeit* (Neuwied, 1965), trans. by Thomas Burger as *The Structural Transformation of the Public Sphere: An Inquiry into a Category of Bourgeois Society* (Cambridge, MA, 1989). Yet, to the contrary, see Oskar Negt and Alexander Kluge, *Public Sphere and Experience: Toward an Analysis of the Bourgeois and Proletarian Public Sphere*, trans. Peter Labanyi et al. (Minneapolis, 1993).

8. With respect to consumer identity, some scholars, like Daniel Miller, Grant Mc-Cracken, and Russell Belk, have suggested that goods help project or mark identity; others, like Pierre Bourdieu, suggest that goods are part of identity; still others, like Jean Baudrillard, argue that goods actually equal identity and thus make identity superficial or inconsequential. Craig Clunas, "Modernity, Global and Local: Consumption and the Rise of the West," *AHR* 104 (1999): 1497–1511; Daniel Miller, *Material Culture and Mass Consumption* (Oxford, 1987), 128; Grant McCracken, *Culture and Consumption* (Bloomington, 1988), 88, 98; Russell W. Belk, "Possessions and the Extended Self," in *Consumption*, ed. Daniel Miller (London, 2001), 1:203–4; Pierre Bourdieu, *Distinction: A Social Critique of the Judgement of Taste* (Cambridge, 1984); Jean Baudrillard, *Simulations*, trans. Paul Foss (New York, 1983), 4, 25, 102.

9. Curiously, the links between buying and using are usually addressed in the analysis of probate inventories, when the analyst admits knowing almost nothing about how goods are acquired, appreciated, or used; all he or she knows is that they were owned. Little more is discussed, because more often than not he or she is not concerned with macroeconomic matters.

10. Sir Hugh Plat, *Delightes for Ladies* (London, 1602), title page; Gervase Markham, *Countrey Contentments; or, The English Huswife* (London, 1623), 142–43; Giles Rose, *A Perfect School of Instructions for the Officers of the Mouth* (London, 1682), 1, 11–14, 108–24. On the "male exclusivity" of inns and coffeehouses, see Shields, *Civil Tongues*, 59; Walvin, *Fruits of Empire*, 40. A similar metropolitan masculinization of production occurred in distilling, brewing, and cidering. Sarah Hand Meacham, "From Women's Province to Men's Domain: Gender, Technology, and Alcohol in the Chesapeake, 1690 to 1800" (PhD diss., University of Virginia, 2003), 38–41, 164.

11. Account with Dawes & Knight, 1667/78–1680, *sub* July 23, 1668, folder 14, Robert Gibbs MSS, AAS; Penn to Logan, 1701, in *Correspondence between William Penn and*

James Logan, ed. Deborah Logan and Edward Armstrong (Philadelphia, 1870), 1:43; Elizabeth Coates Receipt Book, 1702–53, CPP; John Harris Sr. Account Book, 1749–75, fol. 59, John Harris Jr. Recipt Book, 1775–91, fol. 32, HSP; *Carter Diary*, 1:443–44, 523–24, 2:781, 824, 950–51; Hunter D. Farish, ed., *Journal and Letters of Philip Vickers Fithian, a Planation Tutor of the Old Dominion, 1773–1774* (Charlottesville, 1947), 75; *Washington Papers*, Colonial Series, vol. 6 (1988), 235, 248–49; R. W. G. Vail, ed., "A Dinner at Mount Vernon," *New-York Historical Society Quarterly* 31 (1947): 75; Patricia B. Schmit, ed., *Eleanor Parke Custis Lewis's Housekeeping Book* (New Orleans, 1982), 2.

12. Webber, "Journal of Robert Pringle, 21–23, 24–30, 93–112. See also: *Carter Diary*, 1:269, 322, 2:640, 1134; *Records of Purchases at the King George Hotel*, 60, 65, 86, 124; Ledger Book "B," 1766–73, fol. 206, Frey Papers, private collection, Middletown, PA; Allen Day Book, 1771–72, fol. 1, AAS; Cynthia Kierner, "Hospitality, Sociability, and Gender in the Southern Colonies," *Journal of Southern History* 62 (1996): 454–55.

13. Not all decedents' estates were probated, and not all probated estates were inventoried. The old and the wealthy are disproportionately represented. Moreover, when they were inventoried, the lists did not always contain a full or accurate asset reporting. There was no agreement of what constituted a full list. In New England, land was reported and valued, but elsewhere irregularly so. Nor was there any consensus on what constituted fair valuation for items (whether the standard be market, statute, or custom). In some places, legacies left to a widow often escaped the attention of inventory takers. Drink was often excluded from a listing and there is little discussion of why. The silence is probably attributable to local custom: wine may have been lumped among perishables and regarded as belonging by right to survivors, despite the fact that wine generally lasted longer than most food. Probably also key is the fact that inventories tilt evidence toward the sorts of drink people bought in bulk and were expected to store, and away from local supplies needing little cellarage. Whatever the causes, such imperfections distort the distribution of wealth by ignoring the poor or property-less, as well as underrepresenting the value (even existence) of comestibles. On probate analysis and its uses, see Gloria L. Main, "The Correction of Biases in Colonial American Probate Records," *Historical Methods Newsletter* 8 (1974): 10–28; Carole Shammas, "Constructing a Wealth Distribution from Probate Records," *Journal of Interdisciplinary History* 9 (1978): 297–307; Alice H. Jones, "Estimating Wealth of the Living from a Probate Sample," *Journal of Interdisciplinary History* 13 (1982): 273–300; Peter Benes et al., eds., *Early American Probate Inventories* (Dublin, NH, 1987).

14. The construction of the database analyzed here operated on three principles. First, four colonies were selected, largely on the basis of geographical distribution: Massachusetts, New York, South Carolina, and Jamaica. Second, within two of those colonies, a metropolitan county (that housed the seat of government) and a less-developed interior county were selected: for Massachusetts, Suffolk and Hampshire; for New York, New York and Albany. County officials in these two colonies were responsible for the recording of testamentary dispositions, probate inventories, and related deeds. In South Carolina and Jamaica, colony officials were responsible for collecting and

collating such records; sometimes they noted the residence of the decedent, but sometimes not. As a result, it is not always possible to distinguish metropolitan from backcountry decedents. Accordingly, the samples for Carolina and Jamaica were constructed to include inventoried decedents from all counties and parishes. For each jurisdiction, a database of all decedents whose estates were inventoried was compiled for two periods—a decade or half decade near the beginning of the century, and a decade or half decade near the end. Since the survival of probate records has not been uniform across colonies, exact overlap of all four studied regions was impossible to effect. For instance, the Massachusetts county records were culled for the years 1703–7 and 1803–7; New York probe inventories were culled for 1703–12 and 1790–99. Jamaica records are spottier. The earliest years one could derive good data for were 1700–1705 and 1713–16; intervening years are inaccessible. Similarly, since Carolina probates were not recorded until the 1730s; the first decade surveyed is 1732–41. Thus, the data are scattered across time, although enough overlaps have occurred to show trends across regions.

15. On cider consumption and production in the Chesapeake, see Meacham, "From Women's Province," chaps. 1–2.

16. In Pennsylvania, the market prices for a gallon of Madeira and West India rum closely approached each another. Elsewhere, spirits were sometimes priced slightly higher than wine, which makes sense given the higher alcohol content per volume (rum has twice the content of Madeira). The cheapest wines could be 50 percent more expensive than the strongest beers. In Virginia, court-set rates for tavern drinks allowed charging the same for a gallon of rum as for a gallon of Iberian wine, and slightly more for a gallon of rum than for one of French wine. In Maryland, French wine was cheaper by one-third than Madeira and Port, and the latter two were cheaper by one-fourth than imported rum, although, in a twist, rum was cheaper by one-fifth than Malaga and Canary. From colony to colony, there was much variance. Yet, in each, some wines were within the reach of those with money to spend. Whether they could spend it was another matter, for choice was also a function of the innkeeper's selection and inventory, local drinkers' tastes, and the liquor's survival. Some establishments carried no wine. For those for whom just such a tavern was their only source of alcohol, the question of wine selection was moot. William Whitmore, ed., *The Colonial Laws of Massachusetts, Reprinted from the Edition of 1672, with Supplements through 1686* (Boston, 1887), 68–69, 80–82, 251; *The Early Records of the Town of Providence* (Providence, 1892–1915), 2:94; Gallus Thomann, *Colonial Liquor Laws* (New York, 1887), 74, 86–89; 287–88; *The Colonial Laws of New York* (Albany, 1894), 1:39, 100–101, 105–6; William W. Hening, ed., *The Statutes-at-Large* (Philadelphia, 1823), 1:229, 287, 350, 521, 2:234, 263, 287–88, 297, 393, 3:395–400, 6:71–76; York County Deed Books, vol. 13, fols. 61, 211, 1693, 1706/7, 1708/9, State Library of Virginia.

17. David Hancock, "The Price of Wine" (paper presented at the XXth International Economic History Association Congress, Buenos Aires, 2002).

18. Jamaica was one of the exceptions to this "rule."

19. The varieties of wine in New York inventories rose from one to thirteen, but that is partly because "Made Here A" was included—what today one might consider a "Madeira-

flavored beverage"—alongside true wine. The Albany data are aberrant: no wines and spirits appeared. But this cannot have been the case, surely, given the Dutchman's well-known penchant for drink and the numerous references to wine being consumed in Albany's homes and taverns, to spirits being used in its Indian and skin trade, or to cider being made in its vicinity. The absence of drink is probably attributable to an undisclosed recording practice of omitting drinks from probate inventories: perhaps, Albany men and women thought of wine, like food, as perishable, and so more properly the property of the immediate family than of the heir; or perhaps it was just an unstated local convention not to record wine. It is of course always possible that the Dutch in Albany did not customarily keep wine in large amounts—perhaps they drank most alcoholic drinks at taverns and bought and kept only enough for short-run consumption, and that whatever was held at the time of death was used up at the funeral of the deceased. Reinforcing the reason for such custom would be the fact that, in New York, probate inventories were drawn up for only two types of decedents: those who died without a will, largely the poorer sort in society; and those who died with a will but requested an accounting of the property.

20. William Eddis, *Letters from America*, ed. Aubrey C. Land (Cambridge, 1969), 57–58. Hugh Jones had written much the same of Virginia in 1720. *The Present State of Virginia* (London, 1724), 80. Cf. William Smith, *The History of the Late Province of New-York* (New York, 1829), 277.

21. Richard L. Bushman, "American High-Style and Vernacular Cultures," in *Colonial British America: Essays in the New History of the Early Modern Era*, ed. Jack P. Greene and J. R. Pole (Baltimore, 1984), 366. See also the influential work of T. H. Breen, who supports the reigning Anglicization paradigm but argues that Americans "only slowly integrated into the British consumer economy" and that the "key decade" was the 1740s—"An Empire of Goods: The Anglicization of Colonial America, 1690–1776," *Journal of British Studies* 25 (1986): 486, and "'Baubles of Britain': The American and Consumer Revolutions of the Eighteenth Century," *Past and Present* 119 (1988): 85, 90, 97, 103—and the monumental summary by Carson, "Why Demand?" in Carson, Hoffman, and Albert, *Of Consuming Interests*, 687–91, cf. 26, 41, 104, 130, 134, 144, 201–2, 257–60, 275–81, 404, 435, 457.

22. *Pennsylvania Gazette*, May 14, 1730, June 24, 1731; [A Lady of Distinction], *The Mirror of the Graces; or, The English Lady's Costume* (New York, 1813), 40, 26–27, 109–10, 214–19.

23. *Pennsylvania Gazette*, March 4, 1755.

24. I Timothy 5:23; *Franklin Papers*, 1:352, 6:339, 7:279, 11:537, 20:403–4. On medicinal uses generally, see Sarah E. Williams, "The Use of Beverage Alcohol as Medicine, 1790–1860," *Journal of Studies on Alcohol* 41 (1980): 545, 548; Salvatore P. Lucia, *A History of Wine as Therapy* (Philadelphia, 1963), 155–73; Francis R. Packard, *History of Medicine in the United States* (New York, 1963), 1:571–77. Roy Porter, "The Drinking Man's Disease: The Pre-history of Alcoholism in Georgian Britain," *British Journal of Addiction* 80 (1985): 387–89, provides a good overview of British medical opinion.

25. *Laurens Papers*, 8:484, 601, 640, 12:274; Elaine F. Crane, ed., *The Diary of Elizabeth Drinker* (Boston, 1991), 2:1526, 1540; Charles E. Nash, *The History of Augusta*

(Augusta, 1904), 242, 319, 413. See also Captain Peter Drake, *Amiable Renegade: The Memoirs of Captain Peter Drake* (Stanford, 1960), 278; Frye Bayley, "Reminiscences of Colonel Frye Bayley of Newbury and Peacham, Vermont, 1763–1778," *Collections of the Vermont Historical Society* 4 (1943): 36; L. H. Butterfield, ed., *The Book of Abigail and John: Selected Letters of The Adams Family, 1762–1784* (Cambridge, MA, 1975), 151; R. W. Chapman, ed., *The Letters of Samuel Johnson* (Oxford, 1952), 82. On folk practice, see Williams, "Use," 555–58, 563. Popular manuals include William Buchan, *Domestic Medicine*, 16th ed. (London, 1799); Samuel Stearns, *The American Herbal; or, Materia Medica* (Walpole, 1801); Joseph Townsend, *Elements of Therapeutics; or, A Guide to Health*, 2nd ed. (Boston, 1807); James Ewell, *The Planters and Mariners Medical Companion* (Baltimore, 1807). Cf. instances of using wine as medicine in the novels of the American writer Susanna Rowson: *Trials of the Human Heart* (Philadelphia, 1795), 6, and *Charlotte Temple* (Philadelphia, 1797), 132.

26. Elizabeth Coates Receipt Book, 1702–53, CPP; *Carter Diary*, 1:142, 154–55, 168, 170, 173, 216, 218, 220, 236, 2:824–25, 829, 1036, and, on the planting of vines, 1:258, 276, 2:1134–135. Writing of the treatment of slaves in St. Croix in 1788–91, Hans West noted that "Doctor, midwife, medicine, Madeira wine, sago, arrowroot, all are at the disposal of the Negro patient from the moment the illness manifests itself." On another St. Croix estate, slaves received "a whole cask of Madeira wine, or about 400 bottles" during one fever. Hans West, "Description of St. Croix," in *The Kamina Folk: Slavery and Slave Life in the Danish West Indies*, ed. George F. Tyson and Arnold R. Highfield (St. Thomas, 1994), 135, 148. On giving Port to horses, see John Bartlet, *The Gentleman's Farriery* (London, 1753).

27. The importance of knowing how to make wines "equal that of Europe" was stressed early in the century in *The Way to Get Wealth* (London, 1702). For English receipt books and cookbooks, see Elizabeth Raper Grant, *The Receipt Book of Elizabeth Raper* [c. 1756–70] (Soho, 1924); Alice Smith, *Art of Cookery* (London, 1758); Elizabeth Raffald, *The Experienced English Housewife* (Manchester, 1769); Susannah Carter, *The Frugal Housewife* (London, 1772); *Lady's Magazine; or, Entertaining Companion for the Fair Sex* 5 (July 1775): 345–46, (September 1775): 473–74; Richard Briggs, *The English Art of Cookery*, 3rd ed. (London, 1794). For American recipes and cookbooks, see Benjamin Franklin, *Poor Richard*, 1735 (Philadelphia, 1735), and *Poor Richard's Almanack* (Philadelphia, 1757; New York, 1784; Boston, 1806); Richard J. Hooker, ed., *A Colonial Plantation Cookbook: The Receipt Book of Harriott Pinckney Horry*, 1770 (Columbia, 1984), 60; Karen Hess, ed., *Martha Washington's Booke of Cookery* (New York, 1981); Susan Berry, "Household Cookery, Arithmetic & Painting" (c. 1793), MSS Collection, Clements Library, Ann Arbor; Amelia Simmons, *American Cookery*, ed. Mary T. Wilson (Hartford, 1796), 17, 20–25, 28, 30, 32–37, 45. Meacham argues that the production of made wines became masculinized after 1760. "From Women's Province," 161–65. The evidence is less than convincing, but it is clear instructions to men on how to make wine with the aid of technology increased in the late eighteenth century.

28. Byrd, *Secret Diary*, 110; "William Logan's Journal of a Journey to Georgia, 1745," *PMHB* 36 (1912): 5–6; *Carter Diary*, 1:525, 2:824; Fithian, *Journal*, 191; John Hunter,

"An Account of a Visit Made to Washington at Mount Vernon . . . 1785," *PMHB* 17 (1893): 78–79; Joshua Brookes, "A Dinner at Mount Vernon," ed. R. W. G. Vail, *New-York Historical Society Quarterly* 31 (1947): 73, 75.

29. Byrd, *Secret Diary*, 337.

30. *Carter Diary*, 1:252–55, 259, 263, 270, 322, 571, 2:671–72, 737, 781, 824, 1037–60.

31. Barthélmy Faujas de St. Fond, *A Journey through England and Scotland to the Hebrides in 1784*, ed. Sir Archibald Geikie (Glasgow, 1907), 1:37–38; Steven Blankaart, *De borgerlyke tafel* (Amsterdam, 1683); Erasmus Jones, *The Man of Manners; or, Plebeian Polish'd*, 2nd ed. (London, 1737), 678–79; Simmons, *American Cookery*, 3–4; E. Spencer, *The Modern Cook* (Newcastle, 1788), 136–38; Carter, *Frugal Housewife* (1795), 169–80.

32. I would like to thank Jack Larkin for bringing the details of this painting to my attention; it is discussed in David W. Conroy, *In Public Houses: Drink and the Revolution of Authority in Colonial Massachusetts* (Chapel Hill, 1995), 212–13.

33. Evangeline W. and Charles M. Andrews, eds., *Jonathan Dickinson's Journal; or, God's Protecting Providence* (New Haven, 1945), 80; Wayne Andrews, ed., "The Travel Diary of Dr. Benjamin Bullivant," *New-York Historical Society Quarterly* 40 (1956): 61; Black, "Journal," 1:124, 126, 242–43. Drink also marked the close of hospitality on departure. Not accidentally did Samuel Sewall take "a glass of good Madera" with a brother and friends before embarking for London in 1688. Samuel Sewall, "Diary," *Collections of the Massachusetts Historical Society*, 5th ser., vol. 6 (1879): 184.

34. Henry Laurens to John Laurens, September 21, 1779, in *Laurens Papers*, 15:173; Byrd, *Secret Diary*, 5, 54, 80, 106, 125, 165, 188, 190, 265.

35. Kenneth and Anna Roberts, eds., *Moreau de St. Mery's American Journey [1793–1798]* (New York, 1947), 265–66; Samuel Johnston to Henry Jackson, September 29, 1778, in David Fowler, ed., *Guide to the Sol Feinstone Collection of the David Library of the American Revolution* (Washington Crossing, 1994), no. 681; Marquis de Chastellux, *Travels in North America in the Years 1780, 1781 and 1782* (Chapel Hill, 1963), 1:109, 153; Francesco dal Verme, Conte di Bobbio, *Seeing America and Its Great Men*, trans. Elizabeth Cometti (Charlottesville, 1969), 54–55, 57–59; Fithian, *Journal*, 29. Cf. William Priest, *Travels in the United States of America* (London, 1802), 33; Donald Fraser, *The History of Man*, 1st Am. ed. from 3rd Eu. ed. (New York, 1806), 354–56. This supposedly distinctive American practice of drinking after dinner was decidedly similar to British practice by 1789. Johann Wilhelm von Archenholz, *A Picture of England* (London, 1789), 201.

36. Ann Wells Rutledge, "After the Cloth Was Removed," *Winterthur Portfolio* 4 (1968): 49–51. It now hangs in the Henry Francis du Pont Winterthur Museum. Roupell's portrait bears similarity to two later paintings: *The Toast* (1810–15), Nugent Collection, Newburgh, IN (plate 12); Henry Sargent, *Dinner Party* (1821), Museum of Fine Arts, Boston.

37. Felicity Heal, "The Idea of Hospitality in Early Modern England," *Past and Present* 102 (1984): 67, 81.

38. Elite southern women participated in domestic hospitality rituals, and their presence "and the virtues that contemporaries increasingly associated with idealized femininity

... contributed to the development of the public and quasi-public rituals of sociability." Kierner, "Hospitality," 450.

39. "The Sideboard," in [Arnaud Berquin], The Looking-Glass for the Mind; or, Intellectual Mirror (New York, 1804). Cf. H. A. C., The History of Mother Twaddle (Philadelphia, 1809); Rowson, Charlotte Temple, 142; Martha Read, Margaretta (Philadelphia, 1807), 25; The Parlour Companion (Baltimore, 1810), 188; Galateo; or, A Treatise on Politeness and Delicacy of Manners (Baltimore, 1811), 191–93; [A Lady of Distinction], Kelroy (Philadelphia, 1815), 217.

40. Blankaart, Tafel, 81; Sewall, "Diary," 23; Byrd, Secret Diary, 11, 28; Crane, Diary of Elizabeth Drinker, 2:1526–1540; Webber, "Journal of Robert Pringle," 106; Black, "Journal," 1:416; Carter Diary, 1:525, 2:1001; Theodore G. Tappert and John W. Doberstein, trans., The Journals of Henry Melchior Muhlenberg (Philadelphia, 1942), 1:100, 119; Eugene P. Chase, ed., Our Revolutionary Forefathers: The Letters of François, Marquis de Barbé-Marbois (New York, 1929), 123; Philadelphia Monthly Meeting—Arch Street, Minutes, 1765–71, Quaker Collection, Haverford College Library, Haverford, PA; Baron Cromot du Bourg, "Diary of a French Officer," Magazine of American History 3 (1880–81): 209; Benjamin Rush to John Adams, 1808, cited in Louis P. Masur, Rites of Execution: Capital Punishment and the Transformation of American Culture, 1776–1865 (New York, 1989), 90–91; James M. Adair, An Essay on Diet and Regimen, 2nd ed. (London, 1812), 50. For an example of drinking wine at teatime in English fiction, see Eliza Fowler Haywood's History of Jemmy and Jenny Jessamy (London, 1753), 3:151–52. See also Rodris Roth, "Tea Drinking in 18th-Century America: Its Etiquette and Equipage," Contributions from the Museum of History and Technology 14 (1963): 64; Kross, "'If You Will Not Drink,'" 38–40, 47.

41. Heal, "Idea," 85. Arguing that "the offering of hospitality demonstrated both the power and beneficence of these elites whose largesse, in turn, ideally strengthened ties of patronage and dependence between superiors and presumed inferiors," as Kierner does, misses much of what was going on in the eighteenth century. "Hospitality," 451. While the need for patronage and deference may have been great in the South, such an emphasis there and everywhere ignores the fact that most acts of domestic hospitality were not between different orders, as they might have been in earlier centuries à la Heal, but between equals or near equals.

42. This line of inquiry is especially associated with the sociologist Jürgen Habermas. Note 7, above.

43. Deuteronomy 32:14. Mack P. Holt sketches "the intricate links between spirituality and material life" in early modern Burgundy, paying close attention to the liturgical use of wine. "Wine, Life, and Death in Early Modern Burgundy," Food and Foodways 8 (1999): 73–98. Cf. Robert C. Fuller, "Wine, Symbolic Boundary Setting, and American Religious Communities," Journal of the American Academy of Religion 63 (1995): 497–517, and Religion and Wine (Knoxville, 1996), 10–32, 74–82.

44. Kross, "'If You Will Not Drink,'" 28–55. For Catholics in Spanish California, see Giorgio Perissinotto, ed., Documenting Everyday Life in Early Spanish California (Santa Barbara, 1998); Maynard Geiger, Franciscan Missionaries in Hispanic California, 1769–1848: A Biographical Dictionary (San Marino, 1969), x.

45. Quakers did not hold Communion. Had they done so, they would probably not have used "real wine," as it would have been inconsistent with their oft-stated desire to eschew alcohol consumption. Carrying the torch of temperance after the Revolution, they cautioned members not only against using but also retailing liquor. Until then, however, restraints were more internal than external. Edward Shippen Sr. to Edward Shippen Jr., March 20, 1754, in *Letters and Papers relating Chiefly to the Provincial History of Pennsylvania* (Philadelphia, 1855), 25–27; William Cobbett, *A Year's Residence in the United States of America* (Belfast, 1818), 360; Ezra Michener, *A Retrospect of Early Quakerism* (Philadelphia, 1860), 307–22; Sydney James, *A People among Peoples: Quaker Benevolence in Eighteenth Century America* (Cambridge, 1963), 17–22, 255–71, 283.

46. The dietary laws with which observant Jews were expected to comply included strict rules about wine consumption. In principle, they were not to consume "real wine" physically, but could use it liturgically, pouring it out in various acts of thanksgiving, worship, and atonement. When consuming it in service, they used an unfermented alcohol-free beverage. Jonathan Sarna, "Passover Raisin Wine, the American Temperance Movement, and Mordecai Noah," *Hebrew Union College Annual* 59 (1988): 269–88.

47. John Wesley, *Journal of the Rev. John Wesley* (London, 1870), 3:419.

48. William Bray, *A Sermon of the Blessed Sacrament of the Lord's Supper* (London, 1641); Edward Reynolds, *Meditations on the Holy Sacrament of the Lord's Last Supper* (London, 1647); Richard Vines, *A Treatise of the Right Institution, Administration, and Receiving of the Sacrament of the Lord's-Supper* (London, 1657); Francis Fullwood, *The General Assembly* (London, 1667); Ralph Cudworth, *A Discourse concerning the True Notion of the Lord's Supper* (London, 1676); Thomas Beverley, *A Sermon of the True, Spiritual Transubstantiation* (London, 1687); Samuel Willard, *Some Brief Sacramental Meditations Preparatory for Communion at the Great Ordinance of the Supper* (Boston, 1711); Andrew Kippis, *A Concise Account of the Doctrine of the New Testament concerning the Lord's Supper*, 4th ed. (London, 1766); John Wesley, *Duty of Constant Communion* (New York, 1788). On attitudes toward drunkenness, see Karen Stubaus, "'The Good Creatures': Drinking Law and Custom in Seventeenth-Century Massachusetts and Virginia" (PhD diss., Rutgers University, 1984), 12–91.

49. *Journal of Nicholas Cresswell*, 52.

50. Account Book, 1727–31, Account Book 1748–66, box 1, Financial Records, and Ledger, 1719–58, Book, 1747–59, Ledger, 1755, Book, 1755–58, Financial Records, King's Chapel Archives, MHS; Henry W. Foote, *Annals of King's Chapel*, vol. 2 (Boston, 1896), 324–25; Treasurer's Accounts, 1747–1827, Records of the Old South (Third) Church, Congregational Library, Boston.

51. Dutch Reformed records mention "wine for use at the Holy Communion" or Spanish wine "for the deaconry" meetings or for funeral services and receptions. Janny Venema, *Deacons' Accounts, 1652–1674* (Rockport, 1998), 188, 193, 195, 199, 205–7, 211, 218–19, 223–24, 230, 238. The celebration of Communion by the Moravians of Bethlehem, Pennsylvania, constituted "the climax in the monthly devotional cycle"; by the 1750s, yearly purchases were considerable, much more than needed for ser-

vices. Diaconate at Bethlehem Ledger "A," 1743–44, fols. 29, 82; Beverly Smaby, *The Transformation of Moravian Bethlehem: From Communal Mission to Family Economy* (Philadelphia, 1988), 17–18. Salzburgers also used imported wine. George F. Jones, ed., *Detailed Reports on the Salzburger Emigrants Who Settled in America . . . Edited by Samuel Urlsperger* (Athens, GA, 1990), 15:100.

52. In another contemporary print—Sutton Nichols's *An Extempore Sermon*, c. 1680–1741 (London or Boston), a minister offers up his thoughts, holding a treatise on malt aloft in one hand and a wineglass in the other, while an assistant opens a cask of beer or ale. Before them are arranged on a table another glass, a wine bottle, and a beer can. If engraved by Nichols, it was most likely first engraved decades earlier than 1741. The print is reprinted in Peter B. Brown, *Come Drink the Bowl Dry: Alcoholic Liquors and Their Place in Eighteenth-Century Society* (York, 1996), which stipulates 1741 and attributes it to Nichols. Two other anticlerical prints widely disseminated in America commented on ministerial drinking: Carrington Bowles, *The Parson and Captain: A Satire on the Clergy* (c. 1760); Thomas Rowlandson, *The Holy Friar* (1807). Frederic G. Stephens and M. Dorothy George, eds., *Catalogue of Political and Personal Satires Preserved in the Department of Prints and Drawings in the British Museum* (London, 1978), nos. 3,789 and 10,924.

53. Outside services, even Quakers, Catholics, and Jews partook. Although meetings regularly cautioned Quakers against trading in and consuming liquor, Friends kept taverns near the houses, so as to capture the business of other Friends entering or leaving meetings! Jack D. Marietta, *Reformation of American Quakerism, 1748–1783* (Philadelphia, 1984), 19–21; Salinger, *Taverns*, 146. Domestic drinking could be as substantial among Quakers as worldlings. When Madeira trader Richard Bisset visited Philadelphia in 1801 and dined at Moore Wharton's, he drank with five Quakers who were "not dry ones—. . . fully evidenced by . . . drinking no inconsiderable Quantity of Claret and Madeira." He became "literally *bungy*" and "passed a bad night—the Claret and Madeira rioting" through his veins and "exciting a thirst so violent that it appeared as if the waters of the Schuylkill and Delaware would not suffice to assuage it." Journal, 1801, box 32, item 2,882, Museum, Independence National Historical Park, Philadelphia.

Similarly with Jews: New Yorker Abigail Franks sent her son some Madeira for his use in 1735, and Daniel Gomez ordered an annual pipe for himself in the 1740s–60s; Chapman Abram, a Montreal fur trader, personally possessed a dozen wineglasses and two decanters in 1783. Jacob R. Marcus, *American Jewry: Documents, Eighteenth Century* (Cincinnati, 1959), 433–35; Abigail Franks to Naphtali Franks, December 12, 1735, in Leo Hershkowitz and Isidore Meyer, eds., *The Lee Max Friedman Collection of American Jewish Colonial Correspondence: Letters of the Franks Family (1733–1748)* (Waltham, 1968), 44; Daniel Gomez Ledger, 1740–66, fols. 104, 147, 174, 188, 197, American Jewish Historical Society, Newton Centre, MA. Jews imported wines and encouraged American viniculture. *Commerce of Rhode Island, 1726–1800*, 2 vols. (Boston, 1914–15); *Weekly Journal*, June 5, September 18, October 20, 1739, January 24, 31, April 21, 1740; Aaron Lopez Ledger Book, 1768–74, fols. 223, 248, 245, and Hill, Lamar & Hill to Abraham Redwood, July 7, 1759, no. 24, June 5, 1762, no. 35,

November 12, 1763, no. 38, January 31, 1764, no. 39A, May 24, 1766, no. 48, March 31, 1768, no. 57, John Rowe to Abraham Redwood, July 16, 1764, no. 41A, October 21, 1765, no. 44, February 10, 1766, no. 45, folder 4, grey box 654, Abraham Redwood Papers, Newport Historical Society, Newport, RI; Shipping Records of Brig *Industry*, 1768, box 2, folder 4, and of Sloop *Charlotte*, 1769–70, box 4, folder 7, Mercantile Accounts of Joseph Gardoqui & Sons, Madeira, 1780–82, box 11, folder 15, Aaron Lopez Papers, American Jewish Historical Society, Newton Centre, MA; Marcus, *American Jewry*, 370–73, 99.

54. Sewall, "Diary," 323; Joshua Hempstead, *Diary* (New London, 1970), 624; Matthew Patten, *The Diary* (Concord, 1903), 432–33, 440–41; Byrd, *Secret Diary*, 324.

55. Treasurer's Accounts, 1747–1827, June 9, 1755, December 8, 1766, August 31, 1767, November 6, 1779, Records of the Old South (Third) Church, Congregational Library, Boston; Ernest H. Cherrington, *The Evolution of Prohibition in the United States of America* (Westerville, 1920), 29–33.

56. Edward Jenner to Robert Jenner, February 17, 1816, in Genevieve Miller, ed., *Letters of Edward Jenner* (Baltimore, 1983), 91; Edward Dunn, trans., "The Diary of Tutor Henry Flynt" (typescript, 1978), 1:469–75, 485, 495–96, 505–7, 510–14, 519–20, 522–23, 531–33, 2:551, 567, MHS; John Adams to Benjamin Waterhouse, February 19, 1805, Adams-Waterhouse Letters, box 2, folder 1, MHS.

57. "The Laws of Harvard College [1767]," *Publications of the Colonial Society of Massachusetts* 31 (1935): 356; *Publications of the Colonial Society of Massachusetts* 49 (1975): 114–31. Leon Jackson considers late eighteenth-century student drinking to be an expression of "anxious liminality," with students caught between "two competing understandings of friendship and association" shaped by different republican ideologies. "The Rights of Man and the Rites of Youth: Fraternity and Riot at Eighteenth Century Harvard," *History of Higher Education Annual* 15 (1995): 19–20. At Princeton, admission of wrongdoing and a commitment to future good behavior constituted "punishment" before 1790. During the 1790s, the tide shifted. When some students went out drinking in neglect of their studies and exhibited "very indiscreet conduct in the street & a very indecent noise, and disorder in the college," two were expelled. The approach gained acceptance. Punishments increased markedly around 1800. Ruth L. Woodward, "Diary at Nassau Hall: The Diary of John Rhea Smith," *Princeton University Library Chronicle* 46, no. 3 (1985): 269–91, *sub* April 6, 1786; Richard A. Harrison, ed., *Princetonians, 1776–1783: A Biographical Dictionary* (Princeton, 1981), 409; Wesley F. Craven and Ruth L. Woodward, eds., *Princetonians, 1784–1790* (Princeton, 1991), 113, 182, 361, 465–66, 479–82, 489; J. Jefferson Looney and Ruth L. Woodward, eds., *Princetonians, 1791–1794* (Princeton, 1991), 54, 66, 252, 353, 363.

58. Pennsylvania Hospital Accounts, William Redwood Account Ledgers, 1775–1810, 1787–90, HSP; New York Hospital Minutes, 1771–1817, vols. 1–3, Archives, Weill Cornell Medical Center, New York, NY; Philadelphia Dispensary Minutes, 1786–91, Pennsylvania Hospital, Philadelphia; *Account of the Design, Origin, and Present State of the Philadelphia Dispensary* (Philadelphia, 1805), 3–4; Boston Dispensary Minutes, 1796–1815, p. 151, Countway Library, Harvard Medical School, Boston.

59. Augustin Belloste, *The Hospital-Surgeon* (London, 1701), 221; Dr. John Crawford to

Lieut.-Gen. Mathew, c. 1793, box 130, MS Collections of the Medical and Chirurgical Faculty of Maryland, MS 3000, pp. 46–56, 151–58, Maryland Historical Society, Baltimore. Cf. Contract, March 16, 1779, PRO 30/20/18, NA-UK, for diets on the Barbados station, requiring Madeira and Spanish wine, small punch, and old rum.

60. Byrd, *Secret Diary*, 5, 28.
61. Douglas S. Freeman, *George Washington: A Biography* (New York, 1948), 2:320–21; *Washington Papers*, Colonial Series, vol. 5 (1988), 332–37; Black, "Journal," 2:40–49; Byrd, *Secret Diary*, 50, 54, 80, 82, 105–8, 125, 165–67, 181, 188, 190, 233–34, 270–71, 334, 432.
62. *Pennsylvania Archives*, 8th ser., 11 (1931): 1209; "How They Mixed Drinks in Colonial Times," *PMHB* 23 (1899): 410; *Pennsylvania Gazette*, October 31, 1734; Black, "Journal," 1:117–32, 233–49, 404–19; Kierner, "Hospitality," 457.
63. Sewall, "Diary," 593, 693; Hempstead, *Diary*, 35, 47, 52, 56, 66–67, 79, 88, 90–93, 138, 160, 584; Patten, *Diary*, 20–21, 28–29, 34–38, 42, 51, 114, 417, 420–37, 440–45, 448–51, 464–65, 468–70, 476–81, 484–85, 496–97, 502, 510, 514–15.
64. Black, "Journal," 1:117; Isaac Norris Sr. to Benjamin Bartlett, December 1, 1705, June 21, 1721, Norris Letter Books, HSP; Henry W. Foote, ed., *Annals of King's Chapel*, vol. 1 (Boston, 1882), 200; Hempstead, *Diary*, 584; Patten, *Diary*, 21, 441; Nash, *History of Augusta*, 271; *Pennsylvania Gazette*, August 13, 1788, June 29, 1790; Michener, *Retrospect*, 316–22.
65. On the American military, see George Washington to the President of Congress, August 16, 1777, in John C. Fitzpatrick, ed., *The Writings of George Washington*, vol. 9 (Washington, DC, 1993); Alice Earle, *Curious Punishments of Bygone Days* (New York, 1907), 7–9, 88, 92; George Haskins, *Law and Authority in Colonial Massachusetts: A Study in Tradition and Design* (New York, 1960), 210; William Stryker, *The Battles of Trenton and Princeton* (Boston, 1898), 361–64; Mark Lender and James Martin, eds., *Citizen Soldier: The Revolutionary War Journal of Joseph Bloomfield* (Newark, 1982), 68, 74, 78, 88, 96, 101, 103; Theodore Thayer, *Nathanael Greene* (New York, 1960), 237–49; *Pennsylvania Gazette*, February 13, 1782. On the British military, see *London Gazette*, June 12, 1750, June 30, 1752, May 22, 1756, September 19, 1758, February 22, 1762, June 14, August 30, November 30, 1764; Paul Kopperman, " 'The Cheapest Pay': Alcohol Abuse in the Eighteenth-Century British Army," *Journal of Military History* 60 (1996): 445–59, and "The British High Command and Soldiers' Wives in America, 1755–1783," *Journal of the Society for Army Historical Research* 60 (1983): 23; Ira Gruber, ed., *John Peebles' American War: The Diary of a Scottish Grenadier, 1776–1782* (London, 1997), 81, 106, 169–70, 181, 241, 247, 295, 297, 368, 397, 406, 429, 497–98, 502, 508; William Spavens, *The Seaman's Narrative* (Louth, 1796), 45, 115, 123.
66. Campbell Letter Book, 227, Schenectady County Historical Society; Phyn & Ellice Account Book, 1767–68, *sub* September–October 1767, NYSL; Edward Shippen Sr. to James Burd, February 17, March 12, May 14, June 4, July 7, September 30, October 29, 1767, Edward Shippen of Lancaster Letter Books, folder 6 (1761–67), APS; Patten, *Diary*, 450, 481; Nash, *History of Augusta*, 261; Marcus Rediker, *Between the Devil and the Deep Blue Sea* (Cambridge, 1982), 124–38; Daniel Vickers, *Farmers and Fisher-*

men (Chapel Hill, 1994), 94; Dennis Sullivan, *The Punishment of Crime in Colonial New York* (New York, 1997), 50; Wainwright, *Colonial Grandeur,* 35; Harold E. Gillingham, "Some Colonial Ships Built in Philadelphia," *PMHB* 56 (1932): 156–86.

67. Hempstead, *Diary,* 56, 101, 160.

68. Richard Bushman, *The Refinement of America* (New York, 1993), 184–85; Roth, "Tea Drinking," 64; Shields, *Civil Tongues,* 104–20, 314–16.

69. James N. Green, "The Rise of Book Publishing in the United States, 1785–1840," in *Extensive Republic: Print, Culture, and Society in the Early Republic,* ed. Mary Kelley and Robert Gross (Chapel Hill, 2009), 1; Jan Lewis, "The Republican Wife: Virtue and Seduction in the Early Republic," *WMQ,* 3rd ser., 44 (1987): 691–92. Cf. R.G., *The Accomplish'd Female Instructor: or, A Very Useful Companion for Ladies, Gentlewomen, and Others* (London, 1704), 22–23.

70. Daniel Defoe, *The History and Misfortunes of the Famous Moll Flanders* (London, 1722), and *The Fortunate Mistress; or, Roxana* (London, 1724); Samuel Richardson, *Pamela; or, Virtue Rewarded* (London, 1740), and *Clarissa* (London, 1748); Tobias Smollett, *Roderick Random* (London, 1748), 1:183, and *Peregrine Pickle* (London, 1751), 3:244; Henry Fielding, *Tom Jones* (London, 1749), 4:26, 103, 6:296–97, and *Amelia* (London, 1752), 1:134, 2:112; Charles Johnstone, *Chrysal; or, The Adventures of a Guinea* (London, 1760), 2:16–17; Frances Brooke, *Emily Montague* (London, 1769), 103; Henry Mackenzie, *The Man of the World* (London, 1773), 1:216.

71. Martha Read, *Monima; or, The Beggar Girl* (New York, 1802), 79, 163, 455, and *Margaretta; or, The Intimacies of the Heart* (Philadelphia, 1807), 25, 171; Sarah Wood, *Amelia* (Portsmouth, NH, 1802); Nathan Hilton, *The Young Lady and Gentleman's Spelling Book* (Exeter, NH, 1807), 149–51; Elizabeth Somerville, *A Birthday Present* (Boston, 1814), 60, 90; [Lady of Distinction,] *Mirror of the Graces,* 26–28.

72. Gawen Hamilton, *The Raikes Family* (1730–32); Marcellus Laroon, *Dessert Being Served at a Party* (1725), and *Officer and Lady at Supper* (1735). Cf. the more popular John Collet, *Bachelor's Fare; or, Bread and Cheese with Kisses* (1777); George Woodward, *Days of Comfort and Draughts of Delight* (1792); James Gillray, *A Decent Story* (1795); *When Seated with Sal, All My Messmates Around,* in *Nautical Songster; or, Seaman's Companion* (Baltimore, 1798); Martin, *Comic Adventures of Old Mother Hubbard; Unless She Was Sinning,* in Oliver Goldsmith, *Dr. Goldsmith's Celebrated Elegy* (Philadelphia, 1809). The 1819 edition of *Mother Hubbard* has finer engraved prints showing Hubbard clutching a bottle in each hand.

73. In contrast, Spanish American visual culture of the same period commonly depicted in a positive spirit the drinking of alcohol by women of various *castas.* Ilona Katzew, *Casta Painting: Images of Race in Eighteenth-Century Mexico* (New Haven, 2004), 115–16, 120, 170. For the ubiquity of female drinking in Europe, see Brennan, *Public Drinking,* 206–10; Kross, "'If You Will Not Drink,'" 38–40. For drinking in India, where "every lady" drank "at least a bottle" at meals in the 1780s and 1790s, see [Phebe Gibbes,] *Hartly House, Calcutta* (Dublin, 1789), 140, 58; Eliza Fay, *Original Letters from India (1779–1815)* (New York, 1925), 199, 263–68.

74. H. R. McIlwaine, ed., *Minutes of the Council and General Court of Colonial Virginia, 1622–1632, 1670–76* (Richmond, 1924), 151.

75. R. Campbell, *The London Tradesman* (London, 1747), 280.

76. Frederike Charlotte Luise Riedesel, *Letters and Journals relating to the War of the American Revolution and the Capture of the German Troops at Saratoga* (Albany, 1867), 139, 131; Gideon D. Scull, ed., *Voyages of Peter Esprit Radisson* (Boston, 1885), 245. In support of the moderate drinking of girls between ten and fifteen, see Somerville, *A Birthday Present*, 60, 90. See also Webber, "Journal of Robert Pringle,"106; [Gentleman in this City,] *Advice to the Fair Sex* (Philadelphia, 1803), 91, 149; Laroon, *Officer and Lady at Supper* (1735); Collet, *Bachelor's Fare* (1777); Woodward, *Days of Comfort* (1792); Gillray, *A Decent Story* (1795); *When Seated with Sal* (1798).

77. This and the following paragraph draw upon *The Distiller of London* (London, 1652); Sir Kenelm Digby and G. Hartman, *Choice and Experimented Receipts in Physick and Chirurgery* (London, 1668); *Directions for the Use of This Famous, Admirable and Never Failing Cordial Drink* (London, 1673); G. Hartman, *The True Preserver and Restorer of Health* (London, 1695); J.W., *Beauties Treasury; or, The Ladies Vade Mecum* (London, 1705); John Boston, *The Husbandman's Guide* (Boston, 1710); George Cheyne, *An Essay of Health and Long Life* (London, 1724), 53–54, 76; George Smith, *A Compleat Body of Distilling* (London, 1725); Thomas Harward, *Electuaarium Novum Alexipharmacum; or, A New Cordial, Alexiterial and Restorative Electuary* (Boston, 1732); James Jenks, *The Complete Cook* (London, 1768); Friedrich Miller, *Doctor Benjamin Godfrey's Cordial* (Hagerstown, 1796); *A Treatise upon Making of Fine Rich London Cordial Gins . . .* (London, 1806); Samuel Chamberlain, *Auxiliary to Health* (Boston, 1807); Daniel Hopkins, *Cordial Purging Elixir* (Hartford, 1808); Samuel Chamberlain, *Patent Bilious Cordial* (Boston, 1809). On making wine, see Eliza Johnston and Claudia Murphy, *The Accomplish'd Servant-Maid; or, The Whole Art of Cooking Made Easy to the Meanest Capacity* (Edinburgh, 1747); Penelope Bradshaw, *Bradshaw's Valuable Family Jewell* (London, 1748); William Graham, *The Art of Making Wine from Fruits, Flowers, and Herbs* (London, 1776); *The Young Woman's Companion and Instructor* (Manchester, 1806).

78. Byrd, *Secret Diary*, 11; *Pennsylvania Gazette*, March 2, 1732/33, 1–2. For early debate on the merits of tea versus wine, see *Pennsylvania Gazette*, May 31, 1733. Perhaps because tea taking provided opportunities to drink liquor, it became a "female sin" in the years before the Revolution. *The Female Patriot, No. 1, Addressed to the Tea-Drinking Ladies of New York* (New York, 1770). See also Maria Edgeworth, "The Lottery," in *Lame Jervas . . .* (New York, 1800); James M. Adair, *An Essay on Diet and Regimen*, 2nd ed. (London, 1812), 50; Sarah Green, *Good Men of Modern Date* (Philadelphia, 1813), 10.

79. Mercantile Ledger and Petty Ledger, 1771–75, Hook Papers, Duke University Library, Durham; Lorna Simmonds, "The Afro-Jamaican and the Internal Marketing System: Kingston, 1780–1834," in *Jamaica in Slavery and Freedom*, ed. Kathleen Monteith and Glen Richards (Mona, 2002), 273–90; Philip D. Morgan, *Slave Counterpoint* (Chapel Hill, 1998), 142, 413–16; Charles Long, *The History of Jamaica, Civil and Commercial* (London, 1774), 2:492; "Characteristic Traits," *Columbian Magazine* [Kingston] 3 (1797): 108–9; Richard Bickell, *The West Indies as They Are* (London, 1825), 65–67; Daniel Horsmanden, *The New York Conspiracy* (Boston, 1971), 67n.

Restraints were removed several days each year when blacks were allowed to gather openly in public spaces and drink, dance, and celebrate. Dirk Hoerder, *Crowd Action in Revolutionary Massachusetts, 1765–1780* (New York, 1977), 71–78; John F. Watson, ed., *Annals of Philadelphia and Pennsylvania, in the Olden Time* (Philadelphia, 1857), 1:286; Kross, "'If You Will Not Drink,'" 34–38, 41–42; Salinger, *Taverns*, 130–31.

80. Michael Craton and James Walvin, *A Jamaican Plantation* (Toronto, 1970), 136; B. W. Higman, *Slave Population and Economy in Jamaica, 1807–1834* (Cambridge, 1976), 23; Douglas Armstrong, *The Old Village and the Great House* (Urbana, 1990), 158–59; Thomas Thistlewood Diaries, August 30, 1757, January 22, 1759, December 25, 1774, Lincolnshire Archives, Lincoln; Morgan, *Slave Counterpoint*, 142, 413–16; *Carter Diary*, 1:492; Joseph J. Ellis, *His Excellency George Washington* (New York, 2004), chap. 5. For laws on slaves' use of liquor, indicative of European fears of disorder and interracial mixing, see Henry S. Cooley, "A Study of Slavery in New Jersey," in *Slavery, and Constitutional History*, ed. Herbert B. Adams (Baltimore, 1896), 36–67; John R. Larkins, *Alcohol and the Negro: Explosive Issues* (Zebulon, 1965), 6–11.

81. Craton and Walvin, *Jamaican Plantation*, 136; Armstrong, *Old Village*, 158–59; Thistlewood Diaries, December 8, 1755, January 29, September 30, 1757, September 1, 1758, January 16, 1759, January 21, September 23, 1767, May 18, 1770, January 8, 1771, March 19, November 11, 1776, October 14, 1777, April 8, June 20, 1784, May 16, 1786. See also Trevor Burnard, *Mastery, Tyranny, and Desire: Thomas Thistlewood and His Slaves in the Anglo-Jamaican World* (Chapel Hill, 2004). Rum and whisky were fed to Carolina and Virginia slaves as well. *Laurens Papers*, 5:100; Thomas Jefferson, *Memorandum Books: Accounts . . . , 1767–1826* (Princeton, 1997), 1290; Morgan, *Slave Counterpoint*, 412–13.

82. Mercantile Ledger and Petty Ledger, 1771–75, Hook Papers, Duke University Library, Durham; Ann Smart Martin, "Buying into the World of Goods" (PhD diss., College of William and Mary, 1993), 308–9. Such was not the case in wine-rich places like Madeira, where household slaves were frequently described as "inclined to drink," having an "unconquerable passion for wine," or "abandoned to drunkenness," nor was it the case in Portuguese Africa during the 1600s, which was awash in Portuguese wine. James Gordon to Alexander Gordon, October 11, 1761, Letterfourie Papers; John Leacock to William Waddell, November 16, 1764, Spence, Leacock & Spence Letter Book, Leacock Papers; Newton & Gordon to William Kirkpatrick, July 18, 1769, NGL; Lamar, Hill, Bisset to Henry Hill, May 3, 1787, Hill-JJS(A); Curto, *Enslaving Spirits*, 66–78, 90–98, 149–83.

83. Byrd, *Secret Diary*, 53, 56, 338; Hempstead, *Diary*, 262–65, 303; Thistlewood Diaries, February 23, 1757, September 1, 1758, March 15, 1776; *Carter Diary*, 1:363, 527, 2:1145; *Georgia Gazette*, July 11, 1765, 4; Morgan, *Slave Counterpoint*, 365, 415.

84. Although, see a 1776 painting of a French West Indian parlor by Le Mesurier, which suggests that wealthy free blacks in the French Caribbean did play that role. Le Mesurier, *Mulatto with Young White Girl Visiting Black People in Their House at Martinique* (1775), Ministère de l'Outre-Mer, Paris.

85. Bickell, *West Indies as They Are*, 66. Cf. Craig MacAndrew and Robert Edgerton, *Drunken Comportment: A Social Explanation* (Chicago, 1969).

86. Although most of the allegations of drunkenness were made by whites, not all were. In their own songs, Jamaican slaves called attention to too much drinking and through ridicule tried to get women to eschew heavy consumption. "The Drunken Negro's Song," cited in Linda Sturtz, "'None So Fine as the Garnet Ladies': Jamaican Popular Music" (paper presented at the Twelfth Annual Conference of the Omohundro Institute, Quebec, June 2006).

87. Robert Juet, "The Third Voyage of Master Henry Hudson," *Old South Leaflets* 94 (1898): 7–8, which is greatly embellished by Johan Heckewelder in *An Account of the History, Manners, and Customs of the Indian Nations* (Philadelphia, 1819), 73–74.

88. The two seminal historical works on Indians and alcohol are Peter Mancall, *Deadly Medicine: Indians and Alcohol in Early America* (Ithaca, 1995); William E. Unrau, *White Man's Wicked Water: The Alcohol Trade and Prohibition in Indian Country, 1802–1892* (Lawrence, 1996). On Indians and wine in Spanish Florida, see Hale G. Smith and Mark Gottlob, "Spanish-Indian Relationships: Synoptic History and Archaeological Evidence, 1500–1763," in *Tacachale: Essays on the Indians of Florida and Southeastern Georgia during the Historic Period*, ed. J. Milanich and S. Proctor (Gainesville, 1978), 16.

89. Stubaus, "'Good Creatures,'" 78–79; James Axtell, *Beyond 1492* (New York, 1992), 115; Richard White, *The Middle Ground: Indians, Empires, and Republics in the Great Lakes Region, 1650–1815* (New York, 1991), 138; Dean Lloyd Anderson, "Documentary and Archaeological Perspectives on European Trade Goods in the Western Great Lakes Region" (PhD diss., Michigan State University, 1992), 104–52; Mancall, *Deadly Medicine*, 42–43, 49–57, 68, 70–73, 136, 138; Nathaniel B. Shuntleff, ed., *Records of Plymouth Colony Laws, 1623–1682* (New York, 1861), 52; John R. Bartlett, ed., *Records of the Colony of Rhode Island and Providence Plantations, in New England* (Providence, 1856), 1:149, 219, 279, 307; *The Jesuit Relations and Allied Documents*, vol. 9 (Cleveland, 1896), 203–4 (1636), vol. 11 (1898), 194–95 (1637), vol. 22 (1898), 239–41 (1642), vol. 24 (1898), 141–43 (1642–43), vol. 26 (1898), 145–57 (1645), vol. 28 (1908), 30–31 (1646), vol. 30 (1899), 201 (1647), vol. 34 (1899), 38 (1649), vol. 35 (1899), 267–68 (1650), vol. 43 (1899), 77 (1657), vol, 45 (1899), 137–38 (1661), vol. 48 (1899), 62–3 (1662–63), vol. 62 (1900), 126–27 (1681–83), vol. 66 (1910), 24, 27 (1702), 135 (1707–8), 156–57 (1710). If the French specified a wine, it was—surprisingly—usually Spanish, which was preferred, and occasionally Madeira.

90. Bruce M. White, "The Trade Assortment: The Meanings of Merchandise in the Ojibwa Fur Trade," in *Vingt ans après: Habitants et marchands*, ed. Sylvie Dépatie et al. (Montreal, 1998), 130.

91. For earlier gifts, see Emma Helen Blair, trans., *The Indian Tribes of the Upper Mississippi Valley and Region of the Great Lakes* (Cleveland, 1912), 2:22–24; R. C. Dailey, "The Role of Alcohol among North American Indian Tribes as Reported in the Jesuit Relations," *Anthropologica* 10 (1968): 48–50; Axtell, *Beyond 1492*, 35–36. On gifting during the Seven Years' War, see William L. Stone, *The Life and Times of Sir William Johnson, Bart.* (Albany, 1865), 2:403, 422, 425, 444, 450, 459, 3:345; O'Callaghan, *Colonial History of the State of New York* vol. 7, *sub* July 30, 1766; Johnson, *Papers*, 12:150–51. On resumption of present giving in 1764 by the British, a custom banned in

1761, see Jon W. Parmenter, "Pontiac's War: Forging New Links in the Anglo-Iroquois Covenant Chain, 1758–1766," *Ethnohistory* 44 (1997): 623, 635; Bruce M. White, "A Skilled Game of Exchange: Ojibwa Fur Trade Protocol," *Minnesota History* 50 (1987): 240, and "Trade Assortment," 115–37. For later gifts, see *Pennsylvania Gazette*, December 27, 1775; *Michigan Pioneer and Historical Society, Historical Collections* 10 (1886): 632–33; Invoice, June 7, 1782, Porteous Papers, box 1, Buffalo and Erie County Historical Society, Buffalo; *Pennsylvania Gazette*, March 25, 1789; John Boit, "John Boit's Log of the Second Voyage of the *Columbia*," in *Voyages of the "Columbia*," ed. Frederic W. Howay (Boston, 1941), 383–85; Charles Bishop, *The Journal and Letters of Captain Charles Bishop on the North-west Coast of America, in the Pacific and the New South Wales, 1794–1799* (Cambridge, 1967), 71.

92. Stubaus, "'Good Creatures.'" Indicative of the double standard is the Puritan law granting Indians a bounty of wine if they brought in the head of a wolf. Mancall, *Deadly Medicine*, 103–4.

93. Conroy, *Public Houses*; Thompson, "Social History," 11, 453; Shields, *Civil Tongues*, xvi.

CHAPTER 10. "POWER TO GIVE SUDDEN REFRESHMENT" AND RESPECT

1. To comprehend the place of wine drinking in the English Atlantic world, it would be best, here and in the following chapter, to begin with those understandings and conversations that prevailed long before 1640 and persisted well after 1815, and to analyze several empires. The significations reconstructed in the present chapter, however, occurred mainly among English speakers in Britain, India, and America and, to a lesser extent, with sellers residing at the point of production. Not enough material has been uncovered for Portuguese and Brazilian consumption to allow significant comparison, although that which has suggests similar conclusions. Furthermore, as in the preceding chapter, American writings are relied upon primarily, if they existed, and are generally supplemented with English publications. On most medical and health topics, Britons led the way, however, and Anglo-Americans produced comparatively little; London remained the center of English speakers' publishing world. Only after independence did Americans turn to writing about health and medicine in a big way, and even then much of their thought was derivative. As in previous chapters, "consumer" and "consumers" are used here to refer to anyone who bought drink or drank it: importers, wholesalers, and retailers, who recorded the thoughts of those who bought from them and who drank themselves, as well as consumers proper (the drinkers).

2. Richard Short, *Of Drinking Water* (London, 1656), 1; cf. Tobias Whitaker, *The Tree of Humane Life* (London, 1638), 24, 20. This and the following paragraph are drawn from Bernice K. Watt and Annabel L. Merrill, *Composition of Foods*, rev. ed. (Washington, DC, 1963), 16, 75, 181–82; *The Merck Manual of Diagnosis and Therapy* (online version, 2001). If wine has more carbohydrates, the others could have more calories, because the other noncarbohydrates produced greater heat exchange.

3. Richard S. Dunn et al., *The Journal of John Winthrop, 1630–1649* (Cambridge, MA,

1996), 734, 736; John Winthrop to ——Winthrop, July 23, 1630, in Stewart Mitchell, ed., *The Winthrop Papers* (Boston, 1931), 2:303–4; *A Relation of Maryland* (London, 1635), in Clayton Hall, ed., *Narratives of Early Maryland, 1633–1684* (New York, 1910), 93.

4. Stephen Hales, *Philosophical Experiments* (London, 1739), 10–47; Admiral Hawke to Board of Admiralty, August 12, 1759, in Ruddock F. Mackay, ed., *The Hawke Papers* (Brookfield, 1990), 264–65; Joseph François Charpentier de Cossigny, *Essai sur la manière de conserve à la mer l'eau potable, dans les voyages de long cours* (Paris, 1774); *Pennsylvania Gazette*, January 26, 1774; *New York Courant*, July 12, 1774; Riedesel, *Letters*, 29; Médéric-Louis-Elie Moreau de Saint-Méry, *Moreau de St. Méry's American Journey* (New York, 1947), 14; Edward Cutbush, *Observations on the Means of Preserving the Health of Soldiers and Sailors, and on the Duties of the Medical Department of the Army and Navy* (Philadelphia, 1808), 22–25.

5. Cecil Headlam, ed., *Calendar of State Papers, Colonial Series, 1716–1717* (London, 1930), 360; *Pennsylvania Gazette*, February 15, 1731/32, May 9, 1734; Letter Books, Logbooks, and Diary, 1803, Edward Preble Papers, vols. 24, 28, 31, 33, LC; George Hay, "Recollections of the War of 1812," *AHR* 32 (1926): 76. On sailors' rations, see Vitorinho M. Godinho, *Mita e mercadoria* (Lisbon, 1990); Peter Earle, *Sailors* (London, 1998), 86–92; Daniel Vickers, "Work and Life on the Fishing Periphery of Essex County, Massachusetts, 1630–1695," in *Seventeenth-Century New England* (Boston, 1984), 83–115; Rediker, *Between the Devil*, 191–93. On British Navy rations, see Mackay, *Hawke Papers*, 264–65; Contract, March 16, 1779, PRO 30/20/18, and NOSL (Jamaica) Entries, *sub* June 11, 26, 1802, May 14, June 5, 1804, July 7, 1806, NA-UK; Richard B. Sheridan, *Sugar and Slavery: An Economic History of the British West Indies* (Baltimore, 1973), 346–47; Sidney W. Mintz, *Tasting Food, Tasting Freedom* (Boston, 1996), 59–60. On U.S. rations, see Christopher McKee, *A Gentlemanly and Honorable Profession: The Creation of the U.S. Naval Officer Corps, 1795–1815* (Annapolis, 1991), 450–53; Maurice B. Gordon, *Naval and Maritime Medicine during the American Revolution* (Ventnor, 1978), 32–46; Harold D. Langley, *A History of Medicine in the Early U.S. Navy* (Baltimore, 1995), 43; Joan Druett, *Rough Medicine: Surgeons at Sea in the Age of Sail* (New York, 2000), 13–14, 31, 50–53, 66.

6. John Harington, "The Salerne School," in *The Englishman's Doctor* (London, 1607), 8; Samuel Purchas, *Hakluytus Posthumus* (Glasgow, 1905–7), 19:164–67; *A Declaration of the State of the Colony and Affaires in Virginia* (London, 1622); Francis Higginson to a Friend, September 1, 1629, in Everett Emerson, *Letters from New England* (Amherst, 1976), 34; *A Relation of Maryland*, 93. Cf. Penelope Aubin, *The Noble Slaves* (London, 1739), chap. 5; Tobias G. Smollett, *Roderick Random*, vol. 2 (London, 1748), chap. 45; Johnstone, *Chrysal*, 1:14; Thomas Love Peacock, *Melincourt* (1817; London, 1927), 121.

7. Tobias Venner, *Via Recta ad Vitam Longam* (London, 1620), 24; Short, *Of Drinking Water*, 57–61, 93–98; *Journal of Nicholas Cresswell*, 52; Franklin D. Scott, ed., *Axel Klinkowström's America, 1818–1820* (Evanston, 1952), 69. On water contamination, see Sidney A. Norton, *Contaminations of Drinking Water* (Columbus, 1882), 1–9; T. Mitchell Prudden, *Drinking Water* (New York, 1891), 34–47, 54–62; Grant M.

Simon, "Houses and Early Life in Philadelphia," APS, *Trans.*, n.s., 43 (1953): 280–88; George Augustin, *History of Yellow Fever* (New Orleans, 1909), 767–75, 986–92; Georges Vigarello, *Concepts of Cleanliness: Changing Attitudes in France since the Middle Ages* (Cambridge, 1988), chap. 10; Jean-Pierre Goubert, *The Conquest of Water: The Advent of Health in the Industrial Age* (Princeton, 1989), 1–58.

For debates on drinking water, see Charles Lepois, *Selectiorum Observationum et Consiliorum de Praetervisis Hactenus Morbis Affectibusque Praeter Natura* (Boutestein, 1714); John Hancocke, *Febrifugum Magnum* (London, 1722); James Gardner [Daniel Defoe], *Remarks on the Reverend Dr. Hancocke's "Febrifugum Magnum"* (London, 1723); *Remarks upon "Remarks"; or, Some Animadversions on a Treatise Wrote by One Who Calls Himself Dr. Gardner* (London, 1723); *A Counterfeit Detected, and Justly Exposed* (London, 1723); John Smith, *The Curiosities of Common Water; or, The Advantages Thereof in Preventing and Curing Many Distempers* (London, 1723), 3, 39, 44; Cheyne, *Essay of Health*, 42, 48; Etienne Geoffroy et al., *Traité des vertus medicinales de l'eau commune* (Paris, 1725); Johann Z. Platner, *Panegyrin Medicam* (Leipzig, 1738), and . . . *indicit et de pestiferis aquarum petrescentium escpirationibus disserit* (Leipzig, 1747); John Rotheram, *A Philosophical Inquiry into the Nature and Properties of Water* (Newcastle, 1770), 25–26, 47–49, 61–63; Benjamin Rush, "Paper . . . [to the] Committee on Natural History and Chemistry," July 18, 1773, *Proceedings of the American Philosophical Society* 22 (1885): 80; Pierre Thouvenel, "Observations sur les eaux potables," in *Histoire de la société royale de medicine* (Paris, 1777–78), 2:274–89; Wallis, *Works of Thomas Sydenham, M.D.*, 2:228; Corporation of the City of New York, *Proceedings of the Corporation of New-York on Supplying the City with Pure and Wholesome Water* (New York, 1799), 16; Ralph Dodd, *Observations on Water* (London, 1805), 69, 72–76; John Sinclair, *The Code of Health and Longevity* (Edinburgh, 1807), 1:234, 239–42.

8. On undrinkable stream and spring water, see Thistlewood Diaries, *sub* January 16, 1759; William Fleming, "Journal of Travels in Kentucky, 1779–1780," in Mereness, *Travels in the American Colonies*, 630; Thouvenel, "Observations," 275; Benjamin H. Latrobe, *View of the Practicability and Means of Supplying the City of Philadelphia with Wholesome Water* (Philadelphia, 1799), 17.

9. Water polluted by decomposing flesh came to be seen as a significant problem in the 1770s, at first in France, and eventually throughout the English-speaking world. The principal solution—charcoal filters—was expensive, and the ability to chemically analyze water accurately was nonexistent. On wells and sewers, see Pierre-Jean-Claude Mauduyt, "Sur la corruption des eaux infectées par les insectes," in *Histoire de la Société royale de medicine*, vol. 1, pt. 2 (Paris, 1776), 245–59; Benjamin H. Latrobe, *The Journal of Latrobe . . . from 1796 to 1820* (New York, 1971), 97 (1805); Benjamin Rush, "An Inquiry into the Comparative State of Medicine, in Philadelphia, between the Years 1760 and 1766, and the Year 1805," in *Medical Inquiries and Observations*, 2nd ed. (Philadelphia, 1805), 364–405; Sinclair, *Code*, 1:242–67. Comparable to open, feces-filled drains were cemeteries. M. du Tennetar, *Mémoire sur l'état de l'atmosphère* (Nancy, 1778), 23.

10. On lead and lead pipes, see Richard P. Wedeen, *Poison in the Pot: The Legacy of Lead*

(Carbondale, 1984); François Citois, *De Novo et Populari apud Pictones Colico Bilioso Diatriba* (Paris, 1639); Johann Jakob Wepfer, *Miscellanea Curiosa sive Ephemeridum Medio-Physicarum Germanicarum Curiosarum* (Frankfurt, 1688), 70–71; Eberhard Gockel, "Vini Acidi per Acetum Lithargyri," unpublished notes, 1697, cited by Wedeen, *Poison*, 22; Robert Pierce, *Bath Memoirs* (London, 1697), 249–63; William Musgrave, *De Arthritide Symptomatica* (Exon, 1703); "An Act for Preventing Abuses in the Distilling of Rum and Other Strong Liquors" (1723), chaps. 11, 15, in *Acts and Resolves, Public and Private, of the Province of the Massachusetts Bay* (Boston, 1874), 2:302–3, 307; Herman Boerhaave, *A Collection of Reviews and Letters Lately Inserted in the "Daily Journal"* (London, 1730); John and Charles Carter to Hayward & Chambers, November 10, 1733, Carter Letter Book, 1732–82, Alderman Library, University of Virginia, Charlottesville; Thomas Cadwalader, *An Essay on the West-India Dry-Gripes* (Philadelphia, 1745); John Huxham, *Observations . . . [Including] A Short Dissertation on the Devonshire Colic* (London, 1759), 9, 13, 17, 259–65; George Baker, "An Inquiry concerning the Cause of the Endemial Colic of Devonshire" (1767) and "An Examination of Several Means, by Which the Poison of Lead May be Supposed Frequently to Gain Admittance into the Human Body" (1767), in College of Physicians in London, *Medical Transactions*, 3rd ed. (London, 1785), 1:198, 212, 234–36, 258; Thomas Goulard, *A Treatise on the Effects and Various Preparations of Lead* (London, 1769), 115–17, 196–97; Benjamin Franklin to George Baker, cited in College of Physicians, *Medical Transactions*, 1:286, and to Benjamin Vaughan, July 31, 1786, in Smyth, ed., *Writings*, 9:530–33; John Wright, *An Essay* (London, 1795), 41; James Hardy, *A Candid Examination . . .* (London, 1778), 43, 78–83, 91–94; Thomas Dobson, *Encyclopedia* (Philadelphia, 1798), 18:870–71; William Lambe, *Researches into the Properties of Spring Water with Medical Cautions* (London, 1803), 11–15, 20–23, 73–74; Sinclair, *Code*, 1:317.

11. Steven Blankaart, *A Physical Dictionary* (London, 1684), 295.

12. This and the following paragraph draw upon Nicholas Culpeper, *A Physicall Directory; or, A Translation of the London Dispensatory Made by the Colledge of Physicians in London* (London, 1649), 90; Richard Graves, *The Spiritual Quixote* (London, 1773), 1:323; Thomas J. Pettigrew, ed., *Memoirs of the Life and Writings of the Late John Coakley Lettsom* (London, 1817), 3:355; William Northcote, *The Marine Practice of Physic and Surgery* (London, 1770), 1:83, 85, 108, 25, 127–28; *Pennsylvania Gazette*, July 12, 1786; William Smith to Benjamin Rush, March 9, 1803, Benjamin Rush Papers, vol. 22, fol. 52, HSP; Lee Anderson and Gregory Higby, *The Spirit of Voluntarism—A Legacy of Commitment and Contribution: The United States Pharmacopeia, 1820–1995* (Rockville, 1995), 3–13. Other American compendia include John R. Coxe, *The American Dispensatory* (Philadelphia, 1806); James Thacher, *The American New Dispensatory* (Boston, 1817). Two texts were published during the American Revolution, but postwar physicians usually relied upon British texts until the 1800s. For wines being distributed by doctors, see Thomas and Phineas Bond of Philadelphia Ledgers, 1751–70, vol. 2, fols. 13, 15, 20, 57–61, 70, 90, 344, 359, 393, and Theophilus Rogers Recipe Book, 1779–1801, fols. 12, 17, 24, 28–29, 38–39, CPP. On local popular

usage of Madeira, Lisbon, Fayal, and Sherry, see George Frey to Benjamin Pulteney, October 5, 1782, Frey Papers, private collection, Middletown, PA.

13. *Pennsylvania Gazette,* September 26, December 12, 1771; *New-Hampshire Gazette, and Historical Chronicle,* January 11, 1771; *The Virginia Almanack for the Year of Our Lord God 1768* (Williamsburg, 1767), 32–33 and unnumbered pages immediately preceding.

14. Ambroise Paré, *The Method of Curing Wounds Made by Gun-Shot* (London, 1617), 65; John Woodall, *The Path-way to the Surgions Chest* (London, 1628), 2–3; Thomas Sydenham, *Praxis Medica: The Practice of Physick,* 3rd ed. (London, 1716) [trans. of William Salmon, *Processus Integri* (London, 1695)], 282, 285, 296); *A New Tract for the Cure of Wounds Made by Gun-Shot or Otherways* (London, 1701), 4; Augustin Belloste, *The Hospital-Surgeon* (London, 1701), 43–44, 46, 55–57, 144, 148, 182, 207–9, 246; Daniel Turner, *The Art of Surgery* (London, 1722), 329; Lorenz Heister, *A General System of Surgery* (London, 1743), 1:113; John Jones, *Plain Concise Practical Remarks on the Treatment of Wounds and Fractures* (Philadelphia, 1776), 24; John Ranby, *The Nature and Treatment of Gunshot Wounds* (Philadelphia, 1776).

15. John C. Fredriksen, ed., *Surgeon of the Lakes: The Diary of Dr. Usher Parsons, 1812–1814* (Erie, 2000), 112; Paulson, *Hogarth's Graphic Works,* vol. 2.

16. Harington, "Salerne School"; John Woodall, *The Surgeon's Mate; or, Military and Domestique Surgery* (London, 1618), 92, 96; Riedesel, *Letters,* 132. Cf. James E. Gibson, *Dr. Bodo Otto and the Medical Background of the American Revolution* (Springfield, 1937), 218–21, 225–28, 243, 263, 267, 277–79; Whitfield J. Bell Jr., *John Morgan: Continental Doctor* (Philadelphia, 1965), 222–33; Gordon, *Naval and Maritime Medicine,* 32; Druett, *Rough Medicine,* 31.

17. *Colonial Records of the State of Georgia* (Augusta, 1985), 29:212–13; William Buchan, *Domestic Medicine,* 2nd ed. (London, 1772), 662; Rogers Recipe Book, 1779–1801, CPP; Samuel Bard, *A Compendium of the Theory and Practice of Midwifery* (New York, 1807), 112, 132. See also Catherine M. Scholten, *Childbearing in American Society: 1650–1850* (New York, 1985), 26; Michael J. O'Dowd, *The History of Medications for Women* (New York, 2001), 91, 160.

18. John Moyle, *Chirurgus Marinus* (London, 1702), 15, 46–47; Buchan, *Domestic Medicine,* 708; Jones, *Plain Concise Practical Remarks,* 25, 112; John Bell, *Discourses on the Nature and Cure of Wounds,* 1st Am. ed. (Walpole, 1807), 181–83.

19. Belloste, *Hospital-Surgeon,* 246; Jones, *Plain Concise Practical Remarks,* 112–13. Although, contra, see Ranby, *Nature and Treatment of Gunshot Wounds,* 26–27.

20. Thomas Cogan, *The Haven of Health* (London, 1584), 5; John Minsheu, *A Dictionarie in Spanish and English* (London, 1599); Harington, "Salerne School," 5; Whitaker, *Tree of Humane Life,* 20.

21. Thomas Thacher, *A Brief Rule to Guide the Common-People of New England to Order Themselves and Theirs in the Smallpocks, or Measels* (Boston, 1677); Louis Armand de Lom d'Arce, Baron de Lahontan, *New Voyages to North America* (Chicago, 1905), 2:671; William Salmon, *Seplasium* (London, 1693), 926–27, and *Pharmacopeia Londiniensis* (London, 1707), 552–64.

22. Steven Shapin, "Trusting George Cheyne," *Bulletin of the History of Medicine* 77 (2003): 269–70. A contemporary introduction to Galenic thought appears in Nathaniel Hodges, *Vindiciae Medicinae and Medicorum; or, An Apology for the Profession and Professors of Physick* (London, 1665), 145. On the broad changes in medical science, see Roy Porter, *The Greatest Benefit to Mankind: A Medical History of Humanity* (New York, 1998), 201–303. The essays by Andrew Wear, Guenter Risse, and Roy Porter, in Andrew Wear, ed., *Medicine in Society: Historical Essays* (Cambridge, 1992) are helpful, as are Roy Porter, *Patients and Practitioners* (Cambridge, 1985); Mary Lindemann, *Medicine and Society in Early Modern Europe* (Cambridge, 1999); Andrew Wear, *Knowledge and Practice in English Medicine, 1550–1680* (Cambridge, 2000).

23. Louis Lemery, *A Treatise of Foods, in General* (London, 1704), 286, 290. See also Edward Ward, *The London Spy* (London, 1709), pt. xv, p. 377; Peter Shaw, *The Juice of the Grape* (London, 1724), 8, 26–36, 41, 47; Edward Shippen Sr. to John Shippen and James Burd, August 5, 1758, in *Letters and Papers*, 130.

24. John Wesley, *Primitive Physick* (London, 1747), xviii–xx; A Gentleman of the Faculty, *Observations concerning the Medical Virtues of Wine* (London, 1786), 5–7, 10–11. Benefits were not all internal; wine drinkers were supposedly less susceptible to infectious diseases, like plague and smallpox. Nathaniel Hodges, *Loimologia*, 2nd ed. (London, 1720), 184, 217, 225; Cadwalader Colden to Dr. John Bard, July 5, 1758, *The Colden Papers, 1755–1760*, in *Collections of the New-York Historical Society . . . 1921* (New York, 1923) 245; Gerard, Freiherr van Swieten, *A Short Account of the Most Common Diseases Incident to Armies*, 2nd ed. (London, 1767), 2, 45, 58, 65–67; "Extract of a Letter from Cadwalader Colden, Esq. to Dr. Fothergill, October 1768," *American Museum or Repository* 3 (1788): 53, 57–58; John Crawford, *An Essay on the Nature, Cause and Cure of a Disease Incident to the Liver* (London, 1772), 18; *Pennsylvania Gazette*, February 22, June 29, 1775; Gerard, Freiherr van Swieten, *The Diseases Incident to Armies, with the Method of Cure* (Philadelphia, 1776), 158; Frey to Pulteney, October 5, 1782, Frey Papers, private collection, Middletown, PA; Marcus Kuhl's Notes on Adam Kuhn's Lectures on the Materia Medica, 1790s, 2:154, CPP; John Crawford to General Mathew, 1793, MS 3000, Maryland Historical Society, Baltimore; Fraser, *History of Man*, 354–56; John Melish, *Travels through the United States of America* (London, 1818), 45.

25. This and the following paragraph draw on Buchan, *Domestic Medicine*, 378–79; *Pennsylvania Gazette*, August 16, 1775, May 19, 1780, May 29, 1782, July 4, 1787; Benjamin Rush, *An Inquiry into the Effects of Spirituous Liquors upon the Human Body* (Boston, 1790), 12; John Brown, *The Elements of Medicine* (London, 1795), 243–66; David Hosack to John McNeil, June 22, 1808, to John Watts, January 29, 1809, Hosack Letters, 1801–26, New York Academy of Medicine, New York. The Cambridge Female Humane Society purchased three bottles of Madeira in 1819 as "Articles of Nourishment" for those it helped. Annual Report, 1819, Female Humane Society Papers, Schlesinger Library, Cambridge, MA. Bathing babies and invalids in wine was an ancient Greek custom. Richard B. Onians, *The Origins of European Thought* (Cambridge, 1954), 222.

26. George Cheyne, *Observations concerning the Nature and Due Method of Treating the Gout* (London, 1720), 3, 96–97, and *Essay of Health*, 42–43, 47–49; Edward Strother, *An Essay of Sickness and Health*, 2nd ed. (London, 1725), 68–69; James Sedgwick, *A New Treatise on Liquors* (London, 1725).

27. William Cadogan, *A Dissertation on the Gout, and All Chronic Diseases* (London, 1771), 63–70; William Heberden, *Commentaries on the History and Cure of Diseases* (London, 1782), 35, 47–48, 51–52; *A Treatise on the True Effects of Drinking Spirituous Liquors, Wine and Beer, on Body and Mind* (London, 1794), 1–2, 6–7, 16; John C. Lettsom, *Hints Designed to Promote Beneficence, Temperance, and Medical Science* (London, 1797), 1:182–84. The anonymous 1794 *Treatise* allowed exceptions for people "obliged to work sometimes harder than usual, either with their head or body, so that they must have recourse to a little of nourishing drinks"—but only in "cases of utmost necessity."

28. William Cullen, *First Lines of the Practice of Physic* (Philadelphia, 1781), *A Treatise of the Materia Medica* (Edinburgh, 1784), 1:294–305, and *Synopsis Nosologiae Methodicae* (Edinburgh, 1785); Porter, *Greatest Benefit*, 260–61.

29. Joel C. Bernard, "From Theodicy to Ideology: The Origins of the American Temperance Movement" (PhD diss., Yale University, 1983), 100–103; Benjamin Moseley, *Treatise concerning the Properties and Effects of Coffee*, 5th ed. (London, 1792), 74.

30. Benjamin Rush to Benjamin Franklin, 1771, in Rush, "Letters," *PMHB* 12 (1954): 12.

31. Prescriptions at the height of the 1793 yellow fever epidemic in Philadelphia show that the contribution of the experimentalists had had little appreciable effect on daily doctoring. John H. Powell, *Bring Out Your Dead: The Great Plague of Yellow-Fever in Philadelphia in 1793* (New York, 1949), 77. On Kuhn, professor of Materia Medica at the College in Philadelphia and practicing there in 1786–94, see "Notes on the *Materia Medica*," 1786, "Lectures on the Practice of Physic," 1786, Kuhn, "Notes for a Course of Lectures," 1794, National Library of Medicine, Washington, DC; Kuhn, "Lectures on Yellow Fever," 1794, fol. 69, CPP.

32. Porter, *Greatest Benefit*, 231–32. On the cure for scurvy, see Kenneth J. Carpenter, *The History of Scurvy and Vitamin C* (Cambridge, 1996), 44–45, 68; Francis E. Cuppage, *James Cook and the Conquest of Scurvy* (Westport, 1994), 94–95; Christopher Lloyd and Jack Coulter, *Medicine and the Navy, 1200–1900* (Edinburgh, 1961), 3:81–93, 293–328.

33. Interestingly, wines were often stored in leaden containers in the seventeenth and eighteenth centuries. While it is purely speculative that lead may have seeped into the wine (or other alcoholic beverages, for that matter), we do know that high levels of lead from modern occupational exposures may alter the kidney's filtering unit (so-called lead-induced nephropathy), resulting in decreased uric acid excretion and predisposition to gout. J. Claude Bennett et al., *Cecil Textbook of Medicine*, 20th ed., vol. 2 (Philadelphia, 1996); Qing Yu Zeng, "Drinking Alcohol and Gout," *Lancet*, April 17, 2004, 1251–252; William A. N. Dorland, *Dorland's Illustrated Medical Dictionary*, 28th ed. (Philadelphia, 1994), 713; Wedeen, *Poison*; Josef Eisinger, "Lead and Wine," *Medical History* 26 (1982): 279–302; Gene V. Ball, "Two Epidemics of Gout," *Bulletin of the History of Medicine* 45 (1981): 401–8; Michael V. Baker et al., "The Relation

of Serum Uric Acid to Subclinical Blood Level," _Rheumatalogy and Rehabilitation_ 20 (1981): 208–10; Josef Eisinger, "Lead and Man," _Trends in Biochemical Sciences_ 2 (July 1977): 147–50; L. A. Healey, "Port Wine and Gout," _Arthritis and Rheumatism_ 18 (1975): 659–62; Margaret Maclachlan, "Effects of Food, Fast and Alcohol on Serum Uric Acid and Acute Attacks of Gout," _American Journal of Medicine_ 42 (1967): 38–57; John Duffy, _Epidemics in Colonial America_ (Baton Rouge, 1953), 37–38; Carey P. McCord, "Lead and Lead Poisoning in Early America: The Pewter Era," _Industrial Medicine and Surgery_ 22 (1953): 573–77; Maurice A. Schnitker, "A History of the Treatment of Gout," _Bulletin of the Institute of the History of Medicine_ 4 (1936): 89–120. The best history of the subject is Roy Porter and G. S. Rousseau, _Gout: The Patrician Malady_ (New Haven, 1998).

Obesity, hypertension, and consumption of protein-rich products (like red meat and seafood), purine-rich vegetables, and alcoholic beverages are associated with gout. Oral ethanol ingestion increases uric acid synthesis, although different alcoholic beverages seemingly have varying effects. Beer appears to have a stronger association with gout than spirits or wine. Beer contains purines (particularly guanosine), and extrapolation suggests that large-volume consumption of purines may shift usual metabolism in the direction of uric acid overproduction. Today medicine does not believe that "moderate" wine consumption increases the risks of getting gout.

34. Cogan, _Haven_, "Dedication," 5; Daniel Sennert, _Two Treatises: . . . Second Treatise of the Gout_ (London, 1660), 7, 14; Wallis, _Works of Thomas Sydenham_, 2:196, 226–28. Cf. Philander Misaurus, _The Honour of the Gout_ (1699; London, 1735), 51; Cheyne, _Observations_, 3, 96–97, and _Essay of Health_, 42–43, 47–48; Boerhaave, _Aphorisms_ (London, 1724), 372–82; Samuel Richardson, _Letters Written to and for Particular Friends_, 4th ed. (London, 1750), 45–46; Nicholas Robinson, _An Essay on the Gout_ (London, 1755), 147, 158. For later anti-wine writing about gout, see Buchan, _Domestic Medicine_, 490.

35. Cadogan, _Dissertation on the Gout_, 46–47, 66–67; James Hardy, _An Answer to the Letter_ (London, 1780), 5; Porter and Rousseau, _Gout_, 101–5.

36. William Heberden, _Commentaries on the History and Cure of Diseases_ (London, 1802), 35, 47–48, 51–52; Robert James, _Medicinal Dictionary_, vol. 3 (London, 1745), s.v. "vinum"; Benjamin Kent to Benjamin Franklin, January 19, 1766, _Franklin Papers_, 13:49; _Morning Chronicle_, December 22, 1784; John Morgan, Lectures on "The Practice of Physic," MS Lectures, no. 5 (1780s), CPP. One of the main reasons Heberden wrote his 1782 _Commentaries_ was to refute those arguing for the ameliorating effects of wine on gout. For instances of Americans adhering to the pro-wine advice of doctors and experts, see Byrd, _Secret Diary_, 28; Louis B. Wright, ed., _Letters of Robert Carter_, 1720–1727 (San Marino, 1946), 15–16, 30–31; Charles Lowe to Benedict Leonard Calvert, April 5, 1728, in "Letters to Benedict Leonard Calvert," _Maryland Historical Magazine_ 3 (1908): 311–20; William Byrd II, _William Byrd's Natural History of Virginia I_, ed. Richmond C. Beatty (Richmond, 1940), 89; John and Charles Carter to Hayward & Chambers, November 10, 1733, Carter Letter Book, 1732–82, Alderman Library, University of Virginia, Charlottesville; Elizabeth Coates Receipt Book, CPP.

37. Roy Porter, _For the Benefit of All Mankind: A History of Humanity_ (London, 1998),

680; Paul Starr, *The Social Transformation of Medicine* (New York, 1982), 55–56. Of course, since no one could be certain that wine was lead-free, abstinence would still have been advisable: while lead does not contain purines as do some alcohols, chronic exposure to lead is related to decreased urate excretion and an increased incidence of gout secondary to a lead-induced nephropathy. Lead's association with gout is via renal toxicity and alteration in urate handling, not via excess purines. One may naturally extrapolate that a chronic consumer of large amounts of alcohol prepared in leaden containers or sweetened with lead would have been at risk for the same type of renal disease. Byrd, *Secret Diary*, 28, and *Natural History*, 89; Carter, *Letters*, 15–16, 30–31; *Pennsylvania Gazette*, July 24, 1732. Elizabeth Coates, who was much influenced by James's "great dictionary," listed wine as one of the remedies for gout in a "receipt book" of cures she kept in Philadelphia. Coates Receipt Book, CPP. See also Rush to Franklin, 1771, in Rush, "Letters," 12; *Pennsylvania Gazette*, July 12, 1786; Thomas D. Mitchell, "Notes on the Lectures of Dr. Benjamin Rush," 1809–11, 2:45–61, CPP. Men and women in Britain likewise used or avoided wine. G. Eland, ed., *The Purefoy Letters*, *1735–1753* (London, 1931), 1:30; Richardson, *Letters*, 261.

38. *Colonial Laws of Massachusetts*, 202; Nathaniel B. Shurtleff, ed., *Records of the Governor and Company of the Massachusetts Bay in New England* (Boston, 1853–54), 1:76, 2:100, 3:289, 324, 369, 425, 427; *The Colonial Laws of New York* (Albany, 1894), 1:41; *The Early Records of the Town of Providence* (Providence, 1892), 2:45, 83, 97, 3:38–39, 139. "Roistering and gulling in *Wine* with a dear felicity" by the lower sort was noted by John Josselyn, who visited Maine in the 1660s. After unloading their catch, the local fishermen regularly spent a few days, "sometimes a whole week," drinking "two or three Hogsheads of *Wine* or *Rhum* . . . when the merchant is gone." *An Account of Two Voyages to New England* (London, 1674), 160–62.

39. Wesley, *Journal*, 3:419; *Pennsylvania Gazette*, September 30, 1736; William Smith Jr., *The History of the Province of New-York*, ed. Michael Kammen (Cambridge, 1972), 227; "Journal of a French Traveller in the Colonies, 1765, I," *AHR* 26 (1921): 743; Wright, *Essay*, 42; York County Deed Books, State Library of Virginia, Richmond; Arthur H. Cole, *Wholesale Commodity Prices in the United States*, *1700–1861* (Cambridge, MA, 1938).

40. *Early Records of the Town of Providence*, 6:37–39, 76–78, 95, 7:117–19, 10:47–48, 111–12, 12:31–32, 92, 15:235–36, 16:103–5, 110, 112, 114–15, 306–8, 362–64, 394–97, 148–55; Jonathan Pearson, *Early Records of the City and County of Albany* (Albany, 1919), 4:57, 85, 89; George F. Dow, ed., *An Inventory of the Contents of the Shop and House of Captain George Corwin, of Salem, Massachusetts Bay* (Salem, 1910), 18.

41. John Oldmixon, *The British Empire in North America*, 2nd ed. (London, 1741), 1:428; James Birket, *Some Cursory Remarks Made by James Birket in His Voyage to North America*, *1750–1751* (New Haven, 1961), 9–10; George F. Jones, ed., *Detailed Reports on the Salzburger Emigrants Who Settled in America* (Athens, GA, 1990), 15:100.

42. Drake, *Memoirs*, 53–54; John Guerard to William Joliffe, November 14–15, 1753, January 31, 1754, John Guerard Letter Book, SCHS; Henry Laurens to Corsley Rogers & Son, July 8, 1755, Henry Laurens to Harry Thompson, November 8, 1756, in *Laurens Papers*, 1:290, 2:346–47; L. H. Butterfield, ed., *Diary and Autobiography of John*

Adams (Cambridge, 1961), 1:213; Wainwright, *Colonial Grandeur*, 62–63; Catharine Livingston to Matthew Ridley, November 3, 1784, Ridley Papers, MHS. On distinctions among drinks based on a drinker's wealth, see Ann Pinson, *The New England Rum Era: Drinking Styles and Social Change in Newport, Rhode Island, 1720–1770* (Providence, 1980), 16–17; Roy Porter, introduction to Thomas Trotter, *An Essay . . . on Drunkenness* (London, 1804, 1988), x–xi.

43. Oliver M. Dickerson, *The Navigation Acts and the American Revolution* (Philadelphia, 1951), 172, 188; Edmund Morgan and Helen Morgan, *The Stamp Act Crisis* (New York, 1962), 39, 41, 45; R. C. Simmons and P. D. G. Thomas, eds., *Proceedings and Debates of the British Parliaments respecting North America, 1754–1783* (New York, 1982), 1:487–93, 508–11; Chastellux, *Travels*, 1:315.

44. William Lee to Lamar, Hill, Bisset & Co., January 5, 1784, William Lee Letter Books, VHS; Patrick Campbell, *Travels in the Interior Inhabited Parts of North America in the Years 1791 and 1792* (Toronto, 1937), 46; Robert Beverley to William Beverley, August 22, 1794, *Virginia Historical Magazine* 21 (1913): 102; "The Purse," in St. John Honywood, *Poems* (New York, 1801), 5.

45. Matthew Miller to Newton & Gordon, February 2, 1780, unnumbered bundle, box 1780/81, CGP-Guildhall; John O'Keeffe, *The Young Quaker* (London, 1784), act III, sc. 2, p. 23; Newton & Gordon to Thomas Gordon, February 12, 1787, vol. 9, fol. 340, November 24, 1791, vol. 14, fol. 15, NGL; *Pennsylvania Gazette*, November 17, 1790; William Bentley, *The Diary of William Bentley, D.D.* (Gloucester, 1962), 1:299; C. Bruyn Andrews, ed., *The Torrington Diaries* (London, 1934), 4:75-76; John Davis, *Travels of Four Years and a Half in the United States of America [1798–1802]* (London, 1803), 267.

46. The meanings of the words "quality," "elegance," "gentility," "refinement," "respectability," and "superiority" generally overlapped, despite some subtle differences. Bushman, *Refinement*, 61. For the purposes of the argument here—that eighteenth-century British Americans used wine to display their status—the overlap is stressed. On the definition and redefinition of what it meant to be genteel and refined, see Hancock, *Citizens*, 279–81, 320–81; Bushman, *Refinement*, xii–xiii, 61–63; Gordon S. Wood, *The Radicalism of the American Revolution* (New York, 1992), 25, 31–37. Bushman confines his study of refinement to the person, exchanges between refined people and, most innovatively, their environments. He pays little attention to commodities and drinking. Bushman's gentility was inculcated by a cohesive, elite group of gentlemen. Peter Thompson has begun to fill the gap. In colonial Philadelphia, "drinking was crucial to the process by which a gentleman adopted the forms of 'gentility' and demonstrated his gentility to his peers and to society at large"; it "was not an act of release but of definition." Thompson, "'Friendly Glass,'" 459–50. Many more meanings were also conveyed.

47. Mintz, *Tasting Food*, 78; Wood, *Radicalism*, 25, 31–32, 37.

48. Comte de Ségur, *Memoirs and Recollections* (New York, 1825), 335. Cf. Black, "Journal," 1:124–26, 241–44; Alexander Hamilton, *Gentleman's Progress*, ed. Carl Bridenbaugh (Chapel Hill, 1948), 88; Thomas Vernon to Samuel Vernon, 1771, Vernon Papers, box 79, folder 3, Rhode Island Historical Society, Providence.

49. G. B. Warden, *Boston, 1689–1776* (Boston, 1970), 67; *Pennsylvania Gazette*, July 1, 1736, May 15, 1740; *Boston Weekly News-Letter*, October 11, 1750; *American Museum* 2 (May 1787), 379.

50. Fithian, *Journal*, 138. The thinking persisted well into the nineteenth century: William A. Alcott, *The Young Man's Guide*, 3rd ed. (Boston, 1834), 148.

51. Hamilton, *Gentleman's Progress*, 98.

52. Alexander Fraser's transcription of James May's recollection of Detroit in 1778, in *Sketches of the City of Detroit, State of Michigan* (Detroit, 1855), 5–8; John May, *Journal and Letters of Col. John May, of Boston*, ed. William M. Darlington (Cincinnati, 1873), 64–65; Eliza S. Quincy, ed., "[Ann Powell's] Journal [1739]," *Magazine of American History* 5 (1880): 37–47; Campbell, "Travels," 121, 127, 134, 165, 179–80; Heal, "Idea," 66–93. Detroit was well supplied with wine. Ships from Fort Erie brought 151 casks in 1793–94 alone. "Remains of Ordnance, 1789 and 1794," in Michigan Pioneer & Historical Society, *Collections and Reports* 12 (1887), 4–5.

53. John Adams to Abigail Adams, May 22, 1771, in Charles F. Adams, ed., *Letters of John Adams Addressed to His Wife* (Boston, 1841), 1:229.

54. Faujas de St. Fond, *Journey*, 47–49, 182–83, 252–53; Cook, *Sotweed Factor*, 18, 22–23; Fithian, *Journal*, 138. On his second attempt, the hapless inspector, after having "seen a little our Manner," made a toast to *"Ladies, when only Mrs. Carter was in attendance."* Fithian's report replicates the fate of a young 1746 "stripling." *True Patriot*, January 21–28, 1746.

55. Edward Warren, *The Life of John Collins Warren, M.D.* (Boston, 1860), 1:14; *Domestic Management; or, The Art of Conducting a Family* (London, 1800), 73–75; John Trusler, *Principles of Politeness and of Knowing the World*, 16th ed. (London, 1800), 40; Joseph Berchoux, *Gastronomie; ou, L'homme des champs a table* (Paris, 1801), 54–56.

56. On varieties available in England, see César de Saussure, *A Foreign View of England in the Reigns of George I. and George II.* (New York, 1902), 99–107 (1726); William Speechly, *A Treatise on the Culture of the Vine* (York, 1790); Hannah Cowley, "The Town Before You" (1795), in *The Plays*, ed. Frederick M. Link (New York, 1979), 2:22; R. Worthington, *An Invitation to the Inhabitants of England to the Manufacture of Wines* (Worcester, 1812). On varieties in America, see Black, "Journal," 1:126; John Johnson, "Essay on the Culture of the Vine," *Transactions of the Society for the Promotion of Useful Arts in the State of New-York* 2 (1807): 133–61; *An Essay on the Climate of the United States* (Philadelphia, 1809). In Portugal: Vicencio Alarte, *Agricultura das vinhas* (Lisbon, 1712); Constantino Botelho de Lacerda Lobo, "Memória sobre a cultura das vinhas de Portugal," in *Memórias económicas da Academia real das ciências de Lisboa, para o adiantamento da agricultura, das artes, e da indústria em Portugal, e suas conquistas (1789–1815)* (Lisbon, 1991), 2:43, 52–53; Alvares da Silva, "Memória," 2–7; Agostinho Ignacio da Costa Quintella, *Tratado para a cultura das vinhas em Portugal* (Lisbon, 1800). In Spain: Cecilio García de la Leña, *Disertacion en recomendacion y defensa del famoso vino malgueña, Pero Ximen, y modo de formalo* (Malaga, 1792); Francisco María Campuzano, *Oracion que en la abertura de sesiones del dia quince de julio de este año con el objeto de restablecer la Sociedad pa-*

triótica riojana (Logroño, 1815). In France: Jean-Antoine-Claude Chaptal, *Chemistry*, part iv, sec. 5, chap. 6; M. Maupin, *Méthode de Maupin sur la manière de cultiver la vigne et l'art de faire le vin* (Paris, 1798–99); Chaptal, *L'art de faire le vin* (Paris, 1807); Etienne Calvel, *Principes pratiques de la plantation et de la culture du chasselas et autres vignes précoces* (Paris, 1811); André Jullien, *Topographie de tous les vignobles connus* (Paris, 1816).

57. Andrew Boorde, *The Breviarie of Health* (London, 1598), 8; Harington, "Salerne School," 5; Adam Gopnik, "Through a Glass Darkly," *New Yorker*, September 6, 2004, 6.

58. Jacques Savary des Bruslons and Philémon Louis Savary, *Dictionnaire universel de commerce*, 3 vols. (Paris, 1723–30); Malachy Postlethwayt, trans., *The Universal Dictionary of Trade and Commerce*, 2nd ed. (London, 1757), 2:837. As late as 1813, these four traits were regarded as the most important by French oenologists. André H. Jullien, *The Wine Merchant's Companion and Butler's Manual* (London, 1825), 78. Taking cues from English colleagues, Jullien first published a *manuel* in 1813 and a second edition several years later; it was translated into English in 1825. By the early 1800s, *bouquet*—"that aromatic perfume which arises from the wine when it is exposed to the air"—was receiving sustained attention as well.

59. This and the following paragraphs draw on Miller, *Gardener's Dictionary*, s.v. "wines," which includes many of Savary's rubrics; Dennis De Coetlogon, *An Universal History of Arts and Sciences* (London, 1745), 10–12, 679–80; Johnson, *Dictionary*, s.v. "wine"; John Barrow, *A New and Universal Dictionary of Arts and Sciences* (London, 1751), s.v. "wine"; Spence, Leacock, & Spence to John Erskine, June 26, 1762, Leacock Papers; Temple Croker, *Complete Dictionary of Arts and Sciences*, vol. 2 (London, 1765), s.v. "wine"; Diderot and d'Alembert, *Encylopédie*, 17, s.v. "vin"; Thomas Mortimer, *A New and Complete Dictionary of Trade and Commerce* (London, 1765), s.v. "wine"; *Encyclopedia Britannica*, 3:942–43; James Gordon to John Rankine, October 18, 1774, James Gordon Letter Book, 1765–75, fol. 492, Letterfourie Papers; *Treatise of the Materia Medica*, 1: 296–305; John Leacock to William Leacock, October 13, 1795, May 10, 1796, Leacock Papers; *Encyclopedia Britannica*, 18:869–70 (drawing on Chaptal's *Chemistry*, iv.5.vi); Thomas Dobson, *Encyclopedia* (Philadelphia, 1798), 18:869–70; Thomas Murdoch to Pierce Butler, October 18, 1800, vol. 21, fol. 70, NGL; James Walker, *Hints to Consumers of Wines or the Abuses* (Edinburgh, 1802), 1–57; A. F. M. Willich, *Domestic Encyclopedia* (Philadelphia, 1803), 494–97; C. H. Kauffman, *The Dictionary of Merchandise, and Nomenclature* (Philadelphia, 1805), 364; Sinclair, *Code*, 1:307–8.

60. Thomas Newton to Newton & Gordon, October 3, 1758, Thomas Newton Letter Book, CGP-MWC; Daniel Henry Smith to James Gordon, May 2, 1774, Letterfourie Papers; Francis Newton to Newton, Gordon & Johnston, April 12, 1786, box 1786–87, CGP-Guildhall; Newton & Gordon to Crawford & Johnston, April 18, 1785, vol. 8, fol. 237, to Francis Newton, May 4, 1792, vol. 13, fol. 180, to Pierce Butler, October 18, 1800, vol. 21, fol. 70, NGL.

61. Jullien, *Companion*, 1, 3–4, 8, 47–48, 57, 72–79, 86–87.

62. Richard N. Côté, "Fine Wine and Thoroughbreds: The Friendship of Thomas Jeffer-

son and Col. William Alston," *Journal of the American Wine Society* 28 (Winter 1996): 112–14, and *Mary's World* (Mount Pleasant, 2000), 35–39; *Galateo* (Baltimore, 1811), 201.

63. Croft, *Treatise*, 24; McBride, *General Instructions*, 22–46; Wright, *Essay*, 34; *One Thousand Valuable Secrets* (Philadelphia, 1795), 264–80.

64. Isaac Norris Sr. to "Esteemed Friends," Isaac Norris Sr. Letters, 1704–6, in Norris of Fairhill Papers, vol. 6, fol. 3, HSP; Richard Hill to John Smith, April 18, 1746, vol. 1, fol. 180, Hill-JJS(A); Newton & Gordon to Alexander Munro, August 10, 1776, vol. 6, fol. 113, NGL; Lamar, Hill, & Bisset to Henry Hill, October 9, 26, 1784, vol. 9, fol. 88, Hill-JJS(A); Robert Duff to James Duff, December 14–20, 1785, Letterfourie Papers; "How to Fine a Pipe of Madeira," September 28, 1787, Scrapbook, CGP-PC; Newton, Gordon, Murdoch & Johnston to Charles Chambers, December 15, 1787, vol. 10, fol. 93, NGL; Richard Lamar Bisset to Henry Hill, March 3, 1792, vol. 10, fol. 221, Hill-JJS(A); Newton, Gordon & Murdoch to Edward Greathead, March 29, 1792, to Francis Newton, May 4, 1792, to William Mitchell, June 4, 1792, vol. 14, fols. 153, 180, to Henry Heskith, October 15, 1799, vol. 20, fol. 67, to John Gibbes, May 29, 1802, vol. 23, fol. 312, NGL; William Leacock to John Leacock, August 17, 1807, Leacock & Leacock Letter Book, 1807–10, Leacock Papers.

65. For experts on fining, see Charleton, *Mysterie*, 159–65, 195–97; John Houghton, *A Collection of Letters for the Improvement of Husbandry and Trade* (London, 1683), 1:166–67; William Salmon, *The Family-Dictionary; or, Household Companion*, 2nd ed. (London, 1696), 384–86; S.J., *Vineyard*, 69; Hill, *Works*, 2:102–3; Miller, *Gardener's Dictionary*, s.v. "wines"; *Annual Register* 2 (1759): 383; Croker, *Complete Dictionary*, vol. 2, s.v. "wine"; Jenks, *Complete Cook*, 322; James Hardy, *A Candid Examination* (London, 1778), 43, 111; *One Thousand Valuable Secrets*, 266; Dobson, *Encyclopedia*, 18:869–73. By 1800, writers were providing extremely detailed descriptions of fining. Kauffman, *Dictionary of Merchandise*, 364; H. Sabine, *The Publican's Sure Guide; or, Every Man His Own Cellarman* (London, 1807); Gourlay, *Observations*, 19; Jullien, *Companion*, 29–46; William Beastall, *A Usefull Guide* (New York, 1829), 13–156.

66. Defoe, *Review*, bk. 20, pp. 305–11, 321–23; Cadwalader Colden to Amos Garrat, August 13, 1714, in *Collections of the New-York Historical Society for the Year 1917* (1918): 20–21; Neumann, *Chemical Works*, 441–48; Isaac Wikoff, *Broadside* (Philadelphia, 1771). Particularly intriguing is an engraved 1743 representation of a tavern keeper or innkeeper constructed from the various tools and paraphernalia used in the trade. The arms, for example, were made from decanters. Visually, the viewer could learn what one needed to keep and serve wine and spirits. *A Victualler or Publican* (1743), in Stephens and George, *Catalogue*, vol. 3, no. 2471.

67. Jullien, *Companion*, 1, 3–4, 8, 47–48, 57, 72–79, 86–87.

68. While the French led in vinicultural technology, the English led in etiquette innovation. Cf. Henry Fielding, *Miscellanies*, 2nd ed. (London, 1743), 1:119, 123; Jonathan Swift, *The Works*, ed. Sir Walter Scott (Edinburgh, 1824), 11:395 (first published in 1745 in London as *Directions to Servants in General*); *The Complete Servant Man* (London, 1758), 57–78; Faujas de St. Fond, *Journey*, 1:71–73; Matthew Carey, *Mis-*

cellaneous Essays (London, 1830), 318–20; *Encyclopedia Britannica*, 18:870; *Domestic Management*, 73–75; Maria Wilson, *The Complete Confectioner* (London, 1800), 222; Lord Chesterfield and John Trusler, *Principles of Politeness* (London, 1806), 40; Fraser, *History of Man*, 187–89, 250–51, 354–55. In America, room service proceeded less formally than in Europe. Hosts often did the work of servants, and bottles sat on the table. *Galateo*, 191–94; Robert Roberts, *The House Servant's Directory* (London, 1827), 36–37, 59–61. Prescription never reached the hysterically compulsive level demanded in 1825 by the Briton Thomas Cosnett, who specified the exact number and place of wine and water glasses and decanters, the distance between glasses, the array of small glasses for a sideboard, etc. *The Footman's Directory, and Butler's Remembrancer* (London, 1825), 82–88.

69. Gérard de Lairesse, *Groot Schilderboek* (Amsterdam, 1707; Haarlem, 1740), 1:54–55, trans. as *A Treatise on the Art of Painting, in All Its Branches* (London, 1738, 1817), 34, plate 12; Buckner Stith to George Washington, March 22, 1787, in *Washington Papers*, Confederation Series, vol. 5 (1997), 99.

70. Henry Peacham, *The Compleat Gentleman*, 2nd ed. (London, 1661), 215, 222–24.

71. Henry Peacham, *The Art of Living in London* (London, 1642), 3.

72. Thomas Heywood, *Philocothonista; or, The Drunkard, Opened, Dissected, and Anatomized* (London, 1635), frontispiece, 49; Francis Quarles, *Enchiridion* (London, 1644), cent. 2, chap. 74, cent. 3, chap. 14; Edward Bury, *England's Bane* (London, 1677), 4; Jean Gailhard, *The Compleat Gentleman* (London, 1678), 190; A.B., *Humane Prudence* (London, 1682), 82; *The Art of Pleasing in Conversation* (London, 1691), 88–89; Thomas Tryon, *A New Art of Brewing Beer, Ale, and Other Sorts of Liquors* (London, 1791), 10; Baltasar Gratian, *The Complete Gentleman* (London, 1776), 92, 198. For studies of drinking in early modern England, see Archer Taylor, "When Wine Is In, Wit Is Out," in *Nordica et Anglica*, ed. Allan H. Orrick (The Hague, 1968), 53–56; John M. Sullivan Jr., "Women, Wine, and Song: Three Minor Genres of Seventeenth-Century British Poetry" (PhD diss., University of Minnesota, 1981); Dora J. Janson, "Visions of the Vine: A Symbolic History," in *Wine: Celebration and Ceremony*, ed. Hugh Johnson (New York, 1985), 45–74; Robert J. Merrett, "Bacchus in Restoration and Eighteenth-Century Comedy: Wine as an Index of Generic Decline," *Man and Nature* 7 (1988): 177–93, and "Bacchus in Eighteenth-Century Britain: French Wine and Literary Sensibility," *LIT* 8 (1997): 23–59; Anya Taylor, *Bacchus in Romantic England: Writers and Drink, 1780–1830* (London, 1999).

73. Kenneth A. Lockridge, *The Diary, and Life, of William Byrd II of Virginia, 1674–1744* (New York, 1987), 6, 47, 49, 54. In keeping "an exact Diary of all your Actions," Byrd was following the advice of a behavior manual popular during his student days: A.B., *Humane Prudence*, 68–69.

74. Dall W. Forsythe, *Taxation and Political Change in the Young Nation, 1781–1833* (New York, 1977), 40. Reactionary politicos worried about wine drinking's effect on the Republic: alcohol emboldened drinkers, loosening individual restraints, facilitating the questioning of authority and increasing the chance of drunkenness, family neglect, and criminal mischief.

75. Francis Hawkins, *Youths Behaviour* (London, 1663), 30, 33–35; Roger L'Estrange, *The*

Rules of Civility (London, 1671), 107–10. While manuals were addressed to "persons of quality," they had wider influence, helping to "coordinate diverse elements in the population." Lawrence E. Klein, "Politeness for Plebes," in *The Consumption of Culture, 1600–1800*, ed. John Brewer and Ann Bermingham (London, 1995), 365–66.

76. Fielding, *Miscellanies*, 1:119, 123; Swift, *Works*, 11:395; *Complete Servant Man*, 57–58; Faujas de St. Fond, *Journey*, 1:71–73; Carey, *Miscellaneous Essays*, 318–20; *Encyclopedia Britannica*, 18:870; *Domestic Management*, 73–75; Wilson, *Complete Confectioner*, 222; Chesterfield and Trusler, *Principles of Politeness*, 40; Fraser, *History of Man*, 187–89, 250–51, 354–55; Cosnett, *Footman's Directory*, 82–88; Roberts, *House Servant's Directory*, 36–37, 59–61. Imitative of English guidance literature (it is a word-for-word borrowing) is the entry on wine in Dobson, *Encyclopedia*, 18:869–73. Parody appears in *Chesterfield Travestie* (Philadelphia, 1812), 17. See also *Galateo*, 27, 172–73, 192–94, 201.

77. Catholic artists were less free or eager to detail the subject, and so produced far fewer drink paintings. This is certainly the case in Portugal and Spain, the notable exception being Velázquez's *Bacchus; or, The Drinkers* (1628–29). For French elite drinking, see Jean-Baptiste-Siméon Chardin, *Le buffet* (1728), Louvre; Nicolas Lancret, *Le déjeuner de jambon* (1735), and, with corks aflying, Jean-François de Troy, *Le déjeuner d'huitres* (1737), at the Musée de Condé, Chantilly; Charles-André van Loo, *La halte de chasse/Déjeuner de chasse* (1737), Louvre; Jean-Michel Moreau *le jeune*, *Le souper fin* (1776–77), Waddeson Manor. Martine Vasselin, "Des fastes de Bacchus aux beuveries flamandes: L'iconographie du vin de la fin du XVe siècle à la fin du XVIIe siècle," *Nouvelle revue du seizième siècle* 17 (1999): 219–51.

78. Paul Staiti, "Character and Class," in *John Singleton Copley in America*, ed. Carrie Rebora et al. (New York, 1995), 54.

79. There was, of course, nothing rigid about viewing and interpreting art. Understanding it relied on shared language, yet also individual experience.

80. For engravings on the walls of coffeehouses and taverns, see *A London Coffee House* (c. 1668, British Museum); *Coffee-House Mob* (1710, British Museum); *Settling the Affairs of the Nation*, with an engraved portrait of John Wilkes hanging above the entrance door (1794–1800, British Museum). John Lewis Krimmel's painting *Village Tavern* (1814) similarly displays patriotic prints on the walls of an ordinary. Art imitated tavern life: Inventory of Thomas Whatson, of Port Royal, March 11, 1701, liber 5, fols. 103–4, Probate Inventories, IRO; Inventory of Benjamin Backhouse, September 21–22, 1767, vol. X (1765–69), fols. 176–80, of Catherine Backhouse, December 26, 1767, fols. 222–23, Probate Inventories, SCDAH; Inventory of Edward Edes, November 19, 1803, no. 21,977, pp. 670–74, Suffolk County Probate Inventories, MSA.

81. Diana Donald, *The Age of Caricature: Satirical Prints in the Reign of George III* (New Haven, 1996), 48.

82. *Giles Cooke and Family* is on loan to the Baltimore Museum of Art from the Estate of James Cook.

83. There is nothing comparable to the toasting ritual in the consumption of chocolate, coffee, or tea. Central to the present analysis of toasting is the work of Mary Douglas, who saw Kosher rituals as a way to distinguish competent insiders from floundering out-

siders. High elaboration would reveal outsiders pretending to be insiders and provide complex selection and initiation processes for aspirants. Factory, regimental, school, and class rituals were directed towards the same end. According to Douglas, Jews were liturgically repulsed by incomplete, ill-fitting, or inappropriate things. Douglas, *Purity and Danger: An Analysis of the Concepts of Pollution and Taboo* (London, 1966), 53–54.

84. On toasting in England and Scotland, see Faujas de Saint Fond, *Journey*, 1:47–49, 252–53. On toasting by Indians, who used the toast as a mark more of equivalence than of superiority and inferiority, see Mancall, *Deadly Medicine*, 73.

85. Douglas, *Purity and Danger*, 78, 86, and "Deciphering a Meal," in *Implicit Meanings*, ed. Douglas (London, 1975), 249, 260. Theorists who seem to have lost sight of the reinforcing element of ritual include Johan Huizinga, *Homo Ludens* (London, 1949); Arnold Van Gennep, *The Rites of Passage* (London, 1960); Victor Turner, *From Ritual to Theatre* (New York, 1982). Too much is made of Van Gennep's second phase of transition in which at times one can find an inversion of normal life.

86. The toast's origins lie with the ancients. Jews, Greeks, and Romans drank "a little from a full cup of wine" and bestowed it "upon one to whom one wishes well." Onians, *Origins*, 217. In Europe, drinkers swore oaths over wine from the eleventh century. Schivelbusch, *Tastes of Paradise*, 169. In England, see Robert Parsons, *A Conference upon the Next Succession to the Crowne of Ingland* (St. Omer, France, 1594), i.i.3; Fynes Morrison, *An Itinerary* (London, 1617), 151; Peacham, *Compleat Gentleman*, 223; Timothy Gunton, *An Extemporary Answer to a Cluster of Drunkards* (London, 1648), broadside; James Howell, *Epistolae Ho-elianae: Familiar Letters Domestic and Forren* (London, 1650), 2:77; William Congreve, *The Way of the World* (London, 1700), 164. See also Peter Clark, *British Clubs and Societies, 1580–1800: The Origins of an Associational World* (Oxford, 2000), 6, 8, 26–46.

87. Dunn et al., *Journal of John Winthrop*, 109–10; Shurtleff, *Records*, 1:271, 2:121; Durand de Dauphiné, *A Huguenot Exile in Virginia* (New York, 1936), 129; John Dunton, *The Life and Errors of John Dunton* (London, 1705), 1:126–27; Increase Mather, *A Testimony against Severall Prophane and Superstitious Customs* (London, 1687); Louis Armand de Lom d'Arce, Baron de Lahontan, *New Voyages to North America* (Chicago, 1905), 2:671; Cook, *Sotweed Factor*, 21; Samuel Sewall, *The Diary* (New York, 1973), 2:741–43; Edward P. Alexander, ed., *The Journal of John Fontaine: An Irish Huguenot Son in Spain and Virginia, 1710–1719* (Williamsburg, 1972), 106; Cotton Mather, *Advice from the Watch Tower* (Boston, 1713), 34; Francis Goelet, *The Voyages and Travels of Francis Goelet, 1746–1758* (Flushing, 1970), *sub* October 8, November 5, 1750; Byrd, *Secret Diary*, 79–80, 334; Elaine G. Breslaw, ed., *Records of the Tuesday Club of Annapolis, 1745–56* (Urbana, 1988).

88. Chastellux, *Travels*, 1:109–10.

89. Byrd, *Secret Diary*, 79–80, 334; Breslaw, *Records of the Tuesday Club*; Comte d'Estaing to Gabriel de Sartine, November 5, 1778, in Stanley J. Idzerda, ed., *Lafayette in the Age of the American Revolution* (Ithaca, 1979), 2:203; Comte de Ségur, *Memoirs*, 335; Margaret Smith, *What Is Gentility* (Washington, DC, 1828), 59. On the passing of bowls and glasses, see Davis, *Travels*, 142.

90. Earlier representations of toasting in America include several sketches in the manuscript version of the *Records of the Tuesday Club*; George Roupell, *Mr. Peter Manigault and His Friends* (1759). Cf. John Lewis Krimmel, *A Village Tavern* (1814), which shows a group of country folk drinking out of glass tumblers in a rural post house tavern, a corked bottle of red wine standing on the shelf behind the bar; and Henry Sargent, *The Dinner Party* (1821), Museum of Fine Arts, Boston, which depicts a group of men having a drink after dinner, three bottles sitting on the sideboard.

91. One "treatise on politeness and delicacy of manners" printed in Baltimore in 1811 had a separate discussion on how to handle the toasts. *Galateo*, 175–76.

92. *Pennsylvania Gazette*, June 26, 1755, July 26, 1753; *South-Carolina Gazette*, 1753.

93. *New-York Mercury*, September 8, 1755, 3; *Pennsylvania Gazette*, August 5, 1756, November 15, 1759, January 22, 1761, July 28, August 25, 1763; *New-York Mercury*, November 20, 1752, 3; *Pennsylvania Gazette*, November 21, 1765, August 5, 1756; *Boston Gazette*, August 21, 1769.

94. These and the following paragraphs draw on the following sources: *Boston Gazette*, September 16, November 11, 1765; *Pennsylvania Gazette*, November 28, 1765. On the November 5 "Union Feast" in Boston, see Gary B. Nash, *The Urban Crucible*, abr. ed. (Cambridge, 1986), 164–65.

95. For repeal toasts, see *Pennsylvania Gazette*, March 31, May 22, 26, 29 (New York, and Burlington, Vermont), June 2, 5, 12 (Charlestown, Wilmington, North Carolina, Falmouth, Maine, Newport, Rhode Island), June 19, 1766. For later toasts, see *Pennsylvania Gazette*, September 1, 1768, March 23, August 31, 1769, March 26, 1772; *Boston Gazette*, May 26, June 2, 1766, March 23, 1767; *Virginia Gazette* (Purdie and Dixon), June 6, 1766; *Newport Mercury*, May 19, 1766.

96. Staiti, "Character," 54.

CHAPTER 11. ARS BIBENDI

1. In Britain, the incorporation occurred in the 1710s, and in Anglo-America soon thereafter. A similar shift took place in France and the French empire. Catherine Ferland, "Du vin d'Espagne au Champagne: La 'carte des vins' de la nouvelle France au XVIIIe Siécle," *Material History Review* 57 (2003): 15–29. The conversations reconstructed here occurred mainly among English-speaking American, British, and East Indian buyers and, to a lesser extent, with sellers living at the point of production. Not enough material has been uncovered to reconstruct Portuguese and Brazilian consumption, although that which has confirms the argument. As before, "consumer" is used to refer to anyone who bought or drank wine.

2. Richard Steele, *Guardian*, no. 34, April 20, 1713.

3. Erving Goffman, *The Presentation of Self in Everyday Life* (New York, 1959). It is hard to overestimate the importance of Goffman's insights; they shaped the work of sociologists and anthropologists for decades. Fredrik Barth, *Process and Meaning in Social Life* (London, 1981); Victor Turner, *The Anthropology of Performance* (New York, 1987). However, few scholars have followed up the analysis of objects as props, which Goffman alluded to but which was not central to his work. In recent decades, theorists

of social distinction like Pierre Bourdieu (building on Thorstein Veblen and Georg Simmel) and theorists of semiotic value like Arjun Appadurai, Roland Barthes, and Grant McCracken (building on Marshall Sahlins and Mary Douglas) have suggested that goods display class status and convey conscious and unconscious messages about ideology, personality, and gendered and raced positions in society. So construed, these goods are props. It therefore seems appropriate to bring them back into focus. Bourdieu, *Distinction*; Roland Barthes, *Système de la mode* (Paris, 1967), and "Towards a Psycho-Sociology of Food Consumption," *Food and Drink in History* 5 (1979): 166–76; Appadurai, *Social Life of Things*; McCracken, *Culture and Consumption*. See also Sherratt, "Alcohol and Its Alternatives," 12–15.

4. Susan Leigh Star and James R. Griesemer, "Institutional Ecology, 'Translations' and Boundary Objects: Amateurs and Professionals in Berkeley's Museum of Vertebrate Zoology, 1907–39," *Social Studies of Science* 19 (1989): 387–420.

5. Gratian, *Complete Gentleman*, 198; Robert Blair St. George, *Conversing by Signs: Poetics of Implication in Colonial New England Culture* (Chapel Hill, 1998), 3, 7, 9.

6. Star and Griesemer, "Institutional Ecology," 408.

7. Samuel Pepys, *The Diary*, ed. Robert Latham and William Matthews, vol. 4 (Berkeley, 1971), 17–19, 297–98, and vol. 6 (1972), 51; Paulson, *Hogarth's Graphic Works*, vol. 2. On early cellars, see Charleton, *Vintner's Mystery Display'd*, first given as a paper to the Royal Society in 1662 and republished as *Of the Mysterie of Vintners* (London, 1700), 71; Frederick Brache, ed., *Letters of Sir George Etherege* (Berkeley, 1974), 285. By 1700, vaults were common in the London wine trade. Henry Liddell, *The Letters of Henry Liddell to William Cotesworth*, ed. J. M. Ellis (Leamington Spa, 1987), 29; Memo Book, fol. 1v & loose, Merchant's Memos & Accounts, 1708–12, in *Curson v. Shelton*, Masters' Exhibits (Blunt), C 103/168, NA-UK; *Guardian*, September 14, 1713; Drake, *Memoirs*, 316; Miller, *Gardener's Dictionary*, s.v. "wines." Caves, vaults, and cellars abounded in late Georgian London. Jonathan Michie to Mr. Thompson, May 15, 1771, Jonathan Michie Letter Book, 1770–84, Westminster City Archives; Barry, *Observations*, 67–84; Sophie v. la Roche, *Sophie in London*, ed. Clare Williams (London, 1933), 143. According to *Encyclopedia Britannica*, 4:281–82, a cellar differed from a vault; the latter was "deeper, the former being frequently little below the surface of the ground" and "in modern buildings, are the lowest rooms in a house," situated "level with the surface of the ground" or below "the pavement before the house, especially in streets and squares." They were not unique to London. Harold Williams, ed., *The Correspondence of Jonathan Swift* (Oxford, 1965), 4:331; *The Torrington Diaries* (London, 1936), 3:194–95; Truman G. Staffan and Willis W. Pratt, eds., *Byron's Don Juan* [1819] (Austin, 1957), canto 13, stanza 76; Simon Bradley and Nikolaus Pevsner, *The Buildings of England: London, I: The City of London* (London, 1997), 474, no. 41, 479, nos. 12–13, esp. 578, nos. 7–8; A. F. Kelsall, "The London House Plan in the Later 17th Century," *Post-medieval Archaeology* 8 (1974): 80–91; Andrew Byrne, *London's Georgian Houses* (London, 1986), s.v. "basements"; Dan Cruickshank and Peter Wyld, *London: The Art of Georgian Building* (Oxford, 1975), 29, 36, 38–39.

8. McKearin, "Notes," 120–27; Whitmore, Aspinwall Notarial Records, 26; Frederic De Peyster, ed., *The Life and Administration of Richard, Earl of Bellomont* (New York, 1879), vii.

9. William Pittman, "Morphological Variability in Late Seventeenth and Early Eighteenth Century English Wine Bottles" (master's thesis, College of William and Mary, 1990); Richard Carrillo, "English Wine Bottles as Revealed by a Statistical Study," in *The Conference on Historical Site Archaeology Papers—1972*, ed. Stanley South, 7 (1974): 290–306; Ivor Nöel Hume, "Excavations at Clay Bank in Gloucester County, Virginia, 1762–1963," *Contributions from the Museum of History and Technology* 52 (1968): 9–14; Edward P. Alexander, ed., *The Journal of John Fontaine* (Charlottesville, 1972), 85–86; Carter L. Hudgins, "The 'King"s Realm': An Archaeological and Historical Analysis of Robert Carter's Corotoman" (master's thesis, Wake Forest University, 1981), 40, 44, 103, 110–11; Stanley South, "Russelborough: Two Royal Governors' Mansions at Brunswick Town," *North Carolina Historical Review* 44 (1967): 340–72; Graham Hood, *The Governor's Palace in Williamsburg* (Chapel Hill, 1991), appendix; Anne Toogood, *Ephraim Hartwell Tavern: Historic Structure Report* (Denver, 1974), 19; Peter DuBois to Sir William Johnson, November [9,] 1761, Johnson, *Papers*, 3:563; Bentley, *Diary*, 2:25; John May, *Journals and Letters of Col. John May of Boston* (Cincinnati, 1873), 66.

10. *Pennsylvania Gazette*, January 20, March 3, June 25, 1747, September 27, 1750, March 6, April 5, July 19, 1753, June 6, 1754, March 18, 1755, December 9, 1756, June 1, 1757, February 15, December 6, 1759, February 25, 1762, April 12, June 21, 1764, October 5, 1774. An American cellar was usually a subterranean structure, but sometimes "cellar" denoted a store. *Pennsylvania Gazette*, April 29, 1756. Typical small cellars were found in two of three large (each twenty by thirty-six feet) Southwark row houses on the east side of Swanson Street, between it and the Delaware; each had "a vault under the alley" behind the house for holding eight hogsheads. *Pennsylvania Gazette*, December 23, 1762. An advertisement for a house at 78 Walnut Street in Philadelphia reveals a much more commodious cellar. See chap. 7, no. 65, above.

11. Jean Pierre Purry, *A Description of the Province of South Carolina* [before 1731] (London, 1732), 132. For similar arrangements, see Byrd, *Natural History*, 89; Arnold R. Highfield, trans., *J. L. Carstens' St. Thomas in Early Danish Times* (St. Croix, 1997), 108; Côté, "Fine Wine," 112–14; Richard Barry, *Mr. Rutledge of South Carolina* (New York, 1942), 73–77; Croft, *Treatise*, 24; John Wickham Commonplace Book, 1803–38, Wickham Family Papers, VHS.

12. Thomas Murdoch to Henry Heskith, October 15, 1799, vol. 20, fol. 67, NGL.

13. Erving Goffman's thoughts on theatrical props speak directly to the connection between cellars and gentility. The canonical presentation of his dramaturgical, performative approach to understanding interpersonal relations and communications appears in *The Presentation of Self in Everyday Life*. In it, Goffman rejected analyses of peoples' actions and words as entirely internally motivated. He emphasized that people act and speak to others, and that it can be instructive to regard observers and listeners as each other's audience. Their meetings take place on a "front stage." Be-

fore and after interactions, they retire to a "back stage" and prepare for future performances. The physical stage is important, as are the ancillary objects on that stage—sets, props, costumes—that facilitate and enhance the performance.

14. Goffman, *Presentation of Self*, 7.

15. For these and the following three paragraphs, see McKearin, "Notes," 120–27; Samuel Johnson, *The Adventurer* (Troy, 1903), 183; Miller, *Gardener's Dictionary*, s.v. "wines"; Pluche, *Spectacle de la nature*, 305; *Carter Diary*, 2:1134–135; *Encyclopedia Britannica*, 3:232; Robert Shannon, *A Practical Treatise on Brewing, Distilling, and Rectification* (London, 1805).

16. Raphael A. Weed, "Silver Wine Labels," *New York Historical Society Quarterly Bulletin* 13 (1929): 47–67; N. M. Penzer, *The Book of the Wine Label* (London, 1947), 15–31; Michael Clayton, *The Collector's Dictionary of the Silver and Gold of Great Britain and North America* (London, 1971), 342.

17. Drinking with glass containers also gave greater opportunity for profits for retailers. Not only did changing fashion require the purchase of new sets of glasses and decanters, but the objects could be relied upon to break, which necessitated further purchasing. This was a case far better than a planned obsolescence. Moreover, a certain percentage of the drinkers were bound to be drunk, or at least unstable, which fact increased the rate of breakage. Thus both consumers and retailers gained from drinking an intoxicating, perhaps addictive drink in breakable containers.

18. Peter Pope, "Historical Archaeology and the Demand for Alcohol in 17th Century Newfoundland," *Acadiensis* 19 (1989): 72–90; James E. Fitting et al., "Archaeological Excavations at the Marquette Mission Site, St. Ignace, Michigan, in 1972," *Michigan Archaeologist* 22 (1976): 190–93; William M. Kelso et al., *Jamestown Rediscovery V* (Richmond, 1999), nn39–78, describing earthen Spanish jars for olives, wine, and water and French earthenware flasks (bottles) for wine being shipped to Jamestown. Too, Chinese porcelain wine cups were brought to Jamestown by the Dutch and used in Virginia in the 1610s.

19. Thomas Heywood details the variety of wooden, ceramic, metal, and glass drinking vessels available in midcentury London in *Philocothonista*, 45–48. On Venetian glass, see Jutta-Annette Page, *Beyond Venice* (Corning, 2004). On Ravenscroft (1632–83), see Rosemary Rendel, "Who Was George Ravenscroft?" *Glass Circle* 2 (1975): 65–70, and "The True Identity of George Ravenscroft, Glassman," *Recusant History* 13 (1975): 101–5. W. A. Thorpe's account is fuller but occasionally erroneous: *History of English and Irish Glass*, 2 vols. (London, 1929). On Ravenscroft's glass, see R. J. Charleston, *English Glass and the Glass Used in England, c. 400–1940* (London, 1984), 111–15; Thorpe, "English Glassware in the Seventeenth Century," *Glass Notes* 16 (1956): 27–36.

20. A shortage of timber in England in the early 1600s and a 1615 prohibition against its use as a fuel for manufacturing promoted the adoption of coal-fired furnaces. Coal blasts produced a bottle glass that was both stronger and heavier than glass blasted by wood. On glassmaking in England, see Charleston, *English Glass*, chaps. 3–4; Daniel Klein and Ward Lloyd, *The History of Glass* (London, 1984), chaps. 1–5. Good general studies of glass made in Europe, which Ravenscroft's glass eclipsed in the Anglophone

world, include Johan Soetens, *In glas verpakt* (Amsterdam, 2001); Wilfred Buckley and Fernand Hudig, *European Glass: A Brief Outline of the History of Glass Making* (London, 1926). On glassmaking in Venice, see W. Patrick McCray, *Glassmaking in Renaissance Venice* (Aldershot, 1999); in Bohemia, see Edmund Schebek, *Böhmens Glassindustrie und Glashandel: Quellen zu ihrer Geschichte* (Frankfurt, 1969); in Hungary, see Béla Borsos, *Glassmaking in Old Hungary* (Budapest, 1963), 21–49; in France, see Geneviève Sennequier and Denis Woronoff, *De la verrerie forestière à la verrerie industrielle* (Rouen, 1998); Warren Scoville, *Capitalism and French Glassmaking, 1640–1789* (Berkeley, 1950); in Germany, see M. A. Gessert, *Geschichte der Glasmalerei in Deutschland* (Stuttgart, 1939); in the Netherlands, Low Countries, and Flanders, see Henri Schuermans, *Verres à la vénitienne fabriqués aux Pays-Bas* (Brussels, 1993); Robert H. McNulty, "Common Beverage Bottles: Their Production, Use and Forms in Seventeenth- and Eighteenth-Century Netherlands," *Journal of Glass Studies* 13 (1971): 91–119, 14 (1972), 141–47.

21. On glassmaking in America: Frederick W. Hunter, *Stiegel Glass* (Boston, 1914); Stephen Van Rensselaer, *Early American Bottles and Flasks*, rev. ed. (Peterborough, 1926), 50–194; Victor S. Clark, *History of Manufactures in the United States* (New York, 1929), 1:168–69; Dorothy Daniel, *Cut and Engraved Glass, 1771–1905* (New York, 1950), 107–23, 386–89; Helen McKearin and George McKearin, *American Glass* (New York, 1941), and *Two Hundred Years of American Blown Glass* (New York, 1950); Dwight P. Lanmon, "The Baltimore Glass Trade, 1780 to 1820," *Winterthur Portfolio* 5 (1969): 15–48, and "Glass in Baltimore: The Trade in Hollow and Tablewares, 1780–1820" (master's thesis, University of Delaware, 1968); Rosalind Beiler, "Caspar Wistar" (PhD diss., University of Pennsylvania, 1993); Arlene Palmer, *Glass in Early America* (Winterthur, 1993); Kenneth Wilson, *American Glass, 1760–1930* (New York, 1994), 55–64. After the Revolution, glass houses also sprang up in Maryland (Maryland Glass Factory, 1789), in Pittsburgh and its environs (Albert Gallatin, 1797, and James O'Hara & Isaac Craig, 1797), in Woodbury (New Jersey Glass Manufactory, 1799), in Boston (Boston Glass House, 1801), near Albany (Hamilton Glass House, 1801), in Philadelphia (Philadelphia Glass Works, 1801), to name only a few. Rita S. Gottesman, *The Arts and Crafts in New York, 1777–1799* (New York, 1954), 99–104, and *The Arts and Crafts in New York, 1800–1804* (New York, 1965), 129–35.

22. These and the following paragraphs draw upon Star and Griesemer, "Institutional Ecology," 393, 389, 410, 412.

23. Thomas Murdoch to various correspondents, 1794–95, box 41, CGP-Guildhall.

24. Campbell, "Travels," 121, 127, 134, 165, 179.

25. *Vinetum Britannicum* (London, 1676); Franklin, "Verses on the Birthday of Mary Stevenson," June 15, 1767, in *Franklin Papers*, 14:188.

26. Standard sizes for storing finished wine varied in volume. Contemporary references in letters of Madeira distributors and consumers suggest an array of volumes. On one occasion, 60 bottles equaled one-eighth of a pipe (that is, 60 bottles equaled 13.75 gallons, and 1 bottle equaled 0.23 gallons). Most bottles were probably expected to hold about 0.25 gallons (1 quart, 2 pints, or 32 ounces), and, when bottles were designated

by size, they were usually referred to as "quart bottles." According to chapter 3, notes 73–76 above, one cask of Madeira in Madeira equaled one pipe, and one pipe equaled 400 bottles; thus, 1 bottle in Madeira equaled 0.275 gallons, or roughly a quart. Looking at surviving bottles from colonial American archaeological sites, John McCusker has established that the "average bottle" of wine in the eighteenth century contained about 0.22 gallons or 1.75 pints or 28 ounces (0.8175 liters). Today, a standard wine bottle contains about 0.20 gallons or 1.61 pints or 25.76 ounces (0.75 liters). Yet, a bottle could be larger: on another occasion 180 bottles equaled 15 *quartolas* (a *quartola* being a quarter of a pipe, 180 bottles equaled 412.50 gallons, and 1 bottle equaled 2.29 gallons). Moreover, it could be much smaller: in 1772, according to Henry Laurens, since one-half pipe of Madeira would fill 600 bottles, 0.09 gallons should have filled up 1 bottle. McCusker, *Rum and the American Revolution*, 819–20; *Laurens Papers*, 8:383; Lahontan, *New Voyages*, 1:375.

27. Charleston, *English Glass*, 90–98; Klein and Lloyd, *History*, 117–69. Machine-made bottles were first manufactured in the 1820s.

28. William P. Doepkens, *Excavations at Mareen Duvall's Middle Plantation of South River Hundred* (Baltimore, 1991), 139, 142. An analysis of all *Pennsylvania Gazette* announcements advertising the sale of Claret and "French" wine between 1729 and 1762 suggests that only a quarter of all sales involved the sale of such wine in barrels.

29. *Pennsylvania Gazette*, July 31, August 14, December 4, 1729, December 21, 1731, February 8, March 7, 1732, December 18, 1740, June 13, July 4, October 31, 1751, July 30, August 20, November 23, 1752, May 31, 1753, October 10, 1754, August 14, October 30, 1755, October 21, 1756, February 17, April 28, 1757, June 22, 1758, July 19, December 13, 1759, September 23, 1765, March 23, August 10, 1769, June 21, July 12, 1771, January 22, 1773, February 1, 22, March 15, 29, April 12, May 31, August 2, 30, 1775, April 1, 1789, March 3, 1790; James Walker, *Hints to Consumers of Wine on the Abuses Which Enhance the Price of That Article* (Edinburgh, 1802), 19, 56–57. See also George F. Dow, *The Arts and Crafts in New England, 1704–1775* (Topsfield, 1927), 97–104; Gottesman, *Arts and Crafts in New York, 1726–1776* (New York, 1938), 96–99, . . . *1777–1799* (New York, 1954), 99–104, and . . . *1800–1804* (New York, 1965), 129–35; Alfred C. Prime, *The Arts and Crafts in Philadelphia, Maryland and South Carolina, 1721–1785*, vol. 1 (Topsfield, 1929), 13, 132–57, and . . . *1786–1800*, vol. 2 (Topsfield, MA, 1932), 151–63.

30. In England, the earliest intact example divorced from the bottle bears the mark "John Jefferson 1652"; the earliest intact example attached to the bottle has the designation "King's Head Tavern 1657." The earliest dated example of a colonial American bottle seal is tied to a much later site: a squat, olive-colored wine bottle with a seal bearing the legend "Richard Burbydge 1701" was found in a rubbish pit during an excavation of a plantation dwelling house and outbuilding not far from Williamsburg, along with other seals bearing the initials of "FJ" for Frederick Jones, the owner. Sheila Ruggles-Brise, *Sealed Bottles* (London, 1949); Roy Morgan and Gordon Litherland, *Sealed Bottles: Their History and Evolution (1630–1930)* (Burton-on-Trent, 1977). Seals were not peculiar to the English-speaking world. Soetens, *In glas verpakt*, 35–36, 149–50.

31. Planters and merchants often used the same personal initials for their bottle seals as

for their shipping adventures when marking export and import containers. As wine varieties proliferated, some seals even described the contents or volume of the bottle, although this was more often done for other beverages, not wine. This and the following paragraph draw from Doepkens, *Excavations*, 139, 142; Hudgins, "The 'King's Realm,'" 208, 315–16. Discussion of seals in colonial America appears in Ivor Nöel Hume, *Glass in Colonial Williamsburg's Archaeological Collections* (Williamsburg, 1969), 35–37, *A Guide to Artifacts of Colonial America* (New York, 1969), 61–62, 69–71, "Excavations at Rosewell," *Contributions from the Museum of History and Technology* 18 (1963): 173, and "Excavations at Tutter's Neck in James City County, Virginia, 1960–1961," *Contributions from the Museum of History and Technology* 53 (1968): 70.

32. The assurance seals conveyed allowed sellers to charge premium prices for wine-filled bottles marked with seals. Thomas Wharton to Benjamin Franklin, November 18, 1767, in *Franklin Papers*, 14:310.

33. For firm brands, see Newton, Gordon & Murdoch to Samuel & John Span, December 22, 1793, vol. 15, fol. 296, NGL. For examples of firm brand advertising, see *Poulson's American Daily Advertiser*, March 18, April 24, November 30 ("N, G, M" of Madeira), 1801, January 12 ("house of Phelps, Page & Co." of Madeira), July 14, 19 ("Pasleys' Brand" of Tenerife), September 4 ("Pasleys' Brand" of Tenerife), September 21 ("Bulkeley & Sons Brand" of Lisbon), 1815.

34. John Kersey, *Dictionarium Anglo-Britannicum*, 1708 (London, 1708), s.v. "decanter." For poetic mention of the decanter, see Leonard Welsted, *Epistles* (London, 1724), 39. The art of decanting was detailed by Jonathan Swift in 1745. *Works*, 11:395. The evolution of the decanter is described by John M. Bacon, "Bottle-Decanters and Bottles," *Apollo* 30 (1939): 13–15; Charleston, *English Glass*, 163–65; Derek C. Davis, *English Bottles and Decanters, 1650–1900* (London, 1972), 18–21; G. Bernard Hughes, *English, Scottish and Irish Table Glass, from the Sixteenth Century to 1820* (London, 1956), 257–83; Klein and Lloyd, *History*, 153–55.

35. G. Bernard Hughes, "Decanters for the Admiral's Table," *Country Life*, October 6, 1960, 722–23, and "Label Decanters of Georgian Times," *Country Life*, April 6, 1961, 764–65. The Rodney design was an improvement on that of prior ship decanters, which, according to Hughes, "never broke away from the shape of the wine bottles they replaced." Stopper designs changed more readily than decanter designs. Whatever the design, wholesalers and retailers sold decanters in pairs and, from 1760, they were also available in groups of four, six, twelve, and twenty-four. Half-pint, pint, quart and, after 1770, half-gallon and gallon decanters were marketed. Hughes, *Table Glass*, 273.

36. Franklin, "Verses on the Birthday of Mary Stevenson," 188.

37. In 1755, the *Norwich Mercury* was the first to advertise engraved named decanters in Britain: "New-fashioned Decanters" inscribed with the names of various beverages—"Port, Claret, Mountain, White Wine, Lisbon, Madeira, Florence, Rhenish, Burgundy, Hock, Beer and Cyder" and "decorated with Vine Leaves, Grapes, etc." *Norwich Mercury*, December 26, 1755, August 5, 1758. See also Hughes, "Label Decanters of Georgian Times," 764; Ivor Nöel Hume, *Archaeology and Wetherburn's*

Tavern (Williamsburg, 1969), 37, and *Glass*, 26, fig. 15; Sondy Sanford, "Monticello, Archaeological Glass," *Glass Club Bulletin* 139 (Winter 1983): 9–10; R. De Treville Lawrence III, *Jefferson and Wine* (The Plains, 1976), 343. The Arthur Hay decanter, c. 1740–50, and Henry Wetherburn decanter, 1750–56, are kept in the Archaeology Department of Colonial Williamsburg.

This and the following paragraphs are drawn from *Boston Gazette*, June 8, July 6, November 23, 1761; *New-York Gazette*, May 26, June 16, 1760; *New-York Mercury*, April 4, 1763; *Birmingham Gazette*, January 23, 1764; *New-York Gazette*, February 20, June 25, 1764, April 15, 1771; *Pennsylvania Gazette*, August 30, 1764; *Pennsylvania Gazette*, August 30, 1764, December 16, 1775, April 24, 1776; *Virginia Gazette*, July 25, December 18, 1766, February 25, 1768, October 4, 1770, October 31, 1771, May 11, 1776, February 21, 1777, January 23, 1778. Comparing English and American glassware advertisements is problematic. They do not appear in London papers to any great extent. Moreover, there is a difference in advertisement content between the mother country and its colonies: London papers focus on books and pamphlets, followed by drugs, auctions, and ships; colonial papers devote much more space to commodities. It may be that other types of ads were run in a few select newspapers but have not been found, or more likely a different sales and advertisement culture existed in London than in the colonies.

38. A "Madeira Bottle Neck Ring," made by John Reilly, in 1808, was put up at auction by Bonham's in 2003. Engraved around its side was: "This wine was bought at Madeira in 1792 and afterwards traveled round the Southern Promontory of Africa, through the Straits of Sunda, Banka and Formosa through the Corian Sea round the Eastern Extremity of Asia, the Cheatou & Meatou Straits into the Yellow Sea & home again, a distance comprising 30,900 Miles." Bonhams, *Annual Catalogue* (London, 2003). For decanter label advertisements, see *Pennsylvania Gazette*, July 16, 1777. For examples of the use of labels in a household, see the inventory of New York governor Tryon in December 1773, *New York History* 35 (1954–55): 306. Cf. Herbert C. Dent, "Wine, Spirit, and Sauce Labels," *Antiques* 35 (January 1939): 19–21. Paper labels on bottles are noted by Pepys, *Diary*, 3:18. Such labels were sold by retailers and affixed by them throughout the eighteenth century, and were simultaneously used by consumers. However, they achieved wide usage only in the middle of the nineteenth century, when exporters began to find it beneficial to advertise their "brand" through them, something especially important with the increase of wine shops and their display of wine bottles.

39. On heavy balusters, light balusters, and balustroids, see G. B. Hughes, *English Glass for the Collector, 1660–1860* (New York, 1968), 30–32; Klein and Lloyd, *History*, 126–30.

40. On "Silesian," twist, and facet glasses, see Hughes, *English Glass*, 34–44; Jancis Robinson, *The Oxford Companion to Wine* (Oxford, 1994), 343–44; Klein and Lloyd, *History*, 130–49. There is question whether the three post-1750 designs arose simultaneously or seriatim. Robinson alleges the former; Klein and Lloyd the latter.

41. *Pennsylvania Packet*, December 1, 1796.

42. W. A. Thorpe, "Drinking Glasses Commemorative of William III," *Apollo* (1926):

165–70, 210–216. On Jacobite glasses, see Geoffrey B. Seddon, *The Jacobites and Their Drinking Glasses* (Woodbridge, 1995), 95–133. For Loyalist glasses, numerous examples were found at Harveys Wine Museum in Bristol, such as a c. 1770 English glass engraved with "The King & The Friends of His Majesty's American Loyalists." On privateer glasses, see Klein and Lloyd, *History*, 160. On Freemasons glasses, see *Pennsylvania Gazette*, September 5, 1754, June 3, 1762; Chloe Zerwick, *A Short History of Glass* (Corning, 1980), 73, ill. 61; Helen McKearin, "Eighteenth Century Advertisements of Glass Imports into the Colonies and the United States," *Glass Notes* 14 (1954): 14–15. On enameling, see W.A. Thorpe, "The Beilby Glasses," *Connoisseur* (1928): 10–23. On gilding and stippling, see Klein and Lloyd, *History*, 134. Only Britons so decorated.

43. Arlene Palmer, "Glass Production in Eighteenth-Century America: The Wistarburgh Enterprise," *Winterthur Portfolio* 11 (1975): 75–101; Hunter, *Stiegel Glass*, 60–78, 180–90; Lanmon, "Baltimore Glass Trade," 4–48. Stiegel's 1769 output is listed in McKearin and McKearin, *American Glass*, 86. For advertisements of wineglasses made by other American manufacturers, see *Maryland Journal and Baltimore Advertiser*, February 11, 1785 (Amelung), March 14, 1788 (Keener), May 22, 1789 (Amelung). The Connecticut Historical Society has examples of bottles manufactured, c. 1800, at the Pitkin Glassworks in East Hartford.

44. Ivor Nöel Hume disagreed. "Glass shapes continued in use in Williamsburg for a good many years after the styles . . . had ceased being made in England." By comparing advertised glassware to excavated glassware, he also found that "homes in the larger northern cities . . . contained a greater variety of ornamental drinking glasses, decanters . . . , and the like, than did those of Williamsburg." *Glass*, 25–28. His reasoning argues only for the retention of old styles in secondary, nonport towns like Williamsburg that were never central to Atlantic commerce, not the adoption of newer styles.

45. *Pennsylvania Gazette*, 1728–1800, passim. In only one ad was English glassware described as coming from Liverpool. Glassware was infrequently advertised as "American," although there were occasional notices by Richard Wistar and Henry Stiegel. *Pennsylvania Gazette*, March 5, 1741, June 27, 1771. For the Charleston list, see *South Carolina Gazette*, November 20, 1752. Sellers in other towns were not offering as wide an array, often only "beer and wine glasses." Cf. *Boston Evening Post*, April 30, 1750, March 11, May 27, 1751; *New York Evening Post*, June 17, 1751. But by the 1760s, the range had increased in all towns. *Pennsylvania Gazette*, December 28, 1769; *Boston News-Letter*, May 16, 1771, December 31, 1772; *New-York Gazette and the Weekly Mercury*, April 15, December 16, 1771.

46. *Pennsylvania Gazette*, June 4, 1761, October 18, 1764, December 6, 1775, April 24, 1776, November 14, 1778, December 7, 1785; *New-York Gazette and the Weekly Mercury*, April 15, 1771.

47. *Pennsylvania Gazette*, 1754, 1761, 1763, 1767; McKearin and McKearin, *American Glass*, 86.

48. Charleston, *English Glass*, 104–5, 116; Albert Hartshorne, *Old English Glasses* (London, 1897), 230–34, 438–39; William Ramsey, comp., *The Worshipful Company of Glass Sellers of London* (London, 1898), 59–77.

49. Archaeological remains and glass collections suggest that the larger wineglasses usually contained about six fluid ounces, and the more common smaller wineglasses three ounces; an even smaller cordial glass introduced at the end of the seventeenth century held roughly one ounce. Capacity of glasses is delineated in E. Barrington Haynes, *Glass through the Ages*, rev. ed. (Harmondsworth, 1959), 200; Charleston, *English Glass*, 157. Haynes suggested an eighteenth-century wineglass contained two to three ounces. Charleston believed it could hold as little as one and a half ounces. In eighteenth-century France, manufacturers designed three different sizes for four different wine drinks: *grands* for vin ordinaire, *moyens* for vin étranger, and *petits* for liqueurs and eau-de-vie. James Barrelet, *La verrerie en France de l'époque Gallo-Romaine à nos jours* (Paris, 1953), 112. For examples of orders, see Hannah Penn to James Logan, July 24, 1700, in Dunn and Dunn, *World of William Penn*, 3:610.

50. On specialized glassware, see Nathaniel Bailey, *An Universal Etymological English Dictionary* (London, 1724), s.v. "rummer"; Charleston, *Glass*, 140; Butler and Walkling, *Book of Wine Antiques*, 191–214. Differentiation and specialization in Europe set in between 1700 and 1775. Some of the sets had two or three differently sized wineglasses and four water glasses. Distinctions were made between wine, water, and beer glasses. The sets were counterparts to the grand porcelain table services crafted in the first half of the eighteenth century. Jiřina Vydrova, "Les débuts de la différenciation des types de verre de table en Bohême," *Annales* (Congrès international d'étude historique du verre—Liège) 5 (1972): 205–15; Ada Polak, "The 'Ip Olufsen Weyse' Illustrated Price-List of 18th-Century Norwegian Glass," *Journal of Glass Studies* 11 (1969): 100–104. Also see the two-volume trade catalog for a Bohemian glass manufacturer at the end of the eighteenth century, kept in the Manuscript Division, Winterthur Library.

51. For Stansbury's invoice, see Mitchell Papers, PSA. For Newton & Gordon's order of "Madeira glasses," see Newton & Gordon to Thomas Gordon, May 6, 1799, vol. 19, fol. 285, NGL. Also see McKearin, "Eighteenth Century Advertisements, Part II," 17; *Pennsylvania Gazette*, September 25, 1746, June 4, 1761; Order Book, 1772–74, Rhinelander Papers, NYHS; Gottesman, *Arts and Crafts in New York, 1726–1776*, 98–99, and . . . *1777–1799*, 102–3, 197–98; Dructor, "New York Commercial Community," 306–438; Arlene Palmer Schwind, "English Glass Imports in New York, 1770–1790," *Journal of Glass Studies* 25 (1983): 179–85. On India, see John Fryer, *A New Account of East-India and Persia* (London, 1698), 93; Inventory of Ross Belt, May 27, 1788, LAG 34/27/9, vol. 1, fol. 424, as well as LAG 34/27/11, p. 763 (1789), LAG 34/27/13, p. 52 (1790), LAG 34/27/19, p. 9 (1797), IOL; *Asiatic Annual Register* 2 (1800): 123. *Hartly House* (Dublin, 1798), a novel by Phebe Gibbes, whose son had died in India, details Anglo-Indian drinking habits. The oil painting entitled *A Lucknow Dinner Party*, c. 1820, now in the possession of William Dalrymple, London, depicts British and Indian glassware being used together on a table in India. Similar array appears in the painting *Lord and Lady Moira* (1819), IOL.

52. *Charleston Courier*, October 10, 1803, 4. One Philadelphia glass and ceramic seller carried an extensive range of English and German glassware. At his death in 1813, he was offering ring-necked decanters; plain, cut, and engraved half-pint, pint, and

quart decanters; coasters; glass mugs; common goblets; and quart and double-flint tumblers, some covered. Leonard Keehmle, Inventory, November 24–26, 1813, nos. 1813–131, Philadelphia City and County Probate Records, City Hall, Philadelphia.

53. The first record of a drinking suite was an order placed with a Bristol glasshouse by a New Yorker in 1780; nothing more is known about it. The earliest surviving suite was made in Ireland in 1788, but it is unclear if its glasses were keyed to specific wines. More is known of sets made in Waterford around 1800. Honor for the arrival of sets as important fashion items goes to a dinner the Liverpool Corporation gave for the Prince of Wales in 1806. For that dinner, that body ordered large Claret, "wine," and small Port glasses from Perrin & Geddes of Warrington, and later copied them as a gift for the prince. On the New York set, see Schwind, "English Glass Imports," 184. On the Irish sets, see Phelps Warren, "Luxury in English and Irish Cut Glass," *Antiques* (1969): 885–86. On the English sets, see Cherry Gray and Richard Gray, "The Prince's Glasses: Some Warrington Cut Glass, 1806–1811," *Journal of the Glass Association* 2 (1987): 18, 11, 13. A glassmaker's 1794 list appears in *Pottery Gazette*, May 1, 1895, but no suites were offered. Another set made for the Prince of Wales in Staffordshire c. 1806 contained Port, Sherry, Claret, and Champagne glasses. An 1810–24 set made for the Crown had three different wineglasses and two different decanters. R. B. Brown, "The Davenports and Their Glass, 1801–1807," *Journal of the Glass Association* 1 (1985): 32.

Extensive specialized suites—complete sets of a dozen glasses with separate vessels for Madeira, Port, Sherry, Hock, red, white, brandy and cordials, flutes for Champagne and cordials, goblets, and matching decanters and water beakers—did not appear in the States until the 1820s, when glassmakers introduced mechanical pressing. Not until 1859 was a full suite of three wineglass sizes marketed, when McKee & Brothers of Pittsburgh offered champagne, wine, and cordial glasses. Jane Spillman and Lowell Innes, eds., *M'Kee Victorian Glass: Five Complete Glass Catalogs from 1859/60 to 1871* (Corning, 1981); Palmer, "Glass Production," 85. On manufacturers' release of specialized glassware, see Palmer, *Glass in Early America*, 57–84. On mass production of drinking glasses, see Zerwick, *Short History*, 79; Ruth W. Lee, *The History of the Boston and Sandwich Glass Company*, 8th ed. (Northborough, 1939), 89–92, 103–5, 162–66; Frederick Irwin, *The Story of Sandwich Glass and Glassworkers* (Manchester, NH, 1926), 22, 80–87.

54. *Moniteur de la Louisiane*, no. 383, December 19, 1803, no. 376, January 2, 1804. Cf. George Oudard, *Vieille Amérique: La Louisiane au temps des français* (Paris, 1931), 292.

55. Berry Tracy and Mary Black, *Federal Furniture and Decorative Arts at Boscobel* (New York, 1981), 122–23, no. 91.

CODA. "THE PLEASURES OF THE BOTTLE"

1. Matthew Heynes, *A Sermon against Drunkenness* (London, 1701), 20; Daniel Duncan, *Wholesome Advice against the Abuse of Hot Liquors* (London, 1706), 90; Edward Ward, *Wine and Wisdom; or, The Tipling Philosophers* (Dublin, 1751), 9;

George Berkeley, *Alciphron; or, The Minute Philosopher*, 2nd ed. (London, 1732), 104; Edmund Burke, *A Philosophical Enquiry into the Origin of Our Ideas of the Sublime and Beautiful* (London, 1757), 3.

2. This and the following paragraph draw upon John Pomfret, *The Choyce* (London, 1700), 1:5; Homer, *Odyssey*, bk. xiv, l. 520; Gay, *Beggar's Opera*, act III, sc. 8, p. 50; [Franklin,] "Obedient Wives"; John Gay, "Fables" (1738), II, in *The Poetical Works* (London, 1926), 502; "Journal of a French Traveler in the Colonies, 1765, Part II," *AHR* 26 (1921): 73. Literature reinforced such thinking. From 1640 through 1815, characters in operas, plays, and novels were commanded to "fill ev'ry glass, for wine inspires us, and fires us, with courage, love and joy" or "to prop up your spirits with old stout Madeira." Penelope Aubin, *The Noble Slaves* (1722; London, 1739), chap. 9, pp. 72, 79; Henry Fielding, *Jonathan Wild* (London, 1743), chap. 14; Smollett, *Roderick Random*, chaps. 22, 50, 59; Fielding, *Tom Jones*, bk. 8, chap. 12; Smollett, *Peregrine Pickle*, vol. 2, chap. 42; Henry Fielding, *Amelia* (London, 1752), bk. 4, chap. 9; James Boswell, *The Life of Samuel Johnson* (New York, 1950), 828 (echoing the words of Psalm 104:15, and of St. Francis of Sales's 1600 *Treatise on the Love of God*); John O'Keeffe, *The Dead Alive: A Comic Opera* (London, 1783), act II, p. 23; Croft, *Treatise*, 19; Truman Guy Staffan and Willis W. Pratt, eds., *Byron's Don Juan* [1819] (Austin, 1957), canto 13, stanza 76.

3. *The Mirror* (Boston, 1792), 2:11; Horace, *Epistles*, bk. I, epistle V, ll. 25–28 (50 B.C.), in *The Odes, Satyrs, and Epistles*, 2nd ed. (London, 1688), 486; William Shakespeare, *Macbeth* [1605–7], act II, sc. III, ll. 32–40; Henry Peacham, *Minerva Britannia; or, A Garden of Heroical Devises* (London, 1612), 227; Whitaker, *Tree of Humane Life*, 20; *Bacchus Turn'd Doctor*, often attributed to Ben Jonson but more likely the work of Aurelian Townshend—see Townshend's *Journal* (London, 1670), which draws on his *Bacchus Iacchus* (London, 1655); William Congreve, *The Old Batchelour* (London, 1693), act IV, sc. III, ll. 64–65. For a New World variation, see Nicasius de Sille to Maximiliaen van Beeckerke, May 23, 1654, in I. N. Phelps, *The Iconography of Manhattan Island, 1498–1909* (New York, 1922), 4:149.

     Drinking to please oneself stood in contrast to drinking to get drunk. An alarm against drunkenness had been sounded by as early as the late sixteenth century. Philip Stubbes, *The Anatomie of Abuses* (London, 1583), s.v. "gluttonie and drunkennesse"; Thomas Nash, *Pierce Penilesse* (London, 1592); Walter Raleigh, *Sir Walter Raleigh's Instructions to His Sonne* (London, 1632), 81. Early opposition to drinking alcohol focused on the animality induced; although beastliness was always a concern, later attacks highlighted its dimming of wit. Homer, *The Iliad*, trans. Alexander Pope (London, 1717), 342; Thomas Fuller, *Gnomologia* (London, 1732); *Treatise on the True Effects of Drinking Spirituous Liquors*, 11.

4. Boorde, *Breviarie of Health*, 8; Charles Darby, *Bacchanalia; or, A Description of a Drunken Club* (London, 1683), 1; John Wilmot, *Familiar Letters* (London, 1697), 1:26; George Washington, *The Diaries*, ed. Donald Jackson (Charlottesville, 1976), 1:144; St. George Tucker, "Bacchanalian," ll. 1–6, 12, in *The Poems of St. George Tucker of Williamsburg, Virginia, 1752–1827*, ed. William S. Prince (New York, 1977), 71.

5. Horace, *Epistles*, bk. I, epistle V, l. 29, p. 486; Francis Hopkinson, "I've a Thought," ll. 214–29, in *The Miscellaneous Essays and Occasional Writings* (Philadelphia, 1792), 2:228, 236. For a contrary strain suggesting wine "invents nothing; it only tattles," see *Piccolomini* (1799), act II, sc. 14, l. 52, in Samuel T. Coleridge, *Complete Poetical Works* (Oxford, 1912), 67.

6. Attributed to François Rabelais, *The Whole Works; or, The Lives, Heroic Deeds and Sayings of Gargantua & Pantagruel* (1534; Eng. trans., London, 1708); Joseph Addison et al., *The Spectator*, vol. 4 (Oxford, 1965), 543; Ward, *Wine and Wisdom*, 11, 14, 17, 39; Benjamin Franklin to *New-England Courant*, September 10, 1722, in Smyth, *Writings*, 2:4; Georg C. Lichtenberg, *The Reflections* (London, 1908).

7. Thomas Brennan, *Public Drinking and Popular Culture in Eighteenth-Century Paris* (Princeton, 1988), 19; William Shakespeare, *Julius Caesar* (London, 1623), act 4, sc. III, ll. 2071–72; John Fletcher and Ben Jonson, *The Bloody Brother*, 2nd ed. (London, 1629), p. before 1; John Oldham, "The Careless Good Fellow," alternately "The Claret Drinkers Song" (London, 1680), in *Poems and Translations* (London, 1683), 161; George Meriton, *The Praise of York-shire Ale* (London, 1685), 5–6; Henry Aldrich, *Five Reasons for Drinking* (London, 1705); Gay, "Fables" (1738), II, p. 287; Henry Fielding, *Joseph Andrews* (London, 1742), bk. 1, chap. 11; Frances M. Brooke, *The History of Emily Montague* (London, 1769), 1:103–4; Frederick Reynolds, *Management: A Comedy* (London, 1799), act III, p. 39; James Kenney, *Turn Out! A Farce* (London, 1812), act II, sc. III, p. 35.

8. Roth, "Tea Drinking," 71–72; Byrd, *Secret Diary*, 78; Richard Jodrell, trans., *Illustrations of Euripides, on the Ion and the Bacchae* (London, 1781), ll. 774–76; Alexander Pope, *The Wife of Bath* (1714), in *The Works* (London, 1736), 3:172; Smollett, *Peregrine Pickle*, vol. 3, chaps. 82, 89, 90, 83; Richard B. Sheridan, *The School for Scandal* (London, 1777; Dublin, 1780), act III, p. 35; St. George Tucker, "Bacchanalian," ll. 25–30, 37–42. On weddings, see William Eddis, *Letters from America* (Cambridge, 1969), 58. Likewise, the "principal inhabitants" of New London were "entertained liberally with plumb cake & cheese & wine" at the marriage of Miner Hempstead. Hempstead, *Diary*, 624. Similar customs had prevailed during the seventeenth century: wine, spirits, beer, and food were served at funerals in Dutch Albany; often, the wine was in the house at the time of death, but it was sometimes provided by the deacons, as when poor parishioners or church officers were interred. Venema, *Deacons' Accounts*, 224. When the minister of Boston's King's Chapel died in 1736, deacons ordered two gallons of Madeira "for the Burriall . . . & Mourning for his Family"; likewise, when their minister died three decades later, they bought six bottles. Social uses of wine were not peculiar to elites. In 1766, the family of the Lancaster County ferry keeper bought five gallons of wine and six gallons of rum from Shippen & Burd's store for his funeral. Drink lent a formality to almost any rite of passage worth noting. Bill, March 12, 1733, Bills and Receipts, 1736, Financial Records, box 1, folder 8, Financial Records, King's Chapel Archives, MHS; Foote, *Annals of King's Chapel*, 2:35–36; Entry "For the Funeral" of William Wright, February 1766, Shippen & Burd Wine Book, fol. 102, APS.

9. *Pennsylvania Gazette*, November 1752; John Adams to James Warren, October 7, 1775, in Robert J. Tayler, ed., *Papers of John Adams* (Cambridge, 1979), 3:188–91; *Pennsylvania Gazette*, July 1792.

10. Franklin, *Autobiography*, 42–43; Alexander Hamilton, *The History of the Ancient and Honorable Tuesday Club*, ed. Robert Micklus, vol. 1 (Chapel Hill, 1990); "To Horse My Brave Boys," MS 387.1, Homony Club Papers, 1748–73, fol. 22v, Maryland Historical Society; Richard Sheridan, *The Duenna* (London, 1775), act II, sc. II, p. 45; Wolley, *Two Years' Journey*, 66–67; John Pope, *A Tour* (Richmond, 1792), 86.

11. While alternative views of wine consumption ran current (see, for instance, note 3 above, as well as chapter 10—for it was also seen as encouraging drunkenness and bad behavior and as leading to neglect of labor and abandonment of family—these were relatively insignificant perspectives before 1815. It is not that these positions were never staked out—it is just that they were infrequent and slight, at least until the heyday of temperance agitation in the 1820s and 1830s.

12. Brennan, *Public Drinking*, 188; Carol Harrison, *The Bourgeois Citizen in Nineteenth-Century France* (Oxford, 1999), 3; Daniel Gordon, *Citizens without Sovereignty: Equality and Sociability in French Thought, 1670–1789* (Princeton, 1994), 29, 33, 51–52, 55–85. Historians of France have studied sociability best: Ulrich Im Hof, *The Enlightenment* (Oxford, 1994), 105–17; Gordon, *Citizens*; Dena Goodman, "Sociabilité," in, *Le monde des lumières*, ed. Daniel Roche and Vincenzo Ferrone (Paris, 1999), 251–57; Harrison, *Bourgeois Citizen*, 1–15; Pierre-Yves Beaurepaire, *L'espace des francs-maçons: Une sociabilité européenne au XVIIIe siècle* (Rennes, 2003). The most recent study of it in Britain is Peter Clark, *British Clubs and Societies, 1580–1800* (Oxford, 2000). Shields's *Civil Tongues* remains the best examination of the American analogue.

13. Hamilton, *History*, 1:35–36; John Pomfret, *Poems upon Several Occasions* (London, 1735), 3.

14. Darby, *Bacchanalia*, 2; Comte d'Estaing to Gabriel de Sartine, November 5, 1778, in Stanley J. Idzerda, ed., *Lafayette in the Age of the American Revolution* (Ithaca, 1979), 2:203. See also "A Club Formed by the Jews, 1761," *Newport Historical* 4 (1883): 58–60; Morris A. Gutstein, *The Story of the Jews of Newport: Two and a Half Centuries of Judaism, 1658–1908* (New York, 1936), 170–72; Charles Warren, "Samuel Adams and the Sans-Souci Club in 1785," MHS, *Proceedings*, 3rd ser., 60 (1926–27): 233–28; Minutes of the Sub Rosa Club, November 4, 1797, NYHS, for which a new pipe of Madeira was purchased each season.

15. Wolley, *Two Years' Journey*, 65–66, 68; William Gooch to Edmund Gibson, Bishop of London, 1735, *VMHB* 32 (1924): 328; Deodatus Bye to John Loveday, March 1, 1740, in Sarah Markham, *John Loveday of Caversham, 1711–1789* (Wilton, 1984), chap. 16, p. 1; Thomas Hancock to Harris & Crisp, August 23, 1750, Thomas Hancock Letter Book 1750–62, Hancock Papers, HBS; Mary Fisher to Benjamin Franklin, August 14, 1758, vol. 8 (1965), 120, Thomas Livezey to Benjamin Franklin, November 18, 1767, vol. 14 (1970), 309–10, Benjamin Franklin to William Franklin, July 25, 1773, vol. 20 (1976), 328, Peter Allaire to Franklin, January 31, 1780, vol. 31 (1995), 428–29, *Franklin Papers*; Jonathan Williams Jr. to William Temple Franklin, May 18, 1782, photocopy,

Franklin Papers, Yale University, New Haven; Daniel Roberdeau to Fernandes & Co., November 28, 1764, Roberdeau Letter Book, 1764–71, fol. 25, HSP; Frederick Smyth to Aaron Lopez and Jacob Rivera, January 8, 1773, box 14, folder 10, Aaron Lopez Papers, American Jewish Historical Society, Newton Centre, MA; Thomas Jefferson to William Small, May 7, 1775, in Boyd, *Papers of Thomas Jefferson*, 1:165; Chastellux, *Travels*, 1:153; Jacques T. Godbout, *The World of the Gift*, trans. Donald Winkler (Montreal, 1998), 185; John Marsden Pintard to Elias Boudinot, April 3, 1783, Boudinot Correspondence, folder 41, ABS; Anne Grant, *Memoirs of an American Lady* (London, 1808), 272.

16. Bradley C. Brooks, "The Social Functions of Alcohol in Eighteenth-Century Maryland" (master's thesis, University of Delaware, 1987), 33. For recent historical work on the gift, see Avner Offer, "Between the Gift and the Market: The Economy of Regard," *Economic History Review* 50 (1997): 450–76; Godbout, *World of the Gift*; Natalie Z. Davis, *The Gift in Sixteenth-Century France* (Madison, 2000); Ilana Krausman Ben-Amos, "Gifts and Favors: Informal Support in Early Modern England," *Journal of Modern History* 72 (2000): 295–338; Valentin Groebner, *Liquid Assets, Dangerous Gifts* (Philadelphia, 2002), 23–27. Extending hospitality and inducing pleasure through wine gifts became a hallmark of American politics, much as in British. Bernard, "Theodicy," 57; Brooks, "Social Functions," 31; Charles Sydnor, *Gentlemen Freeholders: Political Practices in Washington's Virginia* (Chapel Hill, 1952), chap. 4; J. R. Pole, *Political Representation in England and the Origins of the American Republic* (New York, 1966), 23, 136–37, 149–56; Rhys Isaac, *The Transformation of Virginia, 1740–1790* (Chapel Hill, 1982), 46, 111–14; Edmund Morgan, *Inventing the People: The Rise of Popular Sovereignty in England and America* (New York, 1988), 183–85; John G. Kolp, *Gentlemen and Freeholders: Electoral Politics in Colonial Virginia* (Baltimore, 1998), 28–32.

17. George Washington to John Marsden Pintard, May 20, 1786, to George William Fairfax, June 25, 1786, to William Pearce, November 23, 1794, in John C. Fitzpatrick, ed., *The Writings of George Washington*, vol. 28 (Washington, DC, 1938), 433, 470, vol. 34 (1940), 41–42, 53. On differences in duty and price between Madeira and Claret in Washington's day, see *Columbian Gazetteer*, October 3, November 28, 1794; *American Apollo*, April 24, 1794; *Independent Gazetteer*, March 19, 1794.

18. R. W. G. Vail, ed., "A Dinner at Mount Vernon, from the Unpublished Journal of Joshua Brookes (1773–1859)," *New-York Historical Society Quarterly* 31 (April 1947): 74; George Washington to Mary Ball Washington, February 15, 1787, in Fitzpatrick, *Writings*, vol. 29 (1939), 160.

CONCLUSION. "IF BACCHUS, NOT NEPTUN, WERE GOD OF THE SEA"

1. The difference is hinted at in this conclusion's title, a quote from Charles Sackville, Earl of Dorset, *The New Academy of Complements* (London, 1669), 89 (song 5 of "Songs *Alamode*").

2. "Contracts" in the sense used by economists, that is, agreements among agents that

incorporate quid pro quos, does not imply that there were written legal contracts. Usually there were none.

3. One study, George L. Miller, "Marketing Ceramics in North America," *Winterthur Portfolio* 19 (1984): 1–5, finds many of the same traits.

4. Contemporaries certainly referred to themselves as connected. Royal Humane Society, *Annual Report* (London, 1792), 7.

5. David T. Konig, "Colonization and the Common Law in Ireland and Virginia, 1569–1634," in *The Transformation of Early American History: Society, Authority, and Ideology*, ed. James A. Henretta et al. (New York, 1991), 70–92; Bernard Bailyn, *The Ideological Origins of the American Revolution* (Cambridge, MA, 1967), 94–159.

6. Robert Sidney Smith, "The *Wealth of Nations* in Spain and Hispanic America, 1780–1830," *Journal of Political Economy* 65 (1957): 109–10, 115; Horst Dippel, *Germany and the American Revolution, 1770–1800*, trans. Bernhard A. Uhlendorf (Chapel Hill, 1977), 64–70, 81, 141–44, 159, 162. Blessed with creative interpreters and challenged by Spanish censors, no accurate Spanish translation of the treatise was published before the 1950s.

7. Steele, *English Atlantic*, vii–ix, 5, 44, 63, 113–14, 122–33, 213–14, 275, 278; Mintz, *Sweetness*, 173–83, 187–214; Richard Drayton, *Nature's Government: Science, Imperial Britain, and the "Improvement" of the World* (New Haven, 2000), xiv, xviii, 50, 78–79, 92, 107–8, 220.

8. Adam Smith, *An Inquiry into the Nature and Causes of the Wealth of Nations* (1776), ed. R. H. Campbell et al. (Oxford, 1976), 2:564; John J. McCusker, "Colonial Statistics," in *The Historical Statistics of the United States*, ed. Susan B. Carter et al., 4th ed. (Cambridge, 2006), 5:637–38.

9. Joel Mokyr, *The Lever of Riches: Technological Creativity and Economic Progress* (Oxford, 1990).

10. *Pennsylvania Packet*, December 1, 1796.

11. It is important to understand what is not being claimed here. It is not being claimed that the innovations of the eighteenth century were created for nineteenth-century use; this book has repeatedly emphasized that much of social and economic life is a response to agents' immediate needs and situations, with little long-term foresight. It is also not being claimed that industrialization and globalization could not have occurred in the absence of the eighteenth-century organizational innovations; the scientific and technological discoveries that led to faster transportation and increases in worker productivity would have created these phenomena in some form or another in any case. What is being claimed is that they took the forms they did because they built on the organizations, attitudes, and approaches nineteenth-century people inherited from the men and women of the eighteenth century.

12. Gavin Wright, "Towards a More Historical Approach to Technological Change," *Economics Journal* 107 (1997): 1564; C. K. Harley, "A Review of O'Rourke and Williamson's Globalization and History: The Evolution of a Nineteenth Century Atlantic Economy," *Journal of Economic Literature* 38 (2000): 931.

13. Probably the most famous study group was Birmingham's Lunar Society, which included the manufacturer Matthew Boulton, the physician Erasmus Darwin, the

preacher and scientist Joseph Priestley, the inventor James Watt, and the potter Josiah Wedgwood. They met from 1775 "at each other's houses on the Monday nearest the full moon, to have light to ride home." Jenny Uglow, *The Lunar Men: Five Friends Whose Curiosity Changed the World* (New York, 2002), xiii.

14. Alessandro Nuvolari, "Collective Invention during the British Industrial Revolution: The Case of the Cornish Pumping Engine," *Cambridge Journal of Economics* 28 (2004): 348, 355; R. C. Allen, "Collective Invention," *Journal of Economic Behavior and Organization* 4 (2004): 1–24.

15. Franco Malerba, "Innovation and the Evolution of Industries," *Journal of Evolutionary Economics* 16 (2006): 10.

16. For Kevin H. O'Rourke and Jeffrey G. Williamson, globalization is the "integration of international commodity markets," and global "commodity price convergence" is the test for it. They argue that increased trade and factor movements caused prices of locally scarce factors to fall and factor prices to converge. The eighteenth century, to them, was a "transitional phase sprinkled with trade in furs, tobacco and cotton." While at some factual level this was the case, it is also something of a caricatured straw man that ignores many of the other important shifts and trends of the immediately prior period. "When Did Globalization Begin?" (NBER Working Paper Series, WP 7632, April 2000), 3, 4, 6, and *Globalization and History: The Evolution of a Nineteenth-Century Atlantic Economy* (Cambridge, MA, 1999).

17. Patrick O'Brien, "Provincializing the First Industrial Revolution," *Working Papers of the Global Economic History Network (GEHN)* 17/06 (January 2006): 14, 26.

18. Kerby Miller, *Emigrants and Exiles: Ireland and the Irish Exodus to North America* (New York, 1985). See also Alan Lester, *Imperial Networks: Creating Identities in Nineteenth Century South Africa and Britain* (London, 2001), who shows how settlers in the eastern Cape area of South Africa in the early decades of the nineteenth century built communication networks with settlers in other colonies as a way of gaining greater metropolitan subsidy and support, officials participated in discussion networks and face-to-face meetings to ease the task of governing and promote their individual careers, and missionaries deployed links to and contacts in metropolitan reform movements. Connections in Britain were eagerly deployed to ease tasks along the periphery. Tony Ballantyne, *Orientalism and Race: Aryanism in the British Empire* (Basingstoke, 2002), adumbrates discussion networks linking men and women in different colonies.

19. Rosalind J. Beiler, "Peterstal and Wistarburgh: The Transfer and Adaptation of Business Strategies in Eighteenth-Century American Glassmaking," *Business and Economic History* 26 (1997): 343–53; Jeffrey J. Matthews, "The Pursuit of Progress: The Corning Glass Works, Alanson B. Houghton, and America as World Power, 1851–1929" (PhD diss., University of Kentucky, 2000).

ACKNOWLEDGMENTS

1. William L. Clements to Randolph G. Adams, October 18, 1933, William L. Clements Papers, Clements Library, Ann Arbor.

A NOTE ON CONVENTIONS

1. The most authoritative account of the moneys of Portugal, Spain, Britain, and their Atlantic empires appears in John J. McCusker, *Money and Exchange in Europe and America, 1600–1775: A Handbook* (Chapel Hill, 1978), 107–8, 300–302. For more detailed accounts, see Augusto C. Teixeira de Aragão, *Descripção geral e historica das moedas cunhadagem nome dos reis, regentes e governadores de Portugal* (Lisbon, 1874–80), 2:237–39; Mauro, *Le Portugal*, 395–432.

2. Newton & Gordon to Corrie & Scott, September 20, 1763, vol. 3, fol. 203, to Thomas Gordon, January 20, 1801, vol. 21, fol. 186, NGL; Sydney Parkinson, "Account" [a reworking of Joseph Banks's *"Endeavour" Journal*], 10, typescript, Royal Geographical Society Library, London; *"Endeavour" Journal*, 165; Communication of the Provedor to the King, July 27, 1762, caixa ii, no. 251, AHU; Arbuthnot Letters, fol. 52, NLS.

3. McCusker, *Money and Exchange*, 301.

4. Communication of the Provedor to the King, July 27, 1762, caixa ii, no. 251, AHU; Newton, Gordon & Johnston to Sir Robert Herries & Co., December 15, 1777, vol. 6, fol. 313, NGL. On money and credit before 1700, generally, see Azevedo e Silva, *A Madeira*, 1:451–67.

5. Newton & Gordon to Johnston & Jolly, October 19, 1766, vol. 4, fol. 41, NGL.

6. Newton, Gordon & Murdoch to Thomas Gordon, July 10, September 18, 1794, vol. 16, fols. 7–8, 81, to Evans, Offley & Sealy, September 25, 1794, vol. 16, fol. 98, NGL.

7. On merchants' chit coins, see Newton, Gordon & Murdoch to Thomas Murdoch, October 19, 1805, vol. 27, fol. 149, NGL; John Leacock to William Leacock, November 1, 1801, Leacock Letter Book 1799–1802, Leacock Papers.

8. John Leacock Jr. to William Leacock, November 1, 1801, Leacock Letter Book 1799–1802, fol. 210, Leacock Papers.

List of Unpublished Sources

Archives and libraries consulted in my research containing only one manuscript or collection do not appear in the following list.

BRAZIL

Rio de Janeiro

Arquivo Nacional

Codex 156: Terms of Vessels, vol. 1
Codex 157: Imports and Exports, 1724–1820 — Bonds for Vessels, 1724–1808
Codex 158: Register of Vessel Cargoes, 1820
Junta de comercio, caixas 448–49: Summaries of Charts of Importation, 1808–14

Biblioteca Nacional, Seção de manuscritos

Chart of Goods Exported from the Captaincy, 1803–4
Contracts of the Subsidio grande dos vinhos, 1738, 1739, 1756, 1757
Particular Papers, 1807–9

Salvador de Bahia

Arquivo Publico do Estado da Bahia

Registers of Entry of Merchandise, 1806–11

Municipal Archives

Books of *Entradas*, 1790–1815

DENMARK

Copenhagen

Rigsarkivet

Correspondence of the Consuls in Madeira
Oud notarieel-archief, Notarial Deeds

ENGLAND

Lincoln

Lincolnshire Archives

Thomas Thistlewood Diaries

London (Greater London)

British Library

Banks Correspondence, Add. MSS 33977
Catalogue of Plants, 1690, Sloane MSS 2346/197–99
Hemming and Milner Correspondence concerning Madeira Consulship, 1706–10, Blenheim Papers, vol. 410
India Office Records
 Accountant-General's Records, L-AG
  General Ledgers
  Probate Inventories, 1780–1815
 Court of Directors Minutes, B
 General Correspondence, E
  E1 Home Correspondence
  E3 Dispatches to "the East"
  E4 Dispatches to Madras
 Proceedings and Consultations, P
  Commercial Reports, External, Bengal and Madras
Journal of an Officer, 1764–65, King's 213
Charles Murray Correspondence, Egerton 3504
John Shattocke Description of Madeira, Egerton 2395

Christie's

Auction Catalogues

Guildhall Library

Cossart, Gordon Papers—Loose In-Letters, 1759–1815
Stephen Jackson Day Book of Orders, 1763–65

National Archives of the United Kingdom (formerly Public Record Office)

C 9 — Court of Chancery, Six Clerks Office, Pleadings before 1714, esp. *Brailsford v. Peers & Tooke*

C 11 — Court of Chancery, Six Clerks Office, Pleadings, 1714–58, esp. *Brailsford v. Peers & Tooke*

C 114/70 — Chancery Masters' Exhibits (Unknown), Wine Merchant's Books: Account Book, 1775–77

CO 142/31 — Colonial Office, Jamaica, Miscellanea, Census, 1754

CO 388/1–95 — Board of Trade, Original Correspondence, 1654–1792

FO 63/1–191 — Foreign Office and Predecessor, General Correspondence, Portugal, 1781–1815

SP 89/4–90 — State Papers, Portugal, 1638–1783

Natural History Museum

Francis Masson Letters, 1777

Westminster City Archives

Jonathan Michie Letter Book, 1770–84, and Ledger, 1770–86

Stanstead, Suffolk

Private Collection

Cossart, Gordon Papers, Letter Books and Scrapbook, 1748–1815

FRANCE

Paris

Archives Nationales

Affaires étrangeres, B/I/684–85, B/I/763–65, B/III/385: Correspondence with Consuls in Madeira

Archives de la marine, 3/JJ/86

JAMAICA

Kingston

National Library of Jamaica

William Freeman Letter Book

Spanishtown

Island Record Office

Deed Books

Will Books

Jamaica Archives

Probate Inventories

MADEIRA

Funchal

Arquivo Regional da Madeira

Account Book of the Venda de direitos de agua do Convento de Santa Clara
Acts of the Municipal Chamber (Camâra Municipal)
Jesus Maria José, Book of Current Accounts, 1706–32
Minutes of the Meetings of the Municipal Chamber
Ornelas Vasconcelos Family Archives

Blandy's Head Office, Archives

English Factory Minutes, 1809–48
English Factory Records, 1722–1815

Madeira Wine Company Archives

Cossart, Gordon Papers: Account Books, Letter Books, Letters
Thomas Newton Letter Book

Private Collection

Leacock Papers

Private Collection

Welsh Papers

THE NETHERLANDS

Rotterdam

Gemeentearchief Rotterdam

Oud notarieel archief, Notarial Deeds, 1585–1714

PORTUGAL

Lisbon

Arquivo Histórico Ultramarino, Instituto de Investigação Científica Tropical

Documents concerning the Navigation and Trade of Madeira and Brazil

Arquivo Nacional da Torre do Tombo

Livros dos direitos por entrada, Funchal, nos. 7–8, 21–22, 146–55, 177–91, 220–21, 469
(1717–18, 1727–1815), Provedoria e Junta da Real Fazenda do Funchal, Alfândega do
Funchal

Livros dos direitos por saída, Funchal, nos. 272–326 (1721–23, 1727–29, 1768–1815), Prove-
doria e Junta da Real Fazenda do Funchal, Alfândega do Funchal
Livros dos cobrancas, nos. 306, 308–9 (1650, 1687, 1699), Alfândega do Funchal
Collecção de ministério do negócios etrangeiros, caixas 550, 551, 919: Charts of Goods and
Ships Leaving Portugal, 1700–1815

Biblioteca Nacional
Manuscripts Section, Colecção Pombalina MS 219, no. 29: Various Papers, c. 1780

Oporto
James Symington
Condell, Innes Letter Book, 1789–1807

SCOTLAND
Ballindalloch

Ballindalloch Castle Muniments, Macpherson-Grant Papers, General James Grant Correspondence, Bundle 244: Scott, Pringle & Cheap Letters

Edinburgh
National Archives of Scotland
GD 113/5/92   Wallas Papers, 1816–19
GD 306/1/1   Letter Book of Alexander Oliphant & Co., 1766–71
GD 345/943   Grant of Monymusk Papers, James Duff Letters

National Library of Scotland
Arbuthnot Letters

Private Collection
Gordon of Letterfourie Papers

UNITED STATES
Albany, New York
New York State Archives
Port of New York City Manifest Books, 1743–75

New York State Library
Daniel Campbell Family Papers, Account Books, 1759–69
Phyn & Ellice Letter Book, 1768–75

John Porteous Papers, 2 folders, 1778–99
Abraham Yates Account Book, 1753–90

Albuquerque, New Mexico

University of New Mexico, Special Collections
John Howard March Letter Book, 1815–27

Annapolis, Maryland

Maryland Hall of Records
Anne Arundel/Baltimore County Rent Roll, no. 1
Anne Arundel County Court Land Deeds, 1712–40
Anne Arundel County Quaker Meeting Minutes
Chancery Records, no. 3, 1712–24
Dorsey Collection, Book of Invoices of Goods Shipped by Perkins, Buchanan & Brown of London, for Lancelot Jacques, 1766–74
Naval Officer Port Records, Annapolis, 1742–46

Ann Arbor, Michigan

William L. Clements Library
Shelburne Papers, 1665–1797
Tailyour Papers, 1783–1800

Baltimore, Maryland

Maryland Historical Society
Cheston Galloway Papers, MS 1994, 1749–79

Boston, Massachusetts

Congregational Library
Records of the Old South (Third) Church of Boston: Treasurer's Accounts

Harvard Business School, Special Collections
John and Jonathan Amory Papers
Thomas Coffin Amory Papers
Backus Family Account Books, 1793–1815
Peter Faneuil Ledger, 1725–32
Elisha Ford Day Book, 1771–95
Thomas Hancock Letter Books, Business Papers, and John Hancock Letters
Henry Lloyd Letter Book, 1765–67
William Manning Tavern Books, 1753–78

William Peck Account Book, 1800–1801
Andrew and Joseph Perkins Papers, 1783–1825

Massachusetts Historical Society

Amory Family Papers
   John and Jonathan Amory Accounts, 1761–67
   John and Jonathan Amory Letters, 1765–86
   Thomas Amory Account Book, 1720–28
   Thomas Amory Account Book, 1770–71
Caleb Davis Papers, 6 vols., 1752–65
John Dolbeare Bill of Lading Book, 1718–40
"The Diary of Tutor Henry Flynt," trans. Edward Dunn (transcript, 1978)
Greenough Papers
Jeffries Family Papers
King's Chapel Archives, Financial Records, Books, and Records
Edmund Quincy Papers, 1703–88

Massachusetts State Archives

Suffolk County and Hampshire County Probate Inventories, 1700–1815

New England Historic Genealogical Society

Fayerweather Papers, Thomas Fayerweather Papers, 1737–1818, and Thomas Fayerweather
   Letter Book, 1749–54

Society for the Preservation of New England Antiquities

Codman Papers, John Codman Letter Book, 1785–89

Buffalo, New York

Buffalo and Erie County Historical Society

Porteous Papers

Charleston, South Carolina

South Carolina Historical Society

Chesnut, Miller & Manning Collection, Chesnut Plantation (Kershaw) Papers
John Guerard Letter Book, 1752–54
Henry Laurens Letters
Waring & Hayne Records, 1755–1871

Columbia, South Carolina

Probate Inventories, Charleston and Kershaw counties, 1732–1807

Detroit, Michigan

Detroit Public Library, Burton Historical Collection

John Askin Papers

Durham, North Carolina

Duke University Library

Holker Papers
Hook Papers
Lowrance Ledger

Harrisburg, Pennsylvania

Dauphin County Court House

Session Docket Books, 2 vols., 1785–1815
Tax Lists, 1750–1815

Pennsylvania State Archives

Baynton, Wharton & Morgan Papers
Dorsey & Hughes Receipt Book, 1777–88
John Harris Sr. Receipt Book, 1749–69
John Harris Jr. Receipt Book, 1760–91
William McCord Account Books, 1777–79
John Mitchell Papers
Willing, Morris & Swanwick Papers, 1783–85

Hartford, Connecticut

Connecticut State Library

James Jarvis Papers
New London Ground Levy Roll, 1771

Haverford, Pennsylvania

Haverford College Library

Howland Collection: Hill Family Papers
Quaker Collection

Lawrence, Kansas

Spencer Research Library, University of Kansas

William Bolton Letters, 1702–13

Madison, Wisconsin

Wisconsin Historical Society

Joseph Kershaw Account Book, 1769–74

Newark, New Jersey

New Jersey Historical Society

Stevens Papers

New London, Connecticut

New London County Historical Society

Journal, 1771–1801
Journal of Selectmen, 1764–67
Nathaniel Shaw Jr. Papers, Account Books
John Winthrop Jr. Papers

Newport, Rhode Island

Newport Historical Society

Merchant Collections

Newton Centre, Massachusetts

American Jewish Historical Society

Aaron Lopez Papers

New York, New York

American Bible Society

Boudinot Correspondence, John Pintard and John Marsden Pintard Letters, 1781–99

American Jewish Historical Society

Gomez Family Papers, Daniel Gomez Ledger, 1740–66
Aaron Lopez Papers, 1768–82

Columbia University, Library, Manuscript Division

Isaac Bell Account Book/Letter Book, 1768–1860
John Jay Papers: Letters to Peter Jay

Museum of the City of New York

Charles Crooke Receipt Book, 1737–64

New York Historical Society

Frederick Ashton De Peyster Manuscripts, Account Book, 1723–33
Nicholas Low Collection, 1728–1809
Phyn & Ellice Bills of Lading Book, 1772–73
Lewis Pintard Letter Book, 1795–99
Rhinelander Papers
Peter Stuyvesant Letter Book
Tontine Coffee House Collection, Correspondence, Accounts, 1789–1823
Daniel Wier Letter Book, 1778–80

New York Public Library

Charles Carroll of Carrollton Letter Book, 1771–1833
Philip Cuyler Ledger, 1763–94
Philip Cuyler Letter Book, 1755–60
Diary and Log of a Journey from Kilkenny to Liverpool and Philadelphia, 1789–91
Galloway Papers: Correspondence, 1739–54
John Van Cortlandt Ledgers B–D, 1757–72
John Van Cortlandt Letter Book A, 1762–69
Stephen & John Van Cortlandt Letter Book, 1771–92

New York University

Jacob Leisler Papers

Philadelphia, Pennsylvania

American Philosophical Society

James Burd Business Records and Accounts, 1747–68
Burd-Shippen Papers: Receipts, 1746–92, and Miscellaneous Items, 1708–91
John Leacock Commonplace Book, 1768–1800
Israel Pemberton Jr. Letter Book D, 1744–47
Edward Shippen of Lancaster Letter Books
John Williams Day Book and Ledger, 1773–74

College of Physicians of Philadelphia

Thomas and Phineas Bond Ledgers, 1751–70
Elizabeth Coates Receipt Book, 1702–53
Dreer Collection Manuscript Lectures: Adam Kuhn, John Morgan, Benjamin Rush; and
    Notes on Their Lectures by the Students, 1780–1815
Receipt Books, eighteenth century
Theophilus Rogers Recipe and Prescription Book, 1779–1801
Benjamin Rush Manuscript Bills, Letters, and Notes, 1745–1813
Samuel and Benjamin Shoemaker Account Books

Historical Society of Pennsylvania

James Burd Letter Book, 1756–58
General John Cadwalader Correspondence, 1768–74
John and Peter Chevalier Day Book, 1760–66
Coates Family Papers
   John Reynell Account Book, 1738–61
   John Reynell Day Books, 1728–37
   John Reynell Invoice Book, 1735–58
   London Coffee House and Tavern Journal, 1736–43
Customs House Papers, 1704–89
Thomas Forbes Letter Book, 1722–23, 1729–32
Tench Francis Ledger and Invoice Book, 1759–63
Francis & Relfe Invoice Book, 1759–61
George Frey Survey and Warrant Book, 1763–1806
Benjamin Fuller Papers, 1762–99, 5 vols.
Simon Gratz Collection, Andrew Clow & Co. Letters, 1784–1813
James Hamilton Papers, Letters from George Frey to James Hamilton
John Hamilton & Nathaniel Drew Ledger, 1805–7
John Harris Jr. Ledgers, 1761–75, 1786–91
King of Prussia (Manheim) Tavern and Store Account Book, 1768–69
Martha Morris Laurence Collection, Papers of Thomas Laurence, 1746–54
Logan Papers
   Estate Papers of Mayor Richard Hill
   Isaac Norris Jr. Letter Book, 1735–55
James Logan Account Book, 1720–27
Mifflin & Massey Ledger A, 1760–63
George Morgan Letter Book, 1767–68
Norris of Fairhill Papers
Isaac Norris Sr. and Jr. Letters, 1702–9, 1716–30, and Ledgers, 1724–31, 1731–40, 1709–40
Joseph Ogden "Accounts Receivable" Ledger, 1749–55, 1769–71
Philadelphia Port Captain's Reports, 1797–1802
William Pollard Letter Book, 1772–74
Samuel Powell Letter Books, 3 vols., 1727–47
John Reynell Letter Books, 1744–45, 1745–47, 1752–54
Thomas Riche Letter Book, 1764–71
Daniel Roberdeau Letter Book, 1764–71
Cropley Rose Letter Book, 1779–81
Samuel and Benjamin Shoemaker Ledgers, 1745–51
Edward Wanton Smith Collection
   Lamar, Hill, Bisset & Co. Papers, 4 folders, 1762–1802
Sarah A. G. Smith Collection
   Hill Family Papers, 7 folders, 1757–98
William Trent Sr. Ledger, 1703–8

Wharton Papers, Thomas Wharton Letter Book, 1752–59, and Thomas Wharton Receipt
  Book, 1752–55
John Wister Receipt Book, 1749–54

Library Company of Philadelphia
Jonathan Dickinson Letter Book, 1715–21
John Jay Smith Collections
  "A," Hill Family Papers, 13 vols., 1698–1797
  "B," Hill Family Papers, 1 box and various account books, 1698–1797
John Smith Diaries, 1739–52

Providence, Rhode Island

John Carter Brown Library, Brown University
Brown Papers

Rhode Island Historical Society
Vernon Papers

Richmond, Virginia

State Library of Virginia
Order Books, York County

Virginia Historical Society
Robert Carter Letter Book, 1723–24, 1728–30
William Lee Letter Books, 1783–86
Mutual Assurance Association Papers
John Wickham Commonplace Book

Salem, Massachusetts

Peabody Essex Museum, Essex Institute, James Duncan Phillips Library
Curwen Family Papers
  Samuel Curwen Business Papers, 1734–72
  Samuel Curwen Letter Book, 1771–75
  Samuel Curwen Light and Impost Account Book, 1752–74
Derby Family Papers
  Derby Family Shipping Papers
  Elias Hasket Derby Papers
  Richard Derby Papers

Schenectady, New York

Schenectady County Historical Society

Daniel Campbell Letter Book

Washington, DC

Library of Congress

Amory Papers, Armory Letter Books
Galloway-Maxey-Marcoe Family Papers
Jamieson Papers

Williamsburg, Virginia

Colonial Williamsburg Foundation

Robert Carter of Nomini Hall Letter Books, 1761–68

Winterthur, Delaware

Winterthur Library and Museum

Gardiner's Island (Suffolk County, NY) Glass Catalogs
Museum Collection
Powel Family (Business) Papers, 1730–78: Samuel Powel Day Book, 1735–39
Wister Family Collection, Papers of John Wister and Succeeding Firms

Worcester, Massachusetts

American Antiquarian Society

Allen Family Collection, Thomas Allen Papers, 1750–90
Bossenger Foster Day Book, 1780–83
Cornelius Cuyler Letter Book, 1724–33
Daniel Fisher Papers, 1790–1837: Bills and Receipts
John Hull Letter Book, 1670–83
Daniel Smith Account Book, 1707–11
Artemas Ward Shrewsbury Ledger, 1750–75

WALES

Abergavenny

Clytha Park, Sir Richard Hanbury-Tennison

Wardlaw Ramsay of Tillicoultry Papers

Index

accounting (recordkeeping), 40, 188; books for, xiii–xiv, 180–81, 235, 311; by Portuguese firms, 493nn21, 23; standards for, 181–84. *See also* countinghouses; inventory

Adams, John, 298, 303, 336, 388

Addison, Joseph, 84

adulteration (of wine): by adding brandy, 80, 84–90, 174, 178, 188, 255, 455nn32–33; by adding other substances, 79–84, 155, 299; by blending south- and north-side wines, 60–61, 79, 155. *See also* color: manipulating

advertising: of engraved decanters, 374; of glasses, 382, 383; of Madeira, 477n57; on wine bottles, 371; by wine sellers, 209, 251–54. *See also* branding (of casks)

Africa: and Madeira island, 166; and Madeira wine, xv, xvi, xxi, xxix, 113. *See also* Africans; slave trade; *specific places in*

Africans, 8, 433n46; enslaved, in Anglo-America, 234, 241, 286, 287, 310–13, 400; enslaved, on Madeira, 11–12, 47, 430n29, 543n82

agency. *See* entrepreneurs

agents: defined, 528n84; dismissal of, 489n59; dispersal of, around Atlantic, xvi, 157, 163–66, 197, 395, 402, 403, 406, 488n56, 501n20; exporters as, 133, 173–74, 178, 189; firms' sharing of, 192; importers as, 214, 218, 236; networks of, xv, xx–xxiv, 126–27, 129, 142–44, 146–48, 172, 206, 248, 256, 488n56; and quality control of wines, 177; system of, 126–27, 129; wages for, 184

aging (of wine), 73, 94–97, 100, 104, 187, 215, 357, 395; connoisseurship about, 341, 342, 367–68; heating's effects on, 90, 93

agitating (of wine), 73, 86, 89–90, 102, 104, 395, 458n45

agriculture: local, for global trade, 2; variety of, on Madeira, 7–8, 47–48. *See also* food imports; sugar; viticulture

agua pé, 75

aguardente, 125, 131, 191

Ahmuty, Arthur, 488n56

Alder, William, 485n32

ale, 85, 282, 294, 382

alehouses, 513n12

Alentejo wine, 131

Alexander, James, 467n13

Alexander grape, 111, 467n13

Alfândega. See Customs House

Algarve wine, 131

296, 297; clubs in, 391; glassware in, 366, 374; hospitals in, 299; soldiers' drinking in, 302; stores in, 246, 249, 254; taverns in, 240, 279; toasts in revolutionary, 354; wine agents in, 166; wine brokers in, 219; wine exports to, 151; wine importers in, 201–3, 206–9; wine networks in, 160, 197–98, 237; wine preferences in, 339

bottles: choice of, 342; demand for, 266; display of, 291, 337, 342, 346, 365; medicine, 309; as primary shipping container for French wines, 112, 369; purchasing of, 279, 297, 370, 402; rented, 246, 250, 255, 370; as sales unit, 201, 232; seals for, 255; selling of, 255; shapes of, 367–69; sizes of, 367, 565n26; storage of, in cellars, 361, 367; storing rum in, 280. *See also* bottling; corks; seals

bottle seals. *See* seals

bottling, 341, 369

Boulton, Matthew, 576n13

"boundary objects," xxviii, 356, 365–66, 376

bouquet (of wine), 556n58

Bourdieu, Pierre, 423n19, 529n8, 562n3

Bradick, Isaac Gualter, 140

Bradlee, David, 209

Bradlee, Thomas, 209

Branco, Diogo Fernandes, 113, 146, 191

branding (of casks), 100–102, 371

brands: on firms' wine containers, 100–102, 169–70, 177; iron, for marking wine containers, xiii, 82

brandy (aqua vitae), 318, 454n30; addition of, to wines, 80, 84–90, 174, 178, 188, 255, 455nn32–33; in college rooms, 297; French, xv, xxi, 80, 86, 88–89, 192, 314; glasses for, 381; grapevines for, 445n27; in homes, 288; individuals' purchasing of, 280; loaning of, among export firms, 192, 195; markets for, 314; medicinal uses of, 286, 303; Portuguese, 88–89; for sailors, 319; Spanish, 88; strength of, in Madeira, 85; for water purification,

319; in wine firms' inventory, 186; wine traded for, 131

Braventon, William, 520n46

Brazil: British traders in, 134; currency in, 415; import and export records for, xxvi, 420n4; Madeira imported by, 26, 107, 113–14, 124–26, 171, 196, 474n43; Madeiran emigration to, 9–10; Madeiran slaves from, 12; markets of, opened to Lisbon, 107, 112, 114, 125, 132; networks based in, 146; sugar from, 20, 394, 400; unsuccessful viniculture in, 20, 124; warm wine cellarage in, 91, 92; and wine for Angola, 473n38; wine imported by, xxv, 474n43. *See also specific places in*

Breen, Timothy H., 422n11, 533n21

Brennan, Thomas, 421n6

Brewer, John, xviii

brimstone, 186

British America. *See* Anglo-America

British Caribbean. *See* Caribbean; *specific places in*

British West Indies. *See also* West Indies; *specific places in*

Brito, Francisco de Ornelas de, 190

brokers (of wine), 219–20, 255–59, 263, 396

Brown, John, 327, 328

Brown, Thomas Bayne, 476n54

Brush, Richard, 151, 197–98, 392

Bual grape, 51–53

Buchan, William, 324, 328

Bullivant, Benjamin, 289

bumpers, 350, 353, 385

bungholes, 81, 90, 100

bung plugs, 98

bungs, 97, 100, 170, 174

Burd, James, 303

Burges, Gedley Clare, 163, 185, 189

Burgundy wine, 53, 92, 288

Burke, Peter, 486n44

Burnett, David, 148

Burnett, John, 148

Bushman, Richard, 554n46

business cards, 252–53

pruning (of grape vines), 55, 56

"public sphere": coffee as part of, 294; vs. domestic sphere, 277–78, 299–300; men seen as dominating, 303–4; taverns and stores as part of, 269–70, 276, 277, 294–95, 300

Quakers, 148, 295, 537n45, 538n53; among wine exporters, xix, 102, 141, 145, 479n3; among wine importers, 225; wine networks of, 211

quality (of wine): aging as characteristic of, 96; ascertaining, xxiv, 62–63, 160–61; of auctioned wine, 219; and bottle seals, 371; characteristics of highest, 155–56; educating customers about, 259; heat as increasing Madeira's, 90–94, 112, 230, 359–60, 395; importers' concern for, 222; location of grapes as influencing, 45; of north- vs. south-side Madeiran wines, 60; in *partidas*, 66–67; rain as affecting, 58. *See also* quality control (of wine)

quality control (of wine), 175, 177–78, 188

"quality house," 155–56

quart bottles, 367

quarter-casks, 98, 201, 232, 253, 391

quarto, 98

quartola, 98

Quebec, 237, 313

Quincy, Edmund, Jr., 219

quintas. See villas

Rabelais, François, 387

racking, 341; in adulterating wine, 83; aeration of must while, 76; for changing color of wine, 81; in fining wine, 77, 102; by steam-powered engines, 90

Raffald, Elizabeth, 287

rain (and grape harvest), 58–59

Raleigh, Walter, 110

Randolph, John, 210

Randolph, William, Jr. (colonel), 210, 300

ratafia glasses, 382

Ravenscroft, George, 364, 371, 372, 376, 381, 395, 565n20

Ray, William, 134

Read, Martha, 305

Reade, Lawrence, 205

Reading (Pennsylvania), 264–66

recipes: for compounding drugs with wine, 321–22; for wine fining, 78

recordkeeping. *See* accounting

refinement. *See* gentility

refining (of Madeira). *See* fining (clarifying) (of Madeira)

Rehoboth (Massachusetts), 243

religion: of British exporters, 140–41, 166; networks based on, xvi, 145, 149–50, 211, 249, 394; as separating Madeiran natives from foreigners, 17–18, 29–30; of wine brokers in America, 255; of wine importers in America, 207. *See also* Catholics; identity; Jews; Moors; Protestants

Rennell Current, 2, 393

reputation. *See* trust

residences. *See* homes

retailers, xxvii–xxviii; defined, 499n10; of glassware, 381; individuals as purchasing wine from, 199; Madeira exporters as also, 18, 21, 31, 62, 68, 169, 173, 188, 478n2; in New York, 208; in Pennsylvania, xxi, 245, 246, 248–54, 261–63, 314, 402–3, 517n27; in rural areas, 259–63; specialization in wines carried by, 199, 209, 239, 246, 247, 253–55, 260, 266–67, 402–3; vs. wholesalers, 510n1; wine brokers as, 255–59, 263; wine coopers as, 239, 253, 255, 341, 357, 453n14, 511n4; wine importers as, 206, 236, 238; wine importers as supplying, 220, 239, 248; and wine manufacture, 79. *See also* networks; stores and storekeepers; taverns and tavernkeepers

Reynolds, Frederick, 388

Reynolds, John, 267

Rhenish wine, 83, 118, 119, 127, 258, 288, 323; medicinal uses of, 323, 326

rhetoric (of wine). *See* language: of discrimination about wine
Rhine, xxi
rice, 108, 175, 176, 179, 186, 192, 393, 396
Richbell, Richard, 136, 138, 189
Riche, Thomas, 179
Ricks, Goodman, 303
Riddell, John, 148
Riedesel, Friedrich Adolf, 306
Rio de Janeiro, 125, 126
risk: capitalists' involvement in, 172–73, 197–98; entrepreneurs' acceptance of, xvii, 21, 208, 214, 248; exporters' increasing acceptance of, 178–80. *See also* pilferage; piracy; privateering; shipwrecks; smuggling
rituals: church, using wine, 295–96, 318; diplomatic, with Indians, 314, 315; of social wine drinking, 169, 278, 293–94, 315, 317, 335, 340, 348, 349–54, 372, 374. *See also* deportment; toasts and toasting
Rivera, Jacob Rodriguez, 391
Roanoke Island, 110
Roberdeau, Daniel, 391
Robertson, Andrew, 147
Robertson, Ebenezer, 366
Robertson, Peter, 256
Robie, Thomas, 297
Rocha, Manuel, 190
Rocio, Marcos Gonçalves, 136, 138
Rodney decanters, 372
Roman Catholics. *See* Catholics
Rome (ancient), 90, 92, 94, 371, 560n86
Rorabaugh, William, 529n3
Ross, Robert, 220
Roupell, George, 290–91, 346–47, 561n90
Rowe, John, 159–60, 175
Rowlandson, Thomas, 515n15
Royal African Company, 466n5
Royal Treasury (Funchal), 23–25
Rübenkam, Anna Catharina, 255
rum, 85, 267, 318; alcohol content of, 312, 532n16; in home wine cellars, 280, 284, 290, 336, 367; individuals' purchasing

of, 279–80; manufacturing of, 212–13, 515n17; markets for, 265, 268, 312, 314; price of, 282, 333, 532n16; sailors' drinking of, 275, 302, 319; selling of, 254, 263; size of containers for, 184; social class of drinkers of, 333; in taverns, 242, 243; wages paid in, 302, 303; wine traded for, 218, 400
rummers (specialized wine glasses), 382, 383
Rush, Benjamin, 328, 329, 332
Russia, 131–32
Rutgers, Cornelia, 206
Rutledge, John, 360, 505n59

Sack (Spanish wine), 83, 127, 280, 314, 340; glasses for, 381; medicinal use of, 318–19, 327
sacraments. *See* communion; rituals
Sahlins, Marshall, 562n3
saídas. See ships: departure of, from Madeira
sailors: care of ailing, 195, 318–19; laws regarding wine sales to, 333; rations of, 275, 302, 319
St. Augustine, 289
St. Croix, 121, 154
St. Eustatius, 121
St. Kitts, 149, 151, 179
St. Paul, Frederick, 131
St. Thomas, 121
St. Vincent, 154
Salem (Massachusetts), 160, 202–3, 287
Salle, Abraham, 290
Salmon, William, 326
salt, 81
Salvador de Bahia. *See* Bahia
Sanches, Joaquim José, 193
Sanches, Luis Vicente, 193
San Lucar wines, 122
Santa Clara nuns, 10, 29, 195
Santo Domingo, 154
Sá Pereira, João António de, 61
Sargent, Henry, 561n90